Oxford Historical Society
VOL. LXIX

A CARTULARY OF THE HOSPITAL OF ST. JOHN THE BAPTIST

1.

2.

1. The first seal of the Hospital. S' FRATRVM OSPITALIS S' IOHANNIS DE OXEN'

2. The second seal of the Hospital. S' COMVNE DOMVS HOSPITALIS SCI' IOHIS BAPTISTE EX' PORT' [ ].

Frontispiece.

A CARTULARY OF THE HOSPITAL OF ST. JOHN THE BAPTIST

EDITED BY THE

REV. H. E. SALTER, M.A.

NEW COLLEGE, OXFORD

VOL. III

OXFORD

PRINTED FOR THE OXFORD HISTORICAL SOCIETY

AT THE CLARENDON PRESS

1917

PRINTED IN ENGLAND
AT THE OXFORD UNIVERSITY PRESS

PREFACE

THE Hospital of St. John, like many other hospitals, has left us no record of the way in which it came into being. In the case of a monastery there is usually little doubt when it was founded and who was the founder. It began with a foundation charter in which the founder was named and the first endowments were recited; and this deed was not likely to be forgotten, partly because it had to be shown to the Visitor whenever he made a Visitation of the house, and also for the reason that as the descendants of the founder had special privileges in connexion with the monastery, they would be interested in the preservation of the deed. Furthermore, in the case of a monastery, the laying of the foundation stone, the consecration of the abbey or priory church, and the institution of the first abbot or prior, were events of a kind to be recorded by contemporary chroniclers. But hospitals, many of which had no endowments but depended upon alms, might spring up or pass out of existence, and little notice be taken. This is the case with all the hospitals in Oxford. We know from a notice in the Hundred Rolls of Edward I that the Hospital of St. Bartholomew was founded by Henry I, but we do not know when it was founded or what endowments it received from the king. Of the hospital for lepers which existed on the north side of the church of St. Giles we know neither when it began nor when it ended; all we know is that it was in existence as early as the reign of Henry III and as late as 1390, and that in the next century the site was in the possession of University College. Unendowed hospitals in the parishes of St. Clement and St. Peter in the East are mentioned in the years 1345 and 1338 respectively, when they had permission to beg for alms, but we do not know when they were founded or where they stood; in fact, it is possible that they never advanced beyond the stage of good intentions, for if the faithful withheld their alms, a hospital of that kind must cease to exist. There were three hospitals at Woodstock, two at Banbury, and one at Bicester, but of none do we know the date of their origin, except the Hospital of St. John at Banbury.[1]

It is definitely stated by mediaeval Chroniclers and by royal charters[2] that Henry III was the *fundator* of the Hospital of St. John; but the word *fundator*, when used of a monastic house, had a different meaning from our word *founder*, and did not designate the man who began the house, but the man who had given the land on which the buildings stood. There is a good instance in the Cistercian Abbey of Thame. It was originally founded by a knight named Gay or Gait on land that belonged to him at Oddington; but when the site was found unsuitable, the monastery was moved to Thame and established on land which was given by the Bishop of Lincoln, and although all the endowments which the original founder gave continued to be held by the monks, yet the Bishop of Lincoln was henceforth reckoned to be founder of the abbey, with such rights as belonged to that position. In the same way Henry III became founder of the Hospital of St. John in the year 1234, for the reason that he provided a new site and new buildings for the Hospital, where now Magdalen College stands, part of the land being bought by him[3] and part belonging to him as protector and, as might be said, lord of all the Jews; but he certainly did not originate the Hospital. This Cartulary contains many deeds which show that the Hospital was in existence and owned property before the date of Henry III's foundation.

An earlier founder is reckoned to be Hugo de Malaunay,[4] or de Malo Alneto, a knight of Oxfordshire, whose chief seat was at Chalgrove. No passage has been found in which he is named founder, but his grant (see Vol. I, p. 73) is entered on the first page of the manuscript Cartulary of the Hospital, as though the scribe of the Cartulary considered it to be in some

[1] *Victoria County History* (*Oxfordshire*), vol. i, p. 152.

[2] See vol. ii, p. 436.

[3] See vol. i, p. 78.

[4] In vol. i, p. 73, it has been too readily assumed that Hugo Malaunay's deed is a foundation charter.

sort a foundation charter. It also appears from charter no. 14 (see Vol. I, p. 16) that in the year 1346 there was an idea that Hugo de Malaunay was founder of the Hospital; for just as a monastery, when it was unknown who was the donor of a piece of land, always attributed the gift to its founder, should any question arise about the title, so in this dispute about land in St. Clement's the original gift is attributed to Hugo de Malaunay, although as a matter of fact the land was acquired a hundred years later; and again in charter no. 71 Hugo de Malaunay is mentioned very much as a founder would be mentioned. In the preface to charter no. 70 it is pointed out that if Hugo de Malaunay was a founder of the Hospital, his line died out about 1226, and his property escheated to the king, so that the road was clear for the king to become a second founder. But if charter no. 70 is closely examined it will be noticed that it can hardly issue from one who claimed to be a founder; for it is a sale, not a free grant, and a perpetual rent is also retained; so that in two points it is unlike a foundation charter. And in any case it could not be the origin of the Hospital; for the deed states that the Hospital was already in existence, that it possessed money, and had received a gift from John, Count of Mortain.

It is probable that the earliest charters which mention the Hospital are found in the Cartularies of Godstow Abbey and of the Templars of Sandford. The following deed is taken from the latter source (Bodl. Wood MS. empt. 10, fol. 34):

Uniuersis sancte ecclesie fidelibus fratres hospital*is*[1] sancti Iohannis herbergerie site ad portam orientalem Oxenforde, salutem in uero salutari. Nouerit uniuersitas uestra nos communi consilio & communi assensu ciuium[2] Oxeneforde in placit*is* domini regis apud Oxeneforde concessisse & quietam clamasse Willelmo le Knit[3] terram ubi Radulfus mansit uersus aquilonarem murum Oxenforde cum herbergagio[4] illius terre, ad donandam predictam terram cum herbergagio militibus Templi Ierosolimitani in puram & perpetuam

[1] Possibly, hospital*arii.*

[2] *cū,* MS. The Cartulary is in bad and careless writing.

[3] *Kyrit,* MS.

[4] *herbergagium* seems to mean *house, messuage.*

> elemosinam, solutam & quietam ab omni seculari seruicio. Et quia uolumus quod sciatur & quod perpetuo firmum & ratum permaneat, etiam sigilli nostri munimine corroborauimus; hiis testibus, Philippo Priore sancte Frideswyde, Nigello decano Oxon', Henrico filio Segrim[1] aldermanno, Thoma de Thademerton preposito & multis aliis.

This deed is earlier than November 27, 1195, at which date Philip had ceased to be prior of St. Frideswide's;[2] at present the date of his death is unknown, but it must have been between July, 1191, and November 27, 1195.[3] On the other hand, Nigel did not become dean (i.e. rural dean) of Oxford until about 1185; so that the date of the deed is 1185–1195.

But the following deed which is taken from the Godstow Cartulary,[4] now in the Record Office, seems to be earlier still:—

> Sciant omnes presentes et futuri quod ego Simon presbiter de sancto Petro concessi et dimisi et liberaui Iohanni Kepeharm terram meam que est inter terram meam ubi maneo et terram quam Walterus Crampe tenet de hospitali de Ierusalem, illam terram predictam cum medietate gabuli domus mee ubi maneo, ita quod gabulum erit nobis commune, concessi ut predictum est et dimisi prenominato Iohanni in longum et in latum, sicut camera que est super terram condonat et in profundum usque ad terram quam dedi hospitali sancti Iohannis ad portam orientalem Oxenefordie quam Agamundus le Bolter tenet, [habendum et tenendum][5] illi et heredibus [suis de me et heredibus][5] meis firmiter et stabiliter in feodo et hereditate libere et quiete et honorifice, reddendo inde annuatim unum denarium ad festum sancti Michaelis pro omni seruicio. Et pro concessione et donacione prediuise terre prenominatus Iohannes dedit michi sexaginta solidos de recognicione. Et ego et heredes mei predictam terram warantizabimus predicto Iohanni et heredibus suis contra omnes homines. Et ut prescriptum pactum de me et heredibus meis predicto Iohanni et heredibus suis perpetuo firmum et ratum permaneat, ego Simon presbiter sigilli mei attestacione corroboraui, hiis testibus, magistro Fulcone de

[1] *Segrini*, MS.
[2] *Feet of Fines* (Pipe Roll Soc.), 71.
[3] *V. C. H.* (*Oxfordshire*), p. 100.
[4] K.R., Misc. Books, no. 20, fol. 127.
[5] Omitted by the scribe.

Abyndon, Willelmo diacono filio Randulfi de Lincolnia, Willelmo filio Radulfi, Iohanne fratre suo, Willellmo Coppe, Segar', Rich*er*o nepote prioris.

It is not easy to fix the date of this deed. John Kepeharm died in 1204 or 1205, but the use of the form *Oxenefordia*, not *Oxonia*, suggests a date not later than 1200. The succession of the rectors of St. Peter's in the East during the twelfth century is not known, but 'Simon presbiter de sancto Petro' attests a deed which cannot be later than 1165.[1] Likewise 'Iohannes filius Radulfi de sancto Martino' attests an Oseney deed[2] of the year 1163. Apparently he was brother of Nigel de sancto Martino who died about 1200. Segari, called in Oseney deeds Segari Poie or Segari mercator, appears in deeds of about 1190; and we shall not be far wrong if we assign our deed to 1180–1190.

From this deed, therefore, we learn that the Hospital of St. John was in existence in the latter half of the reign of Henry II. We know of no founder and it need have had none; we may imagine that one or more of the residents in Oxford, seeing that a home was needed for the destitute, whether infirm or not, rented or bought a house outside the East Gate and devoted themselves to this Hospital, and by gifts and legacies property was soon acquired. It may be pointed out that the sudden origin or development of the University about the years 1170 to 1190, bringing a large, and often destitute, population to Oxford, must have made such a hospital necessary; and even in later days, when better preparation had been made for scholars, the Hospital was still reckoned to have been founded for the benefit of 'poor scholars and other miserable persons'.[3]

A change in the importance of the Hospital, though not necessarily in its situation or constitution, was introduced by the grant[4] of Hugo de Malaunay, of which the date must be between 1191 and 1199. By that deed the Hospital purchased all that Peter Boterel had owned in Oxford both within and

[1] *The Godstow Cartulary* (E.E.T.S.), p. 383.

[2] Oseney, S. Giles no. 16.

[3] See vol. iii, p. 7.

[4] Vol. i, p. 73.

without the city (*burgum*). Peter Boterel held three knights' fees of the Honour of Wallingford, situated at Chalgrove[1], or more accurately at Chalgrove, Gangsdown, and Rycote, in the county of Oxford. He must have died in the course of the year ending Michaelmas 1165, and in the Pipe Roll for that year the sheriff accounts for 'xx*s*. iiii*d*. de terra Petri Boterelli extra portam del Est de Oxinford'; this was probably the profit for a portion of a year, for in the next Pipe Roll the amount is £2 12*s*. 4*d*. Next year the sheriff accounts for 'xvii*s*. iii*d*. de terra Petri Boterelli de dimidio anno dum fuit in manu regis'; so that we learn that about Easter 1167 the king had ceased to hold this land. The matter is made more clear by the next Pipe Roll, which states that the king had granted this portion of Peter Boterel's land to Osbertus Janitor and his wife at a rent of ten shillings.

The Pipe Roll of 13 Hen. II records that at Easter 1166 they had also been granted Headington Mill 'ad perficiendas x libratas terre quas Rex dedit eis pro servitio suo'. Osbert seems to have died about Michaelmas 1177;[2] the mill was soon granted to Oliver de Plugeney, and it is likely enough that he also obtained the land of Peter Boterel, paying the rent which in the Pipe Rolls of 1186 and 1189 appears at the figure of 10*s*. 8*d*. By Michaelmas 1189 it seems that Oliver de Plugeney was dead and the sheriff accounts for 49*s*. 2*d*., being the issue of the land of Oliver de Plugeney.[3] In this way the land of Peter Boterel reverted into the king's hands and was once more reunited with the lordship of Chalgrove. When King Richard started for the Holy Land, he granted the Honour of Wallingford to his brother John, who in process of time granted to Hugo Malaunay the manor of Chalgrove and the land of Peter Boterel.[4] As it appears from the deed of Hugo Malaunay that John had already granted to the Hospital a rent of ten shillings from the land of Peter Boterel, no doubt the quitrent of which we hear when the land was granted to Osbert Janitor, we can understand how important to the Hospitallers the deed of Hugo Malaunay

[1] *Testa*, p. 115.
[2] *Pipe Roll*, 24 Hen. II, p. 116.
[3] *Pipe Roll*, 1 Ric. I, p. 111.
[4] Vol. i, p. 72.

was. By means of it they acquired the freehold of the land on which apparently their hospital stood, and of which they already possessed the quitrent; and though it was not a foundation charter, it was of similar value. As the Hospital paid a quitrent on Cowlake to the manor of Chalgrove, we may assume that the land of Peter Boterel extended eastward as far as the parish of St. Clement's.[1]

This land of Peter Boterel seems to have been a small manor outside East Gate, and its boundaries those given in charter no. 71. On the south it was bounded by Paris Mead and the grange of St. Frideswide's, which stood at the south end of Rose Lane; on the west it was bounded by the city wall; on the north by the manor of Holywell, which at that time included the north end of what is now the Grove; on the east the boundary was the branch of the Cherwell which runs from King's Mill to East Bridge.[2] That this was a manor seems to be proved by the *Inquisicio ad quod damnum* which was held when Edmund, Earl of Cornwall, proposed to acquire nine houses between the town wall and Rose Lane, as a site for the Trinitarian Friars. The jury at that time gave as their verdict[3] that the Hospital held the lordship of all these houses, although we know from the Cartulary that it owned the freehold of no more than two of them. The verdict of the jury is confirmed by the statement in the Hundred Rolls of 1279 that the Earl of Cornwall held the site of the Trinitarian Friars 'in capite de magistro Hospitalis',[4] and by another statement in that record, which is now illegible but could be read in Wood's time,[5] that the land of the Hospital extended 'a loco qui dicitur Estbridge et ab insula que dicitur Paris usque ad portam orientalem ex utraque parte vici'.[6] The Cartulary proves that the freehold of the land on the

[1] The statement made in vol. i, p. 72, that Cowlake was within Addison's Walk is incorrect. Cowlake is identical with Great Mead (see vol. iii, pp. 22, 186, 274), which was divided into one portion of $5\frac{3}{4}$ acres called Angel Mead because it was leased with the Angel (vol. iii, p. 381), while the remainder, containing $7\frac{1}{2}$ acres (*ib.* p. 380), was leased with the Greyhound and was called Greyhound Mead. These meadows lie between Addison's Walk and the eastern branch of the Cherwell (vol. i, p. 154).

[2] See vol. i, pp. 72 and 75.

[3] Vol. i, p. 68.

[4] *Hundred Rolls*, ii. 799.

[5] Wood, *City of Oxford*, ii. 520.

[6] *Hundred Rolls*, ii. 803.

north side of the road from East Bridge to East Gate was not acquired by the Hospital until the fifteenth century, but in 1279 it possessed the lordship or the manorial rights. When this lordship ceased to exist, and why, is unknown to us.

Of the situation of this first hospital, which lasted until 1234, and of its constitution we know nothing except what can be deduced from the charters contained in Vols. I and II. As the Hospital was always described as *extra portam orientalem*, we have some idea where it must have been, and fuller information is supplied by charter no. 351[1] (Vol. I, p. 351), where a piece of land in the parish of St. Peter in the East is described as having one end or 'front' in the churchyard of St. Peter in the East, and the other end 'close to (*ad*) the city wall, hard by (*iuxta*) the hospital of St. John.' There can be no doubt that this land extended east and west, so that the buildings of the Hospital must at that time have been in Long Wall Street almost due east of the church of St. Peter, either in the Grove or at the north end of the buildings of Magdalen College School.

A few facts about the constitution and the work of the Hospital in its first stage can be gleaned from the charters which date from before 1234. The Hospital consisted of brethren and sisters, the latter being mentioned in charter no. 266 (Vol. I, p. 266). There is no mention of any master or warden until after 1225, the first instance being in charter no. 558 (Vol. II, p. 71), where *Elyas magister* appears. The date cannot be later than 1231 because John Pady is described as mayor, and for the same reason it is not earlier than 1225. In two deeds of Michaelmas 1232 to Michaelmas 1233 *Elyas capellanus* is described as *custos* (Vol. I, pp. 267, 308). With these exceptions there is no mention of any warden, and it was the custom in these earliest days that leases were granted by the brethren as a body, not by the master or warden.[2] The Hospital is generally described as the Hospital of St. John the Baptist, but in four deeds St. Mary is joined

[1] The deed is undated, but as Torald, who seems to have died about 1226, is one of the witnesses, we know that it is before the rebuilding by Henry III. The names of Cnitwin and Ailwin Tornarius suggest a date before 1220.

[2] See vol. i, p. 291.

with St. John (Vol. I, pp. 229, 266, 303, and Vol. II, p. 244). The nature of the Hospital is shown by the phrase *ad sustentacionem pauperum* (Vol. I, p. 229) and by the mention of the *firmaria* or *domus infirmorum* (Vol. I, p. 266, and Vol. II, p. 206) in which a light was kept burning. While in most of the deeds the foundation is called *hospitalis* or *hospitale*, for the word could be masculine, neuter, or even feminine, in the three earliest charters it is called *herebergeria* (see Vol. I, p. 73, and Vol. II, p. 435). But it seems that there was no distinction of meaning between the two words, and in two of these three charters the terms are used indifferently. Both of the words are vague, and merely state that the foundation was one where men obtained hospitality or harbour, and do not indicate whether the hospitality was temporary or permanent, or whether it was given to the hale or the sick. A hospital with us means a place where the sick are tended and receive medical care until they die or recover, but in the Middle Ages a hospital might be an almshouse where permanent hospitality was given, and the case of the Hospital of St. John of Jerusalem proves that a hospital might be a free inn, a place where temporary hospitality was given to pilgrims, necessitous perhaps but not necessarily sick. We have seen that the Hospital of St. John outside the East Gate is described in early deeds as existing for the benefit of *pauperes* and *infirmi*, and as Matthew Paris substitutes *peregrini* for *pauperes*, we may assume that its purpose was twofold—to receive the infirm like a modern hospital, and to provide lodging for wanderers or tramps. There is no indication that it existed as a permanent almshouse at any time, and it remains to be proved that hospitals of the almshouse type existed as early as the twelfth century, except in the case of leper hospitals. Its constitution shows what was its purpose; for where a hospital was founded as an almshouse, the brethren of the hospital were the aged inmates; but in the case of a hospital which was founded for the temporary shelter of poor and sick, the brethren were permanent residents who took the place of the committee which manages a modern hospital and is in charge of the funds; and such was the case with the Hospital of St. John. The brethren were distinct from the infirm and were in the position of monks in a monastery. It is evident therefore that the Hospital was not of the kind where the aged might settle for life, but was a place where travellers or the sick might be received for a time. Anthony Wood suggests that the Hospital was built for the accommodation of those who made a pilgrimage to the shrine of St. Frideswide; but, as far as we know, such pilgrims were few, and probably they came only at the time of St. Frideswide's fair.

The first indication that King Henry III was interested in the Hospital of St. John is on April 9, 1230, when he commanded Hugh de Neville, his forester, to permit the Hospital to have two loads of dead wood in Shotover Forest daily, as had been the custom heretofore until Brian de Insula stopped it.[1]

On May 5, 1231, the king gave up (*concessit*) to the master and brethren of the Hospital of St. John the garden which had belonged to the Jews outside East Gate, to erect their hospital there, saving to the Jews a suitable spot outside the said garden for the burial of dead Jews; the bailiffs of Oxford are to give seisin to the Hospital.[2] Two months later, when the king granted King's Mill to the Hospital, he renewed the previous grant, adding on this occasion that the garden was to be used for rebuilding the Hospital (*de novo construendum*) and that the spot reserved for the burial of the Jews was to be near the said garden.[3] Though the area is described in the grant as *gardinum* of the Jews it is described as their burial-place in the Hundred Rolls of 1279, where we read that the Hospital was founded by the king 'in area seu curia ubi Iudeorum corpora sepeliebantur'.[4]

[1] *Calendar of Close Rolls*, p. 320.

[2] *Ib.* p. 500.

[3] See vol. i, p. 77; *Calendar of Close Rolls*, p. 530; *Calendar of Charter Rolls*, p. 135. The original grant was issued at Oxford on July 12, and so it appears on the Charter Roll; but in the Close Roll it is dated 'July 14 at Woodstock'. It is noticeable that both the deeds of May 5 and July 12 use *concessit* not *dedit* in connexion with the garden of the Jews; but *dedit* is used of King's Mill.

[4] *Hundred Rolls*, ii. 803. Some of these words are now illegible, but they were read by Wood (see *City of Oxford*, ii. 520).

How or when the Jews obtained this spot is quite unknown. Even if it was their original burial-place, it must have been acquired after 1180; for in that year was drawn up a document recording the mighty works of St. Frideswide, and among other stories it is mentioned that when a Jew of Oxford had recently used slighting words of the saint, not only was he stricken with mortal illness, but also when his corpse was sent to London for burial, as was the custom of the Jews,[1] the cart broke down and the corpse fell out; which shows that Jews at that time were not buried at Oxford. But there is no evidence to show how soon after 1180 it was acquired; nor, again, to show how it became the property of the king. It is likely enough that when the king expressed his desire to have the land, the Jews surrendered it to him to procure his goodwill, only stipulating that a portion should be reserved for their use; accordingly the Jews retained the part on the south side of the road, being 300 feet by 80 or 90 feet, and the Hospital took the rest. If the measurement of 300 feet was from east to west, as seems to have been the case (see Vol. I, p. 38), and if the portion on the north side of the road was of the same width, the garden of the Jews supplied the site for almost the whole of the southern part of the Hospital; for the measurement from the corner by the porter's lodge to the Cherwell is only about 320 feet.[2]

On October 8, 1231, the king gave order to Hugh de Neville that the Hospital of St. Bartholomew was to have five *fusta* from Shotover forest, while the Hospital of St. John and the Friars Preachers and Friars Minors were to have thirteen *fusta*.[3]

On February 24, 1232, Hugh de Neville was commanded to supply the brethren of the Hospital with five oaks from Brill Forest and five oaks from Shotover, for the building of the Hospital; and Thomas de Langele, forester of Whichwood,

[1] Digby MS. 177, fol. 13.

[2] If, as is stated in the *Polychronicon*, the King himself laid the foundation stone of the Hospital, the date would be either July 12 or Oct. 8, 1231, for on those two days the King was in Oxford. The former date is the more probable.

[3] *Calendar of Close Rolls*, p. 568; *fustum* is a beam of some kind (see Ducange).

was to supply three oaks for the same purpose, from the forest that was in his charge.[1]

On May 25, 1232, the king, being at Woodstock, granted to the Hospital without the East Gate of Oxford fifty cart-loads of thorn and underwood, to be supplied by Hugh de Neville.[2] On June 17, 1232, we hear of further building; for on that day Hugh de Neville is commanded to supply to the Hospital of St. John twenty-three *copulas* and beams and *pannas* [3] from the forests in his charge 'for the building of the new chapel of St. Mary which has been begun at the new hospital'; and ten *copule* are to be supplied for the same purpose from the forest of Cornbury.[4]

Between Michaelmas 1232 and Michaelmas 1233 the king acquired through Geoffrey his almoner a tenement, which to judge from the price was not large, to be added to the site of the Hospital. We are able to state that it was where the gate of the Hospital stood,[5] immediately to the east of what was subsequently Magdalen Hall.

The establishment of the Hospital by the king is assigned by Matthew Paris to the year 1233, in these words: 'Simili quoque pietatis spiritu tactus, idem rex quoddam nobile hospitale Oxoniis constituit, non procul a ponte, ut ibidem infirmi et peregrini suae remedium percipiant necessitatis.' [6] But the year according to our reckoning would be 1234. For on January 26, 1234, the king gives notice by Letters Patent that, as patron and founder of the Hospital of St. John without the East Gate of Oxford, he has appointed that of the goods which he has conferred or shall confer on the Hospital, three brethren, chaplains,[7] shall be maintained, of whom one, elected by the brethren in common and presented to the king, shall be over the others, to keep the rule of St. Augustine, which the

[1] *Cal. of Close Rolls*, p. 35.

[2] *Ib.* p. 62. A platform upon a heap of faggots seems to have been used by builders instead of a scaffold.

[3] *panna*, a beam of some kind; see Ducange. He does not give *copula* in any such sense.

[4] *Cal. of Close Rolls*, p. 74.

[5] Vol. i, p. 78.

[6] *Mat. Par.* ii. 263 (Rolls Series). The author drew a picture of the Hospital on the margin of his manuscript; it is reproduced in *The Mediaeval Hospitals of England* by Miss Clay (p. 1).

[7] *capellani* is the regular word for those in priests' orders.

king wishes to be observed by the chaplains and brethren of the Hospital, and to be over them in the administration of the temporalities belonging to the Hospital; and that likewise, of the said goods, six brethren, lay persons, and six sisters shall be maintained who shall tend the infirm and poor of the Hospital and administer necessaries to them. The number of the said chaplains, brethren or sisters, shall not be increased until the goods of the Hospital have so increased that more can be fitly maintained, and when it is necessary for more brethren or sisters to be added to the number, then this shall only be done with the licence of the king or his heirs.[1] We should judge from the statutes of the Hospital which were made in 1246 (Vol. III, p. 1) that the three brethren in priests' orders would be the master, the cellarer, and the sacrist.

But the building of the Hospital was not completed for another year or more. On May 30, 1234, the king issued a general mandate to all those persons through whose lands the king's timber is being brought from Reading to Oxford for the work of the Hospital which the king is building there, that they make not any impediment to the passage of it.[2] We may assume that the timber was being sent by the river. On September 25 he gave an order to the keeper of Savernake forest to supply 100 oak-trees to Geoffrey, the king's almoner, 'for the building of our hospital at Oxford'; the king's

[1] 'Rex omnibus &c. salutem. Ad omnium noticiam uolumus peruenire quod nos tamquam aduocati & fundatores hospitalis nostri sancti Iohannis extra portam orientalem Oxonie pro utilitate eiusdem hospitalis & fratrum in eo conuersantium constituimus quod de bonis que contulimus eidem hospitali, pro salute anime nostre & pro animabus antecessorum & heredum [*sic*], & de bonis que processu temporis a nobis uel heredibus nostris uel ab aliis conferenda sunt, sustententur tres fratres capellani imperpetuum quorum unus de communi prouisione fratrum electus & nobis presentatus presit aliis ad ordinem sancti Augustini custodiendum, quem uolumus in eodem hospitali ab eisdem capellanis & fratribus obseruari, & in administratione temporalium ad idem hospitale pertinentium, & quod similiter inde sustententur sex fratres laici & sex sorores, qui infirmis & pauperibus eiusdem hospitalis deseruiant & necessaria administrent. Prohibemus autem ne numerus predictorum capellanorum, fratrum aut sororum per aliquem augeatur aliquo tempore antequam idem hospitale in bonis creuerit temporalibus, unde plures possint commode sustentari. Et cum necesse fuerit quod plures fratres siue sorores numero predicto addantur, tunc non nisi de licencia nostra uel heredum nostrorum fiat. Et ut hec nostra concessio & prouisio pro nobis & heredibus nostris perpetuam optineat firmitatem, presenti scripto sigillum nostrum fecimus apponi. Teste rege, apud Wintoniam, xxvi die Ianuarii; loquendum.' Patent Roll, 16 Hen. III, m. 16.

[2] *Cal. of Pat. Rolls*, p. 51.

carpenters would select the trees that are most suitable.[1] The last notice of building is on April 12, 1235, when John de Neville is commanded to supply from Shotover forest to the king's almoner four posts, four *pannas*, and the necessary *laqueos* for the building of a kitchen for the Hospital of St. John at Oxford.[2]

It is uncertain who was in charge of the Hospital at this time. We hear of a certain 'J., master of the Hospital of St. John at Oxford' in 1236, who in the month of April appoints William de Mora to be his attorney in a lawsuit about a house in Oxford;[3] and on May 27, 1237, we learn that the archdeacon of Oxford had removed 'brother William', to whom the king had temporarily committed the administration of the spiritual things of the Hospital, and had appointed Elyas to be master.[4] There is no evidence to show who 'brother William' was, but we may conjecture that he was the same as William de Mora. The action of the archdeacon at once raised the question, who had the power of visiting the Hospital and of appointing the master. In the case of most hospitals it was the custom that a visitation should be made by the bishop or an agent of his, when there was a complaint of mismanagement, and for small hospitals probably nothing more was needed than the archdeacon's visitation; but in the case of hospitals that were of royal foundation it was the rule that they were exempt from the interference of the bishop or archdeacon, and that if a visitation was necessary, the king's chancellor would be the visitor. It may be added by way of explanation that whether the bishop or the chancellor was visitor, it was not necessary that they should conduct the visitation in person; but according to law and custom they could delegate their powers to one or more of their clerks. The king in his letter to the archdeacon, dated May 27, says that he marvelled much at the interference; that there could be no question to whom the patronage of the Hospital belonged as 'we founded it for the salvation of our

[1] *Cal. of Close Rolls*, p. 522.
[2] *Ib.* p. 75.
[3] *Close Rolls*, p. 349. Perhaps he was John de Lewknor, the king's almoner, see below.
[4] *Ib.* p. 533.

ancestors and endowed it with our own goods'; and commands him to disturb no more the king's right of patronage. On the same day he writes a similar letter to the Bishop of Lincoln, and demands that the bishop should order the archdeacon to recall his presumptuous act.[1] On the next day the king issued a writ to the brethren that they should be 'intendant' to Simon de Norwico, his clerk, to whom he had appointed the charge of the temporalities of the Hospital for the present.[2] He also informed the archdeacon that should he fulminate a sentence of excommunication against the king's bailiffs, or the brethren of the Hospital, disturbing the king's right of patronage in the Hospital, Simon had been appointed the king's proctor, to make appeal against such excommunication. And another letter was sent to Elyas, that he should be content with the chaplaincy for the present and not interfere with the administration of the temporalities, because on account of an expectation of an apostolical privilege a perpetual master cannot at present be made in the Hospital.[3] If the papal privilege was obtained, we have now no record of it. It may be added that Simon de Norwico was at the same time placed in charge of the Abbey of St. James, Northampton, which was vacant.

Three days later, on May 31, the king sent a letter to the priors of Eynsham and Northampton, who had been appointed by the pope judges delegate to decide a cause in which the Hospital was concerned, and bade them stay the cognizance of the cause until the king was in those parts. For as the king is patron of the Hospital, having founded it and enriched it with his goods, the brethren cannot commence any cause about the goods of the Hospital without the king's consent or enter into any disadvantageous composition. Otherwise, the king appeals to the apostolic see and appoints W., the bearer of the letter, as his proctor to make the appeal. He adds that 'he who bears himself as prior in the said hospital is not prior and has not been presented by the king to the bishop'.[4] We do not know what the cause was about which the judges were to give

[1] *Close Rolls*, p. 533.
[2] *Cal. of Pat. Rolls*, p. 183.
[3] *Ib.* p. 183.
[4] *Ib.*

a verdict, but as it had reached the stage of being referred to judges delegate, it must have been of long standing and must have been begun by Elyas; no doubt it is to him that reference is made in the concluding words.

A week later, on June 7, the king wrote to the archdeacon of Oxford that an agreement which had been made between the brethren of the Hospital and the vicar of St. Peter's in the East was prejudicial to the king, as patron of the Hospital; and he appointed W., the bearer of the letter, to appeal against the agreement, as it had been made without consulting the patron of the Hospital.[1] No doubt the matter was about tithes due to the vicar, and had been settled by Elyas in a manner of which Simon, the king's representative, disapproved.

Not long afterwards the office of master was filled. On July 9, the king writes to the Bishop of Lincoln to admit Robert, who ministered in the king's chapel at Oxford (i. e. at Beaumont palace), to the custody of the king's hospital without the wall of Oxford, which the king has thought fit to commit to him during pleasure.[2] It is possible that the bishop made some difficulty about instituting a man who held the mastership only 'at pleasure'; for on September 2 we find that Robert, the king's chaplain at Oxford, is presented to the Bishop of Lincoln for admission to the perpetual wardenship of the hospital at Oxford;[3] and on the roll of Bishop Grosseteste for the year 1237 is the entry that Robert, chaplain, on the presentation of the king, is instituted warden of the Hospital on the resignation of Elyas, chaplain, who had previously been 'rector'; the archdeacon is to give him induction and the brethren are to obey him as their prior and master.[4] This is the only mention of the Hospital of St. John on the rolls of the bishop, and we must assume that subsequent masters were not presented to him and did not receive institution.

It will be noticed that the title of the head of the house was for a time uncertain. *Magister* was the title which ultimately prevailed, but *custos* was used indifferently during the

[1] Vol. i, p. 394. The deed is also to be found on the Patent Roll.

[2] *Cal. of Pat. Rolls*, p. 189.

[3] *Ib.* p. 195.

[4] *Grosseteste's Institutions*, p. 453 (Cant. & York Soc.).

thirteenth century and, as will be seen, is found frequently on the Patent Rolls to the very end; and the entry in the bishop's register for 1237, and the king's letter of May 31, 1237, show that at first there was a possibility that the title would be 'prior'. In two or three deeds the head of the house is styled *rector*.[1]

On November 8, 1241, Henry de Leuekenore was appointed to the custody of the Hospital, until the return of Robert the chaplain, 'who by licence of the king has gone to the north';[2] perhaps Robert died on this journey, for on April 14, 1242, Henry de Leuekenore is appointed to the custody of the Hospital, which he is to hold 'during pleasure', and a command is given to the brethren and sisters to be obedient to him.[3]

On June 27, 1238, the king granted twenty oaks to the warden of the Hospital, for rebuilding his mills which had been burnt.[4] This no doubt refers to King's Mill; for there is no indication that the Hospital had any other mill.[5] On July 12, 1241, the king's mutton 'of the time of St. Martin' which was at Woodstock was given to the *custos* of the Hospital of St. John for the use of the poor; this was probably the mutton which was salted in November 1240.[6] A gift of twelve oaks for timber is recorded on April 15, 1242, but we do not know what building was in progress then.[7] In the course of the next year the king made two gifts of timber to the Hospital; on May 17, 1243, eight oaks were given[8] to 'the Master of the hospital of St. John outside the East gate of Oxford', and on October 2, 1243, twenty oaks from the wood of Covintry were supplied[9] to John, the king's almoner, 'for the building of the hospital at Oxford'; the probability is that this latter gift was not for St. Bartholomew's, but for St. John's Hospital. Next year there must have been much building at the Hospital; for on March 4, 1244, the king commanded[10] that forty oaks should be supplied to the *custos* of the Hospital of St. John at

[1] e.g. vol. ii, p. 380.
[2] *Cal. of Pat. Rolls*, p. 266.
[3] *Ib.* p. 280.
[4] *Close Rolls*, p. 67.
[5] Wood speaks of Hospital Mill (*City of Oxford*, i. 401), but says that, if it ever existed, it was built by Magdalen College in 1486.
[6] *Close Rolls*, p. 316.
[7] *Ib.* p. 413.
[8] *Ib.* (1242–1247), p. 100.
[9] *Ib.* p. 46.
[10] *Ib.* p. 166.

Oxford 'for the works of the hospital'; five days later he also granted ten oaks to make a barn at Cornberge.[1] Perhaps this year marks the conclusion of building operations; for no timber was granted in 1245, and the ten oaks which were ordered[2] February 22, 1246, were to build a grange, possibly not at Oxford.

Meanwhile the Hospital was provided with a burying ground. We must conclude that originally both the brethren and the patients were buried in the churchyard of St. Peter's in the East; but on July 20, 1245, the king notified to the archdeacon of Oxford that, the pope having given command to the Bishop of Lincoln to provide a cemetery for the Hospital where the brethren and the patients may be buried, provided that there is no damage to the mother church, the king as patron of the Hospital appoints William the chaplain, and Roger subdeacon, brethren of the Hospital, as his representatives, to secure the indemnity of the mother church.[3] A deed must have been drawn up by which the Hospital granted compensation to the rector of St. Peter's in the East for the churchyard which they were allowed to have; but it is not to be found among the muniments of the Hospital. In a papal grant of privileges of October 6, 1245 (Vol. III, p. 7), there is mention of the cemetery of the Hospital and of the *capellas*, one chapel no doubt being for the brethren and the other for the patients. Probably both of these are to be distinguished from 'The Charnel', where we know mass was said.[4] Subsequently there were two cemeteries as well as two chapels; for in the last decade of the thirteenth century a space of ground opposite

[1] *Close Rolls*, p. 168. Is Tornberge (? Thornborough) the right reading?

[2] *Ib.* p. 396.

[3] *Calendar of Patent Rolls* (1232–1247), p. 457, where *subdean* is given as the rendering of *subdiaconum*. As the original is somewhat obscure it is best to give it in full:—'Rex archidiacono Oxon' uel eius officiali salutem. Cum dominus Papa ad instanciam nostram dederit in mandatis Lincolniensi episcopo ut hospitali Oxonie cimiterium prouideret et sepulturam fratrum eiusdem hospitalis et pauperum in eodem hospitali decedentium, prouisa tamen indempnitate matricis ecclesie, et nostra intersit ut patroni eiusdem hospitalis de prouisione facienda de indempnitate ecclesie predicte constituimus ad hoc loco nostro Willelmum capellanum et Rogerum subdiaconum eiusdem hospitalis.' The translation is 'Since the Pope &c., and since it concerns us, as patrons of the hospital, to make provision for the indemnity of the church, we appoint &c.'

[4] Vol. ii, p. 442.

the Hospital was acquired on the south side of the road, where the Bishop of Lincoln gave permission that a cemetery should be consecrated for the patients who died in the Hospital.[1] Wood tells us that many bones were dug up in 1641 between the Physick Garden and East Bridge.[2] On March 23, 1246, the pope wrote to the abbot and the archdeacon of Westminster, who apparently were the *conservatores* of the Hospital, repeating the privileges that he had granted during the previous year; and if we may believe the clause of dating at the end of statutes of the Hospital,[3] it was on the same date that they were issued or at least confirmed; but the clause has so many errors that it cannot have been on the original statutes but must be the invention of the transcriber; it is probable that the original merely contained the statement that the statutes were confirmed by the pope at the request of the king. We do not know by whom they were drawn up; had they been made by the pope there would have been some reference to the abbot and archdeacon of Westminster, who were the papal *conservatores* of the Hospital, and the clause of malediction on those who broke the statutes would have contained the names of St. Peter and St. Paul as well as St. Mary. Probably they were drawn up by some clerk of the king. They profess to be additions to some older statutes, of which we have no knowledge. The brethren were to be clothed alike in dark woollen material, 'chamlet or burnet'; in fine weather they would wear a *pallium* or *mantellum*, i. e. a gown, with a double cross on the left side below the shoulder; in wet weather a *cappa* was worn, which would slip over the head, the cross in this case being in the middle in front. A chapter of the house was to be held not daily but weekly. The canonical hours were to be said, but in a somewhat unusual way; for they began matins at dawn not at midnight, and before the office of the day the matins of Our Lady was said; immediately afterwards they had prime, terce, mass, sext, and none, as it appears; evensong and compline are not mentioned, but were probably

[1] Vol. i, pp. 39–43.
[2] Wood's *City of Oxford*, ii. 522.
[3] Vol. iii, p. 6.

said together at night, so that the whole of the services for the day were accumulated in two groups.[1] The brethren and sisters were to wait upon the infirm, and were not to be more in number than was necessary for this work. It was expected that some of the sisters[2] would have private servants, but as all the brethren and sisters, as it seems, were to be bound by the law of poverty, we cannot understand how any would have had their own servants unless they had obtained a corrody in which this privilege was stipulated. None were to be admitted as patients who suffered from incurable diseases such as leprosy, palsy, dropsy, or insanity.

Some three months later, June 5, 1246, the king granted to the *custos* of the hospital outside East Gate the spring of water in the town ditch, known as Crowell, to convey it by an aqueduct to the Hospital; the sheriff was to allow no one to hinder this.[3] Crowell was at the north-east corner of the town wall, at the top of Long Wall Street. It will be noticed in Appendix III that the latrines of the infirmary of the Hospital were flushed by a small stream which flowed from west to east, and in all probability it is the aqueduct which the brethren were permitted to make from Crowell.

During the years 1242 to 1258 there is difficulty in tracing the succession of the masters of the Hospital; and as the Patent Rolls give little help and the Close Rolls are still unprinted, we must fall back on the deeds of the Hospital, of which some appear in this Cartulary and the rest have been calendared by Dr. Macray. Although, as we have seen, Henry de Lewknor was appointed warden on April 14, 1242, yet we find that John de Lewknor, the king's almoner, was acting as warden on May 31, 1242. In three deeds he is mentioned as *custos* or *rector*, but only one of them is dated, wherein he is described as 'warden of the Hospital under the king'.[4] He was in office the next year; for on August 20, 1243, 'brother John, the almoner' is bidden provide William de Berking, a blind priest, with food and clothing for life in

[1] Vol. iii, p. 5.

[2] Vol. iii, p. 6. They are called *sorores conuerse*, 'lay sisters', but this does not imply that there were sisters of any other kind.

[3] *Close Rolls* (1242–1247), p. 438.

[4] See *Muniments of Magdalen College*, by Dr. Macray, p. 1.

'the hospital at Oxford'.[1] It is true there was another royal hospital at Oxford, St. Bartholomew's, but as it was a leper hospital, it cannot be meant here. The fact is that until about 1263 there was a dual headship of the Hospital; on the one hand the king's almoner or chancellor had the supreme control and could grant leases and make agreements about property, styling himself *custos*, though he did not reside on the spot; on the other hand the chief of the brethren at Oxford, who saw that the rule of the house was observed and the accounts duly kept, was also called *custos* and sometimes *magister*, and had business powers concurrent with the king's representative.

Of Henry de Leuekenore or Lewknor we have a deed as late as May 3, 1246,[2] in which he describes himself as 'Master of the Hospital of St. John and parson of Thorentone'; another undated deed in which he is styled 'formerly rector of Thorentone, Warden of the Hospital of St. John' must be later still. He must have died in 1246 or early in 1247, for we have a deed issued by 'Adam the Chaplain, warden of the Hospital', the date of which cannot be later than Michaelmas 1247.[3] We might have expected that the registers of the Bishop of Lincoln would show when Henry de Lewknor resigned the rectory of Thornton, but though the register of Bishop Hugh Wells mentions that he was instituted rector of Thornton, Bucks., in June 1217,[4] the register of Bishop Grosseteste which runs from 1235 to 1254 has no reference to Thornton. The explanation of this may be that as Henry de Lewknor in 1217 appointed a vicar under him to reside at Thornton, the vicarage and rectory would be consolidated when Henry resigned the rectory, and the bishop's clerks forgot to enter the fact that the vicar became the rector.

Adam the chaplain, who was master before Michaelmas 1247, held the office May 4, 1248, on which day he issued a deed which still survives.[5] Meanwhile John the almoner had been succeeded as head warden by Roger the king's

[1] *Close Rolls* (1242–1247), p. 39.
[2] Thornborough, deed 27.
[3] See vol. i, p. 89.
[4] *Register of Hugo Wells*, i. 36 (Cant. and York Soc.). In Lipscombe's *History of Bucks* the date is wrongly given.
[5] 'Hokeday, 22 Hen. fil. John.' Thornborough, deed 82.

almoner. In this Cartulary we have a deed issued by 'Roger the king's almoner' on June 21, 1246,[1] and another by 'Roger de Cramfeld, the king's almoner', on January 1, 1253.[2] There can be no doubt that these were issued by one man, for Roger the king's almoner, who is frequently mentioned in the Patent Rolls, is given the full name 'Roger de Cramfeld' in an entry of August 16, 1242.[3] On March 28, 1253, he was succeeded by 'Master William de Kilkenni, king's clerk', archdeacon of Coventry, and chancellor or at least keeper of the seal, who on that day was appointed to the custody of St. John's Hospital, a writ being issued to the brethren that they should be obedient to him.[4] He was also appointed master of Ospring Hospital; and that he succeeded to these offices on the death of Roger de Cramfeld is made probable by an entry on the Patent Roll, dated April 26, 1253, 'that Master William de Kilkenny, having undertaken the keeping of the king's hospitals, which Roger, sometime the king's almoner, had from the king, shall be quit of all account and reckoning for the time that he shall hold the said keeping'. None of the deeds of the Hospital which survive make any mention of him as *custos*. On January 1, 1255, he resigned the office of chancellor and was followed by Henry de Wengham, who also succeeded to the office of head warden of the Hospital; for a deed of the Hospital, which we can date by the witnesses to be between January 1, 1255, and November 3, 1258, is attested by 'Henry de Wengham, chancellor of the king and warden of the Hospital of St. John'.[5]

As under warden or acting warden of the Hospital, Adam was followed by a certain Thomas of whom we have two deeds in this Cartulary, one being of the date December 7, 1253, and the other a few months earlier.[6] Other deeds of his are in existence, dated November 30, 1252, and April 28, 1254.[7] Between Michaelmas 1255 and Michaelmas 1256 the master was named Henry,[8] whom we may safely identify with Henry

[1] See vol. ii, p. 141.
[2] See vol. ii, p. 149.
[3] Patent, 26 Hen. III, m. 10.
[4] See the Calendar of the Patent Roll of 37 Hen. III.
[5] Shipton-on-Cherwell, deed B. 3.
[6] Vol. i, p. 396 and p. 335.
[7] See Macray, *Muniments of Magdalen College*, p. 2.
[8] See vol. i, p. 281.

de Wylebi who is named as master in deeds of 1258 and the next few years.[1] On November 2, 1263, as we read in the Patent Roll, 'Henry de Wyleby, master of the Hospital of St. John, received the custody of the same place, as other wardens have been accustomed to have', and the brethren and tenants were commanded to be obedient to him. It will be noticed that Henry is described as already in the possession of the mastership, and what was now given to him was the supreme wardenship which had hitherto been held by the king's almoners or chancellors.

A final concord of November 1264 informs us that the master on that date was named Walter.[2] He is to be identified with Walter de Wyleby or Wilebi, who is mentioned as master in deeds of the Hospital between 1270 and 1280.[3] An entry on the Patent Roll for June 19, 1268, that 'at the instance of Walter de Nevill, Master of the Hospital of St. John without the East gate of Oxford, exemption from being placed on assizes was granted to John de Pontefracto', shows that his full name was Walter de Nevill from Wyleby (i.e. Willoughby in Warwickshire, where the Hospital had land). For a while he was in control of the Hospital of St. Bartholomew as well; for we read in the Patent Roll for November 11, 1265, that the master of the Hospital of St. John at Oxford was commanded to have the care of the Hospital of St. Bartholomew, as Henry his predecessor had, until the king should come to those parts. We have deeds which mention this master after Michaelmas 1278,[4] and an entry on the Close Roll shows that he was master of the Hospital as late as April 19, 1281.[5]

It may be accidental, but it is worth notice, that the king's almoners and chancellors are not styled 'masters' of the Hospital, but 'wardens' (*custodes*). This may be because they could not satisfy the conditions for the mastership laid down in the rule of the house, that the master should be in priest's orders and one of the brethren of the house. But we find

[1] See Macray, p. 2.
[2] North Marston, deed 27.
[3] See *Cartulary of St. Frideswide's*, vol. i, p. 337 (O.H.S.).
[4] See vol. i, p. 52.
[5] Close Roll, 9 Ed. I, m. 7 *d*.

the title *custos* was also used by the resident master; thus Adam the chaplain in one deed describes himself as *custos*, in another as *magister*.[1]

From the year 1281 the succession of the masters is certain. On December 24, 1281, the king appointed Nicholas de Shireveleye, chaplain, 'to the custody of the Hospital of St. John at Oxford, of which he is a brother, founded by King Henry III for the maintenance of the poor'; he is to hold the post for life.[2] The king had shown an interest in him three years earlier; for on January 17, 1278, he wrote to the Bishop of Worcester asking him to confer the orders of deacon and priest upon brother Nicholas de Schreveleck, brother of the Hospital of St. John without the East gate of Oxford, although the same brother is not of the bishop's diocese but because the same Hospital is the king's free chapel where, as in the other free chapels of the king throughout the kingdom, the diocesan ought to exercise no jurisdiction.[3] The name is spelt Nicholas de Schriveley in this Cartulary.[4] In Twyne's time there was in the town archives a roll *de iuratis et assisis apud Oxon' coram Salomone de Roff' 13 Ed. I*, on which was a plea of Robert, prior of St. Frideswide's, *versus Nicholaum magistrum hospitalis sancti Iohannis Oxon'*; Twyne gives no details except *negat Nicholaus se esse magistrum, immo custodem tantum ad voluntatem regis*. Much credence should not be given to such replies in legal proceedings; they are often frivolous and untrue, and the Patent Roll tells us that Nicholas was appointed master for life, not *ad voluntatem*; furthermore, in the Cartulary he styles himself *magister* and *custos* indifferently. But the record is useful as confirming the point already indicated, that one who held the charge of the Hospital temporarily should be called *custos* not *magister*.[5] On December 5, 1295, he was superseded by Robert de Scardeburgh, king's clerk, who was appointed to the custody of the Hospital, during the king's pleasure, by reason of its having

[1] Vol. i, pp. 89 and 132.
[2] Patent Roll, 10 Ed. I, m. 20.
[3] *The Register of Bishop Giffard*, p. 96 (Worcestershire Hist. Soc.).
[4] Vol. i, p. 137.
[5] Twyne MSS. xxiv. 485.

fallen into debt;[1] but on April 1, 1301, Nicholas was reappointed to his office, during pleasure.[2] He was holding the office in January 1316;[3] and in the same month was associated with the Chancellor of the University to make an inquiry into the state of the Hospital of St. Bartholomew;[4] he must have died towards the end of the year, as on November 18, 1316, the king accepted the appointment of William de Ottington, chaplain, to the custody for life of the Hospital of St. John;[5] the appointment had been made by Queen Margaret, widow of Edward I, who held the proceeds of the town of Oxford as part of her dowry. Under this master the Hospital was reported to be ill-governed, and on October 2, 1331, two of the king's clerks, Robert de Stretford and Richard de Chaddesleye, were ordered[6] to make a visitation of the Hospital, which was reported 'to be much decayed for want of good rule'. In a few weeks the master was dead, and on January 28, 1332, Geoffrey Halyweye of Wolsincote, one of the brethren, was appointed to the custody of the Hospital during the king's pleasure,[7] the Hospital being in the king's hands 'by reason of the death of William de Otyndon'. On January 11, 1335, Adam de Lodebroc, one of the brethren, was appointed to the custody of the Hospital, during the king's pleasure.[8] On August 26 in the same year the king commanded Robert de Stratford, archdeacon of Canterbury, John de sancto Paulo, and mag. Richard de Hunsyngore, who was the official of the archdeacon of Oxford, to make a visitation of the Hospital, 'which is reported to be greatly decayed by misrule, some of the brothers, sisters, and servants being disobedient, wasting the goods of the Hospital, quarrelling among themselves, and leading dissolute lives'.[9] We have no details of the visitation, but it appears that Adam, the new master, showed zeal for good rule; for on March 12, 1337, the king granted to Adam de Lodebrok, warden of the Hospital, that in consideration of his industry in the ordering its affairs, he shall hold for life the custody of it, which hitherto he had

[1] Patent Roll, 24 Ed. I, m. 24.
[2] *Ib.* 29 Ed. I, m. 19.
[3] Vol. i, p. 374.
[4] *Collectanea*, iii. 115 (O.H.S.).
[5] Pat. 10 Ed. II, m. 8.
[6] *Ib.* 5 Ed. III, m. 20.
[7] *Ib* 6 Ed. III, m. 30.
[8] *Ib.* 8 Ed. III, m. 5.
[9] *Ib.* 9 Ed. III, m. 23.

only held at the king's pleasure.[1] He was alive on July 10, 1350, when the king issued a commission to hear and settle his complaint that he had been assaulted and robbed by the vicar of Headington,[2] and on October 12 of that year he issued a charter which still survives.[3] Two years later, on October 24, 1352, John de Iddebury, a brother of the Hospital, was appointed to its custody, during the king's pleasure, and the sheriff was commanded to give him induction.[4] On August 12, 1361, Robert de Tewe, priest, having been elected by the brothers and sisters of the Hospital to be a brother and master and warden of the Hospital, which was void by the death of John de Iddebury, the king granted that he should hold the wardenship according to the force and effect of the election.[5] On the death of Robert de Tewe, the king on May 28, 1384, confirmed the election of Adam de Merston, and issued a writ to the brethren and sisters to be obedient to him.[6] Three years later, May 18, 1387, the king confirmed the election of a second John Iddebury, one of the brethren, to be warden in the room of Adam de Merston, deceased, and a writ was issued to the brethren and tenants in the usual form.[7] On December 10, 1392, the king granted that Richard Tewe should hold the wardenship of the Hospital, 'to which he has been elected by the brethren of the house on the death of John Iddebury'; the customary writ of obedience was issued 'to the brethren' of the Hospital;[8] and it is noticeable that there is no mention of 'sisters' either in the writ or in the description of the electors. The next master was William Lodebrok, to whom the king granted on August 28, 1434, that he might hold the mastership to which he had been elected by his fellow brethren on the death of Richard Tewe.[9] He and the next two masters held office but a short time; for on January 28, 1436, Thomas Oxenford, one of the brethren, received the grant of the mastership, having been elected by the brethren on the death of William Lodebrok;[10] and on

1 Pat. 11 Ed. III, m. 23.
2 *Ib.* 24 Ed. III, m. 21.
3 Vol. i, p. 333.
4 Pat. 26 Ed. III, m. 22.
5 *Ib.* 35 Ed. III, m. 7.
6 *Ib.* 7 Ric. II, m. 6.
7 *Ib.* 10 Ric. II, m. 9.
8 *Ib.* 16 Ric. II, m. 16.
9 *Ib.* 12 Hen. VI, m. 12.
10 *Ib.* 14 Hen. VI, m. 15.

March 9, 1438, the king accepted the election of brother Hugh Burton as warden of the Hospital of St. John, in the place of Thomas Oxinford, deceased, and granted to him the said wardenship.[1] The last master was 'brother Richard Vyse', to whom the king granted the wardenship on May 18, 1442, void by the resignation of Hugh Burton.[2]

In these entries the following points may be noticed: The head of the house is entitled indifferently *magister* or *custos* to the very end. It is probable that in every case he was elected by the brethren; for the entry about Hugh Burton in 1438 shows that the statement that a man had received the wardenship by the grant of the king need not imply that there was no election as well. The 'grant' by the king takes the place of 'institution' by a bishop. The 'induction' in the case of the first master was given by the archdeacon, but in all subsequent cases, as far as we know, by the sheriff. It is probable that the brethren could not elect one from outside their number, for we are told that when they wished to elect Robert de Tewe in 1361, before he was elected master they took the step of electing him a brother. It has been indicated that there is no mention of sisters in the Hospital after the year 1384, when they are mentioned in the king's writ; and as we hear nothing of sisters at the time of the dissolution of the Hospital and the notice of the election in 1392 is pointedly silent about them, we may assume that they came to an end between 1384 and 1392. This is confirmed by the record[3] of a court held at Oxford on September 26, 1390, under the Statute of Labourers, at which the master of the Hospital was accused of paying excessive wages to thirteen servants. The last of them, by name Alice Deye and Alice Mey, stated 'quod seruiunt infirmis in dicto hospitali existentibus et multum circa eos uigilant et laborant'. It is not impossible that servants were hired to help the sisters in their nursing, but the more probable conclusion is that there were no sisters. Some of the masters were appointed for life and some

[1] Pat. 16 Hen. VI, m. 1.

[2] *Ib.* 20 Hen. VI, m. 33.

[3] Univ. Archives, Pix Y. no. 15. It is hoped that the record will be soon printed. The names of the servants in 1390 but rarely correspond to those in 1380, given in *Oxf. City Documents*, p. 40 (O.H.S.).

'during pleasure'; it seems that from 1300 to 1352 all the masters were in the first instance appointed 'during pleasure', and that from 1361 to 1442 they were appointed for life; but many of the entries are silent on the matter.

The Hospital of St. John was used by the king, like other monastic houses, as a place where his servants could be provided for, when they were past work. The following entries are taken from the Calendar of Close Rolls: On March 8, 1293, the king sends to the Hospital his servant Nicholas le Ferur, now incapable of work, requesting that he be provided with the necessaries of life as long as he lives; on June 6, 1306, the master of the Hospital is commanded to admit Roger de Braithewell, who has been maimed in the king's service in Gascony, and to provide him with the necessaries of life as long as he lives; on November 26, 1307, the king commands the Hospital to admit Geoffrey de Castre, king's chaplain, whom the king is bound to provide with sustenance in return for his service, as he has refused a benefice involving a cure of souls, and to find him and a clerk serving him fitting sustenance in food, drink, robes, shoe-leather, wood, litter and other necessaries for the term of his life, and to find him a fitting chamber for his residence within the enclosure of the Hospital, as previously commanded by letters under the king's privy seal, to which they have paid no attention; on August 12, 1314, the master of the Hospital is ordered to provide maintenance for John de Sheperton, who has been a servant of the king and is now unable to labour for his living; on January 14, 1342, the king issues to the Hospital a mandate to admit a servant of the king, William de Staveleye or Staneleye, cook, and to provide for him as long as he lives, as he has long served the king and is now infirm; on April 10, 1342, the order is repeated, the name now being given as William le Keu (= cook) of Staneleye or Staveleye; on February 18, 1357, the king sends John de Helmeswell to the Hospital to receive there for his life such maintenance as William Kyngesman, deceased, had there at the king's request. This last entry shows that the Hospital was not expected to provide for an unlimited number of the king's servants, and that a new nomination was not made until there was a vacancy by death.

The Hospital was also occasionally used in the same way for the reception of women. Thus we find on the Close Roll of Henry III that on September 29, 1235, he commanded the brethren of the Hospital to admit Maud, daughter of Geoffrey le Chamberleyn, whom he is sending them, to be one of their sisters; and on May 1, 1236, he sends them a similar order to admit Milisant, widow of Symon le Establer, to whom he has granted that she should be one of the sisters at the Hospital. It may be noticed that these women are to occupy a position different from that of the men whom the king sent to the Hospital; the men were to reside there as guests, but the women were to become sisters, incurring on the one hand the duty of keeping the monastic rule and of helping with the nursing of the sick, on the other the privilege of electing the master and having a voice in the management of the house. In 1341 a woman named Alice fitz-Ralph obtained a writ from the king that she should receive her maintenance for life at the Hospital. Our information is derived from the Patent Roll of 15 Edward III, where we read that Alice on payment of twenty shillings obtained from the king that her complaint should be tried by a commission. She seems to have had difficulty in framing her complaint correctly, and it was first drawn up on May 1, and amended on May 8 and July 3. Her statement was that Adam, master of the Hospital of St. John, Henry de Stodeleye, John le Peyntor, John Peggy, Richard Sclwode, John Alston, John Norton, and others assaulted her in a suburb of Oxford, imprisoned her, afterwards veiled her face, brought her by night so veiled and imprisoned to a street there, threw her into a filthy place, took from her a writ under the privy seal addressed to the master of the Hospital that she should have her sustenance in the Hospital for life at the king's request, took her goods at Oxford and at Shaldeswell, and carried them away. We gather from this that she was a native of Shaldeswell (i. e. Shelswell), and as the residents of Oxford who took part in the assault are known to have been men of high position and the leading men of the town, we may guess that they represented public opinion and that the general feeling was that Alice was unfit to be admitted to the Hospital. We also notice that the writ she received was under the privy seal, which explains why the Close Rolls, of which there are calendars from 1272 for the next hundred years, give none of the writs which nominated women to be received in the Hospital. We do not know what was the result of the inquiry.

Another complaint against the Hospital of St. John occurs on the Patent Roll of 41 Edward III, where we read that on July 6, 1367, the king issued a commission to find by inquisition the names of those who with Robert de Tewe, master of the Hospital of St. John at Oxford, John de Ichendenne, brother of the Hospital, William Hamond and William Cook, imprisoned and ill-treated John Glovere, servant of Ingelram de Coucy, earl of Bedford, at Oxford, took £20 in money which the earl had delivered to him for expediting his business, and compelled him, before he could leave prison, to be condemned in £100 to the said William and William before the chancellor of the University of Oxford, and to be bound to them in another £100 before the mayor of Oxford and the clerk of the recognizances at Oxford; whereby the earl's business remained undone. William Hamond and William Cook were apparently lay servants of the Hospital and are mentioned frequently in these volumes,[1] while John de Ichenden was a brother who was at the head of the business of the house.[2] Reading between the lines we conclude that John Glovere had at some time incurred a debt to William Hamond and William Cook, and that when he journeyed to Oxford he put himself within the power of his creditors, and was taken by them into the chancellor's court and there condemned to pay. If this is so, the proceeding was lawful, though doubtless annoying to the Earl of Bedford.

On more than one occasion the king found it necessary to insist that the Hospital was exempt from episcopal visitation. Pope Innocent III in 1245 forbade any diocesan bishop or

[1] See vol. i, p. 163.

[2] See vol. iii, p. 141.

archdeacon to exact 'procurations' from the Hospital by reason of paying a visitation;[1] but we have seen that as early as 1237 the king had claimed that the archdeacon had no power to make a visitation, and on November 8, 1304, Edward I wrote to the Bishop of Lincoln 'that[2] he permit the Hospital of St. John at Oxford to be quit of payments, procurations, and other exactions of the ordinary, and to release to the Master and brethren of the Hospital any distress that he may have levied in this behalf, as the Hospital, which was founded of the alms of the king's progenitors, has been wholly exempt from all jurisdiction of the ordinary and from all such payments from the time of its foundation, so that no one but the king and his chancellor ought to visit or intermeddle with it'. Again, on April 4, 1320, when the archbishop was visiting the diocese of Lincoln as metropolitan, Edward II wrote[3] to him in almost identical terms, and stated that a letter to the same effect had been sent to the Bishop of Lincoln on November 8, 1304. A third instance is supplied in this Cartulary,[4] King Richard II writing on September 5, 1397, to the Bishop of Lincoln, forbidding a visitation of the Hospital which he proposed to make. It is likely enough that similar letters were sent on other occasions. Whenever the bishop planned to visit a monastic house, a notice was sent giving warning of the day, and whenever the Hospital of St. John received such a notice, they would appeal to the king's chancellor, who would send a letter claiming exemption for the Hospital.

It was not uncommon that when there was quarrelling in a monastery those that were to blame were sent to reside in another monastery. Accordingly in the reigns of Edward II and III, as we learn from their Close Rolls, some of the brethren of the Hospital of Ospring were sent to the Hospital of St. John. On May 16, 1314, Nicholas de Staple, one of the brethren of Ospring Hospital, who quarrelled with the master, was commanded to transfer himself to the Hospital

[1] Vol. iii, p. 7.
[2] *Cal. of Close Rolls* (1302–1307), p. 225.
[3] *Ib.* (1318–1323), p. 226.
[4] Vol. ii, p. 411.

of St. John, where he was to be provided with the necessaries of life, as one of the brethren, until further orders. On March 23, 1327, Nicholas de Staple, who in the meanwhile must have returned to Ospring and had been elected master, was sent to the Hospital of St. John to be admitted as one of the 'chaplain brethren', in the place of brother William de Dewesburi, who is to be sent from Oxford to be admitted at Ospring. On March 26, 1332, Thomas Urre, one of the brethren of Ospring, is sent to the Hospital of St. John, to be there provided with the necessaries of life at the expense of the house at Ospring; and on October 10, 1334, Nicholas de Staple is once more sent back to Ospring, where he is to live as one of the brethren.

In the rolls of Edward III we find many references to the poverty of the Hospital and to exemption from taxation. The charters of liberties granted in 1246 and 1266 released the Hospital from certain payments of fees, such as the sheriff's aid, and from fines which fell on a district, such as *murdrum*, which fell on the hundred, or a fine which fell on the whole county; but no exemption from tallage or other tax was granted.[1] On October 4, 1237, the Hospital was given exemption from a thirtieth that was then being collected,[2] and it was also exempt when the taxation of Pope Nicholas was made in 1291 on all the ecclesiastical revenue of the country. In 1278, when a tallage of a tenth and a fifteenth was granted to Edward I and all the religious houses in Oxford paid a tenth on their rents, the Hospital of St. John paid £11 8*s.* 8*d.* on tenements within the town and 16*s.* on tenements in Northgate Hundred,[3] so that its rental from Oxford at that time must have been £122. On August 30, 1327, Edward III issued a writ to the mayor of Oxford 'quod Prior et fratres hospitalis sancti Iohannis extra portam orientalem Oxonie et homines sui apud Oxoniam liberi et quieti esse debeant de omnibus tallagiis et contribucionibus cum

[1] Vol. ii, pp. 395, 399.

[2] *Close Rolls* (1234–1237), p. 569.

[3] Twyne MSS. xxiii, pp. 222, 440. The roll of taxation was seen by him in the Town Archives, but it has now perished. In Dowell's *History of Taxation* this tallage is described as a fifteenth, but Twyne's extract shows that it was a tenth as well.

communitate ville predicte prestandis'. This writ is not on the Close Rolls, but the original was seen by Twyne in the Archives of the Town, and his copy (Twyne MSS. xxiii, 28) may be trusted. On December 16, 1332, when a tenth and a fifteenth were being levied in Oxfordshire, the collectors were bidden take nothing from the Hospital of St. John without the East gate of Oxford, founded by Henry III of his alms, 'as it is so slenderly endowed that its goods now hardly suffice for the maintenance of the master and brethren and of the weak and infirm therein, and of other almsgiving to be made according to the ordinance of the said king, and if it be charged with the aids granted to the king by the community of the realm, it will be necessary for the master and brethren to diminish the said alms'.[1] Two years later, December 15, 1334, another order was given to the collectors in the same words.[2] On March 14, 1336, the Hospital received a new grant from the king, that it should be exempt from all aids granted to the king whether by laity or clergy, should it be proved that it would be necessary to restrict the chantries and almsgiving of the Hospital, if it was forced to contribute to the tax.[3] On December 12, 1338, the takers and purveyors of wool were commanded to take none from the Hospital of St. John, as it was so slenderly endowed that it would be necessary to reduce its alms, if it was charged with the aids granted by the community of the realm;[4] and on the same day a similar letter was sent to those who were collecting the triennial tenth and fifteenth.[5] A few months later, June 6, 1339, those who were arraying men at arms in Warwickshire, in which county the Hospital had land, were bidden lay no charges upon the Hospital, the same reason being assigned as before,[6] except that there is mention of chantries as well as alms that would suffer if the Hospital was impoverished, thus repeating the language of the charter of 1336. On July 18,

[1] *Cal. of Close Rolls* (1330-1333), p. 513.

[2] *Cal. of Close Rolls* (1333-1337), p. 285.

[3] Vol. ii, p. 406. It is also on the Charter Roll of 10 Ed. III (*Cal. of Charter Rolls*, iv, p. 355).

[4] *Cal. of Charter Rolls* (1337-1339), p. 577.

[5] *Ib.* p. 581.

[6] *Cal. of Close Rolls* (1339-1341), p. 223.

1340, those who were assessing the subsidy of the 'ninth', and those who were collecting, were commanded to take nothing from the three hospitals of *Maison Dieu* at Dover, Ospring, and St. John's at Oxford, in each case the reason being that the alms of the hospitals would be diminished, if they contributed to the tax.[1] A year later, July 12, 1341, the assessors and collectors of wools in the counties of Warwick and Oxfordshire were bidden levy none from the Master and brethren of the Hospital of St. John, 'as they have shown the king that although the Hospital was founded by Henry III for all the poor infirm resorting thither, to remain there until they are healed and to find divers chantries and alms', it is so slenderly endowed that it would be necessary to diminish the alms, if contribution was made to the aids granted to the king.[2] On December 15, 1341, the king wrote to those who were collecting wool in the counties of Oxfordshire, Warwickshire, and Buckinghamshire that they should supersede until a fortnight after St. Hilary's day the exaction they have made upon the Hospital of St. John, so that after deliberation with the council the king may cause what is reasonable to be done, as the Hospital was founded by Henry III for the maintenance of the Master, brethren, and sisters and of the weak and infirm poor, and for maintaining chantries, alms, and other works of piety for the souls of that king and his heirs and of all the faithful departed, and if the Hospital be charged with the aids granted by the clergy on the community of the realm it will behove the Master and brethren to diminish their alms, on which ground the king has granted that the Hospital should be for ever quit of all aids and tallages;[3] this last clause refers to the royal grant of 1336. The decision of the king and council seems to have been that on this occasion the Hospital ought to be exempt; for on May 22, 1342, a mandate of the king and council was sent to the collectors of wool in the same three counties to collect no wool from the Hospital of St. John, otherwise it would be necessary for the Hospital to reduce its alms, 'and they are

[1] *Cal. of Close Rolls* (1339–1341), p. 499. [2] *Ib.* (1341–1343), p. 187.
[3] *Ib.*, p. 355.

discharged of all contributions and taxations as has been testified before the king and his council by John, archbishop of Canterbury, William de Shareshull and other lieges worthy of confidence'.[1] The last clause seems to mean that it was testified that under the present circumstances the Hospital was discharged from all contributions. Perhaps this testimony was not considered adequate, for on October 26 John de Alveton and William Louches were instructed to make an inquisition about the alleged poverty of the Hospital and see whether the burdens incumbent upon it were such that it was unable to contribute its share of the wool which had been voted to the king.[2] On December 15, 1342, the king sent a mandate to the treasurer and barons of the exchequer to postpone until next Easter the demand for wool made upon the Hospital of St. John, as the king has granted by charter that if such payment would make it necessary to diminish the alms of the Hospital, it is to be exempt.[3] Finally, on May 23, 1343, the king ordered the treasurer and barons of the exchequer to supersede their demand upon the brethren and sisters of the Hospital for the tenth, fifteenth, ninth, wool and other aids,[4] as the king has granted by charter that they and their successors should be quit of all manner of aids, contributions, and tallages. As far as the Calendar of Close Rolls reaches, i. e. to 1381, there is no other reference to any exemption of the Hospital; but Twyne saw two other writs among those that were preserved in the Town Archives; of these the former[5] is described as of the seventeenth year of the reign (i. e. 1343) and was 'pro exemptione hospitalis a solvenda taxacione lane atque eciam decime aut decime quinte sive alterius cuiuscumque quote, etiamsi summus pontifex decimam seu quamcumque aliam quotam clero Anglie imposuerit et eam aut aliquam partem eiusdem domino regi concesserit'. Twyne does not say to whom the writ was issued, but there can be no doubt that it is distinct from the writ issued to the exchequer on May 23 of

[1] *Cal. of Close Rolls* (1341–1343), p. 433.

[2] Vol. ii, p. 439. It is also entered on the Patent Roll of 16 Ed. III.

[3] *Cal. of Close Rolls* (1341–1343), p. 668.

[4] *Ib.* (1343–1346), p. 67.

[5] Twyne MSS. xxiii, 218.

the same year. The second writ seen by Twyne[1] was of the eighteenth year (i. e. 1344), and was addressed 'ad Priorem sancte Frideswide, collectorem lanarum, et socios suos ut supersedeat a colligenda lana a fratribus et sororibus hospitalis sancti Iohannis extra portam orientalem racione temporalium suorum in villa Oxonie'. That the prior of St. Frideswide's was a collector of wool we know from a writ of March, 1342, which orders that he should be distrained for delay in collecting the wool.[2] As the king was granted no wool after the year 1341, it appears that the prior of St. Frideswide's must have been collecting his arrears in 1344.

We may insert here two other references to the Hospital of St. John which were copied by Twyne from records which have now perished. The first[3] was a writ:—

> 'Rex vicecomiti Oxon' salutem. Questus est nobis magister hospitalis sancti Iohannis extra portam orientalem Oxonie quod magister Henricus de Seton, custos domus scolarium aule de Balliolo Oxonie, Thomas de Waldeby et Ricardus de Ratford iniuste et sine iudicio disseisiuerunt eum de libero tenemento suo in Oxonia post primam &c. Teste me ipso apud Westmonasterium, XXVIII die Februarii, anno regni nostri XVII^mo^.'

Both Edward I and Edward II were at Westminster on February 28 in the seventeenth year of their reigns, but it is generally assumed that this writ is of February 28, 1324; it seems that by the middle of the next year Richard de Ratford or Retford had ceased to be a member of Balliol.[4] The second was a list of presentments at a view of frankpledge,[5] of which the date is not given, but internal evidence shows that it must be later than 1350: 'magister sancti Iohannis extra portam orientalem Oxonie acrochiavit sibi quandam insulam extra portam orientalem, de antiquo spectantem ad dominum regem et burgenses suos Oxonie.' The presentments are apparently for the north-east ward. If the burgesses of Oxford ever owned an island on the north side of

[1] Twyne MSS. xxiii, 158.

[2] *Cal. of Close Rolls* (1341–1343), p. 507.

[3] Twyne MSS. xxiii, 405.

[4] *Balliol Oxford Deeds* (O.H.S.), p. 285.

[5] Twyne MSS. xxiii, 444.

the bridge, it can only have been as waste land; the waste of the manor belonged to the burgesses as part of the fee-farm of the town. But it is wise to remember that in presentments of this kind reckless accusations were made. Possibly it is merely a repetition of an accusation which was raised and settled a hundred years earlier at the eyre of 1285, when it was stated that 'a certain Henry, Master of the Hospital of St. John, had appropriated, sixteen years before, an island surrounded by the water of Charwell, one pole in extent, worth *6d.* a year; which plot used to pertain to the borough of Oxford'. Whereupon the master appeared in court and agreed to pay to the king an annual rent of sixpence for the island.[1]

A third deed which Twyne has preserved[2] is called by him *arbitramentum sive laudum.* It is the settlement of a dispute between Merton College and the Hospital of St. John in these words:—

'Scilicet quod quidam Brede inter Yrismen poole et aquam de Charwell fiat de novo bene et sufficienter emendat' et reparat' secundum quod hactenus fieri consueuit custibus et sumptibus predictorum magistri et fratrum ista vice tantum, et exinde dicti custos et scolares reparabunt in perpetuum sumptibus suis propriis et emendabunt totiens quotiens necesse fuerit; et insuper quod rivulus currens a dicto le Brede et aqua inde simul, cum piscaria usque ad stagnum molendini predictorum magistri et confratrum sancti Iohannis, de cetero sit aqua cum piscaria dictorum custodis et scolarium; ac insuper quod aqua currens a dicto molendino versus austrum sit communis aqua et piscaria usque quoddam cornerium cuiusdam crofti dictorum magistri et confratrum, et quod pisces inde capti et omnia alia emolumenta equaliter dividantur prout abbas de Oseney et balliui domini regis ville sue Oxonie capiunt et piscantur; proviso semper quod omni tempore ad libitum dictorum magistri et confratrum bene liceat predictis magistro et confratribus facere cariagia in dicta aqua; ac vero insuper quod rivulus et aqua inde currens simul cum piscaria incipiens a dicto cornerio predicti crofti versus orientem et currens versus occidentem

[1] *Oxford City Documents* (O.H.S.), p. 206.
[2] Twyne MSS. xxiii, 192.

in perpetuum sit separalis rivulus cum aqua et piscaria predictorum custodis et scolarium.'

The dictionaries give no suitable meaning for the word *brede*; possibly it means a ditch to carry the overflow from Irishman's Pool (i. e. Parson's Pleasure) to the Cherwell below King's Mill. The complaint may have been that the Hospital of St. John, by damming the water at King's Mill, injured the meadow land of Holywell which lay to the north-west. As the ditch would be made on the land of Holywell, the fishing in it would naturally belong to Merton College. The reference to Oseney is merely brought in as an example of water owned equally by two parties; it does not refer to the Cherwell, but to water of the Thames near Oseney. Twyne thinks that *brede* means *bridge*, but it does not seem likely. Can it mean an *overflow*, which checks or bridles the water?

The Hospital had the right of holding a court for its own tenants, but by what grant is uncertain. The record of it has been preserved by Twyne, who copied the roll of a hustengs court of January 23, 1300, which has now perished.[1] The words are:—

'Curia Oxonie tenta die Lune[2] in crastino sancti Vincencii martiris anno Ed. I XXIX°. Adam de Tywe queritur de Baldewyno le Webbe, quod ubi fuit die dominica proxima post festum Concepcionis beate Marie Virginis anno regni regis Edwardi nunc vicesimo nono post prandium in domo Willelmi le Mercer in parochia sancti Petri orientalis in suburbio Oxonie extra portam orientalem Oxonie, venit dictus Baldewynus et cepit ipsum per pectus & dilaceravit supertunicam dicti Ade a collario usque ad zonam suam, & non eo contentus clausit ostium dicte domus et extraxit cultellum suum et voluit ipsum occidisse, nisi rescussus fuisset per Petrum le Harenger; unde dicit quod deterioratus est et habet dampnum ad valenciam XL solidorum, et hoc paratus est &c. Et Baldewynus venit, et salvo esse ibidem totum defendit. Et super hoc venit frater Willelmus de Otyndon de hospitali sancti Iohannis extra portam orientalem Oxonie et petit curiam suam hospitalis predicti de predictis Ada & Baldewyno, tenentibus hospitalis predicti, et

[1] Twyne MSS. xxiii, 257.
[2] January 23 was a Monday in the year 1300.

concessa est ei; et idem frater Willelmus assignavit partibus predictis diem curie die dominica proximo sequente post hunc diem.'

It is probable that this William de Otyndon was the brother who was elected Master nearly thirty years later. The record leaves us uncertain whether the court of the Hospital was only for those who, like Baldwin and Adam, dwelt outside East gate, or applied to all their tenants in Oxford. We are not aware that the Hospital was granted the right of *sak* and *sok* by the king, but we have suggested that the land of Peter Boterel outside East gate was originally a manor with a manorial court attached to it.

Another right of the Hospital was to take the goods of their tenants who committed suicide or were condemned as criminals. This privilege was granted by Henry III in 1246 and 1266 (vol. ii, p. 399), and we see it used in the case of Edward de Hales, who lived in one of the houses of the Hospital in St. Mary's parish.[1] When he took refuge in a church in 1298 and abjured the realm, the bailiffs seized his goods; but the Hospital obtained a writ from the king according to the tenor of the charter of Henry III, and when the writ was presented to the bailiffs, they surrendered the goods to the Hospital.

A third privilege of the Hospital was to receive forfeited goods of various kinds from the market of Oxford. Perhaps the first instance is in a charter of Edward I, January 10, 1284, by which when forestallers and regraters make purchases contrary to the liberties of the University, the goods are to be taken to the Hospital of St. John and given to the poor and infirm.[2] In 1290 it was decided that putrid meat and fish that was forfeited in the market, and also the amercements for the offence, should be granted in the same way to the Hospital.[3] It need not be assumed that the meat and fish were to be eaten by the patients; there was a demand for flesh of any kind for feeding the fish in fish-ponds, and what

[1] *Oxford City Documents* (O.H.S.), p. 175; *Oxford Coroners' Inquests*, p. 12.

[2] *Oxford City Documents* (O.H.S.), p. 216.

[3] *Munimenta Academica* (Rolls Series), i, p. 52.

was forfeited to the Hospital could be sold for this purpose or used in the fish-ponds of the Hospital. Another extension of this principle was made in 1348, when it was decided that the Hospital should receive one-tenth of the amercements from the assay of weights and measures.[3] A deed of April 1348, recently acquired by the Bodleian Library, shows that this last point was decided by the Archbishop of Canterbury and the Bishop of Chichester, to whom it was referred whether the tenth penny from the amercements and forfeitures of the assay should be given to the Hospital of St. John, or to maintain a light at the morning mass in St. Mary's, or for the repair of Petitpount; the judges selected the first. As far as is known, there survives but one roll of the assay of weights and measures, now in the University Archives (Y. 16, rot. 30), from which we learn that the income from this source was small. It is undated, but is apparently of 1347; whether the court was held yearly or half-yearly we do not know. On this occasion there were but twelve offenders in the whole of Oxford, and though the amount of the amercements is not given, we know that they were always light in the Middle Ages, so that it is not likely that the tenth portion which was given to the Hospital amounted to more than a shilling.

A fourth privilege was the right of sanctuary, which was claimed on one occasion in 1463, and of which we have given details in vol. ii, p. 2. It is hardly credible that all the tenements, or even one tenement, of the Hospital had been granted this right by a papal bull, and it may be noticed that the man who fled to Broadgates did not maintain that it had been granted by any one pope but 'a Romanis pontificibus'; and when the proctor was convinced that the claim was just, it was not by inspection of a papal bull but by instruction (*instructus per custodem*). It was probably an idle tale which sprang up in the middle of the fifteenth century, and it is noteworthy that the proctor had hitherto no knowledge of any such privilege. Hospitals were certainly treated by popes and bishops with special favour above all monastic houses, and some may have started the idea that hospitals and all

[1] *Munimenta Academica* (Rolls Series), i, p. 159.

their properties in old times had the right of sanctuary according to church law, and ought still to enjoy it. The matter was not examined by any court of law, and the proctor, who was evidently very willing to be convinced, was satisfied with the evidence of hearsay. In 1580 it was maintained that all the ground which was included within the wall of the College was sanctuary, 'and that a man being apprehended for felony did claim for sanctuary about 54 years past, and had the same'.[1]

Of the inner life of the Hospital we have little means of judging. There are no complete rentals to show us what was its income, and the Taxatio of Pope Nicholas gives us no help. As there are no computus rolls beyond the fragment printed in this volume, pages 19 to 27, we know little of the names and numbers of the brethren and sisters and how the income was spent. We know that in 1234 it was settled that the Hospital should consist of three brethren in priest's orders, six lay men and six lay sisters, and that when the Hospital was dissolved in 1457 there were five brethren, all of them priests. In 1340 there is some indication that besides the master there were seven sisters and nine brethren,[2] and as eight of the latter are styled 'frater' we are inclined to assume that they were in priest's orders and only one a layman, or possibly a probationer. If some of the eight had been laymen, there would have been some alteration in title to distinguish those who held the higher rank as priests. In all monasteries the lay brethren, which were numerous in the twelfth and thirteenth centuries, disappear subsequently, and the rule arose that all the brethren should be ordained as soon as possible; and it was probably the same with the Hospital. In the register of John Gilbert, bishop of Hereford, there is a notice that on May 23, 1388, Edmund Waterdene of St. John's Hospital outside the East gate of Oxford was ordained subdeacon in Hereford Cathedral,[3] and when other episcopal registers are published we shall have more instances. We have proof that the Hospital was used in the fourteenth

[1] Vol. ii, p. 460.
[2] Vol. iii, p. 18.
[3] *Register of John Gilbert*, p. 178 (Cant. and York Soc.).

century, much as we use modern hospitals, as the place to receive those who were injured. Thus in 1305 Robert Attewyndyate, who lived near the South gate of Oxford, having his finger broken with a blow, was taken to the Hospital of St. John, where he died;[1] and in 1396 a certain Roger, who had fallen into the water from East Bridge, was carried to the Hospital.[2]

The original hospital stood, as has been shown, in Long Wall Street, and its site may be represented by the land which is mentioned in deed no. 149, bounded on the west by Long Wall Street and on the east by the lane which ran between Magdalen Hall and Magdalen College; on the south the boundary was the north wall of the tenements in the 'Gravel Walk', and on the north was 'The Grove' (*virgultum*). For the buildings of the second hospital the reader is referred to Appendix III.

When the plan is consulted at the end of volume i, entitled 'Oxford outside East Gate in 1771', it will be noticed that the line of the property of Magdalen from the porter's lodge to East Bridge is different from the line of the houses from Long Wall Street to Magdalen Hall; and the question arises whether this was so in the days of the Hospital of St. John, or whether the houses were thrown back about 1480, when they were rebuilt. It is certainly the case that roads in the Middle Ages outside the towns were of great width, that carts might be able to avoid the holes and bogs, and it may be the case that the road from East Gate to East Bridge was of the width of 70 or 80 feet, the part over which the traffic might be diverted being on the north side of the road from East Gate to the Hospital and on the south side from the Hospital gate to East Bridge. It is also true that the instances of Balliol College and St. John's show that this extra width of road could be enclosed in later times, when the care of roads made such width unnecessary. But the evidence, such as it is, suggests that in the days of the Hospital the houses stood where now is the line of the street,

[1] *Coroners' Rolls of Oxford*, p. 12 (printed by the *Oxford Chronicle* Co.).
[2] *Ib.* p. 50.

and that the 'Gravel Walk', as it was called, was made when Magdalen College was built. The chief argument is drawn from the rentals, which show that during the years 1478 to 1484 all the houses between Long Wall Street and Magdalen College were pulled down and rebuilt; but it is very unlikely that a dozen contiguous houses would all need to be rebuilt, unless it was intended to alter the frontage and erect the row on a new site. In 1519 it was called 'the Newe Rewe',[1] and though this might mean 'the row of new houses', it more naturally means 'the row in the new position'. Also it must be noted that Balliol did not enclose the northern side of Broad Street until 1683,[2] whereas the Gravel Walk was enclosed with a wall certainly before 1580.[3] The more probable conclusion, therefore, is that the row of houses was thrown back about 1480, to give a view of Magdalen chapel and front gate, and that a low wall was made on the south side of the Gravel Walk, where the wall now is.

It is evident that the high road passed across the burial-ground of the Jews, and that in 1231 the Hospital received the portion which was on the north side of the road, while that which was on the south was retained by the Jews. If it seems strange that the same piece of land should serve as a road and also as a cemetery, it may be pointed out that it was so with several of the Oxford churches, notably St. Mildred's Church and St. Peter's in the East, burials having been found in Brasenose Lane and Queen's Lane. In 1293 the Hospital obtained this southern portion as well, and leaving a width of 26 feet for the road they obtained a strip measuring 64 feet by 300 feet as a cemetery for their own patients. When the road was enclosed in this way, the question arose whose duty it was to repair. In 1331 Edward III issued a writ to the bailiffs and commonalty of Oxford that they should make no claim on the Hospital to repair the road from Pettypont to 'the cross by the gate of the Hospital'.[4] Where this cross stood is uncertain. It will be seen in Appendix III that there was a stone cross opposite the west end of the chapel

[1] Vol. i, p. 150.
[2] *Balliol Oxf. Deeds*, p. 24 (O.H.S.).
[3] Vol. ii, p. 461.
[4] Vol. ii, p. 405.

of St. John the Baptist, but as it seems to have stood within the walls of the Hospital, it is probable that the writ of the king refers to some other cross. Anthony Wood[1] assumes that it stood in 'East Gate Street before the door of St. John's Hospital' (i.e. where now is the gateway to the President's Lodging), but it may be noticed that the writ does not say *ante portam* but *iuxta portam.* The Ordnance Survey places the cross in an impossible position, in the narrow roadway opposite the so-called Pilgrim's Gate. Twyne, who copied the original deed in the Town Archives,[2] and from whom Dr. Langbane made his copy, has these words about the cross:[3] 'whether the cross was at the street gate of the Hospital or at a back gate, perhaps at the bounds of St. Cross's parish, we cannot tell.' That there was a cross at this spot, just within the boundary of Holywell parish, we know from our deeds (see vol. ii, pp. 359, 360), and it is mentioned in an extract that Twyne gives us[4] from a roll of presentments at a view of frankpledge, probably at the end of the fifteenth century: 'The road between the chain outside East Gate and the cross of Holywell is blocked with rubbish by Nicholas Mansyple.' We have no proof that there was a backway into the Hospital from Long Wall Street; but it may be pointed out that the gate which stood in East Bridge Street is described as 'the great gate' of the Hospital,[5] as though there was another gate elsewhere; and to this day there is an old doorway in the wall of Magdalen at the point where Holywell parish begins. There is no evidence to show who repaired this piece of road. Twyne copied from the Town Archives a writ of Edward the Black Prince to the mayor and bailiffs of Oxford that they should repair the road between East Bridge and Crowelle[6] (which was a pond at the north end of Long Wall Street), and a reply of the authorities of Oxford asking that the sheriff may hold an inquest to discover whose duty it is to repair this road, as it

[1] *City of Oxford*, i, p. 291 (O.H.S.).
[2] Twyne MSS. xxiii, p. 454.
[3] Twyne MSS. xxiv, p. 467.
[4] Twyne MSS. xxiii, p. 157.
[5] Vol. iii, p. 206.
[6] Twyne MSS. xxiii, p. 461.

has never been the duty of the mayor and bailiffs.[1] As late as 1580 the matter was still in dispute.[2]

The dissolution of the Hospital seems to have taken place without much warning. Richard Vise was appointed master on May 18, 1442; five years later he obtained from the pope a dispensation to hold with his mastership any benefice with or without cure;[3] on December 4, 1451, the king granted to the Hospital the advowson of Horspath, which might be served by one of the brethren of the Hospital without the endowment of a vicarage or the distribution of alms to the poor parishioners.[4] Hitherto there is no indication that the Hospital was misgoverned; but on May 5, 1456, the king issued[5] a commission to Masters Luke Lancok and John Boteller, doctors of decrees, John Moreton, doctor of laws, William Godeyere, bachelor in either law, and John Wynterburn, bachelor in laws, to visit and survey the Hospital of St. John, wherein by the negligence of masters divine service and works of piety have for no small time ceased, and whereof diverse possessions are withdrawn and wasted, and the chalices, books, vestments, and other ornaments sold by the masters; and to make inquisition touching the behaviour of masters, ministers, and farmers of their possessions. Of the commissioners we know that Lucas Lancok[6] was at one time president of Pekwater Inn, and from 1452 to 1453 rector of St. Michael's South; John Boteler[7] was principal of the School of Canon Law in Little Jewry in 1450; John Moreton[8] was head of the School of Civil Law in 1452; and William Godeyere was principal of White Hall in Cheyne Lane[9] about 1450; nothing is known of John Winterbourn. We cannot tell what was the result of the inquiry, but four months later there seems to have been no idea of suppressing the Hospital; for on September 27, 1456, the king granted permission[10] to the president and scholars of Magdalen Hall to acquire in mort-

[1] Twyne MSS. xxiii, p. 397.
[2] Vol. ii, p. 460.
[3] *Cal. of Papal Registers*, x, p. 11.
[4] *Cal. of Pat. Rolls* (1446–1452), p. 506.
[5] *Ib.* (1452–1461), p. 303.
[6] Wood, *City of Oxford*, i, p. 597; iii, p. 95.
[7] *Ib.* i, p. 602.
[8] *Ib.* i, p. 603.
[9] *Ib.* i, p. 258.
[10] *Cal. of Pat. Rolls* (1452–1461), p. 324.

main lands that belonged to Oseney Abbey, St. Frideswide's, Littlemore Priory, University College, Oriel College, 'the prior and brethren of St. John the Baptist without the east gate', and the mayor and commonalty of Oxford. It seems probable that this grant in the first instance was issued with the view that Magdalen Hall might acquire the block of land between High Street and Merton Street, extending westward to Logic Lane or even farther,[1] the owners of this land being the bodies mentioned in the deed. But in a few days Bishop Waynflete was made chancellor of the realm, and within a month the scheme had been formed to dissolve the Hospital and to grant the site to Magdalen Hall; for on October 27, 1456, the king granted to William, bishop of Winchester, the patronage and advowson of the Hospital of St. John, and the master and brethren had licence to grant to Magdalen Hall all the possessions of the Hospital, including the site;[2] and if this letter be invalid, the chancellor shall issue another, without fine or fee. For some months there were negotiations between Richard Vise and the bishop;[3] and on July 5, 1457, the Hospital with its site and all its possessions was granted by the brethren to the authorities of Magdalen Hall by virtue of the deed of September 27, 1456. Thus the Hospital came to an end, and on August 20, 1457, the president of Magdalen Hall is in possession of the Hospital and on that day grants annual pensions of £10 to Robert Heyys, John Vobe, and John Sylam, priests,[4] three out of the four brethren who in addition to Richard Vise formed the staff of the Hospital at that time.[5] It is noteworthy that these grants bear the seal of the Hospital of St. John, which must by that time have been in the possession of John Hornley, president of Magdalen Hall. Another step was necessary, of which we have a trace in deed no. 970, namely to obtain the permission of the pope to suppress the Hospital. This was obtained on March 14, 1458, and the pope granted that Richard Vise, who already held the living of Faleghe or Fallay, might hold another with it, and

[1] See vol. i, pp. 260, 262.

[2] *Cal. of Pat. Rolls* (1452–1461), p. 343.

[3] *History of Magd. Coll.*, by H. A. Wilson, p. 14.

[4] Vol. ii, p. 449.

[5] Vol. ii, p. 416.

each of the four brethren might hold a living.[1] One of them, John Vobe, held a chantry at Canterbury Cathedral which he resigned on September 22, 1459.[2]

Two references to the Hospital of St. John in its last years may be found in the Chancellor's Register.[3] The first is correctly printed in *Munimenta Academica*, ii. 669, but some words must be wanting in the original. The entry evidently states that on August 16, 1457, Richard Vise, late master of the Hospital of St. John, was banished from Oxford by the chancellor, because on the previous day, when he had been committed to the Castle prison 'for diverse transgressions of enormity', he left the prison without the leave of the chancellor. We do not know what his former offence was, but 'enormity' was used of such a mild offence as failing to appear in court when summoned. The other entry[4] states that on September 19, 1457, dom. Walter, brother of the Hospital of St. John, was convicted of carrying arms, bows and arrows; the chancellor ordered him to be cited, but it was certified that he had withdrawn from Oxford. We may assume that this refers to Walter Rede, who was one of the brethren when the Hospital was dissolved.[5] Perhaps it was because he was known to be a man of unstaid behaviour that no pension was assigned him in the previous month when the other brethren received pensions.[6]

After the extinction of the Hospital, the name occurs in the Chancellor's Register. William Ive, the vice-chancellor, held his court October 8, 1461, 'in collegio beate Marie Magdalene vulgariter nuncupato domus sancti Iohannis extra portam orientalem Oxonie';[7] on November 3, 1461, the spot is described as 'in ecclesia collegii sancte Marie Magdalene';[8] on December 2, 1461, it is 'in capella sancti Iohannis';[9] December 3, 'in domo sancti Iohannis Baptiste'.

One more reference to the Hospital has been found while this Preface was being printed. Twyne (vol. xxii, p. 335),

[1] Vol. ii, pp. 413–416.
[2] *Cal. of Pat. Rolls*, p. 529.
[3] Registrum Aaa in the University Archives.
[4] Aaa, fol. 163.
[5] Vol. ii, p. 416.
[6] Vol. ii, p. 449.
[7] Aaa, fol. 188.
[8] *Ib.* fol. 190.
[9] *Ib.* fol. 191.

giving some extracts from a lost cartulary of Abingdon Abbey, has the following note:

> E libro Abendone, qui in particulas dividitur. Particula quinta, carta 37. 'Omnibus sancte matris ecclesie filiis, ad quos presens scriptum peruenerit, magister Edmundus de Abbendone salutem in domino. Nouerit uniuersitas uestra me concessisse et dedisse et hac presenti carta mea confirmasse deo et hospitali sancti Iohannis de Oxonia ad portam orientalem et fratribus ibidem commorantibus domum cum omnibus pertinentiis, que fuit Reginaldi Diuitis in vico West in villa de Abendone,' &c.

Twyne adds that the deed which followed mentioned that *magister Edmundus* was afterwards archbishop of Canterbury, and no doubt it was the deed by which the Hospital of St. John granted the tenement to Abingdon Abbey. There was a chapel of St. Edmund, of which the remains are still to be seen in West St. Helen's Street, and our deed suggests that it was built on the site of the house of Reginald le Rich, father of Edmund. The land was given to the Hospital about 1220 or 1230, and probably alienated to the Abbey after the death of the donor.

At the conclusion of this work, the thanks of the members of the Oxford Historical Society should be conveyed to the President and Fellows of Magdalen College, who have defrayed the whole expense of this, the longest cartulary that the Society has published; and in particular to the Rev. H. A. Wilson, who has made many suggestions, and to Mr. R. T. Gunther, who has added in Appendix III a most valuable account of what is known about the buildings of the Hospital.

CONTENTS

LIST OF PLATES

ILLUSTRATIONS IN TEXT

CORRIGENDA

VOL. I

p. 72, line 5 from the bottom. Great Mead or Cowlake was east of Addison's Walk; *see* Vol. III, p. xi

p. 313, line 3 from the bottom. *For* 1845 *read* 1835

VOL. II

p. 153, line 24. *For* Benediti *read* Benedicti

p. 234, line 17. *For* II Hen. VII *read* 1483

p. 404, margin. *For* 1321 *read* 1331

p. 445, line 4 from the bottom. The scribe wrote *John* in error for *Richard*

VOL. III

p. 24, line 19. Probably *in manenis* is an error for *in auenis*

A CARTULARY OF THE HOSPITAL OF ST. JOHN THE BAPTIST

I. THE RULE OF THE HOSPITAL.

THE Rule of the Hospital, as far as is known, survives only in a paper MS., now Bodleian MS. Top. Oxon. d. 8, which contains five Papal Bulls or confirmations and a summary of some royal charters. It is in a hand of the middle of the fifteenth century, and the last entry shows that it cannot have been written before 1442. It was formerly in the Ashmolean, and the assumption that it was deposited there with the other MSS. of Anthony Wood is proved by a note of Wood, printed in Wood's *City of Oxford* (O. H. S.), ii. 528. He there states that he had in his possession (1) a copy of the Statutes of the Hospital of St. John; (2) a Roll of Inspeximus of several kings concerning its lands and foundation; (3) an abstract of certain gifts given in the time of Henry III. All these are now in the Bodleian; the copy of the Statutes is what is here printed; the Roll of Inspeximus is Bodleian Roll no. 23, being a copy of Henry V's charter (see charter 942); the 'abstract of certain gifts' is Bodleian Roll no. 24. We do not know how Wood obtained these records. In the account of the Hospital of St. John, which he wrote for his *City of Oxford* before he had seen the muniments of Magdalen, he makes no mention of these records; and the natural assumption is that they were subsequently given to him by the Bursar of Magdalen, probably when Wood obtained leave to inspect the charters of the College.

[1. **The rule of the Hospital drawn up by Innocent IV.**]

In nomine sancte Trinitatis, patris et filii et spiritus sancti. Amen. **Mar. 23, 1246**

De magistro.

Dilectissimi in Cristo fratres, uestram moneo caritatem & exhortor in domino ut [uos][1], qui religionis formam accepistis, que in uobis per habitum exterius preostensa est, mente deuota teneatis eam interius et exequamini et proferatis in actum. Vera enim religio non tantum est in habitu exteriori, sed in executione mandatorum dei. Caueat unusquisque, omni adhibita diligentia, ne hoc euangelicum sibi possit

[1] A hole in the page.

impingi 'Attendite a falsis prophetis &c.'; et quia exortis nouis malis noua adhibenda sunt medicamina, uestigia predecessorum uestrorum magistrorum aliquantulum digressi,[1] ut coarceantur quedam mala de nouo exorta et mala futura cautius possint euitari, statutis antiquis quedam noua uolumus superaddere. Statuimus ergo quod in uestro fratrum collegio frater unus hospitalis sancti Iohannis Baptiste extra portam orientalem Oxonie persona dignior, sapientior et honestior, de parentela libera procreata, legittime a fratribus ad hoc electa, aliis presit fratribus et magistratum teneat, qui semper memor sit nominis sui quod a maioritate accepit, sitque in diuinis operibus assiduus ac deuotus et perseuerans operarius; nichil extra preceptum dei (quod absit) agat, iubeat uel instituat, sed eius iussio et doctrina diuine iusticie sapiat condimentum. Delinquentes subditos pie moneat excessus corrigere, secundum datam sibi regulam uiuere, de bono semper in melius proficere. Caueatque magister ne sub eius cura aliquis fratrum rebellis aut incorrigibilis inueniatur. Pastoris namque culpa esse creditur, quod in grege suo paterfamilias minus inuenit utilitatis. Ideoque si quis fratrum inquietus, rebellis uel inobediens fuerit, omnis sibi diligentia tanquam oui morbide est attribuenda, ut cesset et quiescat et canonicis obediat[2] mandatis, ne eius contagione grex possit infici uel contaminari, sed ut ipse magister tanquam bonus pastor ouium in iudicio domini dicere possit cum propheta 'Iusticiam tuam non abscondi in corde meo'. Magister uero quod discipulos suos facere docuerit, prior ipse id faciat, et quod fugiendum eos monuerit, ut a facie colubri illud effugiat, ne aliis predicans ipse reprobus inueniatur. Fratrem unum plus quam alium magister non diligat, nisi quem in bonis actibus inuenerit meliorem. Equalis caritas dilectionis debetur omnibus.

De celerario.

Frater unus de congregatione, uir maturus, sapiens et honestus, fiat celerarius, de quo magister fiduciam possit obtinere pleniorem, eo quod in multis negociis magistri[3] debet onera portare. Sit eciam sobrius, non multum edax, non elatus, non turbilentus [*sic*], non iniuriosus, non piger, non tenax, non auarus, nec prodigus; sed uir timens deum, qui omni familie uice magistri debet preesse, disponens et ordinans actus eorundem sicut melius uiderit expedire; tamen sine magistri iussione nichil omnino faciat uel incipiat. Si quis autem

[1] This will not construe; perhaps the true reading was 'et a uestigiis predecessorum uestrorum magistrorum aliquantulum digressi estis'.
[2] obedire, MS.
[3] magister, MS.

fratrum irracionabiliter quicquam petierit ab eodem, non spernendo eum contristetur; sed male petita cum humilitate denegabit; nulli se reddat difficilem. Sed si in sua possessione id quod ab eo petitur non habeat, bone responsionis sermo porrigatur, quia [1] sermo bonus super datum optimum; equo animo commissum sibi impleat officium. Horis competentibus que sunt distribuenda distribuat, ne in domo dei perturbetur aut contristetur aliquis.[2] Omni solicitudine curam gerat infirmorum pauperum, hospitum superuenientium.

De Sacrista.

Sacrista itaque sit unus de fratribus fidelis, in obsequio dei deuotus, chorum regens et ornans ecclesiam, in sua possessione habens ornamenta, libros, uestimenta et quecumque ad ecclesiam spectantia, percipiens redditus, oblationes et obuenciones ad ecclesiam spectantes et pauperum extraneorum in firmaria decedentium uestes et alia bona, si qua habuerint; debet idem sacrista libros et uestimenta seruare, reparare et renouare, ceram et oleum inuenire ad lampades ardentes in choro, firmaria et dormitorio. De receptis uero debet in fine anni magistro compotum reddere. Et quia eidem sacriste deputata est cura firmarie, statuimus et firmiter precipimus quod infirmorum admittendorum confessionem audiat priusquam admittantur, si fuerint adulti.[3] Non admittant leprosos, paraliticos, ydropicos, furiosos, morbo caduco laborantes, fistulas aut morbos incurabiles pacientes nec mulieres lasciuas pregnantes nec iuuenculas: sed pocius extra domum aliqua porcio sustentacionis eis assignetur, si indiguerint, cum infirmentur, quoadusque conualuerint.

De fratribus admittendis.

Statuimus quod de cetero nullus admittatur ad habitum ad instanciam quorumcumque nisi ipse ad minus per sex menses steterit in probatione. Peracto tempore probationis supradicte, et si magister et fratres illum approbant, admittantur [*sic*]. Statuimus eciam quod omnes fratres et sorores unusquisque habeat alium commendatum in orationibus suis, sacerdotes in missa, laici et sorores in oratione dominica. Et cum aliquis obierit fratrum siue sororum, quod omnes confratres sui sacerdotes deuote celebrent pro anima illa illo die siue in crastino et quod laici et sorores dicant pro illa anima psalterium beate uirginis, et quod ille mortuus habeat unum de confratribus suis celebrantem pro anima sua, et quod habeat corrodium suum illo anno, adeo integre

[1] The scribe writes 'quia . . . officium' as one clause.

[2] The scribe has begun a new sentence with 'Aliquis'.

[3] The scribe begins a new sentence with 'Si fuerint adulti'.

sicut esset habiturus in uita; et cum dies anniuersarius suus fuerit singulis annis quod habeat plenum seruitium mortuorum cum aliis specialibus orationibus de omnibus fratribus et sororibus. Statuimus et prohibemus quod nullus ad ordinem seu ad confraternitatem admittatur irretitus uiciis incontinencie. Gulosi, ebriosi, luxuriosi, contenciosi, illiterati, persone deformes et defectum membrorum patientes, perpetue infirmitatis laborantes molestia incurabili, omnino repellantur, sed mites et humiles uiri timorati [1], in obsequio dei deuoti, admittantur ad habitum seu ad confraternitatem.

De obedientia fratrum.

Statuimus et statutum esse volumus quod omnes fratres et sorores sint obedientes suo preposito sine contradictione aliqua ita, cum aliquid a preposito imperatum fuerit, ac si diuinitus imperaretur. Moram pati nesciant [2] in faciendo, nec decet eos, qui nichil Cristo carius existimant, pro quo contempserunt uitam mundi propriamque uoluntatem, promittentes uiuere sub alieno arbitrio, et alieno iudicio se submittentes ac imperio, uerba Cristi in corde recolendo 'Non ueni facere voluntatem meam sed eius qui misit me'. Et tunc erit acceptabilis deo et dulcis hominibus, quia obediencia que maioribus prebetur deo exhibetur.

De Silentio.

Rara sit fratribus loquendi licencia, quia mors et uita in manibus lingue. Statuimus igitur quod post completorium fratres in dormitorio teneant silentium a tempore quo eunt cubitum usque ad primam cantatam in crastinum, & eciam in refectione teneant silentium. Loqui tamen et docere magistrum condecet. Tacere et audire discipulis conuenit. Et ideo, si qua loqui compellit necessitas, prius a preposito per signum loquendi cum omni humilitate requiratur licencia, ne quis plus loqui uideatur quam expedit. Scurilitatem uero et uerba ociosa que ad edificacionem non pertinent, sed pocius fratres ad iracundiam mouentia, in omnibus locis dampnamus, et ad huiusmodi uerba subditorum os aperire non permittimus.

De seruitio faciendo.

Statuimus eciam quod omnes fratres sani simul ad matutinas surgant ita tempestiue ut ante auroram uel saltem in aurora matutine possint percantari. Intrantes quidem primo ecclesiam, humiliter crucifixum debent adorare et coram autentico [*sic*] altari cum deuotione beate Marie uirginis maxime [*sic*]. Deinde stantes in stallis matutinas

[1] See Vulgate, Acts viii. 2.

[2] nesciat, MS.

dicant de beata uirgine cum deuotione et consequenter de die; quibus inceptis et dictis usque ad ultimum uersum psalmi primi nullus deinceps frater chorum introeat, sed extra chorum permaneat expectans sue desidie culpam a suo preposito puniendam. Consequenterque prima et tertia percantatis, missa secundum ordinationem sacriste celebretur; qua celebrata cetere hore dicantur, et deinde fratres exeant et negotiis domus intendant, quilibet eorum prout competit officio sibi deputato.

De proprietate.

Ad hec autem superaddimus statuendo ne quis presumat aut aliquid dare aut accipere sine consensu et iussione sui prepositi, neque aliquid habere proprium, nullam omnino rem, quibus non licet nec sua corpora nec suam uoluntatem, in propria habere uoluntate. Omnia sint communia. Et si quisquam hoc nequissimo proprietarii uicio deprehensus fuerit, amonitus semel et iterum, si se non emendauerit graui subiaceat pene sibi infligende. Deinde si quod habuerit proprium, ante septem dies post promulgationem huius statuti illud resignet in manu sui prepositi in utilitatem domus conuertendum. Alioquin ab eodem septimo die ipso facto retentionis proprii fit excommunicatus. Si autem innotescerit [*sic*] aliquem cum proprietate obisse, corpus eius proiciatur extra sepulturam Cristianam et sepeliatur more asini in fimario[1], proiecto super eum eius proprio a fratribus dicentibus 'Pecunia tua tecum sit in perdicionem'.

De modo gerendi.

Omnes simul iaceant in uno dormitorio et de communi omnes cibentur et potentur in uno refectorio; omnes dormiant uestiti femoralibus et indumento quo utuntur loco camisie; nullus discurrat per uillas seu per patrias uel nemora sine comitatu et laudabili testimonio a suo licentiatus preposito. In uilla Oxonie nullus comedat siue bibat, nec ante fores sedeat ad aliquod spectaculum. Nullus ad decios[2] uel ad taxillos[3] ludat. Cum autem domum egredi contigerit, pallio utatur aut cappa.

De indumentis.

Induantur omnes russeto, cameleto uel[4] burneto, ita ut robe omnium sint concordantes. Unus nigram robam non habeat et alius albam. Cappas habeant cruce duplici ante pectus signatas. Similiter et mantella crucibus sint signata ante humerum ex parte sinistra.

[1] fumario, MS.
[2] dice.
[3] *taxilli* were oblong dice with four sides and the ends rounded.
[4] ue, MS.

De uita.

Casti sint omnes et sobrii, lasciuiam domantes, moderati in uictu, cum mulieribus non loquentes seu iocantes, recordantes semper quod mulierum contractus multos fecerunt errare sapientes. Qualibet ebdomada conueniant simul in capitulo et ibidem regulariter fratrum excessus a preposito corrigantur. Teneaturque capitulum absque garrulitate et clamore. Et qui deliquerint humiliter et obedienter canonicam subeant disciplinam. Nullus fratrem suum carnalem aut nepotem exhibeat. Plures fratres aut sorores non admittantur quam necessarii sunt ad seruiendum infirmis. Sorores conuersè uagas non teneant domicillas, sed si quas tenuerint arceantur ne discurrant in locis priuatis domorum aut gardinorum, per quod possit oriri infamia. Si quam familiam fratres habere contigerit, honesta sit, moderata, et casta. Si quis uero de familia ebriosus seu incontinens fuerit, nisi admonitus ab huiusmodi uiciis se subtraxerit, amoueatur. Veraces sint fratres sine iurgio, sine turpiloquio, sine maledicto. Qui maledixerit fratri suo sit ille maledictus, et qui benedixerit benedictionibus repleatur. Si quis fratrum super mendacio possit conuinci, graui pena plectetur. Similiter famuli mendaces a seruitio domus expellantur. Similiter et hi quos super furto conuinci contigerit. Fratres autem omnes et singuli qui in dicto hospitali habent obedientias, de bonis sibi commissis in fine anni reddant compotum suo preposito. Sorores conuerse, secundum quod competit sexui suo, obseruent ea que superius fratribus statuimus obseruanda. Hec nostra statuta seruantibus omnibus gracia et pax a deo multiplicetur in terris ita quod regnum eterne beatitudinis possideant sine fine; contempnentes et contradicentes maledictionis dei et beate Marie uirginis et omnium sanctorum incurrant sentenciam. Amen.

Expliciunt [*sic*] statuta super regulam confirmata a uenerabili et sanctissimo papa Innocentio patre nostro, ad peticionem illustris regis Anglorum Henrici tercii qui fuit fundator istius hospitalis. Data Auinioni[1] x Kalendas Aprilis, pontificatus sui anno tercio. Eo tempore fuit factus Hugo episcopus Lincolnie.[2]

[2. **A bull of privileges by Innocent IV.**]

Oct. 6, 1245 Innocencius episcopus, seruus seruorum dei, dilectis filiis custodi et fratribus hospitalis sancti Iohannis de Oxonia Lincolniensis diocesis

[1] Innocent IV did not stay at Avignon. He was at Lyons at this time. The word should be 'Lugduni'.

[2] This of course is untrue. Hugh was Bishop of Lincoln in the time of Innocent III, but not in the time of Innocent IV.

salutem et apostolicam benedictionem. Pia regum et principum desideria deuotorum gratanter amplectimur, et quanto iocundius in cunctis deo placitis operibus delectemur, tanto libentius ad perfectionem eorum fauorem et graciam impartimur. Cum igitur carissimus in Cristo filius noster, rex Anglorum illustris, feruore diuine pietatis accensus hospitale uestrum[1] ad subleuationem pauperum scolarium et aliarum miserabilium personarum de bonis regiis construi fecerit et dotauit [*sic*]; Nos eiusdem regis supplicationibus inclinati personas uestras et hospitale ipsum, in quo dei et pauperum predictorum estis obsequio mancipati, cum omnibus bonis que in presentiarum racionabiliter possidet, aut in futurum iustis modis prestante domino poterit adipisci, sub beati Petri et nostra protectione suscipimus et presentis scripti patrocinio communimus, auctoritate uobis presentium concedentes ut pro uobis et familiaribus uestris ac pauperibus in hospitali degentibus memorato capellas et cimiterium liceat uobis habere, ac oblationes et obuentiones quas Cristi fideles eidem contulerint hospitali, uel reliquerint testamento, in eius usus conuertere ac pauperum predictorum; et cum interdictum terre fuerit generale, clausis ianuis, excommunicatis et interdictis exclusis, non pulsatis campanis, uoce suppressa, in predictis capellis officia celebrare diuina, dummodo causam non dederitis interdicto; districtius inhibendo ne diocesanus uel archidiaconus loci racione uisitacionis procurationes a uobis exigere aut extorquere presumat, quodque nullus delegatus, subdelegatus, executor, uel eciam conseruator, auctoritate sedis apostolice uel delegatorum ipsius, in personas uestras seu familiarium uestrorum excommunicationis siue interdicti sentenciam audeat promulgare absque mandato sedis apostolice speciali. Nulli ergo omnino hominum liceat hanc paginam nostre protectionis, concessionis et inhibitionis infringere uel ei ausu temerario contraire. Si quis autem hoc attemptare presumpserit, indignationem omnipotentis dei ac beatorum Petri et Pauli apostolorum eius se nouerit incursurum. Dat' Lugduni ii Non. O[ctobris],[2] pontificatus nostri anno tercio.

[3. **The form of oath for the brethren on admission.**]

Profiteor deo omnipotenti et sancto Iohanni, huius ecclesie patrono, me honeste et caste uiuere secundum statuta istius domus, et pauperibus deseruire ut decet in hac domo; sic deus me adiuuet et omnia sancta eius euangelia.

Postea faciat obedientiam magistro.

[1] nostrum, MS. [2] A hole in the MS.

[4. A letter of Innocent IV on behalf of the Hospital.]

Mar. 23, 1246 Innocentius episcopus &c. dilectis filiis abbati & archidiacono Westmonasterii London' salutem &c. Cum dilectos filios custodem et fratres hospitalis sancti Iohannis de Oxonia Lincolniensis diocesis ac hospitale ipsum, quod carissimus in Cristo filius noster rex Anglorum illustris ad sustentacionem pauperum scolarium et aliarum miserabilium personarum fecit construi de bonis regiis et decorari, ad preces ipsius regis cum omnibus bonis que in presentiarum rationabiliter possidet aut in futurum iustis modis prestante domino poterit adipisci sub protectione susceperimus apostolice sedis et nostra; dictis custodi et fratribus concedentes ut pro se ac familiaribus suis et pauperibus in hospitali degentibus memorato capellas et cimiterium liceat ipsis habere ac oblationes et obuentiones quas Cristi fideles eidem contulerint hospitali uel reliquerint testamento in eius usus conuertere ac pauperum predictorum; et cum interdictum terre fuerit generale, clausis ianuis, excommunicatis et interdictis exclusis, non pulsatis campanis, uoce suppressa, in dictis capellis officia possint celebrari diuina, dummodo ipsi causam non dederint interdicto, districtius inhibendo ne diocesanus uel archidiaconus loci racione uisitacionis procurationes ab eis exigere aut extorquere presumat; quodque nullus delegatus, subdelegatus, executor uel eciam conseruator auctoritate sedis apostolice uel delegatorum ipsius in eorum personas seu familiarium suorum excommunicationis seu interdicti sentenciam audeat promulgare absque mandato sedis apostolice speciali; Discrecioni uestre per apostolica scripta mandamus quatinus predictos custodem et fratres non permittatis contra prescriptarum protectionis, concessionis et inhibitionis nostrarum tenorem ab aliquibus indebite molestari, molestatores huiusmodi per censuram ecclesiasticam appellatione postposita compescendo. Quod si non ambo his exequendis potueritis interesse, alter uestrum ea nichilominus exequatur. Dat' Lugdun' x kalendas aprilis, pontificatus nostri anno tercio.

[5. A bull of confirmation by Urban V.]

Apr. 10, 1369 [Urb]anus [1] &c. dilectis filiis magistro et fratribus hospitalis pauperum sancti Iohannis Baptiste Oxoniensis Lincolniensis diocesis salutem &c. Omnes [ ] [2] et immunitates a predecessoribus nostris concessas necnon libertates et exemptiones secularium exactionum

[1] A hole in the MS Probably this is Urban V with the date 1369; if it is Urban VI the date will be 1385.
[2] A hole.

a regibus & principibus et aliis racionabiliter uobis indultas sicut eas iuste et pacifice obtinetis &c. confirmamus. Dat' Rome quarto Idus Aprilis, pontificatus nostri anno septimo.

[6. A bull of confirmation by Gregory XI.]

Gregorius episcopus, seruus seruorum dei, dilectis filiis magistro et fratribus hospitalis sancti Iohannis ante portam orientalem Oxonien[sem] salutem et apostolicam benedictionem. Cum a nobis petitur quod iustum est et honestum, tam rigor equitatis quam ordo exigit rationis ut id per solicitudinem officii nostri ad debitum perducatur effectum. Eapropter, dilecti in domino filii, uestris iustis postulacionibus grato concurrentibus assensu, personas uestras et locum in quo diuino estis obsequio mancipati cum omnibus bonis que inpresentiarum racionabiliter possidetis aut in futurum iustis modis prestante domino poteritis adipisci sub beati Petri et nostra protectione suscepimus; specialiter autem terras, possessiones ac alia bona uestra, sicut ea omnia iuste ac pacifice possidetis, uobis et per uos eidem hospitali auctoritate apostolica confirmamus ac presentis scripti patrocinio communimus. Nulli &c. Dat' Laterani v Kalendas Feb., pontificatus nostri anno quarto. **Jan. 28, 1374**

[7. A summary of a charter of Henry III.]

Henricus &c. Sciatis[1] nos dedisse, concessisse et hac carta nostra confirmasse deo et beate Marie, magistro, fratribus, sororibus et infirmis hospitalis nostri sancti Iohannis extra portam orientalem Oxonie quod ipsi et successores sui imperpetuum habeant et teneant omnes libertates et quietancias subscriptas, uidelicet quod ipsi et omnes homines sui sint quieti in perpetuum de sectis comitatuum, hundredorum &c. Dat' per manum nostram apud Northamptone octauo die Iunii anno regni nostri quinquagesimo. Ista allocancia irrotulatur in rotulo uicesimo in Duk'. **June 8, 1266**

[8. A summary of an Inspeximus by Henry V.]

Carta Henrici quinti.

Henricus &c. Inspeximus litteras patentes domini H. nuper regis Anglie patris nostri in hec uerba: H. &c. Inspeximus literas &c. Ricardi secundi in hec uerba: Ricardus &c. Inspeximus cartam con-

[1] For the full charter see vol. ii, p. 398.

firmacionis Edwardi nuper regis Anglie patris [*sic*] nostri[1] in hec uerba: E. &c. Inspeximus cartam quam dominus H. nuper rex Anglie auus noster fecit magistro et fratribus hospitalis sancti Iohannis extra portam orientalem Oxonie in hec uerba: H. &c. Sciatis nos dedisse et concessisse magistro et fratribus hospitalis sancti Iohannis &c. molendinum &c. in liberam et perpetuam elemosinam ad sustentacionem pauperum et infirmorum eiusdem hospitalis; et quod habeant gardinum quod fuit Iudeorum ad hospitale suum ibidem de nouo construendum. Inspeximus eciam aliam cartam quam idem auus noster fecit deo et sancto Iohanni Baptiste et fratribus ac infirmis hospitalis predicti in hec uerba: H. &c. deo & sancto Iohanni et hospitali nostro et fratribus et infirmis eiusdem hospitalis quandam porcionem bosci in Shothouer' &c. Inspeximus aliam cartam quam idem auus noster fecit custodi, fratribus et infirmis hospitalis predicti &c. Teste meipso apud Westmon' xx die Aprilis anno regni nostri secundo.

[9. **The king confirms the election of Richard Vyse to the post of Master.**]

May 18, 1442

R. omnibus ad quos &c. salutem. Sciatis quod, cum nuper vacante hospitali sancti Iohannis Baptiste extra portam orientalem Oxonie per liberam resignacionem fratris Hugonis Burtone ultimi magistri siue custodis hospitalis predicti, fratres eiusdem hospitalis dilectum nobis in Cristo fratrem Ricardum Vyse confratrem suum magistrum siue custodem hospitalis predicti elegerint, sicut per litteras patentes ipsorum fratrum nobis inde directas nobis constat, nos electionem illam acceptantes uolumus et [concedim]us quod idem Ricardus habeat et teneat custodiam hospitalis predicti cum omnibus iuribus et pertinenciis ad idem hospitale spectantibus iuxta uim, formam et effectum eleccionis supradicte. In cuius &c. Teste R. apud Westmonasterium xxiii die Maii anno &c. regis uicesimo.

[1] For the correct reading see vol. ii, p. 412, where the charter is given.

II. THE PROPERTIES OF THE HOSPITAL IN 1246.

On Aug. 25, 1246, King Henry III confirmed to the Hospital its possessions in Oxfordshire, in Buckinghamshire, in Warwickshire, and in the town of Oxford, and the deed survives on the Charter Roll of 30 Hen. III;[1] that portion of it which deals with the properties in Oxford is here reproduced. After each entry is given in square brackets the page where the original charter of the property may be found in the previous volumes. As only two of the charters are missing (and one of them survives in the Cartulary), it is evident that the muniments of the Hospital of St. John are nearly complete.

Besides the Charter Roll, we have Bodleian Roll no. 24, which gives us the latter half of the list. It is in a hand of the middle of the thirteenth century, and was probably made in 1246 with a view to the king's confirmation. One membrane, containing properties I to XLVIII, is lost, our membrane beginning with number XLIX, but it is noticeable that according to the list on the Charter Roll, the entry which the Bodleian Roll numbers as XLIX is the fiftieth entry. The Bodleian Roll is of use in several places where the Charter Roll is illegible.

It has already been pointed out (see p. 1) that this Roll was at one time in the possession of Anthony Wood, and it bears on the margin some notes in his handwriting.

Charter Roll 30 Hen. III.

De dono Andree Halegod de Oxonia totam terram cum pert. quam emit de Gileberto Caretario Oxonie extra portam orientalem Oxonie. [i. 146.]

De dono Laurencii filii Rocelini feodum cum mesuagio & pert. suis quod tenuit de eodem hospitali & quod Eadmundus le Chapeler & Leticia uxor eius tenuerunt de ipso Laurencio & aliud feodum cum alio mesuagio & pert. suis quod similiter tenuit de eodem hospitali & quod Gilebertus le Bolter & [Ede]lina uxor eius tenuerunt de ipso & unam partem terre non mensuratam que iacet retro curiam que fuit ipsius Edeline & similiter unam partem gardini ipsius Laurencii retro domum suam similiter & totum pratum quod habuit in prato quod uocatur Paris cum pert. extra eandem portam. [i. 84.]

De dono eiusdem quandam domum suam & omnia ad eandem domum pertinencia extra eandem portam. [i. 88.]

De dono Rogeri filii Alwini le Turnur duas partes que ipsum contingebant in prato quod uocatur Paris extra eandem portam. [i. 20.]

De dono Amicie fi[lie Roberti] unum mesuagium proximum mesuagio Iohannis Kepeharm cum omnibus pert. extra eandem portam. [i. 78.]

[1] See *Calendar of Charter Rolls*, vol. i, p. 300.

De dono Matillidis que fuit uxor Rogeri del Ake unum mesuagium quod est inter terram que fuit Willelmi Log & terram que fuit Willelmi Redulf cum pert. extra eandem portam. [i. 71.]

De dono Elene de Blechesdune filie Roberti de Hethe quatuor mesuagia & dimidiam acram terre cum pert. in parochia sancte Crucis de Haliwelle. [ii. 373.]

De dono Iohannis filii Rogeri Beuerage totam terram cum pert. quam habuit in eadem parochia. [ii. 379.]

De dono Ade Cruste de Oxonia totam terram illam cum domibus & omnibus pert. quam Ricardus de Farendone aliquando tenuit & unam acram terre & dimidiam cum pert. in eadem parochia. [ii. 378.]

De dono Galfridi Carpentarii omnes terras & tenementa & omnes redditus que habuit & que habere potuit & que perquirere poterit & que ei uel heredibus suis aliquo iure accidere possint in eadem parochia. [ii. 362.]

De dono Thome Grifin unum mansum cum pert. quod Albricus capellanus aliquando tenuit & uiginti pedes terre in fronte uersus uicum & uiginti & sex pedes terre in profundo uersus curiam que fuit aliquando eiusdem Albrici capellani cum pert. in eadem parochia. [ii. 355.]

De dono Philippi Molendinarii duas solidatas redditus annuatim percipiendas de terra quam Iohannes Scriptor de eo tenuit pro quinque solidis per annum in eadem parochia. [ii. 352.]

De dono Roberti Bodin totam illam terram cum pert. que est inter terram quam Willelmus Curtais & Iohannes Culuerd tenuerunt & murum qui est circa curiam nostram Oxonie uersus occidentem extra portam aquilonarem Oxonie in parochia sancte Marie Magdalene. [ii. 329.]

De dono magistri Iohannis de Northone totam terram illam cum pert. que est inter terram quam Alexander le Mascon aliquando tenuit & terram quam Osmundus Molendinarius tenuit in Bello Monte in eadem parochia. [ii. 325.]

De dono Walteri Cole terras quas Ricardus le Walais, Willelmus Warmete, Robertus filius Ailmari, Eadwardus Aquarius, Walterus Cutel & Robertus le Bere & Adam Ianitor de eo tenuerunt. [ii. 297.]

De dono Symonis Balehorn sexdecim solidatas annui redditus extra eandem portam. [ii. 303.]

De dono Walteri de Bello Monte tres solidatas annui redditus in eadem parochia. [ii. 327.]

De dono Radulfi de Farendone tres solidatas annui redditus in eadem parochia. [ii. 295.]

De dono Amicie que fuit uxor Roberti Waldri totum capitale mesuagium suum cum pert. quod situm est in strata magna infra muros Oxonie in parochia sancti Petri uersus orientem. [i. 277.]

De dono Henrici filii Alwini totam terram quam Ailwinus pater eius emit de Herberto Textore in eadem parochia. [i. 300.]

De dono Gwidonis Sutoris totam terram illam cum pert. que iacet inter terram Henrici filii Fulconis & terram que fuit W[alteri] Inge in eadem parochia. [i. 228.]

De dono Iohannis de Burmingeham illam terram cum edificiis & pert. suis que est inter cymiterium ecclesie sancti Petri uersus orientem & terram Agnetis Log in longitudine & murum terreum quem construi fecit & domum angularem dicti hospitalis iuxta dictum cymeterium in latitudine. [i. 349.]

De dono Dyonisie que fuit uxor Gileberti Borewolde & Roberti filii eiusdem Gileberti totam illam terram que iacet inter terram Henrici filii Symeonis & terram Edithe Deuonisse in Kiboldestrete in eadem parochia. [i. 209.]

De dono Henrici filii Symeonis illud tenementum quod fuit Osberti Fabri cum pert. in eadem parochia. [i. 277.]

De dono Iohannis Pilet duas terras infra muros Oxonie scilicet terram que iacet inter terram que fuit Willelmi Fabri & terram Hugonis Boltarii & terram que iacet inter terram Roberti Kacki & terram Alicie Oliuer cum pert. in eadem parochia. [i. 172.]

De dono Gileberti Martel mesuagium illud cum pert. quod est inter domum angularem ipsius Gileberti & domum Galfridi filii Symonis in eadem parochia. [i. 345.]

De dono Iohannis filii Humfridi de Botele & Matillidis sororis Radulfi filii Symonis Cordewanarii & Theodolfi filii eiusdem Matillidis totam medietatem illius tenementi quod fuit Radulfi filii Symonis Cordewanarii & medietatem seruicii terre que fuit Ernisii le Turnur cum pert. in eadem parochia. [i. 291.]

De dono Henrici filii Symeonis mesuagium angulare cum pert. quod est retro curiam mesuagii quod dedit Henricus filio suo in eadem parochia. [i. 207.]

De dono Thome de Hemtone totam terram quam tenuit de eodem hospitali cum omnibus pert. suis, illam scilicet que iacet inter terram Roberti Sacerdotis filii Danielis de Bamptone & terram Willelmi de Halliwelle in eadem parochia. [i. 407.]

De dono Iohannis Cursy terram que fuit Willelmi de Cofle quam habuit de Matillide Andreu cum pert. in eadem parochia. [i. 329.]

De dono Willelmi filii Elye totam terram quam tenuit de predicto hospitali cum omnibus pert. scilicet illam que iacet inter terram Rogeri Bolle & terram Willelmi de Haliwelle in eadem parochia. [i. 231.]

De dono Ailwini le Tornur mesuagium cum pert. quod habuit in eadem parochia uicinum domui Rogeri Parui. [i. 266.]

De dono Henrici filii Symeonis terram quam Ailwinus le Tornur & postea Henricus filius suus de eo tenuerunt & quam postea emit de Rogero filio predicti Ailwini in eadem parochia. [i. 303.]

De dono Henrici filii Symeonis omne quod habuit in tenemento quod fuit Acei le Mercer quod de eo tenuit in parochia sancti Iohannis et omne quod habuit in tenemento quod fuit Wydonis Sutoris in parochia sancti Petri uersus portam orientalem, & omne quod habuit in tenemento quod fuit Nicholai Nigri in eadem parochia. [i. 238.]

De dono Radulfi Halegod terram cum pert. quam emit de Henrico filio Humfridi Mercerii & de Thoma fratre eius & de Margeria matre eorum in parochia sancti Iohannis. [ii. 112.]

De dono Cecilie de Gundeuil mesuagium cum pert. quod habuit in uico sancti Iohannis. [i. 224.]

De dono Alicie filie Segrimi redditum duorum solidorum de quadam domo in eodem uico. [ii. 112.]

De dono Alexandri Knicht unum mesuagium & quandam partem terre cum pert. in uico de Kiboldestrete. [ii. 106.]

De dono Hugonis de Hakeburne & Alicie uxoris eius terram illam cum pert. que iacet inter terram Gerardi Waterman & Felicie Bolle in eadem parochia. [i. 233.]

De dono Willelmi filii Elye totam terram quam tenuit de eodem hospitali que iacet inter terram Rogeri Bolle & terram Willelmi de Halliwelle in eadem parochia. [i. 231.]

De dono Thome filii Gileberti de la Hyde mesuagium cum terra quod emit de Alexandro le Knicht in uico de Kyboldestrete.[1]

De dono Emme de Ailebur', Ricardi filii eius & Iuliane filie eiusdem Emme totum tenementum in Kiboldestrete cum pert. quod tenuit de eodem hospitali. [i. 212.]

De dono Ade filii Iohannis totum tenementum quod tenuit de eodem hospitali in uico qui uocatur Cropecunte lane. [ii. 98.]

De dono Elie Brodfot terram que iacet inter terram Iohannis Ailnoth & Benedicti Ailnoth & terram que fuit Hugonis Rufi in Cattestrete in parochia sancte Marie. [i. 447.]

[1] This deed is missing; see ii. 106.

De dono Iohannis Pilet terram quam habuit in Cattestrete inter terram Iohannis Seui & terram Petri Illuminatoris. [i. 432.]

De dono Phillippi Molendinarii totam medietatem tocius illius terre cum pert. in Cattestrete que ipsum contingebat & que fuit aliquando Benedicti Ailnoth. [i. 451.]

De dono Roberti de Derby illuminatoris quandam domum suam [ ] in eodem uico. [i. 433.]

De dono Thome le Verrer totum mesuagium cum omnibus seldis adiacentibus & omnibus aliis pertinenciis suis quod habuit ex parte occidentali ecclesie beate Marie. [i. 420.]

De dono Iuliane que fuit uxor Walteri de Oseneia totum capitale mesuagium & alterum mesuagium retro illud mesuagium cum pert. in uico & parochia Omnium Sanctorum. [ii. 17.]

XLIX. De dono Albrede que fuit uxor Radulfi filii Arnebur' totam illam terram cum pert. que iacet inter terram Iohannis le Hore[1] & terram que fuit aliquando Stephani Siman in eadem parochia. [ii. 56.]

L. De dono Willelmi filii Stephani totum illud mesuagium cum pert. quod est inter duos furnos iuxta cymeterium ecclesie Omnium Sanctorum. [ii. 21.]

LI. De dono Aluredi[2] filii Goldiue[3] totam terram cum pert. quam habuit inter terram Walteri Pille & terram Henrici Unwas in parochia sancte Mildride. [ii. 70.]

LII. De dono Henrici Unwas totam illam terram que iacet inter terram Thome de Godestowe[4] & aliam terram ipsius Henrici in eadem parochia. [ii. 72.]

LIII. De dono Emmingi[5] de uico sancti Iohannis terram quam tenuit de feodo Stantone[6] in magno uico Oxonie in parochia sancti Michaelis ad portam aquilonarem. [ii. 271.]

LIIII. De dono Symonis filii Iohannis seldam que est inter seldam que fuit Audoeni filii Radulfi & seldam que fuit Iohannis le Stiward in magno uico in corueiseria.[7]

LV. De dono Roberti filii Laurencii Boidin duas solidatas redditus de terra quam Hugo Aurifaber de eo tenuit in parochia sancti Martini. [ii. 77.]

LVI. De dono Hugonis Harding illas quatuor seldas iuxta magnum

[1] Hoore, Bodl. Roll.
[2] Alfredi, Bodl. Roll.
[3] Goldwine, Bodl. Roll.
[4] Godstou, Bodl. Roll.
[5] Hemingi, Bodl. Roll.
[6] Stantonie, Bodl. Roll.
[7] This deed survives only in the Cartulary, where *Ricardi* is wrongly given for *Radulfi*; see ii. 271.

uicum inter terram que fuit Maugeri Vinetarii & terram que fuit Iohannis Sewy in eadem parochia. [ii. 79.]

LVII. De dono Walteri filii Galfridi Aurifabri duas solidatas redditus de tenemento quod Robertus Owein[1] de eo tenuit in parochia sancti Petri uersus Castrum Oxonie & duodecim denaratas redditus de terra quam Adam Rufus de eo tenuit in eadem parochia & tres solidatas redditus de terra quam Andreas de Wolgaricote de eo tenuit extra portam aquilonarem Oxonie.[2]

LVIII. De dono Rogeri le Veirs sex denaratas redditus de quadam domo in eadem parochia inter domum Ricardi de Uptone[3] & domum Iohannis Ioie. [ii. 265.]

LIX. De dono Ailwini filii Martini totam illam terram que iacet inter terram Nicholai filii Philippi & terram Willelmi Iouusdi[4] in parochia sancte Abbe. [ii. 234.]

LX. De dono Symonis persone ecclesie sancte Abbe tenementum cum pert. quod tenuit de Hugone de Berecote & de Anna matre eius extra paruam portam uersus aquam in eadem parochia. [ii. 244.]

LXI. De dono Lawrentii filii Ade de Gutinges duodecim denaratas redditus de terra quam Phillippus le Granger tenuit in eadem parochia. [ii. 242.]

LXII. De dono Willelmi Parmentarii totam illam terram cum pert. in eadem parochia quam emit de Maugero filio Iacobi Scriptoris. [ii. 231.]

LXIII. De dono Roberti Caschefreins duas solidatas annui redditus de terra que iacet inter terram Willelmi Lowedyn[5] & terram Henrici Virun in parochia sancti Aldadi. [ii. 132.]

LXIIII. De dono Dyonisie Burewald terram illam quam Radulfus le Waunter[6] de ea tenuit in eadem parochia. [ii. 147.]

LXV. De dono Roberti le Minnot[7] totam terram cum pert. quam habuit in eadem parochia cum quatuordecim solidatis & sex denaratis redditus & omnibus aliis pert. suis et duodecim solidatas annui redditus cum pert. in parochia Omnium Sanctorum. [ii. 139.]

LXVI. De dono Galfridi Iussel sex denaratas annui redditus quas habuit de tenemento quod Adam le Mare macon aliquando tenuit in parochia sancte Fritheswiþe. [ii. 128.]

[1] Owan, Bodl. Roll.

[2] This deed exists no longer, nor is it in the Cartulary; in 1248 the Hospital restored to the donor the rents in the parish of St. Peter-le-Bailey in return for a rent in Holywell (see ii. 257), and at the same time received a new charter for the rent in the parish of St. Mary Magdalen (see ii. 333).

[3] Optune, Bodl. Roll.

[4] Ioiesdi, Bodl. Roll.

[5] Loudin, Bodl. Roll.

[6] Gaunter, Bodl. Roll.

[7] Myngnot, Bodl. Roll.

LXVII. De dono Ricardi filii Henrici filii Cristine duodecim denarios redditus de quadam domo in eadem parochia. [ii. 127.]

LXVIII. De dono Walteri de sancto Eadmundo quondam officialis Oxonie terram cum edificiis & pert. suis quam habuit in eadem parochia iuxta domum Vincencii le Taillur, de dono Ade quondam archidiaconi Oxonie. [ii. 125.]

LXIX. De dono Dyonisie que fuit uxor Gileberti Burewald duodecim denarratas redditus quas magister Walterus quondam officialis Oxonie ei reddere solebat pro terra quam Adam quondam archidiaconus Oxonie aliquando tenuit in eadem parochia. [ii. 126.]

LXX. De dono Alicie que fuit uxor Willelmi Chipman[1] sex denaratas redditus de terra que fuit Iohannis le Turnur in uico qui uocatur Suthbrigestrete in parochia sancti Michaelis ad portam australem. [ii. 207.]

LXXI. De dono Galfridi Aurifabri Oxonie duas solidatas redditus in eadem parochia. [ii. 206.]

LXXII. De dono Philippi de sancta Elena totam terram cum pert. & omnibus edificiis quam tenuit de Andrea Halegod inter Castrum Oxonie & abbathiam Oseneye. [ii. 432.]

LXXIII. De dono Hugonis de Malaunai totam terram & omnia tenementa intra burgum Oxonie & extra que Petrus Boterel tenuit die qua fuit uiuus & mortuus. [i. 73.]

LXXIIII. De dono Willelmi filii Walteri Pille pratum cum pert. quod habuit iuxta Culake infra limites prati eiusdem hospitalis. [ii. 72.]

LXXV. De dono Willelmi le Cupere et Nicholai filii & heredis eius quatuor solidatas annui redditus pro quadam terra que iacet inter terram Hardin Palmarii & terram Symonis filii Iohannis. [i. 304.]

LXXVI. De dono Thome filii Thome quandam domum cum pert. que iacet inter domum que uocatur Meidenchalle & domum Iohannis de Westgate. [i. 368.]

LXXVII. De dono magistri Zacharie de Chebeseye terram & domus quas habuit de dono Willelmi filii Guidonis de Londoniis. [ii. 121.]

LXXVIII. De dono Ade filii Iohannis redditum sex solidorum quem tenuit de eodem hospitali in feodo. [ii. 98.]

LXXIX. De dono Roberti filii Rogeri de Swineshulle duodecim denarratas redditus de terra illa que iacet inter terram Walteri de Swineshulle & inter[2] terram Thome Cappe. [ii. 206.]

LXXX. De dono Thome Fullonis sub muro nouem solidatas

[1] Sypman, Bodl. Roll.

[2] This word is omitted in Bodl. Roll.

redditus & quatuor denarratas de terra quam Humfridus de Chiltone cepit de eo sub muro Oxonie, & octo solidatas & quatuor denarratas redditus de terra quam Iohannes Brito cepit de eo, & quatuor solidatas redditus de terra quam Osbertus Smart de eo cepit que fuit Elie Waynpayn. [ii. 237.]

LXXXI. Et de dono Henrici Operarii terram illam que iacet inter terram Willelmi de Fossa & inter[1] terram Augustini presbiteri de Wudeperi. [i. 352.]

III. A COMPUTUS ROLL OF 1340.

None of the computus rolls of the Hospital survive except the following fragment. It is one roll, but the writing begins at each end, and it appears that the first part contains the expenses for shoes for the brethren from Jan. 18 to Sept. 21, 1340, with the farming expenses on the back; and the second part, which begins at the other end of the roll, runs from Sept. 21, 1340, to Sept. 21, 1341, and gives the servants' wages (£8 8*s.*), the payment of rents (£5 0*s.* 5*d.*), and the 'necessary expenses' (£22 19*s.* 1¼*d.*). The roll is in bad condition and badly written, and part of it is illegible.

The first account shows that, besides the Master and Nicholas the Clerk, the Hospital contained nine members, eight of whom are styled brethren; there is no mention here of the number of the sisters; but as the next account records that 16*d.* was paid at Easter for gloves for the brethren and the sisters, it is probable that the House contained sixteen members in all, apart from the Master. There were also the 'free servants', as they would then have been called, Nicholas the Clerk, who went to London for writs, John Gay, and Adam the Writer; and the domestic servants, a carpenter, 'sclatters', a carter, a baker, and, if the roll were legible, we should probably find that there was a washerwoman and a dairy-woman. These all received board, lodging, and perhaps clothing, and a small wage besides. The 'oblations of the servants' at Christmas cost 4*s.* 6*d.*, and the same amount was paid at Easter for 'offertories', but it is hard to believe that the servants were fifty-four in number.

On the back of the first account are the expenses of the harvest of 1340, for the Hospital farmed the adjacent land. The mowing of Parys Mead cost 12*d.*, of Cowlake 5*s.* 6*d.*, of Cowlese 7*s.*, of King's Mead 4*s.* 6*d.*, of Cowelake Rowayn 4*s.*; and the reaping of the corn, grown probably where the Grove now is, was done by forty hired labourers in three and a half days.

The most noteworthy expenses of the year are £1 paid to Mag. William de Stafford, a local doctor, for healing the hand of Brother Thomas

[1] This word is omitted in Bodl. Roll.

de Kylmesham; 12*s.* for making a fishpond; 5*d.* for collars for the swans; and various expenses for making a new missal for the chapel, more than 16*s.* being spent on what is called parchment velym or parchment, while ink, vermilion, and azure were purchased. There is no payment to the writer, and we may assume that it was done by Adam Scriptor, one of the servants of the Hospital.

Solucio pro sotularibus a festo sancte Prisce uirginis usque ad festum sancti Mathei immediate sequens anno xiiii° [1]

Fratri Willelmo de Hunsingore pro sotularibus

Item in septimana Purificacionis beate Marie solut' eidem vi d.; circa festum Pentecosten vi d.

Item pro emendacione sotularium

In septimana sancti Cedde solut' eidem pro emendacione ii d.

Fratri Willelmo de Wottone pro sotularibus

Item in septimana sancti Valentini solut' eidem vi d.; ad festum Phasc' vi d.; item in septimana sancte Petronille vi d.; item in septimana Assumpcionis beate Marie vi d.

Item pro emendacione sotularium

In septimana Conuersionis sancti Pauli i d. ob.; in septimana Seyn Marke i d. ob.; in septimana sancti Barnabe apostoli ii d. ob.

Fratri Thome de Chadleshunte pro sotularibus

Item in septimana sancti Valentini vi d. pro sotularibus; ad festum Phasc' vi d.; item in septimana sancte Petronille vi d.; item in septimana sancti Kenelmi vi d.; item in septimana Exaltacionis sancte Crucis vi d.

Item pro emendacione sotularium

In septimana Conuersionis sancti Pauli i d. ob.; in septimana sancti Marci ob.

Fratri Godefrido pro sotularibus

In septimana sancte Agathe uirginis vi d. pro sotularibus; ad festum Phasc' vi d.; item in septimana sancte Petronille vi d.; item in septimana sancti Kenelmi vi d.; in septimana Exaltacionis sancte Crucis vi d.

Item pro emendacione sotularium

In septimana sancti Georgii ii d. ob.; in septimana Assumpcionis beate Marie iiii d.

[1] Jan. 18 to Sept. 21, 1340.

Fratri Iohanni de Kent pro sotularibus

Item in septimana sancti Valentini solut' eidem pro sotularibus vi d.; ad festum Phasc' vi d.; in septimana Translacionis sancti Thome vi d.

Item pro emendacione sotularium

In septimana Conuersionis sancti Pauli i d. ob.

Fratri Iohanni de Erdintone pro sotularibus

Ad festum Phasc' vi d.

Item pro emendacione sotularium

[*blank*]

Fratri Waltero le Rokaile pro sotularibus

Ad festum Pasc' vi d.

Item pro emendacione sotularium

In septimana Conuersionis sancti Pauli i d.; in septimana sancti Georgii i d.

Fratri Thome d Kilmesham pro sotularibus

Item in septimana sancti Augustini vi d. pro sotularibus; ad festum Pasc' vi d.; item in septimana sancte Petronille vi d.; item in septimana Translacionis sancti Thome martiris vi d.; item in septimana Exaltacionis sancte Crucis vi d.

Item pro emendacione sotularium

In septimana Conuersionis sancti Pauli ob.; in septimana ante festum Pasc' i d. ob.; item in septimana Translacionis sancti Thome i d.

Iohanni Ticly pro sotularibus

Ad festum Pasce vi d.; circa festum Pentecost' vi d.; in septimana sancti Barnabe apostoli vi d.; in septimana sancti Petri quod dicitur Aduincula vi d.; item in septimana Exaltacionis sancte Crucis vi d.

Item pro emendacione sotularium

In septimana sancti Georgii iiii d. ob.; in septimana Assumpcionis beate Marie iii d.

Nicholao clerico pro sotularibus

Item in septimana Translacionis sancti Thome vi d.

tem pro emendacione sotularium

In septimana ante festum sancte Marie iii d. ob.

Summa sotularium xviii s. ix d. ob.

R[otulus] fratris Ade de Lodbroke magistri hospitalis sancti Iohannis et fratris Thome de [de] solucione [stipendiorum fa]mulorum[1] & resolucione reddituum forincecorum & aliorum necessariorum factarum [*sic*] anno [regni Anglie regis] Edwardi [tercii post] conquestum quartodecimo, Francieque primo.

Solucio stipendii famulorum termino sancti Michaelis

Ricardo Sclatter termino Michaelis iii s. et xiiii d. pro ceruisia sua. Item Waltero famulo

[*the rest is illegible*]

Solucio stipendii famulorum termino sancti Thome apostoli

Iohanni Carpentario v s.; Roberto le Sclattere iii s. & xii d. pro ceruisia; Willelmo le Sclattere ii s. vi d. & vi d. [pro ceruisia]; Henrico famulo Sclattere xviii d. & v d. pro ceruisia; Roberto socio suo xviii d. & v d. pro ceruisia; Roberto operario xxi d. & x d. pro ceruisia; Iohanni socio suo xviii d. & v d. pro ceruisia; Willelmo Kalder vii d.; Thome Baker xii d.

Summa xix s. xi d.

Solucio stipend[ii] famulorum termini beate Marie

Item solut' Iohanni Carpentario v s.; item Roberto le Sclattere xii d. & pro ceruisia . . . [*the rest is illegible*]

Summa xxxv s. ii d.

Solucio stipendii famulorum termini sancti Iohannis Baptiste

Item solut' Iohanni Carpentario pro stipendio suo vs.; item solut' Roberto le Sclattere iii s. et pro ceruisia xii d.; item solut' Henrico famulo suo xviii d. & pro ceruisia vi d.; item Willelmo Sclattere ii s. vi d. et pro ceruisia [*blank*]; item Waltero famulo suo xviii d. et pro ceruisia v d.; item solut' Roberto famulo Sclattere xviii d. et pro ceruisia v d.; item solut' Hugoni le Sclattere operanti super aulam infirmorum iii s. et pro ceruisia xii d.; item Iohanni famulo suo xviii d. et pro ceruisia v d.; item Roberto operario de uilla xxi d. et pro ceruisia vi d.; item Iohanni socio suo xviii d. et pro ceruisia v d.; item solut' Andree Carectario vi d.; item Ricardo Baker xii d.

Summa xxviii s. xi d.

Item solut' Nicholao Clerico pro roba [sua] x s.; item solut' Ade Scriptori iii s. iiii d.; item solut' Iohanni Gay pro stipendio suo per

[1] The words within square brackets are guessed.

totum annum x[ ]; item solut' Ade Scriptori termino sancti Iohannis Baptiste iii s. iiii d.

Summa totius stipendii famulorum viii li. viii s.

Resolucio reddituum annis supradictis

In primis solut' apud Hedingdon pro redditu vi d. termino sancti Michaelis; item solut' ecclesie sancti Petri in oriente pro minutis decimis iii s. iiii d.; item solut' apud Couele pro redditu termino sancti Michaelis x s.; item solut' Iohanni de Brehull de tenemento Wareyn[1] iii s. iiii d.; solut' apud Castrum[2] Oxon' pro redditu de [quadam] placia que uocatur Goseholt vi d.; solut' Iohanni de Brehull de tenemento le Hore[3] vii s.; solut' apud Halliwell de termino sancti Michaelis viii s. viii d.; item preposito de Chalegrave x s.;[4] item solut' apud Eynesham pro redditu cuiusdam tenementi quod uocatur Graunger pro arreragiis iiii s.;[5] item solut' lumini sancte Lucie ad domum sancte Frydeswyde pro anno isto & pro anno preterito xvi d.;[6] item solut' apud Coldenorton pro redditu de anno xiii^mo^ v s.;[7] item solut' apud Godestowe de tenemento Metebourne xviii d.;[8] item solut' ibidem iiii d. ob. de tenemento Bultras;[9] item solut' ecclesie sancte Crucis de termino sancti Michaelis xii d.

Summa lvi s. iii d. ob.

Item solut' apud Haliwelle viii s. viii d. de termino beate Marie; item solut' Iohanni Wyard ii s. vi d. q.; item solut' Iohanni de Brehull vii s. de domo Alicie de Neubury;[10] item solut' apud Coueley x s.; item solut' luminari ecclesie de Hedyndon iiii d. de anno preterito; de anno isto iiii d.; item solut' Iohanni Aurifabro[11] iii s. de termino

[1] Henry Simeon had a rent of two shillings from domus Wareyn (see ii. 213) and 16*d.* from the adjacent tenement (see ii. 216). These rents descended to John de Brehull and ultimately to John de Northampton (see ii. 220).

[2] A rent paid at the Castle would be a rent paid to the sheriff; probably Goseholt was not in Oxford but somewhere in the county.

[3] The quitrent from Hore's tenement was originally eight shillings (see ii. 56 and the rental of 1328). In this year fourteen shillings were paid.

[4] The rental of 1328 says this was due for the meadow called Cowlake.

[5] There was a quitrent of 12*d.* a year due to Eynsham from Granger's tenement (see ii. 234).

[6] A rent of 5*s.* 8*d.* was due to St. Frideswide's from Swinbrook's (see ii. 46). Of this sum 8*d.* was due to the light of St. Lucy (see *Cart. St. Frid.* i. 291).

[7] For the rent due to Coldnorton Priory see i. 451, 452.

[8] The rental of 1328 says that there was a rent of five shillings due from this tenement to Godstow; probably the figure here should be 15*d.*, which would be a quarter's rent, and would make the total tally with the items.

[9] The rental of 1328 says that there was a rent of nine pence due from this tenement to Godstow.

[10] Another name for Hore's tenement which has been mentioned already.

[11] The rental of 1328 records a rent of three shillings payable to the heirs of Walter Aurifaber 'pro prato Pille'.

sancti Baptiste anno x[; item solut'] procuratoribus Magdalene xv d. de termino Michaelis; item solut' ecclesie Mildrede ii d. de anno preterito;[1] item s[olut' de anno isto ii d.]; item solut' ecclesie sancte Crucis xii d. de termino beate Marie; item ecclesie sancti Petri in oriente pro m[inutis decimis ad] terminum Annunciacionis beate Marie iii s. iiii d.; item solut' domo [*sic*] sancte Frideswyde pro redditu de tenemento [Simonis de] Gloucestr'[2] ii s. vi d.; item solut' apud Godestowe de tenemento Metebourne pro duobus terminis ii s. [& vi d.]; item solut' ibidem pro tenemento Bultras de termino Annunciationis beate Marie iiii d. ob.; solut' apud Abindone de redditu tenementi [de anno] isto xii d.[3]

Summa xliiii s. i d. ob. q.[4]

Summa resolucionis redditum hoc anno c s. v d.

Expense necessarie pro annis supradictis

Item in septimana sancti Matthei apostoli in pergameno empto vii d.; in cera empta pro sigillacione ii d.; in panno empto ad faciendum caligas pro forestario de Schottore iii s.; solut' clamatori de hustengo[5] pro duobus annis xvi d.; in uelym empt' pro uno missale faciendo pro capella iiii s.; in uermilom empt' pro eodem ii d.; item in una naui[6] empta xxvi s. viii d.; in uno saler empto i d. ob.; in uno caballo conducto pro fratre Galfrido[7] ix d.; solut' pro purgacione bladi i d. ob.; item in uno uase pandoxali empt' qui uocatur une maschfat ix s.; solut' pro factura candelarum ix d.; item solut' pro factura unius lacus pro pisse[8] staurando xii s.; item allocatur Iohanne de Perschore pro aula sancti Willelmi[9] vii s.; solut' apud Lond' pro breuibus perquirendis x d.; item in panno empto pro caligis faciendis pro bedellis iii s. iiii d.; item solut' pro tonsura p[anni] iii d.; in causto empto i d.; item solut' pro purgatione bladi xi d.; solut' le couperc iiii d.; solut' pro tawyng unius corci v d.; item allocatur pro scolis in Cattestret xix d.; in uasis de bosco emptis xiiii d.; solut' pro uentilacione bladi i d.; solut' pro dikyng unius fosse ii d. ob.; item solut'

[1] The rental of 1328 states that this rent was due from St. Mildred's Hall, afterwards known as Deep Hall.

[2] The rental of 1339 shows that Simon of Gloucester was the tenant of Swinbrook's, in All Saints, from which there was a rent of five shillings a year due to St. Frideswide's.

[3] The Hospital paid to Abingdon a rent of 12*d.* a year from a house in St. Aldate's (see ii. 153).

[4] This total is correct, if the conjectural figures within square brackets are accepted.

[5] The Town Crier.

[6] Probably a barge or punt.

[7] Brother Geoffrey is not mentioned in the list of the brethren at the beginning of the roll.

[8] =*pisce*.

[9] St. William's Hall had just been acquired from Joan de Pershore (see ii. 65).

domo [*sic*] sancte Frideswyde pro arreragiis a retro existentibus xx s.; in pergameno uelym empto pro missale iiii s.; in pergameno i d.; in una sera empta pro naui ii d.; in expensis Iohannis Gay[1] per duos dies apud Abyndone ii d.; allocatur ad domum Luce le Gardiner[2] iii d.; item in septimana sancte Katerine in una acra bosci empta ix s.; in tawyng unius corei v d.; solut' Iohanni Coco vii d.; in pergameno i d.; solut' magistro Iohanni de Furlond pro salario suo de anno preterito vi s. viii d.; in speciebus emptis per diuersas uices pro magistro & fratribus vi s.; in una sera empta iii d.; Iohanni Bedeman pro emendatione sotularium suorum ii d. ob.; item in pergameno uelym empto pro missale ii s. x d.; in tawyng unius corei v d.; in candelis ii d.; in uno tunne ii s.; in sex paribus caligarum emptis pro fratribus iiii s. ii d.; solut' Cristiane le Deye pro sotularibus vi d.; in cla*uibus* iii d. ob.; solut' Waltero le Barbour pro rasura fratrum pro dimidio anno ii s.; solut' pro tonsura panni viii d.; item in septimana Natalis Domini dat' per preceptum magistri garcionibus domini regis iii s. ix d.; solut' pro oblacionibus famulorum in die Natalis Domini iiii s. vi d.; solut' bedell' de uilla[3] pro oblacionibus suis ii s.; item solut' balliuis de uilla xviii d.; in (?) manenis emptis xii d.; in pisis emptis pro columbellis vii d.; solut' pro tonsura panni xii d.; solut' pro conductione caballorum per diuersas uices xx d.; item dat' famulis in uigilia Epiphanie per preceptum magistri vi d.; solut' pro misis apud Hedingdone; in sacc' empt' ii s.; solut' pro emendacione caligarum fratrum viii d.; in pergameno ob. qua.; solut' le quernebit*er*e i d.; solut' magistro Willelmo de Stafford in parte solucionis sanacionis manus fratris Thome de Kylmesham vi s. viii d.; solut' pro sanacione porcellorum iiii d.; in pergameno pro missale ecclesie iii s.; item datum Roberto Bedello per preceptum magistri xii d.; solut' pro exemplario missal' vi d.; in septimana conuersionis sancti Pauli in panno empto pro caligis faciendis pro balliuis de uilla & clericis & amicis de uilla vii s. i d.; in uno pari caligarum empto pro fratre Iohanne de Erdintone vi d.; in cotun empto pro candelis faciendis & factura candelarum solut' xxiii d. qua.; solut' fratri Willelmo de Hunsingore pro expensis suis circa Wodestoke & Otyndone ii d. ob. qua.; solut' pro pistrinacione panis in uilla pro amicis de uilla comedentibus cum magistro i d. qua.; item datum Thome Coco quia laborauit per unum diem in coquina, quando magister habuit secum

[1] Mentioned ii. 65, apparently the servant or agent of the Hospital.

[2] A house outside East Gate on the south side; see rentals of 1328 and 1339.

[3] This probably means the serjeants or sub-bailiffs of the town.

uicecomitem Oxonie ad prandium vi d.; item dat' Ade de Dene iii s. v d.; item liberat' Nicholao garcioni magistri pro breuibus perquirendis xxii d.; in pergameno i d.; in pergameno uelym pro missale ecclesie xvii d.; in uermilon ii d.

Summa ix li. vi s. viii d. ob. qua.

Item in septimana sancte Agathe uirginis in petris emptis iii d. ob.; solut' pro tonsura panni ii d.; item datum garcioni Ade de Dene vi d.; in uno (?) spur empto iii d.; in duabus [*sic*] colariis [1] emptis pro cignis v d.; in causto i d.; in uino empto pro uno exhennio misso Ricardo de Hastang ix d.; in pane empto pro eodem ix d.; solut' Iohanni de Bibury de tenemento quondam Isabelle Kepharm [2] pro quadam pensione annuali termino sancti Thome v s.; item allocatur Iohanne de Perschore de aula sancti Willelmi vi s. iii d.; solut' magistro Willelmo de Stafford pro sanacione manus fratris Thome de Kylmesham vi s. viii d.; solut' fratri Thome de Chadleshunte pro expensis suis uersus uillam de Stontone i d.; item in septimana sancti Augustini in duabus acris bosci emptis xx s.; in stramine empto & misso Ricardo de Hatecombe xx d.; solut' pro tawyng unius corei uitulini i d. ob.; solut' pro uulling panni ii d.; in expensis fratris Willelmi de Hunsingore uersus Abyndone ob.

Item in bosco empto x s.; in una naui empta xviii s.; solut' le Coupere ii d. ob.; in uno uomere empto x d.

Item in filo empto ad retia iii d. ob.; in emendacione unius crebri qua.; in filo empto ad retia x d. ob.; solut' operario retium ii d.; solut' i d. ob.

Item solut' Willelmo de Stafford pro fratre Willelmo de Hunsingore infirmo vi s. viii d.; in caustio [*sic*] empto i d.; in cartcloutus emptis xi d.; item solut' pro pueris ad scolas x d.; in pilo [*sic*] empto ad retia viii d.; in a bulter iiii d.; item solut' Heyward de Bekebroke iii d.

Item in emendacione cerorum & clauorum [*sic*] x d.; in Aschoueletr' i d.; in cirotecis emptis pro fratribus & sororibus erga festum Pasce xvi d.; item solut' [*illegible*] ii d.; item solut' operario retium iiii d.; item querne betere i d.

Item in ferrura equorum & aliis rebus ibidem factis vii s. vi d.; solut' pro offertoriis circa festum Pasce iiii s. vi d.; in cirotecis emptis pro carpentariis iii d.; item in thure empt' pro exenio uicecomitis Oxon' vi d.; item solut' Waltero Barbitonsori xii d.; in uno lamine ferri

[1] *colarium* meaning a collar occurs below.

[2] This tenement was in St. Aldate's; see the rental of 1339.

empto v d.; in tarre i d.; item allocatur pro aula sancti Willelmi vi s. iii d.; item solut' Iohanni Byburi de tenemento Kepharm v s.; in uno skelyng[1] empto in una domo vii s.; in uno pari caligarum pro Nicholao clerico vii d.

Item in frettiis (? frettus) iiii d.; solut' retario i d.; in candelis emptis i d.; in emendacione maceriarum celerii ii s. viii d.; item in i pari caligarum pro Iohanne Gay viii d.; in filo empto ad retia xii d.; item solut' Iohanni Biburye de aula Blaunckeney[2] v s.; item in i pouche empto, quod magister dedit uicecomiti Oxon' iiii s.; item in caligis scilicet tres pares [*sic*] pro Willelmo Catesbye & duobus sosiis [*sic*] iii s.; pro famulis eorundem in caligis xviii d.; item allocatum est Waltero Deyar per preceptum magistri xiii s. iiii d. quia pro domo multum laborauit; item in lan' [. . . . .] x s.; in panno tincto ii s. ii d.; in panno tincto vi d.; in panno tincto xii d.; Cristiane de Deford in emendacione sotularium illius i d. ob.; item in filo i d. ad emendendum [*sic*] colers[3]; in i par de trayse ii d.; solut' operario retium iiii d.; allocatur principali de Brodegates[4] retro ecclesiam Omnium Sanctorum ii s. iiii d.; solut' operario de plomis per duos dies & dimidium v d.; item in septimana sequente ante festum 'ante portam Latinam' in talewe empto viii d.; in i par caligarum pro fratre Willelmo Wotton viii d.; in dealbacione duabus [*sic*] coreis ii d.; in incaust' & uermilun empto ad missale iii d.; in cartcloutus viii d.; item in pergamen' i d.; in emendacione fenestrarum (?) uelar' glasse i d.; frater Willelmus H. & Wotton quando fuerunt extra uillam apud Chetwode expenderunt iii d. ob.; item solut' operario de plomis conducto xi d.; in cartcloutus ii d.; in frettus iii d.; solut fretter' i d.; in blado empto pro columbellis vi d. ob.; item solut' le quariours xii d.; in pisis emptis pro columbellis xi d. ob.; solut' pro tonsura ouium ix d.; item in septimana sancte Petronille in pisis emptis pro columbellis xi d. qua.; solut' fratri Willelmo de Hunsingore pro expensis suis in villa i d.; in uno colario empto pro uno equo vi d. ob.; in pisis emptis pro columbellis iii d. ob.; in causto empto i d.; item in septimana sancti Barnabe in duobus caballis conductis extra uillam viii d.; solut' cuidam homini pro factura unius retis ad piscan-

[1] A *skelyng* seems to be what we call a 'lean-to shed'.

[2] This was in the parish of St. Michael North; see rental of 1339.

[3] Collars.

[4] Broadgates, afterwards known as Amsterdam, was not behind All Saints Church, and at this time was known as Burwaldescot (see rental of 1339). The hall that is here mentioned was on the site of Crust's tenement (see ii. 14), and in the rental of 1339 is called 'The hall behind All Saints Church'.

dum ii s.; in pisis emptis pro columbellis vii d.; item in septimana apostolorum Petri & Pauli in pisis emptis pro columbellis vii d. ob. qua.; item datum Thome Coco pro labore suo vi d.; item in uino empto & misso filio Guidonis Bretone iiii d. ob.; item solut' pro pergameno empto pro missale iiii s. vi d.; item in septimana Translacionis sancti Martini in pisis emptis pro columbellis vii d.; in auenis iiii d.; solut' pro tawing unius corei equini iiii d.; allocatum Gilberto Cary pro diuersis speciebus emptis pro magistro & fratribus xiii s. iiii d.; item solut' Isabelle seruienti infirmos xii d.; in panno empto viii d.; in uno pari cirotecarum empto pro fratre Thoma Chadleshunte i d.; item in septimana sancti Thome in pergameno iii d.; in emendacione unius sere iii d.; item in septimana sancti Kenelmi allocatum Iohanne de Perschore pro aula sancti Willelmi vi s. iii d.; item solut' Iohanni de Bibury de domo Kepharm v s.; item solut' cuidam garcioni pro custodia duorum iumentum [*sic*] in bosco vi d.; item solut' pro purgatione stagni de molendino ad tascam x s.; item viii d. ob. pro eadem; item solut' fratri Galfrido in parte solucionis unius rethis vi s. viii d.; in uno burso empto pro uxore Galfridi de Aston ii s.; in pisis emptis iiii d.; item solut' Iohanni Bibury de tenemento Blaunkeneye v s.; in pergameno empto pro missale xii d.; in uno colario empto iiii d. ob.; in azure pro missale ii d.; in iiii paribus caligarum pro hominibus domini Iohannis seint Pol ii s. iiii d.; in duobus caballis conductis pro fratre Willelmo Hunsingore & fratre Thoma Chadleshunte xii d.; solut' fratri Galfrido pro expensis suis circa London' pro negociis domus x s.; in uno caballo conducto pro eodem xviii d.; item in candelis ii d. ob. qua.; in cirotecis emptis v d.; in crebro ob.; item in candelis i d. ob. qua.; in corio albo i d. qua.; in uino empto & misso domino Iohanni Seint Pol pro exhennio iii s. vii d.; in pane xix d. ob.; in uno porco ii s. x d.; in uno uitulo pro eodem xxii d.; solut' Nicholao garcioni pro breuibus perquirendis ii s.; solut' le Coupere pro emendacione uasarum vi d.

Summa xiii li. xii s. iiii d. ob.

Summa omnium expensarum necessariorum [*sic*] xxii li. xix s. i d. qua.

IV. RENTALS OF THE HOSPITAL.

It is fortunate that many rentals of the Hospital survive, and for the period that they cover they are of much value for giving the names of the tenants, the variations of rent, and also to some extent the situation of the tenements; for the rentals occasionally give notes which show where the tenements were.

A mediaeval rental was a list of what the tenants ought to pay, not a list of what was actually paid, and it was drawn up at the beginning of the year, not at the end. Consequently a rental that is dated Michaelmas, 1360, would give the tenants and the rents for the year ending Michaelmas, 1361, not Michaelmas, 1360. Many of these rentals have rough notes of the amounts which were collected, but they are not worth printing; sometimes more was received than was due for the year, because the rent had been in arrears, but generally less than was due; for in the Mediaeval Ages bad debts were common.

In many of the rentals, as also in the rentals of Oseney Abbey, the entries are marked either with A. or F.; these letters stand for *annualis redditus* and *feodum* respectively, the latter word being used in the sense of a fee or fixed payment. In some rentals, instead of placing F. before the entry, the scribe adds *libere* at the end, or *tenet libere*, showing that the freehold belonged to the tenant, not to the Hospital, and that the rent was what we should call a quitrent. In a few cases the scribe makes a mistake when he deals with a tenement held on lease at a fixed rent, and puts F. before the entry instead of A.; but such cases are evidently errors.

The method of the Hospital of St. John, unlike the method of Oseney, was to group the *domus clericorum* at the end of each parish or at the end of the whole roll. These are either Schools or Academic Halls, which were let by a peculiar tenure, on the one hand the tenant being bound to produce some security for his rent, and on the other hand the landlord being bound to perform all necessary repairs as soon as notice was given to him; if he was dilatory, the tenant might carry out the repairs and deduct the cost when he next paid his rent. There was also the peculiarity that, if the tenant and landlord could not agree what was a fair rent, the matter was settled by four *taxatores* or assessors, two from the Town and two from the University, and their decision was to hold good for five years.

In the rentals from 1385 to 1394 we have some interesting information about the letting of houses; for the tenants are divided into those who hold *per annum*, and those who hold *per indenturam* or *ad terminum*. We learn that in the majority of cases a house was not let by lease or indenture but by an agreement for a year; we do not know how much notice had to be given by either side if the agreement was to be terminated.

Both from the rentals of the Hospital and from the rentals of Oseney we learn that there was a steady dwindling of the population of Oxford down to the reign of Queen Mary or Elizabeth, and a steady decline in the rent of houses. In the next section of this volume, where we give the Fine Books of the College, an attempt is made to trace the rise and fall in the values of houses from the beginning of the fourteenth century to modern times by taking certain instances of which we have full records; but in this section we will deal with only the period from 1300 to 1500 and notice the total of the rental from year to year. In 1293 the Oxford rents of the Hospital produced £129 1*s.* 9*d.*; the following table shows how this total decreased:—

	1325	1346	1356	1366	1376	1384	1394	1426	1478
	£ *s.* *d.*	£ *s.* *d.*	£ *s.* *d.*	£ *s.* *d.*	£ *s.* *d.*	£ *s.* *d.*	£ *s.* *d.*	£ *s.* *d.*	£ *s.* *d.*
St. Clement's	18 0	19 6	1 1 0	1 13 4	2 5 0	2 5 4	2 13 0	2 7 5	1 18 0
St. Peter's in the East	24 9 9	28 16 6	16 7 5	21 2 11	24 7 9	29 2 8	29 3 6	27 19 2	32 7 2
St. Mary's	9 6 8	10 12 2	5 18 2	7 10 6	9 3 10	9 4 6	9 2 6	8 17 2	7 4 10
All Saints	7 3 4	9 2 4	6 6 2	6 8 4	8 6 6	8 7 2	8 3 0	9 4 4	7 12 8
St. Martin's	1 10 8	3 7 8	2 11 10	2 10 5	3 9 8	3 14 0	3 3 8	1 12 8	1 6 0
St. John's	1 19 0	1 14 0	1 3 1	1 8 1	1 5 0	1 3 0	1 14 4	14 0	—
St. Michael's South	2 17 0	3 7 0	1 8 8	2 0 4	1 17 0	1 14 4	1 15 0	2 7 4	1 2 8
St. Aldate's	6 17 11	8 0 6	5 17 0	6 15 5	6 16 4	9 12 8	8 13 0	9 7 8	9 8 4
St. Ebbe's	4 14 4	3 14 0	1 9 4	2 2 6	2 17 4	2 4 0	2 16 9	2 14 0	1 0 8
St. Michael's North	2 14 4	3 19 0	1 8 0	1 6 8	1 6 8	1 6 8	1 6 8	2 0 0	1 3 4
St. Mary Magdalene	3 3 0	3 11 0	2 9 10	2 13 11	2 1 8	1 19 0	2 12 4	2 4 4	2 15 0
Houses of Clerks	32 19 1	34 10 0	11 0 0	20 4 11	19 9 8	18 0 0	17 5 4	16 18 0	13 4
Total	98 13 1	111 13 8	57 0 6	75 17 4	83 6 5	88 13 4	88 9 1	86 6 1	66 12 0

These figures are only approximate, for in some cases the clerk has forgotten to enter the amount of rent due from a tenement and an estimate has to be made from previous or following rentals, but this can affect the total of a rental by only a few shillings. It will be observed that there was a drop in rents between 1293 and 1325, some portion of which was recovered in 1346. In 1349 came the Black Death and for a year or two there was chaos, and even seven years later the rental was barely half what it had been in 1346. There was a steady improvement in 1366, 1376, and 1384. Then for ten years there is little change; but in 1426 there is a fall, and in 1478, which is the date of the next rental, the total is little more than half what it was in 1293. And in reality the figures are worse than they appear, as the Hospital had been acquiring new properties all the time and parting with none. The following is a list of the tenements acquired by the

Hospital between 1300 and 1489, with their approximate values, and it is probable that there are others of which we have no records:—

					s.	*d.*	
1.	In 1300.	Perle's (i. 465)	value	about	10	0	yearly.
2.	,, 1302.	Four selds in St. Clement's (i. 5)	,,	,,	18	0	,,
3.	,, 1302.	A shop (i. 112)	,,	,,	4	0	,,
4.	,, 1302.	Three selds by East Gate (i. 140)	,,	,,	14	0	,,
5.	,, 1302.	A messuage and a forge (i. 139)	,,	,,	19	4	,,
6.	,, *c.* 1303.	A house in Pennyfarthing Street (ii. 142)	,,	,,	4	0	,,
7.	,, 1305.	A rent in Cat Street (i. 428)	,,	,,	3	0	,,
8.	,, 1337.	Aula Pille (i. 52)	,,	,,	12	0	,,
9.	,, 1339.	St. William's Hall (ii. 65)	,,	,,	20	0	,,
10.	,, 1349.	Boster Hall (i. 156)	,,	,,	16	0	,,
11.	,, 1354.	Domus Pille (i. 51)	,,	,,	16	0	,,
12.	,, 1360.	Faunt's (i. 438)	,,	,,	10	0	,,
13.	,, 1364.	The Angel (i. 171)	,,	,,	12	0	,,
14.	,, 1370.	Domus Auerham (i. 194)	,,	,,	5	0	,,
15.	,, 1376.	Domus Septima (i. 94)	,,	,,	5	0	,,
16.	,, 1411.	Wild's Entry (ii. 230)	,,	,,	16	0	,,
17.	,, 1413.	Two tofts (ii. 289)	,,	,,	5	0	,,
18.	,, *c.* 1420.	Land by Aristotle Hall (ii. 119)	,,	,,	2	0	,,
19.	Before 1450.	No. 80 High Street (i. 186)	,,	,,	10	0	,,
20.	In 1451.	Land in Castle Street (ii. 247)	,,	,,	60	0	,,
21.	,, 1465.	Domus octaua (i. 103)	,,	,,	13	4	,,
22.	,, 1489.	The site of White Hall (i. 315)	,,	,,	2	0	,,

According to this estimate the rental should have increased about £14 between 1300 and 1489, and this estimate is under the mark, if we may trust the evidence supplied by two lay subsidies or tenths collected in Oxford in 1383 and 1418.[1] It must be explained that in 1291 an ecclesiastical taxation was made throughout England, and lands and houses which were held at that date by ecclesiastical houses paid for the future to ecclesiastical, not to lay subsidies, but whatever a religious house acquired after 1291 paid its due to lay subsidies. In 1334 a new step was taken, and from that date the assessment or valuation of a town did not alter. In collecting a tenth in Oxford the method was to demand first of all a tenth from the endowed chantries, all of which were founded after the thirteenth century, and then from the Colleges and from the monastic houses as far as they had acquired tenements since 1291, the date of Taxation of Pope Nicholas. Now in 1383, when half a tenth was being collected, there are two entries about the Hospital of St. John:

'De magistro et fratribus S. Iohannis extra portam orientalem 9*s.* 1½*d.*
De magistro et fratribus S. Iohannis, Oxon, de antiqua 26*s.* 0*d.*'

[1] Twyne iv. 180 and xxiii. 435.

This seems to mean that in 1334 the Hospital was reckoned to have acquired, subsequently to 1291, lands and tenements in Oxford to the yearly value of £26, and those acquired between 1334 and 1383 were reckoned to be of the yearly value of £9 5*s*. These figures are much higher than those in our list, but it must be remembered that the estimate for the taxation runs from 1291 and ours from 1300, and that in the year 1293 alone the Hospital received Swinbrook's (ii. 47), Punchard's (i. 318), and Bodin's houses (ii. 322), which are reckoned to be worth about £9 10*s*. in the rentals of the beginning of the reign of Edward III. The estimates therefore are not utterly inconsistent. In 1418 the estimate was reduced and the acquisitions of the Hospital since 1291 were reckoned to be worth £30 a year, in other words, about a third of the rental of the Hospital at that time. We may therefore reckon that out of the total of £70 in the rental of 1478, quite £20 represents acquisitions made after the year 1293, and the real fall in prices between those two dates is represented by the figures 129 and 47.

The rentals supply other evidence of the continual decay of Oxford in the many tenements which sank to be gardens and finally were absorbed by their neighbours. This naturally occurred not so much in the main streets as in the corners of the town, the north-east and the south-east corners in particular. Before the Black Death the site of New College was becoming depopulated, and four Academic Halls, bordering the churchyard of St. Peter's, mentioned in the rental of 1293, are gardens in the next rental; but the Black Death hastened the decay, and the rentals show that in the south-east corner of the town a dozen cottages or more, the property of the Hospital, lying in Merton Street, Harehall Lane, and facing the city walls, became waste ground, and the site was not occupied again by buildings until the reign of Charles II. George Street (Irishman Street), the north side of which was occupied by houses in the thirteenth century, was deserted even before 1349 and became a piece of waste ground and was called Brokenhayes, perhaps from the fragments of hedges which marked the old sites. Even in High Street near the East Gate some of the tenements ceased to be occupied in the time of Henry VII and Henry VIII, e.g. White Hall (i. 315), when in addition to the Plague, which never died out, there was the visitation of the Sweating Sickness.

Notice should also be taken of the tenements which pass from the F. class to the A. class without any deed of gift to explain the change; for they are an indication of the decay of Oxford. In such cases the solution is that as rents and values fell, in time the owner of a house who had to pay a large quitrent found that it was cheaper to allow his house to be forfeited to the Hospital than to pay his quitrent. We have an instance where a house passed through this stage twice (ii. 100–105), having about 1320 lapsed to the Hospital for non-payment of the quitrent, and again in 1367 after it had been let at a lesser quitrent.

The houses in the rental are strictly in geographical order, and we can trace the course of the rent-collector as he went round each parish. It was his rule to collect one side of the street at a time, and not to cross from side to side. His arithmetic is so often at fault that no attempt has been made to correct it.

Some interesting light is thrown on familiar names in these rentals, for some rent-collectors described the tenants by the names that were used in daily talk. Thus a tenant near Carfax in the rentals of 1367 to 1376 is called Bartole, Bartele, Bartolot, and Bartelot; finally in 1385 his correct name is given, viz. Bartholomew the Taverner, but in daily life he was probably known as Bartle or Bartlot. Again, the Cesse Shapster of 1371 becomes Cecilia Spinster in 1374 and Cessota Shapster in 1375; so that her familiar name was Cesse or Cessot.[1] The Marieria Taylour of 1371 is the Magota Taylour of 1374 and the Marioria Taylour of 1394. Her name Margaret or Margery[2] was shortened to Mag, and then as Emma makes Emmota and Maria makes Mariota, so Mag makes Magota. In the rental of 1293 Edecus Lotrix, unless the name is an error of the scribe, is a form of Edith, as the next rental shows, and Bele Lotrix of 1293 is Isabella in the subsequent rolls. In 1325 we have the curious name Pulin the Barber which in 1328 is Ipolitus Barbitonsor; apparently the name was shortened to Pul and the termination -in, which appears in Janyn, Huggin, &c., was added. That Pernell and Petronilla are identical is proved by the rentals of 1351 and 1356, if it needs proof.

The rental of 1426 when compared with the preceding rental shows that in the last thirty years the Hospital had lost, or more probably sold, several small quitrents, especially in St. Martin's parish; there is no record that gives any explanation of it.

1. A rental of 1287–1293.

The first rental is a fragment, both the beginning and the end of the roll being wanting. The beginning would have recorded the tenements outside East Gate, also those in High Street within East Gate on the north and the south sides, and the rents 'contra muros uille uersus Kybaldstret', as the phrase is in the next rental, i.e. the rents in what is now King Street, running from High Street to the east end of Merton Street, and in the east part of Kibald Street. The remainder of St. Peter's parish and St. Mary's and All Saints in full are given, but the rest is missing.

The date must be after 1285 because there is mention of *domus Swinbrook*, which was not acquired until that year (see ii. 44), and after 1287 when *domus Canis* in the parish of St. Peter in the East was given to the

[1] This explains the name William Cusseblancpain which occurs in the Cartulary of St. Frideswide (i. 101) and in Oseney deeds; it is William, son of Cecilia Blancpain.

[2] That Margareta, Margeria, and Marioria are identical is undoubted.

Hospital. On the other hand the date must be before 1293, as a comparison with the rental of that year clearly shows.

Villa Oxon. 9.

In uico sancti Iohannis.

De Roberto le Waterman ad iiii terminos. iiii s. vi d.

De Alicia le Waterman que fuit uxor Iohannis de Esefeld ad iiii terminos. iiii s.

De Rogero Carpentario ad iiii terminos. iiii s.

De Bele loctrice [*sic*] ad iiii terminos. vi s.

De domo proximius aule Nitigale, de Alicia de sancto Egidio ad iiii terminos. iiii s.

De domo que fuit Iohannis Pochet. iiii s.

Contra murum a porta Stephani Ligatoris uersus cimiterium.

De Ricardo le Poleter. iii s. vi d. ad iiii terminos.

De Matilda Pulche ad iiii terminos. v s.

De Celena de muris[1] in angulo. xii d.

De Radulpho Balistario pro domo sua ad iiii terminos. ii s. i d.

In cimiterio.

De Henrico Gubiun pro muris in cimiterio sancti Petri. ii s.

De Waltero Scoil. ii s.

De noua domo proximius Waltero Secil. v s.

Ex alia parte ecclesie.

De domo quam Hugo le Norcis [*sic*] tenuit v s. ad iiii terminos, quam domum tradidimus uicario sancti Petri.

De Iohanne de Abrebur' de domo que fuit Ade Cementarii ad iiii terminos. iiii s.

De domo illa que fuit incluse; Symonis Escambiatoris. iiii d.

De domo Kokerel que iacet proximius aule Puellarum, Ioh[annes] de Abresbury. iiii s.

De aula Puellarum. vi d.

De tribus domunculis nouis ad iiii terminos. xii s.

De Margeria de Cudesdune. xvi d.

Contra murum.

De pergamenario contra murum de domo Canis iiii s. ad iiii terminos.

[1] This is not part of Celena's name, for in the next rental it is *pro muris*. Possibly it was a payment for permission to build upon walls which belonged to a tenement of the Hospital.

De terra Giliane de Swindone. iiii s.

De una placea quam magister de Hembur' tenet. vi d.

De duabus seldis in cimiterio sancti Petri in oriente quarum Henricus Gubiun tenet unam & uxor que fuit Willelmi Traci aliam ad iiii terminos. xiiii s.

De domibus clericorum in parochia sancti Petri in oriente.

De uico sancti Iohannis; de aula cum camino. iiii marcas.

De aula Nitigale. xxix s.

De aula in angulo contra murum. xviii s.

Kybaldestrete.

De aula iuxta uenellam[1] que tendit ad uicum sancti Iohannis. xxviii s.

De aula Nigra. xxix s.

De aula Vinee. xviii s.

De aula que uocatur Horsmulle Halle. ii marcas & dimid.

In cimiterio sancti Petri.

De domo in qua uicarius manebat. xxiii s.

De aula media. xviii s.

De aula uersus aquilonem. xix s.

De aula Martel.[2] xxv s.

De cameris.

De iiii cameris in domo Canis; unaqueque camera, quando possunt locari. iiii s.

De una camera propius porte magistri Willelmi de Monteforti; taxata v s. per annum.

Omnes domus suprascripte sunt de parochia sancti Petri in oriente.

De parochia sancte Marie.

In magno uico ex parte australi, de Matilda de Hely. xii d.

De Galfrido le Drouere de domo Plente ad iiii terminos. xxiiii s.

De eodem tenemento de Henrico Fabro. x s.

In cimiterio.

De Ricardo le Barber. xxviii s.

De Rogero Medico. xii s.

De Radulpho Balistario ad iiii terminos. xxx s.

[1] The collector begins at the east end of Kybald Street 'next the lane which leads to St. John's Street', i.e. King Street leading to Merton Street.

[2] Marcel, MS.

In Cattestar' [*sic*].

De Symone ligatore ad iiii terminos. xxx s.

De Radulpho Illuminatore. iiii s.

De terra que fuit Christes-Churche quam Galfridus de Hedingdone tenet simul cum una selda. vii s. vi d.

De domo Iohannis Faunt. x s.

De terra Yonis [*sic*] filii Willelmi Ligatoris. xxiiii s.

De domo quam Robertus Notur tenet. ix s.

In speciario.

De terra Iohannis de Wicumbe. xii d.

De domibus clericorum.

De Inghalle. iiii marc.

De Magna Scola in Castestrete [*sic*]. xl s.

De v cameris infra predictam scolam; unde de magna camera. x s.

Item de alia camera ex transuerso curie. viii s. vi d.

Item de celario. viii s.

Item de solario. viii s.

Item de camera proximius scole. ix s.

Item de domo Scoleg' in Cattestr' quam Prior sancte Frideswide tenet. iiii s.

De parochia Omnium Sanctorum.

De Thoma Ypothecario. xxviii s.

De Godefrido de Hedindune in cimiterio Omnium Sanctorum. iiii marcas.

De Galfrido de Hengsesheye ex parte australi vii s.; unde percipimus annuatim unam marcam de Waltero le Cha[1] apud Magnum Pontem quousque arreragie sint persolute.

De eodem tenemento de Gileberto le lokiere. ix s.

De eodem tenemento de una selda. ix s.

De Roberto le Herbeler & de quadam muliere de duabus seldis sub magna camera de Burwaldescote. ii marcas.

De domo que fuit Roberti de Swinbroc. v marcas.

De domo que fuit Hugonis le Hore in Bucheria. xxviii s.

De iiii seldis eidem domui[2] pertinentibus. iiii marcas.

De aula Burwaldescote. x marcas.

[1] See ii. 37.

[2] This refers to *domus Swinbroc*; this is certain, for the Hospital received from the house of Hugh le Hore nothing but a quitrent of 28*s*.

2. A rental of 1293 or 1294.

Down to the year 1359 no rental states when the year was reckoned to begin; from 1359 to 1367 the date is either Sept. 21 or Sept. 29, but subsequently Dec. 21. If the heading of the roll for 1293 is accurate, it is probable that it runs from Dec. 21, 1293, to Dec. 21, 1294; for the date is 'anno xxii incipiente', and the years of Edward I begin on Nov. 20. On the other hand, the heading of the rentals of 1371, 1374, &c., show that *incipiente* was supposed to agree with *rentale*; in which case this rental might be of Michaelmas 1294.

On the back of the roll is the list of *redditus resoluti* which is found on the roll of 1328 and printed there. It is in the same hand, but not the same ink, as the face of the roll, and may be a few years later. The roll has been much altered and erased, and probably by means of corrections was made to serve for several years.

Rotulus fratris Willelmi de Otyndone de redditibus assise Oxonie anno regni regis Edwardi xxii incipiente.

Extra portam orientalem Oxonie ex parte australi; de parochia sancti Petri.

A. vi s. De domo iuxta pratum de Parys.
A. v s. De domo prox. ubi Bate le Sclattere nunc manet.
A. iiii s. De domo prox. ubi Douce textrix manet.
A. v s. De domo ubi Willelmus Plumbator manet.
A. iii s. De domo prox.
F. xx d. De domo que erat quondam Radulfi Bix, tenenda libere.
F. iiii s. De duobus tenementis que quondam Willelmus Pille tenuit libere.
ii s. De domo que sita est iuxta portam sancte Fredeswyde,[1] quam Prior sancte Fredeswyde tenet.
ii s. De itinere uersus grangiam sancte Fredeswyde[2].
unam libram turis. De tenementis que erant uendita comiti Cornybie.

Extra portam aquilonarem.

F. iiii s. De domo Oliueri Sissoris, tenenda libere.
A. vi s. De domo quam Thomas Sissor tenet.
F. ii s. De domo quam Adam Sissor & Edelina uxor tenent ad terminum uite predicte Hedeline.

[1] i. e. a gateway at the north end of Rose Lane.
[2] A line is drawn through this entry.

F. ix s.	De domo quam Matildis uxor Walteri Tingtoris tenet libere.
F. vii s.	De domo prox. quam I. Mareschall quondam tenuit libere.
	De tenemento quod erat quondam Walteri Godecnaue; nichil inuenimus.
iii s.	De tenemento quod erat quondam Mathey Boltere.
F. viii s.	De tenemento quondam Ricardi Marschall, quod Matilda Ioye nunc tenet libere.
iii s.	De tenemento quod Philippus Clericus quondam tenuit.
xii s.	De duobus tenementis que I. Mareschallus quondam tenuit.

Infra portam orientalem.

F. xxx s.	De domo Stephani Ligatoris librorum; libere.
F. xviii d.	De magna porta ad introitum curie predicti Stephani contra muros uille; libere.
A. x s.	De domo ubi relicta Hugonis Molendinarii manet.
A. xviii s.	De domo ubi Hugo de Rouboru manet.
iiii s.	De celda.
A. xx s.	De domo que erat Thome Ponchard.
F. xiiii d.	De domo quam I. Log tenet libere.
F. x d.	De domo quam Alicia le Mercer tenet libere.
F. xxxii s.	De domo Thome de Benham que uocatur Chapelhalle; libere.
	De quadam selda.
A. xvi s.	De domo quam Henricus Gobiun de nobis tenet cum una celda.
A. iii s.	De eodem tenemento de una celda, quam quidam scriptor tenet.
A. iii s.	De alia celda prox. de eodem tenemento.
F. x s.	De una celda quam I. de Leychamstede tenet ad terminum uite.
A. xvi s.	De eodem tenemento de una celda quam Celena tenet.
vii s.	De eodem tenemento de una celda quam I. Quocus tenet.
F. xl d.	De domo Log in qua Egidius de Stocwelle manebat libere.
F. x s.	De alia domo quam Iohannes Log tenet libere.
F. ii s. x d.	De quadam domo quam Alicia le Mercer tenet libere.
A. xii s.	De duabus celdis de domo Waldri.

F. xx s. De domo que fuit Iohannis Fylekynge, ad terminum uite Agnetis Fylekyn.
A. xiiii s. De duabus celdis iuxta domum Fylekyng.
A. ii s. De solario iuxta curiam quam uicarius de Helsefeld de nobis tenuit.[1]
A. xviii s. De duabus celdis simul cum uno solario de predictis ten*ementis*.

Infra portam ex parte australi.
F. iiii s. De Martyno Exemplatore de domo le Combar'.
i d. De domo Iohannis Fylekyng de eodem Martyno.
F. vi s. De domo Iohannis Kepharm; libere.
F. xxiiii s. De terra quam Willelmus de Borstalle de nobis tenuit libere.[2]

Contra muros uille uersus Kybaldestret.
A. iiii s. De Alicia le Rous.
A. iii s. De domo prox.
iii s. De tercia domo. [*Inserted in another hand.*]
F. iii s. De Thoma Ypotecario; libere.
A. iiii s. De prima domo in Kybaldstret.
A. x s. De domo prox. [Pro anno futuro iii s., *in another hand.*]
A. iii s. De domo quam Iohannes Longe de nobis tenuit.[3]
A. iii s. De relicta Thome Sclattere.
A. iiii s. De domo ubi Robertus de Hauwe manet.
A. iiii s. De domo proxima portam Aule cum Camyno.
F. x s. De Thoma de Orliens de terra que fuit Stephani Sementarii; libere.
A. vi s. De Edecus [*sic*] lotrice.

Contra muros uille a porta Stephani Ligatoris uersus cimiterium sancti Petri.
A. iii s. vi d. De quadam lotrice.
xviii d. De quadam porta Steffani Ligatoris. [*In another hand.*]
A. viii s. De domo quam Matilda Pilche de nobis tenuit.
A. xii d. De Celena pro mur' que assignantur capelle dicti hospitalis.
F. ii s. i d. De Radulfo Balestario pro domo sua; libere.

[1] See i. 266 and 272.

[2] Subsequently xxiiii has been altered to x: this would be after Aug. 22, 1295; see i. 157.

[3] This and the next two houses were subsequently connected by a bracket as though they were let as one tenement.

A. ii s. De uacua placia quam Iohannes de Leychamstede de nobis tenet.

A. iiii s. vi d. De relicta Alani Masoun.

A. x s. De domo prox. quam Hugo le Noreys de nobis tenet.

Adam de Spalding de domo prox.; alocatum uikarie sancti Petri. [*This entry is a later insertion.*]

Ex parte alia ecclesie.

A. v s. De domo quam tradidimus uicario de sancto Petro.

F. iiii s. De Iohanne de Abberburi de domo que fuit Ade Sementarii; libere.

F. iiii d. De domo illa que fuit inclusa; libere.

F. iiii d. De domo illa que fuit Simonis Excambiatoris; libere.

F. iiii s. De domo Kokerel que iacet proxima Aule Puellarum, de I. de Abberburi.

F. vi d. De aula Puellarum; libere.

A. xii s. De tribus domunculis nouis.

A. xvi d. De Margareta de Codesdone.

A. xii d. De domo Canis.

A. iiii s. De terra Iuliane de Swindone solebamus accipere & est in manu nostra.

A. iii s. De una placia quam magister Ricardus de Hambyri de nobis tenuit.

A. viii s. De duabus celdis in cimiterio sancti Petri quas Adam Golde de nobis tenet.

A. vi s. viii d. De Ric. de Suttone pro una selda. [*This is in a later hand.*]

De domibus clericorum in parochia sancti Petri in oriente.

A. xxxii s. De aula Waldry: [taxata per mag. I. de Caunpeden & mag. I. de Wakfeld, et per borgenses W. de Hedyndone & W. de Colesbourne anno r. r. E. xxiii, *in other ink*].

A. xxviii s. De aula ubi uicarius solebat manere de Helsefeld; taxata anno r. r. E. xxii per magistros, scilicet mag. Will. de Euerewyke & mag. I. de Persore & W. de Hedindone & W. Colesbourne, burgenses.

A. xxvii s. De alia curia quam uicarius predictus de nobis tenuit: [taxata per mag. I. de Caunpedene & mag. I. de Wakefeld anno r. r. E. xxiii, et per borgenses scilicet W. de Hedyndone & W. Colesbourne, *in other ink*].

A. iiii marc'. De aula cum camino in uico sancti Iohannis.

A. xxi s. De aula Nittingale: [taxata per mag. Rob. de Thorwaldeby & mag. I. de Retforde, burgenses Adam Spalding & Iohannem de Arderne anno r. r. Edwardi xxiii, *in other ink*].

A. vi s. viii d. De aula in angulo contra murum:[1] [pro anno futuro ix s., *in other ink*].

A. xxvii s. De aula iuxta uenellam que tendit ad uicum sancti Iohannis.[2]

A. xxii s. De aula Nigra in Kybaldstrete.

A. xvii s. De aula Vinee per annum.

A. xxvi s. viii d. De aula que uocatur Horsmullehalle.

In cimiterio sancti Petri.

A. xx s. De aula que uocatur Hayschehalle.[3]

A. xviii s. De aula in angulo.

A. xviii s. De aula media.

A. xviii s. De aula Wlpis uersus aquilonem.

A. xxv s. De aula Martel.

A. iii s. De una camera in domo Canis.

A. v s. De una camera propius porte ubi mag. Will. de Monteforti manebat.

In uico sancti Iohannis.

A. iiii s. vi d. De Thoma le Waterman.

A. iiii s. De domo prox.; de Alicia le Waterman.

A. iiii s. De domo ubi Rogerus Carpentarius solebat inhabitare.

A. vi s. De Bele lotrice.

A. } x s. { De domo prox. aul' Nittyngale.
A. } { De domo que fuit Iohannis Peiet.

In parochia sancte Marie.

F. xii d. In magno uico ex parte australi de Matilda de Hely.

F. xxviii s. De Ricardo le Barber, de domo Plente.

F. xxviii s. De relicta Ricardi le Barber.

A. xi s. De celd' & solario in cimiterio sancte Marie.

F. xxxv s. De Radulfo Balestario.

In uico Cattestrete.

F. xvi s. De Symone ligatore librorum [pro anno futuro xx s., *in other ink*].

[1] Probably Cross Hall: see i. 227.
[2] See i. 219.
[3] See i. 348.

F. iiii s. De Radulfo Illuminatore.
F. vii s. vi d. De terra que fuit Cristischurche quam Galfridus de Hedyndone tenet simul cum una selda.
F. x s. De domo Iohannis Faunt.
F. xxiiii s. De terra Yonis filii Willelmi ligatoris.
F. x s. De domo quam Robertus Notur tenet.
F. xii d. De speciario;[1] de terra Iohannis de Wycumbe.

De domibus clericorum.
A. iiii marc'. De aula Ygke.[2]
A. xl s. De magna schola in Cattestrete.
A. x s. De quinque cameris infra predictam scholam, unde de magna camera.
A. viii s. Item de alia camera ex transuerso curie.
A. iiii s. Item de celario.
A. vi s. Item de solario transuerso.
A. iiii s. Item de camera proxima schole.
A. iiii s. De domo Scholog' in Cattestret' quam Prior sancte Fredeswyde tenet. Non est spes.

De parochia Omnium Sanctorum.
ii marc'. De Thoma Ypotecario.
F. iiii marc'. De Godefrey de Hedindone in cimiterio Omnium Sanctorum.
F. vii s. De Galfrido de Heygseye ex parte australi; unde percipimus annuatim i marcam.
A. ix s. De eodem tenemento de una celda proxima ubi Robertus Lokyere manet.
A. ix s. De eodem tenemento de alia celda.
F. v s. De domo que fuit Roberti de Swynebrok.
A. iiii marc. De quatuor seldis eidem domo pertinentibus; [de i selda de Willelmo de Comenore; de i selda de Geliane Balt; pro ii seldis de Rogero le Cotiler, *in other ink*].
F. xxviii s. De domo que fuit Hugonis le Hore in Bocherya.
A. x marc'. De aula de Borouwaldescote.
A. i marc'. De duabus celdis sub magna camera de Borouwaldescote de Iwone Ipotecario.
[i marc'. de Scimond Lacatiner de una selda, *in other ink.*]

1 In the previous roll it is *in speciario*, so that the word probably here means *spicery*, not *spicer*, as we should expect.
2 i.e. Ing Hall.

De parochia sancti Martini.

F. iiii s. De domo ubi Thomas de Orliens manet.
F. ii s. De domo ubi Alicia de Welles manebat.
F. v s. De introitu Nicholai de Kingestone.
F. xiiii s. De duabus celdis traditis Roberto de la More.
A. ix s. De celda proxima.
F. x s. De una celda quam Nicholaus de Garsindone tenet in Suteria.
F. ii s. De uno solario quod fuit quondam Henrici Gamage quod Ricardus Ouerhee tenet.
F. ii s. De uno solario quod fuit quondam Galfridi Submuro, & est aretro.[1]
F. vi s. viii d. De una celda quam Iohannes de Heyford tenet.
[iiii s. De Ricardo Ypotecario de domo in qua Rosa le Chandeler manet, *in other ink.*]

De parochia sancti Iohannis.

F. iiii s. De heredibus Musso de Binne de Herthalle.
A. iiii s. De domo in Kybaldestrete ubi Ricardus Hayl manebat.
F. xvi s. viii d. De tenemento quod fuit quondam Petri Pistoris.
F. ii s. De terra Marlyni[2] quam mag. Ric. de sancta Fredeswyda tenet.
F. viii s. De terra quam Thomas Balle tenuit.[3]

De domibus clericorum.

A. xxx s. De aula Dosiare.
A. xxii s. De aula Militis.

De parochia sancte Fredeswyde.

F. xviii d. De terra la Mare contra angulum cimiterii.
xii d. De domo Radulfi capellani, que sita est infra portam cimiterii. Non est spes.

De parochia sancti Michaelis apud portam australem.

[De celda iiii s. & solario iii s.; de solario infra curiam iii s.; de celario ob' per septimanam; de alia domo iii s.; de alia domo iii s. *This in other ink.*]

De terra quam habuimus de Sarra tinctrice quam Thomas le Verrur adhuc tenet.

[1] 'in arrears'.
[2] Probably an error for Mazalini; Merton Deed no. 213 shows that John Mazalin held land at this spot about 1240; see iii. 51.
[3] This tenement was really in St. Mary's parish; see i. 471.

A. xx s. De domo Willelmi de Metebourne que fuit quondam Isabelle de Dorkcestria.
A. xvi s. De domo de Feryndone quam Robertus Boletras tenuit.
F. xii d. De terra Roberti Iat apud Swyneshulle.
F. ii s. De terra quam uxor Walteri de la Pylere tenuit.

De parochia sancti Aldati.
F. ii s. De Radulfo Plumbatore de terra Molendinarii.
A. xx s. De domo in cimiterio sancti Aldati ubi Thomas le Ȝernmogare manet.
xiii d. De Roberto de Driffeld in paruo Iudaysmo.
F. ii s. De Bissop Sauwyar.
A. xii s. De domo ubi Galfridus Faber manebat in Iudeysmo.[1]
A. xxiii s. De magna domo prox.
A. xi s. De una celda prox.
A. vii s. De alia celda prox.
A. vii s. De alia celda prox.
F. xvi s. De Iohanne Payn de domo prox. celd'.
xii s. De domo prox. Iohanne [*sic*] Payn.
A. xi s. De Iohanne Wayteschaþe.
A. xxiiii s. De domo prox.
A. xxx s. De domo prox. ubi Iohannes de Herdyntone manet.
A. vii s. De celd' in cornario prox. cimiterio sancti Aldati.
A. xxxiii s. iiii d. De aula Minot.

De parochia sancte Ebbe desuper muros uersus fratres predictos.
F. viii s. iiii d. De terra quam Iohannes Plumbator tenet.
F. viii s. De terra le Brumstare.
F. xvi d. De terra prox. que fuit Willelmi le Seriaunt.

Infra portam.
A. iiii s. De terra le Graunger quam Robertus Sissor tenet.
A. iiii s. De celda prox.
A. iiii s. De celda prox. solario de eadem terra.
A. vi s. De solario ultra predict' celd'.
A. xxi s. De domo Noyf.
A. v s. De terra Waryn.
[vii s. De selda & solario ; *in other ink.*]
F. xviii s. De tenemento quod fuit Walteri de Kyngestone, ubi Nicholaus de Lincolnia manet.

[1] Great Jewry was another name for Fish Street; this house was at the corner of Pembroke Street.

De parochia sancti Petri in occidente.

F. ii d. In cimiterio sancti Petri de tenemento Adam Loudyn.

F. vi d. De pistrina Walteri Palmarii solebamus recipere, & est aretro. Non est spes.

De parochia sancti Michaelis ad portam aquilonarem.

F. xxiii s. De terra que fuit Simonis Excambiatoris quam Fulc' Medicus tenet.

[xxi s. De tribus seldis, *in other ink.*]

De parochia sancte Mildrithe.

A. xxii s. De aula prox. ecclesiam ex parte orientali.

F. iii d. De terra Cole. Non est spes.

F. viii d. De terra quam Willelmus Pille tenuit uersus Smytgate, & sunt aretro. Non est spes.

F. iii d. De terra Henrici Unwas & sunt aretro. Non est spes.

De parochia sancti Thome.

F. i marc'. De terra quam Willelmus de Wotesdone tenet.

De parochia sancte Marie Magdalene.

F. xx s. De terra quam Robertus de Welles tenet.

F. ii s. De eodem feodo de una celda & uno solario que Iohannes Kyng & Florentia uxor eius tenuerunt.

F. ii s. De eredibus Rogeri le Sauser pro uno solario contra ecclesiam Marie Magdalene.

F. xii d. De una celda que fuit Radulfi Aurifabri.

F. iii s. De domo quam Walterus de Wingornia [*sic*] tenet, que iacet uicina domui que fuit Nicholai de Erneborou.

De dimidia placia que uocabatur Morcote nichil inuenimus. Non est spes.

Ex parte orientali.

F. vii s. De domo de Bramtone.

F. iii s. De terra le Waleys quam Rogerus de Schiptone & Iohannes de Dodeford tenent. [De Rogero Bost, *in other ink.*]

F. xii d. De terra Dodeling.

F. xxiiii s. De domo contra ecclesiam Magdalene quam Galfridus Fikeys & Margareta uxor sua tenent ad terminum uite.

Versus aulam regis.

A. vi s. De noua domo proxima stabulo domini regis.

Terra Willelmi Longy & Henrici Ode adquisita est per placitum in Undredo & remanent [*sic*] uacua.

Terra Rogeri le Benchar similiter adquisita per placitum stat uacua.

[iii s. De tenemento quod quondam Hugo de Meres tenuit; *in other ink.*]

De domibus Clericorum.

viii s. De Thoma de Welleburii [*crossed out*].
A. xxv s. De aula Bodyn iuxta aulam Periculosam.
xxiiii s. De alia aula de eodem tenemento.
A. xxx s. De aula que uocatur Brackele Halle.
A. ii marc' & dim. De aula que uocatur Depehalle.

De parochia sancti Egidii.

viii s. De domo Walteri de Moumbrai.
F. xvi d. De terra que fuit Ricardi Politarii in Stocwellestrete.
F. xx d. De terra Iohannis Randulf in eodem uico.

In magno uico uersus ecclesiam sancti Egidii.

F. v s. De noua domo iuxta Robertum de Broutone.
F. vi d. De terra quam uxor Iohannis de Curtlingtone tenet ex parte orientali.

De parochia sancte Crucis.

A. vii s. De tenemento quod Iohannes de Walton tenuit.
F. xviii d. De terra quam Chasse tenuit.
A. v s. De terra quam Iohannes le Tascur tenet.
A. iiii s. De terra quam Ricardus de Merstone tenet.
A. v s. De terra quam Adam de Gloucestre tenet.
A. ix s. De terra quam Adam de Grantedene tenet.
F. ii s. De terra quam uxor Iohannis Kyng tenet.
A. iiii s. De terra quam Willelmus de Walsingham tenet.
A. x s. De domo Griffini.
A. xii s. De domo Maynard in qua Rogerus de Walton manet.
A. xiii s. De duobus cameris in eodem tenemento.
A. xii s. De aliis duobus cameris de eodem tenemento.
A. x s. De duobus cameris ad introitum.
[A. iii s. De tenemento contra ecclesiam sancte Crucis, *in other ink.*]

Summa totalis Oxon cxxix li. xxi d.

De parochia de ȝyfteleye.

F. ii s. De molendino de ȝifteleye quam Iohannes Culuerd tenet.

F. ii s. De Coleman le Mercer.

De parochia de Northbroke.

F. ii s. De Ada Carpentario de Northbroke.

De parochia de Cadewelle.

F. i d. De Germano de Caddewelle.

Ric. Calbel de Chalfgraue; i paria scyratecas.

De parochia de Ode Bartone.

F. v s. De Roberto le Ieuene de eadem.

De uilla de Combe.

3. An undated rental.

The next rental must be after 1302, in which year was acquired the property in St. Clement's with which the roll begins; but as so many of the names are the same as in the rental of 1293, the date cannot be much later than 1302.

De parochia sancti Clementis.

vi s. De selda proxima uenellam.

iiii s. De selda proxima.

iiii s. De tercia selda.

iiii s. De quarta selda.

De una placea uacua iuxta cursum aque.

Extra portam orientalem ex parte australi.

vi s. De domo iuxta pratum de Paris.

v s. De domo proxima ubi Bate le sclattere manebat.

iiii s. De domo proxima ubi Douce textrix manebat.

v s. De domo ubi Willelmus Plumbator manebat.

iiii s. De domo proxima.

xx d. De domo quondam Radulfi Bix; tenenda libere.

iiii s. { De duobus tenementis que quondam Willelmus Pille libere tenuit.
De aula Pille. }

ii s. De domo que sita iuxta portam sancte Fredeswide quam prior eiusdem loci tenebat.

De itinere uersus grangiam sancte Frideswide.

i lb. turis. De tenementis que erant uendita Comiti Cornubie.

Ex parte aquilonari.

iiii s. De domo Oliueri Scissoris; tenenda libere.
vi s. De domo quam Thomas Cissor tenebat.
vi s. De domo quam Adam Cissor tenebat.
v s. De domo quam Matilda tynctoris [*sic*] tenebat.
xvii s. De domo proxima que I. le Marchal tenebat libere.
viii s. De tenemento quondam Ricardi Marchal, quod Matildis Ioye tenebat libere.
vii s. De tenemento quod quondam Philippus Clericus tenuit.
xii s. De duobus tenementis que I. Marchal quondam tenuit.
xiii s. iiii d. De Iohanne Tyngewic.

Infra portam orientalem.

xv s. De tribus schopis in porta.[1]
xxx s. De domo quondam Stephani ligatoris librorum; libere.
xviii d. De magna porta ad introitum curie predicti Stephani contra muros uille.
xix s. De domo ubi relicta Hugonis Molendinarii manebat.
xxii s. De domo ubi Hugo Ruboruz manebat.
xx s. De domo que erat Thome Punchard.
x d. De domo que Alicia le Mercer tenebat libere.
xxxii s. { De domo quondam Thome Beneham que uocatur Chapelhalle libere. De quadam selda. }
vi s. De domo quam Henricus Gobiun de nobis tenebat.
viii s. { De eodem tenemento de una selda quam quidam scriptor tenebat. De alia selda proxima de eodem tenemento. }
xvi s. De una selda quam I. de Leychamsted tenebat.
xii s. De eodem tenemento de una selda quam Celena tenebat.
vi s. De eodem tenemento de una selda quam I. Cocus tenebat.
xl d. De domo Log in qua Egidius de Stocwell manebat libere.
[x s.] De alia domo quam I. Log tenebat libere.
ii s. x d. De quadam domo quam Alicia le Mercer tenebat libere.
xii s. De duabus seldis de domo Waldri.

[1] These shops were really outside the East Gate, but attached to it.

xx s. De domo que fuit I. Filkyng ad terminum uite Angnetis Fylkyng.

xiiii s. De solario iuxta curiam quam uicarius de Helsefelde de nobis tenuit.

xx s. De duabus seldis simul cum uno solario de predic*to* ten*emento*.

Infra portam ex parte australi.

iiii s. De domo le Combar quam Martinus Exemplator quondam tenebat.

i d. De domo quondam I. Fylkyng quam predictus Martinus tenebat.

vi s. De domo quondam Kypharm; libere.

xii s. De terra quam Willelmus de Borstall de nobis tenuit libere.

Contra muros uille uersus Kybaldestrete.

iiii s. De Alicia le Rous.

iii s. De domo proxima.

iii s. De Thoma Ypotecario; libere.

iiii s. De prima domo in Kybaldestret.

iii s. De domo proxima.

vi s. De domo ubi I. de Hamsted manebat.

v s. De domo proxima.

x s. De Thoma de Orliens de terra que fuit Stephani Sementarii [*sic*]; libere.

vi s. De Editha Lotrice.

Contra muros uille a porta Stephani ligatoris uersus cimiterium sancti Petri.

De quadam lotrice.

De domo quam Matilda Pylche de nobis tenuit.

De Celena pro mur' que assignantur capelle dicti hospitalis.

De domo Radulfi Balistarii pro domo sua; libere.

De uacua placia quam I. de Leychamsted de nobis tenebat.

De domo ubi Alanus le Masun manebat.

De domo proxima quam Hugo le Noreys de nobis tenebat.

De Adam Spalding.

Ex parte alia ecclesie.

ix s. De domo quam tradimus uicario de sancto Petro.

iiii s. De I. de Abburberi de domo que fuit Ade Sementarii; libere.

iiii d. De domo illa que fuit inclusa; libere.

v s. De domo illa que fuit Simonis Excambiatoris; libere.

iii s. De domo Kokerel que iacet proxima aule Puellarum de Abburberi.

De aula Puellarum; libere.

De tribus dominiculis [*sic*] nouis.

xvi d. De Margareta de Codesdone.

ii s. De domo Canis.

De terra Iuliane de Swudun solebamus accipere & est in manu nostra.

De una placea quam Ricardus magister de Hamburi de nobis tenuit.

De domibus clericorum in parochia sancti Petri.

xxxii s. De aula Waldri.

xxviii s. De aula ubi uicarius de Helesefelde solebat manere.

xi s. x d. De alia curia quam predictus uicarius de nobis tenuit.

iiii marc'. De aula cum camino in uico sancti Iohannis.

xxii s. De aula Nyttingale.

De aula in angulo contra murum.

De aula iuxta uenellam que tendit ad uicum sancti Iohannis.

xv s. De aula Nigra in Kybaldstrete.

vi s. De aula Viner'.

xx s. De aula que uocatur Horsmelnehalle.

De domo que uocatur Haukeshalle.[1]

xii s. De aula in angulo.

xx s. De aula media.

De aula Wilp uersus aquilonem.

xxv s. Aula Martel.

In uico sancti Iohannis.

iii s. { De domo ubi Thomas le Waterman manebat.
De domo proxima de Alicia le Waterman. }

iiii s. De domo ubi Rogerus Carpentarii [*sic*] manebat.

vi s. De domo Isabelle Lotricis.

[1] Hayschhall in the rental of 1293.

x s. { De domo proxima aule le Nittingale Hall.
De domo que fuit I. Peyt. }

xii d. De quadam placia quam Philippus le Quilter de nobis tenet.

xiiii s. De Cros Hall cum duabus schopis.

In parochia sancte Marie in mangno uico ex parte australi.

De domo Matilda Hely.

xxviii s. De domo Plente.

xlvi s. De domo ubi Ricardus le Barber manebat.

vi s. De selda & solario in simiterio sancte Marie.

xxix s. De domo Radulfus Balistarius quondam manebat.

xx s. De Simone ligatore librorum.

iiii s. De domo Radulfus Illuminator quondam manebat.

vii s. vi d. De terra que fuit Christcherche quam Galfridus de Hedindone tenebat cum una selda.

x s. De domo I. Faunt.

xxvi s. viii d. De terra Yonis, filius [*sic*] Willelmi Ligatoris.

x s. De domo quam Robertus le Notur tenebat.

xii d. De speciar*io*; de terra I. de Wycumbe.

De domibus clericorum.

xlv s. De Aula Ynge.

xxx s. De Mangna scola in Cattesstret.

xiii s. vi d. De quincque cameris infra predictam scolam.

De alia camera extrauerso [*sic*] curie.

De celario.

De solario trauerso [*sic*].

De domo Scolag' in Kattesstret quam prior sancte Fredeswide tenet.

De parochia Omnium Sanctorum.

ii marc'. De Thoma Ypothecario.

iiii marc'. De Godefrido de Hedindone.

vii s. De Galfrido de Hencseye.

viii s. De eodem tenemento de una selda proxima ubi Robertus le Lokyer man*et*.

viii s. De eodem tenemento de alia selda.

De domo que fuit Robertus de Swinebroc.

xxxix s. De quatuor seldis eidem domo [*sic*] pertinentibus.

xxviii s. De domo que fuit Hugonis le Hore in Bocheria.

viii marc'. De aula de Borewaldescot.
ii marc'. De duabus seldis sub mangna camera de Borewaldescot.

De parochia sancti Martini.
iiii s. De domo ubi Thomas de Orliens manebat.
ii s. De domo ubi Alicia de Welles manebat.
xv s. { De introitu ubi Nicholaus de Kyngestun manebat.
De duabus seldis traditis Roberto de la More.
De selda proxima. }
x s. De una selda quam Nicholaus de Garsindun ten*et* in suteria.
ii s. De uno solario quod quondam fuit Henrici Gamage, quod Ricardus Ouerhee tenet.
ii s. De uno solario quod quondam fuit Galfridi Submuro & est aretro.
vi s. viii d. De una selda quam I. de Heyuord tenet.
iiii s. De domo Ricardi Ipotecarii apud Karefouk.

De parochia sancti Iohannis.
iiii s. De heredibus Musso de Bynne de Herthall.
iiii s. De domo in Kybaldestret ubi Ricardus Hayl manebat.
xv s. De tenemento quondam fuit Petri Pistoris.
vi s. De terra Mazelini quam magister Ricardus de sancta Fredeswida tenet.
viii s. De terra quam Thomas Balle tenuit.
De una selda.
De alia selda.

De domibus clericorum.
xxii s. De aula Dosiere.
xx s. vi d. De aula Militis.

De parochia sancte Frideswide.
De terra le Mar' contra angulum cimiterii.
De domo Radulfi Capellani que sita est infra portam cimiterii.

De parochia sancti Michaelis apud portam australem.
De introitu super magnam [*sic*] pontem (*an addition*).
xviii s. De terra quam habuimus de Sarra tinctrice & quam Thomas le Verrur adhuc tenet.
xx s. De domo Willelmi de Meeteborun que fuit quondam Isabelle de Dorccestria.

xvi s. De domo de Feryndun quam Robertus Boletras tenuit.
xii d. De terra Roberti Iat apud Suineshulle.
ii s. De terra quam uxor Walteri de la Piler' tenuit; pro aula de Lutlemor.

De parochia sancti Aldati.

ii s. De Radulfo Plumbatore de terra Molendinarii.
x s. De domo in cimiterio sancti Aldati ubi Thomas le Irmongere manet.
xiii d. De Roberto de Driffeld in paruo Iudaismo per annum.
xviii d. De Bissop Sawyer.
xii s. De domo ubi Galfridus Faber manebat.

v marc' vi s. viii d. {
De magna domo proxima.
De una selda proxima.
De alia selda proxima.
De alia selda proxima.
}

De domo ubi I. Payn manebat.
De domo proxima.
De domo ubi I. Wayteschathe manebat.
xxxiiii s. De domo proxima.

xxx s. {
De domo proxima ubi I. Herdyntun manebat.
De selda in cornario proxima cimiterium sancti Aldati.[1]
}

ii marc' vi s. viii d. De Aula Minote per annum.

De parochia sancte Ebbe desuper muros uersus fratres predicatores.

viii s. iiii d. De terra quam I. Plumbator tenebat.
viii s. De terra le Brumstere.
iiii s. (? iiii d.) De terra proxima que fuit Willelmi le Seriaunt.

xviii s. {
De terra le Granger quam Robertus Cissor tenebat.
De selda proxima.
De selda proxima solario de eadem terra.
De solario ultra predictam seldam.
}

xvi s. De domo Noyf.
xii s. De terra Waryn.
xviii s. De tenemento quod fuit Walteri de Kyngestune, ubi Nicholaus de Lyncolne manebat.

De parochia sancti Petri in occidentalem [*sic*].

ii d. In cimiterio sancti Petri de tenemento Ade Loudon.

[1] These two are bracketed in the rental, but they were not adjacent; the corner seld was on the south side of Pennyfarthing Street, while the house of I. Herdyntun was on the west side of St. Aldate's Street, north of Pennyfarthing Street. Perhaps the bracket means that one tenant paid for both.

De parochia sancti Michaelis ad portam aquilonarem.
xli s. De terra que fuit Simonis excambiatore [*sic*] quam Fulcus [*sic*] Medicus tenet.

De parochia sancte Mildride.
xxii s. De aula proxima ecclesiam ex parte orientali.

De parochia sancti Thome.
xiii s. iiii d. De terra quam Walterus de Wodesdun tenet.

De parochia sancte Marie Magdalene.
xx s. De terra quam Robertus de Well' tenet.
ii s. De eodem feodo de una selda & uno solario que I. Kyng & Florence uxor eius tenuerunt.
ii s. De heredibus Rogeri le Sauser pro uno solario contra ecclesiam predictam.
xii d. De una selda que fuit Radulfi Aurifabri.
iii s. De domo quam Walterus de Wyngorn tenet, que iacet uicin' domus Nicholai de Herneboru.

Ex parte orientali.
vii s. De domo de Bramthon.
iii s. De Rogero Bost.
xii d. De terra Dodelyng.
xxiiii s. De domo contra ecclesiam Magdalene quam Galfridus Fykeys & Margeria uxor eius tenent ad terminum uite.

Versus aulam Regis.
iiii s. De noua domo proxima stabular' domini regis.
iii s. De tenemento quod quondam Hugo le Mercer [1] tenebat.
xvi d, xx d. De duabus celdis in Stokwellstrete.

De domibus clericorum.
De aula Bodin iuxta aulam Periculosam.
De alia aula de eodem tenemento.
xxiiii s. De aula que uocatur Brackele.
xxii s. De aula que uocatur Depehalle.

De parochia sancti Egidii.
xvi d. De terra que fuit Ricardi Politarii in Stockewellestrete.
xviii d. De terra I. Randulf in eodem uico.

[1] rectius 'Hugo de Merse'.

In magno uico uersus ecclesiam sancti Egidii.

v s. De noua domo iuxta Robertum de Brentone.[1]

vi d. De terra quam uxor I. de Curlynthon tenet ex parte orientali.

De parochia sancte Crucis.

De tenemento quod I. de Walthon tenuit.

De terra quam I. Casse tenuit.

De terra quam I. le Tascur tenebat.

De terra quam Ricardus de Mersthone tenebat.

De terra uacua quam Adam de Glousestre tenebat.

De terra quam Adam de Grantedene tenebat.

De terra quam Willelmus de Walsingham tenuit.

De domo Griffini.

De domo Maynardi in qua Rogerus de Walthone manet.

De domo proxima.

De Thoma le Gangfurmer.

De duabus cameris de eodem tenemento.

De aliis duabus cameris de eodem tenemento.

De duabus cameris ad introitum.

De tenemento contra ecclesiam Sancte Crucis.

4. A rental of 1325, probably Dec. 21, 1325, to Dec. 21, 1326.

Rentale hospitalis sancti Iohannis extra portam orientalem Oxonie anno regni regis Edwardi filii regis Edwardi decimo nono.

In parochia sancti Clementis.

vi s. De celda prox. uenellam.

iiii s. De celda prox.

iiii s. De tercia celda.

iiii s. De quarta celda.

Summa xviii s.

Extra portam orientalem ex parte australi in parochia sancti Petri.

vi s. De domo iuxta pratum de Paris.

v s. De domo prox. ubi Bate le Sclattere manebat.

iiii s. De domo prox. ubi Douce Textrix manebat.

v s. De domo prox. ubi Willelmus Plumbator manebat.

iiii s. De domo prox. Ade le Werceman.

[1] rectius ‘Broutone’.

xx d. De domo quondam Randulfi Bixe; libere.
ii s. De domo Pille; libere.
ii s. De aula Pille; libere.

Summa xxvii s.[1] viii d.

Ex parte aquilonari.

iiii s. De domo quondam Oliueri Cyssoris.
vi s. De domo Ade le Welere.
v s. De domo prox. quam Ioh' le Turnur tenet.
vi s. De domo quondam Ade Cyssoris; Ioh' le Couper tenet.
ix s. De Hugone de Pydyngton.
v s. De celda & solario prox. Galfrid' Coci [*sic*].
xii s. De relicta Galfridi Coci.
viii s. De Iohanne Goye.
vi s. De domo quondam Philippi Clerici.
iiii s. De una celda quondam Thome le Marichal.
iiii s. De alia celda de eodem tenemento.
vi s. De solario ultra dictas seldas.
xiii s. iiii d. De celda cum le forge.
v s. De celda prox. portam orientalem.
v s. De celda prox.
v s. De tercia celda.

Summa v li. ii s. iiii d.

Infra portam orientalem.

xxx s. De domo quondam ligatoris librorum.
xviii d. De magna porta.
[ii s. De una placea: *an addition.*]
v s. De proxima celda; le Mulmongere.
ii s. De introitu le Mulmongere.
xiiii s. { De media celda de eodem tenemento.
De celda prox. Pulin le Barber. }
iiii s. De celda Pulyn le Barber.
xviii s. De domo Ruboreus.
xx s. De domo Punchard.
xxxii s. De domo quondam Thome de Benham cum una celda.
vi s. De domo Gobiun.
iii s. De una celda de eadem domo.
iii s. De media celda.
ii s. De tercia celda.

[1] It should be xxix s.

xvi s. De celda in cornario sancti Petri.
xii s. De celda Celena.
vi s. De tertia celda, uidelicet prox.
iii s. iiii d. De domo Stocwelle.
[xii s. De duabus subtus aulam : *an addition.*]
xx s. De domo quondam I. Filekyng, quam W. Barber tenet.
xiiii s. De duabus seldis subtus Georgehall.
xxiiii s. De duabus seldis Willelmi Buffard.
Summa xi li. ii s. x d.

Infra portam ex parte australi.
iiii s. De Thoma Habraham ; libere.
i d. De domo quondam Martini Exemplatoris.
vi s. De domo quondam Kepharm.[1]
Summa x s. i d.

Contra muros uille uersus Kybaldestrete.
iiii s. De domo quondam le Sitoler.
iii s. De domo prox. quod [*sic*] Emma le Mosuld tenet.
iii s. De domo prox. sequente ; Brekebone.
iiii s. De prima domo in Kybaldesstrete.
iii s. De domo secunda, uiz. domo prox.
v s. De domo Alicie Lotricis.
vi s. De domo quondam Ioh' de Haustet.
iiii s. De domo quondam Edithe Lotricis.
ii s. De una celda.
x s. De domo Thome de Orlience.
iii s. De domo quondam Thome Ipotecarii.
vi s. De aula Vine quod [*sic*] I. de Waston tenet.
Summa liii s.

Contra muros uille a porta Stephani Ligatoris Librorum.
iiii s. De domo contra ecclesiam sancti Petri quam quondam W. Buffard tenuit ; nichil quia uacua.
v s. De domo quam I. Watele tenet.
iii s. De domo Thome Boxe.

Contra domum uicarii[2] sancti Petri.
v s. De domo quondam relicte Roberti de Wylabi.

[1] Bostar Hall is omitted, probably by accident.
[2] The vicarage was at the north-east corner of the church ; see Loggan's map of Oxford.

iiii s. De domo quondam I. de Abburberi.
iiii d. De domo inclusa.
iiii d. De domo Simonis Excambiatoris, Aula Mariol.
xvi d. De domo Margareta de Codesdone. (*In a later hand* 'Wytewong'.)
ii s. De domo Canis.
iii s. vi d. De selda prox. magnam portam[1] in cimiterio sancti Petri.
iii s. vi d. De selda prox. de eodem tenemento.
[xviii d. De terris Iuliane de Swyndone; *in a later hand.*]

In uico sancti Iohannis.

v s. De domo Philippi le Quilter & i placea.
vi s. De aula Crucis.
iii s. De una selda de eadem aula.
iiii s. De alia selda de eadem aula cum una placea uacua.
xii d. De una placea uacua.
vi s. De domo prox. aulam cum camino.
v s. De domo prox. aulam de Nyttyngale.
v s. De domo prox.; de Pistrino.
[iiii s. De magistris de aula Baylof pro Hertshedhalle; *another hand.*]

In parochia beate Marie.

xxviii s. De domo quondam Henrici le Barber.
xx s. De domo quondam Isabelle le Barber.
xx s. De celda & solario; I. Basyng.
x s. De celda prox. quam Ric. de la corner tenet.
xxix s. De domo Alani le Staciner.
vi s. De celda & solario in cimiterio beate Marie.
xvi s. De domo quondam Will' de Lodelowe de nobis tenuit.
iiii s. De domo Wareham; libere.
vii s. vi d. De domo quondam Adam de Houton; libere.
x s. De domo Faunt.
xxvi s. viii d. De domo quondam Iuonis; Thomas de Haluton tenet.
x s. De domo Iohannis de Lokyntone; libere.
xii d. De domo Ricardi le Sauser; libere.

Summa ix li. vi s. viii d.

[1] A tenement on the site of Queen's College Chapel had a large gate, and appears to have been known as Broadgates Hall about this time.

In parochia Omnium Sanctorum.

iiii marcas. De tenemento quondam Gofridus de Hedyngtone.
xxvi s. viii d. De celda & solario; Robertus le Staciner.
vii s. De tenemento Hencseye iuxta le Lokieres.
viii s. De celda Thome Chichele.
viii s. De celda Iohannis de Boreword.
x s. De prima celda Suenebroc: I. Cotiler.
x s. De alia celda de eodem tenemento: Isabella Chaundelar.
x s. De celda Balche.
x s. De quarta celda; quondam Iuliana de Paris tenuit.
xxviii s. De domo quondam Hugonis le Hore.
xxvi s. viii d. De duabus celdis subtus magnam cameram de Borewaldescote.

Summa vii li. iii s. iiii d.

In parochia Sancti Martini.

iiii s. De domo quondam Thome de Orlience.
ii s. et de i placea xii d. De domo quondam Alicie de Wellis, quam I. Ouerhee tenet.
De introitu quondam Nicholai de Kyngestone. } uacua.
De celda prox. }
x s. { De tercia celda.
De quarta celda.
x s. De celda in suteria: uacua.
ii s. De solario quondam Henrici Gamage.
ii s. De celda & solario quondam Philippi Cissoris.
vi s. viii d. De celda quondam I. de Heyword; Gilbertus de Wynchekumbe tenet libere.
iiii s. De Ricardo Ipotecario in Quarefuc; tenet libere.

Summa xxx s. viii d.

In parochia sancti Iohannis.

iiii s. De domo quondam Ricardi Hayl.
vii s. vi d. De domo in cornario; Henricus le Luminur.
vii s. vi d. De domo proxima; de Thoma de Hedyndone.
iiii s. De domo Henrici le Gayler.
iiii s. De domo prox., uidelicet de Aula Gayler.
ii s. De aula quondam Ricardus de sancta Fredeswida.
iiii s. De superiore celda Balle.
iiii s. De inferiore celda Balle.
ii s. De i placea prox. inferiorem celdam Balle.

In parochia sancti Michaelis ad portam australem.

vii s. De domo Ricardi le Masun pro celda & solario.
iii s. De uno solario infra prox.
ii s. De uno celario sub eodem solario; uacua.
iiii s. De una domo infra.
iii s. De domo prox. Racke.
xii d. De Racke.
xx s. De domo quondam Willelmi de Meteburne.
xvi s. De domo Boletras, quam Ioh' Brusebos ten'.
ii s. De domo Lutlemor, uiz. Aula Margarete.
xii d. De terra Sueneshulle.

Summa lvii s.

In parochia sancti Aldathi.

xiii d. De magistris de Aula Baylof pro quodam tenemento in Paruo Iudeismo.
ii s. De tenemento Plumbatoris.
xviii d. De domo in cimiterio sancti Aldathi.
lxxiii s. iiii d. De Isabell' Kepeharm.
xxx s. De Rob. le Marchal.
xxx s. De Rob. Treweloue.

Summa vi li. xvii s. xi d.

In parochia sancte Ebbe.

viii s. iiii d. De Thoma de Alstone.
iiii s De tenemento le Bremstar.
iiii s. De celda in cornario le Graunger.
iiii s. De celda prox. quam Petrus Hobbe tenet.
iiii s. De celda prox. solario quod Will' de Schiptone tenet.
vi s. De solario le Graunger.
xviii s. De domo Noyf quam R. Pistor tenet.
xviii s. De curia Lincolnie.
iii s. De celda Warini iuxta uicum.
iii s. De solario ultra dictam celdam: uacua.
v s. De domo infra de eodem tenemento.

Summa iiii li. xiiii s. iiii d.

In parochia sancti Michaelis ad portam aquilonarem.

x s. De domo Excambiatoris; quondam Willelmus de Wodestoke.
vii s. De celda proxima.
vii s. De secunda celda.

vii s. De tercia celda.

xiii s. iiii d. De tenemento, quondam Willelmus de Wodesdone.[1]

Summa liiii s. iiii d.

In parochia beate Marie Magdalene.

ii s. De tenemento quondam I. Doklyntone.

ii s. De Willelmo Mek, pro terra le Sauser.

xii d. De Dudeford pro celda Aurifabri.

iii s. De tenemento Walteri de Wigornia quod I. de Abyndone tenet.

vii s. De domo Bremtone.

iii s. De Rogero Bost.

xii d. De terra Dodelyng.

xxiiii s. De Willelmo de Stoward.

iiii s. De Willelmo Perel pro tenemento iuxta aulam regis.

iii s. De procuratoribus Magdalene.

[De domo Iohannis Beuerle in Stocwellestrete: *erased.*]

In parochia sancti Egidii.

F. xii d. De tenemento de Godestowe.

xvi d. De terra que fuit Ricardi le Politer in Stocwellestrete.

xx d. De terra que fuit I. Randulf, Walterus de Mideley nunc tenet.

v s. De domo prox. Rob. de Brutone, quam I. Tie tenet.

iiii s. De curia Maynard.[2]

[*On the dorse in another hand*]

Rentale de domibus clericorum anno regni regis Edwardi tercii post conquestum primo.

De aula Katerine

xxviii s. De aula Georgii.

liii s. iiii d. De aula cum camino.

xxii s. De aula Nytingale.

xxii s. De aula Nigra.

xxvi s. viii d. De aula Leporis.

xxv s. De aula Martel.

xx s. vi d. De aula Militis.

xxii s. De aula Aristotil.

lxi s. De aula Hynge.

xl s. De scola in Cattestrete.

v s. vi d. De magno solario infra scolam.

[1] This was in St. Thomas's parish.

[2] This was in Holywell parish.

v s. De paruo solario in scola.
iiii s. vi d. De una camera iuxta scolam.
ii s. De selario inferiori.
v li. vi s. viii d. De aula Burwaldescote.
xxxiii s. iiii d. De aula Minote.
xxvi s. De parua aula Boydin.
xxiii s. De alia aula Boydin.
xxviii s. De aula Brakeley.
iiii s. ii d. De paruo solario in Brecham Curt'.
vii s. viii d. De magno solario in eadem curia.
iii s. ix d. De paruo solario in eadem curia.
vii s. De magno solario in eadem curia.
xxxii s. De aula Profunda super Chandyche.
xxii s. De aula Mildride.

5. A rental of 1328.

Rentale domus sancti Iohannis de domibus laycorum in Oxonia, anno regni regis Edwardi tercii post conquestum secundo.

In parochia sancti Clementis.
vi s. De selda proxima uenellam.
iiii s. De selda proxima.
iiii s. De tercia selda.
iiii s. De quarta selda proxima.
Summa xviii s.

Extra portam orientalem ex parte australi.
vi s. De domo proxima prato Paris.
v s. De relicta Batte.
iiii s. De domo quondam Dauid Galas.
v s. De Lucia Gardiner.
iiii s. De domo quondam Ade Werkeman.
F. xx d. De domo Bix.
F. ii s. De domo Pille.
F. ii s. De aula Pille.
Summa xxix s. viii d.

Ex parte boriali.
F. iiii s. De domo quondam Olíueri Scissoris.
vi s. De domo Adam Rotarii.
vi s. De domo quondam Adam Scissoris.
v s. De domo quondam Iohannis le Turnur.
ix s. De domo Hugonis de Pydyngton.

xii d. De una placea.
vi s. De scelda & solario proxima domus quondam Galfridi Coci.
xii s. De domo quondam Galfridi Coci.
F. viii s. De Iohanne Ioye.
vi s. De domo quondam Philippi Clerici.
iiii s. De scelda quondam Thome le Marchale.
iiii s. De alia scelda proxima, uiz. Rogeri Lasmaker.
vi s. De solario ultra easdem sceldas.
xiii s. iiii d. De domo in cornario cum le forge.
x s. De duabus sceldis proxima [*sic*] porte orientali.
v s. De tercia scelda proxima.
Summa v li. v s. iiii d.

Infra portam orientalem.
F. xxx s. De domo ligatoris librorum.
F. ii s. De una placia.
F. xviii d. De magna grangia.
v s. De una scelda iuxta domum le Melmounger.
xiii s. De domo quondam Hugonis le Melmounger.
xviii s. De domo quondam Hugonis Ruburth'.
iiii s. De scelda Ipolit' Barbitonsoris.
xx s. De domo Puncharde.
xxxii s. De domo Beneham cum una scelda.
ii s. De scelda proxima tenemento Gobiun.
iii s. De alia scelda proxima.
iiii s. De uno solario ultra easdem sceldas.
xii s. De scelda in cornario sancti Petri.
xii s. De scelda Celena.
vi s. De scelda proxima, uiz. tertia scelda.[1]
xx s. De domo quondam Iohannis Fylekyng.
xiiii s. De duabus sceldis subtus Georgehalle.
xxiiii s. De domo Willelmi Buffarde.
Summa xi li. iiii s. vi d.

Infra portam ex parte australi.
F. iiii s. De Thoma Habram.
F. i d. De Martino exemplatoris [*sic*].
F. vi s. De aula Kepeharm.
Summa x s. i d.

[1] Some rents are omitted by the scribe at this point.

Contra muros uille & uersus Kybaldstrete.

	iiii s.	De domo quondam Sytolir'.
	iii s.	De domo Emme Mosyeld.
	iii s.	De domo Brekebone.
F.	iii s.	De domo Paternoster.
	iiii s.	De prima domo in Kybaldestrete.
	iii s.	De domo proxima.
	vi s.	De domo quondam Iohannis Hausted.
	v s.	De domo proxima, uiz. Alicie Lotricis.
F.	x s.	De domo quondam Thome Orliens' in Kybaldestrete.
	iiii s.	De domo quondam Edithe Lotricis.
	ii s.	De domo proxima.
	vi s.	De aula Vinie.

Summa liii s.

Circa ecclesiam sancti Petri orientalis.

	v s.	De domo Iohannis de Weyteley.
	iii s.	De domo proxima.
F.	v s.	De relicta quondam Roberti de Weleby.
F.	iiii s.	De domo Iohannis de Abburberi.
F.	iiii d.	De domo inclusa.
F.	iiii d.	De aula Mariolis.
F.	xvi d.	De tenemento quondam Margarete de Codusdone nunc Willelmus Wytewong.
	ii s.	De domo Canis.
	xviii d.	De una placia quondam Iuliane de Swynesdone.
	viii s.	De duabus seldis Ledeberi.

Summa xxx s. vi d.

In uico sancti Iohannis.

	v s.	De Philippo le Quilter cum una placia.
	vi s.	De aula Crucis.
	iii s.	De quadam scelda proxima.
	iiii s.	De alia scelda proxima aulam Crucis cum una placia.
	vi s.	De domo proxima aulam cum camino.
	v s.	De pistrina in uico sancti Iohannis.
	v s.	De domo proxima.
F.	iiii s.	De Herttehewede Halle.

Summa xxxviii s.

In parochia sancte Marie Virginis.

F. xxviii s. De domo quondam Henrici le Barbur.
xx s. De domo quondam Isabelle le Barbur.
vi s. De scelda & solario in cimiterio sancte Marie.
xx s. De domo Iohannis Basyng.
x s. De scelda proxima.
xxix s. De domo Alani le Stacinere.
F. xvi s. De domo quondam Willelmus Lodelawe.
F. iiii s. De domo Waram.
F. vii s. vi d. De domo quondam Adam de Howetone.
F. x s. De domo Willelmi Faunt.
xxvi s. viii d. De tenemento quondam Iuonis, nunc Thomas de Halleton tenet.
F. x s. De domo Iohannis de Lokyntone.
xii d. De tenemento quondam Ricardus le Grasiere.
ii s. De uno gardino infra scolam de Cattestrete.

Summa ix li. x s. ii d.

In parochia Omnium Sanctorum.

F. iiii marc'. De tenemento quondam Galfridus de Hedyngton.
xxvi s. viii d. De scelda quondam Robertus le Stacinere, nunc Gilbertus Kar' tenet.
F. vii s. De tenemento Hayngesey.
vii s. De scelda quondam Thome Checheley.
viii s. De scelda Iohannis Burford.
x s. De prima scelda Swynebroke; Iohannes le Cotelir' tenet.
x s. De alia scelda Swynebroke; Isabella Chaundelir' tenet.
ix s. De tercia scelda Swynebroke.
x s. De quarta scelda Swynebroke proxima.
F. xxviii s. De tenemento quondam Hugonis le Houre.
xxvi s. viii d. De duabus sceldis sub magna camera Burwaldescot.

Summa ix li. xiiii s. viii d.

In parochia sancti Martini.

F. iiii s. De domo quondam Orliens in Ballio.
F. iii s. De domo quondam Alicia de Welles cum una placea uersus fratres Carmeli.
x s. De introitu Nicholai Kyngkestone.
iii s. De scelda proxima.
De tercia scelda.
De quarta scelda.

F. x s. De scelda in suteria.
F. ii s. De solario quondam Henr*icus* Gamage.
F. ii s. De scelda & solario quondam Philippus Scissor.
F. vi s. viii d. De scelda quondam Gilbertus de Wychecombe.
F. iiii s. De domo Ricardus Ipotecar' in quadreuio.

Summa xliiii s. viii d.

In parochia sancti Iohannis.

iiii s. De domo quondam Ricardus Hayle.
F. viii s. {De domo quondam Henricus Lummenur'.
De domo proxima.
F. viii s. {De domo Henrici Gayler, uiz. de Aula Gayler.
De domo proxima.
F. ii s. De Aula Grimmested.
iiii s. De inferiora [*sic*] scelda Balle.
iiii s. De superiora scelda Balle.
ii s. De una placia proxima Balle.

Summa xxxii s.

In parochia sancti Michaelis ad portam australem.

vii s. De Ricardo latomo super magnam [*sic*] pontem.
iii s. De solario prox.
ii s. De scelda prox. subtus solarium.
iii s. De domo prox., uiz. Iuliana de Brehulle.
iii s. De inferiori domo prox. Rake.
xii d. De le Rake.
xx s. De domo quondam Willelmi Meteburne.
xvi s. De domo quondam Bultras Robert'.
F. ii s. De Aula Margarete.
F. xii d. De Swyneshulle.

Summa lviii s.

In parochia sancti Aldathi.

F. xiii d. De tenemento in Paruo Iudaismo magistrorum Baylof [*sic*].
F. ii s. De tenemento Plumbatoris.
F. xviii d. De domo quondam Bissop Saweor' iuxta cimiterium sancti Aldathi.
lxxiiii s. De domo Isabelle Kepeharm.
xxxiiii s. De domo Roberti le Marchalle.
xxx s. De domo Robertus Trewelof.

Summa vii li. ii s. viii d.

In parochia sancti Michaelis ad portam borialem.

xvii s.	De domo Blaunkeney.
xvi s.	De prima scelda in eodem tenemento.
xvi s.	De secunda scelda proxima.
xiii s. iiii d.	De tercia scelda in eodem tenemento.

} Magister habet illum redditum.

Summa xvii s.[1]

In parochia sancti Thome.

F. xiii s. iiii d.	De tenemento quondam Willelmi de Wodusdone.

In parochia sancte Ebbe.

F. viii s. iiii d.	De tenemento quondam Thome de Hallestone.
F. iiii s.	De tenemento Bremmester.
iiii s.	De prima scelda in cornario le Graunger.
iiii s.	De scelda proxima.
vi s.	De solario le Graunger.
iiii s.	De scelda subtus solarium le Graunger.
xx s.	De domo quondam Noyfe.
iii s.	De scelda Varayn proxima uia [*sic*].
iiii s.	De solario ultra dictam sceldam.
v s.	De domo infra.
xviii s.	Curia Lincoln.

Summa iiii li. iiii d.

In parochia sancte Marie Magdalene.

F. ii s.	De tenemento quondam Iohannis de Dokylintone; nunc Iohannes Seterton tenet.
F. xii d.	De Duddeford pro scelda Aurifabri.
F. ii s.	De Willelmo Mike pro solario quondam le Sauser.
F. iii s.	De tenemento quondam Walteri de Wygornia; Iohannes de Abyngdon nunc tenet.
F. vii s.	De curia Henrici de Bramptone.
F. iii s.	De domo Rogeri Bost.
F. xii d.	De tenemento Dodeling.
xxiiii s.	De domo Willelmi Stoford.
iiii s.	De domo Willelmi Perelle, proxima Aula Regis.
iii s.	De domo Marie Magdalene.

Summa l s.

In parochia sancti Egedii.

F. xx d.	De terra que fuit Iohannes Randulf in Stokewelstret. Walterus Mideley tenet.

[1] i.e. omitting the master's share.

F. xvi d. De duabus sceldis in Stokewelstret que fuerunt Ricardus le Pulletir; nunc Iohannes de Abyngdon tenet.

F. v s. De domo proxima Rob*erto* de Bronton; nunc Iohannes de Teye tenet.

F. xii d. De tenemento abbatisse de Godestawe [*sic*].

Summa ix s.

In parochia sancte Crucis.

iiii s. De curia Maynarde super Candyche.

Summa totalis istius rentalis lxvii li. iiii s. x d.

Rentale de domibus clericorum anno regni regis Edwardi tercii post conquestum secundo.

xxxii s. De aula Katerine.
xxviii s. De aula Georgeii.
liii s. iiii d. De aula cum camino.
xxii s. De aula Nyttingale.
xxii s. De aula Nigra. xiii s. non plus occupata.
xxvi s. viii d. De aula Leporis.
ix s. vi d. De aula Martel.
xx s. vi d. De aula Militis.
xxii s. De aula Dosiere.
lxi s. De aula Ingge.
xl s. De scola in Cattestret.
iiii s. vi d. De camera proxima scola [*sic*].
v s. De solario in introitu scole.
v s. vi d. De magno solario infra scolam.
iiii s. De selario subtus solarium proxima [*sic*] latrina.
v l. vi s. viii d. De aula Burwaldescote.
xxxiii s. iiii d. Aula Minote.
xxvi s. De aula Boydin proxima aula Periculosa.
xxiii s. De alia aula Boydin.
xxviii s. De aula Brakeley.
iiii s. ii d. De paruo solario in Brecham Curt'.
vii s. viii d. De magno solario in Brecham Curt'.
iii s. ix d. De paruo selario in Brecham Curt'.
vii s. De magno selario in Brecham Curt'.
xxxii s. De aula Profunda super Candiche.
xxii s. De aula Mildride.

Summa xxxii li. ix s. vii d.

Hii sunt redditus quos fratres hospitalis sancti Iohannis tenentur persoluere capitalibus dominis.

In primis apud Chalgraue ad festum sancti Michaelis. x s.
Item preceptori de Samford ad ii terminos. xx s.
Item pro terra de Hedyngdon domino regi. vii s.
Item heredibus Bodin.[1] iiii s.
Vicario sancti Petri pro minutis decimis. vi s. viii d.
Luminari ecclesie beati Petri pro diuersis tenementis. iii s. viii d.
Predicte ecclesie pro domo Punchard.[2] xii d.
Domino Episcopo Wynton' pro terra le Comber. viii d.
Item de domo Iohannis Philekynk heredibus Henrici le Riche.[3] vi s. viii d.
Pro domo Waldri.[4] vi d.
De domo que fuit Wicarius de Helesfeld heredibus Feteplace iii s. & Alicie le Merser. i d.[5]
Galfrido de Stocwell. ii s.

Parochia sancte Marie.

De Yngehalle. vi d.
Pro terra le Verer; rectori ecclesie beate Marie.[6] xxii d.
Pro selda iuxta portam de Boruwaldescote ecclesie sancte Fridewide [*sic*]. vii s.
De terra que fuit Agnetis Plente, rectori ecclesie beate Marie. xx d.
Luminari eiusdem ecclesie. v d.
Priori de Cantuaria.[7] x d. qua.
Priori de Coldenorton. v s.

Parochia sancti Iohannis.

De duabus seldis in cimiterio sancti Petri heredibus le Riche.[8] xx d.
De aula le Dosier domui de Merton. ii s.
De eodem tenemento heredibus Galfridi de Hengeseye. xii d.
Pro prato Pille heredibus Walteri Aurifabri.[9] iii s.

Parochia sancti Martini.

Pro iii seldis monialibus de Stodle.[10] x s.

[1] See i. 33.
[2] See i. 319.
[3] See i. 278.
[4] See i. 291.
[5] See i. 273. The list on the dorse of the roll of 22 Ed. I adds after this: —De domo Canis ecclesie sancti Edwardi. xviii d.
[6] In i. 419 it appears that half the tenement paid 11*d*.
[7] See i. 451 for this and the next rent; but it looks as if x d. must be an error for iii d.
[8] See i. 344. The tenement was not in St. John's parish.
[9] See ii. 72 *n*.
[10] This is probably the rent of 10*s*. due in 1234 to Robert Oein; see ii. 79.

Parochia Omnium Sanctorum.
De terra Hugonis le Hore, heredibus le Riche.[1] viii s.
De domo Roberti de Sunebroc priori ecclesie Frideswyde.[2] v s.
Luminari ecclesie sancte Frideswyde. viii d.

Parochia sancti Aldati.
De terra Ade Stanford in cimiterio sancti Aldati luminari ecclesie.[3] viii d.

Parochia sancte Abbe.
De terra Iohannis Plumbatoris ecclesie sancte Abbe. ii d.
Pro terra le Granger apud Eynesham.[4] xii d.
De terra Warini; heredibus le Riche.[5] ii s.
Pro terra que fuit Walteri de Kyngestone, Laurence Kepeharme.[6] iiii s.

Parochia sancti Michaelis uersus austrum.
De terra de Fardon heredibus le Ryche.[7] iii s. et ii altilia.
De eodem tenemento apud Godestowe. ix d.
De eodem tenemento ecclesie sancti Michaelis. iii d.
De terra Isabelle de Dorsestria, heredibus Bernard. xii d.
Pro eadem terra apud Godestowe.[8] v s.
De eadem, Andree de Couele ad terminum uite sue. vii s.
De introitu quem habuimus de Sara tinctrice priori sancte Frideswide. iii s.

Parochia sancti Michaelis ad portam aquilonarem.
De terra que fuit Symonis excambiatoris domino H. Wad.[9] xxxi d. ob.
Item luminari eiusdem ecclesie. viii d.

Parochia Marie Magdalene.
De tenemento quod fuit quondam R. Bodin heredibus le Riche.[10] ii s.
De aula Brakkeley ecclesie sancte Frideswyde.[11] iii s.
Pro tenementis in hundredo balliuis in festo sancti Martini. xiiii d.
Pro Depehalle, heredibus le Riche.[12] ii s. ii d.
Ecclesie Magdalene. xiiii d.

[1] For this rent see ii. 56. Henry Simeon the first seems to have been known as Henry le Rich.
[2] For the rents to St. Frideswide's see ii. 46.
[3] See ii. 137 *n*.
[4] See ii. 234.
[5] See ii. 213.
[6] See ii. 232.
[7] The rent was actually 4*s*. not 3*s*.; see ii. 194.
[8] For the two rents from this tenement see ii. 198.
[9] See ii. 271.
[10] See ii. 322.
[11] See ii. 318.
[12] See ii. 309.

Pro nobis & omnibus tenementis nostris balliuis de hundredo pro Foreualseluer. viii d.

Parochia sancte Mildrede.

Eidem ecclesie. ii d.

Parochia sancte Crucis.

Rectori ecclesie sancte Crucis pro diuersis tenementis. xv s. iiii d.

De terra Toma[n] riparia. xviii d.

Pro eodem tenemento luminari eiusdem ecclesie. iii d.

De terra Cas luminari eiusdem ecclesie. ii d.

De terra le Bolur luminari eiusdem ecclesie. vi d.

Parochia sancti Aldati in Iudaismo.

Conuersis Londonie de magna domo cum iiii shopis.[1] x s.

De ii aliis tenementis ad firmam uille que uocatur langable. viii d. ob.

Abbati de Abyndone pro alia domo. xii d.

De tenemento Beneyt de la Corner pro quondam tenement' [*sic*] heredibus Walteri Feteplace. iii s. iiii d.

6. A rental of 1339.

Rentale domus sancti Iohannis Oxon factum de domibus laicorum anno regni regis Edwardi tercii post conquestum terciodecimo.

In parochia sancti Clementis.

vi s. De selda iuxta uenellam.
iiii s. De selda proxima.
iiii s. De tercia selda proxima.
iiii s. vi d. De quarta selda proxima.
Summa xviii s. vi d.

Extra portam orientalem ex parte australi.

vi s. De domo iuxta Parys.
v s. De domo Bate.
iiii s. De domo Galeys.
v s. De domo Gardinar.
iiii s. De domo Werkeman.
xx d. De domo Byx.
ii s. De domo Pille.
xvi s. De aula Pille.
Summa [*blank*].

[1] For this and the next three rents see ii. 153.

Extra portam orientalem ex parte boriali.

F. iiii s.	De domo Oliueri Cissoris.
vi s.	De domo Rotarii.
vi s.	De domo Philippi Cissoris.
v s.	De selda proxima.
v s.	De secunda selda proxima.
ix s.	De domo uinee.
ii s.	De domo proxima.
vi s.	De selda & solario proxim' domum Galfridi Coci.
xv s.	De domo Iohannis le Webbe.
F. viii s.	De domo Iohannis Ioye.
vii s.	De domo Philippi Clerici.
iiii s.	De selda quondam Thome Mareschal.
iiii s.	De selda proxima.
vi s.	De solario ultra dictas seldas.
xiii s. iiii d.	De domo cum le forge.
v s.	De selda prox. portam.
v s.	De alia selda prox.
v s.	De tercia selda prox.

Summa cxv s. iiii d.

Infra portam orientalem ex parte boriali.

F. xx s.	De domo ligatoris librorum.
F. x s.	De domo Sibille Colesbourn.
F. xviii d.	De magna porta.
ii s.	De una placia prox.
xxiii s.	De domo le Melmaker.
v s.	De selda Ypoliti Barbour.
xxii s.	De domo Ruburth.
xxiii s.	De domo Puncharde.
F. x d.	De aula cum camino.
xxxii s.	De domo Benham cum selda proxima.
iii s.	De selda prox. domum Gobiun.
iii s.	De alia selda prox.
iii s.	De solario ultra dictas seldas.
xii s.	De selda in cornario sancti Petri.
xii s.	De selda quondam Celena.
vi s.	De selda prox.
F. iii s. iiii d.	De domo le Nezerwyndmulle.
F. ii s.	De domo Nicholai de Glatton.

xvi s.	De duabus seldis subtus aulam Katerine.
viii s.	De domo quondam Willelmi Barbour.
xvi s.	De duabus seldis subtus aulam Georgii.
xiiii s.	De domo Buffard.
xii s.	De selda proxima.
F. xii d.	De tenemento Gobiun.
	Summa xii li. iiii s. viii d.

Infra portam orientalem ex parte australi.

F. iiii s.	De domo Thome Habraham.
F. i d.	De domo Martini Exemplatoris.
F. vi s.	De aula Kepharm.
	Summa x s. i d.

Contra muros uille uersus Kybaldestret.

iiii s.	De selda quondam Roberti le Cetoler.
iii s. viii d.	De domo Mosield.
iii s.	De domo Brekebon.
F. iii s.	De domo Paternoster.
iiii s.	De prima domo in Kybaldestret.
iii s.	De secunda domo prox.
vi s.	De domo Hausted.
vi s.	De domo prox. cum una placia.
x s.	De domo Orliens.
iiii s.	De domo quondam Edithe Lotricis.
ii s.	De parua domo prox.
vi s.	De aula Vinee.
	Summa liiii s. viii d.

Circa ecclesiam sancti Petri in oriente.

viii d.	De uno gardino quondam uicarii.
v s.	De domo Iohannis de Whatele.
iii s.	De domo prox.
iiii s.	De uno gardino ubi tres aule fuerunt.
F. iiii d.	De domo inclusa.
F. iiii d.	De aula [Mario]l.
F. xvi d.	De tenemento Wytewong.
F. xxiiii s.	De aula Borstall.[1]
ii s.	De domo Canis.
xviii d.	De una placia Iuliane de Swynesdone.

[1] This is inserted here by mistake; it should occur in the parish of St. Peter in the East on the south side of High Street.

iiii s. De uno gardino iuxta ecclesiam sancti Petri.
v s. De prima selda Ledbury.
v s. De alia selda.
vi s. De selda iuxta domum Stephani de Abyndone.
vi s. De alia selda prox.
vi s. De tercia selda prox.
vi s. De quarta selda prox.

Summa iiii li. xiiii d.

In uico sancti Iohannis.

iiii s. vi d. De domo Philippi le Quilter.
vi s. De Aula Crucis.
iii s. vi d. De selda in eadem aula.
ii s. De selda prox. aulam Crucis.
iiii s. De alia selda prox. cum una placia.
vi s. De domo prox. aulam cum camino.
x s. De pistrino in uico sancti Iohannis
F. iiii s. De Herteheudhalle.

Summa xliiii s. iiii d.

In parochia beate Marie uirginis.

xxviii s. De domo quondam Iohannis Pumfreit.
lvi s. De domo Isabelle Barbour.
xx s. De domo Iohannis Basyng.
xxxix s. De quondam Alani le Staciner cum selda.
F. xvi s. De domo Lodelowe.
F. iiii s. De domo Warham.
F. vii s. vi d. De domo Ade de Houtone.
F. x s. De domo Willelmi Faunt.
xxvi s. viii d. De domo quondam Thome de Halton.
F. x s. De domo Lokyntone (*this is erased*).
F. xii d. De domo Ricardi Grasier.
iiii s. De uno gardino infra scol'.

Summa xi li. ii s. ii d.

In parochia Omnium Sanctorum.

xxvi s. viii d. De domo quondam Roberti le Staciner.
F. vii s. De tenemento Hengseye.
viii s. De selda Iohannis Boreford.
viii s. De selda quondam Thome Chicheleye.
xiii s. iiii d. De domo Simonis de Gloucestre.
F. xxviii s. De domo Alicie de Neubury.

	xiii s. iiii d.	De selda quondam Iohannis le Bewer.
	xiii s. iiii d.	De selda prox.
		Summa viii li. xi s.[1]

In parochia sancti Martini.

F.	iiii s.	De domo Thome Orliens.
F.	iii s.	De domo Alicie de Welles cum una placia.
	x s.	De selda iuxta introitum de Kyngestone.
F.	ii s.	De selda in suteria.
F.	vi s. viii d.	De selda Gilberti de Wynchecombe.
F.	ii s.	De solario Henrici Gamage.
F.	iiii s.	De selda in Quadriuio.
F.	ii d.	De selda sancti Petri in Ballio.[2]
		Summa xxxi s. x d.

In parochia sancti Iohannis.

	v s.	De domo Ricardi Hayl.
F.	viii s.	De Henrico Illuminatore.
F.	viii s.	De Aula Gayler.
F.	ii s.	De Aula Grimsted.
	iiii s.	De inferiori selda Balle.
	v s.	De superiori selda Balle.
	ii s.	De una placia prox.
		Summa xxxvi s.

In parochia sancti Michaelis australis.

	ix s.	De domo Ricardi le Mascon cum selda.
	iii s.	De solario prox.
	ii s.	De selda subtus solarium.
	iiii s.	De domo Iuliane de Brehull.
	ii s.	De domo prox.
	iii s.	De domo iuxta le Rakke.
	xii d.	De una [*sic*] Rakke.
	xx s.	De domo Metebourne.
	xviii s.	De domo Bultras.
F.	ii s.	De Aula Mariol'.
F.	xii d.	De tenemento Swyneshulle.
		Summa lxv s.

[1] To make this total correct we must add £2 13*s.* 4*d.* to the rent of Simon of Gloucester. Previous rentals show that that tenement had four shops as well as a house, and that in favourable years the shops were let at a rent of a mark each.

[2] A quitrent from a tenement on the west side of the church of St. Peter le Bailey; it was not in the parish of St. Martin.

In parochia sancti Aldati.

F. xiii d. De uno tenemento in paruo Iudaismo.
F. ii s. De tenemento Plumbatoris.
F. xviii d. De una placia iuxta cimiterium.
lxxiiii s. De domo quondam Isabelle Kepharm.
xxxiiii s. De domo quondam Roberti le Mareschal.
xxxiiii s. De domo quondam Roberti Treweloue.

Summa vii li. vi s. vii d.

In parochia sancte Ebbe.

F. viii s. De tenemento Bremster.
F. xviii d. De tenemento prox. Nicholaum de Pepplisbury.
F. viii s. iiii d. De tenemento quondam Thome de Allestone.
iiii s. De selda in cornario le Graunger.
iiii s. De selda prox.
vi s. De solario le Graunger.
iiii s. De selda subtus solarium.
ii s. De domo Spalding.[1]
xxxiiii s. De domo Stanlake cum tenemento Warein.
F. xii s. De domo quondam Iohannis Dokelintone.[2]
xviii s. De curia Lincolne.

Summa iiii li. xvii s. x d.

In parochia sancti Michaelis borealis.

xl s. De aula Blaunkeneye.
xvi s. De prima selda Blaunkeneye.
xvi s. De secunda selda prox.
xiii s. iiii d. De tercia selda prox.
xiii s. iiii d. De tenemento Wodesdone.

Summa iiii li. xviii s. viii d.

In parochia sancte Marie Magdalene.

F. ii s. De tenemento Iohannis Dokelintone.
xx s. De domo Willelmi de Welles.
F. xii d. De tenemento Dodeford.
F. ii s. De solario le Sauser.
F. iii s. De domo Iohannis de Abyngdon.
F. vii s. De introitu Henrici de Brampton.
F. iii s. De domo Rogeri Bost.
F. xii d. De tenemento Dodeling.

[1] This was in St. Aldate's; see the rental of 1351.
[2] This was in St. Aldate's.

xxiiii s.	De Willelmo de Stouford.
v s.	De duabus seldis iuxta Aulam regis.
F. iii s.	De domo Magdalene.
	Summa lxxi s.

In parochia sancti Egidii.

F. xvi d.	De duabus seldis in Stokewellestrete.
F. xx d.	De duabus seldis ibidem.
viii s.	De domo quondam Iohannis de Tye.
F. xii d.	De tenemento abbatisse de Godestowe.
	Summa xii s.

In parochia sancte Crucis.

vi s. viii d.	De curia Maynard.
F. xviii d.	De domo Iohannis Tye.
	Summa viii s. ii d.

De domibus clericorum anno xiii ut infra :—

cviii s. vi d.	De aula Borewaldescot.
xxxii s.	De aula Katerine.
xxviii s.	De aula Georgii.
xlv s.	De aula cum camino.
xxii s.	De aula Nithingale.
xxii s.	De aula Nigra.
xxvi s. viii d.	De aula Leporis.
xx s.	De aula Militis.
xxvi s.	De aula Dosier.
lvii s.	De aula Ingge.
xl s.	De scolis in Cattestret.
v s.	De paruo solario sub introitu scole.
iiii s. vi d.	De magna camera prox. scole.
v s. vi d.	De magno solario infra scolam.
iiii s.	De celario prox. latrinam.
xxxiii s. iiii d.	De aula Mignote.
xxvi s.	De parua aula Boydin.
xxii s. vi d.	De magna aula Bodin.
xxviii s.	De aula Brakkele.
xxxii s.	De aula Profunda super Candiche.
xx s.	De aula Mildred.
xxvii s.	De aula sancti Willelmi.
xviii s vi d.	De aula Martel.
xxxi s. xi d. ob.	De aula retro ecclesiam Omnium Sanctorum.

xiii s. iiii d. De scolis proximis.
iii s. iiii d. De uno gardino prox. scol'.
Summa xxxiiii li. v d.

Rentale de Halliwelle.

iii s.	De una placia iuxta Crowell.
v s.	De prima domo in Halliwelle.
ii s.	De cotagio proximo.
ii s.	De cotagio prox. Henric' Okham.
iii s. ix d.	De domo Henrici Okham.
xviii d.	De una placia retro domum Okham.
iiii s.	De una placia prox. uenellam.
xii d.	De una placia prox. Sawer.
iiii s.	De domo Sawer.
ii s.	De parua domo iuxta ecclesiam.
iiii s.	De domo prox.
iiii s.	De tercia domo prox.
vi s.	De domo quondam Henrici Brakkele.

Summa cxiii s.[1] viii d.

7. A rental of 1346.

Rentale domus sancti Iohannis extra portam orientalem Oxonie in anno uicesimo per fratrem Thomam de Erluscot procuratorem.

In parochia sancti Clementis.

vi s.	De selda iuxta uenellam.
iiii s.	De selda prox.
iiii s.	De tercia selda prox.
iiii s. vi d.	De quarta selda prox.
xii d.	De una placia prox.

Extra portam orientalem ex parte australi.

vi s.	De domo iuxta Parys.
vi s.	De domo prox.
iii s.	De domo quondam Galeis.
iii s.	De domo Iohannis Slattere.
vi s.	De domo prox'.
F. xx d.	De tenemento Bix.
F. ii s.	De domo Pille.
xvi s.	De aula Pille.

[1] Perhaps an error for cxiii li.

Extra portam orientalem ex parte boriali.

F. iiii s.	De introitu Oliueri Sissoris.
iii s.	De domo prox.
vi s.	De secunda domo prox.
	De tercia domo prox.
	De domo Vine.
	De domo prox. Vine.
vi s.	De selda prox. Thomam le Webbe.
xv s.	De domo Webbe.
	De domo Iohannis Ioye.
vii s.	De domo Philippi Clerici.
iiii s.	De selda quondam Thome le Marechale.
iiii s.	De selda prox.
vi s.	De solario ultra dictas seldas.
xiii s. iiii d.	De domo cum le forge.
v s.	De celda prox. portam.
v s.	De media celda.
v s.	De tercia celda.

Infra portam orientalem ex parte boriali.

xxvii s.	De domo Bokebinder.
x s.	De celda Coleborne.
xviii d.	De magna porta.
ii s.	De una placea prox.
xxvii s.	De domo quod [*sic*] Henricus Skiptone tenet.
v s.	De celda Ipoliti Barbur.
xxii s.	De domo Ruborwe.
xxiiii s.	De domo Punchard.
x d.	De aula cum camino.
xxxii s.	De domo Benham.
iii s.	De domo Gobiun.
iii s.	De domo prox.
iii s.	De solario ultra seld'.
xii s.	De celda in cornario sancti Petri.
xii s.	De celda Celena.
vii s.	De celda prox. Celena.
iii s. iiii d.	De domo quod uocatur Netherwynmulle.
ii s.	De domo Nicolai de Glattone.
xii s.	De duabus seldis desuper Aule Katerine.
viii s.	De domo Willelmi Barbur.

viii s. De celda prox.
ix s. De secunda celda prox.
xxiiii s. De domo Buffard.
xii s. De celda prox. Buffard.

Infra portam orientalem.
iiii s. De domo Abraham.[1]
i d. De Martini Amplexatoris [*sic*].
vi s. De aula Kepharme.

Contra muros uille.
iiii s. iii d. De domo Citoler'.
iii s. De domo prox.
ii s. De tercia selda prox.
ii s. De cotagio Paternoster. }
v s. De domo prox. } Paternoster.
vi s. De alia domo prox. }
iiii s. De prima domo in Kibaldstret.
De [ ][2] prox.
iii s. De secunda domo prox.
vi s. De domo Haustede.
vi s. De domo prox. Haustede.
x s. De domo Orlians.
ii s. De secunda domo prox. aulam Vin'.
iiii s. De domo prox. aulam Vin'.
vi s. De aula Vin'.

Circa ecclesiam sancti Petri in oriente.
viii d. De uno gardino iuxta cimiterium.
F. iiii d. De domo inclusa.
F. viii d. De duabus aulis Mariolus.
F. xvi d. De tenemento Wytewonge.
F. xxiiii s. De aula Borstalle.[3]
ii s. De una placea quod uocatur Hou*er*ehouse.
[ ] De una placea Iuliane de Swyndon.
iiii s. De uno gardino iuxta ecclesiam.
iiii s. De uno gardino retro[4] ecclesiam.
xi s. De duabus celdis Ledebury.
vi s. De celda prox. domum Stephani de Abyngdon.

[1] The occupant was really named *Averham*.
[2] Illegible.
[3] Inserted out of its order, as in the previous rental.
[4] Indistinct.

vi s. De celda prox.
vi s. De tercia celda prox.
iii s. De quarta celda prox.

In uico sancti Iohannis.
iiii s. De domo le Quilter.
vi s. De aula Crucis.
iii s. vi d. De celda in eadem aula.
iiii s. De parua domo prox. cum una placea.
vi s. De domo prox. aule cum camino.
x s. De pistrino in uico sancti Iohannis.
F. iiii s. De magistris aule de Balliolo.

In parochia beate Marie Virginis.
xxviii s. De domo; quondam tenuit Pumfrett.
xxxvi s. De domo; quondam Couto*n* tenuit.
x s. De celda prox.
x s. De secunda celda prox.
xx s. De celda quondam Basyng.
ix s. vi d. De celda prox.
ix s. vi d. De secunda celda prox.
xx s. De selda Iohannis Latoner.
xvi s. De domo Lodelowe.
F. iiii s. De tenemento Waram.
F. vii s. vi d. De tenemento Ade Howton.
F. x s. De domo Faunt.
xxvi s. viii d. De domo W. Levurton.
F. xii d. De domo quondam R. Gracier.
iiii s. De uno gardino infra scolam.

In parochia Omnium Sanctorum.
xxvi s. viii d. De celda quondam Gilberti Cary.
F. vii s. De tenemento Hencsey.
viii s. De domo Iohannis Buruord.
viii s. De celda Chichelye.
iiii l. De domo Simonis Gloucestrie.
F. xxviii s. De domo Alicie de Neubury.
xxvi s. viii d. De duabus celdis Burwaldescot.

In parochia sancti Martini.
F. iiii s. De domo Orliens.
F. iii s. De domo Alicie de Welles cum placea.

F. x s. De selda iuxta introitum de Kyngistone.
F. ii s. De selda in sutoria.
F. ii s. De solario quondam Henrici Gamage.
xviii s. De prima celda Crockesford.
xviii s. De celda prox.
F. vi s. viii d. De celda Gilberti Wynchecombe.
F. iiii s. De selda in quadriuio.
F. iii d. De tenemento Ade Long'.[1]

In parochia sancti Iohannis.

v s. De domo Hayle.
F. viii s. De domo H. Illuminatoris.
F. viii s. De aula Gayler.
F. ii s. De aula Grymsted.
iiii s. De inferiori selda Balle.
v s. De superiori selda Balle.
ii s. De una placea prox.

In parochia sancti Michaelis ad portam australem.

ix s. De domo Webbe.
iii s. De solario prox.
ii s. De celario desuper.
iii s. De domo quondam Brehulle.
ii s. De secunda domo prox. le Rake.
iii s. De domo prox. le Rake.
xx s. De tenemento Meteborne.
xx s. De domo Bultras.
F. ii s. De aula Mariole.
F. xii d. De tenemento Swyneshull.
F. ii s. De tenemento Plumbatoris.[2]

In parochia sancti Aldati.

F. xiii d. De uno tenemento in Paruo Iudaismo.
xviii d. De una placia iuxta ecclesiam sancti Aldati.
lxxiiii s. De domo Kepeharm.
xxxviii s. De domo le Mareschal.
xxxiiii s. De domo Truweloue.
F. xii s. De domo Dokelinton.

[1] Probably an error for Loud'; see rental of 1293.

[2] This tenement was in St. Aldate's; see rental of 1339.

In parochia sancte Ebbe.

F. viii s. De tenemento Bremster.
F. xviii d. De una placea prox.
F. ix s. iiii d. De domo Iohannis Allestone.
iiii s. De celda in cornario le Graunger.
De celda prox.
iiii s. De solario desuper.[1]
vi s. De solario ultra[2] dict' celd'.
xxiiii s. De domo Stanlake cum tenemento Wareyn.
xviii s. De curia Lincoln'.

In parochia sancti Michaelis ad portam borialem.

xl s. De aula Blaunckeney.
xiiii s. De prima celda Blaunckeney.
xiiii s. De secunda celda Blaunckeney.
xi s. De tercia celda Blaunckeney.
F. xiii s. iiii d. De tenemento Wodesdone.

In parochia beate Marie Magdalene.

[F. ii s.] De domo quondam Dokelinton.
xx s. De domo Willelmi de Welles.
F. xii d. De tenemento Dodeuord.
F. ii s. De solario le Saucer.
F. iii s. De domo quondam Iohannis Abyngdon.
F. vii s. De introitu H. Bramptone.
F. iii s. De tenemento Bost.
F. xii d. De tenemento Dodelyng.
xxiiii s. De domo Stouuord.
v s. De domo Perel.
F. iii s. De domo Magdalene.
F. xvi d. De duabus celdis in Stocwellstret.
F. xx d. De duabus celdis ibidem.
viii s. De domo Tye.
F. xii d. De tenemento Godestow.

De domibus clericorum.

iiii li. xiii s. iiii d. De aula Burwaldescot.
[ ] De aula Katerine.

[1] There is some error here; previous and subsequent rentals show that there were three selds and one solar at this corner. Probably the scribe entered the solar twice by mistake. *Desuper* here means *above* (see also p. 109); sometimes it means *below*, as in the list of *Domus clericorum*.

[2] *ultra* means *above* in medieval Latin.

[ ] De aula Georgii.
xlv s. De aula cum camino.
xxii s. De aula Philomene.
xxii s. De aula Nigra.
xxvi s. viii d. De aula Leporis.
xix s. De aula Militis.
xxix s. viii d. De aula Aristotilis.
lvii s. De aula Yng.
xxxv s. De scol' in Cattestret.
v s. De paruo solario.
iiii s. vi d. De camera prox. scolam.
v s. vi d. De magno solario.
iiii s. De celario desuper.
xxxi s. De aula Minot.
xxvi s. De parua aula Bodyn.
xxii s. vi d. De magna aula Bodyn.
xxviii s. De aula Brackeley.
xxxii s. De aula Profunda.
xix s. De aula Mildrede.
xxvii s. De aula sancti Willelmi.
xix s. De aula Martel.
xxxii s. De aula retro Omnium Sanctorum.
xiii s. iiii d. De scolis ibidem.
ii s. De una domo prox.

Summa collecta per fratrem Thomam de Erluscote xiiii li. xvi s. ix d.
Summa collecta per fratrem Willelmum de Wotton proximo anno xxxix li. xv s. x d.

8. A rental of 1351.

Although when this rental was made it was two years from the outbreak of the Plague, yet many traces of that calamity may be noticed. In the first place the rents were very low, and in the second place many of the tenements, in particular the Halls, were vacant and could not be let. In five cases we have the entry 'Mayr Oxon tenet', which might be taken to mean that the mayor, in virtue of his office, was the occupant of the tenement, either as guardian of a minor or as trustee until the true owner was found. But in all probability it is not so; the mayor in this year was John de Bereford, and the following rentals show that in the case of three out of the five tenements he continued to be the tenant after he had ceased to hold the office of mayor.

Rentale domus sancti Iohannis de domibus laycorum in Oxonia anno regni regis Edwardi tertii post conquestum xx^mo quinto.

In parochia sancti Clementis.

viii s. De domo iuxta uenellam quam Willelmus Thame nunc tenet.

ii s. De celda proxima quam Robertus Bedemon nunc tenet.

iii s. vi d. De secunda celda prox. quam Walterus Pinner nunc tenet.

vii s. De tercia celda cum quarta quas Iohannes Dorset nunc tenet.

viii s. De domo iuxta Charewelle cum celda annexa quas Henricus Tapster nunc tenet.

Extra portam orientalem; ex parte australi.

xii d. De domo iuxta Parys.

vi s. vi d. De domo prox. cum secunda domo prox. quas Iohanna Copster nunc tenet

vii s. { De domo quarta quam Willelmus Molton nunc tenet. De domo quinta. }

De domo Bix.

De domo Pille.

De aula Pille.

De domo quondam Reginaldi Deyher.

Ex parte boriali.

De domo proxima porte nostre quam Nicholaus Poure tenet.

iii s. De domo prox. quam Robertus Bosseby nunc tenet.

ii s. De tercia domo prox. quam Petrus Werkemon nunc tenet.

xii d. De quarta domo prox. quam I. Carter nunc tenet.

ii s. De domo quam Agnes Deyher nunc tenet.

vi d. De celda iuxta domum Philippi Taylour.

v s. De domo Philippi Taylour.

De domo prox. quondam Iohannis Ioye quam Iohannes Faber nunc tenet.

iiii s. De tercia domo quam Willelmus Bocher nunc tenet.

De duabus celdis quas Iohannes Faber nunc tenet.

De domo cum le forge quam idem Iohannes nunc tenet.

De domo prima iuxta portam.
ii s. vi d. De secunda domo prox.
De tercia domo prox.

Infra portam orientalem ex parte boriali.

v s. De domo in cornario quam Iohannes Lokyer tenet.
F. vi s. viii d. De domo Coleborn quam Willelmus Honte tenet.
iiii s. De celda prox. quam idem W. tenet.
xii s. De domo prox. quam Willelmus Webbe tenet.
ii s. De celda prox. quam Rogerus Taylour tenet.
x s. De domo prox. illi celde quam Ricardus Louteborouhe nunc tenet.
xiii s. iiii d. De domo prox. quam Iohannes Abyndone tenet.
F. x d. et ii s. pro uno gardino. De aula cum camino quam Ricardus Coke nunc tenet cum gardino.
xx s. De domo prox. quam Nicholaus Heytesbury tenet.
iii s. De prima celda prox. aule Regine quam Iohannes Taylour tenet.
iii s. De secunda celda prox.
iiii s. De tercia celda prox. quam Iohannes Tanner tenet.
ii s. De quarta celda prox. quam Amic' Howyf tenet.
ii s. De quinta celda prox. quam Alic' Abyndon tenet.
De sexta celda prox.
ii s. De solario ultra dict' celd' quod Hugo de Helesfeld tenet.
xiii s. vi d. De duabus celdis in cornario quas Petronilla Coke nunc tenet cum uno gardino iuxta ecclesiam.
v s. vi d. De celda prox. quam Thomas Litelmor tenet.
F. iii s. iiii d. De domo uocata Netherwynmulle.
F. ii s. De domo quondam Nicholai Glatton quam procuratores luminis sancti Thome tenent.[1]
x s. De duabus celdis desuper aulam Katerine.
De domo quondam Willelmi Barbour.
xxvi s. viii d. De aula sancti Georgii cum duabus celdis desuper dictam aulam quas Ricardus Coutone tenet.
x s. De celda prox. quam Willelmus Drouthdalehalle tenet.
De secunda celda quam Robertus Carpunter tenet.

[1] In 1349 Alan de Kylingworth left to his wife for her life a rent of twenty shillings from the tenement of Nicholas de Glatton with remainder to the Chantry of St. Thomas in the church of St. Mary (*Book of Wills*, p. 47).

Ex parte australi.

F. iiii s. De domo Habraam quam Willelmus Longe tenet.

F. i d. De domo Martini Exemplatoris.

F. vi s. De domo Kepharme quam Ricardus Wyte tenet.

v s. De uno gardino quam idem Ricardus nunc tenet in uico sancti Iohannis.

In parochia beate Marie Virginis.

xvi s. De domo Punfrett' quam Rogerus Northwode tenet.

De duabus celdis in cimiterio beate Marie.

xxiii s. iiii d. De domo quam Thomas Latoner cum celd' tenet.

x s. De celdis quas Robertus Barbour tenet.

In Cattestrete.

vi s. viii d. De domo Willelmi Beumount.

vi s. viii d. De domo prox. quam Iohannes More tenet.

De celda proxima.

De uno gardino quam Iohannes Poul tenet infra scol' in Catstrete.

x s. De domo quam Willelmus Leuerton tenet.

F. iiii s. De domo Waram quam Willelmus Buffard tenet.

F. vii s. vi d. De domo quondam Ade de Howtone.

F. x s. De domo quondam Willelmi Faunt. Nunc uicarius de Couele tenet.

iii s. De domo Charnelle quam Willelmus Scriptor tenet.[1]

F. xii d. De uno gardino quondam Ricardi le Grasier.

In parochia Omnium Sanctorum.

F. vii s. De tenemento Henkesey quod Iohannes Olleneye tenet.

x s. De domo prox. port' magn' in Spiceryo.

xiii s. iiii d. De duabus celdis desuper cameram dicte aule[2] quas Iohannes Olleney quondam tenuit.

De prima noua celda exoposito ecclesie Omnium Sanctorum.

De secunda celda ibidem.

l s. De domo quondam Symonis de Glouceter cum quatuor seldis quas Iohannes Mesterton tenet.

x s. De domo quondam Alicie Neubury quam Mayr[3] Oxon tenet.

[1] This tenement near Smith Gate was in the parish of St. Peter in the East.

[2] i.e. Broadgates in the Spicery, though the hall was not generally known by this name as yet.

[3] John de Bereford was mayor this year.

In parochia sancti Martini.

F. iiii s.	De domo quondam Thome de Orliens quam Iohannes Bedeford tenet.
F. iii s.	De domo ubi Alicia de Well' manebat.
F. x s.	De introitu quondam Thome de Kyngestone.
x s.	De prima celda Croxford quam Willelmus London sadeler tenet.
x s.	De secunda celda Croxford.
F. ii s.	De celda in sutoria.
F. ii s.	De solario quondam Henrici Gamage quod Ricardus Ouerhee quondam tenuit.
F. vi s. viii d.	De celda quondam Gilberti de Wynchecombe.
F. iiii s.	De celda in quadriuio quam Mayer Oxon tenet.

In parochia sancti Iohannis.

F. viii s.	De domo quondam Henrici Illuminatoris quam Nicholaus Clerke tenet.
F. viii s.	De aula Gayler quam Mayr nunc tenet.
F. ii s.	De aula Grimstede quam Mayr nunc tenet.
	De prima celda Balle.
	De secunda celda Balle.
	De una placea prox.

In parochia sancti Michaelis ad portam australem.

vi s.	De domo quam Thomas Botelmaker tenet.
viii s.	De domo Meteborne quam Walterus Sauterer' tenet.
vi s. viii d.	De domo Bultras quam Walterus Fox tenet.
F. ii s.	De aula Mariolle de Lyttelmor.
F. xii d.	De tenemento Swyneshulle.

In parochia sancti Aldati.

F. xiii d.	De uno tenemento in paruo Iudaismo quod magister de Bayliollalle tenet.
F. ii s.	De tenemento Plumbatoris quod Iohannes Saucer tenet.
	De una placea iuxta cimiterium sancti Aldati quam Iohannes Spaldyng tenet.
	De una placea quam rector ecclesie sancti Aldati tenet.
xl s.	De domo Kepharme quam Henricus Fysher tenet.
xiii s. iiii d.	De domo Fwytewelle quam Willelmus Alston tenet.
x s.	De domo Treweloue quam Willelmus Bristowe tenet.

F. xii s. De domo Iohannis Dokelintone.
De curia Lincoln' quam Iohannes Hales tenet.[1]

In parochia sancte Ebbe.

F. xviii d. De ten. Bremster quondam Nicholai Pepplesbury.
F. viii s. De una placea prox. quam Iohannes sancte Frideswyde tenet.
F. viii s. iiii d. De domo quondam Iohannis de Allestone prox. quam Willelmus Allstone tenet.
De celd' in cornario le Graunger.
De celd' prox.
De solario le Graunger.
De celd' subtus solarium.
De domo Spaldyng [*scratched out*].
De domo Stanlake cum tenemento Waryn.
De domo quondam Iohannis de Dokelynton [*scratched out*].
De curia Lincoln [*scratched out*].

In parochia sancti Michaelis borialis.

De aula Blaunkeneye quam Ricardus Sotton tenet.
vi s. De celda prox. quam Iohannes Ourtone tenet.
vi s. De secunda celda prox. quam Laurentius Taylor tenet.
iii s. De tercia celda prox.
F. vi s. viii d. De tenemento Wodesdone retro castrum.

In parochia sancte Marie Magdalene.

F. ii s. vi d. De tenemento Iohannis Dokelintone quod mayr Oxon tenet.
De domo quondam Willelmi Welles.
F. xii d. De tenemento Dodeford.
De solario le Saucer.
F. iii s. De domo Iohannis de Abyndone.
F. vii s. De introitu Henrici de Bramtone.
F. iii s. De domo quondam Rogeri Bost.
F. xii d. De tenemento Dodelyng.
De domo Walteri de Stouford.
De duabus celdis iuxta aulam regis.
F. iii s. De domo Magdeleyn.

[1] This house was in St. Ebbe's parish.

In parochia sancti Egidii.

F. xvi d., xx d. De duabus celdis in Stokewellestrete quas Iohannes Gruttone tenet

De duabus celdis ibidem.

De domo quondam Iohannis Tye.

F. xii d. De tenemento abbatisse de Godestowe.

In parochia sancte Crucis.

De curia Maynard.

F. xviii d. De domo Iohannis Tye.

De domibus clericorum anno xx^mo^ quinto.

iii li. Aula Borewaldescote quam magister Iohannes Hetyndone tenet.

De aula Katerine.

De aula cum camino.

De aula Nithingale.

De aula Nigra.

De aula Leporis.

De aula Militis.

De aula Dosier.

De aula Yngge.

De scola in Cattestrete.

viii s. De cameris infra introitum dicte scole quas Walterus Clerk tenet.

De aula Minote quam rector ecclesie sancti Aldati tenet.

De parua aula Boydyn super Candiche.

De magna aula Boydyn ibidem.

De aula Brackele.

De aula profunda super Candich.

vi s. viii d. De aula Mildrede.

v s. De aula sancti Willelmi.

De aula Martell.

De aula retro Omnium Sanctorum.

De scolis proximis.

De uno gardino prox. scolis.

xxx s. De aula Borstalle.

9. A rental of 1352.

Rentale domus sancti Iohannis de domibus laycorum in Oxonia, anno regni regis Edwardi tercii post conquestum uicesimo sexto.

In parochia sancti Clementis.

viii s. De domo iuxta uenellam quam Will' Thame tenet.
ii s. De selda prox. quam Rob' Bedeman tenet.
iii s. vi d. De secunda selda prox. quam Walterus Pinner' tenet.
De tercia selda prox.
De quarta selda prox.
viii s. De domo iuxta Charwell cum celda annexa quas Hen' Tapster tenet.

Extra portam orientalem ex parte australi.

xii d. De domo iuxta Parys.
De domo prox.
vi s. De tercia domo prox.
vii s. De quarta domo prox. cum quinta quas Will' Molton tenet.
De domo Bix.
De domo Pille.
ii s. De domo quondam Reginaldi Deyher.
i lib. thuris. De capella sancte Trinitatis.

Ex parte boriali.

De domo prox. porte nostre.
iiii s. De secunda domo prox. quam Rob' Bossebi tenet.
ii s. De tercia domo prox. quam Pet' Werkman tenet.
De quarta domo prox. quam Thomas Carter tenet.
i rosa. De quinta domo prox. quam Agnes Deyher tenet ad terminum uite sue.
ii s. De sexta domo prox. quam Hen. Carpenter tenet.
ii s. De celda iuxta domum Philippi Taylour.
v s. De domo Philippi Taylour.
v s. De domo Ioye quam Ioh' Faber tenet.
De domo prox.
iii s. De duabus celdis quas Ioh' Faber tenet.
xiii s. iiii d. De domo cum le forge quam idem Ioh' tenet.
De prima celda iuxta portam orientalem.
iii s. De secunda celda prox.
iii s. De tercia celda prox.

Infra portam orientalem ex parte boriali.

v s. De domo in cornario quam Ioh' Lokyer ten'.
vi s. viii d. De domo Colleburne quam Will' Honte ten'.
iiii s. De selda prox. quam idem Will' ten'.
xii s. De domo prox. quam Will' Webbe ten'.
xiii s. iiii d. De secunda domo prox. quam Ric' Wyte ten'.
xiii s. iiii d. De tercia domo prox. quam Ioh' Abyndone ten'.
F. x d. De domo Ricardi Coke.
ii s. De uno gardino quem idem Ric' ten'.
xx s. De domo quam Nich' Heytesburi ten'.
iii s. De prima celda prox. aulam Regine ; Ioh' Taylor ten'.
iiii s. De secunda celda prox. ; Matheus Cornys ten'.
iiii s. De tercia celda prox. ; Ioh' Tanner ten'.
iiii s. De quarta celda prox. ; Amicia Howwif ten'.
{xx d. {xviii d. De quinta celda cum sexta prox. quas Alicia Abindon ten'.
ii s. De solario supra dict' seld' quod Hugo Taylour ten'.
xxiii s. vi d. De tribus celdis in cornario prox. quas Petronilla Piemaker[1] ten'.
F. iii s. iiii d. De domo uoc' Netherwinmulle quam Ioh' Dorset ten'.
F. ii s. De domo quondam Nicholai Glatton quam procuratores luminis sancti Thome ten'.
x s. De duabus seldis desuper aulam Katerine ; Will' Bruer ten'.
viii s. De domo quondam Willelmi Barbour ; Ric' Linne ten'.
xxvi s. viii d. De aula sancti Georgii cum duabus celdis desuper aulam predictam quam Ric' Coutone ten'.
x s. De celda prox. quam Will' Drowthdalealle ten'.
De secunda celda prox. quam Rob. Carpenter ten'.
ii s. De uno gardino iuxta cimiterium sancti Petri in oriente.
De uno gardino retro ecclesiam predictam quam Petronilla Coke ten'.
xi d. De uno gardino iuxta murum ; Rob. Hyham ten'.

Ex parte australi.

F. iiii s. De domo Abraam.
F. i d. De domo Martini Exemplatoris quam procuratores luminis sancte Marie ecclesie sancti Petri in oriente tenet.

[1] *Coke* in the previous rental.

F. vi s. De domo Kepharme.
v s. De uno gardino in Kybaldusstret quam Ric' Wyte ten'.

In parochia beate Marie Virginis.

xvi s. De domo Pounfret quam Rog' Northwode ten'.
xx d. De duabus celdis in cimiterio beate Marie.
xxiii s. iiii d. De domo Thome Latoner cum celd' in cornario.
x s. De celdis prox. quas Rob. Barbour ten'.
vi s. viii d. De domo Willelmi Bewmoynt in Cattestret iuxta Thomam Hame.
vi s. viii d. De domo prox. quam Ioh' More ten'.
De celda prox.
x s. De domo quondam Willelmi Leuertone quam Ioh' Shobindone ten'.
F. x s. De domo prox. quondam Willelmi Faunt, quam Cristina Faunt ten'.
F. iiii s. De domo Waram quam Hen. Malmesburi ten'.
F. vii s. vi d. De domo quondam Ade Howtone quam Ioh' Bedeforde ten'.
iiii s. De domo Charnelle iuxta Smithegate quam Will' Scriptor ten'.
F. xii d. De uno gardino quondam Ricardi Grasier quod Nich' Garlount ten'.
ii s. De uno gardino quem Ioh' Poul ten' infra scolam nostram in Cattestret.

In parochia Omnium Sanctorum.

F. vii s. De ten. Henkesey quod Ioh' Ollney ten'.
x s. De celda prox.[1] quam Hen. Danyel ten'.
xiii s. iiii d. De duabus celdis sub aul' Borwalduscote quas Ioh' Olleney ten'.
iiii s. De duabus celdis exopposito ecclesie Omnium Sanctorum; Ioh' Stodeley ten'.
l s. De domo quam Ioh' Mostertone ten' cum quatuor celdis.
F. x s. De domo quondam Alicie Neuburi quam Ioh' Berforde ten'.
De aula retro ecclesiam Omnium Sanctorum cum scola.

[1] This word is a mistake. Henxsey's tenement was on the south side of High Street, Danyel's shop was next to the entrance of Borewaldescote Hall.

In parochia sancti Martini.

F. iiii s. De domo quondam Thome de Orleensse.
F. iii s. De domo quondam Alicie de Welles.
F. x s. De introitu quondam Thome de Kyngestone.
x s. De prima selda Croxforde.
x s. De secunda selda Croxforde.
F. ii s. De celda in sutoria.
F. ii s. De solario quondam Henrici Gamage.
F. vi s. viii d. De celda quondam Gilberti de Winchecombe.
F. iiii s. De celda in quadriuio quam Ioh' Berforde ten'.

In parochia sancti Iohannis.

F. viii s. De domo quondam Henrici Illuminatoris quam Nic' Clerk ten'.
F. viii s. De aula Gayler.
F. ii s. De aula Grimstede.
De duabus celdis Balle.
De una placea prox.

In parochia sancti Michaelis ad portam australem.

vi s. De domo quam Lucia Botelmaker ten'.
viii s. De domo prox. quam Walterus Sawtrer ten'.
vi s. viii d. De secunda domo prox. quam Walterus Fox ten'.
F. ii s. De aula Mariol de Letulmor.
F. xii d. De ten. Suineshelle.

In parochia sancti Aldati.

F. xiii d. De uno tenemento in paruo Iudaismo quod mag. de Aula Baliolle ten'.
F. ii s. De ten. Plumbatoris quod Ioh' Sawcer ten'.
De una placia iuxta cimiterium sancti Aldati quam Ioh' Spaldyng ten'.
vi d. De una placia quam rector ecclesie predicte ten'.
xlvi s. viii d. De domo Kepharm quam Hen' Fysher ten'.
xiii s. iiii d. De domo prox. quam Will' Aston ten'.
x s. De secunda domo prox. quam Will. Brustowe ten'.
F. xii s. De domo Iohannis Dokelintone.
vi s. viii d. De curia Lincoln' quam Ioh' Hales tenet.

In parochia sancte Ebbe.

F. xviii d. De tenemento Bremster quondam Nicholai Peppusburi.
F. viii s. De una placia prox' quam Iohannes sancte Frideswide ten'.

F. v s. iiii d. qua. De domo quondam Iohannis de Allestone quam Will' Allestone ten'.
De celda in cornario le Graunger.
De celda prox.
De solario le Graunger.
De celda sub solario.
x s. De domo Stanlake cum tenemento Wareyn.

In parochia sancti Michaelis borealis.
xiii s. iiii d. De aula Blaynkeneye quam Nic. Lindraper ten'.
vi s. De celda prox. quam Ioh' Wortone ten'.
vi s. De secunda selda prox.
iii s. viii d. De tercia selda prox.
F. xiii s. iiii d. De ten' Wodesdone iuxta pontem de Oseneye.

In parochia sancte Marie Magdalene.
F. ii s. vi d. De ten' Iohannis Dokelintone quod Ioh' Berforde ten'.
De domo quondam Willelmi Welles.
F. xii d. De ten' Dodeford.
F. ii s. De solario le Saucer.
F. iii s. De domo Iohannis de Abindone.
F. vii s. De introitu Henrici de Bramtone.
F. iii s. De domo quondam Rogeri Bost.
F. xii d. De ten' Dodelyng.
De domo Walteri de Stouford.
vi d. De duabus celdis iuxta aulam.[1]
F. iii s. De domo Magdeleyn.

In parochia sancti Egidii.
F. xvi d., xx d. De duabus celdis in Stocwellestrete quas Ioh' Gruttone ten'.
De duabus celdis ibidem.
De domo quondam Iohannis Tye.
F. xii d. De tenemento abbatisse de Godestowe.

In parochia sancte Crucis.
iii capones. De curia Maynard quam Ioh' Hokeland.
F. xviii d. De domo Iohannis Tye.

De domibus clericorum, anno xxvi ut infra.
lxvi s. viii d. De Borwaldescote aula.
xxx s. De aula Ynge.

[1] *aulam regis* is meant, i.e. Beaumont Palace.

xxx s. De aula Borstalle.
vi s. viii d. De aula Katerine.
viii s. De aula Mildrede.
v s. De aula Willelmi.
ii s. De aula Militis quam Leonardus Bedel ten'.
iiii s. De aula Aristotilis.
De aula Minot quam rector ecclesie sancti Aldati ten'.
v s. De scola in Cattustret quam Steph' Bedel ten'.
viii s. De cameris infra scolam quas Walterus le Clerk ten' (*added in another hand* 'in perditione').
De aula cum camino.
De aula Philomene.
De aula Nigra.
xii d. De aula Leporis.
De aula Dosier.
De aula Bodin super Candich.
De parua aula Bodin.
De aula Brackele.
De aula profunda super Candich.
ii s. De aula Martel quam [*blank*] Barbur ten'.
iiii s. De aula Hert[1] quam mag. de aula Baliol ten'.

10. A rental of 1353.

Rentale domus sancti Iohannis de domibus laicorum in Oxonia anno regni regis Edwardi tercii post conquestum xxvii.

In parochia sancti Clementis.
vii s. De domo iuxta uenellam quam Will' Thame nunc tenet.
ii s. De celda prox.
iii s. De secunda celda prox.
De tercia celda prox.
De domo iuxta Charewelle cum celda annexa.
De quarta celda prox.

Extra portam orientalem ex parte australi.
xii d. De domo iuxta Parys.
De domo prox.

[1] Usually called *Hertheved*.

viii s.	De tercia domo prox.
	De quarta domo prox.
	De quinta domo prox.
F. xx d.	De domo Bix.
F. ii s.	De domo Pille.
iii s. vi d.	De domo quondam Reginaldi Deyher.
libra thuris.	De capella sancte Trinitatis.

Ex parte boriali.

vi s. viii d.	De domo prox. portam nostram quam Rob. le Mason nunc ten'.
iiii s.	De secunda domo prox. quam Ioh' Fer tenet ad terminum uite sue.
ii s.	De tercia domo prox. quam Petrus Werkman nunc tenet.
ii s.	De quarta domo prox. quam Thos. Karter nunc tenet.
i rosa.	De quinta domo prox. quam Agnes Deyher tenet ad terminum uite sue.
ii s.	De sexta domo prox. quam Hen. Karpenter ten'.
xvi d.	De celda iuxta domum Philippi Taylour.
v s.	De domo Philippi Taylour.
v s.	De domo Ioye quam Ioh. Faber nunc tenet.
v s.	De domo prox. quam Ioh' Foller tenet.
iii s.	De duabus seldis } quas Ioh' Faber tenet.
xiii s. iiii d.	De domo cum le forge } quas Ioh' Faber tenet.
iii s.	De prima selda iuxta portam orientalem.
iii s.	De secunda selda prox.
ii s. vi d.	De tercia selda prox.

Infra portam orientalem ex parte boriali.

v s.	De domo in cornario; Ioh' Lokyer nunc ten'.
vi s. viii d.	De domo Colleburne; Will' Hunte ten'.
vi s.	De celda prox.
xii s.	De domo prox.; Will' Webbe nunc ten'.
xiii s. iiii d.	De secunda domo prox.; Ric' Wyte ten'.
xiiii s.	De tercia domo prox.; Ioh' Abindone ten'.
F. x d.	De domo Ricardi Coke.
ii s.	De uno gardino quem idem Ric' tenet infra predictam domum.
xxiiii s.	De domo quam Nich' Heytesbury ten'.
iii s. ix d.	De prima selda prox. aule Regine; Ioh' Taylour ten'.

iiii s. De secunda celda prox.; Matheus Cornys ten'.
iiii s. De tercia celda prox.; Ioh' Tanner tenet.
iiii s. De quarta celda prox.; Amisia Howwif tenet.
iii s. ii d. De quinta celda cum sexta quas Alicia Abindone tenet.
ii s. De solario supra dict' celd', quod Hugo Taylour tenet.
xxiii s. vi d. De tribus celdis in cornario prox. quas Petronilla Piemaker tenet cum uno gardino retro ecclesiam sancti Petri.
F. xl d. De domo Netherwinmelne.
F. ii s. De domo quondam Nicholai Glattone.
xi s. De duabus celdis sub aul' Katerine.
viii s. uel meys[1] allec. De domo quondam Willelmi Barbour; Ric' Linne ten'.
xxvi s. viii d. De aula sancti Georgii cum duabus celdis desuper aulam predictam quas Ric' Coutone ten'.
x s. De celda prox. quam Will' Drowthdalealle ten'.
De secunda celda prox. quam Rob' Karpenter ten'.
xi d. De uno gardino iuxta murum quam [*sic*] Rob. Hyham ten'.[2]

In parochia beate Marie Virginis.

xiiii s. De domo Pomfret; Rog' Northwode ten'.
iiii s. De duabus celdis in cimiterio beate Marie; Ioh' More ten'.
xxiii s. iiii d. De domo Thome Latoner cum celda in cornario.
x s. De celd' prox. quas Rob. Barbour ten'.
iiii s. De domo Willelmi Bewmont in Cattestrete iuxta Thomam Hamme; Rob' Bokebinder ten'.
vi s. viii d. De domo prox. } Rob. Bokebinder ten'.
iii s. iiii d. De celda prox. }
xiii s. iiii d. De domo quondam Willelmi Leuerton; Rob. Manciple ten'.
F. x s. De domo prox. quondam Willelmi Faunt; Cristina Faunt ten'.
F. iiii s. De domo Waram.
F. vii s. vi d. De domo quondam Ade Howtone.
iiii s. De domo Charnelle iuxta Smithgate; Will' Scriptor ten'.

[1] A *meys* of herrings is in the rental of 1357 explained as 'a thousand'.
[2] The scribe forgets the houses *ex parte australi*; but inserts them at end.

F. xii d.	De uno gardino quondam Ricardi Grasier; Nich' Garlount ten' infra domum suam.
ii s.	De uno gardino quem Ioh' Poul ten' in Cattestrete infra scolam nostram.

In parochia Omnium Sanctorum.

F. vii s.	De tenemento Hengsheye quod Ioh' Olney ten'.
xvi s.	De celda prox. quam Hen. Daniel ten'.
	De duabus celdis sub aula Borewaldescote; Rob. Scinner ten'.
iiii s.	De duabus celdis ex opposito ecclesie Omnium Sanctorum, quas Ioh' Stodeley ten'.
l s.	De domo quam Ioh' Mosterton ten' cum quatuor seldis.
F. xxviii s.	De domo quondam Alicie Neubury quam Ioh' Berforde ten'.
xiii s. iiii d.	De aula retro ecclesiam Omnium Sanctorum cum scola.

In parochia sancti Martini.

F. iiii s.	De domo quondam Thome Orleensse.
F. iii s.	De domo quondam Alicie de Welles.
F. x s.	De introitu quondam Thome de Kyngeston.
x s.	De prima selda Croxforde.
x s.	De secunda selda Croxforde.
F. ii s.	De celda in sutoria.
F. ii s.	De solario quondam Henrici Gamage.
F. vi s. viii d.	De celda quondam Gilberti de Winchecombe quam Ric' Forster ten'.
F. iiii s.	De celda in quadriuio; Ioh' Berforde ten'.

In parochia sancti Iohannis.

F. viii s.	De domo quondam Henrici Illuminatoris.
F. viii s.	De aula Gayler.
F. ii s.	De aula Grimstede.
ii s.	De duabus celdis Balle.
	De una placea prox.

In parochia sancti Michaelis ad portam australem.

ix s.	De domo, quondam Lucia Botelmaker; Adam Webbe ten'.
viii s.	De domo prox.; Walterus Sawtrez ten'.
vi s. viii d.	De secunda domo prox.; Walterus Fox ten'.

F. ii s. De aula Mariol de Littilmor.
F. xii d. De ten' Suineshelle.

In parochia sancti Aldati.

F. xiii d. De uno tenemento in paruo Iudaismo; mag. de aula Balioll ten'.
F. ii s. De tenemento Plumbatoris; Ioh' Sawser ten'.
De una placea iuxta cimiterium sancti Aldati.
vi d. De una placea quam rector ecclesie predicte ten'.
l s. De domo Kepharme quam Ric' Piper ten'.
xiii s. iiii d. De domo prox. quam Will. Alstone ten'.
x s. De secunda domo prox.; Will' Bristowe ten'.
F. xii s. De domo Iohannis Dokelintone; Ioh' Norton ten'.
vi s. viii d. De curia Lincoln' quam Ioh' Hales ten'.

In parochia sancte Ebbe.

F. xviii d. De tenemento Bremstre quondam Nicholai Peppusbury.
F. viii s. De una placea prox.; Ioh' sancte Fredeswide ten'.
F. viii s. iiii d. De domo quondam Iohannis Allestone; Will' Allestone ten'.
De celda in cornario le Granger. } Nic. Heynus.
ii s. De celda prox. } Nic. Heynus.
ii s. De solario le Granger. } Nic. Heynus.
ii s. De celda sub solario. } Nic. Heynus.
x s. De domo Stanlake cum tenemento Wareyn; Rob. Lardener.

In parochia sancti Michaelis borealis.

xiii s. iiii d. De aula Blankeneye } Steph' Lindraper.
vi s. De celda prox. } Steph' Lindraper.
vi s. De secunda celda prox.; Rob' Muridew.
iii s. viii d. De tercia celda prox.
F. xiii s. iiii d. De tenemento Wodesdone iuxta pontem Oseneye.

In parochia sancte Marie Magdalene.

F. ii s. vi d. De tenemento Iohannis Dokelintone; Ioh' Berforde ten'.
De domo quondam Willelmi Welles.
F. xii d. De tenemento Dodeford.
F. ii s. De solario le Saucer.
F. iii s. De domo Iohannis de Abindone.
F. vii s. De introitu Henrici de Brampton.
F. iii s. De domo quondam Rogeri Bost.

F. xii d. De tenemento Dodeling.
De domo Walteri de Stauford.
De duabus celdis iuxta aulam.
F. iii s. De domo Magdelayn.

In parochia sancti Egidii.
F. xvi d. De duabus celdis in Stocwellestret; Ioh' Gruttone ten'.
De duabus celdis ibidem.
De domo quondam Iohannis Tye.
F. xii d. De tenemento abbatisse de Godestowe.

In parochia sancte Crucis.
De curia Maynard; Ioh' Hokeland ten'.
F. xviii d. De domo Iohannis Tye.

parochia sancti Petri in oriente ex parte australi.
F. iiii s. De domo Abraam quam Ric. Coke ten'.
F. i d. De domo Martini Exemplatoris quam procuratores luminis sancte Marie ecclesie sancti Petri in oriente tenent.
F. vi s. De domo Kepharme.
v s. De uno gardino in Kybaldstrete; Ric' Wite tenet.

De domibus clericorum [*sic*].

11. A rental of 1356.

Rentale domus sancti Iohannis Oxonie de domibus laycorum anno regni regis Edwardi tercii post conquestum tricesimo; frater Robertus de Tewe tunc procurator domus predicte.

In parochia sancti Clementis.
viii s. De selda iuxta uenellam; Willelmus Thame tenet.
iii s. De selda prox. quam idem Willelmus tenet.
ii s. De alia selda prox. quam Robertus Bedeman tenet.
viii s. De domo iuxta Charwelle cum selda quam Henricus Tapster tenet.

Extra portam orientalem ex parte australi.
De domo iuxta Paris.
vi s. De secunda domo cum tercia quas Robertus Molendinarius tenet.
viii s. De quarta domo cum quinta quas Willelmus Moltone tenet.

F. iii s. De domo Pille; Ricardus Deyher tenet.
vi s. viii d. De aula Pille; Willelmus Hamond tenet.
F. xx d. De domo Bix; Iohannes Saunford tenet.
i lb. turis; de capella Trinitatis.

Extra portam orientalem ex parte boriali.
vii s. ii d. De domo Oliueri Cissoris.
iiii s. De domo prox.; Robertus Bosseby tenet.
ii s. De secunda domo prox.; Thomas Carter tenet.
ii s. De tercia domo prox.
una rosa. De domo Vinee; Agnes Deyher tenet.
ii s. De domo prox.; Henricus Carpenter tenet.
xviii d. De celda cum solario iuxta domum Agnetis Deyher; Iohanna Beckele tenet.
v s. De domo prox.; Philippus Taylour tenet.
v s. De domo Ioye; Willelmus Mesturtone tenet.
v s. De domo prox.; Iohannes Welles tenet.
iii s. De duabus seldis prox. quas Iohannes Marescall tenet.
xiii s. iiii d. De domo cum le forge; Iohannes Marescal tenet.
iii s. vi d. De prima selda iuxta portam orientalem.
iii s. vi d. De secunda selda prox.
iii s. vi d. De tercia selda prox.

Infra portam orientalem Oxon.
xii s. De domo in cornario; Iohannes Couper tenet.
vi d. De celda prox.; Iohannes Lokyer tenet.
x s. De domo Coleborne; Rob. Mason tenet.
iiii s. vi d. De selda prox.; Iohannes Sclatter tenet.
xii s. De domo Melemaker; Iohannes Webbe tenet.
xxii s. iiii d. De domo Robourch cum celda; Rob. Notyngham tenet.
xiiii s. De domo Punchard; Iohannes Abindone tenet.
F. x d. De aula cum camino; Ric. Coke tenet.
xx s. De domo Benham cum celda; Nich. Heytesbury tenet.
iiii s. De prima celda iuxta aulam Regine; Iohannes Taylour tenet.
viii s. De secunda celda cum tercia prox.; Iohannes Tanner tenet.
iiii s. De quarta celda; Amicia Howewyf.
iii s. De quinta celda cum solario Alicie Abindone.

xxi s. viii d. De celd' in cornario cum duabus celdis proximis; Pernell Coke tenet.
F. iii s. iiii d. De domo Netherwyndmull.
F. ii s. De domo Nicholai Glatton; Rob. Mauncel tenet.
vi s. De prima celda subtus aulam Katerine; Iohannes Hasele.
vi s. De secunda celda prox.; Thomas Taylour tenet.
i mes allec'. De domo Willelmi Barbour.
xxvi s. viii d. De aula Georgii cum duabus seldis; Ric. Coutone tenet.
x s. De domo Buffard; Alicia Shepster tenet.
x s. De celda prox.; Rob. Carpenter tenet.

Infra portam ex parte australi.
F. iiii s. De domo Abraham; Ric' Coke tenet.
F. i d. De domo Martini Exemplatoris.
F. vi s. De aula Kepharme.
vi s. viii d. De uno gardino in Kibaldestret; Ric. Wyte tenet.

Circa ecclesiam sancti Petri in oriente.
ii s. De duobus gardinis; Pernell Coke tenet.
ii s. De uno gardino iuxta cimiterium; Ric. Coke tenet.[1]
xvi d. De uno gardino prox.; Iohannes Abindone tenet.
iiii s. De alio gardino prox.; Nic. Heytesbury tenet.
iiii d. De domo inclusa.
iiii d. De aula Mariol.
xvi d. De tenemento Wytewong.

In parochia beate Marie Virginis.
xx s. De domo Punfret; Iohannes Bedel tenet.
x s. De domo Roberti Barbour.
xxiii s. iiii d. De domo Basing cum celd'; Thomas Latoner tenet.
vi s. De duabus seldis prox.; Iohannes Capper tenet.

Cattestrete; ex parte aquilonari.
xx s. De domo Lodelowe cum ii celdis; Rob. Bokebinder.
F. iiii s. De domo Abraham;[2] Henricus Malmesbury tenet.

[1] We may assume from the names of the tenants that this and the next two gardens were on the south side of the churchyard, and adjoined Punchard's, Benham's, and Chimney Hall in High Street.

[2] The scribe means Warham.

F. vii s. vi d. De tenemento Ade de Houtone; Iohannes Croke tenet.
F. x s. De domo Cristiane Faunt.
xiii s. iiii d. De domo Willelmi Leuerton; Rob. Maunciple tenet.
F. xii d. De domo Ricardi Grasier; Nicholaus Garlond tenet.
ii s. De uno gardino infra scolam in Cattestrete.

In parochia Omnium Sanctorum.

x s. De domo Wytewong.[1]
vi s. viii d. De prima celda sub Burwaldescot; Rob. Scinner tenet.
vi s. viii d. De secunda celda prox.; Nich. Rokayle tenet.
iiii s. vi d. De duabus celdis subtus domum Iohannis Stodele.
F. vii s. De ten. Hengsey; Ioh' Stodele tenet.
xiii s. iiii d. De aula retro ecclesiam Omnium Sanctorum; Ioh' Brounnele tenet.
l s. De domo Swynebrok; Ioh' Mosterton tenet.
F. xxviii s. De domo Alicie Newbury.

In parochia sancti Martini.

F. iiii s. De domo Thome de Orliens.
F. iii s. De domo Alicie Welles cum una placea.
F. x s. De celda iuxta introitum de Kyngestone.
F. ii s. De celda in sutoria.
F. ii s. De solario Henrici Gamage.
F. vi s. viii d. De celda Gilberti de Wynchecombe; Ric. Forster tenet.
F. iiii s. De celda in quadriuio; Ioh' Bereford tenet.
F. ii d. De domo sancti Petri in Balliuo.
x s. De prima celda Croxford; Ioh' Sadeler tenet.
x s. De secunda celda prox.; Ric' Tewe tenet.

In parochia sancti Iohannis.

i d. De domo Ricardi Hayle; Nic. Manciple tenet.
F. viii s. De domo Henrici Illuminatoris.
F. viii s. De aula Gaylor; Nic. Manciple tenet.
F. ii s. De aula Grimstede.
ii s. De prima selda Balle.

[1] At the entrance to Burwaldescot Hall.

ii s. De secunda selda Balle.
xii d. De una placia prox.

In parochia sancti Michaelis ad portam australem.

ix s. De domo Ricardi Mason; Iohannes Webbe tenet.
x s. De domo Meteborne; Ioh' Scinner tenet.
vi s. viii d. De domo Bultras; Walterus Fox tenet.
F. ii s. De aula Mariol.
F. xii d. De tenemento Swyneshulle.

In parochia sancti Aldati.

xiii d. De uno tenemento in paruo Iudaismo; mag. de aula Baliol tenet.
ii s. De tenemento Plumbatoris; Ioh' Saucer tenet.
De una placia iuxta cimiterium sancti Aldati.
lx s. De domo Kepharme.
xiii s. iiii d. De domo Willelmi Alstone.
xx s. De domo Trewloue; Walterus Houlond tenet.
vi s. viii d. De curia Lincoln'; Ioh' Ales tenet.
xii s. De domo Iohannis Dokelintone.
iiii s. De una celda iuxta uenellam cimiterii sancti Aldati.

In parochia sancte Ebbe.

iiii s. De ten. Bremster.
ix s. iiii d. De ten. Iohannis de Alstone.
viii s. [*blank*].
ii s. De celda in cornario.
ii s. De celda prox. cum solario.
iiii s. De domo Stanlake cum tenemento Wareyn.

In parochia sancti Michaelis ad portam borialem.

xviii s. De aula Blankeneye cum celda prox.; Stephanus Draper tenet.
vi s. De secunda celda.
iiii s. De tertia celda.
xiii s. iiii d. De tenemento Wodesdone iuxta Oseneye.

In parochia sancte Marie Magdalene.

ii s. De tenemento Iohannis de Dokelintone.
xii d. De tenemento Dodeford.
ii s. De solario Iohannis Saucer.

iii s. De domo Iohannis de Abindone; Ioh' Grutton tenet.
iii s. De procuratoribus ecclesie Magdalene.
xvi d. De duabus celdis in Stocwelstret; Ioh' Grutton tenet.
xx d. De duabus celdis ibidem.
De domo Iohannis Tye; Ioh' Tye tenet.
xii d. De tenemento abbatisse de Godestowe.
vii s. De introitu quondam Henrici Bramtone; Ioh' Plummer tenet.
iii s. De domo Roggeri Bost.
xii d. De tenemento Dodelyng.
xiii s. iiii d. De domo Walteri Stoword.
vi d. De duabus celdis iuxta aulam regis; Ioh' Grutton tenet per cartam.

Redditus domuum clericorum Oxon' anno supradicto.

De aula Borwaldescote.
xx s. De aula Katerine.
xxxv s. De aula Yng.
xl s. De aula Borstalle cum aula Leporis.
xx s. De aula Mildrede.
xiii s. iiii d. De aula Mynott.
xxvi s. viii d. De aula cum camino cum aula Philomene.
ii s. De aula Militis; Leonardus Bedel tenet.
ii s. De aula Martel; Rob. Barbour tenet.
v s. De aula sancti Willelmi.
ix s. De aula Profunda super Candiche.
xx s. De aula Brackele.
ii s. De aula Bodyn.
ii s. De parua aula Bodyn.
v s. De scola in Cattestret.
iiii s. De aula Hertehall'; mag' de Baliol tenet.
xii s. De introitu sancti Iohannis in Cattestrete.
ii s. De scola retro Omnium Sanctorum.

Iuxta Kybaldestrette.

iii s. De celda in cornario; Ric' Werkeman tenet.
iii s. De domo prox.; Margareta Clarke tenet.
iii s. De secunda domo prox.; Alicia Launder tenet.

Summa totius rentalis anno xxxi, xlix li. ix s. vii d.

12. A rental of Sept. 21, 1357.

Oxon': Rentale domus sancti Iohannis Oxonie de domibus laicorum anno regni regis Ed. III a conquestu xxxi, factum ad festum sancti Mathei apostoli tempore fratris Iohannis de Iddeburi magistri dicti domus & fratris Ade de Merstone tunc procuratoris.

In parochia sancti Clementis.

viii s. De selda iuxta uenellam quam Willelmus Tame tenet.
ii s. De selda prox.; Rob. Bedman tenet.
iiii s. De tercia selda prox.; Ioh' Daie tenet.
viii s. De domo iuxta Charewelle; Hen. Tappester tenet.

Extra portam orientalem Oxon' ex parte australi.

vi s. De duabus domibus iuxta Parys; Rob. Molendinarius.
viii s. De duabus domibus prox.; Will' Molton tenet.
F. iii s. De domo Pylle; Ric. Deyher tenet.
vi s. viii d. De aula Pylle; Will' Hamon tenet.
F. xx d. De domo Bixe; Ioh' Saunford tenet.

Extra portam orientalem ex parte boriali.

De domo Oliueri Cissoris; Hugo le Cartere modo tenet.
iiii s. De domo prox.; Will' Molendinarius.
ii s. De secunda domo prox.; Thomas Cartere tenet.
iii s. De tercia domo prox.; Walterus Hambermakyer tenet.
i rosa. De domo Vynye; Agnes Deyher tenet.
ii s. De domo prox.; Henricus Carpenter tenet.
xviii d. De selda cum solario; Iohanna Beckeleye tenet.
v s. De domo prox.; Phil' Taillour tenet.
v s. De domo Ioye; Ioh' Mareschal tenet.
vi s. De domo prox.; Ioh' Welles tenet.
iii s. De duabus seldis prox.; Ioh' Mareschal tenet.
xiii s. iiii d. De domo cum le forge; idem Ioh' tenet.
xii s. De tribus seldis iuxta portam orientalem; Ioh' Lokyer tenet.

Infra portam orientalem ex parte australi.

F. iiii s. De domo Abraham; Ric' Couk tenet.
F. i d. De domo Martini Exemplatoris.
F. vi s. De aula Kepeherm; Will' Wytehalle tenet.

Kybaldestret.

iii s. De domo in cornario; Will' Capellanus tenet.
iii s. De domo prox.; Margareta Clerkes tenet.

iii s. De tercia domo prox.; Alicia Langrygge tenet.
iii s. De quarta domo ibidem; Ioh' le Werckeman tenet.
vi s. viii d. De uno gardino ibidem quod Ric' Wyte tenet.[1]
iii s. De alio gardino ex opposito magne porte aule Camyni quod Will' Hunte tenet.[2]
i rosa. De altero gardino ibidem quod idem Will' tenet.

Infra portam ex parte boriali.

xii s. De domo in cornario; Ioh' Coupere tenet.
iiii d. De selda prox.; Ioh' Lokyere tenet.
x s. De domo Coleborne; Rob. Mason tenet.
v s. De selda prox.; Ioh' Webbe tenet.
xv s. De domo Melemakere; idem Ioh' tenet.
xxiiii s. De domo Roburghe cum selda; Rob' Notyngham tenet.
xiiii s. De domo Punchard; Ioh' de Abyngdone tenet.
F. x d. De aula cum camino; Ric' Couck tenet.
ii s. De uno gardino infra dictam aulam quod idem Ric' tenet.
xx s. De domo Benham; Nic. Heytesbury tenet.
iiii s. De prima selda iuxta aulam Regine; Ioh' le Taillour tenet.
viii s. De duabus seldis prox.; Ioh' Tanner tenet.
iiii s. De quarta selda; Amicia Houwyf tenet.
vi s. De quinta selda cum sexta & solario supra; Alicia Abyngdone tenet.
xxi s. viii d. De selda in cornario cum duabus seldis prox.; Petronilla Pyemaker tenet.
F. iii s. iiii d. De domo Nytherwynmulle.
F. ii s. De domo Nicholai Glatton; Rob' Mauncel tenet.
v s. De prima selda subtus aule [*sic*] Katerine; Rog' Porter tenet.
v s. De secunda selda; Thomas Taillour tenet.
F. i mill' allec uel viii s. De domo Willelmi Barbour; Ric' Deyher tenet.
xxvi s. viii d. De aula sancti Georgii cum duabus seldis subtus; Ric' Coutone tenet.

[1] As this garden is within a few years found to be in the occupation of Richard Pencriche, we may assume that it was at the east end of Merton Street on the north side of the road, where Pencriche Hall was.

[2] This and the next garden must have been on the north side of Harehall Lane; in the rental of 1366 they have been united to Kepeham Hall *alias* the Tabard (subsequently Angel) Inn.

x s. De domo Buffard; Alic' Sheppester tenet.
x s. De domo prox.; Rob' Carpenter tenet.

Circa ecclesiam sancti Petri in oriente.

ii s. De duobus gardinis; Petronilla Pyemaker tenet.
iiii s. De uno gardino ibidem; Nic' de Heytesbury tenet.
xvi d. De altero gardino ibidem; Ioh' Abyngdone tenet.
xii d. De altero gardino ibidem; Ioh' Lokyer tenet.

In parochia beate Marie Virginis.

xx s. De domo Pomfreid; Ioh' Bedel tenet.
x s. De duabus seldis; Rob' Barbour tenet.
xxiii s. iiii d. De domo Basyng cum selda; Thomas Latyner tenet.
vi s. De duabus seldis prox.; Ioh' Cappe tenet.
F. xii d. De uno gardino; Nic' Garland tenet infra clausuram suam.

Cattestret.

xx s. De domo Lodelowe cum duabus seldis; Rob' Boucbynder tenet.
F. iiii s. De domo Abraham; Hen' Malmesbury tenet.
F. vii s. vi d. De tenemento Ade de Houtone; Ioh' Crouk tenet.
F. x s. De domo Cristine Faunt; uicarius de Couele tenet.
xiii s. iiii d. De domo Willelmi Leuerton; Rob' Maunciple tenet.
vi s. viii d. De domo Charnel cum selda; Will' Scriptor tenet.
iii s. iiii d. De uno gardino infra scolam de Cattestret; Ioh' Waleys tenet.

In parochia Omnium Sanctorum.

xvi s. De domo Wytewonge; [Stefanus Polmariua tenet, *in other ink*].
vii s. De prima selda Burewaldescote; Iohanna Sheppestere tenet.
vii s. De secunda selda prox.; Ioh' Skynnere tenet.
iiii s. vi d. De duabus seldis subtus domum Iohannis Stoudleyghe.
F. vii s. De tenemento Hengseye; idem Ioh' tenet.
xiii s. iiii d. De aula retro Omnium Sanctorum; Ioh' Bromleighe tenet.
xvi d. De uno gardino prox.; idem Ioh' tenet.
l s. De domo Swenebrouk; Ioh' Mostertone tenet.
xxviii s. De domo Alicie Nyweburi.

In parochia sancti Martini.

F. iiii s. De domo Thome Horlyance.
F. iii s. De domo Alicie Welles cum una placea.
F. x s. De selda iuxta introitum Thome de Kyngestone.
F. ii s. De selda in sutoria.
F. ii s. De solario Henrici Gamage.
F. vi s. viii d. De selda Gilberti de Wynchecombe; Ric' Forster tenet.
F. iiii s. De selda in quadriuio; Ioh' Bereford tenet.
F. ii d. De domo sancti Petri in Balliuo.
x s. De prima selda Croxforde; Adam le Sadeler tenet.
xii s. De secunda selda Croxforde; Ric' Tuwe tenet.
F. ii s. De uno stayre pro ingressu duorum solariorum desuper dictas seldas quos Ioh' de sancta Fredeswyda tenet.

In parochia sancti Iohannis.

i d. De domo Ricardi Hayle; Nic' Maunciple tenet.
F. viii s. De domo Henrici Illuminatoris; Ioh' Gruttene tenet.
F. viii s. De aula Gayler; Nic. Maunciple tenet.
F. ii s. De aula Grimstede.
x s. De duabus seldis Balle cum una placea prox.; Brianus Maunciple tenet.

In parochia sancti Michaelis ad portam australem.

ix s. De domo Ricardi Mason; Ioh' Webbe tenet.
x s. De domo Meteburne; Ioh' Skynner tenet.
vi s. viii d. De domo Boltras; Walterus Fox tenet.
F. ii s. De aula Mariole; Nich' Barker iunior tenet.
F. xii d. De tenemento Sweyneshul; Thomas Sweyneshull sen. tenet.

In parochia sancti Aldati.

F. xiii d. De uno tenemento in paruo Iudaismo; magistri de aula Baliol tenent.
F. ii s. De tenemento Plumbatoris quod Ioh' Saucer tenet.
xii d. De una placea iuxta cimiterium parochie predicte; Ioh' Tounclerk[1] tenet.
F. xii s. De domo Iohannis Dokelyntone.
l s. De domo Iohannis Kepeharm prox.
xiii s. iiii d. De domo Willelmi Alstone prox.

[1] John de Northampton was Town Clerk.

xx s. De domo Truweloue prox.

x s. De curia Lincolnie; Agnes Hales tenet.

iiii s. De una selda iuxta furnum Walteri Houland: Ioh' Maunciple tenet.

In parochia sancte Ebbe.

F. iiii s. De tenemento Bremester; Nic. Hoggestone tenet.

F. viii s. De domo prox.; Rad. Tanner tenet.

F. ix s. De domo quondam Iohannis Alstone prox.; Ioh' Alston tenet.

vi s. viii d. De domo Stanlake cum ten. Waryn; Margeria Stanlake tenet.

viii s. De iii seldis cum uno solario in cornario; Will' Cartere tenet.

In parochia sancti Michaelis ad portam borialem.

xxx s. De aula Blaunkeneye cum tribus seldis proximis quas Stephanus Lyndrapere tenet.

F. xiii s. iiii d. De tenemento Wodesdone iuxta paruum pontem iuxta Hosenye.

In parochia sancte Marie Magdalene.

F. ii s. De tenemento Iohannis Dokelyntone.

F xii d. De tenemento Dodeford quod Ioh' Wauere tenet.

F. ii s. De solario Iohannis Saucer.

F. iii s. De domo Iohannis de Abyngdone; Ioh' Gruttone tenet.

F. xvi d. De ii seldis in Stockwelstret; Ioh' Gruttone tenet.

F. xx d. De ii seldis ibidem; idem Ioh' tenet.

vi d. De domo Iohannis Tye; idem Ioh' tenet.

F. vii s. De introitu quondam Henrici Bramptone; Ioh' Plomber tenet.

F. iii s. De domo Rogeri Bost; [Henricus Malmisberi tenet, *in other ink*].

F. xii d. De tenemento Dodlyng.

xiii s. iiii d. De domo Walteri Stoford.

F. iii s. De procuratoribus ecclesie Magdalene.

F. xii d. De tenemento abbatisse de Godestouwe.

De domibus clericorum.

lxvi s. viii d. De aula Borewoldescote.

xxxv s. De aula Inge.

xxvi s. viii d. De aula Katerine.

l s. De aula Borstalle cum aula Leporis.
xxviii s. viii d. De aula Camini cum aula Philomene.
v s. De aula Nigra.
ii s. De aula Militis.
ii s. De aula Martel.
xx s. De aula Mildrede.
v s. De aula sancti Willelmi.
xii s. De aula Profunda super Candiche.
xx s. De aula Brackele.
ii s. De aula Bodyn.
De parua aula Bodyn; uacat.
xx s. De aula Mynot.
xx s. De scola in Cattestret.
xiii s. De introitu ibidem.
ii s. De scola retro Omnium Sanctorum.
F. iiii s. De aula Herthalle quam magistri aule Baliol tenent.
F. x s. De introitu sancti Nicholai.

xxxix li. xi d.[1]

13. A rental of Sept. 21, 1358.

Oxon. Rentale domus sancti Iohannis Oxonie de domibus laicorum anno regni regis Edwardi tercii post conquestum xxxii factum ad festum sancti Mathei apostoli tempore fratris Iohannis de Iddeburi, magistri dicti domus & fratris Roberti de Tywe tunc procuratoris.

In parochia sancti Clementis.

viii s. De selda iuxta uenellam; Will. Tame tenet.
ii s. De selda prox. quam Rob. Bedeman tenet.
v s. De tercia selda prox.; Walterus Taillour tenet.
viii s. De domo iuxta Charewille; Hen. le Tappestere tenet.

Extra portam orientalem Oxonie ex parte australi.

vi s. De duabus domibus iuxta Parys; Rob' Muleward tenet.
viii s. De duabus domibus proximis; Will' Moltene tenet.
F. iii s. De domo Pulle; Ric. Deyhere tenet.
vi s. viii d. De aula Pulle; Will' Hamond tenet.
F. xx d. De domo Bixe; Ioh' Saunford tenet.

[1] This apparently is what was actually collected.

Extra portam orientalem ex parte boriali.

vii s. De domo Olyueri Cissoris; Hugo le Cartere modo tenet.
v s. De domo prox., quam Will' le Muleward tenet.
ii s. De secunda domo prox.; Thomas le Cartere tenet.
iii s. De tercia domo prox.; Alicia Wodecock tenet.
i rosa rubea. De domo Vynye; Agnes Deyhere tenet.
ii s. De domo prox.; Henricus le Carpenter tenet.
xviii d. De selda cum solario; Iohannes Beckeley tenet.
v s. De domo prox.; Phil' le Taillour tenet.
v s. De domo Ioye; Iohannes le Mareschal tenet.
vi s. De domo prox.; Iohannes Welles tenet.
iii s. De duabus seldis prox.; Ioh' le Marschal tenet.
xiii s. iiii d. De domo cum le Forge; idem Ioh' tenet.
xii s. De tribus seldis iuxta portam orientalem, quas Ioh' Lokyer tenet.

Infra portam orientalem ex parte australi.

F. iiii s. De domo Abraham quam Ric' Couk tenet.
F. i d. De domo Martini Exemplatoris.
F. vi s. De aula Keypeharm quam Will. atte Wytehalle tenet.

Kybaldestret.

iii s. De domo in cornario; Will' Capellanus tenet.
iiii s. De domo prox.; Margareta Clerks tenet.
iiii s. De tercia domo prox.; Alicia Langrich tenet.
iiii s. De quarta domo ibidem; Ric' le Worckman tenet.
vi s. viii d. De uno gardino ibidem quod Alicia Wodecock tenet.
iii s. De alio gardino ex opposito magne porte aule camini, quod Will' Hunte tenet.
i rosa. De alio gardino ibidem quod idem Will. tenet.

Infra portam orientalem ex parte boriali.

xii s. De domo in cornario; Ioh' Coupere tenet.
iiii d. De selda prox.; Ioh' Lokyere tenet.
x s. De domo Coleborne; Rob. Mason tenet.
v s. De selda prox.; Ioh' le Webbe tenet.
xv s. De domo Melemaker; idem Ioh' tenet.
xxiiii s. De domo Roburgh cum selda; Rob' Notyngham tenet.
xiiii s. De domo Punchard; Ioh' de Abyngdon tenet.
F. x d. De aula cum camino; Ric' le Couk tenet.
ii s. De uno gardino infra dictam aulam; idem Ric' tenet.
xx s. De domo Benham; Nic. Heytesbury tenet.

iiii s. De prima selda iuxta aulam Regine; Ioh' le Taillour tenet.

viii s. De duabus seldis prox.; Ioh' Tanner tenet.

iiii s. De quarta selda quam Amicia Hosewyf tenet.

vi s. De quinta selda cum sexta & solario; quas Alicia de Abyngdon tenet.

xxi s. viii d. De selda in cornario cum duabus seldis prox.; Petronilla Pyemaker tenet.

F. iii s. iiii d. De domo Netherwynmulle; Thomas Golstone tenet.

F. ii s. De domo Nicholai Glattone; Rob. Maunsel tenet.

vi s. De prima selda subtus aulam Katerine; Rog' Porter tenet.

vi s. De secunda selda quam idem Rog' tenet.

i mill. allec' uel viii s. De domo Willelmi Barber; Ric' Deyher tenet.

xxvi s. viii d. De aula sancti Georgii cum duabus seldis subtus; Ric. Coutone tenet.

x s. De domo Buffard; Alicia Sheppester tenet.

x s. De domo prox.; Rob. Carpenter tenet.

Circa ecclesiam sancti Petri in oriente.

ii s.
iiii s.
xvi d.
xii d.
} [*As in the last rental.*]

vi s. viii d. De domo Charnel cum selda quas Will' Scriptor tenet.

In parochia beate Marie Virginis.

xxvi s. viii d. De domo Pomfreit quam Ioh' Bockyngham tenet.

x s. De duabus seldis; Rob. Barbour tenet.

xxiii s. iiii d. De domo Basyng cum selda; Thomas Latyner tenet.

vii s. De duabus seldis proximis quas Hen. Staciner ten'.

F. xii d. De uno gardino; Nic. Garland tenet infra clausuram suam.

Cattestret.

xx s.
F. iiii s.
F. vii s. vi d.
F. x s.
} [*As in the last rental.*]

xx s. De domo Willelmi de Leuertone, quam Ioh' Wottone tenet.

De uno gardino infra scolam.

In parochia Omnium Sanctorum.

xvi s. De domo Wytewong quam Steph' Polmeryua tenet.

vii s. vi d. De prima selda Burwaldescote; Ioh' Skynner tenet.

vii s. vi d. De secunda selda Burwaldescote; idem Ioh' tenet.

iiii s. vi d. De duabus seldis subtus domum Iohannis Stoudleghe, quas idem tenet.

F. vii s.
xiii s. iiii d.
xvi d.
l s.
F. xxviii s.
[*As in the last rental.*]

In parochia sancti Martini.

F. iiii s. De domo Thome Orliance; Ioh' de Bedeford nunc tenet.

F. iii s. De domo Alicie Welles cum una placea; — Wakeman tenet.

F. x s.
F. ii s.
F. ii s.
F. vi s. viii d.
F. iiii s.
F i d.
[*As in the last rental.*]

xii s. De prima selda de Croxford quam Adam le Harpour ten'.

xii s.
ii s.
[*As in the last rental.*]

In parochia sancti Iohannis.

i d.
F. viii s.
F. viii s.
F. ii s.
[*As in the last rental.*]

x s. De duabus seldis Balle cum una placea prox', quas Ioh' Bryan tenet.

In parochia sancti Michaelis ad portam australem.

vi s. viii d. De domo Boltras; Walterus Fox tenet.

x s. De domo Meteborne; Ioh' Skynner tenet.

ix s. De domo Ricardi Mason; Ioh' Webbe tenet.

F. ii s. De aula Mariole; Nicholaus Barker iunior tenet.
F. xii d. De tenemento Sweyneshul; Thomas Sweyneshull senior tenet.

In parochia sancti Aldati.

F. xiii d. De uno tenemento in paruo Iudaismo ex opposito magne scole ibidem.
F. ii s. De tenemento Plumbatoris quod Ioh' Saucer tenet.
xii d. De una placea iuxta cimiterium parochie predicte; Ioh' Tounclerk tenet.
xii s. De domo Iohannis Dokelinton, quam idem tenet.
liii s. iiii d. De domo Iohannis Keapeharm, quam idem tenet.
xiii s. iiii d. De domo Willelmi Alstone, quam idem tenet.
xx s. De domo Truweloue proxima, quam Thos. Lardiner tenet.
xxiiii s. De curia Lincoln quam Adam Webbe nunc tenet.
iiii s. De una selda iuxta furnum quam Ioh' Houlonde tenet.

In parochia sancte Ebbe.

iiii s. De tenemento Bremester quod Nic. Hoggestone tenet.
ix s. vi d. De domo prox. quam Ioh' de sancta Frideswida tenet.
ix s. De domo prox. quondam Iohannis Alstone, quam Ioh' Stafford tenet.
viii s. De domo Stanlake cum tenemento Waryn; Margeria Stanlake tenet.
viii s. De tribus seldis cum uno solario in cornario; Will' Carter tenet.

In parochia sancti Michaelis ad portam borialem.

xxx s.
xiii s. iiii d. } [*As in the last rental.*]

In parochia sancte Marie Magdalene.

F. ii s.
F. xii d. } [*As in the last rental.*]
F. ii s. De solario Iohannis Saucer, quod idem tenet.
F. iii s.
F. xvi d.
F. xx d.
vi d.
F. vii s.
F. iii s.
F. xii d. } [*As in the last rental.*]

xiii s. iiii d. De domo Walteri Stoford quam idem tenet.
F. iii s.
F. xii d. } [*As in the last rental.*]

De domibus clericorum.

lxvi s. viii d. De aula Borewoldescote.
xl s. De aula Inge.
xxvi s. viii d. De aula Katerine.
l s. De aula Borstalle.
xxvi s. viii d. De Camina [*sic*] aula.
xv s. De aula Philomene.
v s. De aula Nigra.
xxvi s. viii d. De aula Aristotil.
ii s. De aula Militis.
ii s. De aula Martel.
xxvi s. viii d. De aula Mildrede.
v s. De aula sancti Willelmi.
xxiiii s. De aula Minot.
x s. De aula Profunda super Candich.
De aula Brackeleye.
De aula Bodyn.
vi s. viii d. De parua aula Bodyn.
xx s. De scola in Cattestret.
xiiii s. De introitu ibidem.
ii s. De scola retro Omnium Sanctorum.
F. iiii s. De aula Herthalle quam mag. aule Balliol ten'.
viii s. De introitu sancti Nicholai.[1]

Dat' per copiam.

Pateat uniuersis per presentes quod nos magister & confratres hospitalis sancti Iohannis extra portam orientalem Oxonie recepimus de magistro & scolaribus aule de Balliolo in Oxonia quinque solidos & unum denarium annualis redditus nobis annuatim debitis viz. pro quadam aula uocata Herthalle iiii s. et quodam tenemento in paruo Iudaismo xiii d. de termino sancti Bartholomei apostoli. Dat' Oxon' die sancti Bartholomei anno regni regis Edwardi III tricesimo tercio [Aug. 24, 1359].

[1] The amount of this quitrent, for so it was, should be ten shillings.

14. A rental of Sept. 21, 1359.

Rentale domus sancti Iohannis Oxonie de domibus laicorum anno regni regis Edwardi tercii a conquestu tricesimo tercio factum ad festum sancti Mathei apostoli tempore fratris Iohannis de Iddeburi magistri dicte domus & fratris Roberti de Tywe tunc procuratoris.

In parochia sancti Clementis.

viii s. De selda iuxta uenellam; Will. Thame.
ii s. De selda prox.; Rob. Bedeman.
v s. vi d. De tercia selda quam Ioh. de Abyndon tenet, et de una placia ibidem uacua.
viii s. De domo iuxta Charewell; Hen. le Tappestere tenet.

Extra portam orientalem ex parte australi.

De domo iuxta Parys.
iiii s. De secunda domo, quam Thomas Blynde tenet.
iiii s. De tercia domo, quam Will. Knyght tenet.
viii s. De quarta domo cum quinta prox.; Will. Molton tenet.
F. iii s. De domo Pulle; Ric. Deyhere tenet.
vi s. viii d. De aula Pulle; Will. Hamond tenet.
F. xx d. De domo Bixe; Ioh. Saunford tenet.

Extra portam orientalem ex parte boriali.

De domo Olyueri Cissoris.
v s. De domo prox., quam Will. le Muleward tenet.
ii s. De secunda domo prox.; Thomas le Carter.
iii s. De tercia domo prox.; Ioh. Syneker.
i rosa rubea. De domo Vynye; Agnes Deyher.
ii s. De domo prox.; Henricus le Carpenter.
ii s. De selda cum solario; Iohannes Beckeley.
v s. De domo prox.; Philippus le Taillour tenet.
v s. De domo Ioye; Iohannes le Marschal tenet.
vi s. De domo prox.; Iohannes Welles tenet.
iiii s. De selda prox.; Ioh. Marschal.
iii s. De secunda selda prox.; Ioh. Marschal.
xiii s. iiii d. De domo cum le Forge; idem Iohannes tenet.
x s. De duabus seldis iuxta portam; Ioh. Shethere tenet.
v s. De tercia selda ibidem; Thomas Syneker tenet.

Infra portam orientalem ex parte australi.

[*All as in the last rental.*]

Kybaldstrete.

[*All as in the last rental.*]

Infra portam orientalem ex parte boriali.

[*All as in the last rental, but reading* 'Rob. le Mason' *for* 'Rob. Notyngham'.]

Circa ecclesiam sancti Petri in oriente.

ii s. De duobus gardinis; Petronilla Pyemaker tenet.
iiii s. De uno gardino ibidem; Nic. de Heytesbury tenet.
xvi d. De altero gardino ibidem; Ioh' Abyngdone tenet.
xii d. De altero gardino ibidem; Alicia Wyte tenet.

De parochia beate Marie Virginis.

xxvi s. viii d. De domo Pomfreit quam Ioh. Bockyngham tenet.
x s. De duabus seldis; Rob. Barbour tenet.
xxiii s. iiii d. De domo Basyng cum selda; Thomas Latyner tenet.
viii s. De duabus seldis proximis.
F. xii d. De uno gardino quod Nic. Garland tenet infra clausuram suam.

Cattestret.

xx s. De domo Lodelowe cum duabus seldis; Rob. Boucbynder.
F. iiii s. De domo Abraham; Henricus Malmesbury.
F. vii s. vi d. De tenemento Ade de Houtone; Ioh. Crouk.
F. x s. De domo Cristine Faunt; uicarius de Couele tenet.
xx s. De domo Willelmi de Leuertone, quam Ioh. Wottone tenet.
iiii s. De uno gardino infra scolam, quod Rob. Boucbynder tenet.

In parochia Omnium Sanctorum.

xvi s. De domo Wytewong; Stephanus Polmeryua tenet.
De prima selda Burewaldescote.
De secunda selda proxima.
iiii s. vi d. De duabus seldis subtus domum Iohannis Stoudleghe, quas idem tenet.
F. vii s. De tenemento Hengseye; idem Ioh. tenet.
xiii s. iiii d. De aula retro Omnium Sanctorum; Ioh. Bromleighe.
xvi d. De uno gardino prox.; idem Iohannes tenet.
l s. De domo Swenebrouk; Ioh. Mostertone.
F. xxviii s. De domo Alicie Nyweburi.

In parochia sancti Martini.

F. iiii s. De domo Thome Orliance, quam Iohannes de Bedeford tenet; qui dictus Iohannes cognouit dictum redditum esse debitum die apostolorum Petri & Pauli in presencia Iohannis Olneye, Roberti Maunsel, domini Walteri rectoris ecclesie sancti Aldati & Iohannis Pureye & in eorum presencia soluit ii s. in partem solucionis duodecima [ ]. Et residuum remanet ad soluendum usque aduentum Willelmi de Catesby. Similiter die predicto Iohannes Wakeman soluit & agnouit redditum domus Alicie Welles aretro existentem in presencia predictorum.

F. iii s. De domo Alicie Welles cum una placea; Iohannes Wakeman.

F. x s. De selda iuxta introitum Thome de Kyngestone.

F. ii s. De selda soterie [*sic*].

F. ii s. De solario Henrici Gamage.

F. vi s. viii d. De selda Gilberti de Wynchecombe.

F. iiii s. De selda in quadriuio; Iohannes Bereford tenet.

F. i d. De domo sancti Petri in Balliuo.

xii s. De prima selda Croxforde; Adam le Harpour.

xii s. De secunda selda Croxforde; Ricardus Tuwe.

ii s. De uno stayre pro ingressu duorum solariorum desuper dictas seldas quos Iohannes de sancta Fredeswyda tenet.

De parochia sancti Iohannis.

i d. De domo Ricardi Hayle; Nic. Maunciple tenet.

F. viii s. De domo Henrici Illuminatoris; Ioh. Gruttene.

F. viii s. De aula Gayler; Nic. Maunciple.

F. ii s. De aula Grimstede.

x s. De duabus seldis Balle cum una placea prox., quas Iohannes Bryan tenet.

De parochia sancti Michaelis ad portam australem.

[*As in the last rental.*]

De parochia sancti Aldati.

F. xiii d. De uno tenemento in paruo Iudaismo quod magister de aula Bailoll tenet ex opposito magne scole[1] sancte Fredeswyde ibidem.

[1] i.e. Civil Law School.

F. ii s.	De tenemento Plumbatoris ; Iohannes Saucer.
xii d.	De una placea iuxta cimiterium parochie predicte ; Ioh. Tounclerk.
xii s.	De domo Iohannis Dokelinton, quam idem tenet.
ix s.	De domo Iohannis Kepeherm prox., quam Ioh. Vissher tenet.
xiii s. iiii d.	De domo Willelmi Alstone, quam idem tenet.
xx s.	De domo Truweloue prox. ; Matilda Houland.
xxiiii s.	De curia Lyncolnie quam Adam le Webbe nunc tenet.
iiii s.	De una selda iuxta furnum ; Ioh. Houland.

De parochia sancte Ebbe.

iiii s.	[*As in the last rental.*]
ix s. vi d.	
ix s.	
viii s.	
	De tribus seldis cum uno solario in cornario.

De parochia sancti Michaelis ad portam borialem.

xxx s.	De aula Blaunkeneye cum tribus seldis proximis quas Stephanus Lynnedraper tenet.
xiii s. iiii d.	De tenemento Wottesdone iuxta paruum pontem iuxta Oseneye.

De parochia sancte Marie Magdalene.

F. ii s.	De tenemento Iohannis Dokelyntone.
F. xii d.	De tenemento Dodeford ; Ioh. Wauere.
F. ii s.	De solario Iohannis Saucer, quod idem tenet.
	De domo Iohannis Wellys.
F. iii s.	De domo Iohannis de Abyngdone ; Ioh. Gruttone.
F. xvi d.	De ii seldis in Stockwelstret ; Ioh. Gruttone.
F. xx d.	De ii seldis ibidem ; idem Iohannes.
vi d.	De domo Iohannis Tye ; idem Iohannes tenet.
F. vii s.	De introitu quondam Henrici Bramptone ; Ioh. Plomber tenet.
F. iii s.	De domo Rogeri Bost.
F. xii d.	De tenemento Dodlyng.
xiii s. iiii d.	De domo Walteri Stoford.
F. iii s.	De procuratoribus ecclesie Magdalene.
v s.	De duabus seldis iuxta aulam regis.
F. xii d.	De tenemento abbatisse de Godestouwe.

De parochia sancte Crucis.
vi s. viii d. De curia Maynard.
F. xviii d. De domo Iohannis Teye.

De domibus clericorum.
c s. De aula Borewaldescote.
xl s. De aula Inge.
xxvi s. viii d. De aula Katerine.
l s. De aula Borstall.
xv s. De aula Leporis.
xxvi s. viii d. De aula Camyna.
xv s. De aula Philomene.
v s. De aula Nigra.
xxvi s. viii d. De aula Aristotil.
ii s. De aula Militis.
ii s. De aula Martel.
xxvi s. viii d. De aula Mildrede.
x s. De aula sancti Willelmi.
xx s. De aula Mynot.
xii s. De aula Profunda super Candiche.
De aula Brackeleye.
vi s. viii d. De aula Bodyn.
vi s. viii d. De parua aula Bodyn.
xx s. De scola in Cattestret.
xiii s. De introitu ibidem.
xiii s. iiii d. De scola retro Omnium Sanctorum.
iiii s. De aula Herthalle quam magister aule Baliol tenet.
vii s. De introitu sancti Nicholai.

Rentale de Halewelle.
iii s. De una placea iuxta Crowelle.
v s. De prima domo in Halewelle.
ii s. De cotagio proximo.
ii s. De cotagio proximo Henrici Ocham.
iii s. ix d. De domo Henrici Ocham.
xviii d. De una placea retro domum Ocham.
iiii s. De una placea proxima uenellam.
xii d. De una placea proxima Sayhere.
iiii s. De domo Sayhere.
ii s. De parua domo iuxta ecclesiam.
iiii s. De domo proxima.

iiii s. De tercia domo proxima.
v s. De domo quondam Henrici Brackeleye.

15. A rental of Sept. 29, 1361 or 1362.

Oxonia; rentale domus sancti Iohannis de domibus laicorum anno regni regis Edwardi tercii a conquestu tricesimo sexto quinto [*sic*] factum ad festum sancti Michaelis tempore fratris Ade de Merstone tunc procuratoris.

In parochia sancti Clementis.

xii s. De selda iuxta uenellam; Will' Thame.
ii s. De selda prox.; Rob' Bedeman.
v s. De tercia selda.
De una placea non edificata ibidem.
viii s. De domo iuxta Charewell quam Hen. Tappester tenet.

Extra portam or. ex parte australi.

De domo iuxta Paris.
iiii s. De secunda domo prox.; Thomas Blinde.
iiii s. De tercia domo; Will' Knyt.
viii s. De quarta domo cum quinta; Will' Molton.
De domo Pille.
vi s. viii d. De aula Pille; Will' Hamond.
F. xx d. De domo Bix; Ioh' Saumford.

Extra portam or. ex parte boreali.

viii s. De domo Olíueri Cissoris; Ric' Porter
v s. De domo prox.; Will' Mulward.
ii s. De secunda domo prox.; Thomas Carter.
iii s. De tercia domo prox.; Rob' Tailour.
rubia rosa. De domo Vinee; Agnes Deyher.
ii s. De domo prox.; Hen. Carpenter tenet.
De selda cum solario.
v s. De domo prox.; Ioh' Taylour.
v s. De domo Ioye; Ioh' Mareschal.
vi s. De domo prox.; Nic' Foller.
iiii s. De una selda prox.; Ioh' Mareschal.
iii s. De duabus celdis prox.; idem Iohannes.
xiii s. iiii d. De domo cum le forge; idem Iohannes.
v s. De prima selda iuxta portam orientalem.
iiii s. De secunda selda.
iiii s. De tercia selda.

Infra portam or. ex parte australi.

F. iiii s.	De domo Abraham; Ric' le Couk.
i d.	De domo Martini Exemplatoris.
vi s.	De aula Kepharme.

Kybaldestret.

iii s.	De domo in cornario.
iiii s.	De domo prox. quam Margareta Clericus tenet.
iiii s.	De tercia domo prox. quam Shineker tenet.
iiii s.	De quarta domo prox. quam Ric' Werkeman tenet.
iii s.	De uno gardino ibidem ex opposito magne porte aule Camini; Will' Honte tenet.
v s.	De uno gardino ibidem; Ric' Penchrich tenet.
rubia rosa.	De alio gardino ibidem; Will' Honte tenet.

Infra portam orientalem ex parte boriali.

xiii s. iiii d.	De domo in cornario quam Ioh' Polter tenet.
iiii d.	De selda prox.; Ioh' Lokiere.
x s.	De domo Coleborne; Alicia Busseby.
iii s.	De selda prox.; Iohanna Stenns.
xvi s.	De domo prox.
xx s.	De domo Roborouth cum selda; Will' Webbe.
xiiii s.	De domo Punchard; Alicia Abindone.
F. x d.	De aula cum camino; Ric' Couk.
ii s.	De uno gardino infra dictam aulam; idem Ricardus.
xx s.	De domo Benham; Nic. Heytesbury.
iiii s.	De prima selda iuxta aulam Regine; Ioh' Tailour.
viii s.	De duabus seldis prox. quas Ioh' Tandi tenet.
iiii s.	De quarta selda quam Amicia Houwyf tenet.
vi s.	De quinta selda prox. cum sexta & solario; Alicia Abindone.
xxiii s. viii d.	De selda in cornario cum duabus seldis prox. quas Petronilla Couk tenet.
F. xl d.	De domo Netherwyndmull } magister aule Regine.
F. ii s.	De domo Nicholai Glattone } magister aule Regine.
xx d.	De prima selda subtus aulam Katerine.
xx d.	De secunda selda subtus aulam Katerine.
F. i mes allec.	De domo Willelmi Barbour; Ric' Loutebourouth.
xxvi s. viii d.	De aula Georgii cum duabus seldis subtus aul' predictam quas Ric' Couton tenet.

x s. De domo Buffard quam Ric' Littelmor tenet.
x s. De domo prox. quam Rob' Carpenter tenet.

Circa ecclesiam sancti Petri in oriente.

De duobus gardinis quos Petronilla Couk tenet.
iiii s. De uno gardino ibidem quem Nic' Heytesbury tenet.
xvi d. De altero gardino ibidem quem Ioh' Abyndone quondam tenuit.
xii d. De altero gardino ibidem quem Alicia Wyte tenet.
De domo Charnel cum seld'.

In parochia sancte Marie.

xxvi s. viii d. De domo Pounfret quam Ioh' Bokyngham tenet.
x s. De duabus seldis quas Rob. Barbour tenet.
xxiii s. iiii d. De domo Basyng cum seld' quas Thomas Latoner tenet.
iiii s. De duabus seldis prox. quas Ioh' Kemster tenet.
F. xii d. De uno gardino quem Nic' Garlond tenet infra clausuram suam.

Cattestrete.

xxvi s. viii d. De domo Lodelowe cum duabus seldis.
iiii s. De domo Abraham ; Ioh' Hardy.
vii s. vi d. De tenemento Ade de Howtone ; Ioh' Croke.
xviii s. De domo Cristine Faunt ; Rob. (?) Barswell.
xx s. De domo Willelmi Leuertone ; Ric' Harpour.
De gardino infra scolam.

In parochia Omnium Sanctorum.

xvi s. De domo Wytewong.
[ ] De prima selda Burwaldescote.
[ ] De secunda selda Burwaldescote.
[ ] De duabus seldis subtus domum Iohannis Stoudleigh ; quas idem Iohannes tenet.
F. vii s. De tenemento Hengseye quod idem Iohannes tenet.
xiii s. iiii d. De aula retro Omnium Sanctorum.
xvi d. De uno gardino.
l s. De Swenebrouk quod Ioh' de Mostertone tenet.
F. xxviii s. De domo Alicie Neuberi.

In parochia sancti Martini.

F. iiii s. De domo Orliaunce.
F. iii s. De domo Alicie Wellus.

F. x s. De selda iuxta introitum.
F. ii s. De selda soterie.
F. ii s. De solario Henrici Gamage.
F. vi s. viii d. De selda Gilberti de Winchecombe.
F. iiii s. De selda in quadriuio.
F. i d. De domo sancti Petri in Ballio.
xiii s. iiii d. De prima selda de Croxforde.
xiii s. iiii d. De secunda selda de Croxforde.
ii s. De uno stayre pro ingressu duorum solariorum.

In parochia sancti Iohannis.
F. i d. De domo Ricardi Hayle.
F. viii s. De domo Iohannis Luminatoris.
F. viii s. De aula Gayler; Nic' Manciple tenet.
F. ii s. De aula Grimstede.
F. x s. De duabus seldis Balde [*sic*] cum una placea prox.; Ioh' Brian tenet.

In parochia sancti Michaelis.
x s. De domo Bolsteras; Ioh' Schepard tenet.
xiii s. iiii d. De domo Meteborne; Ioh' Skiner tenet.
xiii s. iiii d. De domo Ricardi Mason; Ioh' Webbe tenet.
F. ii s. De aula Mariole; Nic. Barker tenet.
F. xii d. De tenemento Sweinshulle.

In parochia sancti Aldati.
xiii d. De uno tenemento in paruo Iudaismo quod mag. de aula Baliol tenet ex opposito magne scole sancte Frideswide.
ii s. De ten. Plumbatoris; Ioh' Saucer tenet.
xii d. De una placia iuxta cimiterium.
xii s. De domo Iohannis de Dokelyngtone.
l s. De domo Iohannis Keypeharm prox.; Ioh' Vyssere tenet.
xiii s. iiii d. De domo Willelmi Halston.
xx s. De domo Trueloue; Thos. Lardener tenet.
xx s. De curia Lyncoln; Adam Webbe tenet.
iiii s. De una selda iuxta furnum; Ioh' Houlond tenet.

In parochia sancte Ebbe.
iiii s. De tenemento Bremster.
ix s. vi d. De domo prox.

ix s. De domo prox.
viii s. De domo Stanlake cum tenemento Waryn; Margareta de Stanlake.
xii s. De tribus seldis cum uno solario in cornario.
De uno tofto prox. quod iacet uacuum & non edificatur.

In parochia sancti Michaelis ad portam borialem.
xxx s. De aula Blaunkeneye cum tribus seldis prox.; Steph' Lynedraper.
xiii s. iiii d. De tenemento Wotesdone in parochia sancti Thome.

In parochia sancte Marie Magdalene.
F. ii s. De ten' Iohannis Gybbes.
F. xii d. De ten' Dodeford.
F. ii s. De solario.
De domo.
F. iii s. De domo Iohannis Habindon; Ioh' de Gretton.
F. xvi d. De duabus seldis in Stockwellstrete.
F. xx d. De duabus seldis ibidem.
F. vi d. De domo Teye.
F. vii s. De introitu Henrici Bramptone; Ioh' Plommer tenet.
F. iii s. De domo Rogeri Bost.
F. xii d. De tenemento Dodlyng.
xiii s. iiii d. De domo Walteri Stowforde.
iii s. De procuratoribus ecclesie Magdalene.
v s. De duabus seldis iuxta aulam regis.
xii d. De tenemento abbatisse de Godestowe.

In parochia sancte Crucis.
vi s. viii d. De curia Maynard.
xviii d. De domo Iohannis Tye.

De domibus clericorum.
lx s. De aula Borewaldescote
xiii s. iiii d. De aula Inge.
xiii s. iiii d. De aula Katerine.
xl s. De aula Borstalle.
xv s. De aula Leporis.
xxvi s. viii d. De aula Camina.
xv s. De aula Philomene.
v s. De aula Nigra.
xxvi s. viii d. De aula Aristotil.

v s. De aula Militis.
xv s. De aula Martel.
xxvi s. viii d. De aula Mildrede.
iii s. iiii d. De aula sancti Willelmi.
xiii s. iiii d. De aula Mynot.
De aula Profunda super Candiche.
De aula Brackeleye.
vi s. viii d. De aula Bodin.
De parua aula Bodin.
De scola in Catstreet.
x s. De introitu ibidem.
De scola retro Omnium Sanctorum.
F. iiii s. De aula Herthalle; magister aule Bayliol tenet xv d.
F. viii s. De introitu sancti Nicholai.

16. A rental of Sept. 21, 1363.

Rentale domus sancti Iohannis Oxon' de domibus laicorum anno regni regis Edwardi tercii a conquestu tricesimo vii^mo^ factum ad festum sancti Mathei apostoli tempore fratris Roberti de Tywe magistri dicti [*sic*] domus et fratris Ade de Merstone tunc procuratoris.

In parochia sancti Clementis.
x s. De selda iuxta uenellam; Will' Tame.
ii s. De selda prox'; Rob' Bedeman.
v s. De tercia selda; Ioh' Abyndon; item de una placea uacua.
viii s. De domo iuxta Charewell; Hen' Tappyster.
Summa xxv s.

Extra portam orientalem ex parte australi.
De domo iuxta Parise.
iiii s. De secunda domo; Thomas Blynde.
iiii s. De tercia domo; Will' Cnyte.
viii s. De quarta domo cum quinta domo prox.; Will' Moltone.
xviii s. De domo Pulle; Ric' le Woller.
vi s. viii d. De aula Pulle; Will' Hamunde.
F. xx d. De domo Bixe; Ioh' Saunforde tenet.
Summa xxxiiii s.

Ex parte boriali.
x s. De domo Holyueri Sissoris; Ioh' atte Welle.
iiii s. De domo prox.; Will' le Melewarde.

ii s.	De secunda domo prox.; Thomas le Carter.
iii s.	De tercia domo; Rob. Cissor.
i rosa rubia.	De domo Vinie; Agnes Diere.
ii s.	De domo prox.; Hen. le Carpenter.
	De selda cum solario; Will' le Woller.
v s.	De domo prox.; Phil' Taylur.
v s.	De domo Ioye; Ioh' Marchal.
vi s.	De domo prox.; Will' Woller.
iiii s.	De una selda prox.; Ioh' Marchal.
iii s.	De duabus seldis; Ioh' Marchal.
xiii s. iiii d.	De domo cum forgio; idem Ioh' tenet.
x s.	De duabus seldis iuxta portam; Ioh' le Webbe.
v s.	De tercia selda; Laurencius Horner.

Summa xlii s. vi d.

Infra portam orientalem ex parte australi.

F. iiii s.	De domo Habraham; Ricardus tenet.
F. i d.	De domo Martini Exemplatoris.
F. vi d.	De Kypeharme; quam Thomas Spenser tenet.

De Kybaldustrete.

iii s.	De domo in cornerio; Ioh' Werkeman.
v s.	De domo prox.; Margareta Clerycus.
v s.	De tercia domo prox.; Hen' Mansipull.
v s.	De quarta domo prox.; Ric' le Werkeman.
vi s. viiii d.	De uno gardino ibidem; Ric' Penkeric.
iii s.	De alio gardino exoposito magne porte aule Camini; Will' Honte.
F. i rosa.	De alio gardino ibidem; idem Willelmus.

Summa xxiii s.

Infra port. or. ex parte boriali.

xiii s. iiii d.	De domo in cornario cum selda; Ioh' Pulter.
x s.	De domo Colburne; Rob' Bathe.
v s.	De domo Melemaker cum selda; Ioh' le Webbe.
xx s.	De domo Roburghe; Will' Woller.
xiiii s.	De domo Puncarte; Alisia Abindone.
F. x d.	De aula cum camino; Ric' le Coke.
	De uno gardino infra dictam aulam.
xx s.	De domo Benham; Nic' Hitheberi.
iiii s.	De prima selda iuxta aulam Regine; Ioh' Taylour.
iiii s.	De secunda selda prox.; Rob' Busseby.

iiii s. De tercia selda; Ioh' Tanner.
iiii s. De quarta selda; Ioh' Dipheger.[1]
vi s. De quinta selda cum sexta & solario supra; Ioh' Alwasnewe.
xxi s. viii d. De selda in cornario cum duabus seldis prox.; Thos. Coke.
F. iii s. iiii d. De domo Nethurwinmulle }
F. ii s. De domo Nicholai Glattune } mag. de aula Regine tenet.
F. x s. De introitu sancti Nicholai }
vi s. De prima selda subtus aulam Katerine; Rogerus Porter.
vi s. De secunda selda subtus aulam Katerine; idem Rogerus.
F. i mile allec' vel viii s. } De domo Willelmi Barbur; Ric' Dier.
xxvi s. viii d. De aula Georgii cum duabus seldis subtus; Ric' Coutone.
x s. De domo Buffarde; Ric' Luttulmore.
x s. De domo prox.; Rob. Carpenter.
Summa vii li. xix s. ii d.

Circa ecclesiam sancti Petri in oriente.
ii s. De duobus gardinis quas Thomas Coke.
iiii s. De uno gardino ibidem; Nich' Hyteberi.
ii s. De duobus gardinis quas Will' Fuller.
De domo Charnelle cum selda, quas Will' Scriptor tenet.

In parochia beate Marie.
xxvi s. viii d. De domo Pumfret; Ioh' Bokigham.
x s. De duabus seldis; Rob' le Barbur.
xxiii s. iiii d. De domo Basing cum selda; Thos. Latynner.
viii s. De duabus seldis prox.; Ioh' Kembuster.
F. xii d. De uno gardino quod Nic' Garlant tenet.

Cattustret.
xxiiii s. De domo Lodelowe cum duabus seldis; Thomas Dolle.
iiii s. De domo Habraham quam Hardi tenet.
vii s. vi d. De tenemento Ade de Houtone; Ioh' Croke.
xviii s. De domo Cristine Faunt.
xx s. De domo Willelmi de Leuertone; Rob' Bokebinder.

[1] Sineger in later rentals.

vi s. De uno gardino infra scolam; Thomas Dolle.
Summa vii li. xiiii s. vi d.

In parochia Omnium Sanctorum.

xvi s. De domo Wytwonk; Steph' Polmerepha.
viii s. De prima selda Burwalduscote; Ioh' Hafter.
viii s. De secunda selda Burwalduscote; quam Trenakele tenet.
iiii s. vi d. De duabus seldis subtus Iohannem Stodle; idem[1] tenet.
F. vii s. De tenemento Hegseye; idem Ioh' tenet.
xiii s. iiii d. De aula retro Omnium Sanctorum; Ioh' Brumle tenet.
xvi d. De uno gardino; idem Ioh' tenet.
l s. De Swenebrouk; Ioh' de Musturtone.
F. xxviii s. De domo Alisie Newebury.
Summa iiii li. xix s. ii d.

In parochia sancti Martini.

F. iiii s. De domo Horlihanse quam Henricus Howlont tenet.
F. iii s. De domo Alisie Welles cum una plac' quam Ioh' Wakeman tenet.
F. x s. De selda iuxta introitum Thome de Kynggustone.
F. ii s. De selda soterie.
F. ii s. De solario Anrici [*sic*] Gamage.
feodo vi s. viii d. De selda Gilberti de Winchecombe.
feodo iiii s. De selda in quadriuio quam Ioh' de Bedeford tenet.
feodo i d. De domo sancti Petri in Ballio.
xiii s. iiii d. De prima selda de Croxforde.
xiii s. iiii d. De secunda selda de Croxforde.
ii s. De uno stayre pro ingressu duorum solariorum desuper dictas seldas que Rogerus Norwode tenet.
Summa xxxiiii s. viii d.

In parochia sancti Iohannis.

feodo i d. De domo Ricardi Hayle quam Agnes Clerke tenet.
feod' viii s. De domo Ioh' Luminatoris quam Ioh' Gruttone tenet.
feod' viii s. De aula Gayler quam Agnes Clerke tenet.
feodo ii s. De aula Grimstede quam Ric' Salusberi & Ioh' Saumford tenent.

[1] i. e. John de Stodle.

x s. De duabus seldis Balle cum una plac' prox' quas Ioh' Briant tenet.

Summa xx s. i d.

In parochia sancti Michaelis ad portam australem.

x s. De domo Bolteras; Ioh' Sceperde.

xiii s. iiii d. De domo Meteburne; Ioh' Schinner.

xiii s. iiii d. De domo Ricardi Mason; Iohannes rector ecclesie sancti Michaelis.[1]

F. ii s. De aula Mariol; Nic. Barker.

F. xii d. De tenemento Swenushulle; Thos. Swenushulle.

Summa xxxviii s. viii d.

In parochia sancti Aldati.

xiii d. De tenemento in paruo Iudesmo quod magister de aula Balial tenet ex opposito magne scole sancte Frideswide ibidem.

ii s. De tenemento Plumbatoris; Ioh' Saucer tenet.

xii d. De una placea iuxta cimiterium; Ioh' Tounclerk.

xii s. De domo Iohannis de Doglintone; Ioh' Gybbus.

l s. De domo Iohannis Kypharme; Iohanna Kypharme.

xiii s. iiii d. De domo Willelmi Alstone quam idem tenet.

xx s. De domo Trewloue; Thomas Lardinniere [*sic*] tenet.

xx s. De curia Lincolne; Adam Webbe ten'.

iiii s. De una selda iuxta furrnum; Walt' Schawndeler tenet.

Summa v li. viii s.

In parochia sancte Ebbe.

iiii s. De tenemento Brumster; Nic' Hoggustone tenet.

ix s. vi d. De domo prox.; Rogerus Norwode tenet.

ix s. De domo Alstone; Ioh' Stafford tenet.

viii s. De domo Stanlake cum tenemento Waryn; Margareta Stanlake.

xii s. De tribus seldis in cornario sancte Ebbe; Ioh' Pultere.

In parochia sancti Michaelis ad portam borialem.

xxx s. De aula Blaunkeneye cum tribus seldis prox. quas Steph' Lindraper tenet.

xiii s. iiii d. De tenemento Wottesdone iuxta Oseneye.

[1] John Attehalle, who ceased to be rector in Nov. 1363 (Wood, *City of Oxford*, iii. 94).

In parochia sancte Marie Magdalene.

F. ii s.	De tenemento Iohannis Dokelyngtone.
F. xii d.	De tenemento Dodeforde; Ioh' Wauere.
F. ii s.	De solario Iohannis Sawcer; quod idem tenet.
	De domo Iohannis Wellys.
F. iii s.	De domo Iohannis Abyndone; Ioh' de Grutton.
F. xvi d.	De duabus seldis in Stokwelstrete; idem Iohannes.
F. xx d.	De duabus seldis ibidem; idem Iohannes.
vi d.	De domo Iohannis Teye quam idem Ioh' Gruttone tenet.
F. vii s.	De introitu quondam Henrici Bramptone; Ioh' Plomer.
iii s.	De domo Rogeri Bost; Hen' de Malmisburi tenet.
F. xii d.	De tenemento Dokelyn.[1]
xiii s. iiii d.	De domo Walteri de Stoford quam idem tenet.
iii s.	De procuratoribus ecclesie Magdalene.
v s.	De duabus seldis iuxta aulam Regin'[2] [*sic*].
xii d.	De tenemento abbatisse de Godestouwe
	Summa xxxviii s. viii d.

In parochia sancte Crucis.

vi s. viii d.	De curia Maynard.
F. xviii d.	De domo Iohannis Teye.

De domibus clericorum.

iiii li.	De aula Borwalduscote.
xl s.	De aula Inge.
xiii s. iiii d.	De aula Katerine.
xl s.	De aula Borstalle.
xv s.	De aula Leporis.
xxvi s. viii d.	De aula Camyna.
xv s.	De aula Philomene.
v s.	De aula Nigra.
xxvi s. viii d.	De aula Aristotil.
v s.	De aula Militis.
xv d.	De aula Martel.
xxvi s. viii d.	De aula Mildrede.
iii s. iiii d.	De aula sancti Willelmi.
xiii s. iiii d.	De aula Minot.
viii s. ii d.	De aula Profunda super Candich.
	De aula Brackeleye.
vi s. viii d.	De aula Bodyn.

[1] The name was Dodeling.

[2] 'regis' is meant.

De aula parua Bodyn.
xx s. De scola in Cattustrete.
x s. De introitu ibidem.
iii s. De scola retro Omnium Sanctorum.
iiii s. De aula Herthalle quam magister aule Baliol tenet.
De introitu sancti Nicholai.[1]

Summa xvii li. iiii s. vii d.

Rentale de Haliwelle.

iii s. De una placea iuxta Crowelle.
v s. De prima domo in Halewelle.
ii s. De cotagio prox.
ii s. De cotagio prox. Henric' Ocham.
iii s. ix d. De domo Henrici Ocham.
xiiii d. De una placea retro domum Ocham.
iiii s. De una placea prox' uenellam.
xii d. De una placea prox' Sayhere.
iiii s. De domo le Sayhere.
ii s. De parua domo iuxta ecclesiam.
iiii s. De domo prox'.
iiii s. De tercia domo prox'.
v s. De domo quondam Henrici Brackeleye.

17. A rental of Sept. 21, 1364.

Rentale domus sancti Iohannis de domibus laicorum anno regni regis [Edwardi tercii a conquestu tri[2]]cesimo viii° factum ad festum sancti Mathei apostoli tempore [fratris Roberti de Tywe magis]tri dicte domus & fratris Ade de Merstone tunc procuratoris.

In parochia sancti Clementis.

x s. De selda iuxta uenellam; Willelmus Tame.
iiii s. De selda prox.; Rob. Bedeman.
viii s. De tercia selda; Ioh' Abyndon; item de una placea uacua.
viii s. De domo iuxta Charewell; Henricus Tappyster.

Extra portam orientalem ex parte australi.

De domo iuxta Paris.
[ ] De secunda domo; Iohannes Dounham.

[*The rest as in the last rental.*]

[1] The rent from this tenement has already been entered among the houses of laymen.

[2] The roll is decayed and the words within square brackets are guessed. The resemblance between this rental and the last proves that the date is 1364, not 1354 or 1374.

Extra portam orientalem ex parte boriali.

[As in the last rental except that Iohannes Douneham holds *domus tercia* in place of Rob. Cissor, and Will. Marchal holds *tercia selda* in place of Laurencius Horner.]

Infra portam orientalem ex parte australi.

F. iiii s. De domo Abraham; Willelmus Spysur.

[*The rest as in the last rental.*]

De Kybaldustrete.

[ ] De domo in cornario; Felicia Launder.
[ ] De domo prox.; Iohannes Welsche.
[ ] De tercia domo prox.; Iohannes Campion.

[*The rest as in the last rental.*]

Infra portam orientalem ex parte boriali.

[ ] De domo in cornario; Radulfus Tanner.
[ ] De domo Melemaker cum selda; Iohannes Cardemaker.
[ ] De domo Coleborne; Ioh' Haletaker.

[*Then as in the last rental.*]

[ ] De tercia selda; Alicia Launder.
[ ] De quarta selda; Iohannes Syneger.

[*Then as in the last rental.*]

[ ] De domo Willelmi Barbur; Ricardus Leytteborou.

[*Then as in the last rental.*]

Circa ecclesiam sancti Petri in oriente.

[*As in the last rental.*]

In parochia beate Marie.

[*As in the last rental.*]

Cattustret.

[*As in the last rental and reading* 'De domo Faunt; Ioh' Taylour'.]

In parochia Omnium Sanctorum.

[ ] De domo Witwonke; Willelmus Taylour.
[ ] De duabus seldis iuxta Barwalduscote; Willelmus Begevunye.

[*Then as in the last rental.*]

[ ] De domo Alicie Neubery; Ioh' Herwel tenet.

In parochia sancti Martini.

[As in the last rental except that Rob. Hawe holds *prima selda Croxforde* and Ioh' Gyffarde *secunda selda Croxforde.*]

In parochia sancti Iohannis.

[*As in the last rental and reading* Somurford *for* Saumford.]

In parochia sancti Michaelis ad portam australem.

[ ] De domo Bolteras; Thomas Kembyster.
[ ] De domo Metebourne; Ioh' Schinner.
[ ] De domo Ricardi Mason; Ioh' Snowe.

[*The rest as in the last rental.*]

In parochia sancti Aldati.

[ ] De tenemento in paruo Iudesmo; mag. de aula Balial.
[ ] De tenemento Dokelintone; Ioh' Gibbus.
[ ] De domo Iohannis Kepharm; Iohanna Wischer.
[ ] De domo Willelmi Alstone.
[ ] De domo Trewloue; Ioh' Spenser.
[ ] De tenemento Plumbatoris; Ioh' Saucer.
[ ] De una placea.
[ ] De una placea iuxta cimiterium; Walterus Schandeler.

In parochia sancte Ebbe.
In parochia sancti Michaelis ad portam borialem.
De parochia sancte Marie Magdalene.
In parochia sancte Crucis.

[*As in the last rental.*]

De domibus clericorum.

iiii li. De aula Borwalduscote.
xl s. De aula Inge.
xiii s. iiii d. De aula Katerine.
l s. De aula Borstalle.
De aula Leporis.
xxvi s. viii d. De aula Camyna.
xv s. De aula Philomene.
v s. De aula Nigra.
xxvi s. viii d. De aula Aristotil.
De aula Militis.
xii d. De aula Martel.
xxvi s. viii d. De aula Mildrede.

x s. De aula sancti Willelmi.
xvi s. De aula Minot.
De aula Profunda super Candich.
De aula Brackeleye.
vi s. viii d. De aula Bodin.
De parua aula Bodin.
x s. De scola in Cat Stret.
x s. De introitu ibidem.
De scola retro Omnium Sanctorum.
xvi d. De aula Herthall.
De introitu sancti Nicholai.
Summa totalis lxiii li. vi s. ii d.

18. **A rental of Sept. 21, 1365.**

Rentale domus sancti Iohannis Oxon' de domibus laicorum & clericorum anno regni regis Edwardi tercii a conquestu tricesimo nono factum ad festum sancti Mathei apostoli tempore fratris Roberti de Tewe magistri dicti [*sic*] domus & fratris Ade de Merstone tunc procuratoris.

In parochia sancti Clementis.
x s.
iiii s.
vi s.
viii s.
[*Tenants as in the last rental.*]

Extra portam orientalem ex parte australi.
De domo iuxta Parise.
vi s. De secunda domo; Iohannes Scheperde.
vi s De tercia domo; Will. Cnyte.
viii s. De quarta domo cum quinta; Will. Moltone.
xviii s. De domo Pulle; Ric. le Voller.
[*The rest as in the last rental.*]

Extra portam orientalem ex parte boriali.
x s. De domo Holyueri Sissoris; Reginaldus Faber.
vi s. De domo prox.; Ioh' Hamonde.
ii s. De secunda domo prox.; Thomas Carter.
iiii s. De tercia domo; Ioh' Woller.
i rosa rubea. De domo Vinie; Agnes Diere.
ii s. De domo prox.; Henricus le Carpenter.

De selda cum solario; uacua.
v s. De domo prox.; Phil' Taylur.
v s. De domo Ioye; Ioh' Marchal.
vi s. De domo prox.; Will. Woller.
iiii s. De una selda prox.; Ioh' Marchal.
iii s. De duabus seldis; Ioh' Marchal.
x s. iiii d. De domo cum forgio; idem Iohannes tenet.
x s. De duabus seldis iuxta portam; unam tenet Laurentius Horner, alteram Margeria Bedewoman.
v s. De tercia selda; Willelmus Marchal tenet.

Infra portam orientalem ex parte australi.

[*As in the last rental.*]

De Kybaldestret.

iii s. De domo in cornario; Alicia Lauender.
v s. De domo prox.; Iohannes Welsche.
v s. De tercia domo prox.; Willelmus Marchal.
v s. De quarta domo prox.; Ricardus le Werkeman.
vi s. viii d. De uno gardino exoposito; Ricardus Penkeriche tenet.
iii s. De alio gardino exoposito; Willelmus Honte.
F. i ros' rub'. De alio gardino iuxta; idem Willelmus.

Infra portam orientalem ex parte boriali.

xvi s. De domo in cornario; Iohannes Tailur.
xii s. De domo Colburne; Iohannes Coke.
xvi s. De domo Melemaker cum selda; Iohannes Cardemaker.
xxiiii s. De domo Roburghe; Willelmus Woller.
xiiii s. De domo Puncarte; Alicia Abindone.
F. x d. De aula cum camino; Ricardus le Coke.
xx s. De domo Benham; Nicholaus Hitheberi.
v s. De prima selda iuxta aulam Regine; Iohannes Taylour.
v s. De secunda selda; Robertus Busseby.
v s. De tercia selda; Alicia Lawnder.
v s. De quarta selda; Iohannes Syneger.
vi s. De quinta selda cum sexta et solario; Iohannes Alwasnewe.
xxii s. De selda in cornario cum duabus seldis proximis; Thomas Coke.

F. iii s. iiii d. De domo Nethurwinmulle }
F. ii s. De domo Nicholai Glattune } magister de aula Regine.
F. x s. De introitu sancti Nicholai }
xii s. De duabus seldis subtus aulam Katerine; Rogerus Porter.
feodo mille allec vel viii s. } De domo Willelmi Barbur; Ricardus Louteberur
xvi s. viii d. De aula Georgii cum duabus seldis subtus; Ricardus Coutone.
xii s. De domo Buffarde; Thomas Lyttulmor.
x s. De domo prox.; Robertus Carpenter.

Circa ecclesiam beati Petri.
ii s. De duobus gardinis; Thomas Coke.
iiii s. De uno gardino ibidem; Nic. Hytheburi.
De uno gardino iuxta; Thomas Schandeler.
ii s. De duobus gardinis; Willelmus Woller.
De domo Scharnel cum selda; que stat uacua.

In parochia beate Marie.
xxvi s. viii d. De domo Pomfret; Iohannes Bokigham.
x s. De duabus seldis; Robertus le Barbur.
xxiii s. iiii d. De domo Basing cum selda; Thomas Latynner.
viii s. De duabus seldis proximis; Iohannes Kymber'.
F. xii d. De uno gardino quod Nic. Garlant tenet.

In Cattustret.
xxiiii s. De domo Lodelowe cum duabus seldis; Thomas Dolle.
iiii s. De domo Habraham; Iohannes Hardi.
vii s. vi d. De tenemento Ade de Houtone; Iohannes Croke.
xx s. De domo Cristine Faunt; Stephanus Wade.
xx s. De domo Willelmi de Leuertone; Robertus Bokebinder.
vi s. De uno gardino infra scolam; Thomas Dolle.

In parochia Omnium Sanctorum.
xvi s. De domo Witwonke; Simon Tayler.
xvi s. De duabus seldis iuxta Burwalduscote; Thomas Scenner.
iiii s. vi d. De duabus seldis subtus Iohannem Stodle; idem Iohannes.
F. vii s. De tenemento Hegseye; idem Iohannes tenet.
xiii s. iiii d. De aula retro Omnium Sanctorum; Iohannes Brumle.
xvi d. De uno gardino; idem Iohannes.

l s. De Swenebrouk; Iohannes de Musturtone.
F. xiiii s. De domo Alisie Newebury; Iohannes Hertwel.

In parochia sancti Martini.
F. iiii s. De domo Horlihanse; Emma Howlont.
F. iii s. De domo Alisie Welles cum una placea; Iohannes Wakeman.
F. x d. [*sic*] De selda iuxta introitum Thome de Kyngustone.
F. ii s. De selda soterie.
F. ii s. De solario Henrici Gamage.
F. vi s. viii d. De selda Gilberti de Winchecombe.
F. iiii s. De selda in quadriuio; Iohannes de Bedeford.
F. i d. De domo sancti Petri in Ballio.
xiii s. iiii d. De prima selda de Croxford; Robertus Hawe.
xiii s. iiii d. De secunda selda de Croxford; Iohannes Giffard.
ii s. De uno stayre pro ingressu duorum solariorum desuper dictas seldas que Rogerus Norwode tenet.

In parochia sancti Iohannis.
F. i d. De domo Ricardi Hayle; Agnes Clerke.
F. viii s. De domo Iohannis Luminatoris; Iohannes Gruttone.
F. viii s. De aula Gayler; Agnes Clerke.
F. ii s. De aula Grimstede; Ricardus Salusbury & Iohannes Somurford.
x s. De duabus seldis Balle cum una placea prox.; Iohannes Brihan.

In parochia sancti Michaelis ad portam australem.
x s. De domo Bolteras; Thomas Kymber.
xiii s. iiii d. De domo Meteburne; Iohannes Schynner.
xiii s. iiii d. De domo Ricardi Mason; Iohannes Snowe.
F. ii s. De aula Mariol; Nicholaus Barker.
F. xii d. De tenemento Swenushulle; Thomas Swenushulle.

In parochia sancti Aldati.
F. xiii d. De tenemento in paruo Iudesmo; magister de aula Balial.
xii s. De domo Iohannis Dokelyntone; Iohannes Gybbus.
lx s. De domo Iohannis Kypharme; Stephanus Lynidraper.
xiii s. iiii d. De domo Willelmi Alston.
xx s. De domo Trewloue; Iohannes Spenser.
xx s. De curia Lincolne; Adam Webbe.

ii s. De tenemento Plumbatoris; Iohannes Sawcer.
xii d. De una placea iuxta cimiterium; Walterus Schaundeler.
iiii s. De una placea exopposito; Iohannes Norhamtone.

In parochia sancte Ebbe.
F. iiii s. De tenemento Brumster; Nicholaus Hoggustone.
F. ix s. vi d. De domo prox.; Rogerus Norwode.
F. ix s. De domo Alstone; Iohannes Stafford.
x s. De domo Stanlake cum tenemento Waryn; Margareta Stanlake.
xii s. De tribus seldis in cornario sancte Ebbe; Iohannes Pultere.

In parochia sancti Michaelis ad portam borialem.
xxvi s. viii d. De aula Blaunkeneye cum tribus seldis; Iohannes Somurford.
xiii s. iiii d. De tenemento Wottesdone iuxta Oseneye.

In parochia sancte Marie Magdalene.
[*As in the next rental.*]

De domibus clericorum.
iiii li. De aula Borwalduscote.
xl s. De aula Inge.
xvi s. De aula Katerine.
xl s. De aula Borstalle.
s. De aula Leporis.
xxvi s. viii d. De aula cum Camino.
xv s. De aula Philomene.
v s. De aula Nigra.
xxvi s. viii d. De aula Aristotil.
De aula Militis.
De aula Martel.
xxvi s. viii d. De aula Mildrede.
vi s. viii d. De aula sancti Willelmi.
xvi s. De aula Minot.
De aula Profunda super Candich.
De aula Brackeleye.
De aula Bodin et de parua aula Bodin.
xx s. De scola in Cattustret.
x s. De introitu ibidem.
vi s. viii d. De scola retro Omnium Sanctorum.

xv d. De aula Hertealle.
De introitu sancti Nicholai.

19. A rental of Sept. 21, 1366.

Rentale domus sancti Iohannis Oxonie de domibus laicorum et clericorum anno regni regis Edwardi tercii a conquestu quadragesimo factum ad festum sancti Mathei apostoli tempore fratris Roberti de Tewe magistri dicte domus et fratris Iohannis de Hychyntone tunc procuratoris.

In parochia sancti Clementis.
x s. De domo iuxta uenellam quam Willelmus Tame tenet.
iiii s. De selda prox. quam Rob. Bedeman tenet.
vi s. De tercia selda quam Iohannes Habyndone tenet; item de una placia ibidem uacua.
xiii s. iiii d. De domo iuxta Scharewel quam Iohannes Pydintone tenet.
Summa xxxiii s. iiii d.

Extra portam orientalem ex parte australi.
vi s. De domo iuxta Parys quam Alicia Lauender tenet.
vi s. De secunda domo quam Willelmus Knyt[1] tenet.
viii s. De tercia domo cum quarta quas Will. Molton tenet.
xviii s. De domo Pylle quam Ricardus Foller tenet.
vi s. viii d. De aula Pylle quam Willelmus Haumon tenet.
xx d. De domo Byx quam Iohannes Saumforde tenet.
Summa xlvi s. iiii d.

Extra portam orientalem ex parte boriali.
xii s. De domo Olivueri Cissoris quam Iohannes Taylur tenet.
vi s. De domo iuxta quam Iohannes Haumond tenet.
v s. De domo secunda quam Thomas Carter tenet.
iiii s. De tercia domo quam Iohannes Hamtone tenet.
unam rosam rubiam. De domo Vinee quam Agnes Dier tenet.
ii s. De prox. domo quam Henricus Carpenter tenet.
v s. De selda cum solario.
v s. De domo prox. quam Philyppus Tailur tenet.
v s. De domo Ioye quam Iohannes Marchal tenet.
vi s. De domo prox. quam Nicholaus Woller[2] tenet.
v s. De una selda prox. quam Iohannes Pouchemaker tenet.

[1] Kynt, MS. [2] Weller, MS.

iii s.	De duabus seldis quas Iohannes Marchal tenet.
x s. iiii d.	De domo cum forgio quam idem Iohannes tenet.
v s.	De prima selda iuxta portam orientalem quam Iohannes Horner tenet.
v s.	De secunda selda prox. quam Henricus Webbe tenet.
v s.	De tercia selda ibidem quam Iohannes Werkeman tenet.
	Summa iiii li. iiii s.

Infra portam orientalem ex parte australi.

	De domo Habraham.
F. i d.	De domo Martini Exemplatoris.
F. xviii s.	De domo Kypharme quam Thomas Spencer tenet.
iii s.	De Kybaldustret. De domo in cornario quam Alicia Lauender tenet.
v s.	De domo prox. quam Iohannes Walche tenet.
v s.	De tercia domo quam Willelmus Marchal tenet.
v s.	De quarta domo quam Ricardus Werkeman tenet.
vi s. viii d.	De uno gardino exoposito quod Ric. Penkeryche tenet.
	Summa xxxviii s. ix d.

Infra portam orientalem ex parte boriali.

xvi s.	De domo in cornario quam Iohannes Scriptor tenet.
xii s.	De domo Colborne quam Iohannes Coke tenet.
xx s.	De domo Melemaker cum selda quam Iohannes Cardemaker tenet.
xxiiii s.	De domo Roburge quam Willelmus Woller tenet.
xiiii s.	De domo Poncard quam Alicia Habyngdon tenet.
F. x d.	De aula cum camino quam Ricardus Cok tenet.
xx s.	De domo Benham quam Nicholaus Hytebery tenet.
v s.	De prima selda iuxta aulam Regine quam Iohannes Taylur tenet.
v s.	De secunda selda quam Robertus Busseby tenet.
v s.	De tercia selda quam Alicia Lauender tenet.
v s.	De quarta selda quam Iohannes Syneger tenet.
ix s.	De quinta selda cum sexta & solario.
xxii s.	De selda in cornario cum duabus seldis proximis quas Thomas Cok tenet.
F. iii s. iiii d.	De domo Nethurwynmulle quam mag. de aula Regine tenet.
F. ii s.	De domo Nicholai Glattone quam idem magister tenet.
F. x s.	De introitu sancti Nicholai quem idem magister tenet.

i s. De duabus seldis subtus aulam Katerine quos Rogerus Porter tenet.

F. Milia Allec' vel viii s. De domo Willelmi Barbur quam Ricardus Louteborou tenet.

xxvi s. viii d. De aula Georgii, cum duabus seldis subtus, quas Ricardus Coutone tenet.

xii s. De domo Buffard quam Thomas Lyttulmor tenet.

x s. De domo prox. quam Robertus Carpynter tenet.

Circa ecclesiam beati Petri in oriente.

ii s. De duobus gardinis que Thomas Cok tenet.

iiii s. De uno gardino ibidem quod Nicholaus Hytebury tenet.

ii s. De alio gardino quod Thomas Schaundeler tenet.

ii s. De duobus gardinis que Willelmus Woller[1] tenet.

De domo Scharnel cum selda que stant uacue.

Summa xii li. xx d.

In parochia beate Marie.

xxvi s. viii d. De domo Pumfret quam Iohannes Bokyngham tenet.

x s. De duabus seldis quas Robertus Barbur tenet.

xxiii s. iiii d. De domo Basigge cum selda quas Thomas Latynner tenet.

x s. De duabus seldis proximis quas Iohannes Kembester tenet.

F. xii d. De uno gardino iuxta, quod Nicholaus Garlont tenet.

Summa iii li. xi s.

In Cattustret.

xxiiii s. De domo Lodelowe cum duabus seldis quas Thomas Dolle tenet.

iiii s. De domo Habraham quam Iohannes Hardi tenet.

vii s. vi d. De tenemento Ade de Houtone quod Iohannes Crock tenet.

xx s. De domo proxima Cristine Faunt quam Stephanus Wade tenet.

xx s. De domo Willelmi Leuerton quam Robertus Bokebynder tenet.

vi s. De uno gardino infra scolam quod Thomas Dolle tenet.

Summa iii li. xix s. vi d.

[1] Weller, MS.

In parochia Omnium Sanctorum.

xx s. De domo Wytwonke quam Symon Taylor tenet.

xviii s. De duabus seldis iuxta Borwalduschot quarum Thomas Schynner tenet unam & Willelmus Taylur alteram.

iiii s. vi d. De duabus seldis subtus Iohannem Stodle quas idem Iohannes tenet.

vii s. De tenemento Hengseye quod idem Iohannes tenet.

xiii s. iiii d. De aula retro Omnium Sanctorum quam rector eorundem [*sic*] tenet.

xvi d. De uno gardino quod idem rector tenet.

l s. De domo Swenebroke quam Iohannes Musterton tenet.

F. xiiii s. De domo Alicie Newebery quam Iohannes Herwell tenet.

Summa vi li. viii s. iiii d.

In parochia sancti Martini.

F. iiii s. De domo Heliaunse[1] quam Hemma Halont tenet.

F. iii s. De domo Alicie Welles cum una placia quam Iohannes Wakeman tenet.

F. x d. [*sic*] De selda iuxta introitum Thome de Kyngustone.

F. ii s. De selda soterie.

F. ii s. De solario Henrici Gamage.

F. vi s. viii d. De selda Gylberti de Wynchecombe.

F. iiii s. De selda in quadriuio quam Henricus Castel tenet.

F. i d. De sancti Petri in Balliuo.

xiii s. iiii d. De prima selda de Croxford quam Robertus Hawe tenet.

xiii s. iiii d. De secunda selda Croxforde quam Iohannes Gyffard tenet.

ii s. De uno staire pro ingressu duorum solariorum de supradictis seldis quas Rogerus Norwode tenet.

Summa l s. v d.

In parochia sancti Iohannis.

F. i d. De domo Ricardi Hayle quam Agnes Clerk tenet.

F. viii s. De domo Iohannis Luminatoris quam Iohannes Grutton tenet.

F. viii s. De aula Gayler quam Agnes Clerk tenet.

F. ii s. De aula Grymstude quam Ricardus Salusbury & Iohannes Somurford tenent.

[1] The name was originally Orleans, and was corrupted to Heliaunse.

x s. De duabus seldis Balle cum una placia proxima quas Iohannes Bryan tenet.

Summa xxviii s. i d.

In parochia sancti Michaelis ad portam australem.

x s. De domo Bolstres quam Thomas Kymber tenet.

xiiii s. De domo Meteborne quam Iohannes Cappemaker tenet.

xiii s. iiii d. De domo Ricardi Mason quam Iohannes Snowe tenet.

F. ii s. De aula Mariol quam Nicholaus Barker tenet.

F. xii d. De tenemento Swnsulle quod Thomas Swynshulle tenet.

Summa xl s. iiii d.

In parochia sancti Aldati.

F. xiii d. De uno tenemento in Paruo Iudeismo quod magister de aula de Baileal tenet ex opposito magne scole sancte Frideswide ibidem.

xii s. De domo Iohannis Dokelyndone quam Iohannes Gybbus tenet.

lx s. De domo Iohannis Kypharme quam Stephanus Lyndraper tenet.

xiii s. iiii d. De domo Alstone quam Iohannes Spenser tenet.

xxii s. De domo Treweloue quam Iohannes Spenser tenet.

xx s. De curia Lincolniensi quam Adam Webbe tenet.

ii s. De tenemento Plumbatoris quod Iohannes Sawcer tenet.

iiii s. De una placia iuxta cimiterium quam Walterus Schaundeler tenet.

xii d. De una placia exoposito quam Iohannes Norhamtone tenet.

Summa vi li. xv s. v d.

In parochia sancte Ebbe.

F. iiii s. De tenemento Brumstede quod Nicholaus Hoggustone tenet.

F. ix s. vi d. De domo prox. quod Rogerus Norwode tenet.

F. ix s. De domo Alstone quam Iohannes Stafford tenet.

x s. De domo Stanlake.

x s. De tribus seldis in cornario sancte Ebbe quas Iohannes Polter tenet.

Summa xlii s. vi d.

In parochia sancti Michaelis ad portam borialem.

xxvi s. viii d. De aula Blankenye cum tribus seldis proximis quas Iohannes Somurford tenet.

xiii s. iiii d. De tenemento Wodusdone iuxta paruum pontem iuxta Osenye in parochia sancti Thome quod idem abbas de Osenye tenet.

In parochia sancte Marie Magdalene.

F. ii s. De tenemento Iohannis Dokelyntone.

F. xii d. De tenemento Dodeford quod Iohannes Wauer tenet.

F. ii s. De solario Iohannis Saucer quod idem tenet.

De domo Iohannis Welles.

F. iii s. De domo Iohannis Habyndone quam Iohannes Grutton tenet.

F. xvi d. De duabus seldis ibidem quas idem Iohannes tenet.

F. iii d. De domo Iohannis Tye quam idem Iohannes Grutton tenet.

F. vii s. De introitu quondam Henrici Bramtone quam Iohannes Plomer tenet.

F. iii s. De domo Rogeri Bost quam Hen. de Malmusbury tenet.

F. xii s. De tenemento Dokelyn.

xiii s. iiii d. De domo Walteri Stauford quam idem tenet.

iii s. De procuratoribus ecclesie Magdalene.

v s. De duabus seldis iuxta aulam regine [*sic*].

xii d. De tenemento abbatisse de Godestowe.

In parochia sancte Crucis.

vi s. viii d. De curia Maynarde.

xviii d. De tenemento Iohannis Tye.

De domibus clericorum.

iiii li. xii s. De aula Borewalduschote.

xl s. De aula Inge.

xxvi s. viii d. De aula Katerine.

xl s. De aula Borstalle.

x s. De aula Leporis.

xxvi s. viii d. De aula cum camino.

xv s. De aula Philomene.

v s. De aula Nigra.

xxvi s. viii d. De aula Aristotil.

viii s. De aula Militis.

De aula Martel.

xxvi s. viii d. De aula Mildrede.
xiii s. De aula sancti Willelmi.
xxii s. De aula Minot.
vi s. viii d. De aula Profunda super Candych.
De aula Brackele.
De aula Bodyn & de parua aula Bodyn.
xxvi s. viii d. De scola in Cattustret.
xii s. De introitu ibidem.
vi s. viii d. De scola retro Omnium Sanctorum.
xv d. De aula Herthalle quam magistri aule Baliol tenent.

Summa totalis domibus clericorum & laicorum anno supradicto lxvi li. iiii s. v d.

Rentale de Halewelle.

De una placia iuxta Crowell.
De prima domo in Halewell.
De cotagio proximo.
De cotagio prox. Henr' Ocham.
De domo Henrici Ocham.
De una placia retro domum Ocham.
De una placia prox. uenellam.
De una placia prox. Sayhere.
De domo le Sayher.
De parua domo iuxta ecclesiam.
De domo proxima.
De alia domo proxima.
De domo quondam Henrici Bracheleye, &c.

20. A rental of Sept. 21, 1367.

Rentale domus sancti Iohannis Oxonie de domibus laicorum et clericorum anno regni regis Edwardi tercii a conquestu quadragesimo primo factum ad festum sancti Mathei apostoli tempore fratris Roberti de Tewe magistri dicte domus & fratris Iohannis de Hychyntone tunc procuratoris.

In parochia sancti Clementis.

x s. De domo iuxta uenellam quam Willelmus Tame tenet.
iiii s. De selda prox. quam Rob. Bedeman tenet.
vi s. De tercia selda quam Ioh' Abyndone tenet.
xiii s. iiii d. De domo iuxta Charewelle quam Ioh' Pydyntone tenet

Summa xxxiii s. iiii d.

L 2

Extra portam orientalem Oxonie ex parte australi.

vi s. De domo iuxta Parys quam Thomas Carter tenet.
vi s. De secunda domo prox. quam Will' Knyt tenet.
viii s. De tercia domo prox. cum quarta quas Will' Molton tenet.
xviii s. De domo Pylle quam Ric. Follere tenet.
vi s. viii d. De aula Pylle quam Will' Haumon tenet.
xx d. De domo Byx quam Ioh' Saunford tenet.

Summa xlvi s. iiii d.

Extra portam orientalem Oxonie ex parte boriali.

x s. De domo Oliueri Cissoris quam Ioh' Carter tenet.
vi s. De domo iuxta quam Ioh' Haumond tenet.
vi s. De domo secunda quam Ioh' Hamptone tenet.
v s. De tercia selda quam Radulfus Sutor tenet.
unam rosam rubiam. De domo Vinie quam Agnes Dier tenet.
ii s. De prox. domo quam Henricus Carpenter tenet.
v s. De selda cum solario quam Ioh' Couper tenet.
v s. De domo prox. quam Philippus Taylour tenet.
v s. De domo Ioye quam Ioh' Couper tenet.
vi s. De domo prox. quam Nic. Follere tenet.
v s. De selda prox. cum solario quam Agnes Godhale tenet.
iii s. De duabus seldis prox. quas Ioh' Mareschal tenet.
xiii s. iiii d. De domo prox. cum forgio quam idem Ioh' tenet.
v s. De prima selda iuxta portam orientalem quam Alicia Irysche tenet.
v s. De secunda selda prox. quam Thomas Blynde tenet.
v s. De tercia selda prox. quam Alicia Deuenysche tenet.

Summa iiii li. vi s. iiii d.

Infra portam orientalem.

De domo quondam Thomas Habraham.
xiiii s. De domo Kepharme quam Thomas Kloptone tenet.
de feodo i d. De domo quondam Martini Exemplatoris quam Ricardus Sheffeld tenet.

De Kybaldustret.

iii s. De domo in cornario quam Alicia Lauender tenet.
v s. De domo prox. quam Ioh' Walsche tenet.
v s. De tercio domo quam Will' Mareschal tenet.

v s. De quarta domo quam Ric. Werkeman tenet.
vi s. viii d. De uno gardino ex opposito quod mag. Ricardus Penkeryche tenet.

Infra portam orientalem ex parte boriali.

xx s. De domo in cornario quam Will' Manciple tenet.
xii s. De domo Colborne quam Andreas Carpenter tenet.
xvi s. De domo Melemaker cum selda quam Will' Prentice tenet.
xxiiii s. De domo Roburge quam Will' Prentice tenet.
xiiii s. De domo Poncard quam Alicia Abyndone tenet.
de feodo x d. De aula cum camino quam Ric' Cook tenet.
xx s. De domo Benham cum selda quam Nic. Heytesbury tenet.
v s. De prima selda iuxta aulam regine quam Ioh' Taylur tenet.
v s. De secunda selda quam Rob. Bosseby tenet.
v s. De tercia selda quam Alicia Lauender tenet.
v s. De quarta selda quam Ioh' Taylour tenet.
ix s. De quinta selda cum sexta & solario que Ioh' Cornwayle tenet.
xxii s. De selda in cornario cum duabus prox. quas Petronilla Coke tenet.
xl d. De domo Nethurwynmulle quam prepositus aule Regine tenet.
ii s. De domo Nicholai Glatton quam idem tenet.
x s. De introitu sancti Nicholai quem idem tenet.
xii s. De duabus seldis subtus aulam Katerine quas Will' Coke tenet.
i mill' allec' uel viii s. De domo Willelmi Barbour quam Ric. Lowtebury tenet.
xxvi s. viii d. De aula Georgii cum duabus seldis subtus quas Ric. Coutone tenet.
xiii s. iiii d. De domo Buffard quam Hugo Coke tenet.
De domo prox. quam Rob. Carpenter tenet.

Circa ecclesiam beati Petri in oriente.

ii s. De duobus gardinis que Thomas Coke tenet.
iiii s. De uno gardino ibidem quod Nic. Heytesbury tenet.
ii s. De alio gardino iuxta quod Thomas Chaundeler tenet.

uacat. De duobus gardinis.
uacat. De domo Scharnel cum selda.

In parochia beate Marie.

xxvi s. viii d. De domo Punfret quam Ioh' Bokyngham tenet.
x s. De duabus seldis quas Alicia Croppe tenet.
xxiii s. iiii d. De domo Basyng cum selda quam Thos. Latoner tenet.
x s. De duabus seldis quas Rob. Barbour tenet.
xii d. De uno gardino quod Nic. Garlond tenet infra domum suam.

Cattustret.

xxiiii s. De domo Lodelowe cum duabus seldis quas Thos. Dolle tenet.
iiii s. De domo Habraham quam Ioh' Hardy tenet.
vii s. vi d. De tenemento Ade de Houtone quod Ioh' Bokyngham tenet.
xx s. De domo Cristine Faunt quam Steph. Wade tenet.
xx s. De domo Willelmi de Leuertone quam Rob. Bokebynder tenet.
iiii s. De uno gardino infra scolam quod Thomas Dolle tenet.

In parochia Omnium Sanctorum.

xx s. De domo Wytwonk quam Will' Taylour tenet.
ix s. De prima selda Burwaldescote quam Thos. Stafford tenet.
ix s. De secunda prox. quam Thos. Trenakle tenet.
iiii s. vi d. De duabus seldis subtus Iohannem Stodlee quas idem tenet.
F. vii s. De ten. Hengseye quod idem Ioh' tenet.
xiii s. iiii d. De aula retro Omnium Sanctorum quam rector ecclesie Omnium Sanctorum tenet.
xviii d. De uno gardino quod idem Rector tenet.
l s. De Swenebrouk quam Mosturtone tenet.
xxviii s. De domo Alicie de Newebery quam procuratores ecclesie Omnium Sanctorum tenent in bocheria.

In parochia sancti Martini.

F. iiii s. De domo Heliaunse quam Hen. Blodd tenet.
F. iii s. De domo Alicie Welles cum una placea quam Ioh' Wakeman tenet in Ballio.

F. x s. De selda iuxta introitum Thome de Kyngustone.
F. ii s. De selda Soterie.
F. ii s. De solario Henrici Gamage.
F. vi s. viii d. De selda Gilberti de Wynchecombe quam Will' Bergeyuene tenet.
F. iiii s. De selda in quadriuio quam Bartolot tenet.
F. i d. De sancti Petri in Balliuo.
xiii s. iiii d. De prima selda de Croxford quam Rob. Hawe tenet.
xiii s. iiii d. De secunda selda de Croxford quam Ioh' Gyffard tenet.
De uno staire pro ingressu duorum solariorum de supradictis seldis quam Rog' Northwode tenet.

In parochia sancti Iohannis.
i d. De domo Ricardi Hayle quam Agnes Clerk tenet.
F. viii s. De domo Iohannis Luminatoris quam Simon Gruttone tenet.
F. viii s. De aula Gayler quam Agnes Clerke tenet.
F. ii s. De aula Grymstude quam rector ecclesie Mertonehalle tenet.[1]
x s. De duabus seldis Balle cum una placia prox. quas Iohannes Buset tenet.

In parochia sancti Michaelis.
xiii s. iiii d. De domo Bolstres quam Ioh' Snowe tenet.
xiiii s. De domo Meteborne quam Ioh' Cappere tenet.
x s. De domo Ricardi Mason quam Thos. Kembere tenet.
F. ii s. De aula Mariole quam Nic. Barkere tenet.
F. xii d. De tenemento Swnsulle quod Thos. Swnsulle tenet.

In parochia sancti Aldati.
F. xiii d. De uno tenemento in Paruo Iudeismo quod scolares de Balliole halle tenent ex opposito magne scole in Iudeismo.
xii s. De domo Iohannis Dokelyndone quam Ioh' Gibbes tenet.
lx s. De domo Iohannis Kypharme quam Stephanus Lynedraper tenet.
xiii s. iiii d. De domo Alstone quam Will' Alstone tenet.
xxii s. De domo Treweloue quam Ioh' Spenser tenet.

[1] In the rental of 1369 'Rector aule Mertone'.

xx s. De curia Lincolniensi quam Adam Webbe tenet.
F. ii s. De tenemento Plumbatoris quod Hen. Cobeler tenet.
iiii s. De una placia iuxta cimiterium quam Will' Saundres tenet.
vi d. De una placea ex opposito quam Ioh' Tounclerk tenet.

In parochia sancte Ebbe.
iiii s. De ten. Brumsted quod Nic. Hoggestone tenet.
ix s. vi d. De domo prox. quam Reginaldus Tanner tenet.
ix s. De domo Alstone quam Ioh' Stafford tenet.
xii s. De domo Stanlake cum tenemento Warein quas Margareta Stanlake tenet.
De tribus seldis in cornario sancte Ebbe quas Margareta Rynges tenet.

In parochia sancti Michaelis ad portam borialem.
xxvi s. viii d. De aula Blankenye cum tribus seldis prox. quas Iohannes Somerford tenet.
xiii s. iiii d. De tenemento Wodusdone iuxta paruum pontem iuxta Oseneye in parochia sancti Thome quod abbas Oseneye tenet.

In parochia sancte Marie Magdalene.
F. ii s. De tenemento Iohannis Dokelintone.
F. xii d. De tenemento Bodeford [*sic*].
F. ii s. De solario Iohannis Saucer, quod uxor eius tenet.
iii s. iiii d. De domo Iohannis Welles, quam Ioh' Hostyler tenet.
F. iii s. De domo Iohannis Habyndone, quam Ioh' Gruttone tenet.
F. xvi d. De duabus seldis ibidem quas dictus Ioh' tenet.
F. xx d. De duabus seldis in Stokwellestrete quas Ioh' Gruttone tenet.
vi d. De domo Iohannis Tye.
F. vii s. De introitu quondam Henrici Bramtone quam Ric. Corcer tenet.
F. iii s. De domo Rogeri Bost quam Ioh' Hardy tenet.
De tenemento Bokelyn [*sic*].
xiii s. iiii d. De domo Walteri Stanford quam idem Walterus tenet.
F. iii s. De procuratore ecclesie Magdalene.
uacat. De duabus seldis iuxta aulam Regine.
F. xii d. De tenemento abbatisse de Godestowe.

In parochia sancte Crucis.
De curia Maynard.
De tenemento Iohannis Tye.

De domibus clericorum.
iiii li. xii s. De aula Burwaldescote.
xl s. De aula Inge.
xxvi s. viii d. De aula Katerine.
xl s. De aula Borstalle.
x s. De aula Leporis.
xxvi s. viii d. De aula cum camino.
xv s. De aula Philomene.
v s. De aula Nigra.
xxvi s. viii d. De aula Aristotil.
xx s. De aula Militis.
De aula Martel.
xxvi s. viii d. De aula Mildrede.
x s. De aula sancti Willelmi.
xxii s. De aula Minot.
uacat. De aula Profunda.
uacat. De aula Brakele.
uacat. De aula Bodyn.
xxvi s. viii d. De scola in Cattustret.
xii s. De introitu ibidem.
vi s. viii d. De scola retro Omnium Sanctorum quam Ioh' Holewey tenet.
F. xv d. De aula Herthalle quam magister aule Baliole tenet in uico sancti Iohannis ex parte australi.

Rentale de Halewelle.
De una placea iuxta Crowelle.
De prima domo in Halewelle.
De cotagio prox.
De cotagio prox. Henr' Ocham.
De domo Henrici Ocham.
De una placea prox. uenellam.
De una placea prox. Sayhere.
De domo le Sayhere.
De parua domo iuxta ecclesiam.
De domo prox.
De alia domo prox.
De domo quondam Henrici Bracheleye.

21. A rental of Dec. 21, 1367.

Rentale domus sancti Iohannis extra portam orientalem Oxonie de domibus laicorum & clericorum anno regni regis Edwardi tercii post conquestum primo[1] incipiente in festo sancti Thome apostoli anno supradicto durante usque ad idem festum proximo sequens anno futuro tempore fratris Iohannis Ichintone tunc procuratoris.

In parochia sancti Clementis.

x s. De domo iuxta uenellam quam Will' Thame tenet.
iiii s. De selda prox. quam Rob. Blynde tenet.
vi s. De secunda selda prox. quam Ioh' Abyndon tenet.
xiii s. iiii d. De domo iuxta Charewell, quam Ioh' Pydintone tenet.

Extra portam orientalem ex parte australi.

vi s. De domo iuxta Paris quam Thomas Carter tenet.
vi s. De secunda domo quam Will' Knyt tenet.
viii s. De tercia domo prox. quam Will' Moltone tenet.
xviii s. De quarta domo cum quinta prox. quas Ric. Follere tenet.
viii s. De aula Pylle cum selda quas Will' Hamond tenet.
F. xx d. De domo Bix prox. quam Ioh' Saumforde tenet.

Extra portam orientalem ex parte boriali.

xii s. De domo Oliueri Cissoris iuxta portam nostram quam Rob. Carpinter tenet.
vi s. vi d. De domo prox. quam Ioh' Hamond tenet.
vi s. vi d. De secunda domo prox. quam Thomas Bruhere tenet
v s. De tercia domo prox. quam Rad. Sutor tenet.
unam rosam rubiam. De domo Vinee prox. quam Walter Follere tenet.
ii s. De domo prox. quam Will' Mileward tenet.
v s. De una selda cum solario; Ioh' Couper tenet.
v s. De domo prox. quam Phil' Taylor tenet.
v s. De domo Ioye quam Ioh' Mareschall tenet.
vi s. De domo prox. Ioye, quam Nich' Follere tenet.
v s. De selda prox. quam Iuliana Berstelawe tenet.
iii s. De duabus seldis prox. quas Ioh' Mareschall tenet.
xiii s. iiii d. De domo cum le forge quas idem Ioh' tenet.

[1] *Sic*, but outside it is endorsed in the original hand 'xl^mo primo'.

v s. De prima selda iuxta portam orientalem quam Amicia Spinter [*sic*] tenet.
v s. De secunda selda prox. quam Thomas Blynde tenet.
v s. De tercia selda prox. quam Ioh' Follere tenet.

Infra portam orientalem ex parte boriali.

xx s. De domo in cornario quam Will' Manciple tenet.
xii s. De domo Coleborne quam Andreas Carpenter tenet.
xx s. De domo Molemaker [*sic*] cum seld' quas Ioh' Cardemaker tenet.
xxiiii s. De domo Roborowe quam Will' Prentice tenet.
xiiii s. De domo Punchard quam Alicia Abyndone tenet.
F. x d. De aula cum camino quam Ric' Coke tenet.
xx s. De domo Benham; Nich' Heytesbury tenet.
v s. De prima selda iuxta aulam Regine quam Agnes Taylour tenet.
v s. De secunda selda prox. quam Rob. Bosseby tenet.
v s. De tercia selda prox. quam Will. Coke tenet.
v s. De quarta selda prox. quam Will. Glouer tenet.
iiii s. De quinta selda prox. quam Cecilia Spinster tenet.
viii s. De sexta selda cum solario quos Adam Bedeford tenet.
xxii s. De selda in cornario cum duabus seldis prox. quas Petronilla Coke tenet.
F. iii s. iiii d. De domo Netherwinmulle quam prepositus aule Regine tenet.
F. x s. De introitu sancti Nicholai quam idem prepositus tenet.
F. ii s. De domo quondam Nicholai Glatton quam idem prepositus tenet.
xii s. De duabus seldis subtus aulam Katerine quas Lucia de Hedyndone tenet.
xxxiii s. iiii d. De domo quondam Willelmi Barbour quam Ric' Louteborowe tenet.
xxvi s. viii d. De aula Georgii cum seld' quas Ric' Coutone tenet.
xiii s. iiii d. De domo Buffard quam Ioh' Coke tenet.
vi s. viii d. De domo prox. quam Robertus Carpenter tenet.

Infra portam orientalem ex parte australi.

xii s. De domo Abraham, super quam sunt due shope edificate: de prima shopa quam Alicia Spinster tenet.
xii s. De secunda shopa quam Will' Coke tenet.

xiiii s. De domo Kepharme quondam Iohanne Brayles, quam Thomas Cloptone tenet.

F. i d. De domo Martini amplexatoris [*sic*] quam Ric' Sheffeld tenet.

Kybaldestrete.

iii s. De domo in cornario quam Ric' Pencriche tenet.

v s. De domo prox. quam Ioh' Wales tenet.

v s. De secunda domo quam Will' Faber tenet.

v s. De tercia domo quam Ric' Werkeman tenet.

vi s. viii d. De uno gardino ibidem ex altera parte quam Ric' Pencriche tenet.

Circa ecclesiam sancti Petri in oriente.

ii s. De duobus gardinis quos Thomas Coke tenet.

iiii s. De uno gardino quem Nich. Heytesbury tenet.

ii s. De uno gardino quem Thomas Chaundelere tenet.

De duobus gardinis uacuis ibidem.

De aula Martel.

De domo Charnel.

In parochia sancte Marie Virginis.

xxvi s. viii d. De domo Punfret quam Ioh' Grasiere tenet.

x s. De duabus seldis in cimiterio ecclesie antedicte quas Thomas Latoner tenet.

xxiii s. iiii d. De domo Basing quam idem Thomas tenet.

x s. De duabus seldis prox. quas Rob. Barbour tenet.

F. xii d. De uno gardino infra clausuram Nicholai Garlond quam idem Nicholaus tenet.[1]

In parochia Omnium Sanctorum.

xx s. De domo Wytewong quam Will' Taylor tenet.

xviii s. De duabus seldis Burwaldescote quas Ioh' Trenacle tenet.

iiii s. vi d. De duabus seldis subtus domum Iohannis Stodele quas idem Ioh' tenet.

F. vii s. De ten. Hengseye quod Ioh' Stodele tenet.

xiii s. iiii d. De aula retro Omnium Sanctorum quam rector ecclesie Omnium Sanctorum tenet.

xviii d. De domo prox. quam idem rector tenet.

l s. De domo Sunnebroke quam Ioh' Mosturton tenet.

[1] The scribe has forgotten all the tenements in Cat Street.

F. xxviii s. De domo Alicie Newburii quam procuratores ecclesie Omnium Sanctorum tenent in Bucheria.

In parochia sancti Martini.

F. iiii s. De domo Orliauns quam Hen. Blod tenet.
F. iii s. De domo Alicie Welles cum una placia iuxta fratres Carmelitas quas Ioh' Wakeman tenet.
F. ix s. De introitu quondam Thome Kyngestone.
F. ii s. De selda in sutoria.
F. ii s. De solario Henrici Gamage.
F. vi s. viii d. De selda Gilberti Wynchecombe quam Will' Bergeyne tenet.
F. iiii s. De selda in quadriuio quam Bartolot tenet.
F. i d. De domo sancti Petri in Ballio.
xiii s. iiii d. De prima selda Croxford quam Rob. Hawe tenet.
xiii s. iiii d. De secunda selda Croxford quam Will' Gyffard tenet.
ii s. De uno stayhe [*sic*] inter dictas seldas quod Rog' Northwode tenet.

In parochia sancti Iohannis.

i d. De uno gardino quod Agnes Clerk tenet.
De domo Henrici Illuminatoris nunc est gardinum quod Ioh' Rede tenet.
F. viii s. De aula Gayler quam eadem Agnes tenet.
F. ii s. De aula Grimstede quam Adam Sclatter tenet.
x s. De duabus seldis Balle cum una placia prox. quas Ioh' Boseit tenet.

In parochia sancti Michaelis australis.

xiii s. iiii d. De domo Bultras quam Ioh' Snow tenet.
xiiii s. De domo Meteborne quam Thomas Cappere tenet.
x s. De domo Mason quam Thomas Kembere tenet.
F. ii s. De aula Mariolle quam Will' Borowe tenet.
F. xii d. De tenemento Suyneshulle.

In parochia sancti Aldati.

F. xiii d. De uno tenemento in Paruo Iudaismo quod scolares aule Balliol tenent.
xii s. De domo Iohannis Dokelynton quam Ioh' Gybbes nunc tenet.
l s. De domo Kepharme quam Ric' Bassett tenet.
xlii s. iiii d. De domo prox. quam Will' Alston tenet.

xxii s. De domo prox. quam Ioh' Spencer tenet.
xx s. De curia Lincoln' quam Adam Webbe tenet.
F. ii s. De tenemento Plumbatoris; abbas Regalis [1] tenet.
De una placia iuxta cimiterium sancti Aldati ex parte australi.
iiii s. De una domo in Paruo Iudaismo quam Will' Saunders tenet.

In parochia sancte Ebbe.

F. iiii s. De tenemento uno extra murum uille.
F. viii s. De domo prox. quam Rogg' Northwode tenet.
F. ix s. iiii d. De tenemento prox. quondam Iohannis Alestone quam Reginaldus Tanner tenet.
xiii s. iiii d. De domo Stanlake quam Rob' Wytele tenet cum tenemento Wareyn.
De domibus in cornario quas Margareta Rynges tenet.

In parochia sancti Michaelis borialis.

xxvi s. viii d. De aula Blaunkeneye cum seld' quas Ioh' Somorworde tenet ad terminum uite.

In parochia sancti Thome iuxta Hoseneye.

F. xiii s. iiii d. De tenemento Wodesdone situato iuxta paruum [pontem] [2] de Oseneye, quod abbas Oseneye tenet.

In parochia sancte Marie Magdalene.

F. ii s. De tenemento Doklyntone.
F. xii d. De tenemento Dodeford; Ric' Oxenford tenet.
F. ii s. De solario Iohannis Saucer quod uxor eius tenet.
iii s. iiii d. De domo Welles quam Ioh' Hostelere tenet.
F. iii s. De domo quondam Iohannis Abyndone quam Ioh' Gruttone tenet.
F. xx d. De duabus seldis in Stokwelstrete quas idem Ioh' tenet.
F. xvi d. De duabus seldis ibidem quas idem Ioh' tenet.
vi d. De domo Tye quam Ioh' Wroth, syneker, tenet.
F. vii s. De introitu quondam Henrici Bramptone quam Ric' Wytewell tenet.
F. iii s. De domo quondam Roggeri Bost quam Ioh' Hardy tenet.
F. xii d. De tenemento Dokelyn.

[1] Regalis Loci is meant, i.e. Rewley.
[2] Omitted by the scribe.

xiii s. iiii d. De domo quam Walterus Stoword tenet retro ecclesiam parochie antedicte.

F. iii s. De procuratoribus ecclesie Magdalen.

De una placia iuxta paruam portam fratrum Carmel. Vacat.

F. xii d. De tenemento abbatisse de Godestowe.

Rentale de Haliwelle eodem anno.

xiii s. iiii d. De una placia iuxta Crowelle cum domo prox. quam Ioh' Kente tenet.

iiii s. De domo prox. quam Ioh' Mileward tenet.

xii d. De secunda domo prox. quam Will' Scynner tenet.

ix d. De gardino prox. gardinum iuxta uenellam que se extendit ad molendinum de Haliwelle quod Will' Sclatter senior tenet.

De uno gardino proximo uenell'. Vacat.

iiii s. De una domo exopposito cimiterio ecclesie de Haliwelle quam Stephanus Triturator tenet.

vi d. De duabus buttis terre arrabilis quas Will' Sclatter senior tenet.

xii d. De una acra terre arrabilis iuxta gardinum fratrum Augustin' in Bellomonte quam Will' Scriptor tenet.

De uno crofft̄o iuxta molendinum de Haliwelle.

De domibus clericorum anno supradicto.

iiii li. xii s. De aula Borwaldescote.

xl s. Aula Ynge.

xxvi s. viii d. Aula Katerine.

xl s. Aula Borstalle.

x s. Aula Leporis.

xxvi s. viii d. Aula cum camino.

xv s. Aula Philomene.

v s. Aula Nigra.

xxvi s. viii d. Aula Arstotil.

xx s. Aula Militis.

xxvi s. viii d. Aula Mildrede.

Aula sancti Willelmi. Vacat.

xxx s. Aula Minote.

Aula Profunda super Candiche. Vacat.

Aula Brackele ibidem. Vacat.

Aula Bodyn et aula Bodyn. Vacant.

xxvi s. viii d. De scola in Cattestrete.
xii s. De introitu ibidem.
vi s. viii d. De scola retro Omnium Sanctorum.
F. xv d. De aula Hertehalle in uico sancti Iohannis ex parte australi.
Magistri aule Balliole debent soluere pensionem inde.

22. A rental of Dec. 21, 1368.

Rentale domus sancti Iohannis Oxonie de domibus laicorum et clericorum anno regni regis Ed. III quadragesimo secundo, incipiente in festo sancti Thome apostoli anno supradicto.

In parochia sancti Clementis.
[*As in the last rental.*]

Extra portam orientalem ex parte australi.
vi s. De domo iuxta Paris; Thomas Carter.
vi s. De secunda domo; Will' Knyt.
viii s. De tercia domo cum quarta; Will' Molton.
xviii s. De quinta domo cum domo Pille; Ric' Follere.
viii s. De aula Pille cum selda; Will' Hamond.
F. xx d. De domo Bix; Ioh' Saumforde.

Extra portam orientalem ex parte boriali.
x s.
vi s. vi d.
vii s.
v s.
[*As in the last rental.*]
i rosa rubia. De domo Vinee; Walterus Foller tenet de Agnete Deyhere.
ii s.
v s.
v s.
v s.
vi s.
v s.
iii s.
xiii s. iiii d.
[*As in the last rental.*]
v s. De prima selda iuxta portam orientalem; Amycia Toukere.
v s.
v s.
[*As in the last rental.*

Infra portam orientalem ex parte australi.

xii s. De domo Abraham; de prima shoppa, Alysia Spinster.
xii s. De secunda shoppa; Will' Coke.
xviii s. De domo Kepharme; Thomas Cloptone.
F. i d. De domo Martini Amplexatoris; Ricardus Sheffolde.

Infra portam orientalem ex parte boriali.

xx s. De domo in cornario cum selda; Willelmus Manciple.
xii s. De domo Coleborne; Andreas Carpenter.
vi s. De selda proxima; Iohanna Spinster.
xviii s. De domo Melemaker; Iohannes Cardemaker.
xx s. De domo Roborowe; Willelmus Prentice.
xiiii s. De domo Punchard; Alicia Abyndone.
F. x d. De aula cum camino; Ricardus Coke.
xx s. De domo Benham; Nicholaus Heytesbury.
vi s. De prima selda iuxta aulam Regine; Agnes Taylour.
vi s. De secunda selda prox.; Robertus Bosseby.
vi s. De tercia selda prox.; Willelmus Coke.
vi s. De quarta selda prox.; Willelmus Glover.
iiii s. De quinta selda prox.; Cecilia Spinster.
viii s. De sexta selda cum solario; Adam Bedeford.
xxii s. De selda in cornario cum duabus seldis prox.; Petronilla Coke.
F. iii s. iiii d. De domo Netherwinmulle }
F. x s. De introitu sancti Nicholai } prepositus aule Regine.
F. ii s. De domo quondam Nicholai Glatton }
xiiii s. De duabus seldis subtus aulam Katerine; Lucia de Hedyndone.
xxxiii s. iiii d. De domo quondam Willelmi Barbour; Ricardus Louteborowe.
xxvi s. viii d. De aula Georgii cum seld'; Ricardus Coutone.
xiiii s. De domo Buffard; Robertus Coke.
xvi s. De domo prox.; Iohannes Manciple.

Kibaldstrete.

v s. De domo in cornario; magister Ricardus Pencrik.
v s. De domo prox.; Iohannes Wales.
v s. De secunda domo; Willelmus Faber.
v s. De tercia domo; Ricardus Werkeman.

Circa ecclesiam sancti Petri in oriente.

ii s. De duobus gardinis; Thomas Coke.
iiii s. De uno gardino; Nicholaus Heytesbury.
ii s. De uno gardino; Thomas Chaundelere.
uacat. De duobus gardinis ibidem.
De aula Martel.
ii s. De domo Charnel; Ricardus Bidul.

In parochia sancte Marie Virginis.

xxvi s. viii d. De domo Punfret; Iohannes Bokyngham.
xii s. De duabus seldis in cimiterio; Thomas Latoner.
xxiii s. iiii d. De domo Basing; idem Thomas.
x s. De duabus seldis prox.; Robertus Barbour.
F. xii d. De uno gardino infra clausuram Nicholai Garlond; idem Nicholaus.
xxiiii s. De domo Lodelowe cum duabus seldis quas Thomas Dolle tenet.
F. iiii s. De domo Abraham; Iohannes Hardy.
F. vii s. vi d. De tenemento Ade Howton; Iohannes Bokyngham.
xxvi s. viii d. De domo Faunt; Iohannes Manciple.
xx s. De domo Leuerton; Robertus Bokbynder.
iiii s. De uno gardino infra introitum sancti Iohannis cum una domo; Thomas Dolle.

In parochia Omnium Sanctorum.

xx s. De domo Wytewong; Willelmus Taylor.
xviii s. De duabus seldis Burwaldescote; Iohannes Trenacle.
iiii s. vi d. De duabus seldis subtus domum Iohannis Stodle; idem Iohannes.
F. vii s. De tenemento Hengseye; Iohannes Stodle.
xiii s. iiii d. De aula retro Omnium Sanctorum; rector ecclesie Omnium Sanctorum tenet.
xviii d. De domo prox.; idem rector.
l s. De domo Sunnebroke; Iohannes Mosturton.
F. xxviii s. De domo Alicie Newbury quam procuratores ecclesie Omnium Sanctorum tenent in Bocheria iuxta Henricum Bathe.

In parochia sancti Martini.

[*As in the last rental.*]

In parochia sancti Iohannis.

i d.	De uno gardino; Agnes Clerk.
iiii s.	De domo Henrici Illuminatoris; Iohannes Rede.
F. viii s.	De aula Gayler, quam eadem Agnes tenet.
F. ii s.	De aula Grimstede; Adam Sclatter.
x s.	De duabus seldis cum una placea; Iohannes Boseit.

In parochia sancti Michaelis australis.

xiii s. iiii d.	De domo Bultras; Iohannes Snow.
xv s.	De domo Meteborne; Thomas Cappere.
x s.	De domo Mason; Thomas Kembere.
F. ii s.	De aula Mariolle; Willelmus Borowe.
xii d.	De tenemento Swyneshulle; Thomas Swyneshulle.

In parochia sancti Aldati.

F. xiii d.	De uno tenemento in Paruo Iudaismo quod scolares aule Balliol tenent.
xii s.	De domo Iohannis Dokelynton; Iohannes Gybbes.
lv s.	De domo Kepharme; Ricardus Bassett.
xiii s. iiii d.	De domo prox.; Willelmus Alston.
xxii s.	De domo prox.; Iohannes Spencer.
xx s.	De curia Lincoln; Adam Webbe.
F. ii s.	De tenemento Plumbatoris; abbas Regalis Loci tenet.
vi d.	De una placea proxima quam idem abbas tenet.
iiii s.	De una placea iuxta uenellam proxima pistrinum; Will' Saundres.

In parochia sancte Ebbe.

F. iiii s.	De tenemento uno extra murum.
F. viii s. vi d.	De domo prox.; Rogerus Northwode.
F. ix s. vi d.	De tenemento prox.; Reginaldus Tanner.
xxvi s. viii d.	De domo Stanlake cum tenemento Wareyn; Robertus Wytele.
	De domibus in cornario quas Margareta Rynges tenet libere ad terminum vite sue.

In parochia sancti Michaelis borialis.
In parochia sancti Thome. } [*As in the last rental.*]

In parochia sancte Marie Magdalene.

F. ii s.
F. xii d.
F. ii s.
iii s. iiii d.
F. ii s.
F. xx d.
F. xvi d. [*As in the last rental.*]
vi d.
F. vii s.
F. iii s.
F. xii d.
xiii s. iiii d.
F. iii s.

uacat. De duabus seldis iuxta aulam regis.
F. xii d. De tenemento abbatisse de Godestowe.

Rentale de Haliwelle.

x s. { De una placea iuxta Crowelle.
De domo prox.; Willelmus Sclatter iun. tenet.
v s. De secunda domo prox.; Iohannes Pistor.
iiii s. De tercia domo prox.; Willelmus Scynner.
ix d. De uno gardino iuxta uenellam; Willelmus Sclatter sen.
iiii s. De una domo ex opposito ecclesie de Haliwelle; Stephanus Thressher.
vi d. De duabus buttis terre arabilis; Will' Sclatter sen.
xii d. De una acra terre arabilis; Will' Scriptor.

De domibus clericorum.

iiii li. xii s. Aula Borwaldescote.
xl s. Aula Ynge
xxvi s. viii d. Aula Katerine.
xl s. Aula Borstalle.
x s. Aula Leporis.
xxvi s. viii d. Aula cum camino.
xv s. Aula Philomele.
v s. Aula Nigra.
xxvi s. viii d. Aula Aristotil.
xx s. Aula Militis.
uacat. Aula Martel.
xxvi s. viii d. Aula Mildrede.

Aula sancti Willelmi.
xxx s. Aula Minote.
viii s. Aula Profunda super Candiche.
uacat. Aula Brakkele.
uacat. Aula Bodyn.
xxvi s. viii d. Scola in Cattestrete.
xii s. De introitu ibidem.
vi s. viii d. De scola retro Omnium Sanctorum.
F. iiii s. De aula Hertehalle; magistri aule Balliol debent soluere pensionem inde xvi d.

23. A rental of Dec. 21, 1369.

Rentale domus Sancti Iohannis extra portam orientalem de domibus laycorum anno regni regis Ed. III post conquestum quadragesimo tercio incipiente in festo sancti Thome apostoli anno supradicto, durante usque ad idem festum anno futuro tempore fratris Roberti de Tewe tunc magistri domus predicte.

In parochia sancti Clementis.
x s. De domo iuxta uenellam; Will' Thame.
v s. De selda prox.
vi s. De secunda selda prox.
xiii s. iiii d. De domo iuxta Charewell; Ioh' Pydintone.

Extra portam orientalem ex parte australi.
iiii s. vi d. De domo iuxta Parys.
vi s. De secunda domo iuxta Paris; Will' Knyt.
viii s. De tercia domo cum quarta; Will' Molton.
viii s. De quinta domo cum sexta.
viii s. De aula Pille cum selda; Will' Hamond.
F. xx d. De domo Byx prox.; Agnes Keye.

Extra portam orientalem ex parte boreali.
De domo Oliueri Cissoris iuxta portam nostram; Rob' Carpenter.
vi s. viii d. De domo prox.; Rad' Sutor.
vii s. De secunda domo prox.; Thos. Carter.
v s. De tercia domo prox.; Ioh' Hampton.
unam rosam. De domo Vinee prox.; Walt' Foller.
ii s. De domo prox.; Will' Milleward.
v s. De una selda cum solario; Ioh' Couper.

v s.	De domo prox.; Phil' Taylour.
v s.	De domo Ioye prox.; Ioh' Mareschall.
vi s.	De domo prox.; Nich' Follere.
v s.	De selda prox. cum solario; Iuliana Berstelawe.
iii s.	De duabus seldis prox.; Ioh' Mareschall.
xiii s. iiii d.	De domo cum le forge; idem Iohannes.
v s.	De prima selda iuxta portam orientalem Oxonie.
v s.	De secunda selda prox.
ii s. vi d.	De tercia selda prox.

Infra portam orientalem ex parte australi.

xii s.	De domo Abraham, super quam sunt duo shope; de prima shopa.
xii s.	De secunda shopa.
xviii s.	De domo Kepharme; Thos. Clopptone.
F. i d.	De domo Amplexatoris [*sic*]; Ric' Sheffeld.

Kybaldstrete.

v s.	De domo in cornario; Ric' Penkriche.
v s.	De domo prox.; Ioh' Wales.
v s.	De secunda domo prox.
vii s. viii d.	De tercia domo prox.
	De uno gardino ibidem; Ric' Pencrike.

Infra portam orientalem ex parte boreali.

	De domo in cornario.
xii s.	De domo Coleborne; Andreas Carpenter.
xii s.	De domo Melemakere.
xx s.	De domo Roborowe; Will' Prentice.
xiiii s.	De domo Punchard; Alic' Abyndone.
F. x d.	De aula cum camino quam Bele Coke tenet.
xx s.	De domo Benham; Nic' Heytesbury.
vi s.	De prima selda iuxta portam aule Regine; Agnes Taylor.
vi s.	De secunda selda prox.; Rob. Bosseby.
vi s.	De tercia selda prox.
vi s.	De quarta selda prox.
iiii s.	De quinta selda prox.
iiii s.	De sexta selda cum solario.
xxii s.	De selda in cornario cum ii seldis prox.; Pernelle Coke.

F. iii s. iiii d. De domo Netherwynmulle; scolares aule Regine tenent.
F. x s. De introitu sancti Nicholai; scolares aule Regine tenent.
F. ii s. De domo quondam Nicholai Glatton; scolares aule Regine tenent.
xiiii s. De duabus seldis subtus aulam Katerine.
xxxiii s. iiii d. De domo quondam Willelmi Barbour; Bels [1] Halton tenet.
xxvi s. viii d. De aula Georgii; Ric' Coutone tenet.
xiiii s. De domo Buffard proxima.
xvi s. De domo prox. aule Droutedale [2]; Ioh' Coke.

Circa ecclesiam sancti Petri in oriente.
iiii s. De uno gardino; Nich' Heytesbury.
ii s. De uno gardino; Thomas Chaundeler.
ii s. De duobus gardinis; Thomas Coke.
De aula Martel.
ii s. De domo Charnel iuxta aulam Nigram; mulier Ricardi Bedel tenet.

In parochia sancte Marie Virginis.
xxvi s. viii d. De domo Punfreit; Ioh' Grasiere.
xii s. De duabus seldis in cimiterio sancte Marie; Thos. Latoner.
xxiii s. iiii d. De domo Basing; idem Thomas.
x s. De duabus seldis prox.; Rob. Barbour tenet.
F. xii d. De uno gardino infra clausuram Nicholai Garlond.

In Cattestrete.
xxiiii s. De domo Lodelowe; Thos. Dolle.
F. iiii s. De domo Abraham; Ioh' Hardy.
F. vii s. vi d. De tenemento Ade Howtone; Ioh' Bokyngham.
xx s. De domo Faunt; Ioh' Manciple.
xx s. De domo Leuertone; Rob. Barbour.
iiii s. De uno gardino infra introitum sancti Iohannis; Thos. Dolle.

In parochia Omnium Sanctorum.
xx s. De domo Wytewong; Will' Taylour.
xviii s. De duabus seldis Borwaldescote; Thos. Trenacle.

[1] In a subsequent rental the name is Bele, short for Isabella.
[2] i.e. Drouda Hall.

iiii s. vi d. De duabus seldis subtus domum Iohannis Stodle; idem Iohannes.

F. vii s. De tenemento Hengseye; idem Iohannes.

xiii s. iiii d. De aula retro Omnium Sanctorum; rector ecclesie dicte tenet.

xviii d. De domo prox.; idem rector.

l s. De domo Swynebroke; Ioh' Musturtone.

F. xxviii s. De domo Alic' Neubury; procuratores ecclesie predicte tenent.

In parochia sancti Martini.

F. iiii s. De domo Orliauns; Hen' Blod tenet in ballio.

F. iii s. De domo quondam Alicie Welles & una uacua placea iuxta fratres Carmel', quas Ioh' Wakeman tenet.

F. ix s. De introitu quondam Thome Kyngestone.

F. ii s. De selda in suteria.

F. ii s. De solario quondam Henrici Gamage.

F. vi s. viii d. De selda quondam Gilberti Wynchecombe; Will' Bergeyne.

F. iiii s. De selda in quadriuio; Bartelott' tenet.

De domo sancti Petri in Ballio.

xiii s. iiii d. De prima selda Croxforde; Rob. Hawe tenet.

xiiii s. viii d. De secunda selda Croxforde; Rob. Letecombe tenet.

ii s. De uno stayre stante inter dictas seldas; uxor Rogeri Nortwode tenet.

In parochia sancti Iohannis.

i d. De uno gardino; Agnes Clerc'.

v s. De domo quondam Henrici Luminatoris; Ioh' Rede.

F. viii s. De aula Gaylere; eadem Agnes.

F. ii s. De aula Grimstede; rector aule Mertone tenet.

x s. De duabus seldis Balle cum una placea prox.; Ioh' Bosett'.

In parochia sancti Michaelis australis.

xvi s. De domo Bultras.

xv s. De domo Meteborne; Thomas Cappere.

x s. De domo Masone; Thos. Kembere.

F. ii s. De aula Mariole; Will' Borowe.

F. xii d. De tenemento Swyneshulle.

In parochia sancti Aldati.

xxv s. De domo Kepharme.[1]

xiii s. iiii d. De domo quam Will' Alstone tenet.

xx s. De domo prox. quam Will. Spencer tenet.

xiii d. De uno ten' in paruo Iudaismo; magistri Baliolhalle tenent.

xii s. De domo quondam Iohannis Dokelintone; Ioh' Gybbes.

xx s. De curia Lincoln'; Adam Webbe.

F. ii s. De ten' Plumbatoris; abbas Loci Regalis tenet.

iiii s. De una placea in cimiterio ecclesie sancti Aldati; idem abbas.

iiii s. De una domo iuxta uenellam Pinneferthingstre; Will' Saundres.

In parochia sancte Ebbe.

iiii s. De tenemento Brunster extra portam Predicatorum[2] sub muro uille.

viii s. viii d. De domo prox.; uxor Rogeri Northwode.

ix s. vi d. De domo prox. quondam Iohannis Alstone; Reginaldus Tanner.

De domo Stanlake.

v s. De tenemento Wareyn in paruo Ballio.

De domibus in cornario quas Margareta Ringes tenet ad terminum uite quiet' de redditu.

In parochia sancti Michaelis borialis.

xxvi s. viii d. De aula Blaunkeneye cum seld'; Ioh' Hamptone.

In parochia sancti Thome.

xiii s. iiii d. De tenemento Wodesdon; abbas Oseneye.

In parochia sancte Marie Magdalene.

F. ii s. De tenemento Dokelintone.

F. xii d. De tenemento Dodeword; Ric' Oxenford.

F. ii s. De solario quondam Iohannis Saucer quod uxor eius tenet.

iii s. iiii d. De domo Welles; Ioh' Hosteler.

F. iii s. De domo quondam Iohannis Abyndone; Ioh' Gruttone tenet.

[1] The rent of this tenement was usually about fifty shillings, but it was probably being rebuilt this year, as the next rental shows a new arrangement of houses at this spot.

[2] Possibly a name for Littlegate or Watergate, the gate in the Town Walls below St. Ebbe's church. No doubt the Preaching Friars had a gate of their own further south where the road crossed Trill Mill, but such a gate would not be so near the tenement in question.

F. xx d. De duabus seldis in Stocwelstrete; idem Iohannes.
F. xvi d. De duabus seldis ibidem; idem Iohannes.
vi d. De domo Tye; Ioh' Syneker.
F. vii s. De introitu quondam Henrici Brampton.
F. iii s. De domo quondam Rogeri Bost; Ioh' Ardy.
F. xii d. De tenemento Dodelyn.
xiii s. iiii d. De domo quam Walterus Stoword tenet retro ecclesiam Marie Magdalene.
F. iii s. De procuratoribus ecclesie antedicte.
uac. De una placea uacua iuxta paruam portam fratrum Carmel'.
F. xii d. uac. De uno tenemento abbatisse de Godestowe.

De domibus clericorum.[1]

De aula Borwaldescote. iiii li. xii s.
De aula Ynge. xl s.
De aula Katerine.
De aula Borstalle. xx s.
De aula Leporis.
De aula cum camino.
De aula Filomene.
De aula Nigra.
De aula Arstotilis. xx s.
De aula Militis.
De aula Mynote. xix s.
De aula Mildrede. xx s.
De aula sancti Willelmi.
De aula Profunda super Candyche.
De aula Brakkele.
De duabus aulis Bodyn.
De scola in Cattestrete. xx s.
De introitu ibidem.
De scola retro Omnium Sanctorum. iii s. iiii d.
De aula Herthalle in uico sancti Iohannis ex parte australi.

[1] The rental shows that many of the smaller halls were unoccupied this year, and those that were occupied paid a low rent. It was a time of dearth as we learn from the register of Bishop Brantyngham, Bishop of Exeter, who on June 20, 1370, granted ten shillings from the common chest to each of the Fellows of Exeter College, as they were unable to live on their allowance, and on November 13 granted an addition of fourpence a week to the weekly allowance, to be continued for the next forty weeks. (*Registrum Coll. Exon.* O.H.S. p. lv.)

24. A rental of Dec. 21, 1370.

This rental is in bad condition, and though the names of the tenants are legible, the rents they paid cannot be deciphered.

Rentale domus sancti Iohannis extra portam orientalem anno regni regis Edwardi III post conquestum XL quarto, incipiente in festo sancti Thome apostoli.

In parochia sancti Clementis.
De domo iuxta uenellam; Willelmus Thame.
De selda proxima; Math' Taylour.
De secunda selda; Willelmus Spicer.
De tercia selda.
De quarta selda.
De domo iuxta Charewell; Iohannes Pydinton.

Extra portam orientalem ex parte australi.
De domo iuxta Parys; Willelmus Bishoppe.
De domo prox.; Willelmus Knyt.
De duabus proximis; Agnes Molton.
De alia domo prox.; Henricus Cartere.
De alia domo prox.; Iohannes Swelere.
De domo Pille cum selda; Willelmus Hamond.
De domo Bix prox.; Agnes Keye.

Extra portam orientalem ex parte boriali.
De domo Oliueri Cissoris; Robertus Carpenter.
De domo prox.; Henricus Sutor.
De secunda domo prox.; Thomas Carter.
De tercia domo prox.; Iohannes Hampton.
De domo Vinee prox.; Iohannes Foller.
De domo prox.; Willelmus Milleward.
De una selda cum solario; Iohannes Couper.
De domo prox.; Philippus Taylour.
De domo Ioye prox.; Iohannes Mareschall.
De domo prox.; Nicholaus Follere.
De selda prox. cum solario; Iuliana Kareles.
De duabus seldis prox.; Iohannes Mareschall.
De domo cum le forge; idem Iohannes.
De prima selda extra portam; Alicia Bedeman.
De secunda selda extra portam; Thomas Blynde.
De tercia selda extra portam.

Infra portam orientalem ex parte boriali.

De domo in cornario.
De domo Coleborne ; Iuliana Leper.
De selda prox. ; Cristina Otindone.
De domo Roborowe ; Willelmus Prentice.
De domo Punchard ; Alicia Abyndone.
De aula cum camino quam Bele Coke tenet.
De domo Benham ; Nicholaus Heytesbury.
De prima selda iuxta portam aule Regine ; Agnes Taylor.
De secunda selda ; Rob. Bosseby.
De tercia selda.
De quarta selda.
De quinta selda.
De sexta selda cum solario.
De selda in cornario cum ii seldis prox. ; Pernelle Coke.
De domo Netherwynmulle }
De introitu sancti Nicholai } prepositus aule Regine.
De domo Nicholai Glatton }
De prima selda subtus aulam Katerine ; Hugo Manciple.
De secunda selda.
De domo quondam Willelmi Barbour ; Bele Haleton.
De aula Georgii ; Ricardus Coutone.
De domo Buffard ; Iohannes Taylour.
De domo prox. ; Iohannes Manciple.

Infra portam orientalem ex parte australi.

[*As in the last rental.*]

Kybaldstrete.

De prima domo.
De secunda domo ; Iohannes Wales.
De tercia domo ; Iohanna Spinster.
De quarta domo ; Ricardus Werkeman.
De uno gardino ibidem ; mag. Ricardus Pencrix.

Circa ecclesiam sancti Petri.

De duobus gardinis ; Thomas Coke.
De uno gardino ; Nicholaus Heytesbury.
De uno gardino prox. ; Thomas Chaundelere.
De domo Charnel ; Ricardus Bidel.

In parochia sancte Marie Virginis.

[*As in the last rental.*]

In parochia Omnium Sanctorum.
De domo Wytewong; Willelmus Cherstone.
[*The rest as in the last rental.*]

In parochia sancti Martini.
De domo Orliauns; Iohannes Blod.
[*The rest as in the last rental.*]

In parochia sancti Iohannis.
De uno gardino; Agnes Clerc.
De domo quondam Henrici Luminatoris; Iohannes Rede.
De aula Gaylere; eadem Agnes.
De aula Grimstede; Adam Sclatter.
De duabus seldis Balle cum una placea; Iohannes Bosett'.

In parochia sancti Michaelis australis.
De domo Bultras; Iohannes Lally.
[*The rest as in the last rental.*]

In parochia sancti Aldati.
De uno tenemento in paruo Iudaismo; magistri aule Balliol tenent.
De domo Iohannis Dokelyntone; Iohannes Gibbes.
De domo Kepharme; Agnes Cnaphalle.
De una shopa; Henricus Fisshere.
De domo Wytewelle; Willelmus Allestone.
De domo prox.; uxor Iohannis Brustowe.
De curia Lincoln; Adam Webbe.
De tenemento Plumbatoris; abbas Regalis Loci.
De uno gardino iuxta cimiterium sancti Aldati; idem abbas.
De una domo iuxta furnum; Willelmus Saundres.

In parochia sancte Ebbe.
De domo quondam Iohannis Allestone; Reginaldus Tanner.
De domo prox.; Robertus Curriour.
De [ ][1]; Iohanna Vielond.
De duabus seldis uoc' Graunger, quas Margareta Rynges tenet.

In parochia sancti Michaelis borialis.
In parochia sancti Thome.
} [*As in the last rental.*]

In parochia sancte Marie Magdalene.
De domibus clericorum.
} [*Illegible.*]

[1] As the rental is illegible it is impossible to say whether this is *tenementum Brunster*, or *domus Stanlake*, or *tenementum Wareyn*; but the rental of 1374 suggests that it is the first.

25. A rental of Dec. 21, 1371.

Rentale domus sancti Iohannis extra portam orientalem de domibus laycorum anno regni regis Edwardi III post conquestum xl quinto incipiente in festo sancti Thome apostoli anno supradicto, durante usque ad idem festum prox. sequente, tempore fratris Iohannis de Ichintone tunc procuratoris.

In parochia sancti Clementis.

x s. De domo iuxta uenellam; Will' Thame.
iiii s. iiii d. De selda prox.; Ioh' Ston' tenet.
vi s. De alia selda prox.; Rob' Sutor.
De alia selda prox.
iii s. iiii d. De alia selda prox.; Will' Sutor.
xiii s. iiii d. De domo iuxta Charewelle; Ioh' Pydyntone.

Extra portam orientalem ex parte australi.

vi s. De domo iuxta Parys; Rob. Mason.
vi s. De domo prox.; Will' Knyt.
viii s. De duabus domibus proximis; Agnes Moltone.
iiii s. De domo prox.; Hen. Carter.
x s. De alia domo prox.; Ioh' Barette.
viii s. De domo Pille cum selda; Will' Hamound.
F. xx d. De domo Bix; Agnes Keye.

Extra portam orientalem ex parte boriali.

iii s. iiii d. De domo Olíueris [*sic*]; Rob. Carpenter.
vi s. viii d. De domo prox.; Hen. Sutor.
vii s. De alia domo prox.; Thos. Cartere.
v s. De alia domo prox.; Ioh' Hamptone.
una rosa. De domo Vinee prox.; Agnes Deyer tenet ad terminum uite.
ii s. De domo prox.; idem [*sic*] Agnes tenet ad terminum uite.
v s. De domo quam Ioh' Couper[1] tenet.
v s. De domo prox.; Phil' Taylour.
v s. De domo Ioye prox.; Ioh' Mareschall.
vi s. De domo prox.; Nich' Follere.
v s. De domo prox.; Iuliana Kareles.
iii s. De duabus seldis prox.; Ioh' Mareschall.
xiii s. iiii d. De domo cum le forge; idem Iohannes.

[1] Caper, MS. It is Couper in the next rental.

ii s. vi d. De prima selda iuxta portam orientalem; Bele Bedeman.
v s. De selda prox.; Thos. Blinde.
v s. De selda prox.; Amys Howyf.

Infra portam or. ex parte bor.
viii s. De domo in cornario; Ioh' Webbe.
xii s. De domo Coleborne; Iuliana Leper.
v s. De selda prox.; Cristina Otyndone.
xii s. De domo Molemakere prox.; Ioh' Wroxstone.
xxiiii s. De domo Roborowe; Will' Prentice.
xviii s. De domo Punchard; Alicia Stanweye.
F. x d. De aula cum camino; Bele Coke.
xx s. De domo Benham prox.; Nich' Heytesbury.
vi s. De prima selda iuxta aulam Regine; Alicia Taylour.
vi s. De secunda selda; Rob. Bosseby.
vi s. De tercia selda; Petronilla Lander.
vi s. De quarta selda; Cesse[1] Shapster.
v s. De quinta selda; Marieria Taylour.
iii s. De sexta selda; Iuliana Hosse.
uacat. De solario supra dict' seld'.
xxii s. De seld' in cornario quas Petronilla Coke.
F. iii s. iiii d. De domo uocata Netherwynmulle }
F. x s. De introitu sancti Nicholai } prepositus aule Regine.
F. ii s. De domo Nicholai Glattone }
vii s. De prima selda subtus aulam Katerine; Hugo Coce.
v s. vi d. De secunda selda prox.; Iohanna Shapster.
xxxiii s. iiii d. De domo Willelmi Barbour; Bele Alton.
xxvi s. viii d. De aula Georgii cum seld'; Ric' Coutone.
xiiii s. De domo Barbour prox.; Thos. Suanefeld.
xvi s. De domo prox.; Ioh' Manciple.

Infra port. or. ex parte australi.
viii s. De domo Abraham; de prima shopa; Will' Sutor.
viii s. De secunda selda inde; Ioh' Coke.
xviii s. De domo Kepharme; Thos. Cloptone.
F. i d. De domo Martini Amplexatoris; Ric' Spencer.

Kebaldestrete.
De prima domo.
v s. De secunda domo; Ioh' Wales.

[1] Short for Cecilia: see the next rental.

v s. De tercia domo; Ioh' Launder.
v s. De quarta domo; Ric' Werkeman.

Circa ecclesiam sancti Petri in oriente.
ii s. De duobus gardinis; Thomas Coke.
iiii s. De uno gardino; Nich' Heytesbury.
ii s. De uno gardino prox.; Thomas Chaundelere.
ii s. De domo Charnel iuxta aulam Nigram ex parte occidentali; Ric' Bidel ten'.

In parochia sancte Marie Virginis.
xxvi s. viii d. De domo Punfrett; Ioh' Grasiere.
xii s. De duabus shopis retro ecclesiam sancte Marie.
xxiii s. iiii d. De domo Basyng prox.; Thos. Latoner.
x s. De duabus shopis prox.; Rob. Barbour.
F. xii d. De uno gardino infra clausuram Nicholai Garlond.

Cattestrette.
xx s. De domo Leuertone; Rob. Bokbynder.
xx s. De domo Faunt; Hen. Manciple.
F. vii s. vi d. De tenemento Ade de Houtone uocato Grampounthalle; Ioh' Bokyngham tenet per mulierem suam.
F. iiii s. De domo Abraham prox.; Ioh' Hardy per mulierem suam.
xxiiii s. De domo Lodelowe; Thos. Dolle.
iiii s. De uno gardino infra scolam; idem Thomas.

In parochia Omnium Sanctorum.
xx s. De domo Wytewong; Will' Taylour.
xviii s. De duabus shopis subtus magne camere [*sic*] aule Borwaldescote, quas Trenacle tenet.
x s. De prima shopa subtus dom' Iohannis Stodele; Will' Cheselehamptone.
x s. De secunda shopa; Emma Shapster.
F. vii s. De ten. Galfridi Hengesey; Ioh' Stodele.
xiii s. iiii d. De aula retro Omnium Sanctorum; uxor Iohannis Bromele.
xviii d. De uno gardino prox. quem eadem tenet.
l s. De domo Swynebroke; Ioh' Mostertone.
xiiii s. De domo Alicie Neubury quam procuratores cantarie ecclesie Omnium Sanctorum tenent ad terminum sexaginta annorum, & septem sunt preteriti inde.

In parochia sancti Martini.

F. iiii s. De domo Orliauns; Ioh' Blod tenet in Ballio.

F. iii s. De domo Alicie Welles cum una placea iuxta fratres Carmel'; quas Ioh' Wakeman tenet.

F. ix s. De introitu quondam Iohannis Kyngestone; Ric' Forster.

F. ii s. De selda in suteria.

F. ii s. De solario quondam Henrici Gamace.

F. vi s. viii d. De seldis quondam Gilberti Wynchecombe; Will' Bergeyne.

F. iiii s. De selda in quadriuio; Bartelote ten'.

F. i d. De domo sancti Petri in Ballio.

xiii s. iiii d. De prima selda Croxford; Rob' Hawe.

xvi s. De secunda selda Croxford.

ii s. De uno stayhere inter dictas seldas; Emma Northwode.

In parochia sancti Iohannis.

i d. De uno gardino quem Agnes Clerk tenuit ad capud gardini sui.

v s. De domo Henrici Illuminatoris: Ioh' Rede.

F. viii s. De aula Gaylere prox. quam Nich' Clerke quondam tenuit.

F. ii s. De aula Grimstede prox. quam custos aule Mertone tenet.

x s. De duabus seldis in Gropelane cum una placea; Ioh' Bosette.

In parochia sancti Michaelis australis.

xvi s. De domo Boltras; Ioh' Lally.

[ ] s. De domo Meteborne prox.; Reginaldus Bocher.

x s. De domo Mason prox.;[1] Thos. Kembere.

F. ii s. De aula Mariole; Will' Borowe.

F. xii d. De tenemento Swyneshulle.

In parochia sancti Aldati.

F. xiii d. De uno tenemento in paruo Iudaismo ex opposito magne scole quod magistri aule Balliole tenent.

xii s. De domo Iohannis Dokelyntone; Ioh' Gibbes.

xl s. De domo Kepharme; Agnes Spicer.

xiii s. iiii d. De una shopa; Hen. Fishere.

[1] This instance shows that *prox.* does not always mean 'adjoining', for *domus Mason* and *domus Meteborne* did not adjoin one another.

xiii s. iiii d. De domo Wytewelle; Agnes Allestone.
xx s. De domo prox.; uxor Iohannis Shrowesbury.
xx s. De curia Lyncolne; Adam Webbe.
F. ii s. De tenemento Plumbatoris prox. domui quondam Iohannis Benham; abbas Regalis tenet.
viii d. De uno gardino iuxta cimiterium sancti Aldati; uxor Iohannis Benham tenet.
iiii s. De una domo iuxta furnam in paruo Iudaismo;[1] Will' Saundres tenet.

In parochia sancte Ebbe extra muram [*sic*] iuxta aquam.
F. ix s. iiii d. De domo quondam Iohannis Alestone; Reginaldus Tanner.
F. viii s. iiii d. De domo prox.; Emma Northwode.
F. iiii s. De tenemento Bremster prox.
xiii s. iiii d. De duabus seldis uocatis Graunger; Margareta Rynges.
vi s. De domo quondam Marierie Stanlake; Ric' Hengseye.
ix s. De tenemento Wareyne in paruo Ballio ex opposito domui Nicholai Hogestone; Ioh' Bruher.

In parochia sancti Michaelis ad portam borialem.
xxvi s. viii d. De aula Blankeneye cum shopis; Ioh' Hamptone chaundeler.
xiii s. iiii d. De tenemento Wodesdone iuxta paruum pontem Oseneye ex parte occidentali; abbas Oseneye tenet.

In parochia sancte Marie Magdalene.
F. ii s. De tenemento Dokelynton.
F. xii d. De tenemento Dodeford; Ric' Oxenford.
F. ii s. De solario Iohannis le Saucer.
iii s. iiii d. De domo Welles; Ioh' Hosteler.
F. iii s. De domo quondam Iohannis Abyndone; Ioh' Gruttone.
F. xx d., xvi d. De quatuor seldis in Stocckewellestrete; idem Iohannes.
vi d. De domo Tye; Ioh' Wroth syneker.
F. vii s. De introitu quondam Henrici Bramptone; Ioh' Manciple.
F. iii s. De domo quondam Rogeri Bost; Ioh' Hardy.
F. xii d. De tenemento Dodelyng.
xiii s. iiii d. De domo Stoword; Walterus Fawlore tenet.

[1] This means Pennyfarthing Street, which was occasionally called Little Jewry because it was at right angles to Great Jewry; see the next rental.

F. iii s. De procuratoribus ecclesie Marie Magdalene.
uacat. De una placea iuxta portam fratrum Carmel' ex parte occidentali.
F. xii d. De tenemento abbatisse de Godestowe.

De domibus clericorum.
iiii li. xii s. De aula Burwaldescote.
xl s. De aula Ynge.
xvi s. De aula Katerine.
xl s. De aula Borstalle, sed alocatur iiii s. pro camera iuxta introitum gardini.
xvi s. De aula Leporis.
De aula Camini.
De aula Philomene.
De aula Nigra.
xxvi s. viii d. De aula Arstotil.
x s. De aula Militis.
xx s. De aula Mildrede.
uacat. De aula sancti Willelmi.
xxvi s. viii d. De aula Mynote.
x s. De aula Profunda super Chandyche.
ii s. De aula Brakkele & Bodyn ibidem.
xl s. De scola in Cattestrete.
x s. De introitu sancti Iohannis.
vi s. viii d. De scolis retro Omnium Sanctorum quas Ioh' Holewey tenet.
F. iiii s. De aula Hertehalle in uico sancti Iohannis, que est de colegia [*sic*] aule Baliole & ipsi magistri colegie antedicte debent soluere redditus nobis inde xv d.

26. **A rental of Sept. 29, 1374.**

Rentale domus sancti Iohannis extra portam orientalem Oxonie de domibus clericorum & laycorum anno regni regis Edwardi tertii post conquestum quadragesimo o[ctau]o, incipiente in festo sancti Michaelis archangeli anno supradicto, tempore fratris Roberti de Tewe tunc magistri domus antedicte & fratris Iohannis Cambrugg' tunc procuratoris.

Parochia sancti Clementis.
x s. De domo iuxta uenellam cum shopa quas Will' Thame tenet.

vi s. De selda prox. quam Ric. Sadeler tenet.
vi s. De alia selda prox. quam Walterus Sutor tenet.
vi s. viii d. De alia selda prox. quam Will' Chappeman tenet.
vi s. De alia selda prox. quam Will' Taylor tenet.
xiii s. iiii d. De domo iuxta Charewell cum shopa quas Ioh' Pydintone tenet.
Summa xlviii s.

Extra portam orientalem Oxon' ex parte australi.
vi s. De domo iuxta Parys quam Ioh' Verere tenet.
vi s. De domo prox. quam Will' Knyt tenet.
viii s. De duabus domibus prox. quas Agnes Molton tenet.
viii s. De alia domo prox. quam Henricus Carter tenet.
xii s. De alia domo prox. quam Reginaldus Webbe tenet.
viii s. De domo Pille cum shopis quas Will' Hamond tenet.
F. xx d. De domo Byx prox. quam Agnes Keye tenet.

Extra portam orientalem Oxonie ex parte boriali.
ii s. De domo prox. portam nostram.
vi s. viii d. De secunda domo prox. quam Ioh' Barette tenet.
vii s. De tercia domo prox. quam Thomas Carter tenet.
v s. De quarta domo prox. quam Ioh' Hamptone tenet.
iiii s. vi d. De domo Vinee prox. quam Will' Webbe tenet.
xxi d. De domo prox. quam Will' Milleward tenet.
De domo prox. quam Thomas Fleccher tenet.
v s. De shopa prox. quam Ioh' Couper tenet.
v s. De domo prox. quam Phil' Taylor tenet.
v s. De domo Ioye prox. quam Ioh' Mareschall tenet.
vi s. De domo prox. quam Nich' Follere tenet.
v s. De selda prox. quam Iuliana Careles tenet.
iii s. De shopis prox. quas Ioh' Mareschal tenet.
xiii s. iiii d. De domo cum forgio quos idem Ioh' tenet.
v s. De prima selda iuxta portam orientalem Oxonie quam Will' Coke tenet.
v s. De secunda selda prox. quam Thomas Blynde tenet.
v s. De tercia selda prox. quam Amys Hosewyf tenet.

Infra portam orientalem Oxon' ex parte australi.
De domo Abraham ubi due shope sunt edificate.
x s. De prima shopa inde quam Ioh' Coke tenet.
x s. De secunda shopa inde quam Alicia Denys tenet.
xviii s. De domo Thome Cloppetone.

F. i d. De domo quam Ric' Spencer tenet.
v s. De prima domo Kybaldestrete quam Thomas Blynde tenet.
v s. De secunda domo prox. quam Margareta Wales tenet.
v s. De tercia domo prox. quam Iohanna Launder tenet.
v s. De quarta domo prox. quam Alicia Launder tenet.
viii s. viii d. De uno gardino quam Ric' Pencriche tenet.

Infra portam orientalem ex parte boriali.
x s. De domo in cornario quam Ioh' Bruher tenet.
xii s. De domo prox. quam Elisabet Paxestone tenet.
xx s. De domo Molemaker [*sic*] cum shopa prox. quas Will' Foller tenet.
xxiiii s. De domo Robowrou prox. quam Will' Prentice tenet.
xx s. De domo Punchard prox. quam Alic' Stauneweye tenet.
F. x d. De aula Camini quam Thomas Bere tenet.
xx s. De domo Benham, quam Henricus Tewe tenet.
vi s. De prima selda iuxta aulam Regine.
vi s. De secunda selda prox. quam Rob' Besseby tenet.
vi s. De tercia selda prox. quam Ioh' Bakere tenet.
vi s. De quarta selda prox. quam Cessilia Spinster tenet.
v s. De quinta selda prox. quam Magota[1] Taylour tenet.
iiii s. De sexta selda prox. quam Pernel Spinster tenet.
vi s. viii d. De solario ibidem quem Nich' Clerc' tenet.
xxii s. De duabus shopis in cornario quas Pernel Coke tenet.
F. x s. De introitu sancti Nicholai quem scolares aule Regine tenet.
F. iii s. iiii d. De domo uocata Netherwynmulle quam idem scolares tenent.
F. ii s. De domo quondam Nicholai Glattone quam idem scolares tenent.
vii s. De prima selda subtus aulam Katerine, quam Hugo Coke tenet.
vii s. De secunda selda ibidem quam Hedda Spinster tenet.
xxiii s. iiii d. De domo Willelmi Barbour prox. quam Will' Southam tenet.
xxvi s. viii d. De aula Georgii prox., quam Ric' Coutone tenet.
xiiii s. De prima selda prox. quam Ioh' Coke tenet.
xvi s. De secunda selda ibidem quam Ioh' Manciple tenet.

[1] She is *Marjery* in the previous rental; *Marjory* in the subsequent.

Circa ecclesiam sancti Petri in oriente.

vi d. De uno gardino quem Hen' Tewe tenet.
iiii s. De uno gardino quem idem Hen' tenet.
ii s. De duabus [*sic*] gardinis quos Pernel Coke tenet.
De uno gardino quam [*sic*] scolares aule noui collegii [1] tenent.
ii s. De uno gardino ex opposito Swygate [2] [*sic*] quem uxor Ricardi Bedel tenet.

Cattestrete ex parte australi.[3]

xx s. De domo Leuertone quam Rob' Bokbynder tenet.
xx s. De domo Faunt prox. quam Will' Lymnour tenet.
F. vii s. vi d. De domo quondam Ade Howetone uocata nunc Aula Graunpount, pro qua Ioh' Bokyngham soluet.
F. iiii s. De domo Abraham prox. pro qua nunc soluit Ioh' Hardy.
xxiiii s. De domo Lodelowe quam Thomas Dolle tenet.
iiii s. De uno gardino infra scolam in Cattestrette quam idem Thomas tenet.

Parochia sancte Marie Virginis.

xxvi s. viii d. De domo Punfrette quam Ioh' Grasihere tenet.
xiii s. iiii d. De duabus shopis in cimiterio sancte Marie quam [*sic*] Hen' Garlond tenet.
xxiii s. iiii d. De domo Basing prox. cum shopis quas uxor quondam Thome Latoner tenet.
x s. De duabus shopis prox. quas Rob' Barbour tenet.
F. xii d. De uno gardino infra domum Nicholai Garlound.

Parochia Omnium Sanctorum.

F. vii s. De tenemento Hengseye, viz. de domo Iohannis Stodele.
xxv s. De domo Wetewong quam Steph' Taylour tenet.
ix s. De prima shopa subtus aulam Burwaldescote.
ix s. De secunda shopa ibidem.
xiii s. iiii d. De aula retro ecclesiam Omnium Sanctorum quam Rector ecclesie tenet.
xviii d. De domo prox. quam idem Rector tenet.

[1] This is the earliest occurrence of the phrase 'New College', and possibly the earliest mention of the College. The garden in question was probably the site of *Aula Martel.*

[2] i.e. Smithgate.

[3] This cannot mean 'beginning at the south', for the rental begins at the north end of the street. Occasionally *australis* means 'west'; so here.

xiii s. iiii d. De prima shopa subtus domum Iohannis Stodele quam Willelmus Chileshamptone [*sic*] tenet.

xiii s. iiii d. De secunda shopa ibidem quam idem Will' tenet.

l s. De domo Swynebrok quam Ioh' Musturtone tenet.

F. xxviii s. De domo quondam Alicie Newbury in bocheria quam Thomas Aylesbury spicer tenet de procuratoribus ecclesie Omnium Sanctorum, & ipsi tenent de nobis ad terminum sexaginta annorum pro xiiii solidis, & decem anni inde sunt preteriti.

Parochia sancti Martini.

F. iiii s. De domo Orliauns in ballio quam Ioh' Blod tenet.

F. iii s. De domo quondam Alicie Welles ex opposito domus predicti Iohannis quam Ioh' Wakeman tenet.

F. x s. De introitu quondam Thome Kyngestone quam Thomas Somoursete nunc tenet.

xx s. De prima shopa Croxford quam Ioh' Hurle tenet.

xvi s. De secunda shopa ibidem quam Will' Letecombe tenet.

ii s. De uno stayh' [*sic*] inter shopas predictas quam uxor Iohannis sancte Fredeswyde tenet.

F. ii s. De selda in sutoria.

F. ii s. De solario quondam Henrici Gamage.

F. vi s. viii d. De seldys quondam Gilberti' Wynchcombe quas Will' Bergeyne tenet.

F. iiii s. De selda in quadriuio quam Bartele [1] tenet.

F. i d. De domo sancti Petri in Ballio.

Parochia sancti Iohannis.

v s. De domo quondam Henrici Luminatoris in Gropecountelane quam Ioh' Rede tenet.

i d. De uno gardino ibidem.

F. viii s. De aula Gaylere quam Rector aule Mertone tenet.

F. ii s. De aula Grymste [*sic*] prox. quam idem Rector tenet.

x s. De duabus shoppis ex opposito quas Ioh' Bosette tenet cum una placea ibidem.

Parochia sancti Michaelis australis.

xvi s. De domo Boltras quam Ioh' Lally, scynner, tenet.

viii s. De domo Meteborne prox' quam Ioh' Couper tenet.

1 Bartele or Bartelot was apparently Bartholomew the Taverner or Vintner; see subsequent rentals.

x s. De domo Mason quam Thomas Kember tenet.
F. ii s. De aula Mariolle quam Will' Borowe bocher tenet.
F. xii d. De tenemento Swynehulle.

Parochia sancti Aldati.
F. xiii d. De uno tenemento in paruo Iudaismo ex opposito magne Scole pro quo mag' aule Ballio [*sic*] sol'.
F. xii s. De domo Iohannis Doklintone pro quo Ioh' Gibbes soluit.
xlvi s. viii d. De domo Kepharm cum shopis quas Roggerus Maunciple tenet.
xiii s. iiii d. De una shopa ibidem quam Iohanna Sapster tenet.
xiii s. iiii d. De domo prox. quam Agnes Allestone tenet.
xxii s. De domo in cornario prox. quam Hen' Herong tenet.
xx s. De curia Lincoln' quam Adam Webbe tenet.
F. ii s. De tenemento Plumbatoris pro quo abbas Loci Regalis soluit.
iiii s. De una domo iuxta furnam sancti Aldati pro qua Will' Saundres soluit.

Parochia sancte Ebbe.
F. ix s. iiii d. De domo quondam Iohannis Allestone; Reginaldus Tanner tenet.
F. viii s. iiii d. De domo prox.
F. iiii s. De uno gardino prox. quam Iohanna Wylonde ten'.
xiii s. iiii d. De duabus shopis in cornario parui Iudaismi[1] quas Margareta Rynges tenet.
xiii s. iiii d. De domo Staunelake quam Ric' Hegenseye tenet.
ix s. De tenemento Wareyn in paruo Ballio quod Ioh' Bruher tenet.

Parochia sancti Michaelis borialis.
xxvi s. viii d. De aula Blaunkeneye cum shopis quas Ioh' Chaundelere tenet.
F. xiii s. iiii d. De ten. Wodesdone iuxta paruum pontem de Oseneye pro quo abbas Oseneye soluit.

Parochia sancte Marie Magdalene.
F. ii s. De tenemento Dokelyntone.
F. xii d. De tenemento Dodeford.
F. ii s. De tenemento Iohannis Saucer; Ric' Tornour tenet.
iii s. iiii d. De domo Welles quam Ioh' Hosteler tenet.

[1] i.e. Pennyfarthing Street.

F. iii s. De domo Iohannis Abyndone; Ioh' Gruttone.
F. iii s. De quatuor seldis in Stoccwelstrete quas idem Ioh' tenet.
ii s. De domo Tye quam Rob. Bathe carpenter tenet.
F. vii s. De introitu Henrici Bramptone.
F. iii s. De domo Rogeri Bost.
F. xii d. De tenemento Dodelyng.
xiii s. iiii d. De domo Stoword quam Nic. Carpenter tenet.
F. iii s. De procuratoribus ecclesie Magdalene.
uacat. De una placea ad portam fratrum Carmel'.
F. xii d. De tenemento abbatisse de Godestowe.

Rentale domorum in Haliwelle.
vii s. De prima domo iuxta Crowelle quam Ioh' Kent tenet.
De secunda domo prox.
De tertia domo prox.
iii s. iiii d. De domo iuxta ecclesiam cum una acra terre & duas buttas terre.

De domibus clericorum anno supradicto.
iiii li. xii s. De aula Burwaldescote quam mag. Edmundus Stafford tenet.
xlvi s. viii d. De aula Ynge quam dominus Iohannes canonicus Oseneye tenet.
xxvi s. viii d. De aula Katerine quam Ioh' Heylesham de Cornewayle tenet.
xl s. De aula Borstalle quam Ioh' Heylesham tenet.
x s. De aula Leporis.
xxvi s. viii d. De aula Camini quam Ric' Pencriche tenet.
xv s. De aula Philomene quam idem Ric' tenet.
uacat. De aula Nigra.
De aula Aristotilis.
xii s. De aula Militis quam mag. Pet. de Almania tenet.
xxvi s. viii d. De aula Minote quam mag. Ric. Wolfe tenet.
xxvi s. viii d. De aula Mildrede quam mag. Will. Wakefeld tenet.
xx s. De scola in Cattestrete quam mag. Ioh' Frensce tenet.
x s. De aula Profunda super Candych quam Ioh' Sauhih' tenet.
ii s. De aula Brackele cum duabus aulis Bodyn quas Ioh' Maunciple tenet.
xii s. De introitu sancti Iohannis in Cattestrette quam Stephanus Clericus tenet.

vi s. viii d. De scola retro ecclesiam Omnium Sanctorum quam Ioh' Holeweye tenet.

F. iiii s. De Hertehalle in uico sancti Iohannis pro qua magister aule Ballioll soluit.

Summa de aulis clericorum xvii li. xv s. vii d.

Summa partis superioris lxi li. ii s. ii d.

Summa totalis lxxviii li. xvii s. iiii d. [*sic*].

Redditus forinseci soluendi diuersis dominis.

xlvii s. v d. Domino de Hedyndone pro terris & tenementis ibidem.

xlvi s. viii d. Domino de Saunford pro uno molendino & terra.

x s. Domino de Challegraue pro Coulake.

v s. Domino regi pro Wodestoke.

ii s. vi d. Domino de Staunton Harecourte pro domo quam Ioh' Chaundel' tenet, & ecclesie sancti Michaelis viii d.[1]

xvi s. vi d. Domino de Haliwelle pro diuersis tenementis ibidem.

xx s. Priori de Walyngford pro manerio de Gersindon.

v s. viii d. Priori sancte Fredeswyde pro domo Iohannis Mosturtone.[2]

vii s. viii d. Eidem priori pro aula retro Omnium Sanctorum.[3]

v s. Priori de Coldenortone pro domo Lokyntone in Cattestrete.[4]

iii s. iiii d. Iohanni Touneclerke pro tenemento Wareyn quam Ioh' Bruher tenet in Paruo Ballio.[5]

vi s. viii d. Eidem Iohanni pro domo quam Will' Southam tenet.[6]

xii d. Camerariis uille Oxon' pro tribus shopis iuxta portam orientalem.[7]

viii d. ob. Balliuis pro Langabele.[8]

xiii d. Balliuo hundredi extra portam borialem.

vi s. viii d. Vicario sancti Petri in oriente pro minutis decimis.

xx s. Eidem uicario pro decimis prati.

xii d. Abbati de Abindone pro domo quam Agnes Alstone tenet.[9]

xii d. Abbati de Eynsham pro shopis quas Margareta Rynges tenet, et ecclesie ibidem.[10]

[1] See ii. 271.
[2] See ii. 46.
[3] See ii. 20; the amount originally due to St. Frideswide's was viii s. viii d.
[4] See i. 451.
[5] See ii. 220.
[6] See i. 278.
[7] See i. 140.
[8] See ii. 153.
[9] See ii. 153.
[10] See ii. 234.

ix d. Abbatisse de Godestowe pro domo quam Ioh' Lalle, scinner, tenet ii d.[1]

ii d. Ecclesie sancte Mildrede pro aula ibidem.[2]

vii d. ob. Ecclesie de Hedyndone.

xvii d. Domino de Hedyndone pro Halhalewuhene.

x s. Conuersis London' pro domo Kepharme.[3]

27. A rental for Sept. 21, 1375.

Rentale domus sancti Iohannis extra portam orientalem Oxonie de domibus laycorum & clericorum anno regni regis Edwardi tercii post conquestum quadragesimo nono, incipient' in festo sancti Mathei apostoli & durant' usque ad idem festum prox. sequens, tempore fratris Roberti de Tewe tunc magistri domus predicte & fratris Ricardi de Wyleby tunc procuratoris. Recepcio per fratrem de Wyleby de redditu Oxon; item recepcio de redditu Oxon per fratrem Iohannem Ichintone.

In parochia sancti Clementis.

x s. De domo iuxta uenellam quam Will. Thame tenet.

v s. De domo prox.

v s. De secunda domo prox.

vi s. viii d. De tertia domo prox. quam Will' Leche tenet.

vi s. De quarta domo prox.

xiii s. iiii d. De domo iuxta Charewelle quam Ioh' Pydinton tenet.

Extra portam orientalem Oxon ex parte australi.

De prima domo iuxta Parys quam Iohanna Laund' tenet.

De secunda domo prox. quam Will' Knyte tenet.

viii s. De tercia domo cum quarta prox. quas Agnes Molton tenet.

iiii s. De quinta domo prox. quam Hen. Carter tenet.

xii s. De sexta domo prox. cum shopa quas Reginaldus Webbe tenet.

viii s. De domo Pille prox. cum duabus shopis quas Will' Hamond tenet.

Extra portam orientalem ex parte boriali.

x s. De domo iuxta portam nostram quam Ioh' Werkeman tenet.

[1] i.e. in St. Michael's South; see the *resoluciones* for 1328.

[2] i.e. St. Mildred Hall.

[3] See ii. 153.

vi s. viii d. De domo prox. quam Ioh' Barette tenet.
vii s. De secunda domo prox. quam Thomas Carter tenet.
v s. De tercia domo prox. quam Ioh' Hampton tenet.
xx s. De domo Vinee prox. quam Will' Webbe tenet.
vii s. De domo prox. quam Will' Milleward tenet.
v s. De selda quam Ioh' Couper tenet.
xiii s. iiii d. De domo prox. quam Nic. Manciple tenet.
v s. De domo Ioye prox. quam Eua Mareschall tenet.
vi s. De domo prox. quam Nich. Follere tenet.
v s. De celda prox. quam Iuliana Kareles tenet.
xxi s. vi d. De domo cum forgio & shopis quas Ioh' Mareschall tenet.
v s. De prima shopa iuxta portam orientalem Oxon quam Will' Mareschall tenet.
v s. De secunda shopa prox. quam Thomas Blinde tenet.
v s. De tercia shopa prox. quam Isabella Howewyfe tenet.

Infra portam orientalem Oxon' ex parte boriali.

x s. De domo in cornario quam Thomas Manciple tenet.
De domo Coleborne prox. quam Alicia T*ri*nite tenet.
xx s. De domo Molemaker prox. cum seld' quas Will' Follere tenet.
xxiiii s. De domo Roborowe prox. cum seld' quas Will' Prentice tenet.
xx s. De domo Punchard prox. quam Alicia Stanweye tenet.
F. x d. De aula camini quam Katerina Bere tenet.
xx s. De domo Benham prox. ; Thomas Bruhere tenet.
vi s. De prima selda iuxta aulam Regine quam Agnes Bocke tenet.
vi s. De secunda selda prox. quam Rob. Bosseby tenet.
vi s. De tertia selda prox. quam Ioh' Bakere tenet.
vi s. De quarta selda prox. quam Cessota [1] Sapster tenet.
v s. De quinta selda prox. quam Marioria Taylour tenet.
iiii s. De sexta selda prox. quam Iohanna Bere tenet.
iii s. De uno solario supra seldam predictam quod scolares tenent.
xxii s. De duabus seldis prox. in cornario quas Petronilla Coke tenet.

[1] As Margeria forms Margota, so Cecilia forms Cessota.

F. x s. De introitu sancti Nicholai in eadem parte pro quo magister aule Regine soluet.

F. iii s. iiii d. De domo prox. uocata Netherwynmulle pro qua idem magister soluet.

F. ii s. De domo prox. quondam Nicholai Glatton pro qua idem magister soluet.

vii s. De prima shopa subtus aule Katerine quam Hugo Coke tenet.

uacat. De selda prox.

xxiii s. iiii d. De domo prox. quam Will' Southam tenet.

xxvi s. viii d. De aula Georgii prox. cum shopis quas Ric. Coutone tenet.

xiiii s. De prima shopa prox. quam Iohanna Shapster tenet.

xiiii s. De secunda shopa prox. quam Will' Taylour tenet.

Circa ecclesiam sancti Petri in oriente.

ii s. De duobus gardinis quos Thomas Coke tenet.

De duobus gardinis ibidem (uacant).

De uno gardino quem scolares aule Nigre [1] tenent.

ii s. De domo Charnel prox. aul' predicte quam uxor Ricardi Bisshele [2] tenet.

Infra portam orientalem Oxon ex parte australi.

De domo Abraham ubi nunc sunt due shope edificate; de prima shopa inde quam Iohannes Coke tenet.

De secunda ibidem quam Iohanna Matelowe tenet.

xviii s. De domo Cloppetone quam Iohannes Cheddesle tenet.

F. i d. De domo Martini Exemplatoris quam Ric' Spencer tenet.

Kybaldestrete.

De domo in Kibaldestrete.

v s. De domo prox.; Margareta Wales tenet.

v s. De alia domo prox. quam Iohanna Laundere tenet.

iii s. ix d. De alia domo prox. quam Iohannes Coke tenet.

viii s. viii d. De uno gardino ibidem quem dominus Ric' Pencriche tenet.

Cattestrete.

xx s. De domo Leuertone quam Rob' Bokebyndere tenet.

xx s. De domo Faunt prox. quam Ioh' Lymnour tenet.

[1] William of Wykeham's scholars were lodged in Black Hall while New College was building.

[2] 'Bidel' is meant.

F vii s. vi d. De domo quondam Ade Howtone pro qua uxor Iohannis Bokyngham soluet.

F. iiii s. De domo Abraham prox., pro qua uxor Iohannis Hardy soluet.

xxiiii s. De domo Lodelowe quam Thomas Dolle tenet.

iiii s. De uno gardino infra scolam ibidem quem idem Thomas tenet.

In parochia sancte Marie Virginis.

xxvi s. viii d. De domo Basing [1] quam Iohannes Grasihere tenet.

xiii s. iiii d. De duabus shopis retro ecclesiam sancte Marie pro quibus Henricus Garlond soluet.

xl s. De domo prox. cum shopis quas uxor Thome Latoner tenet.

x s. De duabus shopis prox. quas Robertus Barbour tenet.

F. xii d. De uno gardino infra domum Nicholai Garlond.

In parochia Omnium Sanctorum.

xxiiii s. De domo Wytewong quam Stephanus Taylour tenet.

xviii s. De duabus shopis subtus aulam Bourwaldescote pro quibus Thomas Baldewyne soluet.

xiii s. iiii d. De aula retro Omnium Sanctorum pro qua rector ecclesie Omnium Sanctorum soluet.

xviii d. De domo prox. pro qua idem rector soluet.

xxvi s. viii d. De duabus shopis subtus domum Iohannis Stodele quas Iohannes Cheleshamptone tenet.

F. vii s. De tenemento Hengseye prox., quam Iohannes Stodele quondam tenuit.

l s. De domo Swynebroke cum shopis quas Iohannes Mosturton tenet.

F. xxviii s. De domo quondam Alicie Neubury in bocheria, pro qua procuratores ecclesie Omnium Sanctorum soluent ad terminum lx annorum quatuordecim solidos argenti annuatim, & de termino predicto undecim anni sunt preteriti.

In parochia sancti Martini.

F. iiii s. De domo Orliauns in balliuo quam Iohannes Blod tenet.

F. iii s. De domo quondam Alicie Welles cum una placea iuxta fratres Carmelitas quam Iohannes Wakeman tenet.

[1] A mistake; the scribe means *Pomfret*; see previous rentals.

F. x s. De introitu quondam Thome Kyngestone quam Thomas Somerset tenet.
xx s. De prima shopa Croxford proxima.
xvi s. De secunda shopa Croxford quam Ioh' Gyffard tenet.
ii s. De uno stayhere inter dictas shopas.
F. ii s. De selda in suteria.
F. ii s. De solario quondam Henrici Gamage.
F. vi s. viii d. De seldis quondam Gilberti Wynchcombe quas Will' Bergeny tenet.
F. iiii s. De selda in quadriuio quam Bartelote tenet.
F. i d. De domo sancti Petri in Ballio.

In parochia sancti Iohannis.

v s. De domo Henrici Illuminatoris quam Ioh' Rede tenet.
F. viii s. De aula Gaylere prox. cum shopis.
F. ii s. De aula Grimstede proxima.
x s. De duabus seldis cum una placea in Gropecountelane quas Iohannes Bosette tenet.

In parochia sancti Michaelis australis.

xvi s. De domo Boletras quam Iohannes Laylly tenet.
viii s. De domo Meteborne prox. quam Ioh' Mason tenet.
x s. De domo Masone quam Thomas Kember tenet.
F. ii s. De aula Mariolle ex altera parte quam Will' Borowe tenet.
F. xii d. De tenemento Swyneshulle.

In parochia sancti Aldati.

F. xiii d. De uno tenemento in Paruo Iudaismo ex opposito magne scole, pro quo magistri aule Balholl soluent.
F. xii s. De domo Iohannis Dokelinton, pro qua Ioh' Gibbes soluet.
xlvi s. viii d. De domo Kepharme prox. cum seldis quas Rogerus Manciple tenet.
xiii s. iiii d. De una shopa prox. quam Iohanna Shapster tenet.
xiii s. iiii d. De domo prox. quam Agnes Alston tenet.
xxii s. De domo in cornario prox. quam Hen. Heryng tenet.
xx s. De curia Lincoln' quam Adam Webbe tenet.
F. ii s. De tenemento Plumbatoris quod Abbas Regalis tenet.
De uno gardino in cimiterio sancti Aldati.
iiii s. De una domo iuxta furnam quam Will' Saundres tenet.

In parochia sancte Ebbe.

F. ix s. iiii d. De domo quondam Iohannis Alstone quam Reginaldus Tanner tenet.

F. viii s. iiii d. De domo proxima.

F. iiii s. De uno gardino prox. quam Iohanna Wylond tenet.

xiii s. iiii d. De duabus shopis quas Margareta Rynges tenet.

xiii s. iiii d. De domo quondam Mariorie Stanlake quam Ric' Hengseye tenet.

ix s. De tenemento Wareyn in paruo ballio quod Ioh' Bruhere tenet.

In parochia sancti Michaelis ad portam borialem.

xxvi s. viii d. De domo Blankeneye cum shopis quas Ioh' Hamptone tenet.

xiii s. iiii d. De tenemento Wodesdone situato iuxta paruum [pontem][1] de Oseneye ex parte occidentali quod abbas Oseneye tenet.

In parochia sancte Marie Magdalene.

F. ii s. De tenemento Dokelintone.

F. xii d. De tenemento Dodeford quod Ric' Oxenford tenet.

F. ii s. De solario quondam Iohannis Sauser quod Ric' Tornur tenet.

vi s. viii d. De domo Welles quam Ioh' Hostelere tenet.

F. iii s. De domo Iohannis Abyndone quam Ioh' Gruttone tenet.

ii s. De domo Tye quam Robertus Bathe carpinter tenet.

F. iii s. De quatuor seldis in Stocwellestret quas Ioh' Gruttone tenet.

F. vii s. De introitu Henrici Bramptone.

F. iii s. De domo Rogeri Bost quam Ioh' Hardy tenet.

F. xii d. De tenemento Dodelyn.

xiii s. iiii d. De domo nostra retro ecclesiam ex parte orientali quam Thomas Mason tenet.

uacat. De una uacua placea iuxta portam fratrum Carmel' ex parte occidentali.

F. xii d. De tenemento abbatisse de Godestowe.

Rentale de Haliwelle eodem anno.

vii s. De domo iuxta Crowell quam Ioh' Kente tenet.

iiii s. De domo prima proxima.

[1] Omitted by the scribe.

iii s. iiii d. De secunda domo proxima.

iii s. iiii d. De uno gardino cum terra ad capud gardini predicti & una acra terre arrabilis iacente in bello campo iuxta gardinum fratrum Augustin' ex parte orientali que Petrus Balliuus tenet.

De domibus clericorum anno supradicto.

iiii li. xii s. De aula Borwaldescote.

xl s. De aula Ynge.

xvi s. De aula Katerine—uacat.

xl s. De aula Borstalle.

x s. De aula Leporis.

xxvi s. viii d. De aula Camini.

xv s. De aula Philomene.

De aula Nigra—uacat.

xxvi s. viii d. De aula Arstotilis.

xiii s. iiii d. De aula Militis.

xxvi s. viii d. De aula Mynote.

xxvi s. viii d. De aula Mildrede.

xxvi s. viii d. De scola in Cattestrete.

x s. De aula profunda super Candych; Ioh' Sauhih tenet.

ii s. De aula Brackele ibidem cum ii aulis Bodyn quas Iohannes Manciple tenet.

xii s. De introitu sancti Iohannis in Cattestrete.

vi s. viii d. De scolis retro Omnium Sanctorum.

F. iiii s. De Hertehalle in uico sancti Iohannis pro qua magistri de collegio Balliolo super Candich soluent per annum xv d.

28. A rental for Sept. 21, 1376.

Rentale domus sancti Iohannis extra portam orientalem Oxonie de domibus laicorum & clericorum anno regni regis Edwardi tercii post conquestum quinquagesimo, incipiente a festo sancti Mathei apostoli.

In parochia sancti Clementis.

x s. De domo iuxta uenellam cum shopa; Will' Thame.

De domo prox.

De alia domo.

xii s. De duabus domibus prox. quas Thomas tenet.

xiii s. iiii d. De domo iuxta Charewelle quam Iohannes Pydington tenet.

Extra portam orientalem ex parte australi.

vi s.	De domo iuxta Parys quam Radulfus Sutor tenet.
vi s.	De domo prox. quam Willelmus Knyt tenet.
viii s.	[*As in the previous rental.*]
iiii s.	
xii s.	
viii s.	
F. xx d.	De domo Bix quam Agnes Keye tenet.

Extra portam orientalem ex parte boriali.

x s.	[*As in the previous rental.*]
vi s. viii d.	
vii s.	
v s.	De tercia domo prox. quam Alicia Hampton tenet.
xx s.	De alia domo quam Cokke, webbe, tenet.
vii s.	De domo prox., quam Willelmus Milleward tenet.
v s.	De schopa quam Iohannes Couper tenet.
xiii s. iiii d.	De domo prox. quam Nicholaus Manciple tenet.
v s.	De domo Ioye quam Elena Deye tenet.
vi s.	De domo prox. quam Nicholaus Follere tenet.
iiii s. viii d.	De selda prox. quam Iuliana Kareles tenet.
xvi s. viii d.	De domo cum forgio & shopis ; Iohannes Mareschall.
v s.	De prima shopa iuxta portam orientalem ; Iohannes Mareschall.
v s.	De secunda shopa prox. ; Thomas Blinde.
v s.	De tercia shopa prox. ; Amy Hosewyf.

Infra portam orientalem ex parte boriali.

x s.	De domo in cornario ; Iohannes Coke.
xii s.	De domo prox. ; Thomas Knauefeld.
xx s.	[*As in the last rental.*]
xxiiii s.	
xx s.	
F. x d.	
xx s.	
vi s.	De prima selda iuxta aulam Regine.
vi s.	De secunda selda ; Rob. Bosseby.
vi s.	De tercia selda ; Ioh' Kaker.
vi s.	De quarta selda ; Magota Taylour.
v s.	De quinta selda ; Cessota Shapster.
iii s.	De sexta selda ; Iohanna Bere.

ii s. De solario supra.

xxii s.
F. x s.
F. iii s. iiii d.
F. ii s.
vii s. } [*As in the last rental.*]

vii s. De secunda selda quam Agnes Taylour tenet.

xxiii s. iiii d.
xxvi s. viii d.
xiiii s. } [*As in the last rental.*]

xvi s. De secunda shopa prox.; Willelmus Taylour.

Circa ecclesiam sancti Petri in oriente.

ii s. De duobus gardinis ibidem quos Thomas Coke tenet.
De uno gardino; scolares aule Nigre tenent.
De duobus gardinis iuxta cimiterium predictum.
ii s. De domo Charnel quam uxor Ricardi Bedel tenet.

Infra portam orientalem ex parte australi.

viii s. De domo Abraham; de prima shopa; Willelmus Taylor.
viii s. De secunda shopa; Iohannes Fleccher.
xviii s. De domo Cloptone.
F. i d. De domo Martini Exemplatoris.

Kibaldstrete.

v s. De domo quam Margareta Wales tenet.
v s. De domo prox., quam Iohannes Coke tenet.
v s. De alia domo quam Iohanna Launder tenet.
uacat. De domo in Kibaldstret.
viii s. viii d. De uno gardino quem Ricardus Pencrix tenet.

In parochia sancte Marie uirginis.

xx s. De domo Leuertone; Rob. Bokebyndere.
xx s. De domo Faunt prox.; Iohannes Lymnour.
F. vii s. vi d. De domo quondam Ade Howton, pro qua Iohannes Bokyngham soluet.
F. iiii s. De domo Abraham prox.; Iohannes Manciple.
xxviii s. De domo Lodelawe cum uno gardino infra scolam; Thomas Dolle.
xxvi s. viii d. De domo Basing;[1] Iohannes Grasihere.

[1] The previous rentals prove that 'Pomfret' is meant.

xiii s. iiii d. De duabus shopis retro ecclesiam, pro quibus Henricus Garlond soluet.

liii s. iiii d. De domo prox. cum shoppis, quas Iohannes Peyntur tenet.

x s. De duabus shopis prox.; Robertus Barbour.

F. xii d. De uno gardino infra domum Nicholai Garlond.

In parochia Omnium Sanctorum.

xxiiii s.
xviii s.
xiii s. iiii d.
xviii d. } [*As in the last rental.*]

xxvi s. iiii d. De duabus shopis subtus domum Iohannis Stodle; Willelmus Cheslehamptone.

F. vii s. De tenemento Hengseye; Iohannes Stodle.

l s. De domo Swynebrook cum shopis; Iohannes Mosturtone.

xxviii s. De domo quondam Alicie Neubury; Henricus Haylesbury.

In parochia sancti Martini.

F. iiii s.
F. iii s.
F. xii d.
xx s. } [*As in the last rental.*]

xvi s. De secunda shopa Croxford; Iohannes Taylor.

ii s. De uno stayhere inter shopas antedictas; Prior sancte Frideswide soluet.

De selda in suteria.

De solario quondam Henrici Gamage.

F. vi s. viii d. De selda quondam Gilberti Wynchcombe; Willelmus Bergeny.

F. iiii s. De selda in quadriuio, quam Bartole Vintere tenet.

F. i d. De domo Petri in Ballio.

In parochia sancti Iohannis.
In parochia sancti Michaelis australis. } [*As in the last rental.*]

In parochia sancti Aldati.

F. xiii d.
F. xii s.
xlvi s. viii d.
xiii s. iiii d.
xiii s. iiii d. } [*As in the last rental.*]

xxiiii s. De domo in cornario; Henricus Heryng.
xx s. De curia Lincolne; Adam Webbe.
iiii s. De parua domo iuxta pistrinum in cimiterio sancti Aldati; Will' Saundres.
F. ii s. De tenemento Plumbatoris iuxta domum quondam Iohannis [*sic*].
De uno gardino in cimiterio sancti Aldati.

In parochia sancte Ebbe.

F. ix s. iiii d. De domo quondam Iohannis Astone; Reginaldus Tanner.
F. viii s. iiii d. De domo proxima pro qua Prior sancte Fridiswide soluet.
F. iiii s. De tenemento Bremster prox.; Iohanna Wylond.
xiii s. iiii d.
xiii s. iiii d. } [*As in the last rental.*]
ix s.

In parochia sancti Michaelis ad portam borialem.

xxvi s. viii d. De domo Blaunkeneye cum shopis; Iohannes Chaundeler.
xiii s. iiii d. De tenemento Wodesdone.

In parochia sancte Marie Magdalene ex parte occidentali.

F. ii s. De tenemento Dodeling.[1]
F. xii d. De tenemento Dodeford.
F. ii s. De solario quondam Iohannis Saucer.
vi s. viii d. De domo Welles; Iohannes Hostelere.
F. iii s. De domo Iohannis Abyndone; Iohannes Gruttone.
ii s. De domo Tye; Robertus Bathe carpenter.
F. iii s. De quatuor seldis in Stocwellestret; Iohannes Gruttone.

Ex parte orientali.

F. vii s. De introitu Henrici Bramptone.
F. iii s. De domo quondam Rogeri Bost.
F. xii d. De tenemento Dodeling.
x s. De domo retro ecclesiam ex parte orientali; Thomas Mason.

[1] *Dokelinton* is meant.

De una uacua placea iuxta portam fratrum Carmel' ex parte occidentali.

F. xii d. De tenemento abbatisse de Godestowe.

Rentale de Haliwelle eodem anno.

viii s. De domo iuxta Crowell; Iohannes Hamond.

vi s. De domo prox.; Willelmus Saleman.

iiii s. De tercia domo; Alicia Lander.

De una uacua placea ibidem.

iiii d. De una uacua placea ex opposito cimiterii ecclesie ibidem ex parte occidentali cum duobus bottis ad caput placee predicte; Iohannes Bosette tenet.

viii d. De una acra iacente in Bello Campo iuxta fratres Augustinenses, quam idem Iohannes tenet.

De terra iacente in crofto iuxta molendinum.

De domibus clericorum.

iiii li. xii s. De aula Borwaldescote.

xl s. De aula Ynge.

De aula Katerine.

xl s. De aula Borstalle.

xii s. De aula Leporis.

xxvi s. viii d. De aula Camini.

xv s. De aula Philomene.

De aula Nigra.

xxvi s. viii d. De aula Aristotelis.

xiii s. iiii d. De aula Militis.

xxvi s. viii d. De aula Mynote.

x s. De aula Profunda super Candich.

ii s. De aula Brakkele cum ii aulis.

xl s. De scola in Cattestrete.

viii s. De introitu sancti Iohannis ibidem.

vi s. viii d. De scola retro Omnium Sanctorum.

xxvi s. viii d. De aula Mildrede.

F. iiii s. De Herthalle in uico sancti Iohannis, pro qua magistri aule Balliolle soluent xv d.

29. A rental of Dec. 21, 1384.

Rentale ville Oxonie de domo sancti Iohannis extra portam orientalem per fratrem Willelmum de Stauerton tunc procuratorem ibidem in festo sancti Thome apostoli anno regni regis Ricardi secundi post conquestum octauo usque ad idem festum in anno tunc proximo reuoluto.

Parochia sancti Clementis.

xii s. De duabus seldis iuxta uenellam quas Willelmus Thame tenet.
iiii s. De tercia selda prox. quam Rogerus Cobeler tenet.
vi s. De quarta selda prox. quam Ricardus Gynge tenet.
xii s. De ii seldis prox. quas Thomas Thame tenet.
xiii s. iiii d. De domo prox. quam Iohannes Pydyngtone tenet.

Parochia sancti Petri extra portam orientalem ex parte australi.

xviii d. De domo prox. prato Paris quam Iohannes Sawer tenet.
vi s. De domo prox. quam Stephanus Carter tenet.
vi s. De domo prox. quam Thomas Iordone tenet.
xiii s. iiii d. De domo prox. quam Isabella Lotrix tenet.
vi s. viii d. De domo prox. quam Willelmus Muleward tenet.
xiii s. iiii d. De domo prox. quam Iohannes Webbe tenet.
xiii s. iiii d. De domo Pylle cum schopa quam Bayly tenet.
F. xx d. De domo Bix quam olim Agnes Keye tenuit.

Extra portam orientalem ex parte boriali.

xiii s. iiii d. De domo prox. port' quam Iohannes Londone tenet.
ix s. De secunda domo quam Iohannes Bruer tenet.
ix s. De tercia domo quam Iohannes Skynner tenet.
x s. De quarta domo prox. quam Thomas Carter tenet.
x s. De quinta domo prox. quam Iohannes Clerk tenet.
xx s. De sexta domo quam Iohannes Mason tenet.
De septima domo prox. quam Nicholaus Sclatter tenet.
v s. De selda quam Nicholaus Kent tenet.
xvi s. De domo quam idem Nicholaus tenet.
xii s. De domo prox. quam Thomas Clerk tenet.
vi s. viii d. De domo prox. quam Agnes Colles tenet.
v s. De selda prox. quam Iohannes Hamond tenet.
xxvi s. viii d. De domo prox. cum ii schoppis quam Iohannes Smyth tenet.

v s. De prima selda iuxta portam orientalem quam Iohanna Chemester tenet.
v s. De secunda selda quam Thomas Blynde tenet.
v s. De tercia selda quam Iohannes Scot tenet.

Infra portam orientalem ex parte australi.

viii s. De selda quam Margareta Fullere tenet.
viii s. De selda prox. quam Iohannes Flescher tenet.
xviii s. De domo Cloptone quam Rogerus Chyddesle tenet.

Kybaldestrete.

v s. De domo quam Margareta Sthephene tenet.
v s. De domo prox. quam Nicholaus Fullere tenet.
v s. De domo prox. quam Iohannes Gardyner tenet.
iii s. De domo in uenella quam Agnes Bocke tenet.

Infra portam orientalem ex parte boriali.

xiii s. iiii d. De domo cum schoppis iuxta uenellam quam Thomas Katur tenet.
xii s. De domo prox. quam Iohannes Carpenter tenet.
xviii s. iiii d. De domo prox. cum schopa quam Isabella Mason tenet.
xxv s. De domo prox. cum schopa quam Philippus Carpenter tenet.
xx s. De domo prox. cum schopa quam Alicia Stanewey tenet.
F. x d. De domo Katerine Bere.
xxvi s. viii d. De domo prox. quam Thomas Bruere tenet.
iiii s. De gardinis quos uicarius ecclesie sancti Petri tenet.
vi s. De selda prox. Aule Regine quam Alicia Fairwomman tenet.
vi s. De selda prox. quam Iohannes Bruere tenet.
vi s. De selda prox. quam Willelmus Bruere tenet.
vi s. De selda prox. quam Iohannes Mason tenet.
v s. De selda prox. quam Adam Cobeler tenet.
iiii s. De selda prox. quam Alicia Baker tenet.
vi s. De alta camera supradicte selde quam Rogerus Mason tenet.
xxvi s. viii d. De domo cum ii schoppis quam Petrus Mason tenet.
x s. De introitu sancti Nicholai quem } prepositus Aule Regine tenet.
iii s. iiii d. De domo prox. quam } prepositus Aule Regine tenet.
ii s. De domo Glattone prox. quam } prepositus Aule Regine tenet.

xxii s. De aula Katerine cum ii seldis & gardino quem Hugo Cok tenet.

xxiiii s. iiii d. De domo prox. cum schop[is] quas Willelmus Southam tenet.

xxxii s. iiii d. De domo prox. cum iii schopis quam Robertus Polford tenet.

xiii s. iiii d. De selda prox. quam Ricardus Coke tenet.

xvi s. De selda prox. quam Iohannes Sawer tenet.

ii s. De domo Charnell quam Agnes Bedel tenet.

Parochia sancte Marie Virginis.

xx s. De domo Leuertone quam Robertus Bocbyndere tenet.

xx s. De domo Fawnt quam Willelmus Luminour tenet.

F. vii s. vi d. De domo Howtone quam Iohannes Bokyngham tenet.

F. iiii s. De domo Abraham quam Iohannes Gynes tenet.

xxx s. De domo Lowdelowe cum i gardino infra scolas sancti Iohannis quam T. Dol tenet.

xxvi s. viii d. De domo quam Iuliana Grasiere tenet.

xiiii s. De ii seldis in cimiterio beate Marie quas Iohannes Cook tenet.

xxiii s. iiii d. De domo Basyng cum schopis quam Iohannes Peyntour tenet.

xxviii s. De ii seldis proximis quas Rogerus Latoner tenet.

x s. De ii seldis proximis quas Robertus Barbour tenet.

F. xii d. De uno gardino infra domum Iuliane Garlonde.

Parochia Omnium Sanctorum.

xxiiii s. De selda Wytwong quam Stephanus Polmorua tenet.

xxiiii s. De ii schopis quas Iohannes Hed tenet.

xiii s. iiii d. De aula retro ecclesiam Omnium Sanctorum quam idem tenet.

xviii d. De domo prox. quam idem tenet.

vi s. viii d. De scola ibidem quam Iohannes Holwey tenet.

xiii s. iiii d. De i selda subtus Stodley quam Iohannes Cheslamtone tenet.

xiii s. iiii d. De alia selda in eodem loco quam Willelmus Borow tenet.

F. vii s. De tenemento Henkseye quod Trysylyan[1] tenet.

c s. De domo Swynebroke quam Adam de la Ryuer tenet.

[1] i.e. Sir Robert Tresilian. On his death, William of Wykeham bought his property. It still belongs to New College.

xxviii s. De domo Alicie Nubury in Bocheria quam Iohannes Manciple tenet de procuratoribus ecclesie Omnium Sanctorum et ipsi tenent de nobis ad terminum xl annorum pro xiiii s. annuatim & inde sunt iam elapsi xxiii.[1]

Parochia sancti Martini.

F. iiii s. De domo Orliens quam Iohannes Blode tenet.
F. iii s. De domo Alicie Welles quam Iohannes Wakeman tenet.
F. x s. De introitu Kyngestone quam Thomas Somersete tenet.
xix s. De selda Croxforde quam Iohannes Sadeler tenet.
xx s. De alia selda Croxforde quam Willelmus Harpour tenet.
F. ii s. De i gradu inter schopas predictas pro quo prior Frideswyde soluet.
F. ii s. De solario Henrici Gamage.
F. iii s. iiii d. De selda in sutoria quam Ricardus Forster tenet.
F. vi s. viii d. De Wychecombe quem [*sic*] Willelmus Bergeyny tenet.
F. iiii s. De selda in quadriuio quam Bartlot Tauerner tenet.
F. i d. De domo in ballio sancti Petri.

Parochia sancti Iohannis.

v s. De domo Henrici Luminour quam Iohannes Rede tenet.
F. viii s. De aula Gailer prox. cum schop' quam Trysylyan tenet.
F. De aula Tremstede [*sic*] quam idem tenet.
De domo Hayle in Kybaldstrete.
x s. De ii schopis cum placea edificata quam Iohannes Boset tenet.

Parochia sancti Michaelis australis.

xiii s. iiii d. De domo Boltras quam Rogerus Harpmaker tenet.
viii s. De domo Meteburne quam Iohannes Mason tenet.
x s. De domo Mason quam Thomas Kymber tenet.
F. ii s. De aula Mariol ex parte occidentali quam Margareta Underwall tenet de Priorissa de Lytelmore.
F. xii d. De tenemento Swyneshulle.

Parochia sancti Aldati.

F. xiii d. De tenemento exoposito scole in Iudaismo pro quo prepositus Baylyhall soluet.

[1] According to the rentals of 1371, 1374, and 1375, the number here should be xx, not xxiii. The rental of 1388 drops one of the years in excess, the rental of 1391 drops another, while the rental of 1392 drops two more, so that the numbering then runs into error on the side of defect.

F. xii s. De tenemento Duclyngtone pro quo Iohannes Gibbes soluet.

xlvi s. viii d. De domo Kepharme quam Rogerus Irlond tenet.

xiii s. iiii d. De selda proxima quam Iohannes Tailour tenet.

xx s. De selda proxima quondam Agnetis Allestone.

xxx s. De domo prox. ibidem quam Iohannes Marlebourghe tenet.

xvii s. De selda prox. quam Iohannes Manciple tenet.

xxiiii s. De domo prox. quam Knauefeld tenet.

xx s. De curia Lincoln quam Adam Webbe tenet.

vi s. viii d. De parua domo iuxta paruam uenellam cimiterii.

F. ii s. De tenemento Plumbatoris quod Abbas de Regali Loco tenet.

De domo nouo [*sic*] edificato [*sic*] iuxta cimiterium sancti Aldati.

Parochia sancte Ebbe.

F. ix s. iiii d. De domo sub muro uille quam Reginaldus Tanner tenet.

F. viii s. iiii d. De domo prox. ex parte occidentali pro quo Prior Frideswyde soluet.

F. iiii s. De tenemento Brymster quod est gardinum quod Iohanna Weylond tenet.

De ii schopis quas Margareta Ryng tenet.

xiii s. iiii d. De domo Stanlake quam Willelmus Manciple tenet.

ix s. De tenemento Waryn in Balliolo quod Iohannes Hyne tenet.

Parochia sancti Michaelis borealis.

xxvi s. viii d. De aula Blanckeneye quam Iohannes Hamptone tenet.

xiii s. iiii d. De tenemento Wodesdone quod abbas Oseneye tenet.

Parochia sancte Marie Magdalene ex parte occidentali.

F. ii s. De tenemento Duclyngtone.

F. xii d. De tenemento Dodeford.

F. ii s. De solario Iohannis Sawcer.

x s. De domo Welles quam Iohannes Hostler tenet.

F. iii s. De domo Abyngdone quam Iohannes Gruttone tenet.

iiii s. De domo Tye quam Iohannes Ropere tenet.

De una placia vacua iuxta portam fratrum Carmelitarum.

De alia placia vacua extra portam eorundem fratrum quam Iohannes Wakeman tenet.

Ex parte orientali.

F. iiii s. De introitu Henrici Bramptone quam Willelmus Cook tenet.

F. iii s. De domo Rogeri Bost iuxta Cardinalhatte.[1]

F. xii d. De tenemento Duclyngtone.[2]

x s. De domo quam Thomas Masone tenet.

Parochia sancti Egidii.

F. xx d. De terra que fuit Iohannis Randulf in Stokwellstret.

F. xvi d. De ii seldis ibidem que fuerunt Ricardi de [*sic*] Pulter.

F. xii d. De tenemento abbatisse de Godestowe.

Parochia sancte Crucis.

iii s. De i placea iuxta Crouwelle.

v s. De domo prox. in Halywelle.

ii s. De cotagio prox.

ii s. De cotagio prox. Henrico Okkam.

iii s. ix d. De domo Henrici Okkam.

xviii d. De i placia retro domum Okkam.

iiii s. De i placia prox. uenellam.

xii d. De i placia prox. Sawer.

iiii s. De domo le Sawer.

ii s. De parva domo iuxta ecclesiam.

iiii s. De domo prox.

iiii s. De domo tercia.

De domo quinta [*sic*] quondam Henrici Brackeley.

xx d. De i placia inclusa exopposito cimiterii eiusdem ecclesie cum ii bottes in Bellomonte situatis.

xviii d. De domo cum i acra terre arabilis in Bellomonte situata inter terram aule Martonis.

viii s. De domo iuxta Crouwelle quam Iohannes Hamond tenet.

vi s. viii d. De domo prox. quam Iohannes Bocher tenet.

iiii s. De tertia domo quam Iohannes Salman tenet.

De domibus clericorum.

ii li. xiii s. iiii d. De aula uocata Burwaldescote quam magister Iohannes Treuam[3] tenet.

[1] For the Cardinal's Hat see *Balliol Deeds*, pp. 73, &c. (O. H. S.); this is the earliest occurrence of the name.

[2] Dodeling is meant.

[3] The name is spelt Treuaur in the next rental. John Trevaur or Treffnan became bishop of St. Asaph in 1395.

ii li. vi s. viii d. De aula uocata ȝynghalle quam magister Thomas Mockyng tenet.

xl s. De aula uocata Bosterhalle quam mag. Rob. Aylesham tenet.

xvi s. De aula uocata Harehalle quam Petrus tenet.

iii li. iii s. iiii d. De aula uocata Chymynehalle cum magno gardino & alia aula uocata Nyghtyngalehalle cum gardino quam Thomas Londone tenet.

xxvi s. viii d. De aula uocata Arsstotelhalle quam mag. Iohannes Stone tenet.

vi s. viii d. De aula uocata Knyghalle quam mag. Walterus Romesey tenet.

xxvi s. viii d. De aula uocata Mynotehalle quam mag. Ric. Wolffe tenet.

xiii s. iiii d. De aula uocata Depphalle super Candych quam Ricardus Skynner tenet.

xxvi s. viii d. De aula uocata Myldredehalle quam Iohannes Alayn tenet.

ii s. De aula uocata Brackeleyhalle cum aliis duabus aulis uocatis Boydynhalle super Candyche quam Iohannes Manciple wallicus tenet.

xl s. De Magna Scola in Cattesstrete quam canonicus Oseneye tenet.

xiii s. iiii d. De introitu sancti Iohannis quem Thomas Dol tenet.

F. iiii s. De aula uocata Herthalle in uico sancti Iohannis situata pro qua prepositus Baylyhalle soluet. xvi d.

30. A rental of Dec. 21, 1385.

Rentale uille Oxonie de domo sancti Iohannis extra portam orientalem per fratrem Willelmum de Stauertone tunc procuratorem ibidem a festo sancti Thome apostoli anno regni regis Ricardi secundi post conquestum nono usque ad idem festum in anno tunc prox. reuoluto.

Parochia sancti Clementis.

xii s. De duobus seldis iuxta uenellam quas Will' Thame tenet ad terminum.

iiii s. De tercia selda prox. quam Rogerus Cobelere tenet per annum.

vi s. De quarta selda prox. quam Ric' Gynge tenet per annum.

xii s. De duabus seldis prox. quas Thos. Thame tenet ad terminum.

xiii s. iiii d. De domo prox. quam Ioh' Pydyngtone tenet ad terminum.

Summa xlvi s. iiii d.

Parochia sancti Petri extra portam orientalem.

xviii d. De domo prox. prato Paris quam Iohannes Sawer tenet ad terminum.

vi s. De domo prox. quam Steph' Carter tenet per annum.

vi s. De domo prox. quam Thos. Iurdon tenet per annum.

xiii s. iiii d. De domo prox. quam Isabella Lotrix tenet per annum.

vi s. viii d. De domo prox. quam Will' Mulnward tenet per annum.

xiii s. iiii d. De domo prox. quam Ioh' Webbe tenet per annum.

xiii s. iiii d. De domo Pylle cum schopa quam Iohannes Bayly tenet ad terminum.

F. xx d. De domo Bix quam olim Agnes Keye tenuit, pro qua Prior Frideswyde soluit.

Ex parte boriali.

xiii s. iiii d. De domo prox. ad magnam portam quam Will' Deyere tenet per annum.

ix s. De secunda domo prox. quam Ioh' Bruere tenet per annum.

ix s. De tercia domo prox. quam Rob. Deyere tenet per annum.

ix s. vi d. De quarta domo prox. quam Thos. Carter tenet per annum.

De quinta domo prox. quam nullus occupauit.

xvii s. De sexta domo prox. quam Ioh' Mason tenet ad terminum.

De septima domo prox. quam Nic. Sclatter tenet ad terminum.

v s. De selda quam Nic. Kent tenet per annum.

xvi s. De domo prox. quam idem tenet per annum.

xii s. De domo prox. quam Thomas Clerk tenet per annum.

vi s. viii d. De domo prox. quam Agnes Colles tenet per annum.

v s. De selda prox. quam Ioh' Hamptone tenet per annum.
xxvi s. viii d. De domo prox. cum ii schoppis quam Ioh' Smyth tenet ad terminum.
v s. De prima selda iuxta portam orientalem quam Iohanna Kemester tenet per annum.
v s. De secunda selda quam Thos. Blynde tenet per annum.
v s. De tercia selda quam Ioh' Webbe tenet per annum.

Infra portam orientalem ex parte australi.
viii s. De selda quam Rob. Fullere tenet per annum.
viii s. De selda prox. quam Ioh' Fleccher tenet per annum.
xviii s. De domo Cloptone quam Rogerus Chyddesle tenet ad terminum.

Kybaldestrete.
v s. De domo quam Ioh' Cook tenet per annum.
v s. De domo prox. quam Will' Carpenter tenet per annum.
v s. De domo prox. quam Ioh' Cook tenet per annum.
iii s. De domo in uenella quam Will' Knyght tenet per annum, nichil soluendo.

Infra portam orientalem ex parte boriali.
xiii s. iiii d. De domo cum schop' iuxta uenellam quam Thos. Catur tenet ad terminum.
xii s. De domo prox. quam Ioh' Carpenter tenet per annum.
xviii s. iiii d. De domo prox. cum schopa quam Isabella Mason tenet per annum.
xxv s. De domo prox. cum schopa quam Phil' Carpenter tenet ad terminum.
xx s. De domo prox. cum schopa quam Alicia Stanewey tenet ad terminum.
F. x d. De domo Katerine Bere.
xxvi s. viii d. De domo prox. quam Thomas Bruere tenet per annum.
v s. De gardinis quos uicarius ecclesie sancti Petri tenet ad terminum.
vi s. De selda prox. aule Regine quam Alicia filia Truloue tenet.
vi s. De selda prox. quam Ioh' Bruere tenet per annum.
vi s. De selda prox. quam Will' Bruere tenet per annum.
vi s. De selda prox. quam Ioh' Mason tenet per annum.
iiii s. De selda prox. quam Adam Cobelere tenet per annum.

iiii s. De selda prox. quam Alicia Baker tenet per annum.

iiii s. De alta camera supra dictam seldam quam Rob' Workman tenet per annum.

xxvi s. viii d. De domo cum ii schoppis quam Thos. Pymaker tenet per annum.

x s. De introitu sancti Nicholai }
iii s. iiii d. De domo prox. } prepositus aule Regine tenet ad terminum.
ii s. De domo Glatton prox. }

xvi s. De aula Katerine cum ii seldis & gardino quam Hugo Cook tenet ad terminum.

xxiiii s. iiii d. De domo prox. cum i schop' quas Will' Southam tenet ad terminum.

xxxii s. iiii d. De domo prox. cum iii schop' quam Rob' Pulford tenet ad terminum.

xiii s. iiii d. De selda prox. quam Ric. Cook tenet per annum.

xvi s. De selda prox. quam Ioh' Sawer tenet per annum.

ii s. De domo Charnelle quam Agnes Bedel tenet per annum.

Summa xvii li. iii s. vi d.

Parochia sancte Marie Virginis.

xx s. De domo Leuertone quam Rob. Bocbyndere tenet ad terminum.

xx s. De domo Fawnt quam Will' Lumynour tenet ad terminum.

F. vii s. vi d. De domo Howgtone quam Ioh' Bokyngham tenet.

F. iiii s. De domo Abraham quam Ioh' Gynge tenet.

xxx s. De domo Lodelowe cum i gardino infra scolas in Catstrete quam T. Dol tenet ad terminum.

xxvi s. viii d. De domo quam Iuliana Graciere tenet ad terminum uite & per annum postea.

xiiii s. De ii seldis in cimiterio beate Marie quas Iohannes Cook tenet per annum.

xxiii s. iiii d. De domo Basyng cum schop' quam Ioh' Peyntour tenet per annum.

xxviii s. De ii seldis prox. quas Rog' Latoner tenet ad terminum.

x s. De ii seldis prox. quas Rob' Barbour tenet ad terminum.

F. xii d. De i gardino infra domum Iuliane Garlond.

Summa viii li. xv s.

Parochia Omnium Sanctorum.

xxiiii s. De selda Wytwongg quam Steph' Polmorua tenet ad terminum.

xxiiii s. De ii schoppis quas Ioh' Hed, cordewayner, tenet ad terminum.

xiii s. iiii d. De aula retro ecclesiam Omnium Sanctorum quam idem tenet.

xviii d. De domo prox., quam idem tenet.

vi s. viii d. De scola ibidem quam Ioh' Holewey tenet ad terminum.

xiii s. iiii d. De selda subtus Stodeley quam Ioh' Cheslamtone tenet per annum.

xiii s. iiii d. De alia selda ibidem quam Will' Bourge tenet per annum.

F. vii s. De tenemento Henkseye quod Tysylyan [*sic*] tenet.

c s. De domo Swenebrok cum schoppis quam Adam de la Riuer tenet ad terminum.

xiiii s. De domo Alicie Nubury in Bocheria quam Ioh' Manciple modo tenet de procuratoribus ecclesie Omnium Sanctorum & ipsi tenent de nobis ad terminum xl annorum pro xiiii s. annuatim, & inde sunt anni iam elapsi xxiiii.

Summa x li. x s. ii d.

Parochia sancti Martini.

F. iiii s. De domo Orlyens quam Ioh' Blode tenet.

F. iii s. De domo Alicie Welles quam Ioh' Wakeman tenet.

F. x s. modo xii d. De introitu Kynggestone quem Thomas Somersete tenet ad terminum.

xix s. De selda Croxforde quam Ioh' Sadeler tenet ad terminum.

xx s. De alia selda prox. quam Will' Harpour tenet ad terminum.

F. ii s. De i gradu inter schoppas predictas, pro quo Prior Frideswyde soluit.

F. ii s. De solario Henrici Gamage.

F. iii s. iiii d. De selda in sutoria quam Ric. Forster tenet.

F. iiii s. De selda in quadriuio quam Bartholomeus Tauerner tenet.

F. i d. De domo in Ballio sancti Petri.

Summa xl s.

Parocbia sancti Iohannis.

v s. De domo Henrici Lumynour quam Ioh' Rede tenet ad terminum.

F. viii s. De aula Gailer prox. cum schopa quam Trysylyan tenet.

F. ii s. De aula Trymstede quam idem tenet.

De domo Hayle in Kybaldestrete & extendit ad finem eorundem tenementorum.

De domo Bosett.

Summa xv s.

Parochia sancti Michaelis Australis.

[De domo Boltras quam][1] Rogerus Harpmaker tenet.

[De domo Meteburne quam] Ioh' Mason tenet ad terminum.

[De domo Mason quam] Thomas Kymber tenet ad terminum.

[De aula Mariol] ex parte occidentali quam Margareta Underwalles tenet de priorissa de Lytelmore.

[De ten. Swineshu]lle.

Summa xxxiii s. iiii d.

Parochia sancti Aldati.

[De tenemento in Iudaismo, pro quo] prepositus Baylyhall soluit.

[De tenemento Duclyngton, pro quo] Ioh' Gybbes soluit.

[De domo Kepharme, quam] Rog' Irlond tenet ad terminum.

[De selda proxima, quam] Ioh' Tailour tenet ad terminum.

[De selda quondam] Agnetis Alestone; modo tenet Thomas Dagworthe barbour; tenet ad terminum.

[De domo prox. quam] Ioh' Marlebourghe tenet per annum.

[De selda prox. quam Ioh'] Manciple tenet per annum.

[De domo prox. in cornerio quam Ioh'] Clanefeld tenet ad terminum.

[De curia Lincoln, quam] Adam Webbe tenet ad terminum.

[De parua domo iuxta pistrinum] quam Ioh' Cook tenet per annum.

[De tenemento Plumbatoris qu]od Mercer tenet de abbate de Regali Loco.

[De domo noua] iuxta cimiterium sancti Aldati quondam Bhissupsawour.

Summa vii li. xiiii s. v d.

[1] The roll is wanting at the left-hand side; the words in brackets are guessed.

Parochia sancte Ebbe.

[De curia Lincoln, quam Adam] Webbe tenet ad terminum.[1]

[De duabus schopis, quas] Margareta Ryng tenet in cornario.

[De domo Stanlake,] quam Will' Manciple tenet ad terminum.

[De tenemento Waryn] quod Ioh' Hyne tenet per annum.

[De domo] sub muro uille quam Reginaldus Tanner tenet ad terminum.

[De domo prox.] ex parte occidentali pro quo Prior Frideswide soluit.

[De tenemento] Bremster quod est gardinum ; Iohanna Weylond tenet.

Summa xlix s.

Parochia sancti Michaelis borealis.

[De aula] Blaunkeneye quam Ioh' Hampton tenet ad terminum.

Summa xxvi s. viii d.

Parochia sancti Thome.

[De tenemento] Wodesdone quod abbas Oseneye tenet ad terminum.

Summa xiii s. iiii d.

Parochia sancte Marie Magdalene.

[De tenemento Duclintone.]

[De tenemento Dodeford.]

[De solario] Iohannis Sawcer.

[De domo] Welles quam Ioh' Hostiler tenet ad terminum.

[De tenemento] quondam Walteri de Wygornia quam Ioh' Gytton tenet.

[De domo Tye] quam Ioh' Roper tenet ad terminum.

[De una placea uacua] iuxta portam fratrum Carmelit'.

[De alia placea uacua] extra portam eorundem quam Ioh' Wakeman tenet.

[De introitu] Henrici de Brompton quam Will' Cook tenet.

[De domo] Rogeri Bost iuxta Cardinalhatte.

[De tenemento Du]clington.

[De domo Willelmi] Stofford quam Ioh'[2] Mason tenet ad terminum.

Summa xxxi s.

[1] This entry has occurred before in St. Aldate's parish, but it is placed rightly in St. Ebbe's.

[2] The previous and subsequent rentals suggest that *Ioh'* is an error for *Thomas*.

Parochia sancti Egidii.

[De terra que] fuit Iohannis Randalff in Stokwellestrete.
[De ii seldis] que fuerunt Ricardi le Pultir.
[De domo prox.] Roberti de Brompton.
[De tenemento] abbatisse de Godestowe.

Parochia sancte Crucis.

[*Apparently as in the last rental.*]

De domibus clericorum.

iii li. vi s. viii d. De aula uocata Burwaldescote quam mag. Ioh' Treuaur tenet.
ii li. vi s. viii d. De aula uocata Yngehall quam mag. Thos. Mockyng tenet.
xl s. De aula uocata Bosterhalle quam mag. Rob. Alesham tenet.
xvi s. De aula uocata Harehalle.
iii li. iii s. iiii d. De aula uocata Chymeneyhalle cum magno gardino & alia aula uocata Nightyngalehalle cum paruo gardino quam Thomas Mere tenet.
xxvi s. viii d. De aula uocata Arstotelhalle quam mag. Ioh' Stone tenet.
vi s. viii d. De aula uocata Kynghhalle quam mag. Walterus Ramesye tenet ad terminum.
xiii s. iiii d. De aula uocata Mynothalle quam mag. Ric. Wolffe tenet.
xiii s. iiii d. De aula uocata Depphalle super Candyche quam Ric' Parchemener tenet ad terminum.
xxvi s. viii d. De aula uocata Mildredehalle quam mag. Alayn tenet.
ii s. De aula uocata Brackeleyhalle cum duabus aulis uocatis Boydenhalle super Candyche quas Ioh' Manciple wallicus tenet.
ii s. De aula uocata Williamhalle.
xvi s. viii d. De magna scola in Catstrete quam canonicus Oseneye tenet.
xiii s. iiii d. De introitu sancti Iohannis quam Thomas Martyn tenet.
F. iiii s. De aula uocata Herthalle in uico sancti Iohannis pro qua prepositis Baylyhall soluet per annum.

Summa xvii li. xiiii s. vii d.

31. A rental of Dec. 21, 1388.

Rentale uille Oxonie de domo sancti Iohannis extra portam orientalem per fratrem Willelmum de Stauertone tunc procuratorem ibidem a festo sancti Thome apostoli anno regni regis Ricardi secundi post conquestum duodecimo usque ad idem festum anno tunc proximo reuoluto.

Parochia sancti Clementis.

xii s. De duabus seldis iuxta uenellam quas Will' Thame tenet per indenturam.

iiii s. De tercia selda quam Rogerus Allutarius tenet per annum.

vi s. De quarta selda quam Ricardus Gynge tenet per annum.

xii s. De duabus seldis prox. quas Thomas Thame tenet per indenturam.

xiii s. iiii d. De domo prox. quam Iohannes Pydyngtone tenet per indenturam.

Parochia sancti Petri extra portam orientalem.

[ ] De Parys quod Will' Dyer tenet per annum.

[ ] De domo prox. Parys; Ioh' Sawer tenet per indenturam.

[ ] De domo prox.; Will' Knyght tenet per annum.

[ ] De domo prox.; Ioh' Cornyshe tenet per annum.

[ ] De domo prox.; Ioh' Mancipul tenet per annum.

[ ] De domo prox.; Will' Mulnward tenet per annum.

[ ] De domo prox.; Ioh' Webbe tenet per annum.

[ ] De domo Pille cum shopa; Ioh' Bayly tenet per indenturam.

[ ] De domo Byx, que situata est iuxta portam sancte Frideswyde, pro qua Prior Frideswyde soluit.

De itinere uersus grangiam sancte Frideswyde; idem Prior.

i lib. thuris. De tenementis uenditis comiti Cornubie; Frater de Trinitate soluit.

Ex parte boriali.

xii s. De domo proxima porte domus nostre; Will' Grimmisby tenet per annum.

viii s. De secunda domo quam Ioh' Bruer tenet per annum.

viii s. De tercia domo quam Ioh' Hickes tenet per annum.

[ ] De quarta domo quam Thomas Carpinter tenet per annum.

[ ] De quinta domo quam Henricus Sutor tenet per annum.

xvi s. De sexta domo quam Ioh' Asscheham, mason, tenet per annum.

viii s. De septima domo; Nicholaus Sclatter tenet ad terminum uite.

v s.
xvi s.
xii s.
vi s. viii d.
v s. } [*As in the last rental.*]

xxvi s. viii d. De domo prox. cum ii shoppis; Ioh' Wady, smith, tenet per indenturam.

v s. De prima selda extra portam orientalem; Nic' Fuller tenet per annum.

v s.
v s. } [*As in the last rental.*]

Infra portam orientalem ex parte australi.

viii s. De selda quam Nic' Fuller tenet per annum.

viii s. De selda prox. quam Ioh' Fleccher tenet per annum.

xiii s. iiii d. De domo Cloptone quam Rogerus Chyddesle tenet per indenturam.

Versus Kybaldstrete.

v s. De domo quam Margeria Stephene tenet per annum.

v s. De domo prox. quam Willelmus Carpunter tenet per annum.

v s. De domo prox. quam Ioh' Gardener tenet per annum.

iii s. De domo cornerii iuxta uenellam in Kybaldstrete quam Will' Knyt tenuit.

Infra portam orientalem ex parte boriali.

xiii s. iiii d. De domo cum schopa iuxta uenellam [1] quam Thomas Catur tenet per indenturam.

xii s. De domo prox. quam Ioh' Fleccher tenet per annum.

xviii s. De domo prox. cum schopa quam Thomas Carpunter tenet per annum.

[1] i.e. the lane which ran northward inside the wall of the City.

xxv s. De domo prox. cum schopa quam Phil' Carpunter tenet per indenturam.

xx s. De domo prox. cum schopa quam Ioh' Sawer tenet per annum.

F. x d. De domo Katerine Bere.

xvi s. viii d. De domo prox. quam Thomas Bruere tenet per annum.

v s. De gardinis iuxta cimiterium ecclesie sancti Petri ex parte orientali quos uicarius eiusdem ecclesie tenet per indenturam.

vi s. De selda prox. aule Regine quam Ioh' Swon tenet per annum.

vi s. De selda prox. quam Ioh' Coke tenet per annum.

vi s. De selda prox. quam Ioh' Coke tenet per annum.

vi s. De selda prox. quam Will' Carter tenet per annum.

v s. De selda prox. quam Ioh' Bruer tenet per annum.

iiii s. De selda prox. quam Alicia Baker tenet per annum.

v s. De alta camera supra dictam seldam, quam Ioh' Coke tenet per annum.

xx s. De domo cornerii; Isabella Schepester tenet per annum.

viii s. De selda proxima; Iohannes tenet per annum.

x s.
iii s. iiii d. } [*As in the last rental.*]
ii s.

xxii s. De aula Katerine cum ii seldis & gardino quam Hugo Burgeys tenet per indenturam.

xxiiii s. iiii d. De domo prox. cum schopa quam Will' Southam tenet cum paruo gardino de tenemento Roberti Pulford per indenturam.

xxxii s. iiii d. De domo prox. cum iii schopis, quam Rob. Pulford tenet per indenturam.

xiii s. iiii d. De selda prox., quam Ricardus Irishe, coke, tenet per indenturam.

xvi s. De selda prox., quam Iohannes Staynthorpe, scriptor, tenet per annum.

ii s. De domo Charnel cum selda ex opposito Smythgate quam Agnes Bedel tenet per annum & gardinum est.

Parochia sancte Marie Virginis; in Cattestrete.

xx s. }
xx s. } [*As in the last rental.*]

F. vii s. vi d. De tenemento Ade de Howtone quod Ioh' Dosier tenet.

F. iiii s. De domo Abraham quam Ioh' Gynes tenet.

xxx s. De domo Lodelowe cum i gardino infra scolas in Catstrete quam Robertus Conyng tenet per indenturam.

xxvi s. viii d. De domo quam Iuliana Graciere tenet ad terminum uite & per annum postea.

xiii s. iiii d. De duabus seldis in cimiterio quas Ioh' Kooke tenet per annum.

xxiii s. iiii d. De domo Basyng cum schop' quam Ioh' Peyntour tenet per annum.

xxviii s. De duabus seldis prox. quas Rogerus Latoner tenet per indenturam.

x s. De duabus seldis prox. quas Robertus Barbour tenet per indenturam.

F. xii d. De i gardino infra domum Iuliane Garlond.

Parochia Omnium Sanctorum.

xxiiii s. De selda Wytwongg quam Steph' Polmorua tenet per indenturam.

xx s. De ii schoppis quas Ioh' Heed tenet per indenturam.

xxiii s. iiii d. De aula retro ecclesiam Omnium Sanctorum in angulo quam Robertus Goldsmith tenet per indenturam.

viii s. viii d. De domo proxima iuxta uiam[1] quam Nicholaus Goldsmyth tenet per uxorem Iohannis Bromleye per indenturam.

vi s. viii d. De scola quam Ioh' Holeweye sclatter tenet per indenturam.

xiii s. iiii d. De selda subtus Stodeley quam Will' Borow tenet per annum.

xiii s. iiii d. De alia selda ibidem quam Ioh' Chesleshampton tenet per annum.

F. vii s. De tenemento Hengseye quondam Iohannis Stodleye in cornerio quod extendit se iuxta uenellam que ducit ad ecclesiam sancti Edwardi.

[1] i.e. Turl Street.

c s. De domo Swenebrok cum schoppis quam Adam de la Riuer tenet per indenturam.

xiiii s. De domo Alicie Nubury in Bocheria quam Iohannes Manciple modo tenet de procuratoribus ecclesie Omnium Sanctorum et ipsi tenent ad terminum xl annorum, de quibus xl annis fluxerunt xxvi et remanent xiiii anni.

Parochia sancti Martini.

F. iiii s. De domo Orlyens quam Ioh' Blode tenet.

F. iii s. De domo Alicie Welles quam Ioh' Wakeman tenuit.

F. x s. De introitu Kyngestone quam Thomas Somersete tenet per indenturam.

xix s. De selda Croxforde quam Ioh' Sadeler tenet per indenturam.

xvii s. De selda Croxforde quam Ric' Browne tenet per annum.

F. ii s. De i gradu inter schoppas predictas, pro quo Prior Frideswyde soluit.

F. ii s. De solario Henrici Gamage.

F. vi s. viii d. De selda in sutoria Gilberti de Winchcombe quam Ric' Forester tenet per cartam.

F. iiii s.
F. i d. } [*As in the last rental.*]

Parochia sancti Iohannis.

viii d. De domo Ricardi Hayle in Kybaldestret; modo est gardinum iuxta aulam Willelmi.

v s. De domo Henrici Luminatoris quam Ioh' Rede tenet per indenturam.

F. viii s. De aula Gayler prox. cum schopa quam Alicia Perys tenet.

F. ii s. De aula Trymstede prox., quam eadem tenet.

x s. De ii seldis Balle cum una domo infra edificata, quam Ioh' Boset tenet per indenturam.

Parochia sancti Michaelis australis.

xvi s. De domo Bolstras quam Ioh' Abyndone tenet per annum.

viii s. De domo Meteburne quam Ioh' Sclyford masoun tenet per indenturam.

x s. De domo Ricardi Mason quam Thomas Kymber tenet per indenturam.

F. ii s. De aula Mariol ex parte occidentali quam Margareta Underwalles tenet.

F. xii d. De domo Swyneshulle.

Parochia sancti Aldati.

F. xiii d. De tenemento ex opposito scole in Iudaismo pro quo prepositus Baylyhalle soluet.

xii s. De tenemento Duclyngton, pro quo Iuliana Gibbes soluet & tenet per cartam.

xlvi s. viii d. De domo Iohannis Kepeharme; Rogerus Cosoure tenet per indenturam.

xiii s. iiii d. De selda prox., quam Ioh' Taylour tenet per indenturam.

xx s. De selda prox. quam Agnes Allestone quondam tenuit & modo tenet Thomas Dagwerthe barbour per indenturam.

xxvi s. viii d. De domo prox. quam Will' Fyscher tenet per annum.

xvi s. De selda prox. quam Ioh' Manciple tenet per annum.

xxiiii s. De domo prox. in cornerio quam Ioh' Clanfeld tenet per indenturam.

vi s. viii d. De parua domo iuxta pistrinam quam Ioh' Cooke tenet per annum.

F. ii s. De tenemento Plumbatoris quod Ric' Garston, alias mercer, tenet de Regali Loco.

xvi s. De domo noua iuxta cimiterium sancti Aldati quam Thomas Kary tenet per annum.

Parochia sancte Ebbe.

xviii s. De curia Lincoln' quam Ioh' Lymnowr tenet per annum.

i d. De ii schopis quas Margareta Ryng tenet in cornerio cum uacua placia.

xiii s. iiii d. De domo Stanlake quam Will' Mancipul tenet per indenturam.

ix s. De domo Waryn in paruo Ballio quod Ioh' Baker tenet per annum.

vi s. viii d. De domo sub muro quam Reginaldus Tanner tenet per indenturam.

F. viii s. iiii d. De domo prox. ex parte occidentali, pro quo Prior Frideswyde soluit.

F. iiii s. De tenemento Brymstere quod est gardinum quod Ioh' Croydon tenet.

Parochia sancti Michaelis borialis.

xxxiii s. iiii d. De aula Blankenye cum ii seldis quam Will' Daguyle tenet per indenturam.

Parochia sancti Thome.

xiii s. iiii d. De tenemento quondam Willelmi Wodesdon iuxta paruum pontem quod abbas de Oseneye tenet per indenturam.

Parochia beate Marie Magdalene.

F. ii s. De tenemento Duclyntone.

F. xii d. De tenemento Dodeford.

F. ii s. De tenemento Iohannis Sawcer quod idem Iohannes tenet.

x s. De domo Welles quam Ioh' Hosteler tenet per indenturam.

F. iii s. De tenemento quondam Walteri de Wygornia quod Iohannes Gyrtone tenet.

De una placia uacua iuxta portam fratrum Carmel'.

De alia placia uacua ex opposito porte de Brokenheys quam Iohannes Wakeman [1] tenuit.

Ex parte orientali.

F. vii s. De introitu Henrici Bramptone quem Will' Cooke tenet modo.

F. iii s. De domo Bost iuxta Cardinalhatte.

F. xii d. De tenemento Duclynton.

x s. De domo Willelmi Stafford quam Thomas Mason tenet per indenturam.

xiii s. iiii d. De domo que quondam uocabatur Dephalle super Candych, quam Ric' Parchemynyr tenet per cartam.

Parochia sancti Egidii.

F. xx d. De terra Iohannis Randulf in Stockwellstrete.

F. xvi d. De ii seldis ibidem que fuerunt Ricardi le Pulter.

[1] Blakeman, MS.

F. iiii s. De domo prox. Roberti de Browtone quam Iohannes Roper tenet per indenturam.

F. xii d. De tenemento abbatisse de Godestowe.

Parochia sancte Crucis.

xviii d. De curia Maynarde super Candych cum i acra terre arabilis in Bellomonte situata inter terram aule Mertonis, quam Will' Carpenter tenet per indenturam.

viii s. De domo prima iuxta Crowell quam Ioh' Hamond tenet per annum.

vi s. viii d. De secunda domo prox. quam Ioh' Furneys bocher tenet per annum.

iiii s. De tercia domo prox. Henr' Okam, quam Ioh' Salman tenet per annum.

xviii d. De uno gardino retro domum Okam.

iiii s. De una placia uacua prox. uenelle ex parte australi.

xii d. De una placia uacua prox. uenelle ex parte boriali cum terra.

iiii s. De domo prox. le Sawer.

ii s. De secunda domo iuxta le Sawer.

ii s. De parua domo iuxta ecclesiam.

De domo una quondam Henrici Brakleye cum terra.

xviii d. De i domo de nouo edificata ex opposito cimiterio ecclesie predicte cum ii buttis in Bellomonte.

De domibus clericorum.

iii li. vi s. viii d. De aula uocata Burwaldescote quam mag. Ioh' Cotesford tenet.

xlvi s. viii d. De aula uocata Inghalle quam mag. Thomas Mockyng tenet.

xl s. De aula uocata Bostarhalle quam mag. Laurentius tenet.

xvi s. De aula uocata Harehalle.

xlvi s. viii d. De aula uocata Chymenyhalle cum magno gardino.

xviii s. De aula uocata Nyghtyngalehalle quam Iohannes tenet.

xxvi s. viii d. De aula uocata Haristotilhalle quam mag. Ioh' Stoneham tenet.

xvi s. De aula uocata Knyghthalle quam Ioh' Ardynton tenet.

xx s. De aula uocata Mynothalle quam Ioh' Russell tenet.

xx s. De aula uocata Depehalle quam Ioh' Lane tenet.
ii s. De aula Willelmi quod est gardinum iuxta aulam Scakcarii.
ii s. De aula uocata Brackeleyehalle cum aliis ii aulis super Candych quam Ioh' Mancipul, wallicus, tenet.
xl s. De magna scola in Cattestreet.
xiii s. De introitu sancti Iohannis quam Iohannes Coke tenet.
xvi d. De aula uocata Herthalle in uico sancti Iohannis pro qua prepositus Baliolhalle soluit.
iii s. iiii d. De aula uocata Hamurhalle quam mag. Galfridus Wyke tenet.

32. **A rental of Dec. 21, 1391.**

Rentale ville Oxonie de domo sancti Iohannis extra portam orientalem, factum per fratrem Ricardum Tuwe tunc procuratorem ibidem a festo sancti Thome apostoli anno regni regis Ricardi ii post conquestum quintodecimo usque ad idem festum in anno tunc proximo sequente.

Parochia sancti Clementis.

[ ] De domo iuxta uenellam ; Henricus Chapman tenet per annum.

[*The rest as in the next rental.*]

Parochia sancti Petri extra portam orientalem ex parte australi.

[*The first seven tenements as in the next rental.*]

vi s. viii d. De domo prox. quam Symon Syneker tenet per annum.
xvi s. De domo Pille quam Galfridus Scriptor tenet per annum.
F. xx d.
i lib. thuris } [*As in the next rental.*]

Ex parte boriali.

[*The first seven tenements as in the next rental.*]

v s. De selda quam Nicholaus Kent tenet per annum.

[*The next five tenements as in the next rental.*]

iiii s. De prima selda extra portam orientalem quam [*blank*].
iiii s. De secunda selda quam Henricus Swon tenet per annum.
iiii s. De tercia selda quam Ricardus Bromfeld, cobeler, tenet per annum.

Infra portam orientalem ex parte australi.

[*As in the next rental.*]

Contra muros uille uersus Kybaldestret.

iiii s. De domo quam Iohannes Lyncoln, coce, tenet per annum.

[*The rest as in the next rental.*]

Infra portam orientalem ex parte boriali.

xiii s. iiii d.
xii s.
xiii s. iiii d. } [*As in the next rental.*]

xxv s. De domo prox. cum shopa quam Philippus Carpunter tenet per indenturam.

[*The next eight tenements as in the next rental.*]

iiii s. De quinta selda prox. quam Iuliana [*blank*].

ii s. De sexta selda prox. quam Alicia Baker tenet per annum.

iiii s. De alta camera supra dictam seldam quam Ioh' Coce tenet per annum.

xx s. De domo cornarii quam [*blank*].

viii s.
x s.
iii s. iiii d.
ii s.
xvi s.
xxiiii s. iiii d.
xxxii s. iiii d. } [*As in the next rental*].

xiii s. iiii d. De selda prox. quam Ricardus Yrysche, coce, tenet per annum.

xvi s. De selda prox. quam Iohannes Staynthorp, scriptor, tenet per annum.

De domo Charnel ex opposito Smithgate.

Parochia sancte Marie; in Cattestrete.

xx s. De domo Leuertone quam Rob. Bokebynder tenet per indenturam.

xx s. De domo Faunt quam Will' Hereford, lymnour, tenet per indenturam.

F. vii s. vi d.
F. iiii s.
xxx s.
xxvi s. viii d. } [*As in the next rental.*]

v s. De selda in cimiterio beate Marie quam Ioh' Spenser, alutarius, tenet per annum.

[*The rest as in the next rental.*]

Parochia Omnium Sanctorum.

xx s. De domo Wytewonge quam Urinus Cissor tenet per annum.

viii s. De shopa subtus cameram Burwaldescote quam Philippus Huphold tenet per annum.

[*The rest as in the next rental.*]

Parochia sancti Martini.
Parochia sancti Iohannis. } [*As in the next rental.*]

Parochia sancti Michaelis australis.

xvi s.
viii s. } [*As in the next rental.*]

x s. De domo Ricardi Mason quam Thomas Kymber tenet per indenturam.

F. ii s.
F. xii d. } [*As in the next rental.*]

Parochia sancti Aldati.

F. xii d.
xii s.
xlvi s. viii d. } [*As in the next rental.*]

xiii s. iiii d. De selda prox. quam Iuliana Hulle tenet per indenturam.

[*The rest as in the next rental.*]

Parochia sancte Ebbe.
Parochia sancti Michaelis borealis.
Parochia sancti Thome.
Parochia sancte Marie Magdalene.
Parochia sancti Egidii.
Parochia sancte Crucis. } [*As in the next rental.*]

De domibus clericorum.

liii s. iiii d. De aula Burwaldescote quam Edwardus Dawndeseye tenet.

xxxvi s. viii d. De aula uocata Inghalle quam Thomas Mockyng tenet.

xl s. De aula uocata Borstalhalle quam Thomas Duffeld tenet.

xvi s. De aula uocata Harehalle quam Iohannes Furede tenet.

xxxvi s. viii d. De aula uocata Chymnyhalle quam Laurentius Samborne tenet.

x s. De gardino annexo quem idem Laurentius tenet.

xvi s. De aula uocata Niȝthyngalehalle quam Thomas Smyth tenet.

xxiiii s. De aula uocata Aristotilhalle quam Iohannes Gambulgeye tenet.

xiii s. iiii d. De aula uocata Knyȝthalle quam Iohannes Ardyntone tenet.

xx s. De aula uocata Minothalle quam Will. Botener tenet.

xx s. De aula uocata Dephalle[1] quam Iohannes Lane tenet.

ii s. De aula Willelmi quod est gardinum, quam Thomas Turke tenet.

De aula uocata Brackelehalle super Candiche cum aliis duabus aulis uocatis Boydynhalle maiore & minore, iam unicum gardinum quam Iohannes Manciple, wallicus, tenet.

xl s. De scola in Cattestret quam Iohannes Fayrewode tenet

vi s. viii d. De introitu sancti Iohannis quem Ricardus Sawlo tenet.

xvi d.
iii s. iiii d. } *[As in the next rental.]*

33. A rental of Dec. 21, 1392.

Rentale uille Oxon de domo sancti Iohannis extra portam orientalem factum per fratrem Hugonem tunc procuratorem ibidem, a festo sancti Thome apostoli anno regni regis Ricardi secundi post conquestum sextodecimo.

Parochia sancti Clementis.

ix s. In primum de domo iuxta uenellam quam Iohannes Bratford tenet per annum.

vi s. viii d. De schopa prox. quam Iohannes Hasele filius Thome Hasele tenet per annum.

iiii s. De secunda schopa prox. quam Rogerus Alutarius tenet per annum.

vi s. De tercia schopa prox. quam Thomas Hasele tenet per annum.

[1] i. e. formerly Mildred Hall.

xii s. De duabus schopis prox. quas predictus Thomas tenet per indenturam.

xiii s. iiii d. De domo prox. cum schopa quam Iohannes Pidyngton tenet per indenturam.

Parochia sancti Petri extra portam orientalem ex parte australi.

xviii d. De domo proxima prato uocato Parys quam Iohannes Sawer tenet per indenturam.

De domo prox. quam Willelmus Knyȝthe pro amore dei tenet.

vi s. viii d. De domo prox. quam Alicia Dey tenet per annum.

vi s. viii d. De domo prox. quam [*blank*].

vi s. viii d. De domo prox. quam Robertus Baker tenet per annum.

vi s. viii d. De domo prox. quam Willelmus Mulward tenet per annum.

xiii s. iiii d. De duabus domibus quas Iohannes Stabeler, webbe, tenet per annum.

vi s. viii d. De domo prox. quam Ricardus Palfreymon tenet per annum.

xvi s. De domo Pille prox. quam Iohannes Spyrewit tenet per annum.

F. xx d. De domo Byx situata iuxta portam sancte Frideswide, quam Prior Frideswide soluit.

i lib. thuris. De tenementis uenditis comiti Cornubie, pro quibus frater sancte Trinitatis soluit.

Ex parte boriali.

xii s. De domo prox. porte domus nostre.

viii s. De secunda domo prox. quam Willelmus Bruwer tenet per annum.

viii s. De tercia domo prox. quam Iohannes Hykkes tenet per annum.

viii s. De quarta domo prox. quam Thomas Carpunter tenet per annum.

viii s. De quinta domo prox. quam Henricus Stanweye allutarius tenet per annum.

xvi s. De sexta domo prox. quam Iohannes Thacham tenet per annum.

De septima domo prox. quam Nicholaus Sclatter tenet ad terminum uite.

iv s. De selda quam Nicholaus Kente tenet per annum.

xvi s. De domo prox. quam idem Nicholaus tenet per annum.
xii s. De domo prox. quam Iohannes Coce tenet per annum.
vi s. viii d. De domo prox. quam Agnes Collus tenet per annum.
v s. De selda prox. quam Iohannes Hampton tenet per annum.
xxvi s. viii d. De domo prox. cum schop[is] quam Iohannes Wady, faber, tenet per indenturam.
iiii s. De prima selda extra portam orientalem quam Willelmus Telby tenet.
iiii s. De secunda selda quam Henricus Swon tenet per annum.
iiii s. De tercia selda quam Iohannes Smeth tenet per annum.

Infra portam orientalem.

xi s. De schopa quam Thomas Coce tenet per annum.
xi s. De secunda schopa quam Iohannes Coce tenet per annum.
xii s. iiii d. De domo Cloptone quam Rogerus Chiddesle tenet per indenturam.

Contra muros uille uersus Kybaldestret.

iiii s. De domo quam [*blank*] tenet per annum.
iiii s. De domo prox. quam Iohannes Excetre tenet per annum.
iiii s. De domo prox. quam Robertus Coce tenet per annum.
ii s De domo cornerii in Kybaldstret quam Thomas Belle tenet per annum.

Infra portam orientalem ex parte boriali.

xiii s. iiii d. De domo cum schopa iuxta uenellam quam Hugo Drake tenet per annum.
xii s. De domo prox. quam Thomas Coton tenet per annum.
xiii s. iiii d. De domo prox. cum schopa quam Matyld' Clynton tenet per annum.
xxv s. De domo prox. cum schopa quam Philippus Carpenter tenet per annum.
xx s. De domo prox. cum schopa quam Thomas Geddyg clerk tenet per annum.
F. x d. De domo Katerine Bere.
xiii s. iiii d. De domo prox. quam Thomas Bruwer tenet per annum.
v s. De gardinis iuxta cimiterium ecclesie sancti Petri ex parte orientali quos uicarius eiusdem ecclesie tenet per indenturam.

vi s. De prima selda iuxta aulam Regine quam Thomas Bruwer tenet.

vi s. De secunda selda prox. quam Willelmus Carpunter tenet per annum.

vi s. De tercia selda prox. quam Iohannes Coce tenet per annum.

vi s. De quarta selda prox. quam Thomas Chaundeler tenet per annum.

iiii s. De quinta selda prox. quam Alicia tenet per annum.

ii s. De sexta selda prox. quam Alicia Baker tenet per annum.

iiii s. De alta camera supra dictam seldam.

xx s. De domo cornerii quam Thomas Stafford tenet.

viii s. De selda proxima quam Iohannes Hupholde tenet per annum.

x s. De introitu sancti Nicholai quem prepositus aule Regine tenet per indenturam.

iii s. iiii d. De domo prox. quam idem prepositus tenet per indenturam.

ii s. De domo Glattone prox. quam idem prepositus tenet per indenturam.

xvi s. De aula Katerine cum duabus seldis & gardino quam Hugo Burgeys tenet per indenturam.

xxiiii s. iiii d. De domo prox. cum schopa & cum paruo gardino de tenemento Roberti Pulford quam W. Sowtham tenet per indenturam.

xxxii s. iiii d. De domo prox. cum schop' quam Robertus Pulford tenet per indenturam.

xiii s. iiii d. De selda prox.

xvi s. De selda prox. quam Iohannes Staynthorp scriptor tenet per annum.

De domo Charnel exoposito Smythgate.

x s. De shopa prox. Blakhalle.

xii s. De secunda shopa.

xiii s. De tercia shopa.

Parochia sancte Marie Virginis; in Cattestrete.

xx s. De domo Leuertone quam Robertus Bokbynder tenet per indenturam.

xx s. De domo Fawnt quam W. Luminor tenet per indenturam.

F. vii s. vi d. De tenemento Ade Howtone quod Iohannes Dosyer tenet.

F. iiii s. De domo Habraham.

xxx s. De domo Lodlowe cum schop' & cum uno gardino infra introitum sancti Iohannis quam Robertus Conyng tenet per indenturam.

xxvi s. viii d. De domo quam Iuliana Grasier tenet ad terminum uite & per unum annum post.

v s. De selda in cimiterio beate Marie.

v s. De selda proxima quam Iohanna Kydewelly tenet per annum.

xxiii s. iiii d. De domo Basyng cum schopa quam Iohannes Peyntur tenet per annum.

xx s. De duabus seldis in cornerio quas Rogerus Latoner tenet per indenturam.

x s. De duabus seldis prox. quas Robertus Barbour tenet ad terminum uite.

F. xii d. De uno gardino infra clausuram Iuliane Garlond quam idem Iuliana tenet, soluend' ad festum Michaelis.

Parochia Omnium Sanctorum.

xx s. De domo Wytewonge quam Urinus Cissor tenet per annum.

viii s. De schopa subtus cameram Burwaldescote quam Robertus Marchant tenet per annum.

viii s. De schopa prox. quam Iohannes Ware tenet per annum.

xxiiii s. De aula retro ecclesiam Omnium Sanctorum quam Willelmus Brasyer tenet per annum.

viii s. iiii d. De domo iuxta uenellam quam Nicholaus Goldsmyth tenet per annum.

vi s. viii d. De scola quam Iohannes Holewey tenet per indenturam.

viii s. De selda subtus Stodle quam Iohannes Brasyer tenet per annum.

x s. De alia selda quam Iohannes Chislamptone tenet per annum.

F. vii s. De tenemento Hengseye quondam Iohannis Stodley in cornerio quod extendit se in uenellam que ducit ad ecclesiam sancti Edwardi.

c s. De domo Swynbrok cum schop' quam Adam Riuer tenet per indenturam.

xiiii s. De domo Alicie Newbury in bocheria quam Iohannes Botestone tenet de procuratoribus ecclesie Omnium Sanctorum, pro qua domo idem procuratores reddere debent post terminum lx annorum xxviii s.; de quibus annis fluxerunt xxvii anni.

Parochia sancti Martini.

F. iiii s. De domo Thome Orliente quam Iohannes Blode tenuit olim.

F. iii s. De domo Alicie Welles quam Iohannes Wakeman tenet cum una placia uacua iuxta fratres Carmel'.

F. x s. De introitu Kyngestone quam Thomas Somerset tenet.

xvii s. De selda Croxford quam Willelmus Furbur tenet per indenturam.

xv s. De selda prox. quam Galfridus Stillyntone tenet per annum.

F. ii s. De uno gradu inter schopas predictas pro quo Prior sancte Frideswide soluere deberet.

F. ii s. De solario Henrici Gamage.

F. vi s. viii d. De selda in sutoria Gylberti de Wynchecombe quam Lambertus Forester tenet per indenturam.

F. iiii s. De selda in quadriuio quam Bartholomeus Tauerner tenet.

F. i d. De domo in ballio sancti Petri.

Parochia sancti Iohannis.

viii d. De domo Ricardi Hayle in Kybaldestret: modo est gardinum iuxta aulam Willelmi quam Iuliana Attecorner tenet.

v s. De domo Henrici Illuminatoris quam Iohannes Rede tenet per indenturam.

F. viii s. De aula Gaylier prox. cum schopa quam Alicia Perys tenet.

F. ii s. De aula Trimstede [*sic*] quam eadem tenet.

x s. De duabus seldis Balk' [*sic*] cum quodam curtilagio adiacente quam Iohannes Boset tenet per indenturam.

Parochia sancti Michaelis australis.

xvi s. De domo Bolstras quam Iohannes Abyndone tenet per annum.

viii s. De domo Meteburne quam Iohannes Slyford tenet per indenturam.

x s. De domo Ricardi Masun quam Thomas [*ends*].

F. ii s. De aula Mariol ex parte occidentali quam Margareta Manciple tenet.

F. xii d. De tenemento Swyneshulle.

Parochia sancti Aldati.

F. xii d. De tenemento exoposito schole in Iudaysmo pro quo prepositus Baliolhalle soluit ad terminum Marie Magdalene.

xii s. De tenemento Bokelintone [*sic*] pro quo Iuliana Gybbes soluit & tenet per indenturam.

xlvi s. viii d. De domo Iohannis Kepeharm quam Rogerus Euerard, corsur, tenet per indenturam.

xiii s. iiii d. De selda proxima.

xx s. De selda prox. quam Edmundus Barbur tenet per indenturam.

xxi s. De domo prox. quam Rogerus Kouele, fyscher, tenet per annum.

xvi s. De selda prox. quam Iohannes Hood, cotoler, tenet per annum.

xxiiii s. De domo prox. in cornerio quam Iohannes Clanfeld tenet per indenturam.

vi s. De parua domo iuxta pistum quam Nicholaus Coce tenet per annum.

F. ii s. De tenemento Plumbatoris quod Ricardus Garston[1] tenet.

xvi s. De noua domo iuxta cimiterium sancti Aldati quam Iohannes Selle capellanus tenet per annum.

Parochia sancte Ebbe.

xviii s. De curia Lincoln' quam Iohannes Wapyngburi, limnour, tenet per indenturam.

i d. De duabus schoppis in cornerio quas Margareta Ryng tenet.

xiii s. iiii d. De domo Stanlake quam Willelmus Wanting, manciple, tenet per indenturam.

viii s. De tenemento Waryn in paruo ballio quod Willelmus Rowe, bruwer, tenet per annum.

[1] Written Grafton, but apparently altered.

vi s. viii d. De domo Allestone sub muro uille quam Reginaldus Tanner tenet per indenturam.

F. viii s. iiii d. De domo prox. ex parte occidentali pro qua Prior sancte Frideswide soluit.

F. iiii s. De tenemento Brymster quod Reginaldus Tanner tenet.

Parochia sancti Michaelis borealis & sancti Thome.

xxxiii s. iiii d. De aula Blankenye cum ii seldis quam Willelmus Daguyle tenet per indenturam.

xiii s. iiii d. De ten[ementis] quondam Willelmi Wodesdone iuxta paruum pontem inter Castrum & Osnye, que abbas de Osney tenet per indenturam.

Parochia sancte Marie Magdalene ex parte occidentali.

F. ii s. De tenemento Duclyntone.

F. xii d. De tenemento Dudeford.

F. ii s. De tenemento I. Sawser.

x s. De domo Welles quam Agnes Hosteler tenet per indenturam.

F. iii s. De tenemento quondam Walteri de Wygornia.

De una placea uacua iuxta portam fratrum Karmel'.

De alia placea uacua exoposito porte de Brokynheyis quam Iohannes Wakeman tenet.

Ex parte orientali in eadem parochia.

F. vii s. De introitu Henrici Bramptone quem Willelmus Coce tenet.

F. iii s. De domo Rogeri Bost iuxta Cardinalhat.

F. xii d. De tenemento Douckelyntone.

x s. De domo Willelmi Stafford quam Thomas Mason tenet per indenturam.

xiii s. iiii d. De domo quondam uocata Dephalle super Candych quam Ricardus Parchiminer tenet per indenturam.

Parochia sancti Egidii.

F. xx d. De terra Iohannis Radulfi in Stokwelstret.

F. xvi d. De secunda selda[1] ibidem que fuerunt Ricardi le Pulter.

iiii s. De domo prox. Roberti de Browtone quam Iohannes Roper tenet per indenturam.

F. xii d. De tenemento abbatisse de Godestowe.

[1] This is an error of the scribe for 'De ii seldis', as other rentals show.

Parochia sancte Crucis.

xviii d. De curia Maynard super Candych cum una acra terre arabilis in Bellomonte situata inter terram aule Mertone quam Willelmus Carpunter tenet per indenturam.

viii s. De prima domo iuxta Crowell quam Iohannes Hamond tenet per annum.

vi s. viii d. De secunda domo prox. quam Iohannes Forneys tenet per annum.

iii s. iiii d. De tercia domo prox. Henric' Okam quam idem Iohannes tenet per annum.

De uno gardino retro domum Okam quod idem Iohannes tenet per annum.

De una placia uacua prox. uenelle ex parte boriali cum terra.

De una placia uacua prox. uenelle ex parte australi.

De domo prox. le Sawer.

De domo secunda iuxta le Sawer.

De parua domo iuxta ecclesiam.

De domo quondam Henrici le [*sic*] Brakkeley cum terra.

xviii d. De una domo de nouo edificata exoposito cimiterio ecclesie predicte cum duabus buttis in Bellomonte quam Iohannes Dosyer tenet per indenturam.

De domibus clericorum.

liii s. iiii d. De aula Burwaldescote quam Edwardus Dawnshey tenet.

xxxvi s. viii d. De aula uocata Inghalle quam Thomas Mockyng tenet.

{ xl s. De aula uocata Borstalhalle quam Thomas Duffeld tenet.
{ xvi s. De aula uocata Harehalle.

{ xxxvi s. viii d. De aula uocata Chymnyhalle.
{ x s. De gardino annexo.
{ xvi s. De aula uocata Niȝthyngale halle.

xxiiii s. De aula uocata Aristotilhalle.

xiii s. iiii d. De aula uocata Knyȝthalle quam Iohannes Ardyntone tenet.

xx s. De aula uocata Minothall.

xx s. De aula uocata Dephalle quam Iohannes Lane.

ii s. De aula Willelmi quod est gardinum.

De aula uocata Brackelehalle super Candiche cum aliis duabus aulis uocatis Boydynhalle maiore & minore, iam unicum gardinum quam Iohannes Manciple, wallicus, tenet.

xl s. De scola in Cattestret quam magister Iohannes Lauyngtone tenet.

vi s. viii d. De introitu sancti Iohannis predicte scole annexo.

xvi d. De aula uocata Herthall in uico sancti Iohannis quam prepositus Baliol tenet, soluend' ad terminum Marie Magdalene.

iii s. iiii d. De aula uocata Hamurhalle iam[1] communis via ex parte australi claustri collegii Wynton' quam custos eiusdem collegii tenet soluendo ad terminum Annunciacionis beate Marie & sancti Michaelis.

Summa totalis rotuli lxxxvii li. xvi s. xi d.

34. A rental of Dec. 21, 1393.

Rentale uille Oxon de domo sancti Iohannis extra portam orientalem, factum per fratrem Willelmum Lodbrok tunc procuratorem ibidem a festo sancti Thome apostoli anno regni regis Ricardi ii post conquestum decimo septimo.

Parochia sancti Clementis.

ix s. In primum de domo iuxta uenellam quam Ioh' Spencer tenet per annum.

vi s. viii d. De schopa prox. quam idem Ioh' tenet per annum.

iiii s. De secunda schopa quam Rog' Alutarius tenet per annum.

vi s. De tercia schopa quam Thomas Hasele tenet per annum.

xii s. De duabus schopis quas predictus Thomas tenet per indenturam.

xiii s. iiii d. De domo prox. cum schopa quam Ioh' Pydyntone tenet per indenturam.

Parochia sancti Petri extra portam orientalem ex parte australi.

xviii d. De domo prox. prato uocato Parys quam Ioh' Sawer tenet per indenturam.

vi s. viii d. De domo prox. quam Will. Knyȝthe tenet per annum.

[1] quam MS.

vi s. viii d. De domo prox. quam Alicia Dey tenet per annum.
vi s. viii d. De domo prox. quam Will. Carter tenet per annum.
vi s. viii d. De domo prox. quam Rob. Baker tenet per annum.
vi s. viii d. De domo prox. quam Will. Muleward tenet per annum.
xiii s. iiii d. De ii schopis quas Ioh' Stabeler, webbe, tenet per annum.
vi s. viii d. De domo prox. quam Magota Stanway tenet per annum.
xiii s. iiii d. De domo Pille quam Ioh' Spyrewyt tenet per annum.
F. xx d. De domo Byx situata iuxta portam sancte Frideswide pro qua Prior Frideswide soluit.
i lib. thuris. De tenementis uenditis Comiti Cornubie pro quibus Prior sancte Trinitatis soluit.

Ex parte boriali.

xii s. De domo prox. porte domus nostre quam Rog' Keruer tenet per annum.
viii s. De secunda domo quam Will' Brwer tenet per annum.
viii s. De tercia domo quam Ioh' Hykkes tenet per annum.
viii s. De quarta domo quam Ric' Coryowr tenet per annum.
viii s. De quinta domo quam Ioh' Sowter tenet per annum.
xvi s. De sexta domo quam Ioh' Thacham tenet per annum.
De septima domo quam Nich. Sclattere tenet ad terminum uite.
vi s. De selda quam Nic. Kente tenet per annum.
xvi s. De domo prox. quam idem Nic. tenet per annum.
xii s. De domo prox. quam Ioh' Coce tenet per annum.
vi s. De domo prox. quam Agnes Colles tenet per annum.
v s. De selda prox. quam Ioh' Hamptone tenet per annum.
xxvi s. viii d. De domo prox. cum schopa quas Ioh' Wady, faber, tenet per indenturam.
iiii s. De prima selda extra portam orientalem quam Ioh' Begger tenet per annum.
iiii s. De secunda selda prox. quam Hen' Swon tenet per annum.
iiii s. De tercia selda prox. quam Ric. Cobeler tenet per annum.

Infra portam orientalem ex parte australi.

xi s. De schopa quam Thomas Coce tenet per annum.

xi s. De secunda schopa quam Ioh' Coce tenet per annum.

xiii s. iiii d. De domo Cloptone quam Rog' Chyddesle tenet per indenturam.

Contra muros uille uersus Kybaldestret.

iiii s. De domo quam Thomas Coce tenet per annum.

iiii s. De domo prox. quam Ioh' Brewer tenet per annum.

iiii s. De domo prox. quam Agnes Typurtone tenet per annum.

ii s. De domo cornerii in Kybaldestret quam Thomas Belle tenet per annum.

Infra portam orientalem ex parte boriali.

xiii s. iiii d. De domo cum schopa iuxta uenellam quam Ioh' Schorier tenet per annum.

xii s. De domo prox. quam Thomas Cook tenet per annum.

xxvi s. viii d. De domo prox. cum scopa quam Ioh' Faber tenet per indenturam.

xxv s. De domo prox. cum schopa quam Phylippus Carpenter tenet per annum.

xx s. De domo prox. cum schopa quam Thomas Geddyng clerk tenet per annum.

F. x d. De domo Katerine Bere.

xxiii s. iiii d. De domo prox. quam Thomas Brwer tenet per annum.

v s. De gardinis cimiterii ecclesie sancti Petri ex parte orientali quos uicarius eiusdem ecclesie tenet per indenturam.

vi s. De i selda iuxta aulam Regine quam Thomas Bruwer tenet per annum.

vi s. De ii selda prox. quam Will. Carpenter tenet per annum.

vi s. De iii selda prox. quam Ioh' Coce tenet per annum.

vi s. De quarta selda prox. quam Thomas Chaundeler tenet per annum.

iiii s. De quinta selda prox. quam Alicia cum uno brachio tenet per annum.

ii s. De sexta selda prox. quam Alicia Baker tenet per annum.

iiii s. De alta camera supra dictam seldam quam cocus aule Regine tenet per annum.

xvi s. De domo cornerii quam Thomas Stafford tenet per annum.

viii s. De selda prox. quam Ioh' Huphold tenet per annum.

x s. De introitu sancti Nicholai quam prepositus aule Regine tenet per indenturam.

iii s. iiii d. De domo prox. quam prepositus aule Regine tenet per indenturam.

ii s. De domo Glattone prox. quam prepositus aule Regine tenet per indenturam.

xvi s. De aula Katerine cum ii seldis & gardino quam Will. Cook tenet per annum.

xxiiii s. iiii d. De domo prox. cum scopa & cum paruo gardino de tenemento Roberti Pulford quam W. Sowtham tenet per indenturam.

xxxii s. iiii d. De domo prox. cum schopa quam Rob. Pulford tenet per indenturam.

xii s. De selda prox. quam W. Sowtham tenet per annum.

xvi s. De selda prox. quam Ioh' Staynthorp tenet per annum.

De domo Charnel exoposito Smythgate.

x s. De i schopa prox. Blakhall quam Ioh' Scriptor tenet per annum.

x s. De ii schopa prox. quam Ioh' Parchemyner tenet per annum.

xiii s. De iii schopa prox. quam Ioh' Gy[rdl]emaker tenet per annum.

Parochia sancte Marie Virginis.

xx s. De domo Leuerton quam Rob. Bokbynder tenet per indenturam.

xx s. De domo Fawnt quam Ioh' Brother, lymnor, tenet per indenturam.

F. vii s. vi d. De ten. Ade Howton quod Ioh' Dosyer tenet.

F. iiii s. De domo Abraham quam Hen. Lymnor tenet.

xxx s. De domo Lodlowe cum schop' & cum i gardino infra introitum sancti Iohannis quam Rob. Conyng tenet per indenturam.

xxvi s. viii d. De domo quam Iuliana Grasyer tenet ad terminum uite & per i annum post.

v s. De selda in cimiterio beate Marie.

v s. De selda quam Iohanna Kydewelly tenet per annum.

xxiii s. iiii d. De domo Basyng cum schopa quam Ioh' Peyntour tenet per annum.

xx s. De duabus seldis in cornerio quas Rog' Latoner tenet per indenturam.

xvi s. De duabus seldis quas Rog' Barbour tenet ad terminum uite.

F. xii d. De i gardino infra clausuram Iuliane Garlond quam eadem Iuliana tenet, soluend' ad festum Michaelis.

Parochia Omnium Sanctorum.

xx s. De domo Wytewong quam Matheus Taylour tenet per annum.

viii s. De scopa subtus cameram Burwaldescote quam Rob. Marchant tenet per annum.

viii s. De schopa prox. quam Ioh' Ware tenet per annum.

xx s. De aula retro ecclesiam Omnium Sanctorum quam Will. Brasyer tenet per annum.

viii s. iiii d. De domo iuxta uenellam quam Nic. Goldsmyth tenet per annum.

vi s. viii d. De scola quam Ioh' Holewey tenet per indenturam.

x s. De selda subtus Stodle quam Will' Borowe tenet per annum.

x s. De alia selda quam Ioh' Chyslamptone tenet per annum.

F. viii s. De tenemento Hengseye quondam Iohannis Stodley in cornerio quod extendit se in uenellam que ducit ad ecclesiam sancti Edwardi.

c s. De domo Swynbrok cum scop' quam Adam Riuer tenet per indenturam.

xiiii s. De domo Alicie Newbury in bocheria quam Ioh' Botestone tenet de procuratoribus ecclesie Omnium Sanctorum, pro qua domo idem procuratores reddere debent post terminum lx annorum xxviii s., de quibus annis fluxerunt xxviii anni.

Parochia sancti Martini.

F. iiii s. De domo Thome Orliente quam Ioh' Blode olim tenuit.

F. iii s. De domo Alicie Welles quam Ioh' Wakeman tenet cum placia uacua iuxta fratres Carmel'.

F. x s. De introitu Kyngestone quam Thomas Somerset tenet.

xvii s. De selda Croxford quam Will' Furbour tenet per indenturam.

xv s. De selda prox. quam Galf' Styllyntone tenet.

F. ii s. De uno gradu inter schopas predictas pro quo Prior sancte Frideswyde soluere deberet.

F. ii s. De solario Henrici Gamage.

F. vi s. viii d. De selda in sutoria Gilberti de Wynchecombe quam Lambertus Forester tenet per indenturam.

F. iiii s. De selda in quadriuio quam Bartholomeus Tauerner tenet.

F. i d. De domo in ballio sancti Petri.

Parochia sancti Iohannis.

viii d. De domo Ricardi Hayle in Kybaldestret modo est gardinum iuxta aulam Willelmi quam Iuliana atte Corner tenet.

v s. De domo Henrici Lymnour quam Ioh' Rede tenet per indenturam.

F. viii s. De aula Gaylier prox. cum schopa quam Alic' Perys tenet.

F. ii s. De aula Trymstede quam eadem tenet.

vi s. viii d. De domo in Gropelane quam Ioh' Baker tenet per annum.

vi s. De i schoppa quam Ioh' Luyde tenet per annum.

vi s. De ii schoppa prox. quam idem Ioh' tenet per annum.

Parochia sancti Michaelis australis.

xiiii s. De domo Bolstras quam Walterus Benet bocher tenet per indenturam.

viii s. De domo Meteburn quam Ioh' Slyforde tenet per indenturam.

x s. De domo Ricardi Masun quam Thomas Warner tenet per annum.

F. ii s. De aula Mariol ex parte occidentali quam Margareta Manciple tenet.

F. xii d. De tenemento Swyneshulle.

Parochia sancti Aldati.

F. xii d. De tenemento ex opposito scole in Iudaysmo.

xii s. De tenemento Bokelyntone [*sic*] pro quo Iuliana Gybbes soluit.

xlvi s. viii d. De domo Iohannis Cepeharm quam Rog' Euerard corsor tenet per indenturam.

xiii s. iiii d. De selda prox.

xviii s. De selda prox. quam Edmundus Barbour tenet per indenturam.

xxi s. De domo prox. quam Rogerus Kouele, fyscher, tenet per annum.

xii s. De selda prox. quam Ioh' Abyndon tenet per indenturam.

xxiiii s. De domo prox. in cornerio quam Ioh' Clanfeld tenet per annum.

vi s. De parua domo iuxta pistum quam Nic. Cook tenet per annum.

F. ii s. De ten. Plumbatoris quod Rog' Grafton [*sic*].

xvi s. De noua domo iuxta cimiterium sancti Aldati.

Parochia sancte Ebbe.

xviii s. De curia Lincoln' quam Ioh' Wapyngbury tenet per indenturam.

i d. De duabus schoppis in cornerio quas Marg' Ryng[1] tenet.

xiii s. iiii d. De domo Stanlake quam Will' Wantyng tenet per indenturam.

viii s. De tenemento Waryn in paruo ballio quod Ioh' Sclatter tenet per annum.

vi s. viii d. De domo Allestone sub muro uille quam Reginaldus Tau*erner* [*sic*] tenet per indenturam.

F. vi s. viii d. De domo prox. ex parte occidentali pro qua Prior sancte Frideswide soluere deberet.

iiii s. De tenemento Brymstere quod Reginaldus Tanner tenet.

Parochia sancti Michaelis borialis & sancti Thome.

xxxiii s. iiii d. De aula Blankenye cum ii seldis quam Will. Daguyle tenet per indenturam.

xiii s. iiii d. De ten. quondam Willelmi Wodesdone iuxta paruum pontem inter castrum & Osney, que abbas de Osney tenet per indenturam.

[1] Kyng, MS. At this time a capital K was much like a capital R, and the clerk in copying the list must have misread the name. Earlier rentals prove that the name was Ryng.

Parochia sancte Marie Magdalene.

F. ii s. De ten. Duclyntone.

F. xii d. De ten. Dudeford.

F. ii s. De ten. I. Sawser.

x s. De domo Welles quam Agnes Hosteler tenet per indenturam.

F. iii s. De ten. quondam Willelmi de Wigornia.

De una placia uacua iuxta portam fratrum Carmel'.

De alia placia uacua exoposito porte de Brokyneheys quam Iohannes Wakeman tenet.

Ex parte orientali in eadem parochia.

F. vii s. De introitu Henrici Bramptone quem Will' Coce.

F. iii s. De domo Rogeri Bost iuxta Cardynalhat.

F. xii d. De ten. Douckelyntone.

x s. De domo Willelmi Stafford quam Thomas Mason tenet per indenturam.

xiii s. iiii d. De domo quondam uocata Dephalle super Candyche quam Ric' Parchymyner tenet per indenturam.

Parochia sancti Egidii.

F. xx d. De terra Iohannis Radulfi in Stokwelstret.

F. xvi d. De ii seldis ibidem que fuerunt Ricardi le Pulter.

iiii s. De domo prox. Robert' de Browtone quam Ioh' Roper tenet per indenturam.

F. xii d. De ten. abbatisse de Godestowe.

Parochia sancte Crucis.

xviii d. De curia Maynard super Candych cum i acra terre arabilis in Bellomonte situat' inter terram aule Mertone quam Will' Carpunter tenet per indenturam.

viii s. De prima domo iuxta Crowell quam Ioh' Hamond tenet.

vi s. viii d. De secunda domo prox. quam Ioh' Forneys tenet per annum.

iii s. iiii d. De tertia domo prox. Henric' Okam quam idem Ioh' tenet.

De uno gardino retro domum Okam quod idem Iohannes.

De una placia uacua prox. uenelle ex parte boriali cum terra.

De una placia uacua prox. uenelle ex parte australi.

De domo prox. le Sawer.

De domo secunda iuxta le Sawer.

De parua domo iuxta ecclesiam.

De domo quondam Henrici le Brakeley cum terra.

xviii d. De una domo de nouo edificata ex oposito cimiterio ecclesie predicte cum ii buttis in Bellomonte quam Ioh' Dosier tenet per indenturam.

De domibus clericorum.

liii s. iiii d. De aula Burwoldescote quam Edwardus Dawnshey tenet.

xxxvi s. viii d. De aula uocata Inghalle quam Thomas Mockyng tenet.

xl s. De aula uocata Borstall Halle quam Thomas Duffeld tenet.

xvi s. De aula uocata Harehalle.

xxxvi s. viii d. De aula uocata Chymnyhalle quam mag. Hamond tenet.

x s. De gardino annexo quem idem magister tenet.

xvi s. De aula uocata Nythyngale Halle quam idem.

xxiiii s. De aula uocata Aristotylle Halle quam Ioh' Gambelgay.

xiiii s. iiii d. De aula uocata Knyȝthall quam Ioh' Ardynton tenet.

xx s. De aula uocata Mynothall quam Pauy tenet.

xx s. De aula uocata Dephall quam Ioh' Lane tenet.

ii s. De aula Willelmi que est gardinum quem rector collegii Exon tenet.

ii s. De aula uocata Brakkelehalle super Candych cum aliis duabus aulis uocatis Boydynhalle maiore et minore iam unicum gardinum quam Ioh' Ma*n*ci,[1] wallicus, tenet.

xl s. De scola in Cattestrete quam mag. Ioh' Lauyngton tenet.

vi s. viii d. De introitu sancti Iohannis predicte scole annexo.

xvi d. De aula uocata Herthalle in uico sancti Iohannis quam prepositus Balliol tenet.

iii s. iiii d. De aula uocata Hamurhalle iam communis uia ex parte australi claustri collegii Wynton quam custos eiusdem collegii tenet.

[1] The previous and subsequent rentals show that this must be an abbreviation for *Manciple*.

[2] quam, MS.

F. iiii s. De aula Hertehalle in uico sancti Iohannis ex parte australi: magistri aule Balliole debent soluere pensionem inde: xv d., quiet'.

35. Part of a rental of Dec. 21, 1394.

Rentale uille Oxon de domo sancti Iohannis extra portam orientalem factum per fratrem Willelmum Lodbrok procuratorem ibidem a festo sancti Thome apostoli anno regni regis Ricardi secundi post conquestum xviii.

Parochia sancti Clementis.

ix s. In primis de domo iuxta uenellam quam Iohannes Spencer tenet per annum.

vi s. viii d. De schopa prox. quam idem Iohannes tenet per annum.

iiii s. De secunda schopa prox. quam Rogerus Alutarius tenet per annum.

vi s. De tertia schopa quam Thomas Hasele tenet per annum.

xii s. De duabus schopis quas predictus Thomas tenet per indenturam.

xiii s. iiii d. De domo prox. cum schopa quam Pydyntone tenet per indenturam.

Parochia sancti Petri extra portam orientalem ex parte australi.

xviii d. De domo prox. prato uocato Parys quam Iohannes Sawer tenet per indenturam.

vi s. viii d. De domo prox. quam Will. Knythe tenet pro amore dei.

vi s. viii d. De domo prox. quam Alicia Dey tenet per annum.

vi s. viii d. De domo prox. quam Ioh. Palfreyman tenet per annum.

vi s. viii d. De domo prox. quam Rob. Baker tenet per annum.

vi s. viii d. De domo prox. quam Will. Muleward tenet per annum.

xiii s. iiii d. De duabus schopis quas Ioh' Stabeler, webbe, tenet per annum.

vi s. viii d. De domo prox. quam Marioria Stanway tenet per annum.

xiii s. iiii d. De domo Pylle quam Ioh' Spyrewyt tenet per annum.

F. xx d. De domo Byx situata iuxta portam sancte Frideswide pro qua Prior Frideswide soluit.

i lib. thuris. De tenementis uenditis Comiti Cornubie pro quibus frater sancte Trinitatis soluit.

Ex parte boriali.

xii s. De domo prox. porte domus nostre quam Rogerus Keruer tenet per annum.

viii s. De secunda domo prox. quam Ioh' Bruwer tenet per annum.

viii s. De tertia domo prox. quam Ioh' Hykkes tenet per annum.

viii s. De quarta domo prox. quam Ric. Coryowre tenet per annum.

viii s. De quinta domo quam Ioh' Sowter tenet per annum.

xviii s. De sexta domo quam Ioh' Brasyer tenet per annum.

De septima domo quam Nicholaus Sclatter tenet ad terminum uite.

v s. De selda quam Willelmus Carter tenet per annum.

xvi s. De domo prox. quam [*sic*].

xii s. De domo prox. quam Ioh' Coce tenet per annum.

vi s. De domo prox. quam Agnes Colles tenet per annum.

v s. De selda prox. quam Ioh' Hampton tenet per annum.

xxvi s. viii d. De domo prox. cum schop' quam Ioh' Wady faber tenet per indenturam.

iiii s. De prima selda extra portam orientalem.

iiii s. De secunda selda prox. quam Ioh' Sowter tenet.

iiii s. De tertia selda prox. quam Ric. Cobeler tenet per annum.

Infra portam orientalem ex parte australi.

xi s. De schop' quam Thomas Coce tenet per annum.

xi s. De secunda schopa quam Ioh' Coce tenet per annum.

xiii s. iiii d. De domo Cloptone quam Rog' Chyddesle tenet per indenturam.

Contra muros uille uersus Kybaldestrete.

iiii s. De domo quam Thomas Coce tenet per annum.

iiii s. De domo prox. quam Ioh' Bruwer tenet per annum.

iiii s. De domo prox. quam Agnes Typurton tenet per annum.

iii s. De domo cornerii in Kybaldestret.

Infra portam orientalem ex parte boriali.

xiii s. iiii d. De domo cum schop' iuxta uenellam quam Ioh' Schoryer tenet per annum.

xii s. De domo prox. quam Thos. Stafforde tenet per annum.

xxiii s. iiii d. De domo prox. cum schop' quam Rob. Marchand tenet per indenturam.

xxv s. De domo prox. cum schop' quam Phil' Carpenter tenet per annum.

xx s. De domo prox. cum schop' quam Thomas Geddyng clerk tenet per annum.

F. x d. De domo Katerine Bere.

xxiiii s. De domo prox. quam Thomas Bruwer tenet per annum.

v s. De gardinis iuxta cimiterium ecclesie sancti Petri ex parte orientali quos uicarius eiusdem ecclesie tenet per indenturam.

vi s. De prima selda iuxta aulam Regine quam Alicia Truloue tenet per annum.

vi s. De secunda selda quam Ioh' Tukker tenet per annum.

vi s. De tercia selda quam Ioh' Coce.

vi s. De quarta selda prox. quam Rog' Alutarius tenet per annum.

iiii s. De quinta selda prox. quam Alicia cum i brachio tenet per annum.

ii s. De sexta selda prox. quam Alicia Baker tenet per annum.

iiii s. De alta camera supra dict' seld' quam Cocus aule Regine tenet per annum.

xviii s. De domo cornerii quam Matilda Gyseborhg tenet per annum.

viii s. De selda prox. quam Ioh' Hupholder tenet per annum.

x s. De introitu sancti Nicholai quam prepositus aule Regine tenet per indenturam.

iii s. iiii d. De domo prox. quam idem prepositus tenet per indenturam.

ii s. De domo Glattone prox. quam idem tenet per indenturam.

xvi s. De aula Katerine cum ii seldis & gardino quam Ioh' Cobeler tenet per annum.

xxiiii s. iiii d. De domo prox. cum schop' & cum paruo gardino de tenemento Roberti Pulford quam Will. Sowtham tenet per indenturam.

xxxii s. iiii d. De domo prox. cum schop' quam Rob. Pulforde tenet per indenturam.

xii s. De selda prox. quam Stephanus Mancyple tenet per annum.

xvi s. De selda prox. quam Ioh' Staynthorp tenet per annum.

i rosa. De selda prox. Blakehall exoposito Smhytgate quam Ioh' Slyford tenet per annum.

x s. De ii selda prox. quam dominus Ric. de Colleg' tenet per annum.

ix s. De iii selda prox. quam Ioh' Scryueyn tenet per annum.

Parochia beate Marie Virginis in Cattestret.

xx s. De domo quam Rob. Bokbynder tenet per indenturam.

xx s. De domo prox. quam Ioh' Brother lymnour tenet per indenturam.

F. vii s. vi d. De tenemento Ade Howton quod Ioh' Dosier tenet.

F. iiii s. De domo quam Hen. Lymnour tenet.

xxx s. De domo cum schop' & cum gardino infra introitum sancti Iohannis quam Rob. Conyng tenet per indenturam.

xxvi s. viii d. De domo quam Iuliana Grasier tenet ad terminum uite & per i annum post.

v s. De selda in cimiterio beate Marie quam Ioh' Kedewelly[1] tenet.

v s. De selda prox.

xxiii s. iiii d. De domo prox. cum schop' quam Ioh' Peyntour tenet.

xxviii s. De ii seldis prox. in cornerio quos Rog' Latoner tenet per indenturam.

xii s. De ii seldis prox. quos Rog. Barbour tenet.

F. xii d. De i gardino infra clausuram Iuliane Garlond quem eadem Iuliana tenet, soluend' ad festum Michaelis.

[*The rest is wanting.*]

[1] 'Iohanna Kedwelly' in the previous rental.

36. A rental of 1395, 1396, or 1397.

The date at the head of the following roll is illegible, but it is certainly subsequent to 1391, for in that year the *Domus Charnel* was still a garden, whereas in this rental, as in the rentals of 1392, 1393, and 1394, it has been rebuilt as three shops. It is earlier than Michaelmas 1398; for the house in the parish of St. Clement, once occupied by John Pydington, is not yet occupied by John of the Chamber (see vol. i, p. 7). This rental is valuable, as it divides the leases into two classes, *cum reparacione* and *sine reparacione*.

Rentale uille Oxonie de domo sancti Iohannis Baptiste extra portam orientalem factum per [fratrem de] Tuwe tunc magistrum ibidem a festo sancti Thome apostoli anno regni regis Ricardi secundi post conquestum [ ] usque ad idem festum in anno tunc prox. reuoluto, fratre Thoma Southam tunc [procuratore ibidem].

Parochia sancti Clementis.

ix s. De domo iuxta uenellam quam Will. Taylour tenet per annum.

vi s. viii d. De selda prox. } quas predictus Willelmus tenet per annum.
iiii s. De secunda selda prox. }

vi s. De tercia selda prox. quam Thomas Hasele tenet per annum.

xii s. De duabus seldis prox. quas predictus Thomas tenet per indenturam.

xvi s. De domo prox. cum shopa quam Ioh' Pydintone tenet per annum.

Parochia sancti Petri extra portam orientalem ex parte australi.

xviii d. De domo prox. Parys quam Ioh' Pope sawer tenet per indenturam.

vi s. viii d. De domo prox.

vi s. viii d. De domo prox.

vi s. viii d. De domo prox.

vi s. viii d. De domo prox.

xiii s. iiii d. De duabus domibus prox. quas Ioh' Stabeler webbe tenet.

vi s. viii d. De domo prox.

xiii s. iiii d. De domo prox.

F. xx d. De domo Bix.

F. ii s. De itinere usque grangiam sancte Frideswyde.

F. i lib. thuris. De tenementis uenditis comiti Cornubie uocatis capella Trinitatis.

Ex parte boriali.

xii s. De domo prox. porte domus predicte quam Ric. Curriour tenet.

viii s. De secunda domo prox.

viii s. De tercia domo prox.

viii s. De quarta domo prox.

viii s. De quinta domo prox.

xvi s. De sexta domo prox. quam Ioh' Manciple tenet per annum.

x s. De septima domo prox. quam Nic' Sclatter tenet ad terminum uite.

xxiiii s. De noua domo cum schopa quam Galf' Taylour tenet per annum.

xiii s. iiii d. De domo prox. quam Thomas Geddynd clerk tenet per indenturam sine reparacione.

vi s. De domo prox. quam Agnes Collus tenet per annum.

v s. De selda prox. quam Ioh' Hampton tenet per annum.

xxvi s. viii d. De domo prox. cum shopa quam Ioh' Wady, smyht, tenet per indenturam cum reparacione.

iiii s. De prima selda extra portam orientalem.

iiii s. De secunda selda.

iiii s. De tercia selda.

Infra portam orientalem ex parte australi.

xi s. De selda.

xi s. De selda prox.

xiii s. iiii d. De domo quam Rog' Chiddesle tenet per indenturam cum reparacione.

Contra muros uille uersus Kybaldestrete.

v s. De domo quam Thomas Cook tenet per annum.

v s. De domo prox. quam Petrus Bruwer tenet per annum.

v s. De domo prox. quam Agnes Tipurtone tenet per annum.

Infra portam orientalem ex parte boriali.

xiii s. iiii d. De domo cum schopa iuxta uenellam quam Will' Shorier carpenter tenet per indenturam cum reparacione, cooperacione excepta.

xii s.	De domo prox. quam Ioh' Catour, souter, tenet.	
xxiii s. iiii d.	De noua domo prox. quam Rob. Marchant tenet per indenturam cum reparacione.	
xxv s.	De domo prox. cum shopa quam Philippus Carpenter tenet per indenturam sine reparacione.	
xxii s.	De domo prox. quam Ioh' Keruer sutor tenet per indenturam cum reparacione.	
F. x d.	De domo quam Katerina Bere tenet.	
xxiiii s.	De domo prox. cum schopa quam Thomas Bruwer tenet per indenturam sine reparacione.	
v s.	De gardinis iuxta cimiterium ecclesie sancti Petri ex parte orientali quos uicarius ecclesie predicte tenet cum reparacione.	
v s.	De prima selda iuxta aulam Regine.	
vi s.	De secunda selda prox.	
vi s.	De tercia selda prox.	
vi s.	De quarta selda prox.	
v s.	De quinta selda prox.	
iiii s.	De sexta selda prox. quam Alicia Baker tenet per annum.	
iiii s.	De alta camera supra dictam seldam.	
xvi s.	De domo cornerii.	
viii s.	De selda prox. quam Ioh' Huphold tenet per annum.	
x s.	De introitu sancti Nicholai	quas prepositus aule Regine tenet per indenturam.
iii s. iiii d.	De domo prox.	
ii s.	De domo Glatton	
x s.	De domo quam Ioh' Hardyng bedellus tenet per indenturam cum reparacione; tamen non habet indenturam.	
xxiiii s. iiii d.	De domo prox. cum shopa quam Will' Southam tenet per indenturam cum reparacione, cooperacione excepta.	
xxxii s. iiii d.	De domo prox. cum shopa quam Rob. Pulford tenet per indenturam cum reparacione.	
xiiii s.	De selda prox. quam Stephanus Manciple tenet.	
xvi s.	De selda prox. quam Ioh' Stanythorp scriptor tenet per annum.	
i rosa.	De selda prox. Blakehall ex opposito Smyhtgate quam Ioh' Slyford tenet per indenturam cum reparacione.	
viii s.	De secunda selda prox.	
viii s.	De tercia selda prox.	

Parochia sancte Marie Virginis in Catstrete.

xx s. De domo cum schopa quam Ioh' Stauerton bocbynder tenet per annum.

xx s. De domo quam Ioh' Brothur lymnour tenet per indenturam cum reparacione.

F. vii s. vi d. De tenemento Ade Howtone quam Ioh' Dosyer tenet.

F. iiii s. De domo Abraham.

xxx s. De domo Lodlowe cum shopa & cum uno gardino infra scolas quam Rob' Conyng tenet per indenturam cum reparacione.

xxvi s. viii d. De domo quam Iuliana Grasyer tenuit; modo Ioh' Grene tenet.

De selda in cimiterio ecclesie beate Marie.

De secunda selda prox.

xxiii s. iiii d. De domo Basyng cum schopa quam Ioh' Peyntour tenet per indenturam sine reparacione.

xxviii s. De ii seldis prox. in cornerio quas Rog. Latoner tenet per indenturam sine reparacione.

xxvi s. De ii seldis prox. quas Rogerus Barbour tenet per annum.

F. xii d. De uno gardino infra domum Iuliane Garlond.

In Gropelane.

vi s. De domo quam Ioh' Stampe tenet per annum.

v s. De selda prox. quam Ioh' Lyde tenet per annum.

v s. De selda prox.

Parochia Omnium Sanctorum.

xvi s. De domo Wyhtwong quam Edmundus Taylour tenet per annum.

viii s. De selda subtus Burwaldescote.

viii s. De secunda selda Burwaldescote.

De domo retro ecclesiam Omnium Sanctorum quam A[. . . . . .].

De domo [. . . .] iuxta uiam quam Nicholaus Goldsmyth tenet.

[De scola ibidem quam][1] Iohannes Holewey tenet.

[De prima selda subtus Stodeley.]

[De secunda selda subtus Stodeley.]

[1] The words in brackets are illegible.

F. vii s. De tenemento Hengseye in cornerio quod extendit se iuxta uenellam que ducit ad ecclesiam sancti Edwardi.

c s. De domo Swynebroke cum shopis quam Adam Ryuer tenet per indenturam cum reparacione.

F. xiiii s. De domo Alicie Newbury in bocheria.

Parochia Sancti Martini.

F. iiii s. De domo Thome Orliente quam Ioh' Blode tenuit.

F. ii s. De domo Alicie Welles quam Ioh' Wakeman tenuit cum una placea iuxta fratres Carmelit'.

F. x s. De introitu Kyngestone quam Thomas Somerset tenet per indenturam.

xv s. De prima selda Croxforde quam Galf' Stillynton tenet per annum.

xvii s. De secunda selda Croxforde quam Will' Furbour tenet per indenturam cum reparacione.

F. ii s. De uno gradu inter shopas predictas pro quo Prior Frideswide soluet.

F. ii s. De solario Henrici Gamage.

F. vi s. viii d. De selda in sutoria quam Ric' Forster tenuit; modo Will' Bergeueny.

F. iiii s. De selda in quatriuio [*sic*] quam Bartholomeus Tauerner tenuit.

F. i d. De domo in ballio sancti Petri.

Parochia sancti Iohannis.

viii d. De uno gardino in Kybaldestrete quod Iohanna Atcorner tenet.

v s. De domo in cornerio quam Ioh' Rede tenet per indenturam cum reparacione.

F. viii s. De aula Gaylier prox. cum shopa quam Alicia Perys tenet.

F. ii s. De aula Trimstede quam eadem tenet.

Parochia sancti Michaelis australis.

xiiii s. De domo Bolstras quam Walterus Bocher tenet per indenturam cum reparacione.

xx s. De domo Meteburne prox. quam Ioh' Laurence, sutor, tenet per indenturam sine reparacione.

x s. De domo quam Thomas Warner tenet.

F. ii s. De aula Mariol ex parte occidentali quam Margareta Manciple tenet.

F. xii d. De tenemento Swyneshulle.

Parochia sancti Aldati.

F. xii d. De tenemento exoposito scole in paruo Iudaismo; prepositus Baliolhall soluet.

xii s. De tenemento Dokelyngtone: Iohanna Gybbes soluet & tenet per cartam.

xlvi s. viii d. De domo Kepharme quam Rogerus [ ]r tenet per indenturam sine reparacione.

xx s. De domo prox. quam Vincencius Taylour tenet.

xviii s. De selda prox. quam Ioh' Barbour tenet.

xxvi s. viii d. De domo prox. quam Ioh' Acham carpenter tenet per indenturam sine reparacione.

xiiii s. De selda prox. quam Ioh' Trenenawnt taylour tenet per annum.

xxiiii s. De domo prox. quam Ioh' Clanfeld tenet per indenturam sine reparacione.

vi s. De parua domo iuxta pistum.

F. ii s. De tenemento Plumbatoris quod Ric. Garston alias Mercer tenet.

xiii s. iiii d. De domo iuxta ecclesiam sancti Aldati quam Rog' Stawntone tenet.

Parochia sancte Ebbe.

xviii s. De curia Lincoln' quam Ioh' Lymnour tenet per indenturam cum reparacione.

i d. De duabus shoppis quas Margareta Ryng tenet in cornerio.

xiii s. iiii d. De domo Stanlake quam Will' Manciple tenet per indenturam cum reparacione.

viii s. De tenemento Waryn in paruo ballio quod Will' Cristemasse tenet per annum.

F. ix s. De tenemento sub muro uille quod Reginaldus Tanner tenet.

F. viii s. iiii d. De domo prox. ex parte occidentali pro quo prior Frideswide soluet.

F. iiii s. De ten' Brymstere.

Parochia sancti Michaelis borialis cum parochia sancti Thome.

xxxiii s. iiii d. De aula Blankeneye cum seld' quam Will' Daguile tenet per indenturam cum reparacione.

F. xiii s. iiii d. De tenemento Willelmi Wodesdone, quod abbas de Oseneye tenet.

Parochia beate Marie Magdalene.

F. ii s. De tenemento Duclyntone.
F. xii d. De ten. Dodeford.
F. ii s. De ten. Iohannis Sawser quod idem Ioh' tenet.
x s. De domo Welles quam Alicia Hosteler tenet per indenturam cum reparacione.
F. iii s. De ten. quondam Walteri de Wygornia quod Ioh' Spront ten'.
De una placia uacua iuxta portam fratrum Carmelit'.
De alia placia uacua exoposito porte de Brokenheys quam Ioh' Wakeman tenuit.

Ex parte orientali in eadem parochia.

F. vii s. De introitu Henrici Bramptone quem Will' Cook tenet.
F. iii s. De domo Rogeri Bost iuxta Cardinalhat.
F. xii d. De ten. Duclyntone.
x s. De domo Willelmi Stafford quam Thomas Mason tenet per indenturam cum reparacione.
xiii s. iiii d. De domo olim uocata Dephalle super Candych quam Ric' Parchyminer tenet cum reparacione.

Parochia sancti Egidii.

xx d. De terra Iohannis Randulf in Stokwelstrete; modo est gardinum.
De duabus seldis ibidem.
iiii s. De domo quam Ioh' Roper tenet per indenturam cum reparacione.
F. xii d. De ten' abbatisse de Godestowe.

Parochia sancte Crucis.

xviii d. De ii domibus super Candyche uocatis olim curia Maynard quas Will' Carpenter tenet per indenturam cum reparacione.
x s. De domo prox. Crowel quam Will' Furneys tenet.
vi s. viii d. De secunda domo prox.
De tercia domo prox. Henrici Okam.
De uno gardino retro domum Okam.
De alio gardino magno prox. uenelle quod Thos. Selby tenet.
xviii d. De i placea uacua prox. uenelle ex parte boriali cum terra.
De domo prox. le Sawer.

De secunda domo iuxta le Sawer.
De parua domo iuxta ecclesiam.
De domo quondam Henrici Brakleye.
xviii d. De domo exoposito cimiterio ecclesie cum ii bottis in Bellomonte quam I. Dosier tenet per indenturam cum reparacione.

De domibus clericorum.
vi marc. & dim. De aula Burwaldescote quam mag. Thomas Heendman tenet.
xlvi s. viii d. De aula Ingehalle quam Thomas Mockyng tenet.
xl s. De aula Bosterhalle quam Nic' Wynbold tenet.
xvi s. De Harehalle.
xlvi s. viii d. De Chymnyhalle cum magno gardino quam Hamundus Gramaticus tenet.
xvi s. De Nyghtyngalehalle.
xxvi s. viii d. De Aristotilhall quam Will' Cook tenet.
xiii s. iiii d. De Knyghthall quam Ioh' Ardyngtone tenet.
xxvi s. viii d. De Mynothalle quam Ioh' Pauy tenet.
xx s. De Deephalle quam Ioh' Lane tenet.
ii s. De aula Willelmi quam rector collegii Exon tenet.
ii s. De Brakelehalle super Candich cum aliis ii, modo gardinum, quam I. wallicus manciple tenet.
xlvi s. viii d. De magna scola in Cattestrete.
xiii s. iiii d. De introitu sancti Iohannis.
xvi d. De Herthalle in uico sancti Iohannis modo gardinum pro qua prepositus Baliolhalle soluit.
iii s. iiii d. De aula uocata Hamurhalle cum uacua placia quam custos noui collegii de Wyntone tenet.

37. **Part of a rental of 1412.**

Rentale uille Oxon de domo sancti Iohannis Baptiste extra portam orientalem anno regni regis Henrici quarti post conquestum Anglie quartodecimo.

Parochia sancti Clementis.
i d. De uno muro capitali prox. uenellam super quam uenellam Iohannes Cator de nouo edificauit.
ix s. De domo prox.
vi s. De shopa prox.
iiii s. De tercia shopa prox.

vi s. De quarta shopa prox.
xii s. De domo prox. quam Iohannes Haseley tenet.
xiiii s. De domo prox. quam Iohannes Carpynter tenet.
Summa li s. i d.

Parochia S. Petri extra portam orientalem ex parte australi.

xviii d. De domo iuxta Paris quam Iohannes Pope tenet.
vi s. viii d. De secunda domo prox.
vi s. viii d. De tercia domo prox.
vi s. viii d. De quarta domo prox.
vi s. viii d. De quinta domo prox.
v s. De sexta domo quam Henricus Glouer tenet.
vi s. viii d. De septima domo quam Ricardus Gardyner tenet.
vi s. viii d. De octaua domo quam Iohannes Stampe tenet.
vi s. viii d. De domo proxima quam Iohannes Brywer tenet.
xiii s. iiii d. De domo prox. quam Willelmus Mauncipylle tenet.
xx d. De domo prox. de capitali redditu prioris sancte Frideswide.
i lib. thuris. De domo sancte Trinitatis.
Summa iii li. xiii s. ii d.

Extra eandem portam ex parte boriali.

xii s. De domo iuxta hospitale quam Iohannes Kynne tenet.
viii s. De domo prox. quam Ricardus Beleouny tenet.
viii s. De domo prox. quam Willelmus Westcote tenet.
viii s. De domo prox. quam Iohannes Panyer tenet.
viii s. De domo prox. quam Willelmus Hawke tenet.
xx s. De domo prox. quam Iohannes Wayne tenet.
x s. De domo prox. quam Nicholaus Sklatter tenet.
vi s. viii d. De shopa iuxta tenementum Iohannis Garsyndone.
xv s. De domo prox.
xiii s. iiii d. De domo prox. quam Thomas Geddyng tenet.
vi s. De domo prox. quam Agnes Colles tenet.
iiii s. De shopa prox.
xxvi s. viii d. De forgia quam Iohannes Wade nuper tenuit.
xii s. De tribus shopis prope portam orientalem.
Summa vii li. xvii s. viii d.

Infra portam orientalem ex parte australi.

x s. De domo quam Robertus Souter tenet iuxta Burgate.[1]

[1] The tenement of Eynsham Abbey next to the house of the Hospital of St. John was called Burgate's (*Cart. of Eynsham*, ii. 246, O. H. S.).

x s. De domo prox.
xiii s. iiii d. De domo quam Rogerus Chiddesley tenet.
v s. De domo contra murum uille Oxon uersus Kybaldstrete quam Robertus Hawuyle tenet.
iiii s. De domo proxima quam Willelmus Skynner tenet.
iiii s. De domo prox. quam Willelmus Lymnour tenet.
Summa xlvi s. iiii d.

Infra portam orientalem ex parte boriali.
xiii s. iiii d. De domo quam Willelmus Shorier tenet.
xi s. De domo prox. quam Willelmus Cook tenet.
xxiiii s. De domo quam Willelmus Hawuyle tenet.
xxvi s. viii d. De domo quam Iohannes Spenser tenet.
xxiiii s. De domo prox. quam Willelmus Lymnour tenet.
F. x d. De domo quam Iohannes Garsyndone senior tenet.
xxiiii s. De domo prox. quam Thomas Briwer tenet.
xvi s. viii d. De tribus gardinis iuxta cimiterium ecclesie sancti Petri in oriente.
v s. De prima domo iuxta aulam Regine.
v s. De secunda domo prox.
vii s. i d. De duabus domibus prox. quas Dauid Tayllour nuper tenuit.
xl s. De tenementis que Ranulphus Mauncipylle tenet.
F. ii s. De domo quondam Glatton quam prepositus aule Regine tenet.
F. iii s. iiii d. De domo prox. quam idem prepositus tenet.
F. x s. De introitu sancti Nicholai quem idem prepositus tenet.
x s. De domo quam Iohannes Hardyng tenet.
liii s. iiii d. De domo quam nuper Willelmus Southam tenuit.
xxvi s. viii d. De domo prox. quam Iohannes Chambre tenet.
viii s. De shopa prox. quam Iohannes Mauncipille tenet.
x s. De secunda shopa prox.
x s. De tercia shopa prox.
viii s. De domo iuxta Blakehalle quam Adam Cook tenet.
viii s. De domo secunda.
viii s. De domo tercia.
Summa xvii li. xiiii s. xi d.[1]

[1] The rest of the rental is wanting.

38. A rental of 1426.

Rentale uille Oxon de domo sancti Iohannis Baptiste anno regni regis Henrici sexti quinto.

In parochia sancti Clementis.

i d. In primis de uno muro capitali prox' uenell' super quam uenellam Iohannes Catour edificauit, quam idem Iohannes Catour tenet per indenturam.

x s. { De domo proxima quam Reginaldus Carpenter tenet. De shopa proxima quam idem Reginaldus tenet. }

xl d. De shopa proxima quam Iohannes Sclatter tenet.

vi s. De shopa proxima quam Thomas Couele tenet.

xiiii s. De domo prox. quam idem Thomas tenet per indenturam.

xiiii s. De domo prox. quam Iohannes Howdan tenet.

In parochia sancti Petri extra portam orientalem ex parte australi.

xiii s. iiii d. De crofto uocato Parys quam Iohannes Lye, bocher, tenet.

iiii s. De gardinis prox. quos Willelmus Euerard tenet, ubi quinque domus combuste fuerunt.

viii s. De domo prox. quam Iohannes Carpenter tenet.

vi s. viii d. De domo prox. quam Nicholaus Fuller tenet.

vi s. viii d. De domo prox. quam Iohannes Stowe tenet.

xiii s. iiii d. De domo prox. quam Willelmus Manciple tenet.

F. xx d. De domo prox., prioris sancte Frideswide.

F. i lib. incense. De tenementis et domo sancte Trinitatis.

Extra eandem portam ex parte boriali.

xi s. De domo iuxta hospitale quam Willelmus Croxford, smyth, tenet.

vi s. viii d. De domo prox.

vi s. viii d. De domo prox. quam Iohannes Snowe tenet.

vi s. viii d. De domo prox. quam Willelmus Carpenter tenet.

vi s. viii d. De domo prox. quam Iohannes Cook tenet.

xiii s. iiii d. De domo prox.

vi s. viii d. De domo prox. quam Henricus Whyte tenet.

iiii s. De shopa iuxta tenementum Iohannis Chamberleyn quam Andreas Carter tenet.

x s. De domo prox.

xii s. De domo prox. quam Symon sadeler tenet.

vi s. De domo prox. quam Alicia Northerne tenet.
iii s. De selda prox.
vi s. viii d. De duabus shopis nuper pertinentibus ad le forge, quas Ricardus Taylour tenet.
De domo cum le forge.
iiii s. De shopa prox. porte orientali.
iiii s. De shopa secunda prox.
iiii s. De shopa tertia prox.

Infra portam orientalem ex parte australi.

x s. De domo prox. tenemento Willelmi Lumnour.
x s. De domo prox. quam Edmundus Kyppyng, taylour, tenet.
xxiii s. iiii d. De domo quam Agnes Chiddesle tenet.
De domo contra muros uille quam Robertus Hauile tenet.
iiii s. De domo prox. quam Willelmus Skynner tenet.
De domo prox. quam Willelmus Lumnour tenet.
iiii s. De gardino exoposito Harehalle.

Infra portam orientalem ex parte boriali.

xiii s. iiii d. De domo.
x s. De domo prox.
xxiiii s. De domo prox. quam Robertus Hauile tenet.
xxvi s. De domo prox. quam Iohannes Galoun tenet.
xxiiii s. De domo prox. quam Willelmus Lumnour tenet.
F. x d. De domo quam Willelmus Euerard tenet.
xxiiii s. De domo prox. quam Alicia Bruwer tenet.
v s. De gardino in cimiterio sancti Petri quem uicarius eiusdem ecclesie tenet.
v s. De gardino prox.
v s. De gardino prox. quem Iohannes Wykham tenet.
v s. De prima domo iuxta aulam Regine.
v s. De secunda domo prox.
vi s. viii d. De tercia domo prox.
viii s. De quarta domo prox. quam Willelmus Kyng tenet.
vi s. viii d. De domo prox.
xxii s. De domo prox. cum shopa in cornerio quam Thomas Taylour tenet cum gardino in cimiterio Petri.
viii s. De shopa prox.

F. ii s. De domo quondam Glatton }
F. iii s. iiii d. De domo prox. } que prepositus aule Regine tenet.
F. x s. De introitu sancti Nicholai }
x s. De domo quam Iohannes Hardyng tenet.
liii s. iiii d. De domo quam Thomas Talbot tenet.
xx s. De domo quam Ricardus Reynald tenet.
vi s. viii d. De shopa prox. quam Matilda Shoper' tenet.
ix s. De secunda shopa prox. quam Rogerus Skybowe tenet.
ix s. De tercia shopa prox. quam Thomas Cook tenet.
vi s. viii d. De prima shopa iuxta Blakehalle quam Iohannes Cook tenet.
vi s. viii d. De secunda shopa quam Margeria Shipster tenet.
vi s. viii d. De tercia shopa quam Iohannes Cook senior tenet.

Parochia beate Marie Virginis in Cattestrete.

xxvi s. viii d. De domo quam Iohannes Skynner tenet cum shopa.
xiiii s. De domo prox. quam Iohannes Skynner tenet.
F. vii s. vi d. De domo Dosier quam Ricardus Parchymyner tenet.
F. iiii s. De domo quam Thomas Dene tenet.
xx s. De domo quam Iohannes Wake tenet.
xxxiii s. iiii d. De domo quam Willelmus Grene tenet.[1]
iiii s. De shopa exoposito ecclesie beate Marie in parte occidentali.
iiii s. De secunda shopa quam Edwardus Grynder tenet.
xxvi s. viii d. De domo prox. quam Agnes Latoner tenet.
xvi s. De domo prox. quam Ricardus Aurifaber tenet.
xx s. De domo prox. quam Willelmus Barbour tenet.
F. xii d. De domo.

Parochia Omnium Sanctorum.

xv s. De shopa proxima le Brodeyates.
x s. { De shopa subtus cameram de Brodeyates } Ric. Chandeler tenet.
{ De secunda shopa }
xviii s. De domo retro ecclesiam Omnium Sanctorum quam [*blank*] Curriour tenet.
x s. De alia domo ibidem.
x s. De domo quam Willelmus Webbe chaloner tenet.
vi s. viii d. De selda exoposito ecclesie Omnium Sanctorum.
vi s. viii d. De alia selda.

[1] This seems to be *domus Plente* on the south side of High Street. The previous five tenements are in Cat Street running from north to south.

iiii li. De domo quam Willelmus Aston tenet.
F. xxviii s. De domo quam Thomas Wychius[1] tenet.

Parochia sancti Martini.
F. x s. De introitu olim Kyngestone quam Thomas Couintre tenet.
viii s. De selda prox.
viii s. De selda secunda prox.
F. vi s. viii d. De selda quam Willelmus Erburfeld tenet.

Parochia sancti Iohannis.
De domo in Gropelane quam Willelmus Grene tenet.
v s. De shopa.
v s. De secunda shopa.
iiii s. De domo prox. quam Iohannes Weston tenet.

Parochia sancti Michaelis australis.
xvi s. De domo quam Henricus Lolly tenet.
xvi s. De domo prox. quam Hugo Bedeford tenet.
xiii s. iiii d. De domo.
F. ii s. De domo Priorisse de Luttilmor' ex altera parte uici.

Parochia sancti Aldati.
F. xii d. De tenemento exoposito scole in Iudaismo quod prepositus Baliolhalle tenet.
F. xii s. De tenemento Dukelyntone quod Thomas Gybbes tenet.
liii s. iiii d. De domo cum shopis quam Iohannes Barton tenet.
x s. De domo prox. quam Nicholaus Grygory taylour tenet.
xiii s. iiii d. De domo prox. quam Margareta Miles tenet.
xxxiii s. iiii d. De domo prox. quam Vincencius Fyschemonger tenet.
xiii s. iiii d. De domo prox. quam Hugo Cobeler tenet.
xxxiii s. iiii d. De domo prox. in angulo quam Robertus Ioie tenet.
viii s. De domo iuxta pistum.
x s. De domo exoposito ecclesie sancti Aldati.

Parochia sancte Ebbe.
xiii s. iiii d. De domo iuxta Powlehalle[2] quam Thomas Stonemason tenet.
v s. De domo in cornerio.

[1] The name was usually spelt Withig or Withick.

[2] Paul Hall, belonging to Oseney, was next to *curia Lincoln.*

v s. De domo proxima annexa.

xvi s. De domo exoposito porte fratrum Minorum.[1]

vi s. viii d. De parua domo in Ballio.

F. viii s. De domo Allestone sub muro uille quam Michael Nortone tenet.

Parochia Michaelis borialis & sancti Thome.

xl s. De domo cum shopis quam Robertus Whitefeld tenet.

F. xiii s. iiii d. De tenementis Wodesdone inter castrum & Osneye in le Hamele uersus Osneye ex parte occidentali que sacrista de Osneye tenet.

Parochia sancte Marie Magdalene.

iiii s. De domo quam Iohannes Clerk tenet.

F. iii s. De tenemento quondam Iohannis Gruttone pro quo Thomas Swan de Oxon soluit.

F. iiii s. De tenemento quod Henricus Berewyk tenet.

xiii s. iiii d. De domo quam Iohannes Cook tenet.

vi s. viii d. { De schopa prox.
De secunda schopa prox.

xiii s. iiii d. De domo super Candyche quam Thomas Ade parchymyner tenet.

Parochia sancti Egidii.

ii s. De domo quam Willelmus Somertone carpenter tenet.

F. xii d. De tenemento abbatisse de Godestowe.

ii s. ii d. De domo quam Iohannes Blakethorne tenet in Stokwellestrete.

Parochia sancte Crucis.

xiii s. iiii d. { De domo quam —— Braybrok tenet.
De domo prox. quam idem tenet.

v s. De domo iuxta ecclesiam sancte Crucis.

viii s. De gardinis iuxta pillory que Willelmus Grene tenet.

De domibus clericorum.

iii l. xv s. De aula uocata Brodeyates.

xl s. De aula uocata Yngehalle.

xl s. De Bostarhalle quam magister Radulphus Perat tenet.

xx s. De Harehalle quam magister Thomas Lowhtbarowe tenet.

[1] This is Wild's tenement. The entry shows that the Greyfriars had a gateway between St. Ebbe's church and Littlegate.

ii marc'. De Chymynyhalle quam magister Thomas Pecy tenet.
ii marc'. De Nyghtyngalehalle.
xxiiii s. De Aristotilhalle.
iiii s. De gardino annexo.
ii s. De gardino olim uocato Knyghthalle.
xxvi s. viii d. De Minothalle quam magister Willelmus Lawle tenet.
xxiiii s. De Depehalle quam magister Thomas Leche tenet.
ii s. De gardino olim uocato Wyllihalle quod rector de Exceter colege tenet.
iiii s. De gardinis super Candych que Henricus Berewyk tenet.
xiii s. iiii d. De scola in Cattestret.
vi s. De introitu sancti Iohannis ibidem quem Clemens Flynt tenet.
xvi d. De Herthalle, modo gardino, iuxta [*blank*] quod magister de Baliolhalle tenet.
xl d. De gardino iuxta nouum collegium olim uocato Hamerhalle quod custos eiusdem collegii tenet.

39. A rental of 1452–4.

The next rental is without heading and is a rough draft and imperfect, written on paper. The entries which deal with Bostar Hall and the adjacent halls show that its date must be between 1448 and 1457, while the first Magdalen Hall was in existence. It must be earlier than Dec. 20, 1454 (see vol. i, p. 361); on the other hand it cannot be earlier than Michaelmas 1452, because among the tenants in St. Mary's parish occurs the name 'Clark, alderman'; he was alderman in 1454, but it is known that he was not alderman in 1448, 1449, 1450, and 1451; the aldermen for 1452 and 1453 are at present unknown.

Parochia sancti Clementis.
i d. Ioh' Barat pro uno muro capitali prox. uenelle, super quam uenellam Ioh' Catour edificauit.
viii s. De Ioh' Angell pro uno tenemento de nouo edificato.
viii s. De Thoma Taylour pro uno tenemento de nouo edificato.
vi s. viii d. De Ricardo Wice alias Carter pro uno tenemento ibidem.

Parochia sancti Petri extra portam orientalem.

[*This portion is missing.*]

Infra portam orientalem ex parte australi.

x s. De proxima domo ten' quam prepositus de aula Magdalene tenet.

x s. De domo prox. quam idem prepositus tenet.

xxvi s. viii d. De domo quam Martinus Fuller inhabitabat.[1]

xxiii s. iiii d. De domo quam Annet' Chiddesley tenet.

iiii s. De domo contra muros uille, quam idem tenet.

iiii s. De domo prox.; quam idem tenet.

iiii s. De domo prox.; quam idem tenet.

iiii s. De gardino exoposito Harrehalle; quam idem prepositus tenet.

xl s. De Bosterhalle; quam idem magister tenet.

xx s. De Harrehalle; quam idem magister tenet.

xxvi s. viii d. De Chymneyhalle; quam idem magister tenet.

xxvi s. viii d. De Nyghtyngalehalle; quam idem magister tenet.

Et pro omnibus istis tenementis iam reddit prepositus per annum vi li. vi s. viii d.

Infra portam orientalem ex parte boriali.

xiii s. iiii d. De domo quam Ric' Carpynter tenet.

x s. De domo prox.; Hugo Dauy.

xxiiii s. De domo prox.; Ioh' Martyn.

xxvi s. De domo prox.; mag. Will' Cooke.

xxiiii s. De domo prox.; Ioh' Mason yrremonger.

F. x d. De domo; Humfridus Euerard.

xxiiii s. De domo prox.; mag. Ioh. Temmys.

v s. De gardino in cimiterio sancti Petri; gardianus de nouo collegio tenet.

v s. De gardino prox. quem idem tenet.

v s. De gardino prox. quod mag. Temmys tenet.

v s. De prima domo iuxta aulam Regine.

v s. De secunda domo; Ioh' Lokeer tenet.

vi s. viii d. De tercia domo; Margeria Coteler tenet.

viii s. De quarta domo; Rog' Carpynter tenet.

vi s. viii d. De domo prox.; Ioh' Saltmerce carpynter tenet.

xvi s. De domo prox. in cornerio cum schopa; Petrus Barbour.

De schopa prox.; idem Petrus: pro istis duobus xiii s. viii d. & omnia honera.

[1] This entry is inserted above the line.

F. { ii s. De domo quondam Glotton; iii s. iiii d. De domo prox.; x s. De introitu sancti Nicholai } prepositus aule Regine.

x s. De domo quam Ric. Marchal (*altered from* Ioh' Hardyng) tenet.

xx s. De domo prox. Petrus Barbour.

liii s. iiii d. De domo uocata le Belle: Hen. Bathe.

xx s. De domo quam Ioh' Mathew tenet.

vi s. viii d. De schopa prox.; idem Ioh'.

ix s. De secunda schopa; Rob. Glouer.

ix s. De tercia schopa; Thomas Bamptone.

vi s. De prima schopa; Ioh' Brat.

vi s. viii d. De secunda schopa; Ioh' Kyng.

Summa xvi li. xiiii s. vi d.

Parochia beate Marie Virginis.

De domo quam Ric' Sutton, glouer, tenet.

De domo prox.; Ioh' Fyscher.

De domo Dosier; Ioh' Clerke aldreman.

De domo quam Thomas Dene stacionere libere tenet.

De domo quam Ioh' Bookebynder tenet.

De domo quam Ioh' Grene tenet.

De schopa ex opposito ecclesie beate Marie in parte occidentali: Annet' Greffyn.

De secunda schopa, quam eadem Annet' tenet.

De domo prox. quam idem [*sic*] Annet' tenet.

De domo prox. quam Thomas Carter taylor tenet.

De domo prox. quam idem Thomas tenet.

De domo Duglyngtone.[1]

Summa viii li. xvi s. ii d.

Parochia Omnium Sanctorum.

De schopa prox. le Brodeyates; Ric. Barbour.

De schopa prox.; Ioh' Heyle.

De secunda schopa; Ioh' Hul ten'.

De domo retro ecclesiam Omnium Sanctorum; Thos. Whyte, manciple.

De alia domo quam idem Ioh' Hul tenet.

De domo quam Philippus Marcham tenet.

[1] This is an error; the house in question never belonged to Ducklington. It was generally called *domus Grasier*.

De selda exoposito ecclesie Omnium Sanctorum.
[De alia selda—*erased.*]
De domo quam Thomas Hall, potycary, tenet.
De domo quam Ioh' Hasschebery tenet.
viii li. xvii s. viii d.

Parochia sancti Martini.

De introitu Kyngestone; Thomas Couentre.
De selda prox.; Thomas Gurdeler.
De secunda selda; Ioh' Mores.
De selda quam Rob. Attewode tenet.
xxxi s. viii d.

Parochia sancti Iohannis.

De domo in Gropelane; Ioh' Grene.
De schopa; in manibus domini.
De secunda schopa; in manibus domini.
De domo prox.; Ioh' Westone tenet.
xxx s.

Parochia sancti Michaelis australis.

De domo quam Ric' Coke, herper, tenet.
De domo prox. quam Ioh' Herreng tenet.
De domo quam Ioh' Mason tenet.
De domo priorisse de Lytilmore.
xlvii s.

Parochia sancti Aldati.

De tenemento exoposito scole in Iudaismo: prepos. Bailihalle.
De tenemento Dukelynton; Rog. Sergent.
De domo cum schopis; Iohanna Bartone.
De domo prox.; Will' Euerard.
De domo prox.; Hugo Cobeler.
De domo prox.; Iohanna Milton.
De domo prox.; Rob. Barbour.
De domo prox.; in manibus domini.
De domo prox.; James Lakoc.
De domo exoposito ecclesie sancti Aldati; Emmota Hasseley tenet.
[De domo quam Nich' Croke tenet; *erased.*]
ix li. vii s. viii d.

Parochia sancte Ebbe.

De domo iuxta Powlehalle; Nich' Croke.

De domo in cornerio; in manibus domini; est ruinosa.

De domo prox. in manibus domini; est ruinosa.

De domo exoposito porte fratrum minorum; in manibus domini; est ruinosa.

De domo parua in ballio; Nich' Blyndman tenet.

De domo Allestone sub muro uille; Ioh' Bronewych bruer.

liiii s.

Parochia sancti Michaelis borialis & sancti Thome.

De domo cum schopis; Rob. Wytfyld.

De tenemento Wodesdon in le Hamele uersus Oseney ex parte occidentali; sacrista de Oseney tenet.

De domo quam Will. Glouer chamberlen libere tenet.[1]

iiii li. xii d.

Parochia sancte Marie Magdalene.

De domo quam Margeria Selham tenet.

De tenemento quondam Ioh' Gurton; in manibus domini.

De tenemento quod Alicia Berrewycke libere tenet.

De domo quam Nich' Feyreman tenet libere.

De gardino quam Iohanna Scarlat tenet.

De domo super Candych; Ezabella Ade tenet.

xliiii s. iiii d.

Parochia sancti Egidii.

De domo quam Ioh' Bayly mason tenet.

De tenemento abbatisse de Godstow; tenet libere.

De gardino quam Ioh' Blackethorn tenuit; in manibus domini.

v s. ii d.

Parochia sancte Crucis.

De domo quam Braybrok tenet.

De dome prox.; idem tenet.

De domo iuxta ecclesiam sancte Crucis; idem tenet.

De gardino iuxta Pillori; Ioh' Grene tenet.

xxvi s. iiii d.

De domibus clericorum.

De aula uoc. Brodeyates in parochia Omnium Sanctorum.

De Arrestotil Halle in parochia sancti Petri.

[1] This entry is an insertion. The tenement cannot be identified; in the earlier and later rentals there is nothing to correspond.

De gardino annexo.

De gardino olim uocato Kny3th Halle.

De gardino olim uocato Wilby Halle; rector de Exeter Coll. tenet.

vii li. ix s. v d.

40. A rental of Sept. 29, 1478.

Rentale de redditibus uille Oxon' renouatum tempore magistri Willelmi Tybard presidentis collegii beate Marie Magdalene extra portam orientalem uille Oxonie anno regni regis Edwardi quarti post conquestum Anglie ad festum Michaelis xviii.

In parochia sancti Clementis.

In primis de Ioh. Barrat pro uno muro capitali proximo uenella [*sic*] super quam Ioh' Cator edificauit i d.; nichil inde.

x s. De domo quam Thomas Warde tenet.

viii s. De domo quam Ioh' Parker tenet.

xx s. De tribus cotagiis que Ioh' Vugle[1] tenet.

In parochia sancti Petri extra portam orientalem ex parte australi.

xxvi s. viii d. De tenemento quod Rob. Perkyns tenet cum uno crofto uocato Parys.

Extra eandem portam ex parte boriali.

viii s. De domo prox. porte collegii quam Ioh' Moleyns nuper tenuit.

vi s. viii d. De secunda domo quam Thos. Iohannez nuper tenuit.[2]

xii s. De tercia domo quam Rob. Baron tenet.

vi s. viii d. De quarta domo quam Ioh' Smarte tenet.

x s. De quinta domo quam Ioh' Marten tenet.

viii s. De sexta domo quam Ioh' Molens tenet.

xxx s. De septima domo quam Ioh' Bowdon tenet.

xiii s. iiii d. De octaua domo quam Walter Karuer inhabitat & reddere solebat.

xiii s. iiii d. De nona domo quam Thomas Adderbery tenet.

x s. De decima domo quam Agnet' Trendeley tenet & reddere solebat.

vi s. viii d. De undecima domo quam Ioh' Karon tenet.

vi s. viii d. De duodecima domo quam Ioh' Grey tenet.

[1] Or Ungle, perhaps identical with Angell; see the previous rental.

[2] In the next rental these first two tenements have been pulled down.

vi s. viii d. De xiii^ma domo quam Nich' Gararde tenet.
xx s. De domo iuxta angulum quam Ioh' Gylle modo tenet.
vii s. De tribus seldis iuxta fontem.[1] Nichil inde.

Infra portam orientalem ex parte boriali & australi.

xii s. De tenemento in quo manet Thomas Iakeson.
x s. De tenemento in quo manet Ioh' Harford.
xiii s. iiii d. De tenemento in quo manet Ioh' Whyte carpintar.
xx s. De tenemento quod Ioh' Whitehede nuper tenuit & reddere solebat.
xx s. De tenemento in quo manet Edmundus Fuller.
F. x d. De tenemento in quo manet Umfridus Euererd, pro quieto redditu.
xx s. Pro aula uocata Gramerhalle quam mag. Broke tenet.
x s. Pro duobus gardinis iuxta cimiterium sancti Petri que gardianus sancte Marie[2] tenet.
xiii s. iiii d. De duobus tenementis que Rob. Lowe tenet.[3]
viii s. Pro tenemento in quo manet Will. Blundell.
xv s. iiii d. De preposito collegii Regine pro diuersis tenementis in parochia sancti Petri in oriente de quieto redditu.
xxxiii s. iiii d. Pro tenemento cum quatuor seldis iuxta angulum sancti Petri, que Ric' Chamberlayn tenet.
xxx s. Pro tenemento in quo manet Will' Smyth.
xliii s. iiii d. Pro tenemento uoc. le Bell in quo manet Will. Addysley.
xxvi s. viii d. Pro tenemento quod Ioh' Ducheman nuper tenuit.
viii s. Pro prox. tenemento in quo manet Ioh' Lamprey.
viii s. Pro prox. tenemento in quo manet Ioh' Taylor.
xx s. De tenemento in quo manet Will. Asshe.[4]
xxvi s. viii d. Pro tenemento uocato Bosterhalle in quo manet Thos. Browne.
xl s. Pro tenemento uocato le Tabard quod Nich. Hewght tenet cum i gardino & reddit xl s.; tamen inde soluimus collegio regali[5] pro quieto redditu xiii s. iiii d.
xl s. Pro tenemento in quo manet Ric. Lex.

[1] i.e. at East Gate.
[2] i.e. the Warden of New College.
[3] This and the next one probably the three shops near Black Hall, on the site of *domus Charnel*.
[4] This is probably Ing Hall in St. Mary's parish. With the next entry we begin the south side of the road and work towards East Gate.
[5] i.e. Oriel.

vi s. viii d. Pro tenemento quod Thos. Iacson nuper tenuit.
vi s. viii d. Pro tenemento in quo manet Ioh' Lynsey barbour.
x s. Pro uno gardino quod Thomas Hall nuper tenuit.
xiii s. iiii d. Pro alio gardino uocato Penkeriche quod Will. Asshe & Will. Wellys tenent.

In parochia beate Marie in Catstret & extra.
xii s. viii d. De tenemento in quo manet Lucia Glouer cum gardino.
x s. De proximo [*sic*] domo in qua manet Glasyer.
F. vii s. vi d. De tenemento quod Ioh' Clerke alderman tenet.
F. iiii s. De prox. domo quam mag. Trapp' tenet; de quieto redditu.
xiii s. iiii d. Pro tenemento in quo manet Ioh' Cornyshe.
xxxiii s. iiii d. Pro tenemento quod Laurencius Taylour nuper tenuit.[1]
xxx s. De tenemento iuxta angulum in quo manet Ioh' Wellys glouer.
xvi s. De prox. domo in qua manet Thos. Bygnell.
xx s. De gardiano & sociis collegii Animarum pro quodam gardino in Catstrete, ubi nuper erat scola et aula dicta Phisikhalle.[2]

In parochia Omnium Sanctorum.
viii s. De domo iuxta Brodeyate quam Nich' Howght tenet.[3]
xxvi s. viii d. De prox. domo uocata Brodeyate in qua manet Rob. Perkyns.
xvi s. De domo pone ecclesiam Omnium Sanctorum in qua manet[4] Percyuallus Thorppe.
viii s. De alia domo ibidem quam Thomas Mase nuper tenuit.
x s. Pro tenemento in quo manet Will. Hore.[5]
viii s. Pro opella ex opposito ecclesie Omnium Sanctorum in qua manet Iohanna Acton.

[1] This is Pomfret's tenement, also known as *domus Plente*; see vol. i, p. 410. The next two tenements were at the west end of St. Mary's church.

[2] In the earlier rentals it is called 'St. John's Entry'.

[3] This is the tenement on the east side of the entrance to Amsterdam; the rent remained at eight shillings, until in the rental of 2 and 3 Phil. and Mary it becomes twenty-four shillings; for subsequent leases see vol. ii, p. 13.

[4] This and the next tenement were on the north side of All Saints Church, and were finally let in one lease; see vol. ii, p. 26.

[5] This tenement was in Turl Street, south of Lincoln College; in 1463, when Hampton Hall was bought by Lincoln, the land on the south, once of the Hospital of St. John, was occupied by William Hore.

xl s. Pro tenemento in quo manet Margareta Halle.

F. xii s. De tenemento in quo manet Ioh' Hychekock draper; de quieto[1] redditu.

F. xvi s. De prox. opella in qua manet Rob. Fyssher; de quieto redditu.

viii s. De opella in qua manet Ioh' Sysam.[2]

In parochia sancti Martini.

x s. Pro introitu olim uocato Kyngestone quem nuper Thomas Dereste tenuit, in quo manet Ric. Lawghtone; nichil inde.

viii s. De prox. opella quam Steph' Glouer nuper tenuit; nichil inde.

viii s. De secunda schoppa[3] in qua manet W. Flecher.

In parochia sancti Michaelis ad portam australem.

iiii s. Pro tenemento cum gardino que Will. Capelond tenet.

x s. De prox. domo quam mag. Walyngford cum gardino tenet.

vi s. viii d. De domo quam Thos. Shefford tenet.

ii s. De domo Priorisse de Litylmor ex altera parte uici quam Ioh' Hauyle bowcher tenet; de quieto redditu.

In parochia sancti Aldati.

xii s. Pro tenemento uocato le Swanne in quo manet Ioh' Goylyn iunior, de quieto redditu.

xl s. De prox. tenemento in quo manet Will' Capelon cum paruo tenemento annexo.

xx s. De prox. tenemento quod nuper Ioh' Alen tenuit.

xxxiii s. iiii d. Pro tenemento in quo manet Ioh' Barbour cum paruo tenemento annexo que Will. Mason[4] habet pro feodo suo.

xxvi s. viii d. De prox. domo in cornerio in quo manet Ric. Bromwyche, quam Will. Mason habet eciam pro feodo suo.

vi s. viii d. Pro tenemento in Pynfarthyngstrete quod Nich. Croke tenet.

[1] This and the next shop form together the tenement of Alice of Newbury which owed a quitrent of 28*s*.

[2] This must have been the shop under Broadgates. The subsequent rentals show that after it had been rebuilt it was let with Broadgates and the whole rent was raised to £3.

[3] Showing that *schoppa* and *opella* are synonyms.

[4] Willelmus Mason is William Orchard; see vol. ii, p. 161.

v s. Pro tenemento exopposito Bulhalle in quo manet Rog. Fermer.[1]

xxvi s. viii d. Pro aula uocata Mynothalle in qua manet mag. Thomas Byrchall.

viii s. Pro tenemento exopposito ecclesie sancti Aldati in quo manet Rob. Feyreman.

In parochia sancte Ebbe.

viii s. De tenemento sub muro uille in quo manet Rob. Hethe; de quieto redditu.

iiii s. De parua domo in Balliolo, in qua manet Thos. Huske.

viii s. De tenemento exoposito porte fratrum minorum in quo manet Ric. Lase.

viii d. De paruo gardino[2] nuper in manu magistri W. Wilcock.

In parochia sancti Petri in occidente.

iii li. vi s. viii d. De tenemento cum i tenemento annexo que Alexander Holywode tenet.

In parochia sancti Michaelis ad portam borialem.

xxiii s. iiii d. De tenemento in quo manet Steph' Glouer.

In parochia sancte Marie Magdalene.

xxvi s. viii d. De tenemento in quo manet Will. Harrys.[3]

F. iiii s. De tenemento in quo manet Isabella Bortone; de quieto redditu.

xiii s. iiii d. De tenemento super Candyche in quo manet Ioh' Ade.

iiii s. De uno gardino in manu relicte Iohannis West.

iii s. De tenemento quod Edwardus Atwodde tenet; de quieto redditu.

iiii s. De tenemento quod magister & socii collegii Balioli tenent.

In parochia sancti Egidii.

iiii s. De domo quam nuper Will. Iohnson tenuit.

De domibus clericorum in parochia sancti Baptiste.

xiii s. iiii d. De aula Aristotil quam nuper mag. Steph' Poyet tenuit.

[1] This is the tenement of which the leases are given in vol. ii, p. 144.

[2] No doubt Granger's tenement at the corner of Little Bailey and Penny-farthing Street.

[3] For leases of this tenement see vol. ii, p. 292.

De domibus clericorum in parochia Omnium Sanctorum.

De gardino olim uocato Wilbyhall[1] quod rector & socii collegii Exon tenent.

41. A rental of Sept. 29, 1480.

Rentale de redditibus uille Oxon' factum tempore magistri Ricardi Mayow nunc presidentis collegii beate Marie Magdalene extra portam orientalem uille Oxon ad festum Michaelis anno regni regis Edwardi quarti uicesimo.

In parochia sancti Clementis.

x s. Thomas Warde: unde solutum est balliuo de Hedingdone xii d.

viii s. Will. Hunte.

xx s. Ioh. Vngull.

In parochia sancti Petri.

xxvi s. viii d. Rob. Perkyns.

i lib. incense: De tenementis & domo sancte Trinitatis: nichil solutum.

Extra eandem portam ex parte boriali.

xii s. De domo prox. porte collegii: Rob. Baron.

vi s. viii d. Ioh' Smert.

x s. Ioh' Marten.

viii s. Ioh' Gylle.

xxx s. Ioh' Bowdon nuper tenuit: uocat quia occupatur cum stauro collegii.

xiii s. iiii d. Ioh' Bowdon.

xiii s. iiii d. Thos. Aderbyry.

x s. Angnes Trenley; nichil inde quia dicta Agnes habuit ex dono.

vi s. viii d. Ioh' Karone.

vi s. viii d. Ioh' Grey.

vi s. viii d. Nich' Garrard, sawyer.

xx s. Hen. Molton.

vii s. De tribus seldis iuxta fontem; nichil quia ruinosum est.

Infra portam ex parte boriali.

xii s. Thomas Iakeson.

x s. Ioh' Wilkyns.

[1] The name of St. William Hall has now been corrupted to Wilby Hall, The hall itself had long ceased to exist.

xiii s. iiii d. Ioh' Whyte, carpenter.
xx s. Ioh' Whythede, cobeler.
xx s. Edmundus Fuller.
F. x d. Umfridus Euerard.
xx s. Gramerhalle; mag. Broke.
xiii s. iiii d. De ii tenementis in quibus manet Rob. Alom.[1]
viii s. De prox. domo in qua manet Iohanna Chyppenham puella.
F. xv s. iiii d. Prepositus collegii Regine.
xxxiii s. iiii d. De domo iuxta angulum cum iii^bus seldis; Ric. Chambyrlen.
xxx s. Will. Smythe.
xliii s. iiii d. Will. Adysley: solutum est collegio Regine vi s. viii d.
xxvi s. viii d. De domo in qua manet Dyryke Dowcheman.
viii s. Ioh' Lamprey.
viii s. Ioh' Bowghey.
xxvi s. viii d. Bosterhalle; Thos. Browne per indenturam.
liii s. iiii d. Le Tabard; Nich' Howghe per indenturam; solutum est collegio regali xiii s. iiii d.
xl s. Ric. Lex.
vi s. viii d. Thos. Ianson.
vi s. viii d. Ioh' Barbur.
x s. Margareta Hall.
xiii s. iiii d. Will. Ashe & Will. Wellys.

In parochia beate Marie.

xii s. viii d. Lucia Glouer.
x s. Ianyn Coke.
vii s. vi d. Ioh' Clerke alderman; nichil inde quia totaliter in decasu; ideo prosequatur breue de cessauit.
iiii s. Mag. Trappe.
xiii s. iiii d. Ioh' Cornyshe.
xxxiii s. iiii d. Ric. Hosyer.
xxx s. Ioh' Wellys glover.
xvi s. Thomas Bygnell.
xx s. De collegio Animarum; nichil inde quia negatur.[2]

[1] This and the next are probably the three shops near Black Hall, on the site of *domus Charnel*.

[2] This is the rent due for Phisick Hall. Ing Hall is omitted entirely.

Parochia Omnium Sanctorum.

viii s. Nic. Howght per indenturam.
xxvi s. viii d. Rob. Perkyns per indenturam.
viii s. De opella; Ioh' Sysam.
xvi s. Percyuallus Thorpe.
viii s. Petrus Carpynter; unde solutum est Priori sancte Frid. viii s.; nichil inde quia totaliter solutum pro quieto redditu.
x s. Will. Hore.
viii s. Iohanna Acton.
xl s. Margareta Hall.
F. xii s. Ric. Kent.
F. xvi s. Rob. Fysher.

Parochia sancti Martini.

vi s. viii d. De opella quam Edwardus Wodeward tenet; nichil inde, quia iacet nescitur ubi.
x s. Ric. Lawghtone; nichil inde quia negatur.
viii s. De proxima opella; in manibus domini pro defectu reparacionis in defectu Prioris de Sancta Frideswida.
viii s. De secunda schoppa; Nich' Flecher.

Sancti Michaelis ad portam australem.

iiii s. Will' Capelond.
x s. mag. Walyngford; unde Prior Frideswide clamat iii s. ut dicit; tamen non solut'.
vi s. viii d. Thos. Shefford.
ii s. Ioh' Hauyle bowcher.

Sancti Aldati.

xii s. Ioh' Goylyn.
xl s. Will. Capelond.
xx s. nuper Hew taylor.
xxxiii s. iiii d.
xxvi s. viii d.
vi s. viii d. } as in 18 Ed. IV.
v s.
xxvi s. viii d.
viii s. Rob. Fayreman; unde solutum est ecclesie sancti Aldati viii d.

In parochia sancte Ebbe.

viii s. Rob. Hethe.
iiii s. Thos. Huske.
viii d. mag. W. Wylcoke.

In parochia sancti Petri in occidente.

iii li. vi s. viii d. Ioh' Dyker.

Sancti Michaelis ad portam borialem.

xxiii s. iiii d. Steph' Glouer; unde sol' est ad ecclesiam sancti Michaelis viii d.

In parochia sancte Marie Magdalene.

xxvi s. viii d. Ioh. Caumey; unde sol' est Iohanni Herle de quieto redditu ii s. vi d.; item balliuo de Northgate xiii d.
iiii s. Will. Coke.
xiii s. iiii d. Isabella Ade.
iiii s. De uno gardino in manu relicte Iohannis Weste.
iii s. Edwardus Wodwarde.
iiii s. Magister & socii Baliol.

Parochia sancti Egidii.

vi s. viii d. Andreas Carpenter.

De domibus clericorum.

xiii s. iiii d. Aula Aristotill; mag. Fynglas.
ii s. De gardino olim uocato Wylbyhalle; rector & socii collegii Exon' tenent; nichil inde quia nescitur ubi iacet.
xl s. De magno prato quod Will. Reynole tenet; unde solut' Barantyne pro quieto redditu x s.
x s. Pro aqua separali; Rob. Baron.
Summa totalis rentalis lxx li. xvi s. viii d.
De quibus est in parcella non solutorum ix li. ii s. iiii d.
Et in tenementis non conductis iii li. xi s. iiii d.
Et in quietis redditibus solutis l s. vi d.
Summa rentalis de claro lii li. viii d.

42. A rental of Sept. 29, 1481.

This is identical with the previous rental except as follows.

Parochia sancti Michaelis australis.

iiii s. Willelmus Capelonde.

x s. Magister Walyngford; unde habet pro feodo suo in anno vi s. viii d.; item solutum est Priori sancte Frideswide de quieto redditu iii s.

vi s. viii d. Thomas Shefford.

ii s. Iohannes Hauyll.

Parochia sancti Aldati.

xii s. Ioh' Goylyn.

xl s. Will' Capelond.

xx s. nuper Heug' Taylor; tamen reddere solebat xxvi s. viii d.

xxxiii s. iiii d. Ioh' Barbur } Willelmus Mason pro feodo
xxvi s. viii d. Ric' Bromwyche } suo.

vi s. viii d. Nicholaus Croke.

v s. Rogerus Fermer ex opposito Bullehalle; unde solutum est abbati de Abindon xviii d.

xxvi s. viii d. magister Byrchalle.

viii s. Robertus Fayreman; unde ad ecclesiam sancti Aldati viii d.

43. A rental of Sept. 29, 1482.

Rentale factum per Robertum Baron de redditibus uille Oxon, renouatum tempore mag. Ricardi Mayhew presidentis collegii beate Marie Magdalene extra portam orientalem uille Oxon, anno regni regis Ed. IV ad festum sancti Michaelis xxii°.

Parochia sancti Clementis [*as in the last rental*].

Parochia sancti Petri extra portam orientalem; ex parte australi.

xxvi s. viii d. Rob. Perkyns.

Ex parte boriali.

x s. De domo prox. scole gramaticali quam Rob. Baron tenet.

viii s. Ioh' Smert.

xxx s. quondam Ioh' Bowdon.

xiii s. iiii d. ubi Ioh' Bowdon habitat.

xiii s. iiii d. Thos. Adderbery.

x s. Ioh' Gylle.

vi s. viii d. Ioh' Karon.
vi s. viii d. Ioh' Grey.
vi s. viii d. Rob. Blake.
xx s. Hen. Molton.
vii s. De tribus seldis iuxta fontem; nichil inde quia ruinosa.

Infra portam orientalem.
xii s. Ioh' Kymber.
x s. Will' West.
xiii s. iiii d. Ioh' Whyte.
xx s. Ric. Stodeman.
xx s. Edmundus Fuller.
x d. Umfrydus Euerard.
xx s. mag. Broke.
x s. De ii gardinis iuxta cimiterium sancti Petri que gardianus collegii sancte Marie tenet; uac'.
xiii s. iiii d. Rob. Alow.
viii s. Thomas Hardewyke.
xv s. iiii d. Prepositus collegii Regine.
xxxiii s. iiii d. Pro tenemento cum iiii seldis; Ric. Chamberleyne.
xxx s. Will. Holden.
xliii s. iiii d. Will. Hadesley.
xxvi s. viii d. Dyryk Rode.
viii s. Ioh. Lampray.
viii s. Ioh' Bowghey.
xx s. Will' Ashe.[1]
xxvi s. viii d. Bosterhall; Nich' Taylor.
xl s. Le Tabard; Nich' Howght; unde collegio regali xiii s. iiii d.
xl s. Ioh' Symson.
vi s. viii d. Rob. Marten.
vi s. viii d. Ioh' Barber.
x s. Margareta Hall.
xiii s. iiii d. Will' Ashe & Will' Wellys.

Parochia sancte Marie.
xii s. viii d. Lucia Glouer.
x s. Ianyn Kocke.
vii s. vi d. Ioh' Clerke.
iiii s. mag. Gorge.

[1] Probably Ing Hall.

xiii s. iiii d. Ioh' Cornyshe.
xxxiii s. iiii d. Ric. Hosyer.
xxx s. Thomas Ufyngton.
xx s. Coll. Animarum.
xvi s. & onera. Thos. Bygnell.[1]

Parochia Omnium Sanctorum.

viii s. & onera. Nic. Howght.
xxvi s. viii d. Rob. Perkyns.
xvi s. Percyuall Thorpe.
xviii s. Ioh' Smyth ; Prior sancte Frideswide recepit inde.
x s. Will' Hore.
viii s. Opella ex opposito ecclesie ; Iohanna Acton.
xl s. Margareta Hall.
xii s. Ric. Kent.
xvi s. Rob. Fysher.
viii s. Opella in qua manet Will. Pypwell.

Parochia sancti Martini.

x s. nuper Thos. Dereste ; uacat.
viii s. nuper Steph' Glouer ; uacat.
viii s. Nich' Flecher ; uacat.
vi s. viii d. De tercia opella ; Ed. Woddewarde.

Parochia sancti Michaelis australis.

iiii s. Will' Capelonde.
x s. mag. Walyngforde.
vi s. viii d. Thos. Shefford.
ii s. Ioh' Hauyle.

Parochia sancti Aldati.

xii s. Ioh' Goylyn iun.
xl s. Will' Capelonde.
xx s. Ioh' Seut*er*.
xxxiii s. iiii d. Ioh' Barbur } Will' Mason.
xxvi s. viii d. Ric. Bromewiche } Will' Mason.
vi s. viii d. Nic. Croke.
v s. Rog. Fermer.
xxvi s. viii d. mag. Byrchall.
viii s. Rob. Fayreman.

[1] This was next to the tenement occupied by Ufyngton.

Parochia sancte Ebbe.
viii s. Rob. Hethe.
iiii s. Thos. Huske.
viii s. Ric. Hosyer.
viii d. Margareta Couper.

Parochia sancti Petri in occidente.
iii li. vi s. viii d. Ioh' Dyker.

Parochia sancti Michaelis borialis.
xxiii s. iiii d. Steph' Glouer.

Parochia sancte Marie Magdalene.
xxvi s. viii d. Ioh' Caumey.
F. iiii s. Will' Howden.
xiii s. iiii d. Alic' Ade.
iiii s. Relicta Iohannis Weste.
iii s. Edwardus Atwodde.
iiii s. Collegium Balliol.

Parochia sancti Egidii.
vi s. viii d. Thomas Iurdan.

De domibus clericorum.
xiii s. iiii d. Aula Aristotill; mag. Broune principalis.
ii s. De gardino olim uocato Wylby Halle; nichil inde.
xl s. De magno prato; Ioh' Lyrpyn.
xx s. De collegio Mertonis pro Kyngs mylle.
x s. De aqua separali; Rob. Baron.
Summa lxxii li. ii s. viii d.
Summa uera rentalis ultra defectus reddituum & uacaciones lxi li. x s. viii d.

44. A rental of Sept. 29, 1484.

Rentale factum per Robertum Baron, collectorem reddit' uille Oxon, renouatum tempore magistri Ricardi Mayhew presidentis collegii beate Marie Magdalene extra portam orientalem uille Oxonie anno regni regis Ricardi tercii ad festum Michaelis secundo.

In parochia sancti Clementis.
xiii s. iiii d. De domo quam Thomas Warde tenet.
viii s. De domo in qua Alen Manyfolde manet.
xx s. De tribus cotagiis que Ioh' Ungull tenet.
Summa xli s. iiii d.

In parochia sancti Petri extra portam orientalem ex parte boriali.

viii s.	De uno tenemento iuxta portam collegii quod Ioh' Molens nuper tenuit.	Nichil hic in onere computantis, quia omnia ista quatuor tenementa trahuntur in edificacionem scole gramaticalis.
vi s. viii d.	De alio tenemento quod Thomas Iouns nuper tenuit.	
xii s.	De alio tenemento in tenura Roberti Baron.	
vi s. viii d.	De alio tenemento nuper in tenura Iohannis Smerte.	
	Summa xxxiii s. iiii d.	

Extra eandem portam ex parte australi.

xxvi s. viii d. De tenemento quod Hen. Molton tenet cum paruo gardino annexo.

Summa xxvi s. viii d.

Item, extra eandem portam ex parte boriali.

x s. De domo prox. scole grammaticali quam Rob. Baron.

xxx s. De secunda domo quam Hen. Peynter nuper tenuit; uacauit per totum annum.

xiii s. iiii d. De tercia domo quam Ioh' Bowdon modo habitat.

xiii s. iiii d. De quarta domo quam Thos. Adderbery nuper tenuit.

x s. De quinta domo quam Ioh' Gylle ten'.

vi s. viii d. De sexta domo quam Ioh' Karon' nuper tenuit.

vi s. viii d. De septima domo quam Ioh' Grey nuper tenuit.

vi s. viii d. De octaua domo quam Rob' Blake nuper tenuit.

xx s. De domo iuxta angulum quam Ioh' Oldeale nuper tenuit xx s.; uac. per totum annum.

vii s. De tribus seldis iuxta fontem; nichil inde quia non edificantur; uac. per totum annum.

Summa vi li. iii s. viii d.

Infra portam orientalem ex parte boriali & australi.

xii s. De domo quam Rob. Karon' tenet.

x s. Pro tenemento in quo manet Rob. Blake.

xiii s. iiii d. Pro tenemento in quo manet Ioh' Whyte carpenter.

xx s. Pro tenemento in quo manet Ioh' Bowcher.

xx s. Pro tenemento in quo manet Edmundus Fuller.

F. x d. Pro domo quam Thomas Mayew tenet: de quieto redditu.

xx s. Pro aula uocata Gramerhalle, quam mag. Broke ten'.

x s. Pro duobus gardinis iuxta cimiterium sancti Petri quos gardianus collegii sancte Marie tenet & reddere solebat x s.; nichil inde.

vi s. viii d. Pro tenemento in quo manet Ric' Griffyth.

vi s. viii d. Pro tenemento in quo manet Nic' Bokebynder; uac. per totum annum.

viii s. Pro tenemento in quo manet Katerina Hardewyke.

F. xv s. iiii d. De preposito collegii Regine pro diuersis tenementis in parochia sancti Petri in oriente de quieto redditu.

xxxiii s. iiii d. De tenemento cum quatuor seldis iuxta angulum sancti Petri que Ric' Chamberleyn tenet.

xliii s. iiii d. De tenemento in quo manet Margareta Goldesmyth uocato le Bell.

xxvi s. viii d. De tenemento in quo manet Ioh' Myssyndene.

viii s. De tenemento in quo manet Hen. Bedell'.

viii s. De proxima domo in qua manet Thos. Coke.

xx s. De tenemento in quo manet Will' Ashe.

xxvi s. viii d. De tenemento in quo manet Nic' Taylor uocato Bosterhalle.

liii s. iiii d. De tenemento uocato le Tabart quod Nic' Howghte tenet cum gardino; tamen inde soluimus collegio regali pro quieto redditu xiii s. iiii d.

xl s. De tenemento in quo manet Ioh' Symson.

vi s. viii d. De tenemento in quo manet Will' Taylor.

vi s. viii d. De tenemento in quo manet Ioh' Lynsey, barbur.

xxx s. De tenemento in quo manet Will' Smythe.[1]

x s. De uno gardino quod Margareta Hall tenet.

xiii s. iiii d. De alio gardino uocato Penkryche Halle quod Willelmus Wellys & Willelmus Ashe tenent.

Summa xxiii li. viii s. x d.

In parochia sancte Marie in Catestrete.

xiii s. iiii d. Pro tenemento in quo manet Ioh' Ashenden, glouer.

x s. De proxima domo in qua manet Ianyn Coke.

F. vii s. vi d. De tenemento quod Ioh' Clerke alderman nuper tenuit & solebat reddere per annum de quieto redditu.

F. iiii s. De proxima domo quam mag. Gorge tenet & reddit de quieto redditu.

[1] This tenement is out of place; it should occur next before *Le Bell*; see previous rentals.

xiii s. iiii d. De tenemento in quo manet Ioh' Glouere.
xxxiii s. iiii d. De tenemento in quo manet Ric. Hosyer.
xxx s. De tenemento iuxta angulum in quo manet Thomas Ufyngton.
xx s. De gardiano & sociis collegii Animarum pro quodam gardino in Katestret; nichil inde.
xvi s. De tenemento in quo manet Thomas Bygnelle.
Summa vii li. vii s. vi d.

In parochia Omnium Sanctorum.

viii s. & onera. De domo iuxta Brodeyat' quam Nich' Howght tenet per indenturam.
xxvi s. viii d. De proxima domo uocata Brodeyat' in qua manet Rob. Perkyns.
xvi s. De domo pone ecclesiam Omnium Sanctorum in qua manet Percyuall' Thorpe.
viii s. De alia domo ibidem quam Ioh' Smythe tenet & reddit per annum viii s. et Prior & conuentus sancte Frideswyde receperunt redditum; nichil inde.
Summa lviii s. viii d.

x s. De tenemento in quo manet Will' Cleche.
viii s. Pro opella ex oposito Omnium Sanctorum quam Ioh' Pengelly tenet.
xl s. De tenemento in quo manet Margareta Halle.
F. xxviii s. De tenemento quam Ric. Kent tenet & reddit de quieto redditu.
viii s. De opella in qua manet Ioh' Armerer.
Summa iiii li. xiiii s.

In parochia sancti Martini.

F. x s. Pro introitu olim uocato Kyngston quem nuper Thomas Dereste tenuit & reddere solebat de quieto redditu; nichil inde quia ipse negat redditum.
viii s. De proxima opella quam Steph' Glouer nuper tenuit; nichil inde quia ruinosa est in defectu Prioris & conuentus sancte Frideswyde.
viii s. De secunda opella ibidem quam nuper Nich' Flecher tenuit & reddere solebat viii s.; nichil inde quia ruinosa est in defectu Prioris & conuentus sancte Frideswyde.

F. vi s. viii d. De tercia opella ibidem quam Edwardus Woddeward tenet & reddere solebat per annum de quieto redditu; nichil inde quia ipse negat redditum.

Summa xxxii s. viii d.

In parochia sancti Michaelis ad portam australem.

iiii s. Pro tenemento cum gardino que Hen. Fuller tenet.

x s. De proxima domo quam mag. Ioh' Walyngforde cum gardino tenet.

vi s. viii d. De proxima domo quam Thos. Shefforde tenet.

F. ii s. Pro domo priorisse de Lytylmore ex altera parte quam Ioh' Hauyle tenet & reddit de quieto redditu.

Summa xxii s. viii d.

In parochia sancti Aldati.

F. xii s. Pro tenemento uocato le Swanne in quo manet Will' Capelonde & reddit de quieto redditu.

xl s. De proximo tenemento in quo manet Ioh' Camney [1] cum paruo tenemento annexo.

xx s. De proximo tenemento in qua manet Ioh' [*blank*]; W. Mason habet pro suo feodo.

xxxiii s. iiii d. Pro tenemento in quo manet Ioh' Barbur cum paruo tenemento annexo, que Will. Mason habet pro feodo suo.

xxvi s. viii d. De proxima domo in cornerio quam Will' Mason habet pro feodo suo.

vi s. viii d. Pro tenemento in Pynfarthingstrete quod Nich' Croke nuper tenuit; nichil inde quia ruinosum est & stetit uacuum per totum annum.

v s. Pro tenemento ex opposito Bullehalle in quo manet Rog' Fermer.

xxvi s. viii d. Pro aula uocata Minothalle in qua manet mag. Thomas Byrchall.

viii s. Pro tenemento ex oposito ecclesie sancti Aldati in quo manet Rob. Fayreman.

Summa viii li. xviii s. iiii d.

In parochia sancte Ebbe.

F. viii s. De tenemento sub muro uille Oxon in quo manet Rob. Hethe & reddit de quieto redditu.

[1] Elsewhere Kanney.

iiii s. & onera. De parua domo in Balliolo in qua manet Thos. Huske.

viii s. De tenemento ex oposito porte fratrum minorum in quo manet Ric. Lase.

viii d. De paruo gardino quod Margareta Couper nuper tenuit.

Summa xx s. viii d.

In parochia sancti Petri in occidente.

iii li. vi s. viii d. De tenemento cum uno tenemento annexo que Ioh' Dyker nuper tenuit.

In parochia sancti Michaelis ad portam borialem.

xxiii s. iiii d. De tenemento in quo manet Steph' Glouer.

In parochia sancte Marie Magdalene.

xxvi s. viii d. De tenemento in quo manet Ioh' Isam.

F. iiii s. De tenemento in quo manet Will. Holden & reddit de quieto redditu.

xiii s. iiii d. De tenemento super Kandiche in quo manet Alicia Ade relicta.

iiii s. De uno gardino ibidem in manu Willelmi Tyrsyn.

F. iii s. De tenemento quod Edwardus Wodwarde ten' & reddit de quieto redditu.

iiii s. De quodam tenemento quod mag. & socii collegii Balioli tenent.

Summa lv s.

In parochia sancti Egidii.

vi s. viii d. De domo in qua Ioh' Iewell manet.

De domibus clericorum.

xx s. De aula Aristotalle in quo manet mag. Kelly principalis ibidem.

ii s.	De gardino olim uocato Wilbyhalle quod rector & socii collegii Exon tenent & solebat reddere.	xxxv s. iiii d.
xxvi s. viii d.	De magno prato quod Thomas Warde tenet.	
vi s. viii d.	De aqua separabili dimissa Roberto Barone.	

For the years 1 Ric. III, 3 Ric. III, 1 Hen. VII, and 8 Hen. VII the Computus gives no details of the rents, but after mentioning what the total should be it gives the *resoluciones* and the *defectus redditus*.

The *resoluciones* are the same in each of these years, viz. 2*s.* 6*d.* from 'le Doubull Key' outside North Gate,[1] paid to William Herle 'armiger'; 8*d.* to the proctors of the church of St. Michael North from the tenement inhabited by John Colet;[2] 13*d.* to the bailiff of Northgate Hundred for suit of court; 2*s.* 4*d.* to the Chamberlain of the Town;[3] 10*s.* to William Barantyne[4] for Great Mead; 1*s.* 6*d.* to the Abbot of Abingdon from a tenement and garden in Pennyfarthing Street occupied by John Fermer; 13*s.* 4*d.* to the King's College from a tenement called le Tabbard; 20*s.* to the manor of Sandford; 8*d.* to the warden of the church of St. Michael at North Gate from the tenement occupied by Stephen Glover;[5] 6*s.* 8*d.* to the Provost of Queen's College from a tenement called le Belle;[6] 10*s.* to the Master of the Rolls for converted Jews; 7½*d.* to the bailiffs of Oxford for landgable. Total, £3 9*s.* 4½*d.*

The *defectus redditus* in 1 Ric. III amounted to £12 5*s.* 2*d.*; no rent was received from the first four tenements next to the Great Gate of the College because they had been made into the Grammar School; the tenement next to the Grammar School 'stetit uacua per iii anni terminos, causa noue edificacionis'; the three selds outside East Gate paid no rent 'quia non edificantur et steterunt desolate per plures annos'; the shop at Carfax late in the tenure of Stephen Glover is 'in decasu, quam Prior sancte Frideswide erigere, exaltare, reparare et construere tenetur';[7] 'item in defectu redditus unius magni prati uocati le Gretmede, quia superundatur annuatim cum aquis, unde male herbe uocate Flagges et alie herbe nociue ibidem accreuerunt et pratum predictum fere destruxerunt'. The *redditus negati* were 20*s.* from All Souls, 2*s.* from Exeter College (i.e. for St. William Hall), 10*s.* from Thomas Durest for Kingston's Entry, and 6*s.* 8*d.* from Edward Atwode (= Woodward) from his tenement in St. Martin's.

In 3 Ric. III the *defectus redditus* were £11 12*s.* 8*d.*; the first five houses next to the gate of the College, including the tenement of Robert Baron, were now The Grammar School, and all the houses as far as the corner, except the house of Thomas Adderbery, had been

[1] The rental of 1480 shows that the Double Key was no. 4, Magdalen Street; apparently William Herle was lord of Northgate Hundred.

[2] This occurs in each of the four years, but it does not occur in 1511 or subsequently. The rentals do not mention John Colet. It is distinct from the quitrent paid to the churchwardens, which occurs below.

[3] i.e. two shillings for Harehall Lane and 4*d.* for the Racke in Grampound.

[4] Lord of the manor of Chalgrove.

[5] i.e. no. 43, Cornmarket.

[6] See vol. i, p. 287.

[7] See vol. ii, p. 79.

vacant part of the year 'causa noue edificationis'; the tenements of Karon, Grey, and Blake had been thrown into one. Aristotle Hall was vacant the whole year. The repairs were £30 18*s.* 3*d.*; the *redditus negati* £2 8*s.* 8*d.*; the *resoluciones* £3 9*s.* 4½*d.*; and as the *redditus assise* were £74 7*s.* 8*d.* the clear amount received by the College was only £25 18*s.* 8½*d.*

In 8 Hen. VII the *defectus redditus* were £8 2*s.* 6*d.* from houses which were vacant 'because no one was willing to hire them'.

45. A rental of Sept. 29, 1487.

Rentale factum per Robertum Baron collectorem redditus uille Oxonie renouatum tempore mag. Ricardi Mayhew presidentis collegii beate Marie Magdalene extra portam uille orientalem Oxonie anno regni regis Henrici VII ad festum Michaelis tercio.

Parochia sancti Clementis.

xiii s. iiii d. Thomas Warde.
viii s. Prox. domus; uacat.
xx s. quondam Ioh' Vngull.

Summa xli s. iiii d.

Parochia sancti Petri; extra portam, ex parte australi.

xxxiii s. iiii d. De tenemento cum crofto uoc. Parys; Hen. Molton.

Summa xxxiii s. iiii d.

Ex parte boriali.

vii s. De domo prox. scole gramaticali quam Rob. Baron tenet.
xl s. De secunda domo; Martinus Bereman.
xx s. De tercia domo; quondam Ioh' Bowdon.
xx s. De quarta domo; Ioh' Taylour.
xx s. De quinta domo; Ioh' Gylle.
xiii s. iiii d. De sexta domo; nichil inde quia non edificatur.
xx s. De septima domo; nichil inde quia non edificatur.
vii s. De tribus seldis iuxta fontem; nichil inde quia non edificantur.

Summa vii li. vii s. iiii d.

Infra portam orientalem.

xii s. Rob. Karon.
x s. Rob. Blake.
xiii s. iiii d. Ioh' Whyt.

xx s. Ioh' Bowcher.
xx s. Edmund Fuller.
F. x d. De domo quam Noui pistor' tenet.
xx s. Gramerhalle; mag. Broke; nichil inde quia ruinosum.
x s. De ii gardinis; gardianus collegii sancte Marie; nichil inde.
xiii s. iiii d. De ii tenementis; Ric. Gryffythe.
viii s. Thomas Hardewyke.
F. xv s. iiii d. De preposito collegii Regine.
xxxiii s. iiii d. Pro tenemento cum iiii seldis; Ric. Chamberleyn.
xl s. le Belle; Ioh' Kamney.
xxx s. Will. Holden alias Smythe.
xxvi s. viii d. Ioh' Myssynden, taylour.
viii s. Iohanna Euererde relicta.
viii s. Thos. Bonde.
xxvi s. viii d. Hen. Lyrpyn.[1]
xxvi s. viii d. Bosterhalle; Nich. Taylour.
liii s. iiii d. le Tabard; Nich' Howghe.
xl s. Ioh' Symson.
vi s. viii d. Rob. Churcheyard.
vi s. viii d. Will' Sareson.
xiii s. iiii d. Pro gardino uocato Penkeriche; nichil.
x s. Pro alio gardino[2]; Will. Manby.
Summa xix li. xvi s. x d.[3]

In parochia sancte Marie.
xiii s. iiii d. Margareta Ashenden, relicta.
x s. Pet. Glouer.
F. vii s. vi d. Ioh' Clerke, alderman; nichil inde.
F. iiii s. De prox. domo, quam mag. George tenet.
xiii s. iiii d. Nuper Iohanna Euererd.
xxxiii s. iiii d. Ric' Hosyer.
xlvi s. De tenemento iuxta angulum; Ric. Norcot.
xx s. De gardiano collegii Animarum.
Summa vii li. vii s. vi d.

In parochia Omnium Sanctorum.
viii s. cum onera. De domo iuxta Brodeyates; Nich. Howght per indenturam.

[1] Probably Ing Hall in St. Mary's.
[2] In the account of repairs at the end of the rental it seems to be 'Nyghtingall garden'.
[3] In this and other cases the items do not answer to the total.

xxvi s. viii d. Rob. Perkyns per indenturam.
xvi s. De domo pone ecclesiam; Ric. Aborow carpentar.
viii s. De domo ibidem, nuper Ioh' Smith; nichil; Prior sancte Frideswide recepit redditus.
x s. De alia domo ibidem iuxta tenementum Iohannis; uacat.
viii s. Opella ex opposito ecclesie; Margareta Knollys.
xl s. Ric. Bolton.
F. xxviii s. De quieto redditu; Ric. Kent.
viii s. De opella; Simon Bache.
Summa iii li. xvi s.

In parochia sancti Martini.
x s. nuper Thomas Dereste; nichil.
viii s. nuper Steph' glouer; nichil.
viii s. nuper Nich. Flecher; nichil.
vi s. viii d. Edwardus Wodewardus.
Summa xxxii s. viii d.

In parochia sancti Michaelis ad portam australem.
xiii s. iiii d. De tenemento cum gardino; Ric. Hewys.
x s. De prox. domo cum gardino; mag. Ioh' Walyngforde.
xiii s. iiii d. De domo prox.; Will' Kenet.
ii s. Ioh' Hauyle.
Summa xxxviii s. viii d.

In parochia sancti Aldati.
F. xii s. Will. Capelonde.
xxvi s. viii d. Cristoforus Coke, bokebynder.
xiii s. iiii d. Ioh' Downe, sadler.
xx s. Hew Afferynton, fuller.
xxxiii s. iiii d. Ioh' Barbur.
xxvi s. viii d. Ioh' Mansepulle.
iii s. iiii d. Nic' Croke in Pynfarthingstrete per indenturam.
v s. Tenementum ex opposito Bullehalle.
xxvi s. viii d. Minothalle; mag. Grey uicarius de Bloxham.
viii s. Rob. Fayrewell [*sic*] ex opposito ecclesie sancti Aldati.
Summa viii li. xv s.

In parochia sancte Ebbe.
F. viii s. Rob. Hethe.
iiii s. & onera. Thos. Huske.

viii s. Ric. Lase.
viii d. De paruo gardino; Ioh' Thurstan gardiner.
Summa xx s. viii d.

Parochia sancti Petri in occidente.
iii li. vi s. viii d. De tenemento cum duobus tenementis annexis Ioh' Whyte carpentar.

Parochia sancti Michaelis borialis.
xxiii s. iiii d. Steph. Glouer.

Parochia sancte Marie Magdalene.
xxvi s. viii d. Ioh' Ysam.
F. iiii s. Rog. Robyns.
xiii s. iiii d. Alicia Ade relicta.
iiii s. In manu Iohannis West fuller.
iiii s. De quodam tenemento; magister & socii collegii Balioli.
Summa lv s.

Parochia sancti Egidii.
vi s. viii d. Ric. Iewell.

De domibus clericorum.
xx s. De aula Arestotil.
ii s. De gardino uocato Wylbyhalle.
xxxiii s. iiii d. De magno prato; Thos. Warde.
xx s. De collegio Mertonis pro Kingsmylle.
iiii s. De aqua separali; Rob. Baron.
Summa totalis lxxiii li. xii s. iiii d.

46. **A rental of Sept. 29, 1507.**

Rentale renouatum anno regni regis Henrici septimi xxiii° per Henricum Hochynson reddituum Oxon' collectorem.

In parochia sancti Clementis.
xiii s. iiii d. Ric. Harme.
xl s. De domo in qua inhabitat Hooper tanner.
xxxiii s. iiii d. De magno prato; Ioh' Baker.
Summa iiii li. vi s. viii d.

In parochia sancti Petri in oriente.
iii li. De domo; Iohannes Gylle.
i lib. incensi; de sacello sancte Trinitatis.

xl s. De aula diue Marie Magdalene.
xxx s. Thomas Pantrey.
xl s. Martinus Bereman.
xiii s. iiii d. Katerina Norrys.
xxvi s. viii d. Will. Campynott.
xx s. Katerina Multon.
xx s. Thomas Cooke.
iii li. vi s. viii d. Ioh' Baker.
x s. De Edmundo Myller; pro aqua piscar'.

Infra portam.
x s. Georgius Hertt.
x s. Rob. Schyrtt.
xx s. Cornyll carpentar.
xx s. Henricus Hochynson.
xx s. nuper Margareta Fuller.
iiii s. le Tymberyerd.
F. x d. Hen. Hudson.
xx s. Gramerhall; Rob. Carow per indenturam.
i lib. piperis. De tenemento cum tribus aliis annexis; Steph. Cook.
xxx s. Rob. Holbeke.
xl s. De ten. voc. ly Belle; Vawhon.
xx s. Rogerus glouer.
ix s. Reg. Leueryk.
viii s. Rog. Taskar.
vi s. viii d. Ioh' Hayborne.[1]
vi s. viii d. Rob. Ionson.
xl s. De pandoxorio in tenura Rob. Carow.
iii li. vi s. viii d. ly Tabard; Thomas Kartar.
xxvi s. viii d. Bowstarhall; Nich' Tayler per indenturam.

Apud Smythgate.
vi s. viii d. Randall Tayler.
vi s. viii d. In tenura magistri An.
viii s. Gilbertus laborator.
Summa xxxv li. xiii s. ii d.

Parochia sancte Marie.
xxvi s. viii d. Georgius Bokebynder.
x s. Ioh' Browne.

[1] Here begins the south side of the road, starting near East Gate.

F. vii s. vi d. Ioh' Egecombe, alderman.
F. iiii s. Legett, glouer.
xiii s. iiii d. De tenemento iuxta Cornysshe; uacat.
xx s. Physykehall; gardianus scholarium collegii Animarum.
xxvi s. viii d. Henricus Lyrpyn.
xxxiii s. iiii d. Ioh' Fustyng.
xlvi s. viii d. Ioh' Husher.
F. xiii s. iiii d. De Booryshede in tenura Caroli Marchell in dominio collegii regalis.
Summa x li. xviii d.

Parochia Omnium Sanctorum.
viii s. Ioh' Symonds, tayler, de quieto redditu, ut per indenturam.
xxiii s. iiii d. Ioh' Walkar, carear.
xvi s. nuper Will' Scissor.
xvi s. Pone ecclesiam; Ric' Boro-wȝght.
x s. Quedam uidua.
vi s. Nuper Edwardus Mortymer.
viii s. De officina ex opposito ecclesie.
xl s. Rob. Teckoo.
F. xxviii s. mag. Ric. Kent.
Summa viii li. vi s.

Parochia sancti Martini.
x s. De introitu Kyngyston; uac.
xl s. Alicia Blunt per indenturam.
Summa l s.

Parochia sancti Michaelis borialis.
ii s. De quieto redditu de Coll. Exon.
xxvi s. viii d. Hen. Sethe.
xiii s. iiii d. De Goodyershowse de quieto redditu ut per compositionem inter coll. Regine & nostrum.
Summa xlii s.

Sancte Marie Magdalene.
xx s. Elyzabethe Tysyn.
iiii s. De gardino ibidem.
iiii s. De collegio Balioli de quieto redditu.
xxvi s. viii d. Ioh' Goodfrey.
iiii s. Rob. Donham de quieto redditu.

iii s. De Will' Bulcum pro quodam quieto redditu exeunte de domo Iohannis Lokyns pistoris.

Summa iii li. xx d.

Parochia sancti Egidii.

xii d. De abbatissa de Godstow.

ii s. iiii d. De gardino Iohannis Blakborne.

vi s. viii d. Ioh' Walle.

Summa x s.

Parochia sancti Petri in occidente.

iii li. vi s. viii d. De pandoxatorio in tenura Alicie Leek cum ii tenementis ibidem.

Summa iii li. vi s. viii d.

Parochia sancti Aldati.

F. xii s. nuper Copplond; le Swan.

xxvi s. viii d. Ioh' Capper.

xiii s. iiii d. nuper Ioh' Downe.

xx s. Ioh' Tayler.

xxiii s. iiii d. Adam Fysher.

xiii s. iiii d. Luter.

xxvi s. viii d. Ric. Barber.

xiii d. Ex opp. scole in Iudaismo; mag. & socii collegii Balliol.

vi s. viii d. Ric. Cooke in Penyferdyngstret.

v s. Sawndres.

xxvi s. viii d. Mynynghall.

xvi s. Ex opposito ecclesie sancti Aldati; Ric. Bobery.

Summa ix li. x s. ix d.

Parochia sancte Ebbe.

F. viii s. Ioh' Heed.

viii s. Ric. Lasy ex opposito Fratrum Minorum.

viii d. De gardino; Will' Caryer.

iiii s. Thomas Leeke.

Summa xx s. viii d.

Parochia sancti Thome.

xiii s. iiii d. De ten. in le Hamell.

Parochia sancti Michaelis australis.

x s. Thomas Aston.

x s. glover.

viii s. Ioh' Palmer.
ii s. Thomas Warden de quieto redditu.
Summa xxx s.

Parochia sancti Iohannis Baptiste.
xxiiii s. De aula Aristotil.
iiii s. De gardino annexo.
iiii s. De gardino, quondam Coll. Ball., modo Mertonis.[1]
vi s. viii d. De Pencryshall.
vi s. viii d. De Nyztynghall.
Summa xlv s. iiii d.

Wyllybyhall de quieto redditu ii s.

47. A rental of Sept. 29, 1511.

Computus Iohannis Renolde collectoris reddituum Oxonie a festo sancti Michaelis archangeli anno regni regis Henrici VIII tercio usque idem festum ex tunc proximo sequens anno dicti domini regis quarto.

Arreragia lxxv li. xv d.

Parochia sancti Clementis pape.
xiii s. iiii d. Domus Ricardi Harme.
xl s. Domus Ricardi Balle, tanner [Willelmi Frere in 1516].
xxxiii s. iiii d. Pro magno prato in tenura Thome Morres [xxxvi s. iiii d. in 1516].
x s. Pro piscaria.

Parochia sancti Petri in oriente.
lx s. Domus relicte Iohannis Gylde.
xl s. De aula beate Marie Magdalene.
xxx s. Domus Thome Pantre.
xl s. Domus Turden, bereman [Nic. Kyrke in 1516].
xiii s. iiii d. Domus Wylkesley [Will. Gateman, 1516; relicta Gateman, 1517].
xxvi s. viii d. Domus Camponet, tayllour.
xx s. Domus Roberti Perrot.
xx s. Domus Thome Cooke [Nic. Kyrke, 1516]. } [The order of these is reversed in 1514 & 1516.]
iii li. vi s. viii d. Domus Thome Morres, baker.
i lib. incensi de quieto redditu exeunte de capella sancte Trinitatis.

[1] i. e. Hertheved Hall.

xii s. Domus Iohannis Cooke [Rob. Boys, 1514; Ioh' Plomer, 1516].

x s. Domus Roberti Boys, carpenter [Ioh' Plomer, 1514; Cornelius carpenter, 1516].

xviii s. Domus Ricardi Tayllour; nuper reddere solebat xx s. [Falowfield, 1513].

xxiii s. iiii d. Domus Gerardi Fuller [Galf' Faber, 1513].

xxiii s. iiii d. Domus in qua manet Rosa relicta Henrici Huchynson; nuper reddere solebat xxvi s. viii d.

vi s. viii d. le Tymber Yard.

x d. De quieto redditu exeunte de domo Henrici Hudson [Ric. Taylor, 1513; Th' Morrys, 1516].

vi s. viii d. De domo in qua manet relicta Wyllyams; tamen reddet in fine termini sui xx s. [in 1516 Rob. Pannett, in domo dimissa Roberto Carewe ad terminum annorum; hoc anno octauo decimo].

i lib. piperis, de quieto redditu exeunte de domo angulari in tenura Stephani Robynson coci [xii d., 1513; xviii d., 1516; xvi d., 1517].

xxx s. Domus Roberti Holbekke.

xxxiii s. iiii d. De le Belle, dimiss' Willelmo Sarseson, set ultimo anno termini sui reddet redditum solitum viz. xl s.

xxvi s. viii d. Domus Rogeri, glouer.

ix s. Domus Rogeri Tasker.

viii s. Domus Ricardi Baker [Agnetis Holbeck, 1514; Ioh' Fuller, 1516].

xxvi s. viii d. Domus Nicholai Sargent.

iii li. vi s. viii d. De signo uocato le Aynegell.

xx s. Domus Roberti Carew, dimissa ad terminum xxx annorum, hoc anno vii^{o}; tamen reddere solebat xl s.

vi s. viii d. Domus Roberti Iohnson.

vi s. viii d. Domus Ricardi Paynter [Rob. Carpenter, 1516].

vi s. viii d. De uno gardino in tenura magistri Fe-Iames.

vi s. viii d. De uno gardino in tenura Nicholai Taylour.

xiii s. iiii d. De duobus tenementis in tenura magistri Anne.

viii s. De domo in tenura Gilberti Hameleton.

Parochia sancte Marie Virginis.

xxvi s. viii d. Domus Henrici Lyrpyn.

xx s. De custode collegii Animarum, pro Phisikhalle.

xx s. Domus Rogeri Taylour; tamen in fine termini reddet redditum solitum viz. xxvi s. viii d. [mag. Mede xxvi s. viii d., 1514; xxiii s. iiii d., 1516].

iiii s. De quieto redditu exeunte de domo in qua manet Will. Wynter coke.

viii s. Domus Henrici Foster; solebat x s. [Ioh' Taylor, 1516].

xx d. De quadam uacua placea, dimissa Willelmo Legat, tamen reddere solebat xiii s. iiii d. [Will. Smith, 1516].

vii s. vi d. De quieto redditu exeunte de gardino magistri Eggecombe.

xl s. Domus Egidii Bokebynder [Egidii Mercer, 1513; Rob. Larke, 1514].

xlvi s. viii d. Domus Iohannis Ussher [Iacobi Collynson, 1514].

xiii s. iiii d. De quieto redditu de le Boryshede in tenura David Potycary.

Parochia Omnium Sanctorum.

viii s. Domus Iohannis Symonds.

xxxiii s. iiii d. Domus Iohannis Walker, caryar.

xvi s. Domus Roberti Wylton [Ric' Wylton, 1514; de nouo edificata in tenura Walker xx s., 1517].

xvi s. Domus relicte Bourroughe [Ioh' Pye, 1516].

viii s. Domus relicte Bocher.

vi s. viii d. De uno gardino, quem nuper tenuit Edwardus Mortymer; reddere solebat xvii s. [xx d., 1514; mag. Goodryk, 1516].

viii s. De quadam opella ex opposito ecclesie Omnium Sanctorum [Ioh' Reynold, 1516].

xl s. De domo Willelmi Frere.

xxviii s. De quieto redditu de duobus tenementis in tenura Ricardi Kent.

Parochia sancti Martini.

xxxiii s. iiii d. De domo in qua Blount manet; reddere solebat xl s. [Ioh' Maderson, 1514].

x s. De introitu uocato le Kyngestone.

Parochia sancti Michaelis in boriali.

xiii s. iiii d. de quieto redditu de quadam domo uocata Goodyers howse.

xxvi s. viii d. Domus Nicholai Postlett.

ii s. De quieto redditu exeunte de aula uocata Willoughby Halle.

Parochia sancte Marie Magdalene.

xxvi s. viii d. Domus Simonis Gaunt [Ioh' Furbour, 1516].

iii s. De quieto redditu exeunte de quodam tenemento Edwardi Wodward, modo magistri Bulcombe.

iiii s. De quieto redditu de domo Roberti Denham.

iiii s. De quieto redditu de tenemento collegii Ballioli.

xxiii s. iiii d. Domus Elbyk, baker [Rob. Hucuale, 1514].

iiii s. De uno gardino ibidem in tenura Thome Coke, noui collegii [in 1513 'aufugit et non potuit aliquid leuari'].

Parochia sancti Egidii.

vi s. viii d. Domus Iohannis Walle.

ii s. iiii d. De gardino nuper in tenura Iohannis Blakehalle.

xii d. De tenemento abbatisse de Godstowe.

Parochia sancti Petri in occidente.

liii s. iiii d. Domus Iohannis Reynold.

vi s. viii d. Domus Iacobi Bruet [Iacobi Dodson, 1512; Ioh' Raby, 1514].

vi s. viii d. Domus Willelmi Derby [Will' Townsend, 1516].

Parochia sancte Ebbe.

viii s. De quieto redditu de domo Iohannis Hede.

viii s. De gardino annexo Aule Bouine.

viii d. De gardino in tenura Willelmi Taillor [xii d., Ioh' Richardson, 1514].

xii d. De gardino in tenura relicte Symonds, nuper ad iiii s. [Ric' Rawlins, 1516].

x s. Domus Willelmi Barkshere.

Parochia sancti Aldati.

xii s. De quieto redditu exeunte de domo uocata le Swan.

xxvi s. viii d. De domo Ricardi Walkelyn.

x s. Domus Iohannis Patryk, nuper ad xiii s. iiii d.

xvi s. Domus Iohannis Taylour [Ioh' Robynson, 1516].

xxiii s. iiii d. Domus Adam Fyssher [Will' Taylor, 1516].

xiii s. iiii d. Domus Thome Barbour [Will' Hale, 1514; Will' Cowper, 1516; Bastian, 1517].

xxvi s. viii d. Domus Iohannis Barbour [Will' Smith, 1514].

xiii d. De quodam tenemento ex opposito scole in Iudaismo, quod prepositus collegii Baliol tenet.

iiii s. De tenemento in Penyferthyngstrete in tenura David Guillam [Ioh' Bowbery, 1517].

x s. De domo exopposito ecclesie sancti Aldati nuper ad xvi s. [viii s. 1514; in tenura Fisher, 1517].

Parochia sancti Michaelis ad portam australem.

viii s. Domus Thome Palmer.

x s. Domus relicte Banastre.

x s. Domus Dauid Morgan.

ii s. De quieto redditu exeunte de domo Priorisse de Litilmore in tenura relicte Warden.

Parochia sancti Iohannis.

Ibidem est aula uocata Aristotille Hall (xxiiii s.) et unum gardinum (iiii d.) sibi annexum, et quoddam gardinum[1] inclusum gardino Mertonis; cum istis computans non oneratur, quia nescitur ubi iacent. [In 1517 it is: ii s. de gardino ubi quondam fuit Aristotyll-hall in tenura magistri Hoper; iiii s. de gardino incluso gardino Mertonis.]

Parochia sancti Thome.

xiii s. iiii d. De tenemento in le hamell iuxta paruum pontem.

Summa totalis lxxvii li. iiii s. i d.

The *resoluciones* are: 2*s.* to William Erley, Esq., for a tenement without North Gate called Le Dobulle Key; 8*d.* from the tenement of Nich. Postlett, skinner, to the proctors of the church of St. Michael North; 13*d.* to the bailiff of Northgate Hundred for releasing suit of court; 18*d.* to the abbot of Abingdon from a tenement in Pennyfarthing Street; 13*s.* 4*d.* to Oriel College for the hospice Le Tabard, now Le Aungell; 4*d.* to magister Wylks;[2] 7½*d.* to the bailiffs of the town for landgable;[3] 13*d.* to Master Darell at his manor of Chalgrove for a quitrent from Great Mead near the bridge; 8*d.* to the churchwardens of St. Aldate's from a house in the tenure of John Baker;[4] 2*s.* 4*d.* to the chamberlains of the City.[5]

[1] The site of Hertheved Hall.

[2] Probably a bursar of New College; in later years the rent was paid to the Warden of New College; it was due from a tenement in Coach and Horses Lane.

[3] In earlier times it was 8½*d.*

[4] i.e. on the south side of St. Aldate's churchyard.

[5] Probably 2*s.* for Harehall Lane and 4*d.* for the Rack in St. Michael's South; after 1515 only 2*s.* is paid.

The following quitrents had not been paid for the previous five years; 10*d.* from the house of Henry Hudson; £1 from Physick Hall; 7*s.* 6*d.* from Edgecombe's garden in St. Mary's; 10*s.* for Kingston's Entry, the rent being denied by John Bishop; 13*s.* 4*d.* from Goodyere's house; 2*s.* from Wilby Hall; 2*s.* 4*d.* from a house in St. Giles's in the tenure of Jeamus; 1*s.* from a tenement of Godstow there; 13*s.* 4*d.* from a tenement in the Hamell; 12*s.* from the Swan; 13*d.* from a garden opposite the school of Civil Law, withheld by Balliol; and 'iiii s. de quieto redditu de quodam gardino [1] prope aulam Vitream nuper in tenura collegii Mertonis; iiii s. de quadam aula [2] iuxta collegium Animarum'.

48. A rental of Sept. 29, 1519.

Computus Iohannis Reynolde a festo sancti Michaelis anno regni regis Henrici VIII undecimo usque idem festum anno duodecimo.

Arreragia lxxxxviii li. ix s. iii d. ob.

Parochia sancti Clementis.

xiii s. iiii d. Ric. Harme.

xl s. Domus uocata le Tanhouse; Ioh' Caxston.

xxxiii s. iiii d. Pro magno prato; Ioh' Smith, nuper Thomas Hewstar [Thomas Hewestar, 1523].

x s. Pro piscaria.

Parochia sancti Petri in oriente.

lx s. Relicta Iohannis Gylle.

xl s. Aula beate Marie Magdalene.

xxx s. Thomas Pantre.

xxvi s. viii d. Rob. Perrett nuper ad xl s. [Porrett, 1521; Parrett, 1523].

xiii s. iiii d. Edwardus Barbour.

xxvi s. viii d. Will. Camponet, taylour.

xviii s. Nich' Kyrke; nuper ad xx s. [Kyrkby, 1523; Kyrby, 1524].

xx s. Nuper relicta Alberti carnificis; dudum Simon organmaker [mag. Chaters Alberti, 1521; mag. Chaters Albertus,[3] 1523].

[1] i.e. Hertheved Hall. It is not known that any adjacent hall was called Glasen Hall; perhaps it was another name for Nun Hall.

[2] In Cat Street. It can hardly have been an Academic Hall at this time, as it was occupied in 1507 by a glover and in 1511 by a cook.

[3] In one rental the name is spelt 'Jaturs'.

iii li. vi s. viii d. Ioh' Smith, nuper Thomas Baker [Thomas Hewster, baker, 1523].
i lib. incensi. Capella sancte Trinitatis.
xii s. Ioh. Plummer.
x s. Cornelius Carpenter.
xviii s. Falowfield; reddere solebat xx s. [Cornell, 1521; Humfridus Hewster, 1523].
xxiii s. iiii d. Garrett smyth.
xxiii s. iiii d. Rosa relicta Henrici Huchynson.
vi s. viii d. le Tymber Yerde.
x d. De quieto redditu, Thomas Morrys.
xx s. Rob. Pannett, mason [Ioh' de Colonia, 1523].
i lib. piperis de domo angulari in tenura Stephani Robynson, coci; hoc anno xx d.
xxx s. Rob. Holbeck.
xxxiii s. iiii d. De le Bell, sic dimiss' Willelmo Sareson ad terminos annorum, et ultimo anno termini sui reddet redditum solitum xl s.
xxvi s. viii d. Ioh' Lee, glover [iii s. iiii d. added in 1524 for a new stable].
ix s. Rog. Tasker.
viii s. Ioh' Fuller.
xxvi s. viii d. Nich. Sargeant [Hen. Freman, 1524].
iii li. vi s. viii d. De signo et hospicio uocato le Aynegelle.
xx s. Rob. Carew [mag. Standish, 1521].
vi s. viii d. De uno gardino nuper in tenura magistri Fe-Jamys & modo magistri Standyshe bedell.
vi s. viii d. De uno gardino in tenura Nicholai Taylor [Nic. Sergeant, 1521; Hen. Freman, 1524].
xiii s. iiii d. De ii tenementis in tenura magistri Anne [Rob. Carpenter, 1521].
viii s. De domo in qua manet Gilbertus Hammolton.
vi s. viii d. Rob. Iohnson.
vi s. viii d. Rob. Carpenter.

Parochia sancte Marie Virginis.

xxvi s. viii d. Hen. Lyrpyn [Ric. Alcock, 1523].
xx s. Gardianus collegii Animarum.
xxiii s. iiii d. Thomas Fuller.
F. iiii s. Will. Wynter, coke.

viii s. Ioh' Taylour; reddere solebat x s.
xx d. Will. Smyth; reddere solebat xiii s. iiii d.
F. vii s. vi d. De gardino magistri Eggecombe.
xl s. Rob. Larke [Iacobus Edmondes, 1523].
xlvi s. viii d. Iacobus Colynson.
xiii s. iiii d. De le Boryshedde in tenura Dauid Poticary.

Parochia Omnium Sanctorum.
viii s. Ioh' Symonds per indenturam.
xxxiii s. iiii d. Ioh' Walker, caryar [Ioh' Brigeman, 1523].
xxvi s. viii d. De noua domo in qua manet Ioh' Briggeman.
xvi s. Ioh' Thurston.
viii s. Relicta Bocher [domus Isabelle Dent modo occupatur cum stauro, 1521].
ii s. De gardino quondam Edwardi Mortymer, modo magistri Gooderyke, reddere solebat xvii s. [Ioh' Brigeman, 1523].
viii s. Opella ex opposito ecclesie Omnium Sanctorum in tenura Iohannis Reynolde [occupatur cum stauro, 1523].
xl s. De domo in qua manebat Willelmus Frere, dimiss' eidem Willelmo ad terminum xvii annorum, hoc anno termini sui sexto.
xxviii s. De quieto redditu, Ric' Kent [Walt. Kent, 1521].

Parochia sancti Martini.
xxxiii s. iiii d. Ioh. Madderson [Matheson, 1521; Mathewson, 1523]; reddere solebat xl s.
x s. De introitu Kyngestone.

Parochia sancti Michaelis in boriali.
xiii s. iiii d. De quieto redditu, de domo uocata Goodegere's house.
xxiiii s. Cristoferus Solby; reddere solebat xxvi s. viii d.
ii s. De quieto redditu de aula uocata Wylloughby Halle.

Parochia beate Marie Magdalene.
xxvi s. viii d. Ioh' Baker, modo Ioh' Reynold.
iii s. De tenemento Ricardi Wodeward, modo magistri Bulcombe.
iiii s. Banestar de quieto redditu.
iiii s. De placea terre inclusa infra muros collegii Balioli.

xxiii s. iiii d. Rob. Hucuale.

iiii s. De gardino nuper in tenura Thome Fuller noui collegii [Rob. Hucuale, 1521].

Parochia sancti Egidii.

vi s. viii d. Ioh' Ball.

ii s. iiii d. De gardino uocato Blakehall.

xii d. De tenemento abbatisse de Godstowe.

Parochia sancti Petri in occidente.

liii s. iiii d. nuper Ioh' Reynolde [Thos. Fuller, 1524].

vi s. viii d. Raby.

vi s. viii d. Will. Townesend.

Parochia sancte Ebbe.

viii s. De quieto redditu; Michael Hethe.

xx d. De gardino annexo aule Bouine; reddere solebat viii s.; modo in tenura Iohannis Leeke.

xii d. De gardino nuper Roberti Rawlyns; nuper ad iiii s.

x s. Will' Barkeshere.

xii d. De uno gardino nuper Ioh' Rychardson.

Parochia sancti Aldati.

xii s. le Olde Swan; de quieto redditu.

xxvi s. viii d. Ric. Walkeleyne.

vi s. viii d. Ioh' Patrykk; reddere solebat xiii s. iiii d.

xvi s. Ioh' Robinson.

xxiii s. iiii d. Will' Taylour.

xiii s. iiii d. Bastyan.

xxvi s. viii d. Will' Smyth.

xiii d. De tenemento exopposito scole Iudaismo; prepositus collegii Balioli.

iiii s. Ioh' Bowbery in Penyferthingstrete.

viii s. De domo exopposito ecclesie sancti Aldati, in tenura Fysher; nuper ad xvi s.

Nichil. De uno gardino in tenura magistri Camby, uocato Mynnett Hall.

Parochia sancti Michaelis ad portam australem.

viii s. Thomas Palmer.

x s. Relicta Banestre.

x s. Dauid Morgan.

F. ii s. Nuper relicta Warden.

Parochia sancti Iohannis.
ii s. De gardino quondam Arestotyll Hall, modo in tenura magistri Hoper [iii s. iiii d. mag Poxwell, 1521].
iiii s. De gardino incluso gardino Mertonis.

Parochia sancti Thome.
xiii s. iiii d. De tenemento in le Hammell.
Summa totalis lxxviii li. xvi s. v d.

49. A rental of Sept. 29, 1535.

Computus Roberti Parrott, collectoris reddituum.

St. Clement.	13/4	Cristoforus glouer.
	40/-	Tanne house; Ioh' Caxton.
	33/4	Thomas Hewester.
	10/-	Piscaria.
St. Pet. in E.	60/-	Euan.
	40/-	Magd. Hall.
	30/-	Nic. Coke.
	26/8	Rob. Parrott.
	13/4	Edward Barbour.
	26/8	[*blank*]
	18/-	——
	20/-	mag. Lee.
	66/8	Will. Nabbe.
	i lib. incensi.	
	12/-	Hen. Edmondson.
	10/-	Cornelius carpenter.
	18/-	Edw. Harpley.
	23/4	Flee, smyth.
	23/4	Rosa relicta Hen. Huchynson.
	6/8	Timber Yard.
	10 d.	Thomas Morrys.
	20/-	Ioh' Snyte.
	i lib. pip.	Steph' Robinson; hoc anno 2/-.
	30/-	Rob. Holbeck.
	33/4	le Bell [*blank*].
	33/4	Ric. Day.
	9/-	Rog. Tasker.
	8/-	Ioh' Payne.

	26/8	Rog. Holden.
	66/8	le Aungell.
	20/-	Mr. Standysh.
	6/8	garden; Hen. Freman.
	8/-	Hammolton.
	13/4	Relicta Poulton.
	6/8	garden; Mr. Fiez James, modo Standishe.
	6/8	Rob. Carpenter.
St. Mary.	26/8	Will. Spene.
	20/-	Phisik hall.
	23/4	Ric. Brigehouse.
	4/-	Will. Wynter.
	8/-	Raynsmor.
	20 d.	Will. Smyth.
	7/6	Mr. Eggecombe.
	40/-	Bartram.
	46/8	Iac. Colynson.
	13/4	Boryshed—David Potycary.
All Saints.	8/-	George Wyllyson—a lease for 13 years more.
	33/4	John Brigeman.
	26/8	John Brigeman.
	16/-	John Thurston.
	8/-	relicta Bocher.
	2/-	once Edw. Mortymer; now Ioh' Brigeman.
	8/-	Storehouse.
	40/-	Rad. Flaxton.
	40/-	A house which was in the tenure of Elena Kent.[1]
St. Martin.	33/4	Ric. Sadler.
	10/-	Kingestowe's entry.
St. Mich.	13/4	Goodyere's house.
	24/-	John Michelson.
	2/-	Willoughby Hall.
St. Mary Mag.	26/8	Thom. Byrd.
	3/-	Rob. Wodeward.
	4/-	Banister.
	23/4	Rob. Hucuale.

[1] The rent was raised from 28*s.* to 40*s.* in 1532.

	4/-	Hucuale; garden; late Rob. [*sic*] Fuller.
	4/-	Balliol College.
St. Giles.	6/8	Will. Hobbes.
	2/4	garden called Blakehall.
	1/-	Godstow.
St. Peter in West.	53/4	Ed. Herste.
	6/8	relicta Baston.
	6/8	Ioh' Cockes.
St. Ebbe.	8/-	Michael Hethe.
	20 d.	garden; Ioh' Leke.
	1/-	garden; late Ioh' Rawlyns.
	10/-	Whyte, slater.
	1/-	John Richardson.
St. Aldate.	12/-	Olde Swanne.
	26/8	Ric. Wakelyn.
	6/8	Will' Gator, cobler.
	16/-	Relict' Barbour.
	23/4	Will' Gubson.
	13/4	Basthyan.
	26/8	Will. Smythe.
	13 d.	Balliol College.
	5/-	Rector Basse in Pennyfarthing St.
	8/-	now included in the Alms House.
	3/4	garden; late mag. Camby.
St. Mich. South.	8/-	John Heron.
	10/-	John Harper.
	10/-	John Beysey.
	2/-	Rob. Warden.
St. John.	4/-	garden.
	4/-	enclosed in Merton College.
St. George [*sic*]	13/4	le Hamell.

50. A rental of Sept. 29, 1545.[1]

Comp. Roberti Porret collectoris reddituum.

St. Clement.	13/4	Cris. Huchynson, glouer.
	40/-	nuper Ioh' Caxton.

[1] The rental for Sept. 29, 1548, is word for word the same.

	33/4	Thom. Hewister.
	10/-	Nich. Markham, barbitonsor.
St. Peter in E.	60/-	Euan Kelleway.
	40/-	Magd. Hall.
	·30/-	Nic. Cook.
	26/8	Mr. Porrett.
	13/4	Hen. Emondson, ianitor collegii.
	26/8	Edw. Bedwarde.
	18/-	[*blank.*]
	20/-	Hen. Mylward.
	66/8	Nyxson.
	i lb. incense.	
	12/-	[*blank.*]
	10/-	widow Preston.
	18/-	Rob. Kettilby.
	23/4	Thomas Flie, smith.
	23/4	Rosa, relicta Hen. Huchinson.
	6/8	Timber yarde.
	10 d.	nuper Rob. Fruen.
	20/-	Rob. Hammon.
	i lib. pip.	Kyrse, barber.
	30/-	Rob. Holbeck.
	30/-	Rog. Hearne, once 40/-.
	30/-	Ric. Day.
	9/-	Rog. Tasker.
	8/-	Ioh' Payne.
	26/8	Mauricius Vaugham.
	66/8	le Angel.
	20/-	mag. Thomas Lee.
	6/8	Garden in tenure of Will. Fruyn & Morrys Vaghan.
	8/-	Ioh' Harryson.
	13/4	Relict' Pulton.
	6/8	Garden of mag. Lee.
	6/8	Rob. Mortimer.
St. Mary.	26/-	Nic. Barbar.
	20/-	Phisickhall.
	23/4	John —
	4/-	Will. Wynter.
	8/-	Will. Raynsmore, once 20/-.

	20 d.	Will. Smyth.
	7/6	Mr. Eggecombe.
	40/-	Barthram.
	46/8	——
	13/4	Borisheheade.
All Saints.	8/-	George Willyson.
	33/4	John Brigeman.
	26/8	John Brigeman.
	16/-	Ioh' Thurston.
	8/-	relicta Bocheour.
	2/-	Garden; once Edw. Mortimer.
	8/-	Shop opposite the church; store-house of college.
	40/-	John —
	40/-	late Helena Kent.
St. Martin.	33/4	Ric. Chapman, sadler.
	10/-	Kingstone's Entry.
St. Michael N.	8/-	Goodyars house; formerly 13/4.
	24/-	John Nicholsone.
	2/-	Willoughbye hall.
St. Mary Mag.	26/8	Darbie.
	3/-	Rob. Wodeward; quitrent.
	4/-	Banyster.
	23/4	Rob. Hucvalle.
	4/-	Rob. Hucvalle; garden.
	4/-	Balliol College.
St. Giles.	6/8	Will. Hewes.
	2/4	Garden called Blackhall.
	1/-	Godstow.
St. Peter in the West.	53/4	late Edw. Herste.
	6/8	relicta Basthian.
	6/8	Ioh' Cokke.
St. Ebbe.	8/-	Michael Hethe.
	20 d.	House of John Bocke and garden next Beef Hall.
	1/-	Garden; late John Rawlins.
	10/-	White, slater.
	1/-	Garden of John Richardson.

St. Aldate. 12/- le Oldeswanne.
26/8 Ric. Walkelyn.
6/8 Will. Cator, cobbler; once 13/4.
16/- relicta Barbour.
23/4 Will. Culston.
13/4 Basthian.
26/8 Will. Smyth.
13 d. De quieto redditu exeunte de quodam tenemento in Penyferthingstrete in ten. rectoris Base.[1]
3/4 Garden; late Mr. Camby.
5/- Base in Pennyfarthing St.
8/- The King's Coll.[2]

St. Michael S. 8/- John Heron.
10/- John Harry.
10/- late John Beysie.
2/- relicta Warden.

St. John. 4/- Garden, once Aristotle Hall, in the tenure of Ric. —.
4/- Garden in Merton College.

St. Nicholas. 13/4.

Total £79 18*s.* 0*d.*

Resoluciones. £3 11*s.* [The 4*d.* to New College (*see* p. 296) is from the tenement of Mr. Lee; only 6*d.* is paid to St. Aldate's from the tenement of John Baker.]

Defectus. Goodyear's house, valued above at 13/4, is let for 8/-.
The tenement, once of Elena Kent, valued at 40/-, is let for 26/8.
Several houses vacant. Total £10 10*s.* 4*d.*

Repairs. £31 9*s.* 9*d.*

Respectuat' £6 17*s.* 8*d.* owing on the house late of Elena Kent, and about £5 of current rents.

51. A rental of Sept. 29, 1554.

Computus Rogeri Herne collectoris.

St. Clement. 13/4 Rodolphus Wilson.
40/- Edouardus Williams.

[1] An error; as the tenement had been removed by Cardinal Wolsey many years before, its site had been forgotten.

[2] i.e. Ch. Ch.

	33/4	Cristiana Hewster & Rob. Fruyn.
	10/-	Rob. Stockhill & Rob. Ardern.
		£4 16*s*. 8*d*.
St. Peter in E.	60/-	Rob. Ardern.[1]
	40/-	Magd. Hall.
	30/-	Rogerus Herne.
	26/8	Alicia Parret; once 40/-.
	13/4	Hen. Emanson, ianitor collegii.
	26/8	mag. Cowper, didasculus.
	18/-	Domus citerior Mr. Gilbert; once 20/-.
	20/-	Domus ulterior Mr. Gilbert.
	66/8	Inn: Cristiana Hewster.
	i lb. incense; chapel of Trinity.	
	12/-	Alexander Cook.
	10/-	Widow Preston.
	18/-	Rob. Ketelbye; once 20/-.
	23/4	Thomas Flye, faber ferrarius.
	23/4	Edw. Abedward; once 26/8.
	6/8	Timberyard.
	10 d.	John Hyll.
	20/-	Rob. Hammon.
	2/-	a lb. of pepper—Kirse, tonsor.
	30/-	Rob. Holbecke.
	33/4	Rob. Tow.
	30/-	Hen. Bolton.
	9/-	Thos. Payne.
	8/-	John Payne.
	26/8	Maurice Vaugham.
	66/8	le Angell.
	20/-	Mr. Hogson.
	6/8	A garden, inter Rob. Fruyn & Mauricium Vaugham.
	8/-	Will' Exham.
	13/4	Two tenements; Will. Smith & John Johnson.
	6/8	John Caponhurste.
	6/8	Will Rodde.
	6/8	A garden; Mr. Hodshon.
		£34 9*s*. 2*d*.

[1] The Computus of 1556 says that the College had held for half a year a cottage next to the tenement of Robert Arden, by the gift of William Standish and Edward Fetteplace; the rent of it was to be 6*s*. 8*d*. a year.

St. Mary.	26/8	Thomas Rilie.
	20/-	Phisick Haule.
	23/4	Inse.
	4/-	Hen. Samon.
	8/-	Alice Bookbynder; once 20/-.
	20 d.	Nich' Markham; once 13/4.
	7/6	Mr. Egecombe.
	40/-	Mr. Goore.
	46/8	Thomas Gyles.
	13/4	Quitrent from le Swanne.
		£9 11*s*. 2*d*.
All Saints.	24/-	Bodington.
	33/4	John Brigeman.
	26/8	John Brigeman.
	16/-	Thomas Poole.
	8/-	Thomas Colpphyn.
	2/-	Garden in the tenure of Baldwyn.
	8/-	Shop opposite All Saints church; Will. Pawle.
	40/-	John Wayte.
	40/-	Robert Grigge.
		£9 18*s*.
St. Martin.	33/4	Thos. Chapman.
	10/-	Kingeston's Entry.
		43/4.
St. Michael N.	13/4	John Ray.
	24/-	Will. Pickaver.
	2/-	Willoughby Haule.
		39/4.
St. Mary Mag.	26/8	Thomas Hynke.
	3/-	Once Will. Marche.
	4/-	Mr. Jamys.
	23/4	Rob. Hucvale.
	4/-	Rob. Hucvale, garden.
	4/-	Ball. Coll.
		65/-.
St. Giles.	6/8	John Johnson.
	2/4	Garden uoc. Blackhall, Huyt.
	1/-	Godstow.
		10/-.

St. Peter in the West. 53/4 Ric. Brigehouse.
6/8 Ric. Brigehouse.
6/8 Nic. Pargenter; once John Cock.
66/8.

St. Ebbe. 8/- Will. Panter.
20 d. Eliz. Rawlins; house & garden next Beef Hall.
1/- Garden; Will. Cod.
10/- Will. Whyte.
1/- Alice Allyn.
21/8.

St. Aldate. 12/- de quieto redditu de domo uoc. le olde Swanne, quam domum cum cellariis & gardino presidens & scolares collegii beate M. Mag. quarto abhinc anno perquisiverunt de Thoma Warren.[1]
26/8 Thomas Pen.
6/8 Pet. Rowe; once 13/4.
16/- John Hunston.
23/4 John Perkins, Will. Fissher, Ric. Williams.
13/4 Ric. Williams.
26/8 Ric. Williams.
13 d. Coll. Ball.
3/4 Myn hawle, a garden, held by principal of Brodegates.
5/- Will. Pawlet; Pennyfarthing St.
8/- Ecclesia Cristi; for Almshouse.
£7 *2s. 1d.*

St. Michael South. 8/- Owin Wykes.
10/- Phil. Geffry.
10/- Phil. Geffry.
2/- John Barton.
30/-.

St. John. 4/- Garden, once Aristotle Hall; Mr. Marshall.
4/- Merton.

St. Nicholas. 13/4 In le Hamelle.
Repairs. £39 *1s. 10½d.*

[1] The Computus of 1556 adds that the College had held for half a year a cottage on the north side of the Old Swan, by the gift of William Standish and Edward Fetteplace. This and the Old Swan were let to Mr. Lant at a rent of £3.

52. Rentals of Sept. 29, 1561, and Sept. 29, 1570.

Computus Rogeri Herne collectoris reddituum.

Sancti Clmentis.

xiii s. iiii d. Rob. Horne [Will. Billingley, 1570].
xl s. Edwardus Williams.
xxxiii s. iiii d. Magnum Pratum; Christiana Hewster & Rob. Fruyn [Hugo Boyden & Will. Ward, 1570].
x s. Piscaria; Rob. Arden & Walt' Amptyll [Edw. Waynwright, 1570].

Sancti Petri in oriente.

lx s. Rob. Arden.
vi s. viii d. De ten. adiacente ex parte occidentali ex dono Willelmi Standisshe & Edwardi Fetiplace.
xl s. Aula B. M. Mag.
xxx s. Rogerus Herne.
xxvi s. viii d. mag. Parret.
xiii s. iiii d. Eliz. Emanson [Mr. Parret xii d. & Mr. Couper xii s. iiii d., 1570].
xxvi s. viii d. mag. Cowper [Mr. Dole, 1570].
xviii s. Citerior domus in tenura magistri Gilbert.
xx s. Vlterior domus in tenura eiusdem.
lxvi s. viii d. Hospitium in tenura Guidonis Pennington.
i lib. incensi. de capella sancte Trinitatis.
xii s. Walterus Amptill.
x s. Ioh' Caponhurst.
xviii s. mag. Ball [Edwardus Ball, 1570].
xxiii s. iiii d. Watkin Jones.
xxiii s. iiii d. Thomas More [Smalman, 1570].
vi s. viii d. le Tymber Yarde.
x d. De domo in qua manet Cox.
xx s. Leonardus Grathill [Edwardus Waynwright, 1570].
ii s. De libra piperis de domo angulari in tenura Kirse tonsoris.
xxx s. Will. Holbeck.
xxxiii s. iiii d. Edwardus Wainwright [Hen. Chapman, 1570].
xxx s. Hen. Bolton.
ix s. Citerior domus in qua mansit Thos. Payne, nunc in tenura Hen. Bolton [Cuthbertus Atkyns, 1570].

viii s. Vlterior domus in qua mansit Thos. Payne, nunc in tenura Hen. Bolton [Cuthbertus Atkyns, 1570].

xxvi s. viii d. Mauricius Vaugham [xxv s. Mauricius Vaugham, xx d. mag. Slithurst pro gardino, ii d. pro licencia extendendi camini sui, 1570].

lxvi s. viii d. Le Angell.

xx s. mag. Hodson [mag. Withington, 1570].

vi s. viii d. Gardinum inter Robertum Fruyn & Mauricium Vaugham [Will. Ward & Mauricium Vaugham, 1570].

viii s. Will. Gaunte.

xiii s. iiii d. Duo tenementa, Ioh' Parkins & Ioh' Iohnson [Ioh' Parkins & Ioh' Hanson, 1570].

vi s. viii d. Will' Ketilbie.

vi s. viii d. Ioh' Widhouse [Ioh' Haywarde, 1570].

vi s. viii d. mag. Hodshon; hortus [mag. Withington, 1570].

Sancte Marie Virginis.

xxvi s. viii d. Thos. Rilie [Vidua Rilie, 1570].

xx s. Phisick Haule.

xxiii s. iiii d. Inse [Will. Jones, 1570].

iiii s. De quieto redditu de domo Hen. Tripley.

viii s. Rob. Amyll.

xx d. De uac. plac.; Ioh' Gore.

vii s. vi d. De quieto red.; nuper Ioh' Edgcombe.

xl s. mag. Gore.

xlvi s. viii d. Thomas Gyles.

xiii s. iiii d. De quieto red. de domo uoc. le Swanne [Old Swanne, 1570].

Omnium Sanctorum.

xxiiii s. Cris. Leuens [Ric. Haule, 1570].

xxxiii s. iiii d. mag. Mathew [Maria Mathew, 1570].

xxvi s. viii d. idem Mathew [Maria Mathew, 1570].

xvi s. Thomas Pole [Ioh' Greneway, 1570].

viii s. Ioh. Sage.

ii s. De gardino Thom. Gyles.

viii s. Opella; Will. Pawle.

xl s. Ioh' Wayte [Will. Perse, 1570].

xl s. nuper Rob. Grigge; nunc Steph. Yewyn [Hen. Aldworth, 1570].

Sancti Martini.
xxxiii s. iiii d. Lenard [Ric. Leonard, 1570].
x s. Tenementum uoc. Kingeston.

Sancti Michaelis borialis.
xiii s. iiii d. Ioh' Ray.
xxiiii s. Will. Peckaver.
ii s. Willoughby Haule.

Beate Marie Magdalene.
xxvi s. viii d. Hen. Smithe [Rog. Whelar, 1570].
iii s. De quieto redditu de tenemento quondam Will. Marsh.
iiii s. De quieto redditu de domo in qua mansit mag. Edwards.
xxiii s. iiii d. mag. Barnes.
iiii s. Gardinum in tenura eiusdem.
iiii s. Coll. Ball.

Sancti Egidii.
vi s. viii d. Geor. Ewyn.
ii s. iiii d. Le gardin' Blackhall in tenura Rogeri Huyt.
xii d. Abbat. de Godstow.

Sancti Petri in occidente.
liii s. iiii d. Richardus Iuery [Walterus Owyn, 1570].
vi s. viii d. Ric. Brighouse.
vi s. viii d. Quondam Ioh' Cox, nunc Coles.

Sancte Ebbe.
viii s. De quieto redditu; Will. Paynter.
xx d. Domus Henrici Milwarde & gardinum annexum aule Bouine.
xii d. Gard. nuper Will. Sparrow [nuper Rob. Denton, 1570].
x s. Will. Philipps.
xii d. Gard. nuper Thom. Comyn.

Sancti Aldati.
liii s. iiii d. Domus in qua manet Mr. Little [Thomas Wode, 1570], que nuper perquisita est de Thoma Warren.
vi s. viii d. Domus contigua ex parte boriali quam Will. Standishe & Edwardus Fetiplace nuper contulerunt collegio predicto.
xx s. Domus ultimo anno perquisita de Simone Parret contigua proximo dicto cotagio ex parte boriali. Et

iam predicte tres domus locate sunt prefato Little [magistro Baylie, 1570] ad terminum 20 ann. pro redd. £4.

xxvi s. viii d. Domus in qua manebat Michael Herne.
vi s. viii d. Domus in qua manet Michael Herne.
xvi s. Ioh. Rawlyns.
xxiii s. iiii d. Domus in qua manet Ioh. Parkins [Ioh. Hunston, 1570], Will. Fisher, Ric. Williams.
xiii s. iiii d. Ric. Williams.
xxvi s. viii d. Ric. Williams.
xiii d. De ten. in Peny farthing strete [*sic*]; de Coll. Ball.
iii s. iiii d. Gardinum uocatum Mynhalle.
v s. Ioh' Nicols in Penyfarthingstrete.
viii s. Christ Church.

Sancti Michaelis australis.
viii s. Owynus Wykes [Norris, 1570].
x s. Bennet.
x s. Bennet.
ii s. In tenura Iohannis Barton.

Sancti Iohannis.
iiii s. Gardinum uocatum Aristotle Haule; modo mag. Will. Marshall.
iiii s. Gardinum inclusum in coll. Merton.

Sancti Nicholai.
xiii s. iiii d. In le hamelle.

Repairs. £30 6*s*. 8*d*. [£22 10*s*. 7*d*., 1570].

53. Rentals of Sept. 29, 1581, and Sept. 29, 1591.

Computus Rogeri Herne [Arthuri Hearne, 1591].

St. Clement. 13/4 Will. Billingsleye.
40/- Edward Williams [William Willyames, 1591].
34/4 Adrian Pennington & Denis; great mead [widow Pennington & Arthur Hearne, 1591].
10/- Edw. Waynwright; fishery [Will. Billingsleye, 1591].

St. Peter in E. 60/- Rob. Arden [Mr. Gibbarde, 1591].
6/8 Rob. Arden [Mr. Gibbarde, 1591].

40/- Mary Magd. Hall.
30/- Rog. Herne.
26/8 Mr. Parrett [James Sommer, 1591].
13/4 nuper Eliz. Emetson; nunc Mr. Parrett 1/- [Mr. Sommer, 1591], Mr. Balgay 12/4 [John Smith, 1591].
26/8 Mr. Balgay [John Smith, 1591].
18/- Citerior domus; Mr. Gilbert [20/- Arthur Hearne, 1591].
20/- Vlterior domus; Mr. Gilbert [Arthur Hearne, 1591].
66/8 Adrian Pennington [widow Pennington, 1591].
i lb. incense.
12/- Will. Whitcotte [Will. Holbecke, 1591].
10/- Ralf Tomlynson.
18/- Mr. Ball [20/- Ric. Poole, 1591].
23/4 Watkin Jones [Will. Price, 1591].
23/4 Will. Smalman [widow Smalman, 1591].
20/- Domus in le Timber yard cum le Timber yard.
10 d. Richard Coxe.
20/- Edward Waynwrighte.
2/- a lb. of pepper from corner ten.; widow Kirse.
30/- Will. Holbecke [Robert Steynhoe, 1591].
33/4 Hen. Chipnam [40/- Nicholas Clare, 1591].
30/- Ric. Potter [Ric. Morgans, 1591].
9/- Citerior domus; Cuthbert Atkinson.
8/- Vlterior domus; Cuthbert Atkinson.
25/- Maurice Vaughan [Ric. Radcliffe, 1591].
20 d. Dr. Slithurste part of a garden [relict of Ric. Slithurste, 1591].
2 d. land for his chimney [relict of Ric. Slithurste, 1591].
66/8 The Angell.
20/- Dr. Withington [Olivar Withington, 1591].
6/8 Gardinum inter Denys & Mauricium Vaughan [Dennishe & Maurice Vaughan, 1591].
8/- Will. Gaunt [The Principal of Hart Hall, 1591].
13/4 Two tenements; John Perkins & John Harison.
6/8 Will. Kittelbye [late Ralf Gorton, 1591].
6/8 James Haywoode [late Ralf Gorton, 1591].

6/8 Dr. Withington; garden [late in the tenure of Olivar Withington, 1591].

St. Mary's. 26/8 Mr. Phetiplace [Mr. Dochen, 1591].
20/- Phisick Hall.
23/4 widow Jones [Mr. Gelibrande, 1591].
4/- quitrent from house of Hen. Tripleye [Bowler, 1591].
8/- Hen. Myles; once 20/-.
20 d. vacant land, John Gore; once 13/4 [13/4 a stable, John Gore, 1591].
7/6 garden; once Mr Edgecombe.
40/- Mr. Gore.
46/8 Thomas Gyles.
13/4 quitrent from le Olde Swanne [late in the tenure of Tyliarde Taylour, 1591].

All Saints. 24/- Leonard Freye.
33/4 Maria Mathewe [Will. Leche, 1591].
26/8 Maria Mathewe [Will. Leche, 1591].
16/- John Grenewode.[1]
8/- John Sonage [where Samson lives, dimised to George Crew, 1591].
2/- garden; Thomas Gyles—once 17/- [7/- Thomas Gyles, 1591].
8/- a shop opposite the church of All Saints—Joseph Barnes.
40/- Michaell Bonnam.
40/- Will. Pearse.

St. Martin. 33/4 Ioh' Wayte.
10/- Kingestowe's Entry [in the tenure of Will. Pickaver, 1591].

St. Michael N. 13/4 Ray.
24/- Will. Pickaver.
2/- Willoughbie Hall.

St. Mary Magd. 26/8 Rog. Wheler [Roger Sherlowe, 1591].
3/- quitrent; once Will. Marshe.
4/- once Mr. Edwards.
23/4 Mr. Barnes [Dr. Barnes, 1591].

[1] Spelt Greneway in 1571, and in the lease of 1583; see vol. ii, p. 26.

4/- garden; Mr Barnes [Dr Barnes, 1591].
4/- Balliol College.

St. Giles. 6/8 George Ewen.
2/4 The garden called Blackhall; Ric. Hewes [Ric. Hewett, 1591].
1/- Godstow.

St. Peter in the West. 53/4 Walter Owen.
6/8 Ric. Brighthowse [Will. Monday, 1591].
6/8 John Coxe [Will. Monday, 1591].

St. Ebbe. 8/- Ric. Brian.
20 d. Hen. Milward's house & garden by Beef Hall—once 8/-.
1/- John Redshawe—once 4/- [Ric. Goffe, 1591].
10/- Will. Philipps [Thomas Mawberley, 1591].
1/- Garden late of Thomas Covin, now Will. Bronde who pays 2/4 more, i. e. 3/4 [6/8 Will. Brande, 1591].

St. Aldate. 53/4, 6/8 } leased to Mr. Johnson [Thos. Fulzeye, 1591].
20/- leased to Mr. Johnson [Henry Buste, 1591].
26/8 John Banks [Richard Banks, 1591].
6/8 Michael Herne [Richard Banks, 1591].
16/- John Rone [George Crewe, 1591].
23/4 John Hunston, Will. Fisher & Ric. Williams [18/- The sons of Gawin Stangar, 5/4 Will. Symonds, 1591].
13/4 Mr. Ric. Williams, 26/8 Ric. Williams } [Will. Symonds, 1591; Isaak Bartilmewe dwells in it].
13 d. Balliol College.
3/4 Myne Hall—principal of Brodyates.
5/- John Nicolls [widow Nicols, 1591].
8/- Christ Church.[1]

St. Michael South. 8/- John Norrys.
10/- Rob. Bennit [Foster, 1591].
10/- Rob. Bennit [Foster, 1591].
2/- John Barton [Will. Barton, 1591].

[1] In 1589 and for the next 20 years the rentals insert here '30/- Donation of John Parratt gent., payable by Christ Church for 21 years'.

St. John. 4/- garden called Aristotle Hall. Mr Atye.
4/- quitrent; garden in Merton Coll.

St. Nicholas. 13/4 le hamel.

Repairs. £8 5*s*. 3*d*. [Nichil, 1591].

54. Rentals of Sept. 29, 1601, and Sept. 29, 1615.

Computus Willelmi Finke [Willelmi Wright, 1615] collectoris.

Sancti Clementis.

xiii s. iiii d. Domus in qua inhabitat Will. Billingsley [Rad. Quenney, 1615].
xl s. Domus in tenura Willelmi Williams [late John Williams. 1615].
xxxiii s. iiii d. Pratum in tenura Eliz. Tyror & magistri Cooke.
x s. Piscaria aquarum iuxta pontem orientalem; Will. Billingsley [George Crew, 1615].

Sancti Petri orientalis.

lx s. Will. Fynke [widow Fynke, 1615].
vi s. viii d. Ten. adiacens ex parte occidentali.
xl s. Aula B. M. Magd.
xxx s. Thomas Grenehill [late Thomas Grenehill, 1615].
xli s. Domus modo Petri Parrett [Mr. Sommer, 1615].
xii s. iiii d. Will. Coxead [Christopher Anderton, 1615].
xxvi s. viii d. Dictus Will. Coxead [Christopher Anderton, 1615].
xx s. Domus citerior; mag. Cooke [Mr. Peto, 1615].
xx s. Domus ulterior; in tenura eiusdem [Mr. Peto, 1615].
lxvi s. viii d. le Greyhound; Ioh' Tiror [widow Tyrer, 1615].
i lib. incensi; capella sancte Trinitatis.
xii s. Domus in qua manet Will. Holbecke.
x s. Domus in tenura Rodolphi Tomlinson.
xx s. Domus in tenura Ric. Poole [Lonsey, 1615].
xxiii s. iiii d. Domus in qua manet relicta Willelmi Price, modo Wilson.
xxiii s. iiii d. Domus in tenura Bowlar, quondam xxvi s. viii d.
xx s. Domus cum le Tymber Yarde; Ric. Weston [Mr. Carpenter, 1615].
x d. de quietu redditu de domo in qua manet Ric. Coxe.
xx s. Domus in tenura Iohannis Hollyns.

ii s. pro libra piperis de domo angulari in qua manet Robinson, tonsor.
xxx s. Domus in qua manet Rob. Staynhoo.
xl s. Domus in tenura Iohannis Poole.
xxx s. Domus in qua manet Ric. Morgan.
ix s. Domus citerior in tenura Cuthberti Atkinson.
viii s. Domus ulterior in tenura eiusdem Cuthberti[1] [8/4, 1615].
xxv s. Domus in ten. Henrici Bust.
xx d. Pro parte horti; mag. Walter.
ii d. De eodem.
lxvi s. viii d. le Angell; mag. Cooke.
vi s. viii d. Pro firma gardini pertinentis dicto hospitio & tenemento Henrici Buste.
xxvi s. viii d. Domus & hortus in tenura Hen. Withington [widow Lilly, 1615].
viii s. Domus in tenura Rob. Muscropp.
xiii s. iiii d. Duo tenementa nuper in tenura Rob. Muscropp.
xiii s. iiii d. Domus in qua manet uidua Hancock.

Summa xxxvi li. xiii s. iiii d.

Beate Marie Virginis.

xxvi s. viii d. Domus in tenura Doctoris Dochen [Dr. Lapworth, 1615].
xx s. Phisicke Haulle; de quieto redditu.
xxiii s. iiii d. Domus nuper in ten. magistri Gellibrand [late Dr. Chennell, now part of the new schools, 1615].
iiii s. De quieto redditu de domo in qua manet West.
xx s. Domus in tenura Myles [late George Boxe, now part of the new schools, 1615].
vii s. vi d. De quieto redditu de gardino nuper magistri Edgcombe.
xiii s. iiii d. De stabulo equino in ten. Henrici Iaxon.
xl s. Domus in qua manet Ric. Dyce[2] [Thomas White, 1615].
xlvi s. viii d. Domus in qua manet Ioseph Barnes.
xiii s. iiii d. De quieto redditu de domo uoc. le olde Swanne, nuper in tenura Tylliard Taylor.

Summa x li. xiiii s. x d.

Omnium Sanctorum.

xxiiii s. Leonardus Fraye.

[1] The rental of 1615 adds here 'V s. Pro firma domus dimisse doctori Eglionby iuxta aulam sancti Edmundi in gardino quondam in tenura Smallman, modo Martini Powdrell'.

[2] Dence according to the lease, see vol. i, p. 411.

xxxiii s. iiii d. Domus in qua manet uidua Leche
xxvi s. viii d. Altera domus in qua manet dicta uidua
[xv lib. Dr. Dale, 1615].

xvi s. Domus in ten. Georgii Crew [Ric. Yenning, 1615].

viii s. Firma alterius domus ibidem in tenura dicti Georgii [Ric. Yenning, 1615].

vii s. De quodam gardino Iosephi Barnes, quondam xvii s. [xii s., 1615].

viii s. Opella ex opposito ecclesie; in tenura Iosephi Barnes [Bernard Banger, 1615].

xl s. Domus in tenura Michaelis Bonham.

xl s. Domus in tenura Willelmi Pearce.

Summa x li. iii s.

Sancti Martini.

xxxiii s. iiii d. Domus in tenura Walteri Payne, quondam xl s. [xl s., 1615].

x s. Ten. uoc. Kingstowe, nuper in tenura Willelmi Pickauer.

Summa xliii s. iiii d.

Sancti Michaelis.

xiii s. iiii d. Goodiere howsse in tenura Willelmi Pickauer.

xxvi s. viii d. Domus altera nuper in tenura dicti Willelmi.

ii s. De Willoughbie Haulle; in tenura Collegii Exon.

Summa xlii s.

Beate Marie Mag.

xxvi s. viii d. Domus nuper Rog. Sherlowe [Dr. Warner, 1615].

iiii s. De quieto redditu de domo Willelmi Marsh.

iii s. De quieto redditu de domo in qua mansit mag. Edwardes.

xxiii s. iiii d. Domus in tenura doctoris Barnes [Ioh' Eueleigh].

iiii s. De gardino in ten. dicti doctoris Barnes.

iiii s. De terra dimiss. Coll. Balliol.

Summa iii li. v s.

Sancti Egidii.

vi s. viii d. Domus in tenura Francisci Moore [Ric' Falkoner, 1615].

ii s. iiii d. De gardino uoc. Blacke Haulle in ten. Ric. Hewett.

xii d. De domo abbatisse de Godstowe.

Summa x s.

Sancti Petri in occidente.

liii s. iiii d. Domus in tenura Walteri Ouen.
vi s. viii d. Domus in tenura Iohannis Featley.
vi s. viii d. Domus in tenura eiusdem.

Summa iii li. vi s. viii d.

Sancte Ebbe.

viii s. De quieto redditu de domo in qua manet Ric. Brian.
iiii s. Domus in ten. Henrici Milwarde, & pro gardino annexo aule Bouine.
xii d. Pro gardino in tenura Ric. Goffe & modo est tenementum.
x s. Domus in tenura Thome Mabberley [Thos. Wheeler, 1615].
vi s. viii d. Pro tenemento & gardino nuper in tenura Willelmi Brande.

Summa xxix s. viii d.

Sancti Aldati.

iii li. Domus in tenura relicte Thome Fulzey.
xx s. Domus in tenura Henrici Buste.
xxvi s. viii d. Domus Ric. Banckes.
vi s. viii d. Alia domus in tenura nuper Michaelis Hearne; olim xiii s. iiii d.
xviii s. Domus in ten. filiarum Gawini Stangar bedelli.
xlv s. iiii d. Domus in qua manet Isacke Bartilmew.
xvi s. Domus in tenura Georgii Crew [Arthur Crewe, 1615].
xiii d. De quieto redditu de ten. in Penyfarthingestrete [*sic*] quondam solut' per Coll. Balliol.
iii s. iiii d. De horto uocato Myne Haulle in tenura principalis de Brodgates.
v s. Domus in tenura uidue Nicoles in Penyfarthingestreete [Andrew Nicholls, 1615].
viii s. Domus exopposito ecclesie sancti Aldati inclusa in domo pauperum ecclesie Cristi.

Summa x li. x s. i d.

Donatio Iohannis Parrett.

Et de xxx s. dat' Collegio per Ioh' Parrett soluend' per decanum et capitulum collegii Aedis Cristi ad terminum xxi annorum quorum xiii effluxerunt anni.

Summa xxx s.

Sancti Michaelis Australis.

viii s. Domus in qua mansit Ioh' Norris.

x s. Domus nuper in tenura Edwardi Foster [Anthony Fyndall, 1615].

x s. Altera domus nuper in tenura dicti Edwardi [Anthony Fyndall, 1615].

ii s. De quieto redditu de domo quondam priorisse de Litlemore nuper collegii sancte Frideswide et modo in tenura relicte Willelmi Barton.

Summa xxx s.

Sancti Iohannis Baptiste.

iiii s. Pro gardino uocato Aristotles haulle in tenura collegii Merton.

iiii s. De quieto redditu de gardino incluso infra Coll. Merton.

Summa viii s.

Sancti Nicholai.

xiii s. iiii d. De quieto redditu de ten. in le Hammell.

Summa xiii s. iiii d.

Respectu.

x d. De domo in qua manet Ric. Coxe[1] negat' per Coll. Regine pro lxxxviii annis.

xx s. De phisicke haulle negat' per Coll. Animarum pro lxxxxiiii annis.

vii s. vi d. Pro gardino nuper Edgcombe[2] negat' pro lxxxxi annis.

x s. Pro Kingestowe's negat' pro lxxxxvii annis.

ii s. Willoughbie Haulle negat' pro lxxxxi annis.

ii s. iiii d. Pro tenemento in tenura Heuet in parochia sancti Egidii negat' pro lxxxxii annis.

xii d. Pro tenemento de Godstowe[3] negat' pro lxxxxvii annis.

xiii d. De collegio Balliol[4] negat' pro lxxxvi annis.

xiii s. iiii d. De le hamelle negat' pro lxxxxi annis.

iiii s. Pro gardino quondam Balliol nunc Merton, negat' pro lxxxii annis.

iii s. De terris nuper Marshall,[5] negat' pro lxxvii annis.

iiii s. Domus in qua mansit mag. Edwardes, nuper mag. James, negat' pro lxvii annis.

[1] In St. Peter's in the East; it still is the property of Queen's College.
[2] In Cat Street.
[3] In St. Giles's.
[4] The rent from Little Jewry.
[5] This and the next were in the parish of St. Mary Magdalen.

55. Rentals of Sept. 29, 1627, and Sept. 29, 1649.

Computus Willelmi Wright [Danielis Fogg, 1649] collectoris.

St. Clement.

0	13	4	Rad. Queney [Eliz. Sherley, 1649].
2	0	0	Eliz. Neighboure, widow [Eliz. Thrall, 1649].
1	13	4	Will. Potter, M.A., & his brothers & sisters [Leonard Bowman & John Slade, 1649].
0	10	0	George Crewe.

£4 16*s*. 8*d*.

St. Peter in E.

3	0	0	Humfrey Ellis.
0	6	8	Humfrey Ellis.
2	0	0	Magd. Hall.
1	10	0	John Tanner.
2	1	0	Mr. Westley.
0	12	4	Will. Hooper, Bach. Theol.
1	6	8	Will. Hooper, Bach. Theol.
1	0	0	Susan Peto, widow.
1	0	0	
3	6	8	le Greyhounde; Will. Potter, M.A., & brothers & sisters [Leonard Bowman, mercer, 1649].
i lb. incense.			
0	12	0	Ric. Holbye.
0	10	0	widow of Ralf Tomlinson [widow of Edward Tomlinson, 1649].
1	0	0	Thomas Clark [Stephen Fairebeard, 1649].
1	3	4	Rad. Wilson [Walter Thinne, gent., 1649].
1	3	4	le Kinges Armes: Gabriel Cracknell [xxvi s. viii d. Anne Hastings & Hen. her son, 1649].
1	0	0	le Tymber Yard; John Carpenter [Joan Carpenter, wid., 1649].
0	0	10	Ric. Coxe.
1	0	0	Ric. Harrison, B.A. [Dr. Airay, 1649].
0	2	0	lb. of pepper; Robinson, tonsor [Ric. Pricket, 1649].
1	10	0	Rob. Steynoe.
2	0	0	John Poole [John Cogan, 1649].
1	10	0	Anne Cracknell, wid. [Anne Hastings & Edward her son, 1649].

0	9	0	Cuthbert Atkinson [Thomas Egerly & Joyce his wife,
0	8	4	1649].
0	5	0	Dr. Englionbie, near St. Edmund's Hall [Anne Hastings, 1649].
1	5	0	Hen. Bust, M.D. [Will. Day, surgeon, 1649].
0	1	10	Mr. Walter, lately dimised to John Butler.
3	6	8	Jane Cooke, widow, & Rob. her son [Will. Day & Ann his wife, dimised to John Slade, 1649].
0	6	8	A garden of that inn dimised to Dr. Bust.
1	6	8	Mary Lillie, widow [Ralf Nicholas & Eliz. Day, 1649].
0	8	0	Rob. Muscroppe.
0	13	4	late wid. Hancock.
0	13	4	Two tens. late in ten. of Rob. Muscroppe, now Thomas Hollowaie.
St. Mary.			
1	6	8	Ed. Lapworth, M.D.
1	0	0	Phisick Hall.
0	4	0	West } quitrents.
0	7	6	late Mr. Egecombe } quitrents.
0	13	4	Stable: Hen. Jackson [Ralf Nicholas, 1649].
2	0	0	Thomas White [John Nixon, gent., 1649].
0	13	4	The Old Swan.
			Dr. Chennell } non in onere.
			George Boxe } non in onere.
1	4	0	Thomas Miller [John Hynde, 1649].
1	0	0	John Addams [Mr. Finmore, 1649].
2	6	8	Barbary Barnes, widow [Mrs. Anne Barnes, 1649].
All Saints.			
1	4	0	Will. Walter [widow Osborne, 1649].
15	0	0	Hen. Punt, gent. [James Parrett, gent., 1649].
0	16	0	Nich. Yenninge [Anne Imings, 1649].
0	8	0	Nich. Yenninge [Anne Imings, 1649].
0	17	0	Garden and tenement; Barbarie Barnes, widow.
0	8	0	Barnard Bangor.
2	0	0	John Tredwell [Thos. Tredwell, now Hen. Silvester, 1649].
2	0	0	Will. Pierce [Jasper Mayne, now Mr. Denys, 1649].
St. Martin.			
2	0	0	relict Walter Payne [Mr. Penne, 1649].
0	10	0	Kingston's.

St. Michael North.

o	13	4	Mr. Rog. Janes [Mr. Joanes, 1649].
1	6	8	John Sare [late John Sare, 1649].
o	2	o	Willoughby Hall.

St. Mary Mag.

1	6	8	Doctor Raleighe [Mr. Holloway, 1649].
o	4	o	Mr. Edwards.
o	4	o	Will. Marshe.
1	3	4	Prudence Eveleigh, widow.
o	4	o	Prudence Eveleigh, widow; a garden.
o	4	o	Balliol College.

St. Giles.

o	6	8	Hen. Peddeslie [John Egley & Eliz. his wife, 1649].
o	2	4	Blackhall, now in ten. of Ric. Hewett.
o	1	o	Godstowe.

St. Pet. in the West.

2	13	4	Walter Owen.
o	6	8	John Fayreclough.
o	6	8	John Fayreclough.

St. Aldate.

3	o	o	Jane Fulzey, wid. [Dr. Clayton, 1649].
1	o	o	Eliz. White, late Hen. Bust, M.D. [John Holloway, 1649].
1	6	8	John Savery, late Ric. Bancks.
o	18	o	Anne Bentley [widow of John Hawks, 1649].
2	5	4	Mary Bartellmewe [Mr. Saunders, 1649].
o	6	8	Michael Hearne; once 13/4.
o	16	o	James Taylor [Thomas Allen, 1649].
o	1	1	Ball. Coll.
o	3	4	Myne Hall.
o	5	o	Andrew Nicholls in Pennyfarthing St.
o	8	o	Christ Church.

St. Ebbe.

o	8	o	Ric. Bryan, quitrent [widow Dewey, 1649].
o	4	o	Hen. Millward for house and for garden by Beef Hall.
o	1	o	Will' Gough [4/o Adkins, 1649].
o	10	o	John Wheeler.
o	6	8	Mr. Owen.

St. Michael South.

o	8	o	Anne Bentlie, late Norrys [John Horne, 1649].
o	10	o	Anthony Findall & Alice his wife.
o	10	o	Anthony Findall & Alice his wife.
o	2	o	Will. Barton [Ric. Hannes, 1649].

St. John.

o	4	o	Merton.
o	4	o	

St. Nicholas.

o	13	4	

Total £101 9*s.* 7*d.*

56. Rentals of Sept. 29, 1659, and Sept. 29, 1680.

Computus Danielis Fogg.

St. Clement.

o	13	4	Mr. Sherley [widow Sherley, 1680].
2	o	o	wid. Greenhill [Zaccheus Smith, 1680].
1	13	4	Will. Day, surgeon, & Jacob Bobert [Dr. Stratford & James Bobert, 1680].
o	10	o	Will. Bayley [Thomas Jarrett, 1680].

Summa £4 16*s.* 8*d.*

St. Peter.

2	o	o	late Latimer Crosse, gent. [widow Crosse, 1680].
1	o	o	Phisick garden; the Univ.
o	6	8	Crosse [widow Crosse, 1680].
2	o	o	Magd. Hall.
1	10	o	Manciple's tenement [Edmund Thurston, 1680].
2	1	o	Mr. Westley [widow Price, 1680].
o	12	4	Mrs. Hooper [Mr. Hooper, 1680].
1	6	8	Mrs. Hooper [Mr. Hooper, 1680].
1	o	o	Eliz. Brockhurst [Mr. Witt, 1680].
1	o	o	Eliz. Brockhurst [Mr. Witt, 1680].
3	6	8	Jacob Bobert.
i lb. incense.			
o	12	o	Daniel Fogge.
o	10	o	Ric. Day [widow Day, 1680].
1	o	o	Eliz. Fairebeard [Stephen Fairebeard, 1680].
1	3	4	James Finch & John Legborne.

1	6	8	Anna Hastings, wid., & Ric. her son [John Edwards, 1680].
1	0	0	le Timber Yard: Mr. Harrison [Robert Lloyd, 1680].
0	0	10	Ric. Coxe.
1	0	0	Mr. Airay.
0	2	0	i lb. pepper—late Ric. Pricket.
1	10	0	Hen. Willis.
2	0	0	John Cogan [Dr. Lane, 1680].
1	10	0	Anne Hastings & Edw. her son [Walter Combes, 1680].
0	9	0	Thomas Egerly & Jocosa his wife } [Ric. Martin, 1680].
0	8	4	Thomas Egerly & Jocosa his wife }
0	5	0	A house near St. Edmund's hall; in tenure of Anne Hastings [The Provost of Queen's, 1680].
1	5	0	Will. Day, surgeon [Dr. Stratford, 1680].
0	1	10	Mr. Walter [Dr. Elliott, 1680].
3	6	8	Will. Day [Dr. Stratford, 1680].
0	6	8	A garden pertaining to the inn, dimised to Dr. Buste [Dr. Stratford, 1680].
1	6	8	wid. Nicholas & John Day [diverse tenants, 1680].
0	8	0	Rob. Muscrop [7/8 Abel Baily, 1680].
0	13	4	late widow Hancock [widow Peirson, 1680].
0	13	4	A ten. in tenure of Rob. Muscropp, dimised to Thos. Halloway [14/0 John Billingsley, 1680].
			£37 2*s.*

St. Mary.

1	6	8	late Mrs. Lapworth [Sir Sampson White, 1680].
1	0	0	Phisick Hall.
0	4	0	} not paid.
0	7	6	}
0	13	4	Mr. Nicholas [Mr. Ewen, 1680].
2	0	0	John Nixon, gent. [Joan Nixon, widow, 1680].
0	13	4	le old Swan, held by Tilliard, taylour.
1	4	0	Thomas Miller [Abel Bailey, 1680].
1	0	0	Mr. Finmore [Abraham White, 1680].
2	6	8	Martin Lypyate [widow Robinson, 1680].
			£10 15*s.* 6*d.*

All Saints.

1	4	0	wid. Osborne [John Newman, 1680].
15	0	0	James Perrott, gent. [Dr. Parrott, 1680].

0	16	0	late Ric. Young, now Mr. Iminge } [diverse tenants, 1680].
0	8	0	late Ric. Young, now Mr. Iminge }
0	17	0	Martin Lypyate [Mrs. Robinson, 1680].
0	8	0	shop; Mr. Young.
2	0	0	Thomas Tredwell, now Elienor Sylvester.
2	0	0	Thomas Dennis, gent. [Mr. Hawkins, painter, 1680].
			£22 13*s*.

St. Martin.

2	0	0	Mr. Payne [Mr. Flexney, 1680].
0	10	0	Kingston's.
			£2 10*s*.

St. Mich.

0	13	4	Mr. Jones [Robert Keate, 1680].
1	6	8	John Croney.
0	2	0	Willoughby Hall.
			£2 2*s*.

St. Mary Mag.

1	6	8	Mr. Philipps.
0	4	0	Mr. Edward } not paid.
0	4	0	Will. Marsh }
1	3	4	Mr. Eveleigh [Margaret Brooks, widow, 1680].
0	4	0	Mr. Eveleigh, a garden [Mr. Finch, 1680].
0	4	0	Balliol College.
			£3 6*s*.

St. Giles.

0	6	8	John Egerly [Charles Cooke, 1680].
0	2	4	Black Hall; Ric. Bowes.
0	1	0	Godstow.
			10*s*.

St. Pet. le Bailey.

2	13	4	Margaret Oven } [Isaac Oven, 1680].
0	6	8	John Fairlong }
0	6	8	John Fairlong [Richard Meeres, 1680].
			£3 6*s*. 8*d*.

St. Aldate.

3	0	0	late Dr. Clayton [Mr. Heron, 1680].
1	0	0	Ric. Halloway, Esq.
1	6	8	Thos. Hudson.
0	18	0	Thos. Fyfeild [John West, Esq., 1680].
2	5	4	wid. Saunders [Thomas Fifeild and Will. Forty, 1680].

o	6	8	Mich. Hearne.
o	16	o	Thos. Allen, Pennyfarthing St. [Thomas Hudson, 1680].
o	1	1	Balliol College.
o	3	4	Mine Hall.
o	5	o	Coxe [Thomas Cox, 1680].
o	8	o	Christ Church.

£10 10*s*. 1*d*.

Donatio Iohannis Parrott—30/- paid by Ch. Ch. once every 21 years; as this is the 8th there is no payment.

St. Ebbe.

o	8	o	late wid. Dewy.
o	4	o	house in the tenure of Hen. Milward & garden dimised to Pembroke College.
o	4	o	Will. Gough, now in tenure of Will. Adkins.
o	10	o	John Wheeler [Richard Hart, 1680].
o	6	8	late Mr. Owen, now Baldwin Hodges.

£1 12*s*. 8*d*.

St. Michael South.

o	8	o	John Horne.
o	10	o	Mr. Miller.
o	10	o	Mr. Miller.
o	2	o	Littlemore tenement, now Ric. Hans, gent. [widow Cave, 1680].

£1 10*s*.

St. John.

o	4	o	Merton College.
o	4	o	

8*s*.

St. Nicholas.

o 13 4

Total £101 15*s*. 11*d*.

The 13*s*. 4*d*. from the Old Swan had been unpaid many years; also 6*s*. 8*d*. quitrent from the house of Michael Hearne, it now being unknown where it was. This latter entry, though reproduced in each year's rental, was an error from the first, as it was not noticed that the holding of Michael Hearne had been united with the next tenement.

V. FINE BOOKS.

UNTIL less than fifty years ago the method under which Magdalen College and the other Colleges let their houses and lands was by 'beneficial leases renewable by a fine', to use the technical term; and although it is still retained to some extent by one College,[1] yet it has been so generally discarded and is so rapidly becoming part of ancient history, that it is unfamiliar even to many College Bursars, and for the sake of the general reader it must be described with some fullness, if the Lease Books and Fine Books of the College are to be understood.

By the beginning of the nineteenth century, when this method had been reduced to a fixed system, the procedure was as follows. Houses in Oxford were for the most part let for a term of 40 years, a longer period being illegal; when 14 years of the period had expired, the tenant brought his lease to the College, surrendered it, and in consideration of a payment of a sum of money received a new lease for 40 years drawn up in the same terms as the previous lease. The custom at Magdalen in later times was to renew leases only on Aug. 6 and Dec. 6, but it was not so originally, nor was it so with other Colleges. The money paid for the new lease was called 'a fine', the word being used not in its modern sense of a penalty, but in its mediaeval sense of a payment in settlement of a dispute or of a bargain. If the value of the property increased, the fine increased, but the rent was not altered, and many tenements in Oxford paid the same rent in 1850 as in 1550. This was not the case at Magdalen, for it will be noticed in the leases that about the years 1812–15 the College gave notice to the tenants that the rents would be increased tenfold or more, and before 1850 these increases were in force; but even so, the rents were small in proportion to the value of the houses and remained at a fixed amount, while the fine varied as the value of houses in Oxford rose or fell. The fine was called an 'arbitrary' fine, and so it was legally, but in practice many College tenants could tell what their fine would be when their lease was renewed; for a custom arose that the fine should bear some proportion to the rack-rent of the house. At Magdalen the rule at the beginning of the nineteenth century was that, if a lease of 40 years was surrendered when 14 years had expired, the fine for renewal

[1] St. John's College.

would be $1\frac{1}{4}$ years' rack-rent;[1] but each College had its own rule, and during the nineteenth century most Colleges raised the fine to $1\frac{1}{2}$ years' rack-rent or even $1\frac{3}{4}$ years.[2] Probably for this there were two reasons; in the first place money was cheaper in the nineteenth century than in the eighteenth, and if a tenant borrowed money to pay his fine, he could get the money on easier terms in the nineteenth century; in other words he could afford to pay a larger fine. And a second reason may be that as the science of building improved, the cost of repairs decreased; for, as will be shown hereafter, the cost of repairs in the Middle Ages was high, being about 40 per cent. of the rent, but in modern times 25 per cent. would be a sufficient allowance, and as the tenant who took the lease undertook the repairs of every kind, his profits were greater as the skill of builders increased, and in consequence his fine was raised.

Though it might be well known that the fine at the end of 14 years should be $1\frac{1}{4}$ or $1\frac{1}{2}$ years' rack-rent, there still remained an uncertainty in some cases; for where the tenant lived in the house he leased, there might be a dispute what its rack-rent would be, if it were let in that way. The valuer of the landlord settled the matter, and there was no appeal from his decision; if the valuation was too high, the tenant could do no more than refuse to renew his lease;[3] but as Colleges were anxious to secure the fines for the renewal of leases, it was not their policy to make the terms too onerous. In many cases there was no need for a valuation, as the rack-rent was well known. Take, for instance, the case of the Angel, of which the Bishop of Chester had a lease in 1694.[4] It need hardly be said that the Bishop did not reside there, but he let it at a yearly rent to an under-tenant; and this was the case with the majority of leases. The tenant who took the lease became an under-landlord and secured an under-tenant, who held under him either by a lease for a term of years or by a yearly agreement. In such cases the rack-rent was known, and it could be reckoned beforehand what the fine would be.

At first sight it seems that the College made a bad bargain, if every fourteen years it received beyond the small annual rent nothing but

[1] To speak accurately it was not the whole rack-rent, but that which remained after the rent due to the College had been paid. Thus if the rack-rent was £21, and the rent to the College was £1, the fine would be £25.

[2] Balliol College demanded 1 year's rack-rent in 1661 (*Balliol Oxford Deeds*, O. H. S., p. 345) and 1671 (*ib.* 341); $1\frac{1}{4}$ years' in 1761 (*ib.* 348), $1\frac{1}{2}$ years' in 1777 (*ib.* 346), 1803 (*ib.* 228), and 1820 (*ib.* 349); $1\frac{3}{4}$ years' in 1832 (*ib.* 349), 1844 (*ib.* 351), and 1846 (*ib.* 211).

[3] For an instance see *Balliol Oxford Deeds*, p. 353.

[4] See vol. i, p. 185.

$1\frac{1}{4}$ years' rack-rent, while the tenant took the rent for $12\frac{3}{4}$ years; but the bargain is not quite as bad as it seems. As an instance we may take the Magdalen tenement in All Saints parish through which the Wheatsheaf Passage runs. The rent was £2, and in 1801, as we learn from the Survey of 1791 which is printed in this volume, it was valued at £45; the fine therefore was $\frac{5}{4} \times$ £43 = £53 15*s*. Now in 1801 the choice before the College was whether for the next 26 years the College would be content with a rent of £2 a year and at the end of that time come into possession of a house which could be let at a rent of £45, or renew the lease and take a fine of £53 15*s*. and another fine in fourteen years' time. If the fine of £53 15*s*. were invested at 5 per cent. compound interest it would amount at the end of 26 years to something more than £150; and a similar fine fourteen years later, if invested for twelve years, would be something less than £100; say the two together would be £250. If, therefore, the College had taken the fines, and invested them instead of spending them, it would at the end of 26 years have had an income of £12 10*s*. a year; by refusing to renew the lease it would in the same number of years be in possession of a house that could be let for £45. From this amount perhaps £12 must be deducted for annual repairs, and something for bad debts, and for the cost of collecting the rent, leaving a net income of £25. It appears, therefore, that a fine set at $1\frac{1}{4}$ years' rack-rent was too easy a bargain for the tenant, but that if he had been charged two years' rent, the arrangement would have been fair to both sides.

The system of letting houses at a low rent with a lease renewable by a fine was not peculiar to Colleges, but it was more general with them than with private owners. Its advantages were many. The College had no trouble about repairs, and it was unnecessary to keep what is now called an Estates Bursar; and there were no bad debts, for as the tenant had paid a fine that he might enjoy the tenement for many years, he would not be so foolish as to withhold his rent and forfeit his lease. The tenant had a lease of such length that it was his best policy to improve his house that he might get a higher rent during his term of forty years; but there was this drawback, that if a man raised the value of the house, his next fine would be higher. But the Fine Books show that in many cases the College granted a lenient fine to a tenant who had improved the College property. The weak point of the system is that it was defrauding posterity; the fine was in reality the rent which the next generation ought to receive, but much reduced on consideration of the fact that it was paid many years before it was due. Private persons, who owned property, in many cases let their leases run out that their children might be better off, but Colleges in the seventeenth and eighteenth centuries had little care for those who were to come.

It is obvious that as a lease drew near its end, the fine for renewal would rise rapidly. If the fine was 1¼ years' rack-rent when one-third of the lease had expired, the fine would be nearly five years' rack-rent when two-thirds had expired. In the Fine Book we see that the fine for Howell's Yard (see vol. i, p. 334) was £13 15*s.* in 1754, when 14 years of the lease had expired, but in 1790 when 36 years were expired the fine was £132. It will be noticed that in the seventeenth century the leases were often renewed at varying intervals; in some cases less than 14 years had passed, in some cases more, and of course the fine varied accordingly. But in process of time it became customary to renew regularly every 14 years; and sometimes in the eighteenth and nineteenth centuries if the lease was renewed when more than 14 years had elapsed, the new lease was antedated and began from the end of the 14 years, and the fine paid was the fine due for a renewal at the end of 14 years, although no doubt the tenant had to pay interest on the money for the years that it was overdue.

The system of beneficial leases produced a curious double ownership in houses; one party owned the freehold and another party owned the lease, and in many cases the lease was much more valuable than the freehold. In 1803 it was reckoned in the case of a house in the parish of St. Mary Magdalen that a lease with 27 years to run was more than twice as valuable as the owner's share of the house.[1] Sometimes the owner of the lease is described as the owner of the house, and in advertisements in Jackson's *Oxford Journal* cases may be found where a man advertises that he will sell what he calls his house, and only adds at the end 'held under — College at a rent of £1, by a lease renewable every 14 years'; often, too, in wills the testator speaks of 'my' house when in reality he only held a lease. It is easy to understand how this mode of speaking arose, when we notice that a lease might be held by members of one family for a hundred years or more; thus the White family held Ing Hall for more than a century (vol. i, p. 464). To buy one of these leases was a way of investing money, and though it was generally the case that

[1] *Balliol Oxford Deeds*, p. 227 (O. H. S.).

the investor was resident in Oxford, and it was desirable that he should be near his house, yet sometimes he was of London or some more distant spot. In all these beneficial leases it is unsafe to assume that the tenant mentioned in the lease was the occupant of the house; in the majority of cases the house was underlet to some one who had not sufficient capital to buy a lease.

It is important to ascertain when this system began; but for the decision of this point the Lease Books and the Fine Books and the College Accounts give us no help. The earliest Fine Book begins about 1649, but it is certain that fines were paid before that time. It is useless to study the College Accounts, for only the rents are recorded there and not the fines, because the fines were what may be called the pocket-money of the Fellows, and did not contribute to the maintenance of the College. The leases give no help for the reason that, though the nineteenth century leases generally mention that a fine was paid and that the old lease was surrendered, it is not so in the eighteenth and the seventeenth centuries, each lease being a reproduction of the original lease, and were it not that we had other sources of knowledge we should assume that the lease before us was an ordinary lease for 40 years at the full value of the tenement. Under these circumstances it may be asked whether there is any proof that the system was not in use in the Middle Ages. It is true that fines are not mentioned in the mediaeval leases or mediaeval rentals, but, as we have seen, neither are they mentioned in post-mediaeval leases and rentals. Yet owing to the fact that the College rentals during the sixteenth century give the expense of repairs each year, we have evidence which shows when the system began. For, as long as the College rentals make mention of repairs, it cannot have been in full working, since the landlord was not responsible for repairs under the system of beneficial leases. In 1544 the repairs were £36 8*s.* 6½*d.*; in 1545, £31 9*s.* 9*d.*; in 1548, £39 2*s.* 8*d.*; in 1554, £39 1*s.* 10½*d.*; in 1561, £30 6*s.* 8*d.* Year after year in the reign of Henry VIII the repairs cost between £30 and £40 on a rental of somewhat less than £80. This may seem a large proportion of the receipts, but the accounts of Oseney Abbey show that the same proportion was paid by Oseney 60 years earlier; no doubt the bad building in the Middle Ages is responsible for the high cost. We may assume, therefore, from the figures given in 1561, that the system of beneficial leases had not begun at that date. But in 1569 the repairs fall to £26 4*s.* 5*d.*, in 1570 to £22 10*s.* 7*d.*, in 1581 to

£8 5*s.* 3*d.*, in 1586 to £1 9*s.* 7*d.*, in 1591 to *nil.* The system, therefore, came into use between 1561 and 1591. Probably at first no fine was paid, but the tenant undertook that if a new lease was granted him he would pay the old rent and also be responsible for the repairs; and as the value of houses increased and he found that he had a good bargain, he would offer the College a fine if his lease might be extended on the same terms or a new lease granted him. The original form of the lease not only bound the tenant to perform all repairs, but also forbade him to alienate the lease without the licence of the College; but in later times it was the universal rule that when a new lease was issued, the tenant received another document called 'the licence', whereby he was allowed to alienate the lease. It might be thought that it would have been simpler to omit the clause in the lease whereby the tenant was forbidden to alienate; probably it was retained because an extra fee was paid to the Bursar or his clerk for issuing a 'licence'.

The end came in 1870. The College appointed a Committee 'to inquire into the expediency of terminating the practice of renewing leases on Fines', and the report was that 'Your Committee regard it as unquestionable that the substitution of the system of Rack-Rent leasing for the system of fines would result in a few years in a very large addition to the revenue of the College, and that independently of this gain, it would be highly desirable that the College should have the actual possession and management of its own estates. Funds for effecting the change of system must be provided by borrowing under the University and College Estates Acts, or by using for the purpose some of the funded property of the College.' This report was adopted at a College meeting held July 21, 1870, and at one stroke the College deprived itself for some years of nearly half its income. Between 1884 and 1891 the leases of the agricultural land of the College ran out, for by the Act of 13 Eliz. a lease of agricultural lands might not be for more than 21 years,[1] but the last lease of house property did not terminate until 1910. Meanwhile to meet current expenses the College had been obliged to raise loans, which it is said reached at one time the total of £250,000.

The records of the fines from 1649 to 1870, preserved at Magdalen in three small books, are worth printing because they show the rise, and in some cases the fall, in the value of houses during that period. When the system of beneficial leases was introduced, it was the fine

[1] See *Enactments in Parl.*, vol. i, p. 176 (O. H. S.).

and not the rent which showed what the house was worth; but unfortunately no College, as far as is known, has preserved a complete list of their fines, and the Fine Books at Magdalen are the best record we have. Of course it must be remembered that the fines were reckoned on different plans at different times, and the first thing is to discover the plan that was in use at Magdalen. The Rental and Survey of 1791, which is printed below, gives us the rack-rent or, as it was called, the improved rent of the tenements in 1791 and for the next twenty or thirty years, and when we refer to the Fine Books we are able to work out the method on which the fines were fixed during that period. From 1791 to 1808 or 1809 the method was to deduct from the improved rent the annual rent due to the College and to fix the fine at $1\frac{1}{4}$ of the remainder. Thus the improved rent of no. 43 Cornmarket in 1800 was £24; from this must be deducted the rent of £1 6*s.* 8*d.* due to the College, leaving £22 13*s.* 4*d.*; the fine therefore was $\frac{5}{4}\times$£22 13*s.* 4*d.* = £28 6*s.* 8*d.* In 1808 or 1809, when the College began to give notice that in 26 years' time the rents of the tenements would be raised, a new method was introduced; the tenant was allowed to deduct from the improved rent not the rent which he paid to the College, but the increased rent which in 26 years' time he would begin to pay, but in return the College raised the fine to $1\frac{1}{2}$ of the sum remaining. At Balliol, as we have seen, a fine of $1\frac{3}{4}$ years' was taken from 1832 onwards, but at Magdalen there was no such rise; the proof of this is that if we take the fines from 1830 onwards and treat them as being $1\frac{1}{2}$ times the improved rent, we obtain for the improved rent a round sum, but if we treat them as being $1\frac{3}{4}$ times the improved rent, we obtain an odd fraction of a penny. By the same method we discover that before 1791 the fine was $1\frac{1}{4}$ times the improved rent *without* deducting the annual rent to the College; but there is some uncertainty at what date the College passed from a fine of one year's rack-rent, which was the custom in the seventeenth century, to $1\frac{1}{4}$ years' rack-rent. The note in the Fine Book about the Angel (tenement no. 7) shows that $1\frac{1}{4}$ was the rule in 1765; and there is a similar note about tenement no. 16. It is probable that the change took place between August and December, 1754; for the fines from the latter date onwards are in a large number of cases a quarter more than the preceding fine, and though it is possible that in some cases the rack-rent had risen by precisely one quarter during the fourteen years, it is unlikely that that would be the exact rise in a large number of tenements. In a few cases the fines in leases after 1754 show no increase, but in these cases the Fine Book often gives the explanation that the tenant had improved his holding, in return for which it was the custom to abstain from raising his fine for the next 26 years, that is until he had had the advantage of his improvements for 40 years. There were other reasons why in certain cases the fine was set low; a widow was sometimes treated leniently, or a charitable body; this may be the explanation why the fine paid by the Feoffees of St. Michael's charities for no. 54 Cornmarket (tenement no. 70) in 1758, 1772, and 1786 was no greater (in fact it was less) than the fine in 1730 and 1744.

By means of the Rentals and Fine Books we are now in a position to show the fluctuations in the value of Oxford houses between 1293 and 1870. We have already shown that from 1293 there was a drop in values for the next fifty years; then in 1349 came the Black Death which increased the fall; afterwards there was a steady recovery for fifty years, though prices did not return to what they had been before 1349. From 1400 onwards to 1480 there was a continual fall, and from 1480 to 1560 things were at their worst. Probably a third of those years were years of Pestilence, and the Rentals of Magdalen College show that in many years a tenth of the houses belonging to the College were unoccupied. The period for which we have least evidence is the century from 1560 to 1660. We have seen that in 1560 the rents represent the true rack-rent at the time, of which the College kept about one-half, the rest being spent on repairs. By 1591 the College was responsible for no repairs, so that we may reckon that houses in 1591 were worth twice as much as in 1560. In reality the rise was rather more rapid; for in 1560 none of the houses were let on beneficial leases, while in 1591 the alteration had taken place in every case, and it is probable that by that date some of the tenants had begun to pay a fine for the renewal of their lease; so that the rise in values between 1560 and 1591 was probably about 2½. From 1591 for the next sixty years we have no evidence; between 1660 and 1690 there was a rapid rise, then for a century values were stationary; but after 1790 prices increased fourfold in forty years. From 1830 to the present time there has been little alteration; tenements in the side streets have decreased in value, no doubt owing to the fact that by the enclosure of the open fields in the neighbourhood of Oxford, there has been a provision of abundant sites for building; but in the main streets, especially near Carfax, prices continued to rise slightly and probably are still rising.

In showing the fluctuations of value by means of the following table, care has been taken to select those houses which have not been divided, or added to, since 1293, and have also been in continual occupation. It would not be fair to take tenements, like some in St. Ebbe's parish, which were uninhabited in the sixteenth century; nor would it be fair to take properties which were occupied as Halls in the Middle Ages; for the fact that Halls were held by a special tenure may have affected the rent at which they were let. Occasionally no doubt the rent or the fine of a tenement is unduly high or unduly low because of the state of repair of the buildings; but by giving as many as eight instances we can eliminate these exceptional causes.

ALTERATIONS IN THE VALUE OF HOUSES, 1293–1870.

Tenement.	14*th century.*	15*th century.*	16*th century.*	17*th century.*	18*th century.*	19*th century.*
1. Swinbrook's, 127–9 High Street.	1293 about £5 1325 about £4 10 0 1346 £4 1357 £2 10 0 1371 £2 10 0 1384 £5 0 0 1395 £5 0 0	1426 £4 0 0 1478 £2 0 0	1507 £2 1535 £2 1561 £2 1591 about £5	1662 about £20 1683 about £45 1697 £42	1700 £40 1725 £42 11 0 1739 £42 11 0 1769 £42 11 0 1783 £42 11 0	1801 £45 1815 £95 1829 £145 1843 £268 1857 £288 1871 £305
2. 38 and 39 Pembroke Street.	1293 £0 18 0 1325 £0 18 0 1346 £0 18 0 1357 £0 10 0 1371 £1 0 0 1384 £1 0 0 1395 £0 18 0	1426 £0 13 4 1478 ——	1507 £0 6 8 1535 £0 10 0 1561 £0 10 0 1591 about £1 5 0	1665 about £4 10 0 1690 £14	1710 about £15 1739 £18 1753 £18 1767 £18 1781 £18 1795 £21	1809 ? £34 1823 £60 1837 £55 1851 £50 1865 £45
3. 43 Cornmarket.	1325 £1 11 0 1346 £3 19 0 1357 £1 10 0 1371 £1 6 8 1384 £1 6 8 1395 £1 13 4	1426 £2 0 0 1478 £1 3 4	1507 £1 6 8 1535 £1 4 0 1561 £1 6 8 1591 about £3 6 8	1664 about £7 1682 about £16 1696 £20	1730 £20 1744 £20 1758 £17 10 0 1772 £17 10 0 1786 £17 10 0	1800 £24 1814 £45 1828 £75 1842 £95 1856 £95 1870 £95
4. Domus Bultras, 17 and 18 St. Aldate's.	1293 £0 16 0 1325 £0 16 0 1346 £1 0 0 1357 £0 6 8 1371 £0 16 0 1384 £0 13 4 1395 £0 14 0	1426 £0 13 4 1478 £0 6 8	1507 £0 8 0 1535 £0 8 0 1561 £0 8 0 1591 about £1	1657 about £4 1670 about £7 1682 about £7 1694 about £8	1708 £9 1722 £11 1736 £11 1759 £11 1799 £18	1813 £42 1827 £63 1841 £65 1881 £45

5. The Bell, 37 and 38 High Street. — Domus Fileking.	1293 £1 0 0 1325 £1 0 0 1346 ?£1 5 0 1357 ——— 1371 £1 13 4 1384 £1 4 3	1412 £2 13 4 1426 £2 13 4 1478 £2 3 4	1507 £2 0 0 1535 £1 13 4 1569 about £3 1590 about £4	1681 about £32 1695 £40	1739 £40 1753 ?£50 1767 £40 1781 £40 1745 £42	1809 £50 1823 £65 1837 £75 1851 £70 1865 £70 1879 £70
6. Chapel Hall, 42 and 43 High Street. — Domus Benham.	1293 £1 12 0 1325 £1 12 0 1346 £1 12 0 1357 £1 0 0 1371 £1 0 0 1384 £1 6 8 1395 £1 4 0	1412 £1 4 0 1426 £1 4 0 1478 £1 0 0	1507 £1 0 0 1535 £1 0 0 1561 £1 0 0 1591 about £2 10 0	1659 about £10 1683 ?£50 1694 about £45	1709 about £32 1723 £34 1737 £34 1751 £34 1765 £34 1779 £34 1793 £42	1807 ?£62 12 0 1821 £135 1835 £125 1849 £120
7. The Coach and Horses, 49 and 50 High Street. — Domus Roboru.	1293 £1 2 0 1325 £0 18 0 1346 £1 2 0 1357 £1 4 0 1371 £1 4 0 1384 £1 5 0 1395 £1 5 0	1412 £1 6 8 1426 £1 6 0 1478 £1 0 0	1507 £1 0 0 1535 £1 3 4 1561 £1 3 4 1566 about £2 6 8	1657 about £14 1671 £20 1686 about £18	1705 about £12 1719 £20 1733 £20 1747 £20 1762 £28 8 0 1776 £28 8 0 1790 £28 8 0	1804 about £40 1818 £65 1832 £83 1846 £93 1860 £77 1874 £77
8. The Light Horseman, 51 and 52 High Street. — Domus Melmaker.	1293 £0 10 0 1325 £0 9 0 1346 £1 7 0 1357 £0 15 0 1371 £0 12 0 1384 £0 18 4 1395 £1 3 4	1412 £1 4 0 1426 £1 4 0 1478 £0 13 4	1507 £1 0 0 1535 £0 18 0 1562 about £1 16 0	1671 £12 1686 £14	1700 £14 1714 £14 1728 £14 1742 £14 1754 £14 1770 £14 1784 £14 1798 £36	1812 £80 1826 ?£92 1840 £100 1880 £100

This table does not give such a good idea of the fall in values between 1300 and 1500, as is obtained from the totals of the rentals year by year (see p. 29). For it was not the case that when the population of Oxford decreased, the rents of all the houses decreased. Those that were needed remained at much the same rent as ever, while those that were not needed were turned into gardens. And as the table we have printed deals only with houses that were continuously occupied, it conveys the idea that there was not much fall in values between 1300 and 1500. But as we have seen, when dealing with the rentals, the rateable value of Oxford in 1500 was less than half what it was in 1300, and probably only a third of what it was in 1250; there was an almost continuous decline for two and a half centuries, and the level at which rents stood in the days of Henry III was not reached again until the end of the reign of Elizabeth.

The following list of fines is made from three Fine Books now at Magdalen. All the columns, except the first, are copied from the originals, including the column headed *Memoranda*; the first column, giving the names of the tenements, is not in the originals. In a few cases the Fine Books reveal the existence of leases which were not copied into the Lease Books; and also in a few cases (e.g. in tenement 39) they assign to the lease a date different from that given in the Lease Book; in such cases the Fine Books are the better authority, for it was essential for the Fine Book to record how much of the lease had elapsed when it was renewed. On the other hand if the Lease Books and the Fine Books do not agree about the name of the tenant, the former is to be followed; for Fine Books were small note-books, somewhat carelessly kept, and the name of the tenant was not essential for their purpose. In some cases no name is given, and in some other cases, where the name has been filled up subsequently, it will be noticed by reference to the leases in the previous volumes that the name given is not the name of the man who paid the last fine, but the name of the man into whose tenure the tenement had passed.

Name of Tenement.	Rent. £ s. d.	Tenant.	Years elapsed.	When renewed.	Fine. £ s. d.	Memoranda.
1. Domus Charnell, part of. See vol. i, p. 389. See also nos. 3 and 5.	0 14 0	John Billingsley	33	July, 1649	10 0 0	In 1685 divided into two leases.
		Ann Billingsley	22½	Jan. 1671	5 0 0	
	0 9 0	Mr. Sellar	14	Dec. 1685	10 0 0	
		Mr. Sellar	14	Dec. 1699	10 0 0	
		Mr. Sellar	14	Dec. 1713	11 0 0	
	0 9 0	Mr. Fortrey	12½	Aug. 1726	10 11 0	
		Mr. Fortrey	14½	Dec. 1740	13 0 0	
		Hartford College	14	Dec. 1754	17 10 0	
		Hartford College	14	Dec. 1768	0 13 4	
2. Howell's Yard, 54, High Street. See vol. i, p. 334.	0 10 0	Richard Day	30	July, 1651	0 13 4	
		Widow Day	17½	Dec. 1668	10 0 0	
		Widow Day	17	Dec. 1685	12 0 0	
		Widow Day	14	Dec. 1699	12 0 0	
		Mr. Day	12½	Aug. 1712	10 0 0	
		Mr. Day	14	Aug. 1726	12 0 0	
		Mr. Day	14	Aug. 1740	12 0 0	
		Mrs. Eliz. Day	14	Aug. 1754	13 15 0	
		Mr. Meyrick	36	Aug. 1790	132 0 0	
		Mr. Meyrick	14	Aug. 1804	18 16 0	
		James Howell	14	Aug. 1818	38 8 0	
		Executors of James Howell	14	Aug. 1832	41 9 0	1872. Fallen in and let to Durran and others.
3. Part of Domus Charnell. See vol. i, p. 389.	0 5 0	Mrs. Prince	14	Dec. 1685	5 0 0	
		Thomas Cookeow	29	Dec. 1714	20 0 0	
		Dr. Newton	38	Dec. 1752	40 0 0	
		Hertford College	14	Dec. 1766	4 0 0	
4. Domus Averam, 78 High Street. See vol. i, p. 199.	0 13 4	John Pearson	21	Dec. 1651	6 13 4	
		Mr. Robert Say	21	Dec. 1672	20 0 0	
		Will. Bromingham	14	Dec. 1686	10 0 0	

Name of Tenement.	Rent. £ s. d.	Tenant.	Years elapsed.	When renewed.	Fine. £ s. d.	Memoranda.
4. Domus Averam, &c., *cont.*		Seymour Cook	14	Dec. 1700	10 0 0	
		Seymour Cook	14	Dec. 1714	10 0 0	
		Edmund Cook	14	Dec. 1728	12 6 8	
		Edmund Cook	14	Dec. 1742	12 6 8	
		John Turner	14	Dec. 1756	15 8 4	
		John Biggs and Turner	14	Dec. 1770	15 8 4	
		John Armborough	14	Dec. 1784	15 8 4	
		Mr. Passand	14	Dec. 1798	26 13 0	
		Mr. Blackwell	14	Dec. 1812	36 0 0	
		Mrs. Blackwell	14	Dec. 1826	45 0 0	
		Mrs. Blackwell	14	Dec. 1840	81 0 0	Not renewed in 1868; sold to the University in 1871.
		James Wilkins	14	Dec. 1854	64 0 0	
5. Part of Domus Charnell. See vol. i, p. 389.	0 7 4	Abell Bayly	22	Jan. 1658	5 0 0	At the renewing in 1702, being the first after the house was new built, the fine was not advanced; but at the next renewing it must be sett according to the improved value.
		Widow Hall	15	Jan. 1673	5 0 0	
		Widow Hall	15	Dec. 1688	5 0 0	
		Mrs. Cutler	14	Dec. 1702	5 0 0	
		Mrs. Cutler	14	Dec. 1716	11 10 0	
		Mr. Finch	14	Dec. 1730	11 10 0	
		Mr. Finch	14	Dec. 1744	11 10 0	
		Hertford College	15	Dec. 1759	16 2 6	
5 A. Site of Hertford Coll. See vol. i, p. 389.	3 15 1	Hertford College		Dec. 1768	0 13 4	It was agreed, July 14, 1768, that the three leases should be united; renewable every 14 years at a fine of 13*s.* 4*d.* and fees. There is a ground plot of this lease taken 1768.
		Hertford College		Dec. 1782	0 13 4	
		Hertford College		Dec. 1796	0 13 4	
6. Leke's tenement; vol. i, p. 193.	1 6 8	Mrs. Nicholas and John Day	22	Jan. 1651	20 0 0	In 1669 divided into 8 tenements and the rent divided.

Day's tenement; vol. i, p. 247.	0 2 0	John Day	18	Jan. 1669	0 13 4	
		Will. Applebee, late Day	14	Dec. 1683	7 10 0	
		Will. Applebee	17	Dec. 1700	10 0 0	
		Edward Applebee	14	Dec. 1714	7 0 0	In 1742 the society abated 14*s*., as he had laid out £20 in repairs, and at present he did not make more of his estate than the fine paid.
		Jane Giles	14	Dec. 1728	7 0 0	
		Mr. Collison	14	Dec. 1742	6 6 0	
		Mrs. Collison	15	Dec. 1757	8 15 0	
Vol. i, p. 247.	0 1 0	Mr. Townsend for part of Collison's	14	Dec. 1785	5 10 0	Included in the lease of late Miss Ward's.
Vol. i, p. 247.	0 1 0	Mr. Shipton the other part		Dec. 1788	8 8 0	Part of what was Shipton's let to Bavin in 1829, rent £5.
7. The Angel; vol. i, p. 185.	3 10 0	William Day	11½	Jan. 1651	16 13 4	
		William Day	10	Dec. 1661	8 0 0	In 1661 the lease was renewed for half the fine, the other half being given him upon his promise to lay out £1,000 in building.
		Dr. Eliot and Dr. Willis	4½	Aug. 1666	5 0 0	
		Dr. Stratford	14	Aug. 1680	65 0 0	
		Bp. of Chester	14	Aug. 1694	70 0 0	
		Dr. Stratford	14	Aug. 1708	70 0 0	
		Dr. Stratford	14	Aug. 1722	75 0 0	July 26, 1765, the quarter's increase was not added to this fine in consideration of Mr. Kemp's engaging to put the house into thorough repair.
		Mrs. Holt	14	Aug. 1736	75 0 0	
		Mary Holt	14	Aug. 1750	75 0 0	
		Mr. James Kemp	14	Aug. 1764	75 0 0	
		William Jackson	14	Aug. 1778	75 0 0	
		Mr. Costar	14	Aug. 1792	93 15 0	
		Mr. Bulley	14	Aug. 1806	195 0 0	In 1806 including stables built in the yard.
		Gillett	14	Aug. 1820	370 8 0	
		Griffith	10	Aug. 1830	358 16 0	For 1830 see Order of Meeting.
		Griffith	14	Aug. 1844	370 0 0	
		Griffith	14	Aug. 1858	329 8 0	In 1866 sold to the University.
8. Parrett's tenement; vol. i, p. 151.	2 1 0	Mr. Westley	10½	Jan. 1651	8 0 0	
		Mrs. Price	20	Jan. 1671	40 0 0	

Name of Tenement.	*Rent.* £ s. d.	*Tenant.*	*Years elapsed.*	*When renewed.*	*Fine.* £ s. d.	*Memoranda.*
8. Parrett's tenement, *cont.*		Mr. Gilman	14½	Aug. 1686	25 0 0	
		Mr. Sherwin	14½	Dec. 1700	25 0 0	
		Mr. Sherwin, &c.	15	Dec. 1715	25 0 0	
		William Tapling	14	Dec. 1729	25 0 0	
		Widow Gillman	14	Dec. 1743	25 0 0	In 1787, in the occupation of William Day.
		William Taylor	14	Dec. 1757	31 10 0	
		Dr. Denison	14	Dec. 1771	31 10 0	Fallen in and built upon by the College.
		Dr. Denison	14	Dec. 1785	31 10 0	
9. Noah's Ark; vol. i, p. 65.	2 6 8	Mr. Latimer Crosse	19	June, 1653	0 13 4	At the renewing in 1685, £5 was abated by reason that the house hath not been inhabited of late for several years.
		Dr. Cross	9½	Dec. 1662	10 0 0	
		Rob. Long, Esq.	9	Jan. 1671	10 0 0	
		Rob. Long, Esq.	14	Dec. 1685	25 0 0	
		Mr. Crosse	16½	Aug. 1702	40 0 0	In 1759 Mr. Berry's estate was lett; Walton and stables £8 1*s*., James Earsley £4, Alice Gardiner £6, John Barnett £5, Shilfox £8, Noah's Ark £23, Rose Lane £8 10*s*., Furthest House £3: Total £65 11*s*. The fine is set so low on account of improvements made on the estate by Mr. Berry's uncle.
		Mr. Crosse	14	Aug. 1716	30 0 0	
		Rob. Hale	15	Aug. 1731	32 0 0	
		Francis Berry	14	Aug. 1745	30 0 0	
		Mr. Berry	14	Aug. 1759	65 0 0	
		Mr. Berry	14	Aug. 1773	73 2 6	
						In 1813 in hand.
						In 1832 pulled down and let to Penson the seedsman at rack-rent.
10. Manciple's tenement; vol. i, p. 148.	1 10 0	Eman. Heath	15	Aug. 1652	0 13 4	[The entry for 1652 is scratched out. Ed.]
		Thomas Frewen	20	Dec. 1660	0 13 4	
		Mr. Edmund Thurstan	13½	Aug. 1674	10 0 0	March 22, 1693; mem. that this

				Mr. Edmund Thurstan	14½	Dec. 1688	20	0	0	lease be not renewed till the
				Mr. Thomas Thurstan	18	Dec. 1706	30	0	0	principall of Magdalen Hall
				Mrs. Coles	14	Dec. 1720	22	0	0	be heard, he having part of
				Walter Beacham	14	Dec. 1734	22	0	0	ground belonging to it.
	1	1	4	Wm. Buckland	14	Dec. 1748	16	0	0	In 1748 this lease was separated
				Dr. Denison	14	Dec. 1762	25	0	0	as in this and the next.
				Dr. Denison	14	Dec. 1776	12	10	0	In 1762 this lease was divided
	0	7	6	Eliz. Gilman	14	Dec. 1748	6	0	0	between Eliz. Rabbond and
				Rob. Cox	14	Dec. 1762	7	10	0	Dr. Denison.
				Rob. Cox	14	Dec. 1776	7	10	0	Now fallen in and built upon, part forming the garden of the President.
11. The Eagle and Child; vol. i, p. 317.	1	0	0	Mr. Harrison	17	Dec. 1652	15	0	0	
				Rob. Lloyd (2 houses)	10	Dec. 1662	10	0	0	
				Mrs. Lloyd	12½	July, 1675	24	0	0	
				Mrs. Lloyd	15	Aug. 1690	30	0	0	
				Mrs. Lloyd	14	Aug. 1704	25	0	0	
				Mr. Phillips	14	Aug. 1718	25	0	0	
				Mr. Phillips	14	Aug. 1732	25	0	0	
				Mr. Phillips	14	Aug. 1746	25	0	0	
				George Webb	14	Aug. 1760	25	0	0	
				Mr. Alleyne	11	Aug. 1771	15	12	5	Sold to Mr. Alleyne.
12. The Greyhound; vol. i, p. 155.	3	6	8	Dan. Waldoe, gent.	10	Oct. 1654	15	0	0	
				Jacob Bobert	2½	Sept. 1657	0	13	4	
				Jacob Bobert	10	Aug. 1667	15	0	0	
				Jacob Bobert	11½	Jan. 1678	12	0	0	
				Jacob Bobert	14	Dec. 1692	26	0	0	
				Jacob Bobert	14	Dec. 1706	30	0	0	
				Mr. Bobart	13½	Aug. 1720	60	0	0	
				Mr. Bobart	14	Aug. 1734	65	0	0	
				Mr. Bobart	14	Aug. 1748	65	0	0	
				Mrs. Hodgkinson	14	Aug. 1762	81	5	0	
				Mr. Bobart	14	Aug. 1776	81	5	0	

Name of Tenement.	*Rent.* £ s. d.	*Tenant.*	*Years elapsed.*	*When renewed.*	*Fine.* £ s. d.	*Memoranda.*
13. Part of Univ. Coll. New Buildings; vol. i, p. 170.	0 1 10	Dr. Zouch	21	Dec. 1652	0 13 4	
		Dr. Elliott	21	Jan. 1673	0 13 4	
		Mr. Elliott	36	Dec. 1708	0 13 4	
		Mr. Smith	18	Dec. 1726	0 13 4	
		Mr. Smith	14	Dec. 1740	0 13 4	
		Mr. Smith	14	Dec. 1754	0 13 4	
		Univ. College	14	Dec. 1768	0 13 4	
		Univ. College	14	Dec. 1782	0 13 4	
		Univ. College	14	Dec. 1796	0 13 4	
		Univ. College	14	Dec. 1810	12 0 0	
		Univ. College	14	Dec. 1824	15 16 0	
		Dr. Browne's trustees	14	Dec. 1838	41 8 0	
			10	Dec. 1848	5 0 0	See Orders of Meeting July 26, 1848. Not renewed in 1876. The fine would have been £31 13*s.*
			14	Dec. 1862	31 13 0	
14. Tenement next to the Greyhound; vol. i, p. 153.	2 0 0	John Hill	18	Aug. 1653	10 0 0	
		Eliz. Brokhurst	6½	Dec. 1659	0 13 4	
		Mr. Witt	15	Jan. 1674	24 0 0	
		Mr. Combes and Mr. Shaw	10½	July, 1685	12 0 0	
			21	Aug. 1706	40 0 0	
		Mrs. Egleton	14	Aug. 1720	18 0 0	
		Mr. Cotes	14	Aug. 1734	18 0 0	
		John Broughton	14	Aug. 1748	18 0 0	In 1832 fallen in, and let to Stevens the Bedmaker.
		John Broughton	14	Aug. 1762	22 10 0	
		Eliz. Broughton	14	Aug. 1776	22 10 0	In 1846 pulled down.
15. High Street, nos. 54 and 55; vol. i, p. 338.	0 12 0	Stephen Prince	11	Jan. 1654	0 13 4	
		Daniell Fogg	11½	July, 1666	10 0 0	This Fogg came to renew, Adit 1661, when £6 13*s.* 4*d.* were set him for a fine, which was then
		Daniell Fogg	14	July, 1680	23 0 0	
		Daniell Fogg	15½	Dec. 1695	20 0 0	

		Mr. Applebee	8	Dec. 1703	10 0 0	thankfully accepted by him, although he came not afterwards either to pay his fine, or have his lease sealed or soe much as made any excuse or other application to the Society.
		Mr. Applebee	14	Dec. 1717	20 0 0	
			14	Dec. 1731	22 0 0	
			14	Dec. 1745	22 0 0	
			14	Dec. 1759	27 10 0	
		Mrs. Seely	14	Dec. 1773	27 10 0	
		Mrs. Seely	15	Dec. 1788	27 10 0	
		Mr. S. Brown	14	Dec. 1802	34 5 0	At the renewing in 1695 £5 was abated by reason of the great fall of rents.
			14	Dec. 1816	54 0 0	
			14	Dec. 1830	76 10 0	
		Jos. Gunning	14	Dec. 1844	129 0 0	
			14	Dec. 1858	96 16 6	Not renewed in 1872. The fine would have been £69. As the fine was not paid in 1858 the lease fell in in 1884.
16. St. George Hall; vol. i, p. 275.	1 10 0	Ann and Edward Hastings	18½	Nov. 1655	55 0 0	This fine (in 1655) was for this and the two following leases.
		Walter Combes	8	Dec. 1663	10 0 0	
			13	Dec. 1676	30 0 0	
			14	Dec. 1690	32 0 0	
		Widow Combes	16	Dec. 1706	42 0 0	
		Mr. Clerke	16	Dec. 1722	47 0 0	
		Mat. Finch and Susan Clarke	14	Dec. 1736	39 0 0	
			15	Dec. 1751	43 10 0	
			14	Dec. 1765	39 0 0	In 1765 the Quarter's increase was not added.
			14	Dec. 1779	39 0 0	
		Mr. Green	14	Dec. 1793	58 2 6	
		Mr. Green	14	Dec. 1807	70 0 0	
			14	Dec. 1821	90 0 0	
			14	Dec. 1835	82 10 0	
			14	Dec. 1849	82 10 0	
			14	Dec. 1863	105 0 0	In 1877 not renewed. The fine would have been £105.

Name of Tenement.	*Rent.* £ s. d.	*Tenant.*	*Years elapsed.*	*When renewed.*	*Fine* £ s. d.	*Memoranda.*
17. The Queen's Arms; vol. i, p. 324.	1 6 8	Anne and Henry Hastings	19	Nov. 1655	0 0 0	
		John Edwards	16	Jan. 1671	12 0 0	
		Provost and Scholars of Queen's	17	Dec. 1688	20 0 0	
		Josiah Pullen	18	Dec. 1706	28 0 0	
		Mrs. Pullen	12	Dec. 1718	25 0 0	
		Mr. Dykes	14	Dec. 1732	25 0 0	
		Dr. Martin	8	Dec. 1740	12 10 0	
		Mr. Musgrove	15	Dec. 1755	34 17 6	
		Mr. Meysey	14	Dec. 1769	26 13 4	
		Mr. Meysey	14	Dec. 1783	30 0 0	
		Mr. Passan	14	Dec. 1797	40 0 0	
			14	Dec. 1811	108 0 0	
		Mr. Rusher	14	Dec. 1825	130 0 0	
			14	Dec. 1839	153 0 0	
			14	Dec. 1853	123 0 0	
		Mr. Brooks	14	Dec. 1867	138 0 0	In 1881 not renewed. The fine would have been £138.
18. Part of Edmund Hall; vol. i, p. 324.	0 5 0	Ann Hastings	19	Nov. 1655	0 0 0	
		The Provost and Scholars of Queen's College in trust for Edmund Hall	17	Dec. 1672	5 0 0	
			16	Dec. 1688	5 0 0	
			16	Dec. 1704	5 0 0	
			16	Dec. 1720	5 0 0	The ground on which the Vice-principal's lodgings are built.
			15	Dec. 1735	5 0 0	
			14	Dec. 1749	5 0 0	
			18	Dec. 1767	7 17 1	Sold to Queen's College in trust for Edmund Hall, 1783.
			15	Dec. 1782	5 0 0	
19. Katherine's Hall; vol. i, p. 299.	1 10 0	Mr. Henry Willis	18	Nov. 1655	5 0 0	
		Mrs. Willis	11	Dec. 1666	4 0 0	

		Henry Willis	14	Dec. 1680	15 0 0	
		Joan Willis	14	Dec. 1694	30 0 0	1694. The whole is worth £44.
		Mr. Willis	13	Dec. 1707	30 0 0	
	4 0 0	Queen's College	2	Dec. 1709	3 0 0	In 1709 the rent was advanced to £4; which is to be paid in liew of a fine.
		Queen's College	14	Dec. 1723	0 13 4	
		Queen's College	14	Dec. 1737	0 13 4	
		Queen's College	40	Dec. 1777	0 13 4	This lease is not renewable but once in 40 years; in 1737 it was renewed by mistake. Sold to Queen's in 1806 under Land Tax Redemption Acts.
20. The Coach and Horses; vol. i, p. 327.	1 3 4	James Finch and Ligborne	13½	Jan. 1657	13 6 0	
		James Finch	14	Jan. 1671	20 0 0	
		James Finch	15	Dec. 1686	20 0 0	
		James Finch Sherwin	19	Dec. 1705	20 0 0	
		Mr. Clarke	14	Dec. 1719	20 0 0	
			14	Dec. 1733	20 0 0	
			14	Dec. 1747	20 0 0	
		Leonard Jefferys	1	Dec. 1748	1 0 0	
			14	Dec. 1762	35 10 0	
		Robert Turner	14	Dec. 1776	35 10 0	
		Robert Turner	14	Dec. 1790	35 10 0	
		Mr. Morrell	14	Dec. 1804	48 0 0	
			14	Dec. 1818	78 0 0	
			14	Dec. 1832	105 0 0	
			14	Dec. 1846	120 0 0	
			14	Dec. 1860	96 0 0	In 1874 not renewed. The fine would have been £96.
21. The Light Horseman; vol. i, p. 331.	1 0 0	Elizabeth Fairbeard	23½	Jan. 1657	2 0 0	
		Stephen Fairbeard	14	Jan. 1671	12 0 0	
		Richard Platt	15	Jan. 1686	15 0 0	
		Sarah Platt	13½	Aug. 1700	13 0 0	
		Mr. Frankling	14	Aug. 1714	14 0 0	

Name of Tenement.	*Rent.* £	s.	d.	*Tenant.*	*Years elapsed.*	*When renewed.*	*Fine.* £	s.	d.	*Memoranda.*
21. The Light Horseman, *cont.*					14	Aug. 1728	14	0	0	
					14	Aug. 1742	14	0	0	
					14	Aug. 1756	17	10	0	
					14	Aug. 1770	17	10	0	
				Mr. Plater	14	Aug. 1784	17	10	0	
					14	Aug. 1798	43	15	0	
					14	Aug. 1812	96	0	0	
				Bartlett	14	Aug. 1826	115	0	0	
				Henry Hall	14	Aug. 1840	126	0	0	Fallen in and let at rack-rent at £100.
22. Link Lodging; vol. i, p. 312.	1	0	0	Christopher Airay	23	Aug. 1659	30	0	0	Three Tenements [worth] £50 per annum, Dec. 1683. The fine was set thus easy upon the account of building and in favour to the orphans.
				Mr. Combes and Applebee	$24\frac{1}{2}$	Dec. 1683	0	0	0	
				Mary Airay	11	Dec. 1694	30	0	0	
				Christopher and John Airay	15	Dec. 1709	34	0	0	
				Mrs. Airay	14	Dec. 1723	34	0	0	
				Francis Airey	14	Dec. 1737	34	0	0	
				Mr. Leaver	14	Dec. 1751	34	0	0	
				Mrs. Leaver and Watson	14	Dec. 1765	42	10	0	
					14	Dec. 1779	42	10	0	
				Mr. Fidler	14	Dec. 1793	51	5	0	
				Mr. Fidler	14	Dec. 1807	91	18	0	
				Mr. Fidler	14	Dec. 1821	162	0	0	
				Rev. E. Hawkins	14	Dec. 1835	147	0	0	
				Griffith	14	Dec. 1849	139	10	0	Fell in in 1889.
23. Boster Hall; vol. i, p. 168.	1	8	4	Dr. Bates	26	July, 1649	25	0	0	
				William Day	16	Aug. 1665	25	0	0	
				Dr. Elliott and Dr. Willis	1	Aug. 1666	0	13	4	
				Dr. Stratford	14	Aug. 1680	35	0	0	
				Now Lord Bp. of Chester	14	Aug. 1694	40	0	0	
				Dr. Stratford	14	Aug. 1708	40	0	0	

	1 8 8	Dr. Stratford	14	Aug. 1722	51 11 4	
		Mr. Harris	11	Aug. 1733	35 0 0	
		Mr. Harris	14	Aug. 1747	50 0 0	
		Dr. Smith	15	Aug. 1762	70 0 0	
		Dr. Smith	14	Aug. 1776	62 10 0	
		Mr. Towsey	14	Aug. 1790	62 10 0	
			14	Aug. 1804	66 8 0	
			14	Aug. 1818	114 0 0	
		Plowman	14	Aug. 1832	232 10 0	In 1847 the property was divided.
			15	Aug. 1847	132 0 0	
			14	Aug. 1861	200 10 0	Not renewed in 1875. The fine would have been £200.
		Slatter	15	1847	380 15 0	
		Slatter	14	1861	246 10 0	Not renewed in 1875. The fine would have been £246.
24. The Bell; vol. i, p. 289.	2 0 0	Dr. Lane	26	Aug. 1664	80 0 0	In 1664 this fine was set so low by reason of a charge he was at in building.
		Mrs. Lane	17½	Jan. 1681	50 0 0	
		Mrs. Lane	14	Dec. 1695	40 0 0	
		Dr. Lane	14	Dec. 1709	40 0 0	
		Provost of Queen's	13	Dec. 1722	36 0 0	
		Provost of Queen's	3	Dec. 1725	6 6 0	
			14	Dec. 1739	40 0 0	
			14	Dec. 1753	50 0 0	
			14	Dec. 1767	50 0 0	
			14	Dec. 1781	50 0 0	
			14	Dec. 1795	50 0 0	
			14	Dec. 1809	50 0 0	
			14	Dec. 1823	82 10 0	
			14	Dec. 1837	97 10 0	
			14	Dec. 1851	90 0 0	
			14	Dec. 1865	90 0 0	In 1879 not renewed. The fine would have been £90.
25. No. 34 High Street; vol. i, p. 271.	0 17 4	Richard Marten	21	Aug. 1665	10 0 0	
		Richard Marten	16½	Jan. 1681	14 0 0	

Name of Tenement.	*Rent.* £	s.	d.	*Tenant.*	*Years elapsed.*	*When renewed.*	*Fine.* £	s.	d.	*Memoranda.*
25. No. 34 High Street, *cont.*				Sir Robert Harrison	14	Dec. 1695	10	0	0	
				Sir Robert Harrison	14	Dec. 1709	10	0	0	
				Mrs. Hudson	10½	Aug. 1720	19	0	0	
				Mr. Boyce	14	Aug. 1734	30	0	0	
				Mr. Wickham	13	Aug. 1747	26	0	0	
					14	Aug. 1761	30	10	0	
					14	Aug. 1775	30	10	0	
					14	Aug. 1789	35	0	0	Purchased in 1795 by Mr. Smith for £1,058 of Mr. Wickham's executors.
				Rev. Mr. Slatter	14	Aug. 1803	42	13	0	
				Mr. Bulley	14	Aug. 1817	78	0	0	
				Miss Bulley	14	Aug. 1831	133	4	0	
				Mathews	14	Aug. 1845	145	10	0	
					14	Aug. 1859	94	10	0	Not renewed in 1873. The fine would have been £94 10*s.*
26. Tanner's Yard; vol. i, p. 241.	0	3	2	William Aldworth	18	Jan. 1669	9	0	0	One tenement out of Day's lease.
				Thomas Dey	21½	Aug. 1691	10	0	0	
				Widow Dye	16	Aug. 1707	8	0	0	
				Mr. Marriner	15	Aug. 1722	15	0	0	
					14	Aug. 1736	12	10	0	
					14	Aug. 1750	12	10	0	
				John Broughton	14	Aug. 1764	12	10	0	
					14	Aug. 1778	12	10	0	
				Mr. Tanner	29	Aug. 1807	45	0	0	Rent raised to £3 10*s.*
				Carolina Coles	22	Aug. 1829	222	0	0	Sold.
27. Nos. 16–18 Merton Street, and 17 King Street; vol. i, p. 236.	0	3	4	William Noble	18	Jan. 1669	18	0	0	Three tenements out of Day's lease.
				William Noble	12	Jan. 1681	12	0	0	
				Mrs. Combes	14	Dec. 1695	14	0	0	
				Executors of Mr. Wright	14	Dec. 1709	14	0	0	
	0	3	0	Executors of Mr. Wright	14½	Aug. 1724	15	0	0	
				Mr. Piddington	7	Dec. 1731	6	0	0	

		Mr. Piddington	14	Dec. 1745	14 0 0	Four tenements are included in this lease. Mrs. Sims £5 10s., late Benwell £5, Mrs. Tomkins £6 10s., Mr. Hall £6 6s. Total £23 6s. One of these tenements is purchased by Mr. Barnet, see below; another by Mr. Hedges, see below.
No. 17 King Street.	0 3 0	Mr. Barnet	37	Dec. 1782	10 0 0	One of Piddington's tenements.
		Mr. Davis	15	Aug. 1797	13 15 6	In 1797 this and Hedges (see below) were consolidated.
		Mr. Mickleham	14	Aug. 1811	20 8 0	In 1811 the leases were separated.
		Mr. Mickleham	14	Aug. 1825	19 0 0	
		Mr. Mickleham	14	Aug. 1839	15 18 0	
		Mr. Mickleham	14	Aug. 1853	14 8 0	
		Mr. Mickleham	14	Aug. 1867	15 18 0	Not renewed in 1881; sold to the University.
No. 18 Merton Street.	0 3 0	Mr. Hedges	38	Dec. 1783	14 0 0	One of Piddington's tenements. See above.
		Thomas Cross	14	Aug. 1797	0 0 0	
		Thomas Cross	15	Aug. 1812	14 16 0	
No. 16 Merton Street.	0 3 0	Mr. James	40	Dec. 1785	60 0 0	One of Piddington's tenements.
		Mr. James	14	Dec. 1799	14 16 0	
		Mr. James	14	Dec. 1813	33 12 0	
		Mr. James	14	Dec. 1827	54 12 0	
		Mr. James	14	Dec. 1841	51 12 0	
		Mr. Wyatt	14	Dec. 1855	59 6 6	Not renewed in 1869. The fine would have been £48 12s.; sold to the University.
No. 17 Merton Street.	0 3 0	Mr. Gould	40	Dec. 1785	14 0 0	One of Piddington's tenements.
		Mr. Maxey	14	Dec. 1799	12 6 0	In 1785 the fine was much
		Mr. Maxey	14	Dec. 1813	26 8 0	underset, the premises being

Name of Tenement.	*Rent.* £ s. d.	*Tenant.*	*Years elapsed.*	*When renewed.*	*Fine.* £ s. d.	*Memoranda.*
No. 17 Merton Street, *cont.*		Simmonds	14	Dec. 1827	20 8 0	much out of repair, the lease having fallen in.
			14	Dec. 1841	35 8 0	
			14	Dec. 1855	30 18 0	In 1869 not renewed. The fine would have been £33 18*s.*; sold to the University.
28. Nos. 13–15 Merton Street; vol. i, p. 233.	0 5 8	Walter Combes	18	Jan. 1669	15 0 0	Three tenements out of Day's lease. Mem. in setting the fine in 1698, the new building was not considered.
		Mr. Combes	16	Dec. 1685	15 0 0	
		Hudson and Combes	13	Dec. 1698	12 0 0	
		Mrs. Combes	14	Dec. 1712	40 0 0	
		Mrs. Combes	14	Dec. 1726	40 0 0	In 1726 the fine was underset, being valued at the parish rate, £42 per annum.
	0 6 0	Mr. Ward	5	Dec. 1731	14 0 0	
		Mr. Ward's daughters	14	Dec. 1745	30 0 0	
		Mr. Townsend	40	Dec. 1785	150 0 0	In 1785, in consideration of the fine being so low, Mr. Townsend is to pay £8 rent.
	1 16 0	Mr. Costar	14	Dec. 1799	12 15 0	One of Townsend's tenements.
	2 16 0	Mr. Rusgrove	14	Dec. 1799	14 0 0	" " "
	2 16 0	Mr. Thos. Dry	14	Dec. 1799	14 0 0	" " "
	7 2 0	Mr. Thos. Dry	14	Dec. 1813	109 0 0	All three tenements. Costar's tenement was added to the Angel subsequently.
No. 13 Merton Street.	2 10 0	Rich. Dry	14	Dec. 1827	65 7 0	
		Rich. Dry	14	Dec. 1841	65 5 0	
		Will. Dry	14	Dec. 1855	57 15 0	In 1869 not renewed. Sold to the University.
No. 15 Merton Street.	1 5 0	Mr. Norris	14	Dec. 1799	6 7 6	One of Townsend's tenements.
		Mr. Norris	14	Dec. 1813	24 0 0	
		Mr. Norris	15	Dec. 1828	32 8 0	

		Mr. Norris	14	Dec. 1842	28 10 0	
		Skinner	14	Dec. 1856	28 10 0	Not renewed in 1870.
29. In Ram Alley; vol. i, p. 242.	0 4 6	Ann Day, widow	18	Jan. 1669	10 0 0	Two tenements taken out of Day's lease.
		Mr. Faulkner	17	Dec. 1686	10 0 0	
		Mr. Faulkner	14	Dec. 1700	7 10 0	
		Mr. Faulkner	14	Dec. 1714	7 10 0	
		Mr. Faulkner	17	Dec. 1731	20 0 0	
		Mrs. Courten	14	Dec. 1745	14 0 0	
		Mrs. Courten	14	Dec. 1759	17 10 0	
	0 3 6	Mr. Walker	34	Dec. 1793	36 15 0	Part of Mrs. Courten's holding.
		Mr. Blackwell	11	Dec. 1804	40 16 0	
	0 2 0	Mr. Heming	9	Dec. 1813	31 15 0	House and garden in Coach and Horse lane part of Blackwell's holding; let on 20 years lease.
			7	Dec. 1820	20 8 0	
			7	Dec. 1827	17 8 0	
			7	Dec. 1834	24 18 0	In 1856 let at rack-rent. In 1870 let to Franklin.
	0 2 0	Mr. Blackwell	9	1813	13 1 6	A house in Ram Alley; part of Blackwell's holding.
		Mrs. Blackwell	7	1820	8 8 0	
		Mrs. Blackwell	7	1827	11 8 0	
			7	1834	11 8 0	In 1840 joined to Cooke's lease.
30. A shop in High Street; vol. i, p. 245.	0 2 0	Stephen Prince	18	Jan. 1669	8 0 0	One tenement, &c., taken out of Day's lease.
		William Applebee	8	Dec. 1677	3 0 0	
		Mrs. Applebee	20	Dec. 1697	14 0 0	
		Seely and Applebee	14	Dec. 1711	7 0 0	
		Seely and Applebee	14	Dec. 1725	7 0 0	
		Applebee	14	Dec. 1739	7 0 0	
		Mr. Seely	14	Dec. 1753	9 0 0	
		Mr. Will. Cooke	18	Dec. 1771	14 0 9	
		William Cooke	14	Dec. 1785	11 5 0	
		William Cook	8	Dec. 1793	30 10 0	A lease for 33 years.
		William Cook	11	Dec. 1804	24 3 6	
		William Cook	11	Dec. 1815	48 0 0	
		William Cook	11	Dec. 1826	55 10 0	

Name of Tenement.	*Rent.* £ s. d.	*Tenant.*	*Years elapsed.*	*When renewed.*	*Fine.* £ s. d.	*Memoranda.*
30. A shop, &c., *cont.*		Eliz. Cook	11	Dec. 1837	126 0 0	In 1837, this is to include the property late Blackwell's.
		William Cook	11	Dec. 1848	112 0 0	
		William Cook	12	Dec. 1860	138 0 0	Sold to the University.
31. No. 22 King Street; vol. i, p. 243.	0 1 8	William Squire	18	Jan. 1669	6 13 4	One tenement, &c., taken out of Day's lease.
		John Vincent	16	Dec. 1685	7 0 0	
		John Vincent	14	Dec. 1699	5 0 0	
		Edward Vincent	14	Dec. 1713	5 0 0	
		William Thomas	14	Dec. 1727	5 0 0	
		Mr. Blackford	14	Dec. 1741	5 0 0	
			14	Dec. 1755	6 5 0	
		Mr. Arnott	14	Dec. 1769	6 5 0	
		Will. Dry	19	Dec. 1788	8 16 0	
			14	Dec. 1802	14 17 6	
		Hollis	14	Dec. 1816	26 8 0	
		Mrs. Gray	14	Dec. 1830	45 18 0	
		Mrs. Gray	14	Dec. 1844	41 6 0	
		Thos. Hill	14	Dec. 1858	35 8 0	Sold to the University.
32. Tenements in King Street and Ram Alley; vol. i, p. 238.	0 4 4	Moses Ford	18	Jan. 1669	20 0 0	Three tenements, &c., taken out of Day's lease.
		Richard Hamlett	8	Jan. 1677	8 0 0	
		Widow Hamlett	14	Dec. 1691	14 0 0	This lease was divided in 1704 to Francis Clarke and Thomas Sheppard.
33. Part of Hamlett's lease; vol. i, p. 239.	0 4 0	Francis Clarke	12½	Aug. 1704	9 6 8	Two tenements out of Hamlett's lease.
		Francis Clarke	14	Aug. 1718	11 0 0	
		Susannah Clarke	14	Aug. 1732	11 0 0	
		Mrs. Smith	14	Aug. 1746	11 0 0	
		Robert Smith	14	Aug. 1760	11 0 0	
		Robert Smith	14	Aug. 1774	11 0 0	
		Mrs. Kimberley	39	Aug. 1813	58 16 0	Two tenements in Ram Alley

		Wise	7	Aug. 1820	10 16 0	and a garden at the back of
		Wise	7	Aug. 1827	10 16 0	Coach and Horses; part of
		Wise	8	Aug. 1835	38 17 0	Smith's holding.
						In 1856 let at rack-rent.
		Mr. Grainge	14	Aug. 1789	6 0 0	A dwelling-house in Coach and
		Mr. Will. Gardiner	14	Aug. 1803	16 2 6	Horse lane, being a moiety
			14	Aug. 1817	16 16 0	of Smith's holding.
			14	Aug. 1831	25 16 0	A small garden belonging to
		Allen	14	Aug. 1845	25 16 6	this estate leased to Mrs. Cook
			14	Aug. 1859	28 16 0	for 33 years.
						Sold to the University.
34. Part of Hamlett's lease, Coach and Horses; vol. i, p. 239.	0 2 0	Tho. Sheppard	$12\frac{1}{2}$	Aug. 1704	4 13 4	A tenement of Hamlett's lease.
		Tho. Sheppard	14	Aug. 1718	7 0 0	In 1704 the new building was
			14	Aug. 1732	7 0 0	not considered in the fine.
			14	Aug. 1746	7 0 0	
		Mr. Clarke	14	Aug. 1760	7 0 0	
		Ben Davis	15	Aug. 1775	7 17 6	
			14	Aug. 1789	7 17 6	
		Mr. Thos Hemming	14	Aug. 1803	13 12 6	
			14	Aug. 1817	26 8 0	
			14	Aug. 1831	26 8 0	
		James Morrell	14	Aug. 1845	45 18 0	
		James Morrell	14	Aug. 1859	54 18 0	Sold to the University in 1871.
35. Site of the College Stables; vol. i, p. 152.	1 19 0	Mrs. Hooper		Aug. 1645	0 0 0	Her brother was then one of the
		John Hooper	$26\frac{1}{2}$	Jan. 1671	20 0 0	fellows but distracted, and
		Mr. Hooper	$11\frac{1}{2}$	June, 1683	10 0 0	the fine thus easy in favour
		Mr. Hooper	12	Aug. 1695	13 0 0	of him.
		Mr. Gardiner	14	Aug. 1709	14 0 0	
		Mr. Wood	$15\frac{1}{2}$	Dec. 1724	24 0 0	
St. Aldate's.						
36. The Wheatsheaf; vol. ii, p. 200.	1 0 0	Eliz. Locsmith	$19\frac{1}{2}$	Aug. 1651	5 0 0	Two tenements.
		Richard Miller	$6\frac{1}{2}$	Jan. 1657	5 0 0	
		Richard Miller	$14\frac{1}{2}$	Aug. 1672	15 0 0	

Name of Tenement.	*Rent.* £ s. d.	*Tenant.*	*Years elapsed.*	*When renewed.*	*Fine.* £ s. d.	*Memoranda.*
36. The Wheatsheaf, *cont.*		Richard Miller	18½	Dec. 1690	20 0 0	
		Richard Miller	14	Dec. 1704	14 0 0	In the fine, anno 1718, the new building was not considered.
		Mr. Townshend	14	Dec. 1718	14 0 0	
		Mr. Townshend	14	Dec. 1732	30 0 0	
		Mr. Ives	14	Dec. 1746	30 0 0	In 1746, at this renewal the College allowed Mr. Ives £5 in consideration of the abatement he is obliged to make his tenant on account of the decrease of business in the inn.
			14	Dec. 1760	30 0 0	
			14	Dec. 1774	30 0 0	
		Mr. Stockford	14	Dec. 1788	30 0 0	
		Mr. Hyde	14	Dec. 1802	48 15 0	
			14	Dec. 1816	72 0 0	
		Widbin	14	Dec. 1830	123 0 0	
		Crozier	14	Dec. 1844	153 0 0	
		Box	14	Dec. 1858	78 0 0	In 1872 not renewed. The fine would have been £78.
37. St. Aldate's Street, nos. 99–102; vol. ii, p. 167.	0 16 0	Thomas Hudson	16½	Aug. 1653	5 0 0	Three tenements.
			15½	Dec. 1668	6 0 0	In 1668, £6 because he built.
	1 16 0	John Hudson	14	Dec. 1682	30 0 0	
			14	Dec. 1696	27 0 0	In 1696 £3 was abated by reason of his improvement by building.
		Mr. Atwood	14½	Aug. 1711	30 0 0	
		Mrs. Lipscomb	16	Aug. 1727	35 0 0	This lease is expired and the houses are let at rack-rent. These tenements were sold to Mrs. Jones postmistress in 1772.[1]
38. Part of the previous holding; vol. ii, p. 168.	0 9 0	Mr. Remmett	15	Aug. 1742	8 0 0	This tenement was bought and taken out of the above lease of Mrs. Lipscomb.
			14	Aug. 1756	8 15 0	
		Mr. Keepe	14	Aug. 1770	8 15 0	

[1] One of the tenements had been made into a separate lease in 1742; see vol. ii, p. 168.

				14	Aug. 1784	8	15	0	
			Mr. Johnson	14	Aug. 1798	9	8	6	
			Mrs. Keepe	14	Aug. 1812	30	0	0	
			Banting	14	Aug. 1826	31	10	0	
			Bennett	14	Aug. 1840	44	4	0	
				14	Aug. 1854	45	0	0	In 1868 not renewed. The fine would have been £37 10*s*.
39. St. Aldate's Street, nos. 101–3; vol. ii, p. 170.	0 26 8		Thomas Hudson	16½	Jan. 1657	3	0	0	One tenement.
			Thomas Hudson	11	Dec. 1668	10	0	0	
	0 7 0		John Hudson	14	Dec. 1682	7	0	0	
			John Hudson	14	Dec. 1696	7	0	0	
			Mr. Dimock	14½	Aug. 1711	7	0	0	
			Mrs. Dimock	14	Aug. 1725	7	0	0	
			Barth. Reynolds	14	Aug. 1739	7	0	0	
			Widow Cradock	21	Aug. 1760	7	0	0	
			Dr. Cust	14	Aug. 1774	6	13	0	
			Dr. Dell	14	Aug. 1788	6	13	0	
			Mr. Etty	14	Aug. 1802	24	11	0	
			Hen. Taunton	14	Aug. 1816	24	0	0	
			Mrs. Taunton	14	Aug. 1830	39	0	0	In 1858 the College refused to renew. Let to Compton in 1870.
40. In Pembroke Street; vol. ii, p. 144.	0 5 0		Thomas Cox	25	July, 1656	1	10	0	
				19	Aug. 1675	1	6	8	
			Widow Cox	15½	Dec. 1690	2	0	0	
			Henry Willett	13	Dec. 1703	2	3	0	
			Dr. Lasher	14	Aug. 1717	2	3	0	The fee simple of this tenement was sold to Mr. Taunton in 1772.
				14	Aug. 1731	2	10	0	
			Mr. Lasher	14	Aug. 1745	2	10	0	
				15	Aug. 1760	3	7	6	
41. St. Aldate's Street, no. 98; vol. ii, p. 166.	0 18 0		Thomas Fifield	19½	July, 1657	8	0	0	
			Mr. Nourse	13	Aug. 1670	15	0	0	
			John West, Esq.	3½	Dec. 1673	0	13	4	

Name of Tenement.	*Rent.* £	s.	d.	*Tenant.*	*Years elapsed.*	*When renewed.*	*Fine.* £	s.	d.	*Memoranda.*
41. St. Aldate's Street, *cont.*				Dr. Conant	12½	Aug. 1686	15	0	0	
				Dr. Conant	½	Dec. 1686	1	10	0	
				Dr. Conant	2	Dec. 1688	4	0	0	
				Dr. Conant	14	Dec. 1702	16	0	0	
				Dr. Lane	14½	Aug. 1717	17	0	0	
					14	Aug. 1731	16	0	0	
				Mrs. Lane	7	Aug. 1738	8	0	0	
					7	Aug. 1745	6	6	0	
					14	Aug. 1759	20	0	0	
				Mrs. Loder	14	Aug. 1773	20	0	0	
					14	Aug. 1787	20	0	0	
				Mr. Banting	15	Aug. 1802	30	19	6	
				Chas. Stevens	14	Aug. 1816	42	0	0	
				Mrs. Stevens	14	Aug. 1830	79	10	0	
					14	Aug. 1844	72	0	0	
				Thos. Sabin	14	Aug. 1858	64	10	0	In 1872 not renewed. The fine would have been £87.
42. St. Aldate's Street, nos. 105 and 106; vol. ii, p. 189.	1	0	0	Ric. Halloway, Esq.	17	Jan. 1657	10	0	0	
				Ric. Halloway, Esq.	15	Dec. 1672	10	0	0	
				Sir Ric. Holloway	9	Dec. 1681	5	0	0	
	2	0	0	Sir Ric. Holloway	8½	Aug. 1690	10	0	0	In 1690 the tenement used for an office was added.
				Mr. Rawlins	11½	Dec. 1701	15	0	0	
				Mr. Rawlins	14	Dec. 1715	20	0	0	
					14	Dec. 1729	20	0	0	
				Widow Rawlins	14	Dec. 1743	20	0	0	
				Mr. Badcock	39	Dec. 1782	200	0	0	
				Mr. Badcock	3	Dec. 1785	2	5	0	
					14	Dec. 1799	41	5	0	
				Mr. Badcock	14	Dec. 1813	85	4	0	
					14	Dec. 1827	136	4	0	
					14	Dec. 1841	218	14	0	

					14	Dec. 1855	233	14	0	
					14	Dec. 1869	270	0	0	April 12, 1879, Mr. Bennett is paying Badcock £150 per annum for his shop and house and now asks £180.
43. The Old Swan; vol. ii, p. 186.	3	0	0	Dr. Clayton	16	Jan. 1657	13	6	8	Two tenements.
				Mr. Hearne	6½	Aug. 1664	0	13	4	In 1664 the fine was set so low in favour of Dr. Clayton.
				Mr. Brooks	14½	Dec. 1678	27	0	0	
	2	0	0	Mr. Brooks	12	Dec. 1690	17	0	0	
				Mr. Brooks	12½	Aug. 1703	18	0	0	
				Mr. Brooks	14	Aug. 1717	20	0	0	
				Mrs. Green	14	Aug. 1731	20	0	0	
					14	Aug. 1745	37	0	0	
				Dr. Kelly	14	Aug. 1759	46	5	0	
				Dr. Cust	14	Aug. 1773	41	0	0	
					8	Aug. 1781	19	0	0	
				Dr. Thompson	4	Aug. 1785	4	0	0	
				Mr. Grosvenor	14	Aug. 1799	62	10	0	
					19	Aug. 1818	156	7	0	
					14	Aug. 1832	199	10	0	
					14	Aug. 1846	184	10	0	In 1874 not renewed. The fine would have been £105. The residue of the lease was purchased in 1878 for £1,750, and a lease given to the Post Office for 99 years at £170 per annum.
					14	Aug. 1860	162	0	0	
44. At the corner of Pembroke Street;[1] vol. ii, p. 164.	2	5	4	Widow Saunders	17½	Dec. 1662	15	0	0	
	1	2	8	Mr. Fifield	17	Jan. 1679	15	0	0	
	1	19	5	Mr. Walker	14½	July, 1694	25	0	0	
	1	19	5	Widow Walker	14	Aug. 1708	25	0	0	

[1] This tenement was divided in 1679, partly reunited in 1694, entirely reunited in 1750, but fines were paid for each part; in 1782 only one fine was paid for the whole. See vol. ii, pp. 164, 165.

Name of Tenement.	*Rent.* £	*s.*	*d.*	*Tenant.*	*Years elapsed.*	*When renewed.*	*Fine.* £	*s.*	*d.*	*Memoranda.*
44. At the corner, &c., *cont.*	1	19	5	Mr. Walker	14	Aug. 1722	25	0	0	
					14	Aug. 1736	25	0	0	
				Wilcox and Kirby	3	Aug. 1739	8	6	8	
					11	Aug. 1750	20	0	0	
				Mr. Blenerhasset	18	Aug. 1768	20	0	0	
				Mr. Parsons	14	Aug. 1782				
					14	Aug. 1796				
					14	Aug. 1810				
45. Wild's tenement; vol. ii, p. 231.	0	4	0	Pembroke College	26	Dec. 1661	0	13	0	[*sic*]
					32	Dec. 1693	0	13	4	
					18	Dec. 1711	0	13	4	
					14	Dec. 1725	0	13	4	
					14	Dec. 1739	0	13	4	
					14	Dec. 1753	0	13	4	
					14	Dec. 1767	0	13	4	
					14	Dec. 1781	0	13	4	Sold to Pembroke College.
46. Part of tenement no. 44, above; vol. ii, p. 165.	1	2	8	Mr. William Forty	17	Jan. 1679	15	0	0	
	0	8	5	Mr. Coles	$14\frac{1}{2}$	July, 1694	5	0	0	
				Mrs. Williams	13	Aug. 1707	5	0	0	
				Dr. Lane	14	Aug. 1721	10	0	0	
					14	Aug. 1735	10	0	0	
				Kirby	15	Aug. 1750	10	0	0	
				Mr. Blennerhasset	18	Aug. 1768	10	0	0	
				Mr. Parsons	14	Aug. 1782	35	0	0	
				Mr. Green	14	Aug. 1796	53	5	0	
				Mr. Parsons	14	Aug. 1810	113	0	0	
					14	Aug. 1824	161	2	0	
				Mr. Greene	14	Aug. 1838	179	2	0	
				Green and Castle	14	Aug. 1852	203	7	0	
				Green	14	Aug. 1866	275	2	0	In 1870, Nov. 4, the College

						granted an extension of 4 years to the lease of the premises of Mr. Green lately destroyed by fire and now being rebuilt. Termination of the lease in 1910. In 1880 the fine would have been £312.
47. St. Aldate's Street, nos. 17 and 18; vol. ii, p. 195.	0 8 0	John Horne	22	Jan. 1657	8 0 0	
			12½	Aug. 1670	6 13 4	
		William Horne	12½	Dec. 1682	6 13 4	
		Mr. Hooper	12	Dec. 1694	7 0 0	
		Mr. Smith	14	Dec. 1708	9 0 0	
		Mrs. Peade	14	Dec. 1722	11 0 0	
		Widow Rooks	14	Dec. 1736	11 0 0	
		Dr. Pitt	9	Dec. 1745	7 0 0	
		Mrs. Pitt	14	Dec. 1759	13 15 0	
		Mr. Moore	26	Dec. 1785	44 18 1	
		Mrs. Grain	14	Dec. 1799	22 0 0	
		Mr. Henry Ward	14	Dec. 1813	50 8 0	
			14	Dec. 1827	81 18 0	
			14	Dec. 1841	84 18 0	In 1881 let to Mr. G. Ward at £45 per annum for 17 years so as to fall in to the College with the Wheatsheaf.
St. Mary's.						
48. Domus Plente; vol. i, p. 411.	2 0 0	Alderman John Nixon	15	Dec. 1652	16 0 0	
		Joan Nixon	15½	Aug. 1668	20 0 0	
		Alderman Fifield	14	Aug. 1682	20 0 0	
		Mr. Fifield	14	Dec. 1696	22 0 0	
		Mr. Allen	14	Dec. 1710	22 0 0	
		Mr. Boyce	9	Dec. 1719	14 0 0	
		Mr. Boyce	14	Dec. 1733	22 0 0	
		Mr. Boyce	14	Dec. 1747	22 0 0	1747, Mrs. Crook rents the

Name of Tenement.	*Rent.* £ *s.* *d.*	*Tenant.*	*Years elapsed*	*When renewed.*	*Fine.* £ *s.* *d.*	*Memoranda.*
48. Domus Plente, *cont.*		Mr. Gilpin	14	Dec. 1761	32 13 0	house at £30; the fine is underset.
		Mrs. Morten	14	Dec. 1775	32 13 0	
		Mr. Richings	14	Dec. 1789	32 13 0	
		Mrs. Benwell	14	Dec. 1803	35 0 0	
		Mr. Jubber	14	Dec. 1817	90 0 0	
			14	Dec. 1831	97 10 0	
			14	Dec. 1845	125 4 0	In 1845 a tenement acquired from the town was added but a tenement held by the principal of St. Mary Hall was removed; see below. In 1873 not renewed; the fine would have been £167 4*s*.
			14	Dec. 1859	167 4 0	
Tenement of the Town	1 6 8	Jubber	15	Nov. 1831	40 0 0	
	0 4 0 for capons	Jubber	14	Dec. 1845	included in	the fine above. This tenement was acquired from the town in Feb. 1845 by exchange.
In Grove Street.	1 10 0	Principal of St. Mary Hall		Dec. 1831		The Principal of St. Mary Hall bought this from Jubber and a lease was granted him in 1831. Not renewed in 1873. The fine would have been £69.
		Speakman	14	Dec. 1845	39 0 0	
			14	Dec. 1859	69 0 0	
49. At the west of St. Mary's church; vol. i, p. 423.	3 3 8	Martin Lypyate	14	Aug. 1652	30 0 0	Including a tenement in All Saints.
		Thomas Robinson	10	July, 1662	20 0 0	
		Eliz. Robinson	14	July, 1676	60 0 0	
		Eliz. Robinson	14	Aug. 1690	60 0 0	
		Mrs. Watson	14	Aug. 1704	70 0 0	

				Mr. Nicholls	14½	Dec. 1715	50	0	0	
					14	Dec. 1729	65	0	0	Sold.
49 A. Outside the walls; vol. i, p. 457.	1	4	0	John Billingsley	14½	Aug. 1656	2	0	0	
50. In Cat Street; vol. i, p. 431.	0	13	4	Prosper Nicholas	16	Dec. 1656	12	0	0	
				Edward Ewen	15	Jan. 1671	20	0	0	
				Widow Ewen	14	Dec. 1685	18	0	0	
				Mrs. Sarah Ewen	14	Dec. 1699	18	0	0	
				Mrs. Law	14	Dec. 1713	18	0	0	
				Mr. Law	14	Dec. 1727	25	0	0	Sold.
50 A. Outside the walls; vol. i, p. 457.	1	0	0	Abraham White	23	Dec. 1660	12	0	0	
51. Ing Hall; vol. i, p. 464.	1	6	8	Sir Sampson White	23	Dec. 1661	25	0	0	
				Sir Sampson White		July, 1662	0	13	4	
				Sir Sampson White	13½	Jan. 1675	14	0	0	
				Mr. White	11	Dec. 1686	12	0	0	
				Mr. White	11	Dec. 1697	15	0	0	
				Mr. White	11	Dec. 1708	15	0	0	
				Mr. White	11	Dec. 1719	20	0	0	
					14	Dec. 1733	35	0	0	
					14	Dec. 1747	35	0	0	
				All Souls Coll.	14	Dec. 1761	35	16	8	
					14	Dec. 1775	35	16	8	Sold in 1775 to All Souls College.
52. Logic School; vol. i, p. 458.	3	0	0	The University	40	Jan. 1685	0	6	8	This lease to be renewed every 14 years paying 6*s.* 8*d.* for the seal and the accustomed fees.
					14	Jan. 1699	0	6	8	
					14½	Aug. 1714	0	6	8	
					14	Aug. 1728	0	6	8	
					14	Aug. 1742	0	6	8	
					14	Aug. 1756	0	6	8	

Tenement.	Rent. £ s. d.	Tenant.	Years elapsed.	When renewed.	Fine. £ s. d.	Memoranda.
52. Logic School, *cont.*			14	Aug. 1770	0 6 8	
			14	Aug. 1784	0 6 8	
			12	Aug. 1796	0 13 4	
			14	Aug. 1810	0 13 4	
			14	Aug. 1824	0 13 4	
			14	Aug. 1838	0 13 4	
			14	Aug. 1852	0 13 4	In 1866 the College refused to renew.
All Saints.						
53. Broadgates; vol. ii, p. 12.	15 0 0	Mr. Perrott	12	Dec. 1649	8 0 0	
		Dr. Perrott	13	Dec. 1662	10 0 0	1662, this fine was in favour because of those new houses which were then lately built.
		Charles Perrott, Esq.	11	Jan. 1673	35 0 0	
		James Perrott	15	Dec. 1688	65 0 0	
		James Perrott	14	Dec. 1702	65 0 0	
		James Perrott	14	Dec. 1716	65 0 0	
		Henry Perrott	14	Dec. 1730	69 0 0	Sold to the Trustees of Radcliffe's Library.
54. At the entrance of Broadgates; vol. ii, p. 13.	1 4 0	John Newman	15	Dec. 1654	8 0 0	
		Wid. Newman	15	Dec. 1669	10 0 0	
		Mr. Hughes	14½	July, 1684	12 0 0	
		Mr. Hughes	30	Aug. 1714	40 0 0	
		Mr. Haynes	14	Aug. 1728	7 6 0	Sold to Radclyffe's Trustees.
55–8. North of All Saints Church; vol. ii, p. 27.	1 4 0	Richard Imings	29	Dec. 1655	10 0 0	Aug. 1677, being forfeited to the University by reason of Mr. Imings being felo-de-se, it was sold to the four tenants in possession who surrendered the old lease and renewed it in several leases with 6*d.* rent increased.
		Richard Imings, jun.	10½	July, 1666	0 13 4	

55. Part of Imings's lease; vol. ii, pp. 27–9.	0 9 0	James Short	11	Aug. 1677	5 0 0	
		Widow Short	14	Aug. 1691	6 13 4	
		Mr. Poland	14	Aug. 1705	6 13 4	
		Mr. Poland	14	Aug. 1719	6 13 4	
		Mr. Tawney	40	Aug. 1760	20 0 0	The following are included in this and in Colborn's lease [no. 58]:—Mrs. Willoughby £2 12*s*., Henry Clark £2 6*s*., Edward Harrison £2 10*s*., Mrs. Barrow £3 12*s*. Total £11. Sold in 1772 to the Rector of Lincoln.
56. Part of Imings's lease; vol. ii, pp. 28, 29.	0 5 6	Thos. Wells	11	Aug. 1677	3 0 0	
		Thos. Wells	14	Aug. 1691	4 0 0	
		Mr. Hedges	14	Aug. 1705	4 0 0	
		Mr. Newman	14	Aug. 1719	4 0 0	
	0 3 0	Mr. Annison	14	Aug. 1733	7 0 0	Divided into two tenements in 1733. Sold in 1772.
	0 2 6	Mr. Warner	14	Aug. 1733	4 0 0	
		Mr. Wise	14	Aug. 1747	4 0 0	
			14	Aug. 1761	5 0 0	Sold in 1772.
57. Part of Imings's lease; vol. ii, pp. 28, 29.	0 6 6	Elinor Davis	11	Aug. 1677	3 10 0	
		Elinor Davis	14	Aug. 1691	4 13 4	
		Widow Curtis	14	Aug. 1705	4 13 4	
		Widow Curtis	14	Aug. 1719	4 13 4	
		Mr. West	14	Aug. 1733	6 0 0	
		Mr. Scanderell	14	Aug. 1747	6 0 0	
		Mrs. Fell	14	Aug. 1761	6 0 0	
			4½	Dec. 1765	1 4 0	Sold in 1772.
58. Part of Imings's lease; vol. ii, pp. 28, 29.	0 3 6	Amy Thompson	11	Aug. 1677	2 3 4	
		Mr. Howell Clerke [*sic*]	14	Aug. 1691	2 13 4	
		Mr. Howell Clerke [*sic*]	14	Aug. 1705	2 13 4	

Name of Tenement.	*Rent.* £ *s.* *d.*	*Tenant.*	*Years elapsed.*	*When renewed.*	*Fine.* £ *s.* *d.*	*Memoranda.*
58. Part of Imings's lease, *cont.*		Mr. Colborn and his wife Mrs. Howell	14	Aug. 1719	2 13 4	This lease expired, and in 1760 was taken by Tawney together with Poland's. See above. Sold in 1772.
59. In Turl Street; vol. ii, p. 26.	0 8 0	Mrs. Leverett	14	Dec. 1743	11 12 0	This tenement was included before in a lease granted to Alderman Nicholls; when he sold his houses to accomodate Dr. Radcliffe's Library, this was sold[1] as above. Sold to the rector of Lincoln 1772.
		Mr. Robinson	19	Dec. 1762	25 0 0	
60. Swinbrooks; vol. ii, p. 54.	2 0 0	Mr. Thomas Dennis	8	Aug. 1653	10 0 0	
		Mr. Hampson	9	July, 1662	10 0 0	
		Mr. Hawkins	9	Aug. 1671	26 0 0	
		Mr. Hawkins	12½	Dec. 1683	40 0 0	
		Mr. Hawkins	14	Dec. 1697	42 0 0	
		Mr. Webb	14	Dec. 1711	40 0 0	
		Mr. Dew	14	Dec. 1725	42 11 0	
		Mr. Dew	14	Dec. 1739	42 11 0	
		Mr. Webb	16	Dec. 1755	56 17 6	
		Ann and Diana Wells	14	Dec. 1769	42 11 0	
		Mrs. Baggs	14	Dec. 1783	42 11 0	
			4	Dec. 1787	11 10 0	
			14	Dec. 1801	53 15 0	
		Giles	14	Dec. 1815	114 0 0	
			14	Dec. 1829	189 0 0	
			14	Dec. 1843	373 10 0	
		Richard Wootten	14	Dec. 1857	403 10 0	In 1871 not renewed; the fine would have been £429.

[1] i.e. to Mrs. Leverett.

61. Hore's; vol. ii, p. 60.	2 0 0	Edward Sylvester	$9\frac{1}{2}$	Jan. 1653	10 0 0	
		Elinor Sylvester	15	Dec. 1668	20 0 0	
		Elinor Sylvester	11	Jan. 1679	0 13 4	1679, only for the seal, because she was burnt out and built anew.
		Pollet and Storey	$23\frac{1}{2}$	Aug. 1703	60 0 0	
		Mr. Wilkins	15	Aug. 1718	25 0 0	
			10	Aug. 1728	18 0 0	
			14	Aug. 1742	23 0 0	
			14	Aug. 1756	28 15 0	
			14	Aug. 1770	28 15 0	
		Mr. Munday	14	Aug. 1784	28 15 0	
		Mr. Paine	14	Aug. 1798	35 0 0	
			14	Aug. 1812	78 0 0	
			14	Aug. 1826	85 0 0	
		Ward	14	Aug. 1840	215 15 6	
			14	Aug. 1854	175 10 0	In 1845 a piece at the south end 24 ft. 3 in. × 25 ft. 5 in. was sold to the city.
			14	Aug. 1868	160 10 0	
62. A shop in High Street; vol. ii, p. 38.	0 8 0	Mr. Younge	17	Aug. 1659	3 0 0	
		Mr. Thos. Younge	16	July, 1675	3 0 0	
		Mr. Thos. Younge	15	Aug. 1690	3 0 0	
		Mr. Smith	$16\frac{1}{2}$	Dec. 1706	4 0 0	
		Mr. Smith	14	Dec. 1720	3 0 0	
		Mr. Waldsworth	14	Dec. 1734	3 0 0	
		King	14	Dec. 1748	3 10 0	
		Mrs. King	15	Dec. 1763	3 0 0	
			14	Dec. 1777	3 0 0	
		Mr. Gunner	15	Dec. 1792	3 15 0	
			14	Dec. 1806	17 13 0	
		Sadler	14	Dec. 1820	18 0 0	
		Taylor	14	Dec. 1834	55 10 0	Exchanged with the City in 1845.
St. Mary Magdalen.						
63. Deep Hall; vol. ii, p. 315.	1 7 4	Mrs. Eveleigh	$15\frac{1}{2}$	Aug. 1654	6 13 4	
		Margaret Brooks, widow	$11\frac{1}{2}$	Dec. 1665	2 10 0	In 1665 this fine was set in charity to the widow.

Name of Tenement.	*Rent.* £ s. d.	*Tenant.*	*Years elapsed.*	*When renewed.*	*Fine.* £ s. d.	*Memoranda.*
63. Deep Hall, *cont.*	0 17 4	Margaret Brooks	10	Dec. 1675	5 0 0	In 1675 the garden by Kettle Hall was separated.
			10	Dec. 1685	5 0 0	
		Mr. Wood	14	Dec. 1699	10 0 0	1699, mem. the house is worth £30 per annum.
		Sir Robert Harrison	16	Dec. 1715	25 0 0	
		Mrs. Hall	14	Dec. 1729	28 0 0	
		Mr. Boyce	14	Dec. 1743	28 0 0	
			14	Dec. 1757	35 0 0	
			14	Dec. 1771	29 10 0	
		Mr. Curtis	8	Dec. 1779	12 11 0	
			14	Dec. 1793	33 18 4	
			14	Dec. 1807	48 6 0	
		Betteris	14	Dec. 1821	78 0 0	
			14	Dec. 1835	100 10 0	In 1835 this fine was taken in consequence of some recent improvements.
			14	Dec. 1849	171 0 0	
		Maffey	14	Dec. 1863	198 0 0	In 1877 not renewed. The fine would have been £198.
64. Magdalen Street, no. 4; vol. ii, p. 292.	1 6 8	John Philips	14	Jan. 1654	10 0 0	
			18	Jan. 1672	25 0 0	
			18	Dec. 1690	25 0 0	
		House and Airay	15	Dec. 1705	18 0 0	
		Mr. House and Mr. Airay	14	Dec. 1719	17 0 0	
		Mrs. Airay	14	Dec. 1733	17 0 0	
		Mr. Leaver	14	Dec. 1747	15 0 0	
		Mrs. Leaver	14	Dec. 1761	10 10 0	
		Mrs. Terry	15	Dec. 1776	11 16 3	
		Mr. Slade	8	Dec. 1784	5 1 0	
		Coleman	17	Dec. 1801	32 8 0	
		Hall and Evetts	14	Dec. 1815	66 0 0	
		Wootton	14	Dec. 1829	111 0 0	
		Wootton	14	Dec. 1843	111 0 0	

		Rebecca Cole	14	Dec. 1857	118 10 0	In 1871 not renewed. The fine would have been £163 10*s*.
65. On the site of Ball. Coll.; vol. ii, p. 308.	0 4 0	Balliol Coll.	exp.	Aug. 1663	0 6 8	
			18½	Jan. 1681	0 6 8	
			16	Dec. 1697	0 6 8	
			14	Dec. 1711	0 6 8	
			14	Dec. 1725	0 6 8	
			14	Dec. 1739	0 6 8	
			14	Dec. 1753	0 6 8	
			14	Dec. 1767	0 6 8	The Fee sold to Balliol in 1774.
66. A garden near Kettle Hall; vol. ii, p. 319.	0 10 0	Mr. Finch	14	Dec. 1689	5 0 0	A garden and a tenement thereupon built.
		Widow Finch	14	Dec. 1703	5 10 0	
		Mr. Finch	14	Dec. 1717	5 0 0	
		Mr. Vicaris	14	Dec. 1731	12 10 0	
			14	Dec. 1745	12 10 0	
			14	Dec. 1759	15 10 0	
		Mr. Paul Bradley	14	Dec. 1773	15 10 0	The Fee sold to Trinity College in 1786.
St. Peter le B.						
67. Castle Street, nos. 2 and 3; vol. ii, p. 251.	1 13 4	Margaret Oven	27	Sept. 1657	20 0 0	
	2 0 0	Isaac Oven	17	Dec. 1674	6 13 4	1674; at this time the house formerly lost was added to this lease and the rent made up to £2.
		Isaac Oven	16	Aug. 1690	15 0 0	
		Isaac Oven	15	Aug. 1705	15 0 0	
		Isaac Oven	14½	Dec. 1719	15 0 0	
	1 10 0	William Grubb	exp.	Aug. 1762	0 6 8	A plot of ground whereon certain buildings were formerly erected.
			15	Aug. 1777	0 6 8	
			15	Aug. 1792	0 6 8	
			14	Aug. 1806	15 15 0	In 1806 the fine was set at £15 15*s*. instead of £22 11*s*., as Grubb had rebuilt the houses since the last renewal.
			14	Aug. 1820	66 0 0	
			15	Aug. 1835	68 5 0	
			14	Aug. 1849	66 0 0	
			14	Aug. 1863	66 0 0	In 1877 not renewed. The fine would have been £66.

Name of Tenement.	*Rent.* £	s.	d.	*Tenant.*	*Years elapsed.*	*When renewed.*	*Fine.* £	s.	d.	*Memoranda.*
68. Castle Street, no. 1; vol. ii, p. 250.	0	6	8	Mrs. Thrift	25	Nov. 1660	12	0	0	
				Richard Meeres	14	Jan. 1674	4	0	0	He pays 13*s*. 4*d*. because he ought to have another house which is charged in the Audite book,
				Mrs. Meeres	14	Dec. 1688	4	0	0	
					14	Dec. 1702	4	0	0	
				John Quelch	14	Dec. 1716	4	0	0	
					14	Dec. 1730	4	0	0	
					16	Dec. 1746	5	1	0	
					25	Dec. 1771	10	10	0	
					14	Dec. 1785	5	0	0	
					14	Dec. 1799	7	1	6	
					14	Dec. 1813	16	16	0	
					14	Dec. 1827	25	16	0	
					14	Dec. 1841	25	16	0	
					14	Dec. 1855	55	16	0	
					14	Dec. 1869	64	16	0	
St. Michael N.										
69. Behind no. 48 Cornmarket; vol. ii, p. 267.	0	13	4	Robert Keate	15	Dec. 1654	4	0	0	
					7	Dec. 1661	1	0	0	
					14	Dec. 1675	3	0	0	
					14	Dec. 1689	3	0	0	
				Mr. Pinnell	6	Dec. 1695	1	10	0	
				Mrs. Pinnell	14½	Aug. 1710	4	0	0	
				Mrs. Pinnell	14½	Dec. 1724	4	0	0	
					16	Dec. 1740	10	2	0	
					14	Dec. 1754	10	0	0	
				Mr. Laurance	14	Dec. 1768	10	0	0	This was sold to Mrs. Nourse and Mrs. Laurance in 1772.
70. Cornmarket, no. 43; vol. ii, p. 276.	1	6	8	John Croney	8½	Aug. 1656	3	0	0	
					8	Aug. 1664	3	0	0	
					7½	Jan. 1671	5	0	0	
					11	Dec. 1682	13	6	8	
					14	Dec. 1696	20	0	0	

		Mr. Wade	19½	Aug. 1716	40 0 0	
		Mr. Baker	14	Aug. 1730	20 0 0	
		The Feoffees of St. Michael	14	Aug. 1744	20 0 0	
			14	Aug. 1758	17 10 0	
			14	Aug. 1772	17 10 0	
				Aug. 1786	17 10 0	
				Aug. 1800	28 6 8	
				Aug. 1814	54 0 0	
				Aug. 1828	99 0 0	
				Aug. 1842	129 0 0	
				Aug. 1856	129 0 0	In 1870 not renewed. The fine would have been £129.
St. Martin's.						
71. South of the Roebuck; vol. ii, p. 88.	2 0 0	William Flexney	9½	Dec. 1653	5 0 0	
			14½	Aug. 1668	13 6 8	
			14½	Dec. 1682	15 0 0	
			14½	Aug. 1697	20 0 0	
		Mr. Adams	14½	Dec. 1711	17 0 0	
		Mr. Adams	14	Dec. 1725	15 12 0	
		George Moore	14	Dec. 1739	15 12 0	
			14	Dec. 1753	16 5 0	
			14	Dec. 1767	16 5 0	
		Charles Moore	14	Dec. 1781	16 5 0	
			14	Dec. 1795	17 10 0	
		Samuel Moore	14	Dec 1809	35 0 0	
		Embling	14	Dec. 1823	94 10 0	
		Dry and Hayes	14	Dec. 1837	102 0 0	
		Spiers	14	Dec. 1851	102 0 0	
		Rose	14	Dec. 1865	109 10 0	Not renewed in 1879. The fine would have been £169 10*s*.
St. Clement's.						
72. See vol. i, p. 10.	0 13 4	Widow Sherley	20½	Dec. 1662	11 0 0	
			14	Dec. 1676	8 6 8	
		Widow Greenway	14	Dec. 1690	8 6 8	
			14	Dec. 1704	8 6 8	

Name of Tenement.	Rent. £ s. d.	Tenant.	Years elapsed.	When renewed.	Fine. £ s. d.	Memoranda.
72. See vol. i, p. 10, *cont.*		Mr. Rouse	14	Dec. 1718	8 6 8	
			14	Dec. 1732	8 6 8	
			12	Dec. 1744	6 10 0	This lease was divided into two parts, and to make up the quit-rent Hedges paid 8*s.* and Harris 5*s.* 4*d.*
			6	Dec. 1750	2 2 0	
	0 8 0	Mr. Hedges	13	Dec. 1763	8 6 8	Sold to the commissioners for paving, improving, &c.
	0 5 4	Harris, late Rouse	14	Dec. 1764	5 0 0	Sold to the commissioners.
73. The Fishing.	0 10 0	Mr. Bayly	29	Dec. 1667	0 13 4	
		Thomas Jarrett	11½	Aug. 1679	0 13 4	
74. See vol. i, p. 11.	2 0 0	Eliz. Greenhill	24½	July, 1657	20 0 0	
		Mr. Smith	11	Aug. 1668	8 0 0	
		Mr. Smith	14	Aug. 1682	12 0 0	1682. In setting the fine the building was not considered. 1695. The holding was divided.
75. Part of Smith's; vol. i, p. 11.	1 0 0	Mrs. Smith	13½	Dec. 1695	0 0 0	Two tenements; part of Smith's. The fine of £10 was abated in charity to Widow Smith.
			14	Dec. 1709	12 0 0	
		Mr. Burrows	14	Dec. 1723	15 0 0	
			14	Dec. 1737	15 0 0	
			14	Dec. 1751	15 0 0	Rent £16 per ann.
	0 14 0	Rebecca Burrows	14	Dec. 1765	15 6 0	One tenement only. Sold to the commissioners.
	0 6 8	Jos. Marygold, late Burrows	14	Dec. 1765	7 13 0	Rent £8 per ann. Sold to the commissioners.
76. Part of Smith's; vol. i, p. 11.	1 0 0	Mrs. Bishop	13½	Dec. 1695	10 0 0	Three tenements; part of Smith's.
		Richard Bishop	14	Dec. 1709	14 0 0	

		Mr. Parker	14	Dec. 1723	14 0 0	
	0 6 8	Mrs. Tubb	14	Dec. 1737	5 0 0	In 1737 this lease was divided into Parcells, having before been injuriously renewed in one lease.
		Mrs. Rogers	14	Dec. 1751	5 0 0	
			14	Dec. 1765	5 0 0	Sold to the commissioners.
	0 6 8	Mr. Penny	14	Dec. 1737	5 13 4	One tenement.
		Will' Beale	15	Dec. 1752	8 15 0	Sold to the commissioners.
	0 6 8	Mrs. Wotton	14	Dec. 1737	5 13 4	One tenement.
		Richard Venn	14	Dec. 1751	5 13 4	
			20	Dec. 1771	10 19 0	Sold to the commissioners.
St. Ebbe's.						
77. Pembroke Street, nos. 38 and 39; vol. ii, p. 233.	0 10 0	Richard Hart	10	Jan. 1651	0 13 4	
			13½	Aug. 1665	4 0 0	
		William Hart	11½	Dec. 1676	3 0 0	
		Mr. Crutch	14	Dec. 1690	6 0 0	1690. The tenement is set at £14 per annum, but lately built.
		Mr. John Wilkins	20	Dec. 1710	28 0 0	
		Mr. John Wilkins	15	Dec. 1725	20 0 0	
			14	Dec. 1739	18 0 0	
			14	Dec. 1753	22 10 0	
			14	Dec. 1767	22 10 0	
		Mr. Loch	14	Dec. 1781	22 10 0	
			14	Dec. 1795	25 12 6	
		Mr. Gould	14	Dec. 1809	42 0 0	
			14	Dec. 1823	77 8 0	
			14	Dec. 1837	69 18 0	
			14	Dec. 1851	62 8 0	
			14	Dec. 1865	54 18 0	In 1865 the fine was not paid.
78. Domus le Granger; vol. ii, p. 236.	0 4 0	John Bowell	15	Dec. 1662	6 0 0	
		Joseph Stacey	20½	July, 1683	12 0 0	
		Mr. Green and Mr. Gaunt	14	Aug. 1697	8 0 0	
		Mr. Stacey	21½	Dec. 1718	16 0 0	
		Mr. Castell	26	Dec. 1744	1 1 0	1744, the fine was set so low

Name of Tenement.	*Rent.* £ s. d.	*Tenant.*	*Years elapsed.*	*When renewed.*	*Fine.* £ s. d.	*Memoranda.*
78. Domus le Granger, *cont.*			14	Dec. 1758	9 0 0	because Mr. Castel was to re-build part of the premises, being ruinous, and to repair the rest.
		Mrs. Castell	14	Dec. 1772	9 0 0	
			15	Dec. 1787	9 0 0	
			14	Dec. 1801	17 5 0	
		Hall and Evetts	14	Dec. 1815	30 0 0	
			14	Dec. 1829	52 10 0	
			14	Dec. 1843	49 10 0	
			14	Dec. 1857	52 10 0	In 1871 not renewed; the fine would have been £52 10*s*.
79. In Little Bailey; vol. ii, p. 214.	0 6 8	Baldwin Hodges	23	Dec. 1645	5 0 0	
			21	Dec. 1666	5 0 0	
			[21½]	[Aug. 1688]		[Lease missing.]
		Feoffees of St. Ebbe's	17	Aug. 1705	5 0 0	
			14½	Dec. 1719	5 0 0	
			14	Dec. 1733	5 0 0	
			14	Dec. 1747	5 0 0	
			14	Dec. 1761	5 0 0	
			14	Dec. 1775	5 0 0	
			14	Dec. 1789	5 0 0	
			14	Dec. 1803	13 6 6	
			14	Dec. 1817	16 16 0	
			14	Dec. 1831	18 6 0	
			14	Dec. 1845	10 16 0	
		Henry King	9	Dec. 1854	0 0 0	1854, this was renewed to Henry King in consequence of having rebuilt the house.
			5	Dec. 1859	10 16 0	 Not renewed in 1873; the fine would have been £43 16*s*.
St. John's.						
80. Site of Aristotle Hall; vol. ii, p. 120.	0 4 0	Merton College	36½	Aug. 1663	0 13 4	
			18	Jan. 1681	2 0 0	
			15	Dec. 1696	2 0 0	

			14	Dec. 1710	2 0 0	
			15	Dec. 1725	3 10 0	
			14	Dec. 1739	3 10 0	
			14	Dec. 1753	4 7 6	
			14	Dec. 1767	4 7 6	
			14	Dec. 1781	4 7 6	
			14	Dec. 1795	4 7 6	
			14	Dec. 1809	16 0 0	
			14	Dec. 1823	17 14 0	
			14	Dec. 1837	25 4 0	In the fine of 1837 no advantage was taken of a recent erection of a house about 11 years since. In 1851 Merton refused to renew. Exchanged for Holywell Mill in 1877.
St. Giles.						
81. St. Giles's, no. 55; vol. ii, p. 343.	0 6 8	John Egerly &c.	21	Dec. 1643	10 13 4	
		Charles Cook	29	Jan. 1672	6 13 4	
		Charles Cook	22	Dec. 1694	4 0 0	
		Charles Cook	30	Dec. 1724	6 0 0	
			10	Dec. 1734	0 6 8	
			14	Dec. 1748	0 6 8	
			15	Dec. 1763	0 6 8	
		Mr. Wood	14	Dec. 1777	0 6 8	
			15	Dec. 1792	2 10 0	
			14	Dec. 1806	17 15 0	In 1807 sold to T. R. Walker for £100 under Land Tax Redemption Acts.
82. The Physick Garden; vol. i, p. 66.	1 0 0	The University	20	Dec. 1658	0 13 4	The lease was for 20 years in each case.
			12½	Aug. 1671	0 13 4	
			20	Aug. 1691	0 13 4	
			20	Aug. 1711	0 13 4	
			11½	Dec. 1722	0 13 4	

Name of Tenement.	*Rent.* £ s. d.	*Tenant.*	*Years elapsed.*	*When renewed.*	*Fine.* £ s. d.	*Memoranda.*
82. The Physick Garden, *cont.*			7	Dec. 1729	0 13 4	
			7	Dec. 1736	0 13 4	
			8	Dec. 1744	0 13 4	
			7	Dec. 1751	0 13 4	
			7	Dec. 1758	0 13 4	
			7	Dec. 1765	0 13 4	
			7	Dec. 1772	0 13 4	
			7	Dec. 1779	0 13 4	
			7	Dec. 1786	0 13 4	
			7	Dec. 1793	0 13 4	
			7	Dec. 1800	0 13 4	
			7	Dec. 1807	0 13 4	
			7	Dec. 1814	1 0 0	
			7	Dec. 1821	1 0 0	
			11	Dec. 1832	1 0 0	
			7	Dec. 1839	1 0 0	
			7	Dec. 1846	1 0 0	
			7	Dec. 1853	1 0 0	
			7	Dec. 1860	1 0 0	In 1867 the lease was not renewed; in Dec. 1880 let to the University at rack-rent at £30 per annum.

VI. A SURVEY OR RENTAL OF 1791.

THE following document is worth printing for the light it throws on the system of fines. It is a survey of the properties of Magdalen College in the town of Oxford, giving the rent of each tenement, and its improved rent, i.e. rack-rent, in 1791; and in many cases is added what the improved rent was reckoned to be in later years. By this means we are able to prove that the system of fines at Magdalen was such as is described in the previous section.

Free tenants.

Magdalen Hall—issuing from the Hall	£2	0	0
Queen's College—a composition for a pound of pepper[1]		2	0
Mr. Robert Tawnay issuing from a house in St. Aldate's[2]		2	8
Mr. Drought, late Dewey, for a house in Brewer's lane. This was recovered to the College in 1684, Mr. Philips the then owner of it compounding with the College for arrears and paying the quitrent for the future. See an account among the Terriers		8	0
Ch. Ch. College for a house included in the Almshouse		8	0
Edmund Hall for a piece of ground taken from the Eagle and Child, then belonging to the College but since sold		1	0
	£3	1	8

Leaseholders.

St. Peter in East.

1. The university for Physic Garden [vol. i, p. 66]; 1 house; old rent £1; improved rent £2 6*s*.

2. Mrs. Berry for Noah's Ark [vol. i, p. 65]; 9 tenements and a coal yard; rent £2 6*s*. 8*d*.; improved rent £77.

3. Gravel Walk; Mrs. Dennison for the New Buildings [vol. i, p. 148]; 1 house; rent 10*s*. 8*d*.; improved rent £10 10*s*.

4. Gravel Walk; Mrs. Eliz. Radbone [vol. i, p. 148]; 3 houses; rent 10*s*. 8*d*.; improved rent £10 10*s*.

[1] See vol. i, p. 307. Redeemed by Queen's College, Aug. 12, 1905.

[2] A note states that this payment was redeemed by Mr. Dore Mar. 25, 1889, but gives no information from what tenement the payment was made. Perhaps it was the quitrent from Littlemore Hall, viz. 2*s*., together with 8*d*. for an acquittance; notice the last entry of this survey.

5. Gravel Walk; the executors of Robert Cox [vol. i, p. 148]; 1 house; rent 7*s*. 6*d*.; improved rent £5 7*s*. 6*d*.

6. Gravel Walk; Mrs. Dennison, late Dr. Dennison [vol. i, p. 151]; 6 houses, being two tenements towards the Gravel Walk and four tenements in a court; rent £2 1*s*.; improved rent £27.

7. Gravel Walk; Mrs. Broughton [vol. i, p. 153]; 1 house; rent £2; improved rent £20.

8. Gravel Walk; Mr. Bobart, the Greyhound [vol. i, p. 155]; rent £3 6*s*. 8*d*.; improved rent £68 6*s*. 8*d*.

9. Mr. Bobart, the Greyhound Meadow, being 7 acres 2 roods 16 perches; rent 16*s*. 8*d*.; improved rent £19 13*s*. 4*d*.

10. Mrs. Siely [vol. i, p. 338]; 2 houses; rent 12*s*.; improved rent £22 12*s*.; and in 1801 valued at £28.

11. Mr. Day, late Mrs. Eliz. Day [vol. i, p. 334]; 2 houses; rent 10*s*.; improved rent £12; in 1801 (? 1807) valued at £16.

12. Mr. Plater, late Anthony Franklyn [vol. i, p. 331]; 4 houses; rent £1; improved rent £15; in 1798 £36; in 1812 £80.

13. Mr. Robert Turner, late Jefferys [vol. i, p. 327]; 4 houses; rent £1 3*s*. 4*d*.; improved rent £29 3*s*.; valued in 1798 at £40. It is two tenements toward High Street; two back tenements, and two lodging rooms.

14. Mr. Meysey, late Musgrove [vol. i, p. 324]; 1 house; rent £1 6*s*. 8*d*.; improved rent £26 6*s*. 8*d*.; then £32; in 1811 valued at £90. It is 156½ ft. long; 31 ft. 6 in. at N. end.

15. Mrs. Leaver and Watson [vol. i, p. 312]; rent £1; improved rent £35; in 1793 £42; in 1807 £45; in 1835 £125.

16. Queen's College, a plot of ground [vol. i, p. 299]; rent £4; improved rent £4; 199 ft. long, 23½ ft. at N., 21 ft. 10 in. at the S.; sold in 1808.

17. The Provost of Queen's [vol. i, p. 289]; 2 houses; rent £2; improved rent £42; in 1809 valued at £50; in 1837 at £75.

18. Mathew Finch and Susan Clark [vol. i, p. 275]; 4 houses; rent £1 10*s*.; improved rent £41 10*s*.; in 1793 £48; in 1807 £58; in 1835 £70.

19. Mrs. Wickham [vol. i, p. 271]; 1 house; rent 17*s*. 4*d*.; improved rent £30; in 1817 £65; in 1835 £70.

20. New Coll. Lane [vol. i, p. 389]; Hertford College; 3 houses; there is a ground plot of this lease 1768, *vide* Lib. fine, page 28; improved rent £36.

21. The Angel Inn [vol. i, p. 185]; Mr. William Costar; 1 house;

rent £3 10*s.*; improved rent £75; in 1806 £160. Costar's tenement, part of holding no. 35, was added to this, and by leave of the College in 1822 was turned into a stable.

22. The Angel Meadow, measuring 5 ac. 3 r. 25 p.; rent 16*s.* 8*d.*; improved rent £16 13*s.* 4*d.*

23. Mr. William Cooke, late Seely [vol. i, p. 245]; 1 house; rent 2*s.*; improved rent £10 10*s.* This house in the High Street together with about two-thirds of the property in Ram Alley formerly belonging to Courtean, lately to Walker, and mentioned at no. 28, together with a garden in Ram Alley attached to Smith and Grange's property mentioned at no. 30, was let on a lease for 33 years in 1794; valued at £19 10*s.* in 1805; at £40 in 1815; at £120 in 1838, but a fine that year was set on £80 only, on account of the new erections in 1831.

24. John Biggs and Robert Turner, late John Turner [vol. i, p. 199]; rent 13*s.* 4*d.*; improved rent £13; in 1812 £30.

25. In Ram Alley [vol. i, p. 247]; Shillingsworth 2*s.*; improved rent £6 6*s.*; £8 in 1802; £22 in 1817. Fallen to the College and leased out again for 20 years to Mr. Bavin at a ground rent of £5, the house being rebuilt by him.

26. Coach and Horses lane; Mr. Benjamin Davis, late T. Clarke [vol. i, p. 239]; 1 house; rent 2*s.*; improved rent £7; valued in 1803 at £11.

27. William Dry, late Arnott, once Blackford [vol. i, p. 243]; 1 house; rent 1*s.* 8*d.*; improved rent £7; £12 in 1802; £22 in 1816.

28. Mrs. Courteen (Richard Walker was the tenant when this rental was made, not Mrs. Courteen; *this in another hand*) [vol. i, p. 242]; 1 tenement in Coach and Horse lane and two others in Ram Alley; rent 4*s.*; improved rent £14. In 1794 this estate was let for 20 years; but about two-thirds of the property in Ram Alley was leased to Mr. Cooke for the term of 33 years; see no. 23. In 1807 this part of the property was valued at £16; subsequently £24 (Blackwell's part £7, Hemmings £17).

29. Mrs. Broughton [vol. i, p. 241]; 2 houses; rent 3*s.* 4*d.*; improved rent £10; subsequently the rent was £3 10*s.*; and improved rent £18; subsequently £102 11*s.* [*sic*].

30. Mr. Robert Smith and Mr. Grange, moieties [vol. i, p. 239]; 1 tenement in Coach and Horse lane and two in Ram Alley; rent 4*s.*; improved rent £12. A small garden belonging to this estate was leased to Mr. Cooke: see no. 23. A moiety of the lease was valued

in 1803 at £13; in 1807 the ground rent increased to £3 10*s.*; soon afterwards rebuilt.

31. Mr. Barnett, late Piddington [vol. i, p. 236]; 1 house; rent 3*s.*; improved rent £8; £11 5*s.* in 1797; in 1811 this tenement, now the Nag's Head, was valued at £11.

32. Mr. Hedges, late Piddington [vol. i, p. 236]; 1 house; rent 3*s.*; improved rent £10; £11 in 1811.

33. Mr. John Gould, late Piddington, opposite Merton Gardens [vol. i, p. 236]; 1 house; rent 3*s.*; improved rent £7; £10 in 1799; £22 in 1813.

34. Mr. James, late Piddington [vol. i, p. 236]; 1 house; rent 3*s.*; improved rent £10; £12 in 1799; £28 in 1813.

35. Mr. Townsend, late Miss Ward's [vol. i, p. 233]; 5 tenements; rent £8 6*s.* In Dec. 1785 it was let to Mr. Townsend at a fine of £150 and an annual rent of £8, exclusive of quitrents, it having in that year run out. Now, in 1799, it consists of four tenements: Costar's valued at £12, Hargrove's £14, Dry's £14, Norris's £6, in all £46. Subsequently it was two tenements: Norris's valued at £20, Dry's at £91.

36. Merton College, a plot of garden opposite Alban Hall [vol. ii, p. 120]; rent £4; improved rent £3 14*s.*; £16 in 1809; £48 in 1837; but the fine was set on £20 only because of the recent erection of buildings, viz. in 1827.

St. Mary's.

37. Mrs. Morten [vol. i, p. 411]; rent £2; improved rent £30; £90 in 1817; in 1831, when part of the premises was built on by the Principal of St. Mary Hall, £97.

All Saints.

38. Mrs. Baggs, late Ann and Diana Wells [vol. ii, p. 54]; 3 houses; rent £2; improved rent £42 11*s.*; in 1801 £45; in 1815 £95.

39. Mrs. King, a piece of ground whereon a shop is built [vol. ii, p. 38]; rent 8*s.*; improved rent £3; £15 in 1806.

40. Mr. Munday, late Wilkins [vol. ii, p. 60]; 1 house; rent £2; valued in 1798 at £30; in 1812 £65.

St. Martin's.

41. Mr. Charles Moore [vol. ii, p. 88]; 2 tenements; rent £2; improved rent £18; in 1795 £16 only; in 1809 £35; in 1837 £75.

St. Michael's.

42. The churchwardens of St. Michael's [vol. ii, p. 276]; 1 house; rent £1 6*s.* 8*d.*; improved rent £17 10*s.*; in 1800 £24.

St. Mary Magd.

43. Mr. Curtis, late Boyce [vol. ii, p. 315]; 1 house; rent 17*s.* 4*d.*; improved rent £28; opposite the theatre; £32 in 1807; in 1835 valued at £120, but the fine was set on £100, as part of the building had been recently erected.

44. Mr. Slade, late Terry, formerly Leaver [vol. ii, p. 292]; 1 house; rent £1 6*s.* 8*d.*; improved rent £10 10*s.*; in 1798 valued at £22; in a subsequent year only £20.

St. Giles.

45. Mr. Daniel, a gateway whereon a house is built, and of which Mr. Wood the brewer is or was undertenant [vol. ii, p. 343]; rent 6*s.* 8*d.*; improved rent £2; valued in 1806 at £15; sold in 1807 for £100.

St. Peter in the West.

46. William Grubb, a plot of ground whereon a woodhouse was or is standing [vol. ii, p. 251]; from N. to S. 120 ft. 9 in.; from E. to W. 44 ft.; in front 39 ft. 6 in.; rent £1 10*s.*; improved rent £1 10*s.*; in 1806 valued at £20.

47. William Grubb, late Carter [vol. ii, p. 250]; 1 house, next to the above on the east; rent 6*s.* 8*d.*; improved rent £4; valued in 1799 at £6; in 1813 £14.

St. Ebbe's.

48. Mrs. Ann Castle [vol. ii, p. 236]; 3 tenements on the north side of the church; in breadth 25 ft., in length 47 ft. 8 in.; on the backside from north to south 31 ft. 2 in.; east to west 33 ft. 1 in.; rent 4*s.*; improved rent £15 8*s.*; in 1801 £18; in 1815 £25.

49. The churchwardens of St. Ebbe's [vol. ii, p. 214]; 1 tenement; rent 6*s.* 8*d.*; improved rent £5; in 1803 £11.

50. Mr. Lock, late Wilkins [vol. ii, p. 233]; 2 tenements; rent 10*s.*; improved rent £18 10*s.* In 1795 the tenement occupied by Mr. Morris was valued at £12, that occupied by Mr. Wise at £9. In 1809 they were valued at £42; in 1833 at £55.

St. Aldate's, Fish Street.

51. Mr. Badcock, late Rawlins [vol. ii, p. 189]; 1 house; rent £2; improved rent £22; in 1799 valued at £35; in 1813 £71.

52. Dr. Thompson, late Kelly [vol. ii, p. 186]; 1 house; rent £2; improved rent £45; in 1799 £52; in 1813 £85.

53. Mrs. Loder, late Lane [vol. ii, p. 166]; 1 house; rent 18*s.*; improved rent £16 18*s.*; in 1801 £23; in 1815 £35.

54. Mr. Keepe, late Mrs. Remmett [vol. ii, p. 168]; 1 house; rent 9*s.*; in 1798 valued at £8; in 1812 £25.

55. Mr. Dell, late Kelley, formerly Craddock [vol. ii, p. 170]; 1 house; rent 7*s.*; improved rent £7; in 1802 valued at £20.

56. Mrs. Parsons, late Gass [vol. ii, p. 164]; 2 tenements; rent 47*s.* 10*d.*; improved rent £35; in 1796 £45; then £113; in 1838 £142.

57. Mrs. Stockford, late Ives, the Wheatsheaf [vol. ii, p. 200]; 1 house; rent £1; improved rent £26; in 1802 £40; in 1816 £90.

58. Mr. Moore, late Pitt [vol. ii, p. 195]; 1 house; rent 8*s.*; improved rent £12; in 1799 £18; in 1813 £42.

59. The Vice-Chancellor for the Logic School [vol. i, p. 458]. This lease described in a map dated 1613 includes the Logic School, part of the Music School and of Cat Street from N. to S. 83½ ft., from E. to W. 81¾ ft., containing 6,826 sq. ft. and ⅛. Rent £3; improved rent £3.

High Street.

60. University College, a small piece of ground [vol. i, p. 170]; rent 1*s.* 10*d.*; valued in 1812 at £12; in 1838 £36.

61. Dr. Smith, late Harris [vol. i, p. 168]; 1 tenement in High Street, and 3 others opposite to Merton Garden; rent 28*s.* 8*d.*; improved rent £50; in 1804 £55.

Total rents	£66	18	3
Free rents	3	1	8
	£69	19	11

Outgoings.

A quitrent to Ch. Ch.	£0	14	10
To the lord of Cowley	1	0	0
To the Chamberlain of the City	0	2	0
An acquittance on this payment	0	0	8
To the College for wine	1	0	0
	£2	17	6

APPENDIX I

THE LIST OF THE DEEDS ABOUT OXFORD CONTAINED IN THE MS. CARTULARY OF THE HOSPITAL OF ST. JOHN

fol. 1	71
	70
	559
	81
fol. 2	16
	153
	69
fol. 3	327
	29
	23
	66
fol. 4	67
	953
	88
	706
fol. 5	80
	82
	72
	89
fol. 6	43
	141
	292
	51
fol. 7	165
fol. 8	14
fol. 9	939
	963
fol. 10	175
	371
	279
	240
fol. 11	326
	307
	349
	360
fol. 12	350
fol. 12	316
	321
	238
fol. 13	213
	345
	293
	216
	301
fol. 14	329
	236
	304
	75
	219
	306
fol. 15	369
	277
	291
	407
	237
fol. 16	276
	266
	640
	353
	348
	214
fol. 17	295
fol. 18	309
	418
fol. 19	434
	433
	420
	421
	583
fol. 20	454
	450
	451
fol. 20	428
fol. 21	469
	422
	478
	479
fol. 22	465
	957
fol. 23	582
	597
	591
	598
	241
	[*sic*] 598
fol. 24	232
	243
	233
	234
	235
fol. 25	586
	242
	611
fol. 26	vacant
fol. 27	753
	755
	744
	741
	756
fol. 28	626
	716
	780
fol. 29	vacant
fol. 30	781
	950
	951
	952
fol. 31	564

fol. 31	566
	567
	563
fol. 32	574
fol. 33	557
	560
fol. 34	785
	786
fol. 35	813
	851
	847
	843
	845
fol. 36	819
	830
	810
fol. 37	836
	811
	850
	797
fol. 38	852
fol. 39	904
	873
	906
fol. 39	899
fol. 40	900
	885
	897
	905
fol. 41	874
	895
	887
	880
	907
fol. 42	85 A
	886
	877
	878
	879
fol. 43	896
fol. 44	858
	857
	856
fol. 45	490
	518
	519
	508
fol. 46	540
fol. 46	489
	541
	504
fol. 47	505
	491
fol. 48	619
	617
	618
	616
fol. 49	706
	747
	707
	690
	710
fol. 50	960
fol. 51	vacant
fol. 52	632
	624
fol. 53	705
	639
	643
	627

APPENDIX II

THE LIST OF THE OXFORD DEEDS IN THE MUNIMENT ROOM OF MAGDALEN COLLEGE, AND WHERE THEY ARE PRINTED IN THIS CARTULARY

St. Clement's

1 =	8
2	6
3	12
4	1
5	3
6	2
7	7
8	5
9	4
10	11

St. Peter's in the East

1 =	211
2	211 *n.*
3	210
4	956
5	651
6	273
7	a Selborne deed
8	399
9	946
10	188
11	252
12	181
13	186
14	481
15	161
16	947
17	346

St. Peter's in the East

18 =	664
19	184, 185
20	14
21	921
22	385
23	222
24	257
25	209
26	262
27	164
28	a summary of charters
29	24
30	208
31	268
32	269
33	32
34	92
35	283
36	403
37	168
38	98
39	170
40	169
41	359
42	266
43	652
44	236
45	373
46	87
47	72
48	83

St. Peter's in the East

49 =	129
50	142
51	76
52	416
53	214
54	162
55	missing
56	652
57	238
58	163
59	227
60	58
61	209
62	254
63	67
64	66
65	108
66	212
67	252
68	255
69	253
70	256
71	112
72	258
73	220
74	218
75	386
76	141
77	368
78	263
79	a Chinnor deed
80	612

St. Peter's in the East. A

1 =	82 *n.*
2	94
3	95
4	93
5	35
6	192
7	19
8	297
9	St. Mich. S. 27
10	306
11	52
12	343
13	203
14	113
15	114
16	117
17	115
18	252
19	23
20	378
21	89
22	27
23	107
24	30
25	362
26	195
27	377
28	104
29	105
30	103
31	60
32	150

St. Peter's in the East. A

33 =	46
34	267
35	153
36	405
37	202
38	139
39	140
40	237
41	292
42	131
43	48
44	384
45	305
46	335
47	382
48	215
49	345
50	319
51	126
52	383
53	307, 308
54	152
55	272
56	159
57	22
58	26
59	294
60	69

St. Peter's in the East. B

1 =	264
2	402
3	314
4	402 *n.*
5	375
6	376
7	357
8	398
9	400
10	200
11	40
12	25

St. Peter's in the East. B

13 =	179
14	372
15	187
16	20
17	379
18	122
19	270
20	34
21	364
22	333
23	213
24	374
25	282
26	299
27	a deed of Oving
28	59
29	654
30	225
31	705
32	44
33	36
34	381
35	353
36	404
37	276
38	75
39	369
40	304
41	640
42	407
43	301
44	394
45	180
46	876
47	311
48	442
49	199
50	57
51	54
52	124
53	53
54	55
55	a deed of Swincombe

St. Peter's in the East. B

56 =	77
57	387
58	118
59	174
60	146
61	221
62	17
63	291
64	175
65	201
66	323
67	120
68	49
69	397
70	240
71	96
72	559
73	278
74	367
75	277
76	321
77	166
78	406
79	118
80	303

St. Peter's in the East. C

1 =	62
2	229
3	68
4	361
5	116
6	298
7	653
8	652
9	90
10	40 *n.*
11	109
12	652
13	261
14	349
15	366

St. Peter's in the East. C

16 =	366 *n.*
17	365
18	42
19	39
20	347
21	284
22	285
23	344
24	351
25	355
26	350
27	360
28	354
29	371
30	61
31	148
32	196
33	341
34	339
35	332
36	342
37	33
38	627
39	652
40	320
41	56
42	106
43	110
44	193
45	265
46	79
47	111
48	330
49	102
50	313
51	18
52	336
53	119
54	80
55	85
56	101
57	204
58	151
59	31
60	21

St. Peter's in the East. C

61 =	652
62	295
63	393
64	948
65	946 *n.*
66	264
67	946 *n.*
68	949
69	945

St. Peter's in the East. D

1 =	317
2	296
3	363
4	45
5	396
6	132
7	133
8	136
9	134
10	135
11	311
12	82
13	316
14	86
15	973
16	183
17	143
18	128
19	127
20	138
21	205
22	100
23	380
24	286
25	280
26	281
27	287
28	986
29	28
30	182
31	176

St. Peter's in the East. D

32 =	130
33	88
34	310
35	125
36	322
37	224
38	395
39	547
40	654
41	324
42	177
43	370
44	327
45	391
46	99
47	123
48	326
49	29
50	13
51	51
52	16
53	302
54	144
55	556
56	191
57	288
58	289
59	309
60	340

St. Peter's in the East. E

1 =	160
2	43
3	228
4	84
5	97
6	167
7	78
8	536
9	582
10	47
11	216

St. Peter's in the East. E

12 =	474
13	178
14	41
15	444
16	401
17	654
18	390
19	589
20	91
21	121
22	356
23	194
24	358
25	279
26	978
27	337
28	974
29	974
30	71
31	189
32	127
33	65
34 }	modern
35 }	
36	784

St. Mary's

1 =	454
2	478
3	428
4	389
5	438
6	437
7	436
8	435
9	445
10	980
11	420
12	456
13	447
14	431
15	448
16	409

St. Mary's

17 =	477
18	410
19	450
20	429
21	433
22	443
23	440
24	480
25	452
26	486
27	439
28	423
29	422
30	451
31	446
32	465
33	479
34	434
35	449
36	482
37	427
38	414
39	485
40	388
41	487
42	483
43	484
44	838
45	425
46	419
47	455
48	441
49	408
50	426
51	464
52	275
53	412
54	466
55	476
56	430
57	475
58	413
59	417
60	418
61	583
62	453

St. Mary's

63 =	471
64	415
65	468
66	469
67	467
68. 1	458
2	459
3	457, 460
69	561

All Saints

1 =	493
2	494
3	495
4	496
5	498
6	546
7	512
8	537
9	492
10	535
11	551
12	552
13	553
14	555
15	542
16	504
17	505
18	506
19	507
20	508
21	489
22	490
23	491
24. 1	529
2	531
25	527
26	532
27	528
28	488
29	545
30	509
31	549
32 =	550
33	539
34	540
35	502
36	never existed
37	503
38	511
39	554
40	541
41	530
42	516
43	515
44	519
45	524
46	520
47	558
48	560
49	557
50	557 *n.*
51	521
52	510
53	522
54	562
55. 1	526
2	525
56	473
57	543
58	518
59	517
60	497
61	547

St. Martin's

1 =	574
2	573
3	573
4	346 A
5	570
6	566
7	568
8	567
9	572
10	571
11 =	577
12	577
13	563
14	580
15	576
16	569
17	565
18	564
19	581
20	578
21	916

St. John's

1 =	588
2	605
3	231
4	608
5	606
6	607
7	602
8	603
9	604
10	587
11	601
12	584
13	585
14	595
15	615
16	609
17	610
18	598
19	230
20	614
21	239
22	599
23	600

St. Aldate's

1 =	638
2	675
3	670
4	668
5 =	672
6	671
7	673
8	636
9	674
10	666
11	677
12	682
13	678
14	665
15	679
16	680
17	685
18	683
19	681
20	646
21	676
22	687
23	688
24	669
25	666
26	667
27	633
28	635
29	684
30. 1	645
2	648
31	641
32	655
33	657
34	642
35	624
36	634
37	658
38	639
39	626
40	656
41	658
42	650
43	629
44	632
45	617
46	630
47	657
48	625
49	643

St. Aldate's

50	missing
51 =	616
52	652
53	652
54	618

St. Michael South

1 =	788
2	703
3	702
4	714
5	696
6	694
7	691
8	690
9	697
10	698
11	691
12	709
13	713
14	789
15	692
16	707
17	701
18	706
19	704
20	693
21	wanting
22	700
23	711
24	712
25	708
26	786
27	793
28	705

St. Ebbe's

1 =	750
2	718
3	719
4	744

St. Ebbe's

5 =	751
6	756
7	755
8	747
9	752
10	754
11	748
12	735
13	737
14	738
15	739
16	716
17	741
18	723
19	749
20	745
21	715
22	724
23	732
24	722
25	725
26	736
27	734
28	726
29	727
30	733
31	728
32	729
33	730
34	731
35	919

St. Peter le Bailey

1 =	760
2	779
3	759
4	761
5	758
6	778
7	775
8	777
9	771
10	772

St. Peter le Bailey

11 =	774
12	773
13	766
14	767
15	764
16	765
17	768
18	769
19	757
20	770
21	776
22	781
23	780
24	a London deed
25	782

St. Mary Magdalen

1 =	849
2	841
3	853
4	795
5	827
6	828
7	832
8	810
9	852
10	855
11	839
12	815
13	820
14	804
15	816
16	830
17	843
18	846
19. 1	812
2	811
20	842
21	817
22	801
23	797

St. Mary Magdalen

24 =	831
25	821
26	814
27	807
28	825
29	829
30	854
31	805
32	845
33	848
34	798
35	836
36	819
37	851
38	847
39	802
40	840
41	850
42	796
43	799
44	833
45	808
46	802
47	803
48	wanting
49	818
50	822
51	813
52	806
53	800
54	835
55. 1	823
2	824

St. Giles's

1 =	861
2	862
3	865
4	859
5	860
6	857
7	856
8	858
9	863

Holywell

1 =	890
2	887
3	905
4	878
5	896
6	879
7	904
8	899
9	871
10	872
11	870
12	894
13	893
14	906
15	874
16	873
17	885
18	895
19	877
20	868
21	883
22	884
23	891
24	888
25	85 A
26	866
27	900
28	914
29	149 A
30	898
31	912
32	881
33	880
34 =	889
35	911
36	892
37	875
38	901
39	867
40	897
41	907
42	909
43	886
44	882
45	903
46	908
47	910
48	869
49	902

Villa Oxon.

1 =	918
2	501
3	207
4	50
5	219
6	690
7	421
8	226
9	a rental
10	472
11	981
12	534
13 =	954
14	794

Hosp. in Gen.

2 =	710
5	961
6	81
11	38
14	958
17	217
21	962

Regie Carte

3 =	924
4	929
6	943
8	73, 937
9	74
10	931
11	940
12	942
13	934
15	927
17	936
24	938
26	932
28	644, 647
29	923
51	944

Carte Concesse

30 =	971
66	968

Mortmains

12 =	534
13	935
14	402

Miscellanea

191 =	917
209	972
259	987
282	977
284	352
332	293
342	920
343	171
346	933
374	965
375	988
380	966
384	967
407	259, 260
411	989
438	970
439	976
440	628

APPENDIX III

ON THE ARCHITECTURE OF THE HOSPITAL OF ST. JOHN

By R. T. Gunther

Compiled from J. C. Buckler's rough notes and from recent original observations.

CONTENTS

It was with peculiar pleasure that I received Mr. Salter's request to furnish some notes upon the Architecture of St. John's Hospital to form an Appendix to his final volume of the *Cartulary*, both because all available materials relating to the Hospital will thereby be brought together and because thus tardy justice will be done to the records and opinions of the two Bucklers, father and son, both of whom may be regarded as architectural pupils of Magdalen College, and whose love for her buildings is shown in the numerous excellent drawings which they made. Buckler senior came early in life to Magdalen to assist the Steward, Richard Fisher, brother to Colonel Fisher who, himself a most admirable draughtsman, encouraged

Buckler to pursue his studies as an artist. President Routh very soon heard of Mr. Buckler's love for ancient buildings and his industry in studying and delineating them. He sent for him, became his patron, and continued all through life an attached friend, transferring these terms of intimacy to the son. Thus incidentally Colonel Fisher's encouragement laid the foundation of the Bucklers' reputation and success in life.

The father, John Buckler, F.S.A., was born at Calbourne, Isle of Wight, in 1770. On leaving Oxford he was articled for seven years to Mr. Cracklow, an architect in Southwark, and practised as a professional architect until 1826, when he retired in favour of his eldest son. From 1796 to 1849 he contributed water-colour drawings yearly to the Royal Academy, many of which were reproduced as aquatint engravings. He died in London in 1851. (*D.N.B.*)

His son, John Chessell Buckler, published several books of views of Churches and Schools between 1822 and 1866. His views were to a large extent worked up from his father's drawings. At Magdalen he is remembered as the author of an anonymous work upon the Architecture of the College, which no doubt also reflected his father's views on the outrages perpetrated by James Wyatt in the Chapel and elsewhere: for instance, for his work of destruction of the ancient roof of the Chapel, this architect found it necessary also to dig up almost the whole area of the floor to a great depth and thus to destroy the greater number of the sepulchral memorials with which the floor was then chiefly paved! Buckler no doubt thought that a College which could permit such wanton injury to its historic associations could be no fit trustee for his literary criticisms and drawings, and bequeathed much that is of the greatest interest to Oxford to the British Museum.

In their profound knowledge of the details as well as of the spirit of Gothic architecture, the Bucklers were in advance of their time: had their advice been followed, the College might have been spared the costly and unworthy additions of the Romantic period, such as the roofs and plaster ceilings of Wyatt, and we at the present day would be freer to devote our energy and treasure to much-needed additions to the College buildings, instead of undoing the work of inferior and unscrupulous architects and restoring the earlier and better style.

Having failed to obtain in Oxford any description of the fabric of the Hospital, when in 1900 I extracted from the wall of the Chapel Porch some fragments of stone molding[1] that had obviously once

[1] Cf. *Proc. Soc. Antiq.* for Dec. 4, 1902.

belonged to that Institution, it was gratifying to find that among the Buckler MSS., which had only recently been made available for study at the British Museum, there was an entire volume of MSS. entitled *Rough Notes concerning the History of the Hospital of St. John the Baptist, situated on the North side of the road without the East Gate of the University and City of Oxford. Superseded in the Fifteenth Century by the College of St. Mary Magdalen.* By J. C. Buckler. Addit. MS. 27963. There were moreover several carefully executed drawings of details drawn to scale.

Guided by Buckler's drawings I ascertained that practically the whole of the shell of an important building of the Hospital is still standing in the High Street, though its walls have been disguised by an outer veneer of new ashlar and by the insertion of new windows: to my astonishment when groping under the basement floor I found Early English corner pillars of a lower chamber of the Hospital still *in situ*: in 1912, when some chambers under the present Home Bursary were being refitted, the old masonry of the walls was stripped of plaster and was once more displayed to the eye for a few hours, but long enough to corroborate the entire accuracy of that part of Buckler's drawing and description. And now while these pages are actually in the printers' hands, two long lost architectural fragments which were sketched by Buckler at Magdalen and believed by him to have been a part of the fabric of the Hospital have been rediscovered at Hertford College, where they are said to have been disinterred in foundations only a few years ago. It is therefore with especial pleasure that I take this opportunity of recalling his long-forgotten labour of love for the College, by printing extracts (rearranged) from his rough notes and by reproducing his drawings. We must always remember that he saw far more of the vestiges of the old Hospital than any man now living will ever see, and was well qualified to judge of the meaning of what he saw. It is unfortunate that his sentences are sometimes involved and that his matter, having apparently been jotted down haphazard, suffers from want of arrangement.

We have now no list of the buildings of the Hospital nor plan of their grouping, though no doubt some clue might be obtained by consideration of other similar foundations of the same period. The Cartulary supplies evidence for the following:

1. A refectory for the brethren and sisters capable of holding about 18.
2. A dormitory for the brethren, to hold about 10.

3. A dormitory for the sisters to hold about 8.
4. A ward for the 'infirm', of whom there were probably never more than 8 or 10.
5. A chapel for the brethren.
6. A chapel for the infirm.
7. Some small rooms, probably 6 to 8, for those who bought corrodies at the Hospital, or were sent by the King to reside there for life; also for the Master.
8. A charnel house.
9. A chapter house.

All the evidence indicates that the area covered by the buildings of the Hospital was practically coextensive with the area of William of Waynflete's College. Buckler gives the measures of the College as 345 feet from east to west and 320 feet from north to south, that is from the North Wall across the Cloister, Chapel and Chaplains' Quadrangle to the south-west angle of the Great Tower. He further suggests that, for the sake of utilizing existing foundations or for grouping the new buildings conveniently with the old, certain dimensions and orientations of the Hospital buildings were perpetuated in the new College.

Mr. Wilson has traced the complicated procedure by which the Hospital buildings were transferred to the College. They would have remained standing in their entirety during the first decade or so of the life of the new College, when they were inhabited by the first President and Scholars, the others continuing to reside in premises where Waynflete had founded the first Magdalen Hall. When the erection of the new buildings of the College was taken in hand, it is hardly likely that more of the fabric of the Hospital was pulled down than was absolutely needful. We imagine that a central site was cleared first for the great buildings round the Quadrangle, while the Hospital buildings nearer the boundary were, so far as possible, left standing as offices and dwellings for the first President and Scholars and workmen, and as a screen or boundary wall. The first wholesale clearing of the site would probably have been begun in 1473, when stone was being collected, and by the 6th of May, 1474, matters were so far advanced that the Foundation stone of the College Chapel could be laid 'in the midst of the high altar'.

It follows that no trace of any original building of the Hospital in a central situation is to be found *in situ*, unless it be of the nature of a foundation or a well, or possibly a *lavacrum in medio Claustri*. Doubtless many of the old stones have been worked into the lower parts of the new walls. On the other hand the buildings near the outside remained standing until much nearer our own times than is commonly supposed; and if only careful records of the vestiges that have appeared from time to time during structural alterations had been kept, our information with regard to the Hospital fabric would by now have attained to respectable proportions. Builders working under architects rarely show respect for the work of earlier and better handicraftsmen than themselves.

Of the Hospital buildings which survived the completion of Waynflete's buildings, four main blocks may be recognized:

I. The Infirmary Block on the North Side of the College Cloister.
II. The Block North of the Infirmary, or the 'Stables' of 1674—c. 1733.
III. The Chapel Building in two storeys (c. 1234).
IV. The Kitchen Block, including the 'Divinity Reader's Lodgings'.

And to these we would add a mention of the Stone Cross opposite to the entrance to the Chapel of the Hospital, destroyed in 1562, the base level of which must now lie deep below the present surface of the ground.

Note on Orientation. In the following description we have, for the sake of brevity, used the points of the compass in their ecclesiastical sense as commonly accepted. It should however be borne in mind that the 'east-west' orientation of the old Chapel of the Hospital is really more nearly a north-south orientation, and that the buildings of the Hospital Infirmary and of the College are orientated almost due north-west and south-east. Thus the 'south' wall of the Hospital Chapel faces west-south-west. The exact orientation of the Hospital buildings may have considerable importance in the determination of their respective ages. We therefore commence our review with an account of those buildings which are more remote from the East Bridge Street (High Street) front, because they, being orientated irrespective of the line of the street, may possibly be older than the buildings erected upon the Jews' Garden given to the Hospital in 1231 and orientated by the line of the street.

In the sequel quotations from the Buckler MS. are indicated by references to the numbers of the folios; the present author's contributions are in square brackets.

FIG. 1. THE NORTH FRONT OF THE CLOISTER BUILDINGS IN WHICH WAS INCORPORATED

A. *Buildings which are believed to have had the orientation of the southern boundary of land given to the Hospital by Hugo de Malaunay in 1194.*

It is suggested that the orientation of these buildings was adopted by Waynflete as the orientation for the Great Quadrangle of Magdalen College.

I. THE INFIRMARY BLOCK

[Our authorities for the details of the old and frequently altered building on the north side of the College Cloister are Buckler, whose descriptions we reproduce, the Bird's-eye View of the College published in the Oxford Almanack of 1730, and certain drawings, now in the College Library, which were made previous to the final demolition of the building in 1822.

These drawings clearly show that the original building, previous to the superaddition of third and attic storeys, was two storeys high and was built, perhaps at different times, for two distinct purposes. For about one quarter of the length of the whole range at the western end, the wall-face was slightly out of line with the rest of the façade,[1] and the elevation is characterized by a row of single-light windows which, in spite of their Perpendicular surroundings, strongly suggest a row of Early English lancet windows. The eastern end was furnished with an elaborate system of isolated sanitary annexes which looked like and were afterwards converted into five large buttresses. It is on account of this unique system of sanitation on the north side of a building which on the other side must have had all the health-giving properties of a south aspect, that we have identified this block with the wards for the infirm of the Hospital. They would have been in two storeys, perhaps one for men and the other for women. The present unnecessary and ill-proportioned buttresses against the north front of the Cloister buildings are therefore a legacy from the old Hospital, with an interesting history. Five of them have been rebuilt by Joseph Parkinson upon the ancient ground-plan, but others have been added unnecessarily on either flank of his new oriel window of the College Library.

The row of single-light windows on the first floor appears to indicate a longish chamber in that position. By appropriate treatment the

[1] This is clearly shown in two water-colour drawings in Magdalen College Library.

older part of this elevation might have been saved and the College might have boasted an architectural view that would have excelled in beauty and interest some of the older work in Merton College.]

f. 27 In point of magnitude the chief remnant of the Hospital spared by Waynflete was the range of building facing North, forming the boundary of the Cloister, the length measuring 194 feet 2 inches from E. to W.
f. 29 The Founder squared all his buildings with this ancient line, and extended and intersected them with mathematical accuracy.

The measure of 194 feet was adequate for the uniform breadth of the College from East to West up to the side of the Chapel and Hall, which together form the South or main limb of the pile; and is advanced Westward about 24 feet beyond the breadth figured.

As this part of the Hospital was distant from observation, the most northern of all the buildings, its aspect was suitable to its position and to its subordination in the interior economy. Its condition and treatment were the same when it became a member of the College. No need appeared to give embellishment to a part of the House beyond common observation. It still faced open ground, meadow or woodland to which there was no direct access except perhaps beyond the West boundary.

f. 30 The Founder preserved nothing more than the North wall of the
f. 31 outermost structure of the Hospital,—the side of a solid building in two stories; but every stone and stick were detached from it, its altitude no less than its length being suitable to his purpose. In breadth and interior disposition, new proportions and divisions were needful, the sturdy old wall lending its strength to the new appliances.

The bulk of the limb thus renewed, gave the measure for the rest. It was sufficient for the depth of the rooms which were in single lines, and in two stories.

In process of time this most meanly treated part of the whole edifice was brought into full view; but however serious, antique and picturesque the prospect it presented, the building gained no favour. No historical associations strengthened the plea for its preservation; and about the same time that Addison's portrait was set up in the Hall, his Chamber and Study at the summit of the North East angle of this range of building were swept away without compunction.

Almost all the windows had been inserted in the place of the original slender apertures. The ashlared wall, the massive buttresses, and the bulky protuberances which supplied recesses to the rooms,

ST. JOHN'S HOSPITAL

combined to produce a venerable monument of builder's work, to which had been added tall chimney-stacks with dormers of various shapes and sizes, pressed together on the parapet in groups as diversified as if they had been heaped up for pictorial effect.

The needless assault upon so interesting a portion of the College, f. 28
proved by its condition as to strength, and uncalled for by reason of its sundry mutilations which a willing mind and a well guided hand could easily have amended, was the resolve of the President,—the grateful recipient of the Founder's beneficence,—the exultant admirer of the accomplished Addison. He turned a deaf ear to pleadings in favour of a building not half worn out, and whose historical interest more than doubled its value as a relic rescued from the hurricane of mischief which swept all else away.

This part of the College, so remarkable for its antiquity and for the significance of its early and its recent history, has assumed an entirely new aspect, but without containing a particle of its former attraction.
The demolition of the North wall [of the Cloisters], which was attended f. 103
with severe disasters, in revenge for the insolent robbery of antiquity, has added a few curious particulars to the stock of information bearing upon the economy of antiquity in domestic arrangements. This example is referred to at the foot of p. 61 [of Buckler's *Observations on the original architecture of S. M. Magdalen College*]: it relates to the Closets of necessity, and the drains connected therewith; and being of the age of the 13th century should be noticed as evidence of habits of decency very superior to those of later periods, and as showing the consideration with which these offices were contrived in
the outer wall of a main building of the Hospital. They are in two f. 104
stories in every instance, but there is no appearance that fresh water was conveyed to them by means of machinery[1] [any more than in the case of the *domicilium necessariorum* annexed to New College. There Bishop Wykeham] went in a straightforward way to work, and seems to have had greater dependence upon manual labour than upon the refinements of science thus applied. The basement of his building is a pit full 80 feet long, and 16 feet wide, with walls 4 feet in thickness: the present depth from the floor to the soil being $14\frac{1}{2}$ feet.

[1] The Science of Hydraulics was very well known and very frequently practised in that century. The writer has examined the underground leaden pipes which conveyed the water to Glastonbury Abbey, and those which the College gave him the opportunity of discovering among the ruins of the College at Brackley. The pipe $1\frac{1}{2}$ in. in diameter took a slant direction from the North-east across the Sanctuary of the magnificent Church to the South-west among the College buildings.

This may not be regarded as a pertinent digression, since the subject which has occasioned its introduction possesses no trace of having been so thoughtfully and so scientifically provided with the means of securing the efficiency of the well contrived drains. As soon as this limb of the Hospital became the property of the College, the purpose of these provisions for health was changed. It became needful to purify the whole system; this being done the recesses were left open, or were enclosed as cupboards by the builder of the College. Plank stones, rough and strong, formed the covering of the drain, which was about 17 inches deep and nearly 2 feet 5 inches in advance of the wall: a branch drain of less capacity joined it from the interior of the College.

In modern days, when the eaves of the roof and grotesque sculptures have ceased to pour the rain water on the ground to disperse itself as it best could, this ancient drain was extended westward, and the whole line brought into use. This part of the discovery was made when the walls were uprooted, and the ground opened for the modern successors of the antique remains: it added to the writer's information upon a feature of the Hospital not before known for a certainty. Single closets[2] in different position are not uncommon in buildings of great age; but a range like this, short though it be, in connexion with the upper and lower floor, is not perhaps to be matched among the remains of the Domestic Architecture of any period previously to the Reformation.

II. THE BUILDING NORTH OF THE INFIRMARY

Being the Stables of 1674 to 1733

[A small group of low two-storeyed buildings formerly stood on the north side of the way leading to the bridge at the entrance to the Walks. It was believed by Wood that certain of these, too, formed part of the Hospital Buildings, though situated beyond the limits of the principal group of edifices.

The oldest view of a building upon this site is that of Agas, who in his oft-quoted map of 1578 represented the north side of a house with the same orientation as the Infirmary. It was a long two-storey

[2] [The nearest approach to them with which we are acquainted are depicted in plan by Dollman in his account of the Hospital of St. Cross at Winchester. There however the closets of dwelling rooms are grouped side by side in pairs. The Infirmary of the Monastery of St. Gall (830–937 A.D.) was provided with excellent *necessaria* for the particular use of the inmates of the Dormitory and of the Ward for Purgations. Withington, *Med. Hist.*, 1894.]

building with a door and five two-light (?) windows to the ground floor rooms and five windows on the first floor,—a middle four-light window flanked by two three-light windows on either side.

Such a house was obviously not a stable: we would suggest that here the Sisters of the Hospital may have resided, though of course in their day the windows may have been less wide than they were a whole century after the foundation of the College. The secluded and pleasant position of this dwelling by the Cherwell, with a garden behind, and perhaps over the bridge, the small enclosed paddock in which was growing the then young Great Oak of Magdalen, all shown in Agas's map, as well as its proximity to the Infirmary and the size of the house, all point to its having been a very likely abode for the Sisters. In elevation the building as it existed in 1578 was not unlike the Scholae Publicae of the University.

According to Loggan's View of the College (1674) some of the rooms of the 'Stables' were heated with fire-places. The buildings were probably removed about 1733 that they might not by their cottagy appearance detract from the grandeur of the New Buildings, then lately erected.]

B. A.

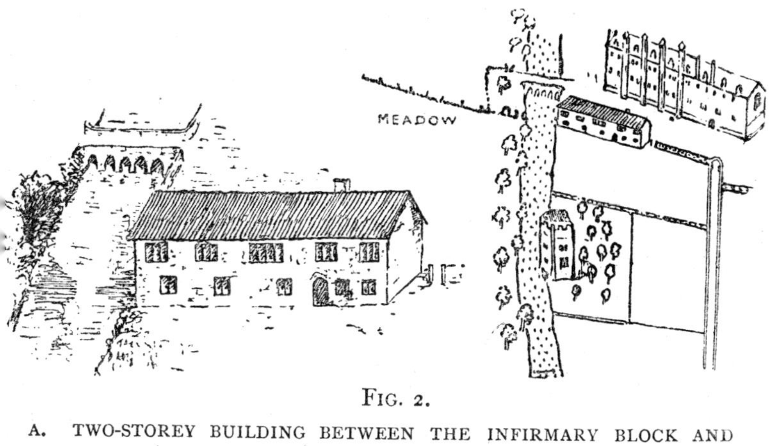

FIG. 2.

A. TWO-STOREY BUILDING BETWEEN THE INFIRMARY BLOCK AND THE 'SONG SCHOOL' AFTER AGAS'S MAP, 1578.

B. THE SAME, ENLARGED.

B. *Buildings with the orientation of the East Bridge Street frontage on land granted to the Hospital by Henry III in 1231.*

III. THE CHAPEL AND CHARNEL HOUSE

Being respectively the Lecture Room and Almshouse of the 16th Century

[An important document respecting this building was drawn up in the form of a Report in 1596, and as it has already been printed in Vol. II, p. 463, we need do no more than quote one or two passages from it.

'2. All the edifices of the sayd Hospitall were in a manner defaced and utterly rased in the founder's time; one chappel only except, wherein we kepe divers lectures and exercises of learning, and under the sayd chappel a stonie vault very low under the ground and thereby unwholesome, which since in common report hath borne the name of the "allmes house" because (as we take it) that only remains of the ruin of the sayd Hospitall.'

As will appear in the sequel the style of architecture of the building accords so closely with that of others which are known to have been erected during the second quarter of the 13th century, that we have no hesitation in referring it to the period of the second foundation of the Hospital by Henry III in 1233. Having arrived at this conclusion on independent grounds, it was particularly gratifying to learn from Mr. Salter that the land upon which this part of the Hospital stands—i.e. the East Bridge Street front—was granted to the Hospital by that King. Several authorities state that the first stone was laid by the King himself.[1]]

f. 43 The figure or ground plan of the Chapel building, which contained a great chamber for secular uses, is a parallelogram whose measures in extreme length and breadth are 57½ ft. and 22 ft. 4 in. respectively. Within the walls on the ground floor, the measures are 50½ ft. by 15 ft. 4 in.; on the upper 51½ by 16 ft. 4 in. [See Plans on pp. 408 and 416.]

As just observed, the building is not simply a Chapel, as was commonly the case. In positions corresponding with the present, the
f. 44 Wayside Chapel was an isolated structure and therefore not necessarily fashioned by the rule of the ancient domestic architecture, in obedience to which the principal chambers were raised upon a basement.

[1] Ranulf Higden, *Polychronicon MS.* Cf. Clark's Wood, *City of Oxford*, ii, p. 519.

VIEW OF MAGDALEN COLLEGE FROM EAST BRIDGE STREET, *c.* 1660

From Skelton, 'Oxonia Antiqua Restaurata', after a Picture in Magdalen College

The Hospital was most probably built on this plan, but if not, the little chapel conformed to the rule for some special advantage in the general arrangement, but of this no account can now be given.

Bridge Chapels received this distinction simply because of the depth of their basements below the level of the public footway. In the example of St. John, the elevation is composed of two stories above the level of the ground, the floor of the Chapel resting upon a chamber groined in stone, and elegantly finished in the details of its architecture. The altitude required for proper proportion in the interior of the Chapel was obtained by a steeply pitched roof of timber which spanned the room with the advantage of consistent ornament as well as of space. The walls have never presented any embellishment beyond that produced by the propriety of the design, and the careful finish of the mason-work.

Of the South or street front of the Chapel a general notion may be f. 50
formed from a large painting on canvas preserved in the President's Lodgings. No other authority is known to exist. In its absence no credit would be given to the statement that the Wayside Chapel retained its exterior design perfect in every member, as if its preservation were a religious obligation, and that harm would occur upon its destruction.

Certain it is that evil befel the College when James Wyatt entered f. 51
the precinct, laid the Chapel in ruins, disturbed the dead in their graves, destroyed their memorials, and turned out all that Bishop Waynflete thought most becoming to the Interior.

The painter of the picture was no flatterer of architecture. His fat representation of the Tower shows that the elegance of proportion offered no charms for his pencil. His partial and undefined view of the Chapel may be easily interpreted with the assistance of the detail of the extant remains. Each tier of windows is shown with distinctness: the sills of the lower are some distance above the footway. One tier is placed symmetrically over the other, the bays being denoted by buttresses, slender, shallow in projection [apparently so much so that the term pilaster-strips might almost be applied to them], and reaching to the parapet which is the plain finish of the elevation.

The Chapel windows [four in number, each with two lights, probably cusped, and with a quatrefoil[1]] were in two compartments, recessed like those of the East window of the ground Chamber, but less wide. The walls on the outside and in every aspect are of rubble, brought

[1] [The windows were very like those of the Hospital of St. Thomas at Canterbury.]

to a nearly smooth surface. In its compact surface were embedded the jambs and arches of the windows, of which sufficient remain to testify to the strength of the construction.

[Elsewhere (Add. MS. 36,431, No. 744) Buckler has a note that the chancel of St. Michael's Church, Greenhill, Lichfield, is of 'early lancet work with this cornice under the sill and upon ye windows. Ye same in ye Chapel of S. John's Hospital on N. and S. sides.' This string course below the windows of the upper storey is indicated in the picture (Pl. II), and Buckler's section of it is given in fig. 10, 4 on page 429, but we do not think that B. could have seen it on the

The Chapel Building of 1234. Building of 1509. Great Tower 1506.

FIG. 3. THE CHAPEL OF ST. JOHN'S HOSPITAL FROM THE STREET.

This view has been reconstructed by the addition of two bays to the end of the woodcut in Ingram's 'Memorials of Oxford'. The original wood block was kindly lent for this purpose by Mr. J. Parker. The ends of the ridge of the roof were probably ornamented with terminal crosses.

North side of the building.] In the absence of the Picture there would not be a particle of evidence to prove that the ashlar now on the outside is of so late a date as the 17th century, unless indeed the carvings in the parapet would be accepted as satisfactory upon this point.

When this view of the College was depicted, the building between the Chapel and the Tower, also the length between the Tower and the extreme eastern angle, had been completed.

f. 59 The North side of the Chapel was left rudely plain, considering that the building was insulated. It was almost a blank surface, and was made more mean by the substitution of eaves for a parapet, and a coat of plaster for honest concrete, or rough mason-work. This side is now completely shrouded by the Ante-chapel of the College, for by a singular coincidence their walls are within a very few feet of each other, and exactly opposite. . . .

To the foregoing general description of the Chapel conjecture can add nothing that will increase its interest. Some of the greater deformities remain to be enumerated. It will then be evident how hopeless the undertaking to adapt a building designed for a special service to employments foreign to its entire organization and to the strictness of its architecture. f. 51

The large vaulted Chamber on the ground floor, being the Charnel of the Hospital, afterwards converted into the Almshouse of the College, and later adapted for use as Cellars, Staircase, Lavatory and Servants' Rooms.

[This Chamber is more completely preserved than any of the other buildings of the Hospital. We must therefore make allowance for the tendency of the architect who laid bare its columns and vaults, to attribute to the room a greater importance than it perhaps deserves. We give his descriptions *in extenso*, but later evidence convinces us that what he calls the 'Strangers' Hall' was not used by 'the classes who solicited temporary repose and refreshment', but by those whose bones required a more lasting resting-place.]

The vaulted basement of the Chapel building was of primary importance in the disposition of the daily charities at the gate. It is indeed the representative of the large chamber or hall to which another position would have been given at a later period. This was the Strangers' Hall, belonging to those classes who solicited temporary repose and refreshment by night and by day; whose numbers were uncertain, whose necessities were various; sometimes their call was simple and brief, and sometimes urgent and prolonged. f. 46

This was an active, incessant, and very important part of the duty of this hospital, but auxiliary to the larger obligations of its endowment as a home for the sick and the aged, and their becoming maintenance. The shrine of St. Frideswide in the Priory church was an object of great attraction; and the gatherings of curious and the devout resembled a perpetual stream, not always equally abundant but at no time exhausted. It had its own eleemosynary; but there were at seasons vast herds who would stop short of the city gate, and prepare themselves for the duty of the morrow. Besides these there were mere wayfarers.

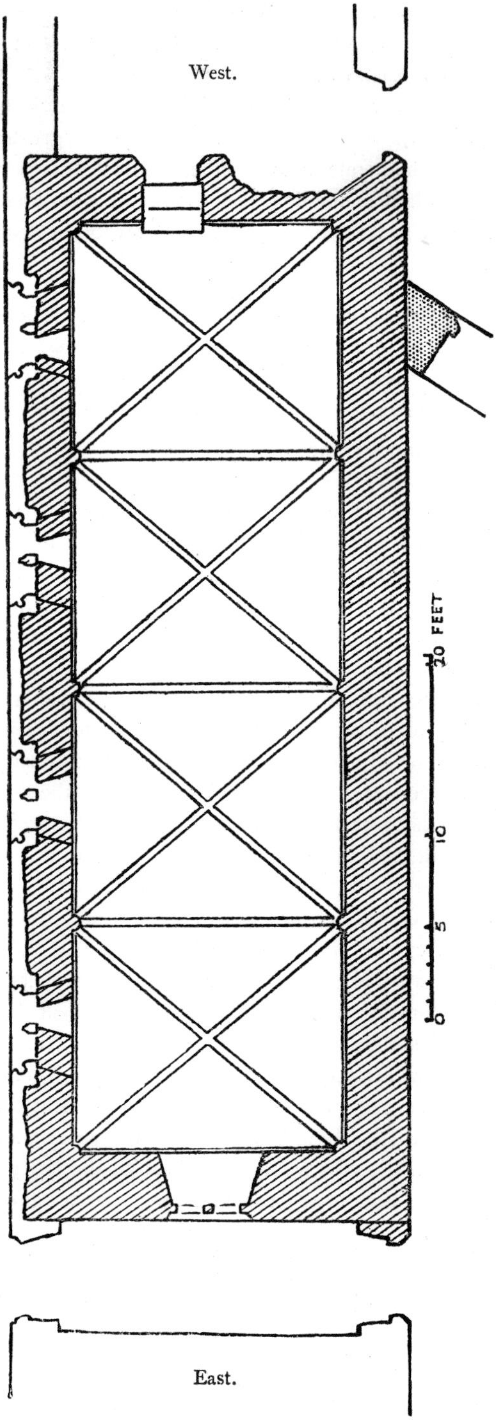

FIG. 4. PLAN OF THE VAULTED BASEMENT OR CHARNEL OF THE CHAPEL BUILDING.

The four two-light windows and the outer casing of the south wall, left white in the plan, were added in 1665.

DOORWAY AND EAST WINDOW OF CHARNEL

After Buckler, with the addition of a quatrefoil light in the window

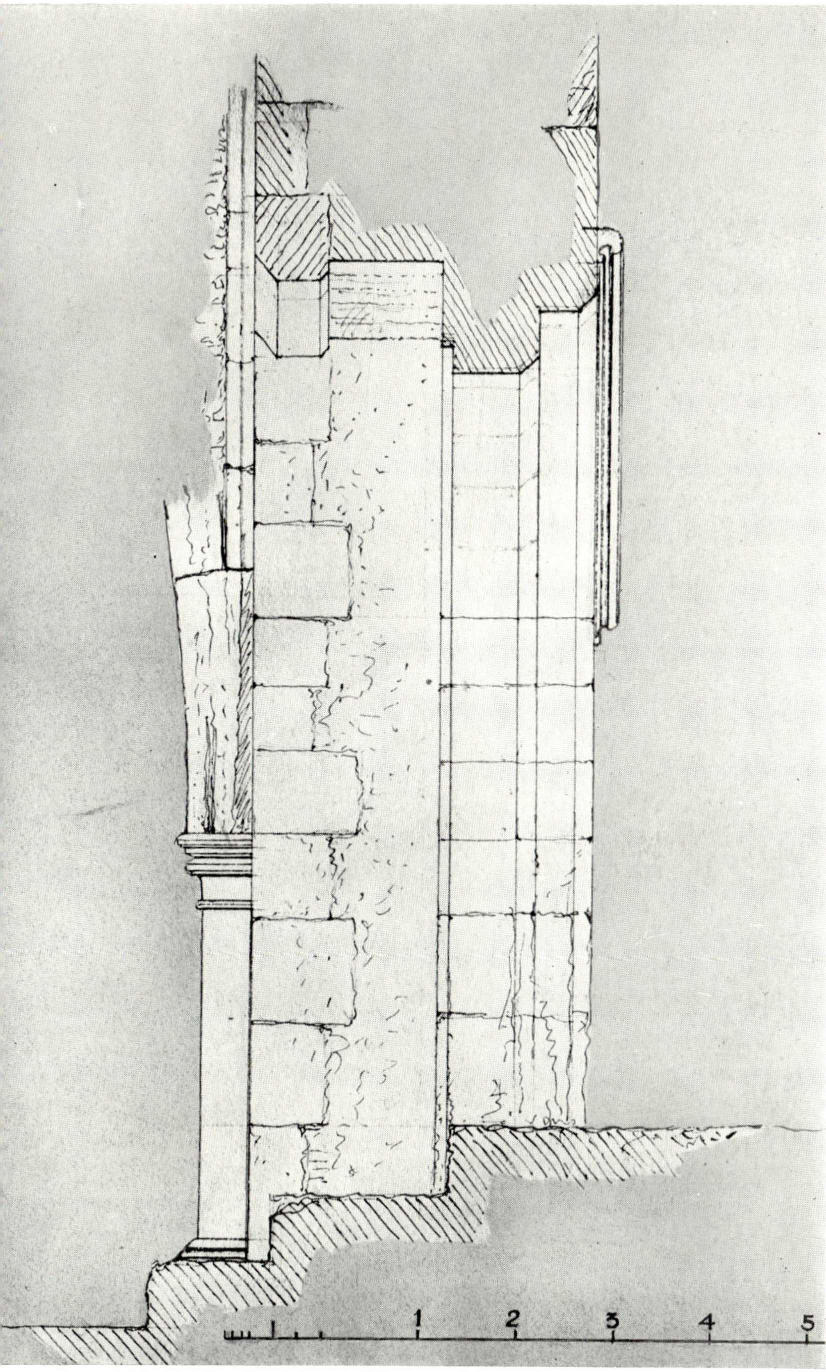

SECTIONAL ELEVATION OF THE ENTRANCE TO THE CHARNEL

After Buckler

[The only entrance was at the West end by a doorway which is shown by its hood-mold to have been originally on the outside of the building. The inner face of the wall is supported by a rear-arch of flattish curvature, to allow headroom for the pointed-topped door to open. The level of the floor inside seems to have been some two

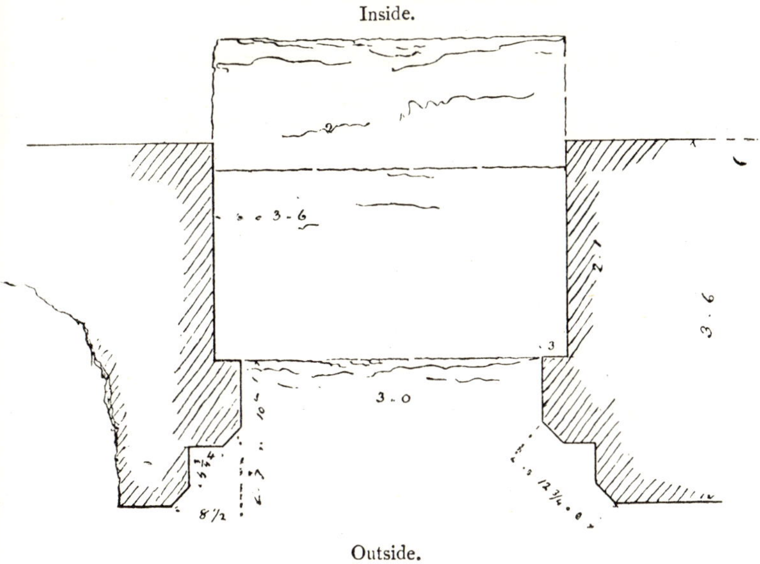

FIG. 5. PLAN OF ENTRANCE TO THE CHARNEL.

feet below the surface of the ground outside, for there were three steps down. The architectural proportions of the doorway are well shown in Plates III and IV.]

The Chamber is arched overhead, and groined in stone, or rather f. 47
was before any part of the interior was devoted to the service of the College, for a vain attempt was made by expelling its elaborate stone-work to introduce the same moderate share of convenience as in the adjoining chambers, but this basement part of the College with a South aspect defied the endeavour, and submitted to its present degradation beyond the reach of memory.

The arch [= vault] spanned the interior of the basement from one side wall to the others. It consisted of a mass of powerfully compacted rubble stone and concrete about fifteen inches in thickness. All the required strength in this arch was of rough workmanship connected with the walls, which were formed of precisely the same mixture. The wall arches were embedded in this coarse material, and held fast by it, as their remnants are at this day. The building as it was taken possession of in the 15th century would, under fair usage, have proved indestructible.

The groin-work was disposed in four bays with diagonal ribs intersected in the centre of the roof, the clustered springers rising from pillars attached to the walls, and to the four angles of the Chamber. The height of the interior from the floor to the vault was 13 feet 9 inches; nearly two-thirds of this measure being occupied by the arch of the roof, which has a solid bearing upon the walls; and with the same precaution the groins extended with elegant uniformity over its surface.

A lancet window appeared in each bay in front, but the back or North wall was blank.

The East window consists of two compartments [= lights] within an arch of singular form, recessed. [The hood-molding, which is carried on across the entire end of the building as a string, is a scroll-molding with a fillet (Plate III). The cusps, of which Buckler found indications in the lights, are soffit-cusps of the kind common in the second quarter of the 13th century.]

The door is at the West end but not in the centre.

The light to the interior was not abundant: it descended from apertures so much above the floor as to prevent inquisitive observations both from within and without. These apertures were perfectly plain on the inside, sloped through the wall from 24 inches to perhaps less than 12 on the outside.

The walls on the inside were ashlared with small stones in courses, even and smooth formerly, but now broken, disjointed, and so much disturbed by the alterations which have been made at different times, as to present a rude appearance. In contrast with this, the large angle-stones of the windows are observable, and remarkable since in the refined architecture of the period great attention was commonly paid to the plain mason-work so as to keep it in agreement with the narrow courses of the design. While time and mischief have roughened the walls, these unsparing powers have operated with a different effect upon the features of the architecture: these may be mischievously mutilated, but as long as any part of the workmanship remains in its original state, merit cannot be disguised.

The bases and capitals of the pillars were wrought with elegance,

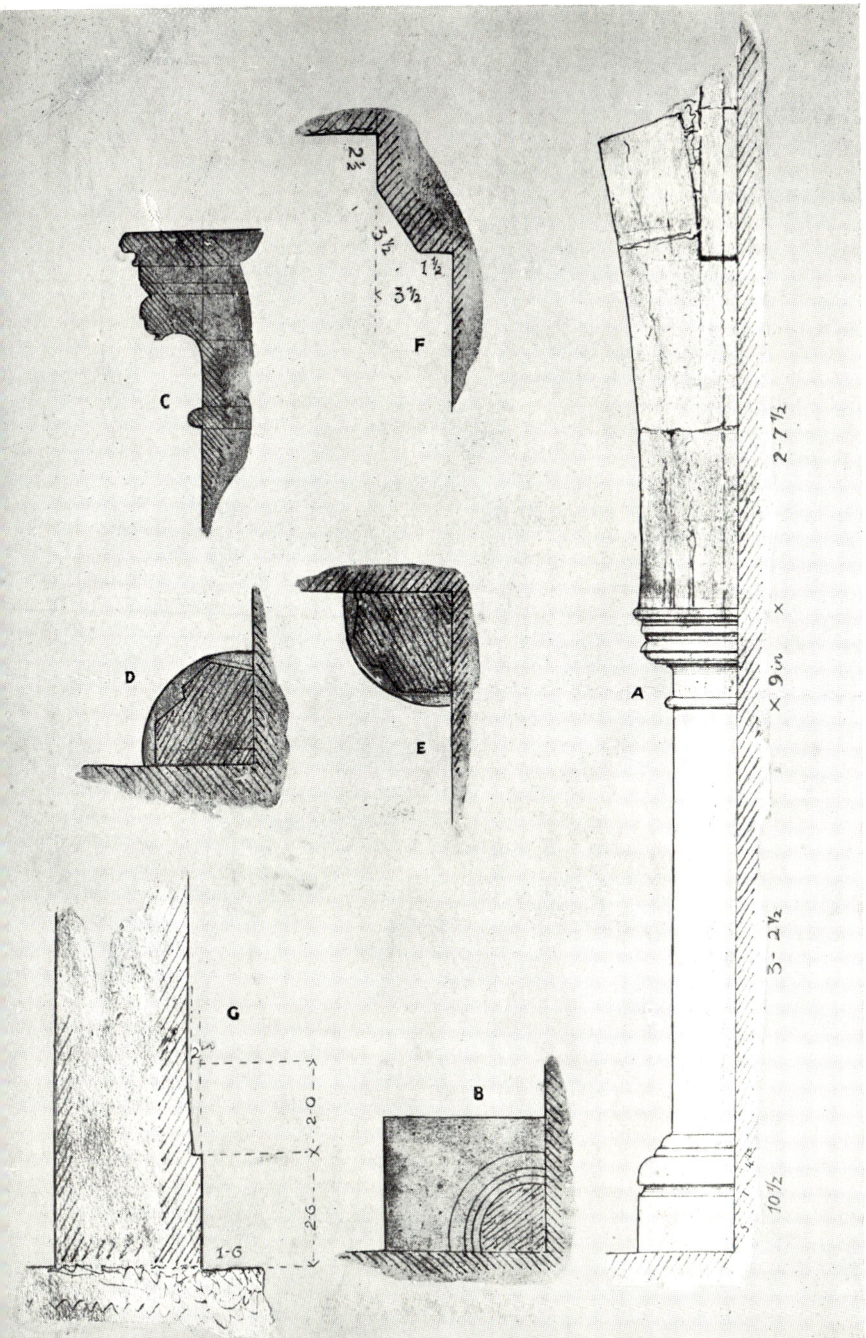

DETAILS OF THE CORNER COLUMNS OF THE CHARNEL

A. Elevation; B. Plan of Base; C. Vertical Section of Capital; D, E. Plans of Springing of Groin Ribs; F. Section of mural Groin Rib; G. Vertical Section of Foundation of Wall.

and the arches and ribs of the roof with care, and in the solid simplicity characteristic of the period.

[The corner columns are of a somewhat unusual type in Early English architecture. The nearest approach to them with which we are acquainted are in the Choir of the Temple Church in London (dated *c.* 1240). The capitals are similar, and in both the bases are worked with a triple roll (Pl. VII).

Notice has been taken of the attempts which were made at different f. 56
periods to raise the floor in the basement of the Chapel proportionate to the increase of the ground on the outside. The accumulation of the earth in towns, singularly conspicuous in the Street front of Magdalen College, is an evil of very ancient date, and one against which no check has at any time proved effectual. The [street] pavement is now [1858] 7 feet 2 inches above the original floor of the Chamber.

The lower chamber has acquired the appellation of a crypt, a term f. 52
as improperly given in this instance as in many which might be named. True it is that the earth had been allowed to accumulate round the walls, and thus to bury them to a considerable depth; but effectually as this clandestine process had deprived the chamber of its former freedom and wholesomeness, the term is not strictly applicable, nor brought so near as to the verge of accuracy, even when the roadway which descended from Carfax to the river without the East Gate was made level to a considerable distance within the fortified boundary.

The floors of Churches cover Crypts, but the term is not faithfully borne out in many instances, since these vaulted basements were not generally built within the ground.

St. John's Hospital occupied a site so slightly out of level that it would have been in danger of floods at certain seasons if its buildings had been based upon Crypts.

It is proved by the entrance to the ground chamber that its floor was sunk within the soil about two feet. This level had not been disturbed when the property fell into the hands of Bishop Waynflete. This appears in the altered level of the floor, the first attempt made to improve the interior, early in the reign of Henry VIII.

As carried out it was a strong indictment against the fine old chamber, —a sweeping measure designed to obliterate its architectural character, and to convert it into lodging rooms in accordance with the rest. The stone roof [i.e. vaulting] was swept away, and with it whatever f. 53
stood in advance of the walls; but as the pillars in the four corners

offered no impediments to the proposed alterations, they escaped with a few accidental mutilations, those at the West end remaining most perfect, indeed so perfect that their shape was very little deformed. The tall, projecting springers of the groins were also in their places.

[At this point Buckler doubtless intended to draw special attention to the two Tudor fire-places which were inserted in the South wall at a height of about 2 feet above the old floor line. They are eloquent testimony that the chamber had become unwholesomely damp, perhaps even flooded when the Cherwell rose high, and to improve matters the

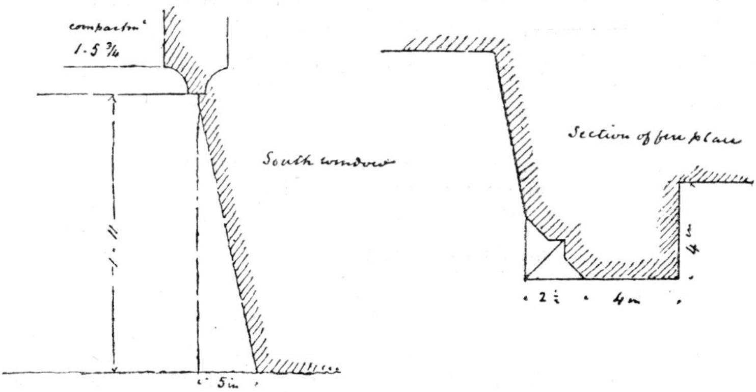

FIG. 6. SECTIONS OF JAMBS OF SOUTH WINDOW AND FIRE-PLACE.

floor was raised and some two or three separate chambers were contrived, one of which being vacant 'about the beginninge of the raygne of King Henry VIII' was furnished at the cost of President Claymond with four beds. So that throughout the sixteenth century the young College in a small way, and aided by an endowment from Claymond for the maintenance of his beds, still kept up the charitable work of the old Hospital. But we imagine that even with the new fire-places the almshouse could not have made a very cheerful abode, and it is on record that in 1507 there were four burials from the *domus pauperum*, and several more in 1508–9.

In 1596 it was reported that 'the usage to intertayne the pore in the said allmeshouse hath bynn from time to time in this sorte. When the President or any of the fellowes doe finde any pore distressed people that are fitt to be pitied, or when any doe come to crave succoure, to the number of one, two or three (butt never above foure)

PLATE VIII

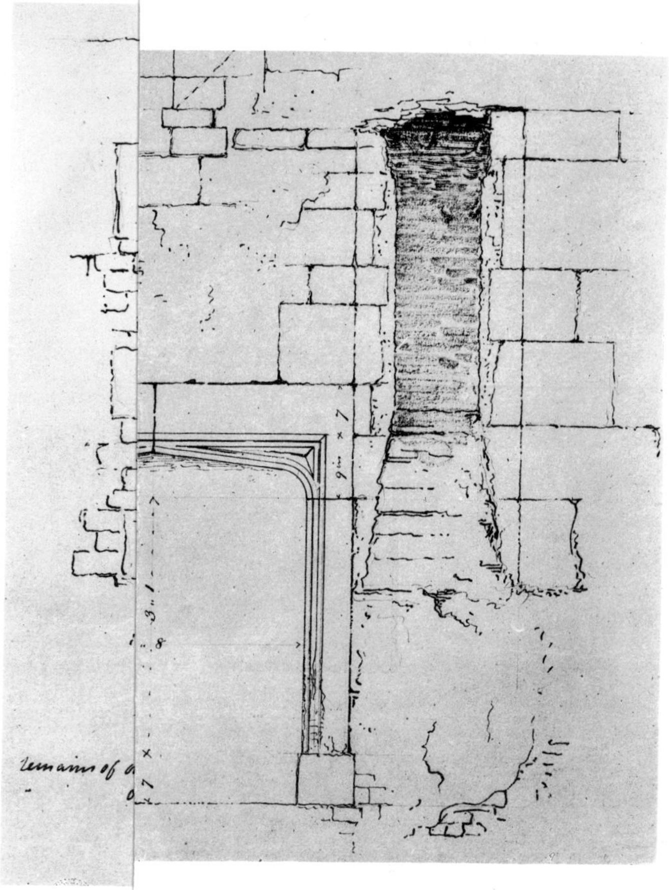

E ALMSHOUSE

they sende them to the keeper of the sayd allmes-house, and there they are lodged for one, two or three nightes as occasion dothe serve, and if theire case be verie pittifull (albeit we have noe allowaunce for victuall ore mayntenaunce for them) yet diverse have bynn relieved with convenient diet by the space of many dayes and weekes at the colledge charges by the consent of the President and officers; in so much as some have bynn mayntayned there to the hower of theire death. In sommer the resort is greater, in winter very smale, bycause of the coldnes and onwholesomenes of the vault; which is in verie deed so moyst and dampish that we have the last yeare removed the beddes into another house not far of, for that everie winter they are subject to rottennes, and have provided some tymber, and meane, God willinge, this spring to provide more, for the bordinge of the floare of the saide Allmes-house, as well for the safetie of our beddes as the health and ease of the poore.'

In 1631–43 Magister Ellis received a salary of £3 as Keeper of the Almonry.]

It is clear therefore that no injury of moment was left for the avidity f. 53
of a later period. The lancet windows were spared, and the interior, thus refashioned, was subdivided, modernised, and perhaps for a short time, inhabited.

All these arrangements, destructive or seasonable, were afterwards undone, but to what end cannot be guessed, seeing that improvement had been driven farther back than before: the fire-places,—needful appendages here—were rendered useless, and neither light nor air refreshed the interior.

The earliest and most fatal alterations included a raised floor 26 inches above the original pavement, and within a few inches of the ground line on the outside.

Under the second assault in the 17th century, the floor was again raised other 24 inches, but not uniformly. It was now placed 7 feet below the glass line of the windows, which were inserted at this time, and have not since been altered.

At the present day [1858] the street pavement is 4 feet 8 inches below the same glass line. But as amendment has not hitherto followed alteration, these changes are not worthy of further notice. Others may, in time to come, sweep all these things out of existence.

[In a further note dated 1866, Buckler draws attention to a cross wall built across the charnel and 2 ft. 4 in. within its west wall. This appears to be the foundation of a fire-place and chimney-stack constructed almost abreast of the pulpit and near the middle of the building.]

f. 54 If the scheme to gut the South buildings in its whole length had been carried out as proposed by the President [Routh], the unwholesome deposits under the ground floor would have been removed, and a rearrangement made of greater value than the present.

Except the Lodge there is not a single habitable room on the ground floor, and it is perhaps owing to this circumstance, and their consignment to neglect and rubbish, that the charnel house beneath has not been detected, and abolished.

f. 55 Some of the wooden partitions and obstructive bulks within the groined chamber were removed, and as much of the unoccupied space as could be dealt with was excavated to the ancient level. But an obstruction of no ordinary kind checked the employment; it was discovered for the first time within human memory, that a great mass of human bones had been deposited against the East wall of the groined chamber, not thrown in promiscuously as if in haste to hide the mortal remains: the act was performed considerately, the bones being sorted and closely packed.

There was no dealing with such objects under the circumstances: the discovery was affecting, and the bones were speedily concealed from view.

Human bones, piled together in the same way, were also found under the floor of the Eastern room of the Lodge. The intermediate space of the building may be occupied in the same manner, the whole length having been excavated for one huge grave as a receptacle for human bones of which no account can be given.[1]

The Chapel building was an excellent specimen of the different kinds of mason-work which its construction included. The builders had not to contend with a dearth of material; on the contrary, stone was used profusely wherever it was required in plain and unmeasured blocks. It was of a quality so durable as not to have been defaced by the weather. But notwithstanding the bounty of its owners, the outer surface of the walls was not ashlared: a concrete composition was preferred, and time has not perceptibly diminished its strength, which was powerfully tested when the front of the wall was torn away as the measure previous to its transformation in unison with the rest of the College front.

[1] For a note on a previous reinterment of bones during Dr. Jenner's presidency, cf. Chandler, *Life of Waynflete*, p. 90.

The exterior was as strongly marked by the solidity of its appearance and the simplicity of its features as the interior by the elegance of the general design and the delicacy of its detail. Such however was the merit of this early style of Pointed architecture (commenced in the preceding reign), owing to the unvarying application of the leading characteristical forms, that the impression upon the mind was certain and stedfast. Cistercian architecture abounds in examples which fortify this remark.

The intrusive windows were very carelessly constructed as to levels and slopes, a remark which applies to the inside only: for them the arches of the lancet windows were destroyed, and for greater convenience the remainders of the apertures were walled up, but they will always be distinctly seen; and it is curious to observe that the second from the altar end is 3 feet wide, the rest being 2 feet.

It is perhaps still more curious to notice that the narrow course f. 57
of ashlar upon which the solid sills of the inserted windows rest denotes the position of the first range of putlogs of the builders' scaffolding. These short lengths of timber upon which the footboards were laid, were of oak, 5 inches by $4\frac{1}{2}$ inches, exactly shaped, placed from 10 to 15 feet apart, and inserted 18 or 20 inches into the wall. When their work was done, the putlogs were not withdrawn, but were cut off to within 3 inches of the face of the ashlar. The fragments thus spared, and now brought to view for the first time since the final alteration of the Wayside Chapel, are more or less decayed. In several instances the putlogs had been wholly removed and the holes filled up with mortar.

The Chapel.

The Chapel was indeed a very conspicuous object on the side of f. 25
the highway when it stood alone, but in process of time it was pressed upon by domestic architecture; the free air could no longer circulate around it, and the only wonder is that the force and fraud of innovation —the uncompromising foe to order and conservative feeling,—left it so long in the enjoyment of its genuine character.

Of the Chapel very little derived from the building can be said. f. 50
Whatever traces of the design may have been spared on the inside are too closely covered up to be examined.

Before proceeding farther . . . it may be well to enquire by what f. 58
means and in what position it [the Chapel] was formerly approached,

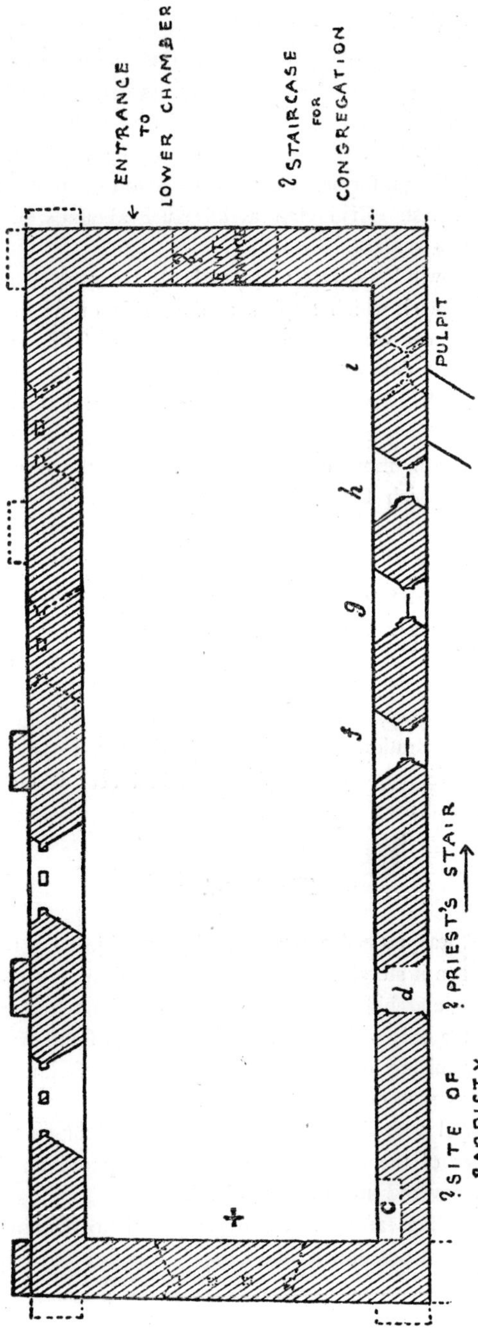

FIG. 7. PLAN OF THE CHAPEL.
Suggested restorations are indicated by dotted lines.

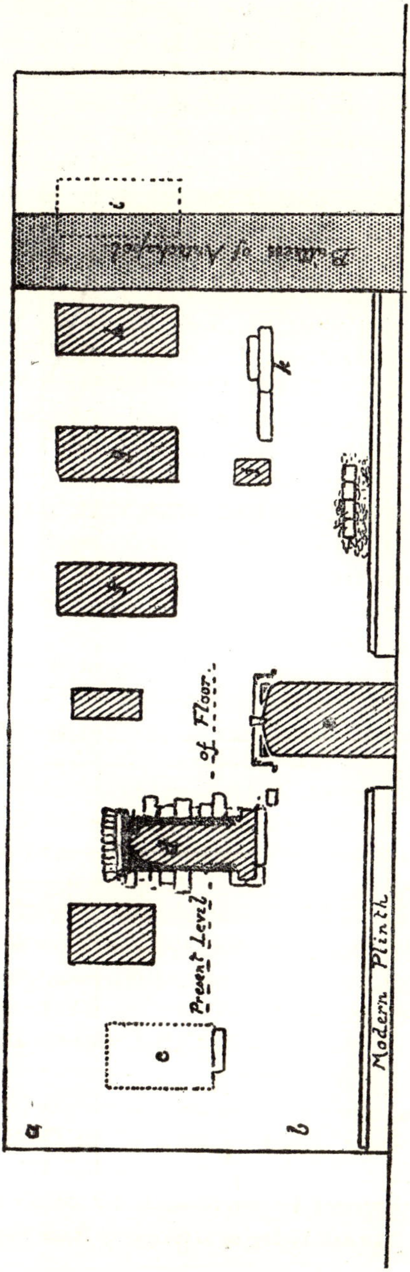

FIG. 8. ELEVATION OF NORTH WALL OF THE CHAPEL BUILDING.

remembering that its destination required that admittance should be obvious, and as direct as could be, its floor being elevated between 13 and 14 feet from the ground. The fair suggestion is that the Chapel, having always been an insulated building, had a Porch, or covered Lobby containing a stair, attached to the West end. This seems more probable than that there should have been an exposed Stone Stair, however common the custom for nearly two centuries
f. 59 after the Anglo-Norman practice had been established. That an appendage of the kind described continued in use up to a late period is scarcely to be doubted on recollection of the very considerable and injurious alteration which was made for the first time in the 17th century for the sole purpose of ascending to the Chapel.

[That the north wall of the Chapel building was continued westwards, and might therefore have served to support a staircase, is apparent from Buckler's observation on p. 419, lines 2 to 7.]

f. 59 At this time a characteristical, but very grotesque door was forced in this back wall of the basement, within which, and at the same time (the groined roof having been previously destroyed), a staircase [1] wholly of timber was framed with great solidity, and it remains to this day unaltered, and gives access to the rooms with which the whole interior of the Chapel is deformed.

. . . But as to the original means of ascent to the Chapel, nothing more can be said than that the ground it occupied was absorbed by the new chambers. The President's judicious scheme, mentioned in another place, would have laid open the Chapel, and no doubt brought to light, from side to side, and from end to end, many intelligible traces of the design. As things remain, a recess in the side wall is the only original feature, belonging to the interior, known to the writer: it was brought to light many years since, during the general survey, but un-
f. 60 accompanied by any other curious discovery. It did not stand within the Clerks' Court, but its east wall being on a line with the same side of the ante-Chapel, a definite inner boundary was given to the Court; and it has often occurred to the writer that the cherished intention of the Founder was to preserve the Chapel, whatever might be its value in the economy of the College.

This notion seems to be strongly corroborated by the care with which the Founder caused the angle of the College Chapel to be connected with the North-west angle of the little Chapel. The union was happily suggested by the necessity for the Pulpit, which is an

1 [The stair leading up to the present Home Bursary.]

attractive feature in a position as favourable for ornament as for its peculiar use. It is important to remark that the flank wall of St. John's Court is attached to the Pulpit, and that this wall to the jamb of the first door, a length of seven feet, is as substantial as the wall of the Chapel, and is indeed a prolongation of it westward thus far; the other jamb of the same door being in a wall 2 feet 8 inches thick, this being the measure of the walls of this flank of the court. The prolonged wall seems to imply an extension of the original buildings along the South boundary, or at least some kind of appendage to the Chapel, but no opportunity was given for discoveries under ground. These remarks have occurred (to the writer) since the revealment of a fragment of the West wall of the Chapel within the wall shown in the ground plan. How it came to pass that this wall was so well defined, as having on one face the pillars and groins in the angles, and on the other the entrance to the groined chamber with a most marked excavation in the wall to give freedom to the door from the court, if it were not in existence at the time, and all these particulars exposed to the light of day, is inexplicable.

When the blank character of the North side of the Chapel was spoken of, the several plain windows which once opened to the Chapel were not overlooked. One was walled up solidly at the time the Pulpit was erected; but the others were retained for the use of the timber Staircase, and give distinctness to objects and incidents prominent in the downward history of the building, while they shed light faintly upon others which in prosperous days were honoured and protected. Formerly, when the Chapel was subdivided by a screen, the three narrow and unadorned windows referred to opened upon the public area before the Sanctuary.[1]

The solution of the various difficulties of this limb of the College might long since have been accomplished but for the selfishness of an individual not upon the foundation, nor in any way connected with elegant taste, yet he baffled the praiseworthy design of the President to economise space, and increase the accommodation of the College. f. 61
Late in life, too late for success to the extent desired, the good President wished to combat with this difficulty, and there can be no doubt that he brought uncommon judgement to bear upon the subject, but he was miserably thwarted, and the plan as a whole was set aside.

[1] [Here Buckler may be mistaken. It is just possible that this north wall, of which he was writing, was originally an inside wall, and that the 'unadorned windows' were inserted after the transference of the Hospital buildings to Magdalen College.]

[Before quoting further from the Buckler MS., it will perhaps make the position clearer if we draw attention to some recent discoveries and give in outline a sketch of the Chapel as we now see it. Since Buckler examined the building the exterior coat of plaster has been removed from the outer north wall and the masonry has been patched and repointed, so that it is now possible to see structural details which were previously concealed.

Above a modern plinth, 17 inches high, the greater part of the wall is faced with small rubble stones, among which window-jamb stones and a few other large stones are conspicuous (fig. 8). There are larger stones (*a . . . b*) all up the eastern end of the wall: here the masonry gives me the impression that a cross wall or buttress has been removed, rather than that this corner is as the builders left it. Excavation might show how far foundations extend. Next, at 9 feet above the present ground-level is a horizontal stone, which appears to be structurally related to the bottom of a large recess, *c*, within the chapel, abreast and north of the altar. This may be a walled-up north doorway leading to a vestry, or it may have been a cupboard. Then, beyond a rectangular modern window with thick wooden sashes of the Wren period, is a walled-up doorway *d* (unknown to Buckler) which formerly opened into the Chapel through Buckler's 'Recess' under a shouldered arch (Plate IX, fig. 1). This doorway is a fact of fundamental importance, because it is absolute proof that the Chapel building originally extended further north than it now does, and that some portion at any rate of its north wall was an inside wall at a time before the College Ante-chapel was erected. It is to be regarded as the priest's entrance to the Chancel, and indicates the former existence of an external, and probably covered, staircase. From the appearance of the masonry I would suggest a landing immediately outside the doorway, and a flight of steps descending westward along the wall. Having regard to the main entrance to the Hospital being west, it would be a natural direction for the approach.

Near the pulpit wall there is again a course of original large masonry, *k*, nearly on a level with the Chapel floor, but the structural significance is not at present clear.

The interior of the Chapel was well lit. Over the altar (where there is now a sitting-room fire-place) there would have been an east window, perhaps with three lights and probably with plate tracery, while we have pictorial evidence that the south wall was pierced with two two-light windows with quatrefoils in the eastern half of its length. West

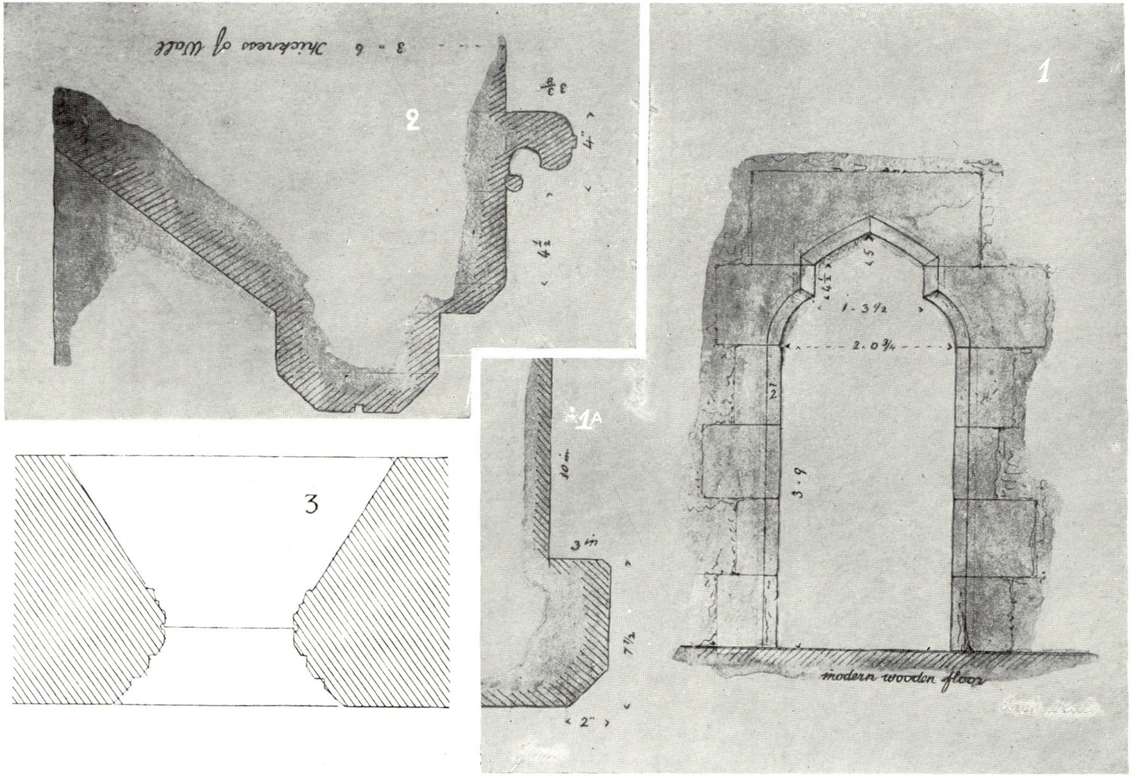

1. Elevation of the Chancel Doorway; 1 A. Section of Jamb of ditto; 2. Section of Jamb and Molding of the East Window of the Charnel; 3. Plan of one of the Windows of the North Wall of the Chapel.

of these there may either have been two other similar windows, making four in all, or else a row of four plain, narrow single-light windows ranged symmetrically with those in the north wall: these would have given light to the nave. The three windows *f, g, h* in their present state with shallow moldings (Pl. IX, fig. 3) on their simple splays do not give one the impression of being contemporaneous with the building, but the exact period of their introduction is quite uncertain. We agree with Buckler in thinking that the entrance for the congregation must have been from the west, and we would urge in this connexion that the lop-sided arrangement of the basement doorway may have been in relation to a staircase which was against the north end of the west wall.

The pulling down of the northern building containing the Priest's stair and the walling-up of the north door of the Chapel may certainly be regarded as a necessary consequence of the adoption by Waynflete of the plan for Transepts to the College Chapel, and of the execution of the idea of building the College on as large a scale as could possibly be worked in between the north wall of the Infirmary, the Kitchen, and the pulpit corner of the Chapel of St. John's Hospital.

In 1490–1, and therefore some years after the completion of the College Chapel, we find it on record that the Chapel of St. John was repaired and that it was furnished with a clock. (Macray, i, p. 22.)

The degradation of the Chapel probably began in the year before the Great Fire of London, for in 1666 an account was settled with one Badger, *caementario operanti in vet. Capella*, 34 *li.* 5*s.* 8*d.*, for making six new chambers within it. (Macray, iv, p. 22.)

The old front was altered at about the same time and was thus forced into line with the 1507–9 building between the Chapel and the Great Tower. Concerning this alteration Buckler was, as usual, outspoken.]

A fire-place excavated on each side of the East wall has taken the f. 50
place of the Altar window; and a cluster of chimneys has rudely supplanted the monitory cross which once appeared on the gable.

The timber roof rose so much above the altitude required by the newer buildings that it could not be pardoned. Mischievous pains were taken to humble the Chapel to the scale and aspect of the rest of the elevation: but whether to this end the original roof was wholly removed, or only in part dilapidated to make it accord with its adjunct, remains uncertain, no portion of it having been opened to view.

But it has never associated cordially with the newer chambers. In f. 25

the forced connexion there could be no agreement, nor any chance of the union ever being satisfactory. The ancient basement was a fine example of the method of treating that part of the Domestic Edifice generally. It contained the best Architecture, but nothing besides for comfortable occupation; it was at all times fireless, of stone throughout, and not over-windowed.

f. 26 When the alteration was made, the passage from the Street to the Clerks' Court [Chaplains' Quadrangle] was made. The archways are of this debased period. But for what purpose is uncertain. They were too late to be of service to the almspeople: the President [Routh] scoffed at the appellation of the 'Pilgrim's Gate'; and he would not entertain the notion that it had ever been used as an entrance to the College. For what purpose then was it made? The question may be answered by supposing that almsgiving survived the destruction of the latest relics of the hospital dwellings, and that this street entrance was the way for the recipients of the last grains of the ancient charity. This seems to be the correct state of the case. The final extinction of this ancient house of charity occurred in the 17th century when this entrance was formed. The little that remained of the royal bounty grew less, and at length passed silently into oblivion. The charity was doubtless maintained while any of the inmates of the old foundation survived its suppression.

[This gate is shown in the aforementioned oil painting (Plate II), and therefore must have been in existence about 1665, before the lowering of the ridge of the Chapel roof. The old oaken door with a peep-hole, that was made to fit the entrance at that time, is now (1917) preserved in the Home Bursary.]

Foundations between the Chapel and the Great Gate.

In an enlargement of the Lodge during the progress of the works undertaken in the front since their commencement anno 1850, the basement of a cross wall of formidable bulk and solidity was dis-
f. 32 covered under the floor, and removed. It resembled a mass of living rock, and for a long time resisted the powerful forces which at length reduced it to fragments.

The writer owns that he felt no regret for the almost hopeless labour of the workmen under his employ, but had much praise to bestow upon the brave fellows of antiquity who placed so much trouble in the way of injurious men and performed such good work in the noble cause of charity.

It was observed that the ancient underground fragments pointed in one direction, that is, perpendicular to the front wall standing on the margin of the footway, but there is nothing more in them for remark. Relics such as these, and others which admitted of different treatment, after being hidden for many generations, appear, as if to give testimony which as far as it reaches is useful, and is instructive as regards the quality of the structure of the 13th century.

[I have failed to find any plan among the Buckler MSS. by which the exact site of this cross wall can be identified. But it would either have belonged to a building joined on to the west end of the Chapel Building or it may have been continuous with the foundations of the Great Gate of the Hospital, which certainly faced west towards the City and was almost certainly provided with a Lodge for a Porter.

It should be remembered that in early days gate-relief may have been given to the poor at this gate instead of at the so-called Pilgrim's Gate, which appears to have been merely a side-door in a wall at the east end of the Chapel until 1506–8 and was in no sense a *porta magna*. There is a record that in 1481 the College Barber (who in after days at any rate was also the College Porter and may have been a pluralist then) had charge of the gate-relief of the poor. The *porta magna* of the Hospital was probably still used as the main entrance in the early days of the College. Its survival would explain why Waynflete does not appear to have thought it necessary to construct a new Gateway for his College.

The exact position of the entrance to the Chapel is a matter of some importance for the determination of the true position of an interesting feature of early Oxford topography, which, I believe, has been misplaced in modern maps,—the large stone Cross, greatly venerated by travellers. 'Nor did any persons whatsoever go over East Bridge, but what paid their respects to the famous Cross of St. John's Hospital.'[1]

In the City Records for 1331 [2] there is a strong suggestion that the Masters, brethren and men of St. John's Hospital had been 'distressed or disquieted by the City authorities . . . for the making and repair of the way which reaches from Little Bridge, even to the Cross near the gate of the Hospital'. Now if the Hospitallers were held responsible for such repairs in their capacity as owners of a street frontage, it

[1] Hearne's Note to Robert of Gloucester's Chronicle, quoted in Holland's *Cruciana*, p. 271. Bloxam, ii, p. lxix.

[2] MS. Twine xxiii, p. 455, quoted by Hurst, *Oxford Topography*.

would only appear reasonable that they should be expected to repair the roadway for the entire length of their frontage.

The commonly accepted position of the Cross does not mark the full extent of the Hospital frontage by several yards. The site of the Cross as indicated in the Town plan published by the Ordnance Survey Office and repeated in the map to Mr. Wilson's *History*, is marked in the middle of the very narrow East Bridge Street on a level with the middle of the Chapel.

Bloxam was, I think, in error in locating the cross 'before the Pilgrims' gate' (*Register*, ii, p. lxix). The objections to a cross upon any such position are that the roadway was very narrow, that there is no indication of a widening or recess in which a large cross could have stood, that it does not mark the limit of the roadway for which the Hospitallers might reasonably have been held responsible, and that in 1562 the College, by ordering its destruction, must have been in possession of its site.

We find a better explanation of its position in two entries in the College accounts, relating to its demolition (Bloxam, ii, p. 277).

'1562 Solut. 20 Martii Gul. Robinson et Johanni Wilks crucem ante januas sacelli Divi Johannis diruentibus et lapides ibidem effodientibus viii s.

— Solut. 25 Martii Jackson et Matthewe locum in quo crux stetit pavimento tegentibus iii s. iiii d.'

The money spent on demolition is a measure of the substantial nature of the fabric. If the *januae sacelli Divi Johannis* were at the west end of the Chapel Building, the cross *ante januas* would naturally have stood still further west and within the line of the street frontage. I would suggest that it stood in the College grounds in the angle between the line of the street frontage and the boundary line between the College and Magdalen Hall, or in other words in the angle between the lines of the present South-facing entrance and of the older West-facing entrance to the College. The Cemetery of the Brethren undoubtedly covered much of this space: the Cross, as Mr. Salter has suggested, may have stood in the Cemetery.

Any one leaving the city by the East gate would have seen the Cross as a conspicuous feature in front of him and would have described it as standing *ante januas sacelli*, with which it would have been in line. Its location on the site indicated would explain why the buildings of Magdalen Hall (1480) came to be placed so far back from the side of the road, and to what good fortune the

College owes that incomparable plot of land (afterwards the Gravel Walk) with greensward and elm-trees by which the beauty of all street views of its buildings was until 1916 so greatly enhanced.]

IV. THE KITCHEN BLOCK, INCLUDING THE DIVINITY READER'S LODGINGS

[The College Kitchen, 'a large and rather gloomy old room, with a very high roof of strong timbers and several contiguous walls,' both by tradition and in the opinion of several antiquaries is ascribed to the Hospital of St. John, and at that the present writer would prefer to leave it, never having had an opportunity of making adequate examination of its walls. To his mind the orientation of the ground-plans both of this building and of the adjoining Divinity Reader's Lodgings on the North side, skew to the near walls of the Cloister Buildings, but parallel to the distant Chapel of St. John, is very strong evidence in favour of their representing constructions older than the College and probably buildings of the 1233 period. If it be surmised that the present College Kitchen is rather large for the size of the Hospital, it may be suggested either that it was used as a Refectory by the Brethren or that large kitchens were usual at that time.

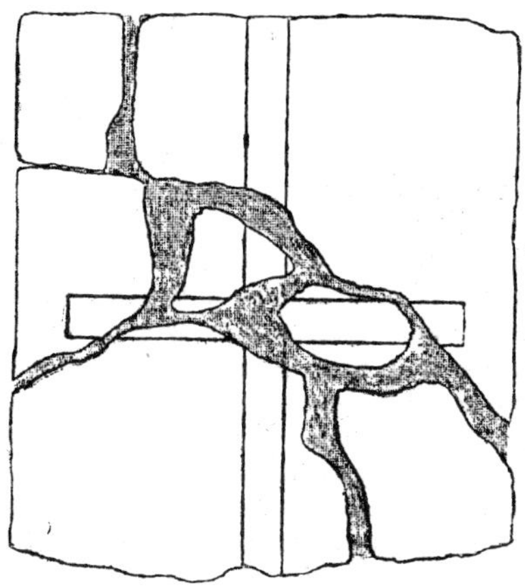

FIG. 9. FRAGMENTS OF GRAVESTONE UNCOVERED IN 1913.

The interesting early carved stone head in the south wall of the Kitchen will be described later (p. 430, Plate X).

The Divinity Reader's Lodgings, regarded as part of the Hospital by Wood,[1] were removed to make way for West's Buildings in 1783. The latter have however inherited their orientation, i.e. the orientation of the 1233 street front.]

[1] Clark's Wood, *City of Oxford*, p. 526.

V. MISCELLANEOUS

a. Gravestone.

[A gravestone of one of the Brethren of the Hospital was unearthed in the summer of 1913 in the middle of St. John's Quadrangle. Unfortunately only some fragments have escaped the navvy's pick, but they are sufficient to show that the upper face of the stone, about 25 inches in width, was slightly sloped off on either side and bore a plain cross lightly chiselled upon the surface. The short arms of the cross are 20 inches in length and 2 inches in width and the stone is about 6 inches in thickness (fig. 9).

The light which this stone throws upon the Cemetery of the Hospital is best explained in a Report to the President from Mr. Poole, who thereby performed his trust more faithfully than most College Bursars would have done.]

From the Keeper of the Archives.

20th September 1913.
Magdalen College,
Oxford.

My dear President,

You will, I think, wish me to give you an account of the discovery of traces of the Cemetery of St. John's Hospital in the course of excavation for the new drainage works in the College. In the middle of last month, when I was acting as Bursar, it was reported to me that the workmen had come upon a gravestone between two and three feet below the present surface of the ground at a spot which I have marked *A* on a very rough plan, which I enclose. The picks unfortunately broke the stone in two, but the smaller half was taken out and I had it placed on the floor of the great Tower. There are indications of a cross on it. Below it was found a skeleton apparently complete and lying *in situ*, but it was necessary to remove the bones as they were above the level of the drain which passed directly through them. I ordered them to be placed in a pocket dug out at the East side of the trench (marked 2 on the plan), where were also collected some other bones from graves (or a grave) in the immediate neighbourhood, which had been disturbed at an earlier date.

A second skeleton was found (and remains) entire just to the West of the grave of E. S. Chaplin (*B*), and a third was partially disturbed at a point which I have marked *C*, but which I rather think was a little nearer to the Lodgings.

I received a request from Mr. Dudley Buxton, of Exeter, who, I understand, is a demonstrator in the department of Human Anatomy, that he might examine the first collection of bones found before they were reinterred; this he did in the presence of the foreman, and then the remains were closed up. I send you Mr. Buxton's letter on the subject.

The extent of ground over which the burials are distributed is surprising: it was far larger than Mr. Salter had inferred from the documentary evidence. The rise of the soil, about 2½ feet, is also noticeable.

Believe me,
Yours very truly,
R. L. POOLE.

b. Fragments of masonry built into the walls of the Chaplain's Quadrangle.

Great use was made by the college builders of the materials on the spot. f. 38

[After the completion of the Great Tower in 1506, work was at once started on the adjacent living rooms, which were three years in building and by which the Chaplains' Quadrangle became enclosed. Their width was governed by the width of the Chapel of St. John, the eastern windows of which, as well as the lower windows of the Tower, they completely covered up. Buckler had an opportunity of ascertaining that these newer walls were largely built of worked stones from the Hospital, a fact which I was able to verify during the recent refitting of the south-east staircase and rooms in 1913, when many architectural details of considerable if neglected interest were once more brought to light.]

The short length of the front beyond the Tower, and the return f. 61 wing of the Clerks' Court, were found to be so much dilapidated in the upper walls and roof as to require amendment without delay, and it was not neglected by the Society.

. . . The antiquarian interest of this Eastern angle of the College is, f. 62 or rather has been, very considerable. That part which incorporates the remains of the Hospital must be referred to with some degree of particularity, since it presents strong testimony in regard to the refined character of the architecture of edifices which have disappeared from among the buildings of the 13th century.

Nowhere else among the College buildings has a discovery been made of the like profuse employment of the materials of desolated walls. The fine finish of the workmanship had been partially injured under the process of re-application, but proof had been given how well 'new works may be constructed of old materials'.

Thus gleams of historical importance burst forth unexpectedly in ancient buildings when necessity leads to their dismemberment; and good feeling should never be wanting to preserve the recollection of their recent existence.

It has perhaps scarcely ever happened that one edifice of distinction has given way to another, without the one yielding, and the other accepting sound materials in stone and timber for the use of the
f. 63 intruder. The builder employed them freely in this inferior part of the building. No outward sign appeared in the upper wall of anything uncommon in the material: the remark was made that the wall differed from the rest in being composed of blocks of stone of uniform size, methodically disposed, the reverse of the method observed in the construction of the rest of the wall. But this particular piece of mason-work was not in quiet repose. Interior alterations and lacerations had disturbed the original compactness of the masonry, which, when opened, exposed fragments of the elegant architecture of the hospital. This curious exhibition made known the deliberation and care with which its walls had been taken to pieces, and the blocks handed over to the builders of the College, and thus employed.

There lay course upon course of single and clustered capitals, massive fragments of arches; of geometrical tracery, and complicated mouldings diverging from the prominent members of the pattern; of jamb mouldings of great depth, and in high relief; clustered pillars of light and robust make; with other fragments which once contributed to the perfection of designs which distinguished the architecture of St. John's Hospital.

The remark should be made that not a single example of sculptured ornament has been discovered: moldings, in all the rich variety of combination they admitted, constituted the ornament of the design.

c. Fragments of masonry built into the wall of the Chapel Porch of Magdalen College.

[The fragments figured in fig. 10 were discovered in the wall of the Chapel Porch in 1900 during the work of shifting the doorway to its original position. The principal fragments then found are now preserved in the Upper Library of the College; they included—

i. A short length of Early English Scroll-molding with a fillet along the scroll (fig. 10, 2). In character it so closely resembles the scroll-moldings *in situ* on the Chapel building, that it may without hesitation be referred to a building of the same age, and it may

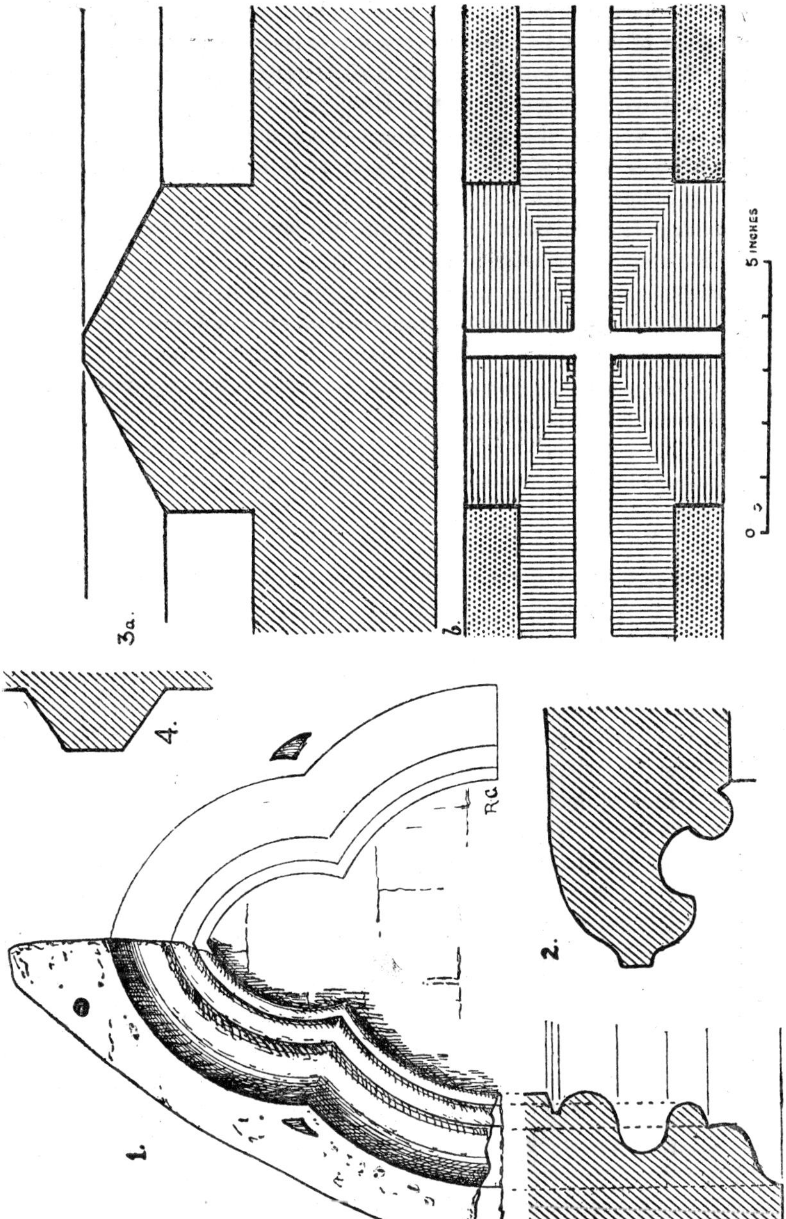

FIG. 10. ARCHITECTURAL DETAILS.

even be identified as part of a hood-molding over one of the south windows of the said Chapel, whence it may have been removed before the 'Perpendicularization' of that front in 1665. It is possible that this and other fragments of the Hospital building were introduced into the wall of the Chapel Porch either during the progress of Inigo Jones' work of ornamentation in 1636 or during the removal of that ornamentation in 1792.

ii. A rudely worked cruciform stone: the junction of a transom with the mullion for a window (fig. 10, 3 a, b).

iii. A portion of a cusped and elaborately molded arch-stone (fig. 10, 1) probably from an ornamental arcade carried on round pillars, or from the arch over a piscina. The deeply cut hollow between two rounds in the molding is characteristic. This fragment had obviously once been part of a building, because its exposed surfaces were coated with three coats of whitewash, and, like the Scroll-molding described above, it probably came from a building of the date (1234) of the Chapel.]

d. Sculptured Fragments.

[i. *The Nun's Head Corbel.* Inserted in the south wall of the Kitchen is a small carved stone head, 6 inches in height, that has every appearance of being coeval with the Hospital (Plate X). It was perhaps originally the corbel of an interior hood-mold: if so it is the sole specimen of the sculpture of the Hospital that is now preserved to us.

A very similar sculptured corbel is to be seen in the Chapter House in Christ Church, where it supports the corner column in the north-west corner of that early 13th-century room.

ii. *St. John's Head.* Perhaps the stone Head reputed to be the Head of St. John the Baptist may also have belonged to the Hospital. It is now standing in a niche in the western gable end of the buildings of St. John's Quadrangle over the present Porter's Lodge, and therefore not far from the supposed site of the Great Gate of the Hospital. Buckler may be referring to this head in his note: 'Some of the sculptures still preserved in the wall of the front court of the College are as ancient as the 12th century' (f. 43).]

e. Fragments of Norman Architecture.

[Among the Buckler drawings there is a sketch (MS. 36,433, No. 256) of two pieces of nicely designed stone-work which were dug up in a Quadrangle in Magdalen College in 1820.

The stones were two of the quoin-stones from the sides or arch of

PLATE X

ANCIENT CORBEL, NOW IN MAGDALEN COLLEGE KITCHEN

QUOIN-STONES FROM A NORMAN ARCH (*c.* 1160-1200)

'Dug up in Quadrangle Magd: Coll: 1820.' Now in Hertford College

After a drawing by Buckler

a window or doorway, probably the latter. The actual corner is formed by a vertical roll-molding, against which abut the points of two chevron moldings which are carved in planes at right angles to one another,—an arrangement that is not very clear from Buckler's drawings (Pl. X). When the stones were in their proper architectural positions, the chevrons including the ornamented triangles would have been in the plane of the wall-face, the other chevrons would have decorated the sides of the aperture or the under surface of the arch, as part of a zigzag ornament. At first sight this chevron or zigzag ornament recalls the late Norman work of which we have such a fine example in Iffley Church (*c.* 1160). Indeed the two beads and beak of one might be a conventionalized form of the bird-heads of the west doorway of that Church, while the 'fleur-de-lys' ornament of the other is paralleled by the foliated foot-ornament on a late Norman base at St. Cross, Winchester (*c.* 1180).[1] At the same time both ornaments were in use in the Early English Style, as at Ringstead, Northants, though we are not aware of their association with chevrons so late as the 13th century.

These two specimens of transition Norman carving are of supreme interest because they alone of all the stones, which we have seen, belonged to a building of a period appreciably earlier than the Charter and Chapel of Henry III. They are the sole material evidence of buildings upon this site as old as, or slightly older than, the charter of Hugo de Malaunay in 1194.[2]

Since the above observations were set up in type, I have had the good fortune to wander into Hertford College and there to find four sculptured stones of late Norman design; two, the arch-stones of a small niche or window, are decorated on two faces with palmette or scallop ornament, and two are *the identical stones from which Buckler's sketches were made.* It is stated that all four stones were found in foundations at Hertford College about 1889, when the demolition of the buildings of 1820–2 was in progress, to make way for the new Library.

If Buckler's note that they were 'Fragments of St. John's Hospital dug up in Quadrangle Magd: Coll: 1820' be correct—at any rate in the matters of place and date, it follows that these stones, after being seen and drawn at Magdalen by him, may have been part of the College contribution to the new buildings for Magdalen Hall on

[1] Parker, *Introd. Gothic Arch.* fig. 50. [2] *Oxf. Hist. Soc.* xvii, p. 533.

the site of Hertford College. The other known contributions made by Magdalen College for this purpose were stone from the College quarry near Shotover by College Order 15 March, 1820, and about £12,600 in money in 1822. It is quite comprehensible that any unwanted fragments which might have been lying about at Magdalen College should have been passed on to the Hertford College site: but that they should have been re-exhumed and be lying exposed for identification during the very week when the proof-sheets of this one and only description of the Hospital Buildings were being read, is little short of miraculous.

Fortunately an account of a find of old stones at Hertford is extant. In 1822 Skelton published a plate[1] of Hertford College buildings with drawings of architectural fragments which he described as 'Curious Norman Capitals and parts of Arches found amongst the stonework of a chimney sometime since removed': these he accepted as proof that a Norman building of importance had once existed on the site of Hertford College. Several of Skelton's sketches represent early capitals, one undoubtedly represents an arch-stone with the palmette or scallop ornament already mentioned, but none represent the Buckler stones, although one sketch represents a stone with chevron moldings, that are so similar that it may have come from the *same arch* as the Buckler stones!

If we are to believe both Skelton and Buckler, it follows that there must have been a substantial building of ornate late Norman work 'somewhere'. Two of its stones were found buried in the Quadrangle at Magdalen in 1820, and in 1889 were again found in Hertford College, where they now are. Another stone, apparently from the same archway, was found with other Norman stones in the old chimney on the Hertford site and was engraved by Skelton in 1822. The Capitals found at the same time are not at present known to me, but two niche-arch stones with palmette ornamentation are illustrated in Skelton's 1822 plate and the originals (after being buried for 67 years) are once more visible in Hertford College.

All these stones were of the time of Hugo de Malaunay. I am in a state of uncertainty as to whether they belonged to his building on the St. John's Hospital site, or to a Norman building on the Hertford site, or to a Norman building on a third site, but I think it likely that they all once belonged to the same structure.]

[1] *Oxonia Antiqua Restaurata*, Pl. 93.

f. The earliest Drawing of the Hospital of St. John.

[The buildings delineated in a manuscript of Matthew Paris so closely resemble those of the *Domus Conversorum*, founded in London by Henry III in 1232 to serve as a refuge for converted Jews, that they were evidently designed by the same master mind, either builder or artist. The windows are also identical with those of the Home for Lepers established near London by 'holy Queen Maud', wife of Henry I, who himself founded the leper-house of St. Bartholomew in Oxford. Representations of both buildings are given in Clay, *Mediaeval Hospitals of England*, 1909. Although one cannot rely absolutely upon the accuracy of the details represented, the drawing reproduced in Fig. 11 may be accepted as evidence for a Tower at the east end and an entrance doorway at the west end of the edifice, but whether these structures are wholly, or at any rate in part, those which we have already described; whether the Tower survived late enough to have suggested Magdalen Tower to the Founder of the College; or whether they stood further back from the street, we must leave to the judgement of others. The simplest theory is that this drawing actually represents the Chapel building of the Hospital at a very early time.]

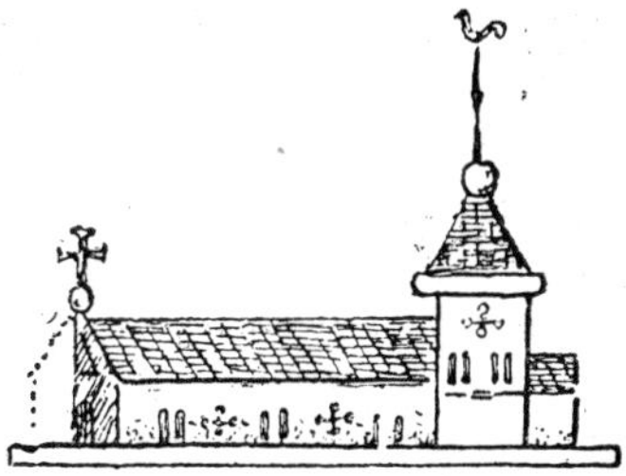

FIG. 11. THE HOSPITAL OF ST. JOHN
After Matthew Paris, *c.* 1250.
Brit. Mus. Roy. MS. 14 C. vii, f. 221.

g. General Conclusions and Notes on Construction. f. 66

So very little of the history of St. John's Hospital is known that the curious in these days must not expect to gather more decisive information as to the quality of its buildings than has been derived from the relics discovered by the several circumstances already mentioned. f. 31

The most diligent search at different times of alteration has not brought to light any fragments of the Hospital walls mingled with those which formed the great bulk of the buildings stretched across the precinct from North to South.

What they were as to shape and extent cannot now be known, but if their strength was equal to that of the remains which have survived to recent years, despair must have overtaken the workmen long before they threw down the side walls of the great chambers of the Hospital.

The builders made choice of a most durable rubble stone, rough and incapable of being reduced to shape, found in the neighbourhood, and forming walls of such extraordinary strength when combined with mortar of the like quality, that the workmen must have been conscious of the almost everlasting firmness of the structures they were raising or the sacred obligation of charity.

f. 66 It was perhaps prudent in the possessor of property thus acquired not to preserve the records of the history, or to proclaim the merit of the buildings devoted to destruction. At no period earlier than that under notice was less compunction felt for the mutilation or the demolition of architecture of superb quality.

The power of doing mischief to this extent was oftentimes purchasable; and was too frequently perpetrated in great Churches for no better reason than to confer upon them the costume of architecture suitable to the taste of the reigning fashion.

The Founder of Magdalen College had no opportunity to indulge a propensity of this kind. The collegiate plan he had prepared for the site could not be engrafted upon the walls of an Hospital, whatever the measures of its buildings. His Master Mason, William Orcheyerd, an expert and able practitioner, had no choice but to throw substantial and beautiful structures into ruins, and to commit the materials to the handicraftsman.

h. Note on the Picture of the Chapel of the Hospital, reproduced on FIG. 3.

Mrs. Poole, who has done such good work in connection with Oxford Historical Portraits, has recently drawn my attention to two unpublished letters in the Bodleian Library which describe the circumstances under which the old picture of the south front of Magdalen College came into the possession of the College.

The first is a letter from Dr. Wm. Holmes, President of St. John's, to Dr. Rawlinson, Feb. 5, 1744/5:

> I must now acquaint you that I have dispos'd of ye Pictures. Dr. Butler will take an opportunity of returning you ye thanks of ye College for ye Picture presented to them, which they received with great pleasure.
>
> *MS. Rawl. Letters*, 29, fol. 75.

The second letter is from Dr. Rawlinson to Thomas Rawlins, June 18, 1745:

> I met with an old painting of Magd. Coll. Oxford at the end of Q. Mary or beginning of Q. Eliz. which appears by the Spanish Habits on the bridge. It pleased them so well that they have given it a place in their Hall.
>
> *Ballard MS.* ii. No. 102, fol. 166.

The picture has been dated *c.* 1660.

1.

2.

3.

4.

5.

6.

7.

1. See vol. ii, p. 381. Hugo le Sclatter.
2. ,, ,, ii, p. 372. Matilda de Haliwelle.
3. ,, ,, i, p. 432. John Pileth.
4. ,, ,, ii, p. 321. Henry Simeon III.
5. ,, ,, ii, p. 151. Mildegoda, Jewess.
6. ,, ,, i, p. 460. Henry Simeon II.
7. ,, ,, i, p. 277. Henry Simeon I.

To face 434.

INDEX

Oxford Historical Society.

PUBLICATIONS.

1884.

1. **Register of the University of Oxford.** Vol. I. (1449–63; 1505–71), edited by the Rev. C. W. Boase, M.A., pp. xxviii + 364. (Price to the public, without discount, and prepaid, 16*s.*)

2. **Remarks and Collections of Thomas Hearne.** Vol. I. (4 July 1705—19 March 1707), edited by C. E. Doble, M.A., pp. viii + 404. (16*s.*)

1884–85.

3. **The Early History of Oxford (727–1100), preceded by a sketch of the Mythical Origin of the City and University.** By James Parker, M.A. With 3 illustrations, pp. xxxii + 420. (20*s.*)

1885.

4. **Memorials of Merton College, with biographical notices of the Wardens and Fellows.** By the Hon. Geo. C. Brodrick, Warden of Merton College. With one illustration, pp. xx + 416. (16*s.*, to members of Merton 12*s.*)

5. **Collectanea, 1st series,** edited by C. R. L. Fletcher, M.A. With 2 illustrations, pp. viii + 358. (16*s.*)

(Contents:—*a.* Letters relating to Oxford in the 14th Century, ed. by H. H. Henson; *b.* Catalogue of the Library of Oriel College in the 14th Century, ed. by C. L. Shadwell; *c.* Daily ledger of John Dorne, bookseller in Oxford, 1520, ed. by F. Madan; *d.* All Souls College *versus* Lady Jane Stafford, 1587, ed. by C. R. L. Fletcher; *e.* Account Book of James Wilding, Undergraduate of Merton College, 1682–88, ed. by E. G. Duff; *f.* Dr. Wallis's Letter against Maidwell, 1700, ed. by T. W. Jackson.)

1886.

6. **Magdalen College and King James II, 1686–88.** A series of documents collected and edited by the Rev. J. R. Bloxam, D.D., with additions, pp. lii + 292. (16*s.*, to members of Magdalen 12*s.*)

7. **Hearne's Collections** [as No. 2 above]. Vol. II. (20 Mar. 1707—22 May 1710), pp. viii + 480. (16*s.*)

8. **Elizabethan Oxford.** Reprints of rare tracts. Edited by the Rev. C. PLUMMER, M.A., pp. xxxii + 316. (10*s.*)

(Contents:—*a.* Nicolai Fierberti Oxoniensis Academiæ descriptio, 1602; *b.* Leonard Hutton on the Antiquities of Oxford; *c.* Queen Elizabeth at Oxford, 1566 [pieces by J. Bereblock, Thomas Nele, Nich. Robinson, and Rich. Stephens, with appendices]; *d.* Queen Elizabeth at Oxford, 1592, by Philip Stringer; *e.* Apollinis et Musarum Eidyllia per Joannem Sanford, 1592.)

1887.

9. **Letters of Richard Radcliffe and John James, of Queen's College, Oxford, 1749–83:** edited by MARGARET EVANS, with a pedigree, pp. xxxvi + 306. (15*s.*, to members of Queen's 10*s.* 6*d.*)

10. **Register of the University of Oxford, Vol. II (1571–1622), Part 1. Introductions.** Edited by the Rev. ANDREW CLARK, M.A., pp. xxxii + 468. (18*s.*)

1887–88.

11. **Ditto. Part 2. Matriculations and Subscriptions.** Edited by the Rev. ANDREW CLARK, M.A., pp. xvi + 424. (18*s.*)

1888.

12. **Ditto. Part 3. Degrees.** Edited by the Rev. ANDREW CLARK, M.A., pp. viii + 448. (17*s.*)

13. **Hearne's Collections** [as No. 2 above]. Vol. III. (25 May 1710—14 December 1712), pp. iv + 518. (16*s.*)

1889.

14. **Register of the University of Oxford, Vol. II, Part 4. Index.** Edited by the Rev. ANDREW CLARK, M.A., pp. viii + 468. (17*s.*)

15. **Wood's History of the City of Oxford.** *New Edition.* By the Rev. ANDREW CLARK, M.A. Vol. I. The City and Suburbs. With 3 Maps and several Diagrams, pp. xii + 660. (25*s.*, to citizens of Oxford 20*s.*; the two Maps of old Oxford separately, not folded, 1*s.* 6*d.*, to citizens 1*s.*)

1890.

16. **Collectanea, 2nd series,** edited by Professor MONTAGU BURROWS. With one diagram, pp. xii + 518. (16*s.*)

(Contents:—*a.* The Oxford Market, by O. Ogle; *b.* The University of Oxford in the Twelfth Century, by T. E. Holland; *c.* The Friars Preachers of the University, ed. by H. Rashdall; *d.* Notes on the Jews in Oxford, by A.

Neubauer; *e.* Linacre's Catalogue of Grocyn's Books, followed by a Memoir of Grocyn, by the Editor; *f.* Table-Talk and Papers of Bishop Hough, 1703–1743, ed. by W. D. Macray; *g.* Extracts from the 'Gentleman's Magazine' relating to Oxford, 1731–1800, by F. J. Haverfield. Appendix: Corrections and Additions to Collectanea, Vol. I. (Day-book of John Dorne, Bookseller at Oxford, A. D. 1520, by F. Madan, including a 'Half-century of Notes' on Dorne, by Henry Bradshaw).)

17. **Wood's History of the City of Oxford** [as No. 15 above]. Vol. II. Churches and Religious Houses. With Map and Diagram, pp. xii + 550. (20*s.*, to citizens of Oxford 16*s.*; Map of Oxford in 1440, separately, not folded, 9*d.*, to citizens 6*d.*)

1890–91.

18. **Oxford City Documents,** financial and judicial, 1268–1665. Selected and edited by Prof. J. E. THOROLD ROGERS, pp. viii + 440 (+ 2 loose leaves for vols. 6 and 16). (12*s.*)

1891.

19. **The Life and Times of Anthony Wood, antiquary, of Oxford, 1632–1695, described by Himself.** Collected from his Diaries and other Papers, by the Rev. ANDREW CLARK, M.A. Vol. I. 1632–1663. With 7 illustrations, pp. xvi + 520. (20*s.*)

20. **The Grey Friars in Oxford.** Part I, A History of the Convent; Part II, Biographical Notices of the Friars, together with Appendices of original documents. By ANDREW G. LITTLE, M.A., pp. xvi + 372. (16*s.*)

1892.

21. **The Life and Times of Anthony Wood** [as No. 19]. Vol. II. 1664–1681. With 10 illustrations, pp. xxviii + 576. (20*s.*)

22. **Reminiscences of Oxford, by Oxford men, 1559–1850.** Selected and edited by LILIAN M. QUILLER COUCH, pp. xvi + 430. (17*s.*, to members of the University 10*s.* 6*d.*)

1892–93.

23. **Index to Wills proved and Administrations granted in the Court of the Archdeacon of Berks, 1508–1652.** Edited by W. P. W. PHILLIMORE, M.A. (Issued in conjunction with the British Record Society.) pp. viii + 200. (10*s.*)

1893.

24. Three Oxfordshire Parishes. A History of Kidlington, Yarnton, and Begbroke. By Mrs. BRYAN STAPLETON. With a coloured map and 2 sheet-pedigrees, pp. xx + 400. (17*s.*, to residents in the three villages 10*s.*)

25. The History of Corpus Christi College, with Lists of its Members. By THOMAS FOWLER, D.D., President of the College. With 3 illustrations, pp. xvi + 482. (20*s.*, to members of Corpus 12*s.* 6*d.*)

1894.

26. The Life and Times of Anthony Wood [as No. 19]. Vol. III. 168½–1695. With 3 illustrations, pp. xxxii + 548. (21*s.*)

27. The Register of Exeter College, Oxford, with a history of the College, and illustrations. By the Rev. C. W. BOASE, M.A. Third edition, enlarged. pp. [8] + clxxxiv + 400. (*Presented to the Society by the author:* 15*s.*, to members of the College 10*s.*)

28. The Cartulary of the Monastery of St. Frideswide at Oxford. Edited by the Rev. S. R. WIGRAM, M.A. With illustrations. Vol. I. General and City Charters. pp. xx + 504 + 6 pages (loose) of corrections to vol. 24. (21*s.*)

1895.

29. The Early Oxford Press, a bibliography of printing and publishing at Oxford, '1468'–1640. With notes, appendixes, and illustrations. By FALCONER MADAN, M.A., pp. xii + 366. (Separate copies can be obtained only from the Clarendon Press, price 18*s.* The Society can only supply it in sets.)

30. The Life and Times of Anthony Wood [as No. 19]. Vol. IV. Addenda With illustrations, pp. xii + 322. (24*s.*)

1896.

31. The Cartulary of the Monastery of St. Frideswide at Oxford. Edited by the Rev. S. R. WIGRAM, M.A. With illustrations. Vol. II. The Chantry and Country Parish Charters. pp. xii + 488 + 8 pages of additions and corrections (loose) to vol. 25. (21*s.*)

32. Collectanea, 3rd series, edited by Professor MONTAGU BURROWS. With illustrations, pp. xii + 450. (21*s*.)

(Contents:—*a*. Some Durham College Rolls, by Rev. H. E. D. Blakiston; *b*. Parliamentary Petitions relating to Oxford, by Miss L. Toulmin Smith; *c*. Poems relating to the riot between Town and Gown, 1355, by Rev. H. Furneaux; Tryvytlam de laude Univ. Oxoniae, by the same; *d*. Wykeham's Books at New College, by A. F. Leach; *e*. Correspondence of Henry Earl of Clarendon and James Earl of Abingdon, 1683–85, by C. E. Doble; *f*. Dr. Newton and Hertford College, by S. G. Hamilton; *g*. Charles Earl Stanhope and the Oxford University Press, by H. Hart.)

1897.

33. A History of Pembroke College, anciently Broadgates Hall. By the Rev. DOUGLAS MACLEANE, M.A. With 4 illustrations, pp. xvi + 544 + 4 pages of Addenda to vol. 32. (21*s*., to members of Pembroke 13*s*.)

34. Hearne's Collections [as No. 2 above]. Vol. IV (15 Dec. 1712 —30 Nov. 1714). Edited by D. W. RANNIE, M.A., pp. x + 466 + [2], with a plate. (1898, 21*s*.)

1898.

35. Epistolae Academicae Oxon., a collection of letters and other documents illustrative of Oxford in the fifteenth century. Edited by the Rev. H. ANSTEY, M.A. With illustrations. Part I, pp. lii + 336. (21*s*.)

36. Ditto. Part II, pp. vi + 389. (21*s*.)

1899.

37. Wood's History of the City of Oxford [as No. 15 above]. Vol. III. Addenda and Indexes, with illustration, pp. x + 476 + [4]. (21*s*., to citizens of Oxford 16*s*.)

38. Old Plans of Oxford, by Agas, Hollar, and Loggan. A portfolio containing 15 plates. (21*s*., to citizens of Oxford 16*s*.)

1900.

39. Oxford Topography, an essay by HERBERT HURST, B.A. With sketch-map, pp. viii + 248. (A companion to No. 38: 21*s*., to citizens of Oxford 16*s*.)

40. The Life and Times of Anthony Wood [as No. 19]. Vol. V, completing the work. Indexes, pp. xvi + 402 + [4]. (21*s*.)

1901.

41. Studies in Oxford History, chiefly in the Eighteenth Century, by the Rev. J. R. GREEN and the Rev. GEO. ROBERSON, edited by C. L. STAINER, M.A. With illustrations, pp. *xx* + xxiv + 382. (21*s.*)

42. Hearne's Collections [as No. 2 above]. Vol. V (Dec. 1, 1714–Dec. 31, 1716). Edited by D. W. RANNIE, M.A., pp. viii + 402 + [6]. (21*s.*)

1902.

43. Hearne's Collections [as No. 2 above]. Vol. VI (Jan. 1, 1717–May 8, 1719). Edited under the superintendence of the Committee of the O. H. S. With an illustration, pp. viii + 432 + [6]. (31*s.* 6*d.*)

1903.

44. The Flemings in Oxford. Vol. I. Edited by the Rev. the PROVOST OF QUEEN'S COLLEGE, pp. xxiv + 592 + [8]. (31*s.* 6*d.*)

1903–4.

45. The Ancient Kalendar of the University of Oxford. Edited by the Rev. CHRISTOPHER WORDSWORTH, pp. xxxii + 294 + [8]. (31*s.* 6*d.*)

1904.

46. Oxford Silver Pennies. Edited by C. L. STAINER, M.A., pp. xlvi + 96 + [8]. With 15 plates. (21*s.*)

1905.

47. Collectanea, 4th series, edited under the superintendence of the Committee of the O. H. S., pp. xii + 346. (31*s.* 6*d.*)

(Contents:—*a.* Description of Oxford from the Hundred Rolls, ed. by Rose Graham; *b.* Oxford Church Notes, by Richard Symonds, 1643–4, ed. by Rose Graham; *c.* Three Consecrations of College Chapels (Lincoln, 1631; Brasenose, 1666; Queen's, 1717), ed. by A. Clark, F. Madan, and J. R. Magrath, D.D.; *d.* Thos. Baskerville's Account of Oxford, c. 1670–1700, ed. by Humph. Baskerville; *e.* Bill of Costs of Charles Ellis, agent in London to the Mayor of Oxford for the Coronation of George IV, 1821, ed. by F. Williams; *f.* Coaching in and out of Oxford, 1820–40, by William Bayzand.)

1906.

48. Hearne's Collections [as No. 2 above]. Vol. VII (May 9, 1719–Sept. 22, 1722). Edited under the superintendence of the Committee of the O. H. S., pp. viii + 428 + [8]. (31*s.* 6*d.*)

1906–7.

49. The Cartulary of the Abbey of Eynsham. Vol. I. Edited by the Rev. H. E. SALTER, pp. xxxvi + 441 + [8]. (31*s.* 6*d.*)

1907.

50. **Hearne's Collections** [as No. 2 above]. Vol. VIII (Sept. 23, 1722–Aug. 9, 1725). Edited under the superintendence of the Committee of the O. H. S., pp. viii + 443 + [8]. (31*s*. 6*d*.)

1908.

51. **The Cartulary of the Abbey of Eynsham.** Vol. II. Edited by the Rev. H. E. SALTER, pp. xcviii + 422 + [8]. (31*s*. 6*d*.)

1909.

52, 53. **Brasenose College Monographs.** Vol. I and Vol. II. Part I. [Only sold in sets of the Society's publications.*]

1910.

54. **Brasenose College Monographs.** Vol. II, Part II. [Only sold in sets of the Society's publications.*]

55. **Brasenose College Register, 1509–1909.** With Lists and Index. [*Presented to the Society by the Editor, Dr. Heberden.* Only sold in sets of the Society's publications.*]

* The two volumes of Monographs are published by Mr. B. H. Blackwell, Broad Street, Oxford, at 10*s*. 6*d*. each: and the Register by the same at 15*s*.

1910–11.

56. **Liber Obituarius Aulae Reginae**, printed in facsimile, with notes, pp. xliii + 153. [*Presented to the Society by the Editor, the Rev. the Provost of Queen's College.*] (42*s*.)

1911.

57. **Catalogue of Oxford Portraits.** Vol. I. By Mrs. R. L. Poole, pp. xxxii + 278. (Additional copies can be obtained only through a bookseller in the ordinary way.)

58. **Enactments in Parliament concerning Oxford and Cambridge.** Vol. I (37 Ed. III—13 Anne), by L. L. SHADWELL, pp. xxxix + 360.

1912.

59–61. **Enactments in Parliament**, Vols. II–IV (1 George I—2 George V), by L. L. SHADWELL. Vol. II, pp. iv + 408; III, pp. iv + 420; IV, pp. iv + 384.

1913.

62. **The Flemings in Oxford.** Vol. II. Edited by the Rev. the PROVOST OF QUEEN'S COLLEGE, pp. xxviii + 418 + [8]. (21*s.*)

63. **A Subsidy collected in the Diocese of Lincoln in 1526.** Edited by the Rev. H. E. SALTER, pp. xvi + 348. [*Presented to the Society.*] (12*s.* 6*d.*)

64. **Balliol Oxford Deeds.** Edited by the Rev. H. E. SALTER, pp. xii + 388 + [8]. [*Presented to the Society.*] (21*s.*)

1914.

65. **Hearne's Collections** [as No. 2 above]. Vol. IX (Aug. 10, 1725–Mar. 26, 1728). Edited chiefly by the Rev. H. E. SALTER, pp. x + 424 + [8]. (21*s.*)

66. **A Cartulary of the Hospital of St. John the Baptist.** Vol. I. Edited by the Rev. H. E. SALTER, pp. xii + 492 + [8]. [*Presented to the Society by the President and Fellows of Magdalen College.*] (21*s.*)

1915.

67. **Hearne's Collections** [as No. 2 above]. Vol. **X** (Mar. 27, 1728–Dec. 16, 1731.) Edited by the Rev. H. E. SALTER, pp. 494 + [8]. (21*s.*)

68. **A Cartulary of the Hospital of St. John the Baptist.** Vol. II. Edited by the Rev. H. E. SALTER, pp. vii + 467 + [8]. [*Presented to the Society by the President and Fellows of Magdalen College.*] (21*s.*)

1916.

69. **A Cartulary of the Hospital of St. John the Baptist.** Vol. III. Edited by the Rev. H. E. SALTER, pp. lvi + 520 + [8]. [*Presented to the Society by the President and Fellows of Magdalen College.*] (21*s.*)

WORKS IN ACTIVE PREPARATION.

The Flemings in Oxford. Vol. III.

The Cartulary of Oseney Abbey. Edited by the Rev. H. E. SALTER.

University Archives. Vol. I; original documents 1214–1377. Edited by the Rev. H. E. SALTER.